IN PRAISE OF *INTERNET LAW AND BUSINESS HANDBOOK*

"The *Internet Law and Business Handbook* is a practical and comprehensive guide to this fast-changing and complicated new world. Industry experts Mark Radcliffe and Dianne Brinson address all the critical topics in a clear, straightforward and highly-accessible manner. Experienced developers and publishers as well as newcomers to the Internet business will benefit by keeping this invaluable resource close at hand."
— *Jim Kennedy, Vice President of Business Affairs, Electronic Arts*

"As the president of a public company whose primary business is focused on the Internet, I know firsthand how difficult and complicated legal issues are in my business. I also know how critical understanding these issues is to the success of my business. Mark Radcliffe has helped me finance and take my company public. I strongly recommend this book to everyone, whether they are doing business on the Internet now or plan to in the future."
— *David Toth, President, Netratings, Inc.*

"I recommend this book to Internet entrepreneurs, business students and marketing professionals. It is packed with practical, hard to find, up-to-date information that is essential for running an Internet business."
— *Sueann R. Ambron, Dean, College of Business Administration*
University of Colorado at Denver

"Mark Radcliffe and Dianne Brinson's 'building block' and 'preventive law' approach provides a practical, easy to understand guide to a complex, dynamic, and evolving area of the law. This book will prove to be enormously useful both to lawyers and nonlawyers engaging in any existing or new Internet business."
— *John Place, Vice President and General Counsel, Yahoo! Inc.*

"Brinson and Radcliffe know their stuff and they've kindly shared the wealth. In a rapidly evolving area fraught with uncertainty, they've demystified much of the Byzantine doctrine, highlighting exactly those areas of greatest interest and importance to those who want to build on the front lines of the Internet and the Web."
— *Jonathan Zittrain, Assistant Professor of Law, Harvard Law School;*
Faculty Co-Director, Berkman Center for Internet & Society

internet
law and business
handbook

internet
law and business
handbook

J. Dianne Brinson

Mark F. Radcliffe

Credits:
The Roberts Group, editing, book design, and production

Some of the material in this book was previously published in the book *Multimedia Law and Business Handbook* by the same authors (Ladera Press 1996).

This publication is designed to provide accurate and authoritative information in regard to the subject matter covered. It is sold with the understanding that the publisher is not engaged in rendering legal, accounting, or other professional service. If legal advice or other expert assistance is required, the services of a competent professional person should be sought.

All products or services mentioned are trademarks or service marks of their respective owners.

Printed in the U.S.A.

Publisher's Cataloging in Publication
(provided by Quality Books Inc.)

Brinson, J. Dianne.
    Internet law and business handbook : a practical guide by J. Dianne Brinson and Mark F. Radcliffe. — 1st ed.
    p. cm.
    Includes index.
    LCCN: 97-71371
    ISBN: 0-9639173-3-1

    1. Internet (Computer network)—Law and legislation—United States. 2. Computer networks—Law and legislation—United States. 3. Business enterprises—United States—Computer network resources—Law and legislation. 4. Business law—United States. 5. Electronic commerce—Law and legislation law—United States. I. Radcliffe, Mark F. II. Title

KF390.5.C6B75 2000   343.09'944
                              QB100-565

CONTENTS

ADDITIONAL ISSUES

APPENDICES

ACKNOWLEDGMENTS

We would like to extend our thanks to all of the individuals who helped us write this book. We wish to thank particularly the partners of Gray Cary Ware & Freidenrich as well as the following contributors: Anna Talerico, iDecisionMaker ("Anatomy of an RFP, chapter 8); Gail L Grant, GLG Consulting (chapter 14); Scott Killingsworth, of Powell, Goldstein, Frazer & Murphy (chapter 17); John D. Gregory, Ministry of the Attorney General, Ontario, Canada, (chapter 19); Jeffrey W. Reyna, of McCutchen Doyle Brown & Enersen (chapter 23); and Eric J. Sinrod, of Duane, Morris and Hecksher (chapter 23).

This book includes our opinions. They should not be interpreted as those of Gray Cary Ware & Freidenrich or its clients. We have done our best to accurately reflect the laws applicable to the Internet and current practices in Internet contracts, but any errors are solely our responsibility.

We would like to thank the following individuals for their assistance:

Warren Adler, Directors Guild of America
Dr. Sueann Ambron, the University of Colorado at Denver
Sue Collins, American Federation of Musicians
Rohn Engh, PhotoSource International
Ned Hearn, Law Offices of Edward R. Hearn
Rebecca Rhine, American Federation of Television and Radio Artists
Barry Young, Gray Cary Ware & Freidenrich
Allen Weingartner, Screen Actors Guild

INTRODUCTION

This book is a comprehensive, practical guide to the legal and business issues that arise in various aspects of using the Internet—setting up business Web sites and personal home pages, putting existing material on the Internet, creating material for the Internet, using material found on the Internet, and e-commerce. The approach taken in this book is what lawyers call "preventive law"—working from a base of knowledge of the applicable laws to create strategies and procedures that will help you avoid future lawsuits and legal complications. (Lawsuits are costly, even if you win.) We have included a number of examples, descriptions of real cases, and checklists to help you understand the issues.

Designed for both nonlawyers and lawyers, the book contains clear explanations of the applicable laws. It uses numerous examples to help you understand how these laws apply to real-world situations. It covers the latest Internet legal developments, including relevant new legislation and regulations (on privacy protection and domain name rights, for example) and recent court decisions.

The book uses a "building block" approach, first clearly explaining the laws that apply to Internet use, then applying the principles to Internet-based activities. Part 1 ("Building Blocks," chapters 1 through 7) will give you an understanding of the laws that apply to use of the Internet—copyright law, other intellectual property laws, copyright ownership rules, contracts law, and the laws of defamation, publicity, and privacy.

Part 2 of the book is called "Creating Web Sites and Web Products" (chapters 8 through 13). This section includes a chapter on Web development agreements and one explaining how to determine when you need permission to use preexisting content in Web sites and Web-based products. It has a chapter explaining how to get licenses to use works owned by others and one describing ownership and licensing practices in the industries that are your most likely sources for preexisting content. The content owner's perspective on licensing is covered in chapter 12 and Web product distribution agreements in chapter 13.

Part 3 is "Web Marketing and E-Commerce Issues" (chapters 14 through 20). This section begins with a chapter on Internet business models by consultant Gail L. Grant. It includes chapters on choosing product names and domain names, e-commerce and sales laws, and linking. It also includes a chapter on privacy policies by Atlanta attorney Scott Killingsworth of Powell, Goldstein, Frazer & Murphy.

Part 4, "Additional Issues," includes chapters on using music on the Web, union issues, service provider liability, and distance learning legal issues. It includes a chapter on the law of email by California attorneys Eric J. Sinrod of Duane, Morris and Hecksher LLP and Jeffrey W. Reyna of McCutchen, Doyle, Brown & Enersen LLP. Chapter 24, "Other Legal Issues," covers legal rules for using trademarks owned by others and laws prohibiting the removal of copyright management information and circumvention of access control devices.

In the appendices, we have included fifteen sample contracts. (The contracts are also on the disk attached to the inside back cover of this book.) Other appendices include an explanation of the U.S. legal system and resource appendices listing rights clearance agencies, search firms, and licensing agents; stock houses and other content sources; and unions and guilds.

HOW TO USE THIS BOOK

Reading this book won't make you a lawyer, but it will enable you to ask appropriate questions and take steps to protect your interests. If you are contemplating taking action based on the principles explained in this book, get the advice of an experienced attorney.

As you probably know, the law of the Internet is still developing. (Every day, the news media run articles on some aspect of Internet law, such as privacy policies, domain name disputes, and linking issues.) As this book goes to press, many legal issues are still unresolved, as we note in the book. New laws are being passed, and cases dealing with crucial issues are being decided. For information on updates to this book, check our Web site, www.laderapress.com.

CHAPTER 1

COPYRIGHT LAW

There are four major intellectual property laws in the United States that are important for Internet users:

- Copyright law

- Patent law

- Trademark law

- Trade secret law

In this chapter, we will discuss copyright law, the most important of the intellectual property laws for Internet users. Patent law, trademark law, and trade secret law are discussed in chapter 2.

Ownership of copyrights and other intellectual property is discussed in chapter 3. Other laws that create rights somewhat like intellectual property law rights—privacy and publicity laws—are discussed in chapter 7. Laws protecting copyright management information and copy prevention devices are covered in chapter 24.

Introduction

Copyright law in the United States is based on the Copyright Act of 1976, a federal statute that went into effect on January 1, 1978. We'll refer to this statute throughout the book as the Copyright Act. The Copyright Act (Title 17 of the United States Code) is available online in Adobe Acrobat PDF format at www.loc.gov/copyright/title17. The United States Copyright Office, part of the Library of Congress, handles copyright registrations (discussed later in this section) and provides information on copyright law on its Web site, www.loc.gov/copyright.

States cannot enact their own laws to protect the same rights as the rights provided by the Copyright Act. 17 USC § 301. For example, a state cannot pass a law to extend copyright protection on works in the state beyond the term of protection given by the Copyright Act. State "copyright" laws exist, but they are limited to works that cannot be protected under federal copyright law. (Requirements for federal protection are discussed in "Standards," later in this chapter.)

Copyright law is important for Internet users for three reasons:

- Much of the material that is on the Internet is protected by copyright, making copyright law a concern for those wishing to use material they find on the Internet. This topic is discussed in "Using Materials from the Web," chapter 9.

- The types of preexisting material used for Web site content—text, graphics, photographs, and music—are copyrightable, and much of this material is protected by copyright. Web site owners and developers and Web product designers and publishers must avoid infringing copyrights owned by others, as explained in chapters 9 and 10.

- Copyright protection is available for Web sites and new Web content. This topic is discussed in "Copyright Protection," chapter 26.

Types of Works Protected by Copyright

Copyright law protects "works of authorship." 17 USC § 102(a). The Copyright Act states that works of authorship include the following types of works:

- **Literary works.** Novels, fictional characters, nonfiction prose, poetry, newspaper articles and newspapers, magazine articles and magazines, computer software, software documentation and manuals, training manuals, manuals, catalogs, brochures, ads (text), and compilations such as business directories.

- **Musical works.** Songs, advertising jingles, and instrumentals.

- **Dramatic works.** Plays, operas, and skits.

- **Pantomimes and choreographic works.** Ballets, modern dance, jazz dance, and mime works.

- **Pictorial, graphic, and sculptural works.** Photographs, posters, maps, paintings, drawings, graphic art, display ads, cartoon strips and cartoon characters, stuffed animals, statues, paintings, and works of fine art.

■ **Motion pictures and other audiovisual works.** Movies, documentaries, travelogues, training films and videos, television shows, television ads, and interactive multimedia works.

■ **Sound recordings.** Recordings of music, sounds, or words.

■ **Architectural works.** Building designs, whether in the form of architectural plans, drawings, or the constructed building itself.

Standards

To receive copyright protection, a work must be "original" and must be "fixed" in a tangible medium of expression. 17 USC § 102(a). Certain types of works are not copyrightable.

Originality

The originality requirement is not stringent: A work is original in the copyright sense if it owes its origin to the author and was not copied from some preexisting work. A work can be original without being novel or unique.

> **EXAMPLE**
>
> John's book, *Designing Web Sites,* is original in the copyright sense so long as John did not create his book by copying existing material—even if it's the millionth book to be written on the subject.

Only minimal creativity is required to meet the originality requirement. No artistic merit or beauty is required.

PRIOR WIDESPREAD USE

While most works make the grade on the originality requirement—because they possess some creative spark, no matter how obvious—a phrase or slogan that has been in widespread use may lack the originality necessary for copyrightability. A federal appeals court held that a music publishing company could not claim copyright in the phrase, "You've got to stand for something, or you'll fall for anything," because the phrase lacked originality. *Acuff-Rose Music Inc. v. Jostens Inc.,* 155 F3d 140 (2d Cir 1998). Short phrases rarely meet the originality requirement and are usually not copyrightable. However, they may qualify for trademark protection, discussed in "Trademark Law," chapter 2.

A work can incorporate preexisting material and still be original. When preexisting material is incorporated into a new work, the copyright on the new work covers only the original material contributed by the author.

EXAMPLE

Web Developer used preexisting photographs and graphics (with the permission of the copyright owners) in a Web design project. The Web site as a whole owes its origin to Developer, but the photographs and graphics do not. Web Developer's copyright on the Web site does not cover the photographs, just the material created by Developer.

Facts owe their origin to no one and so are not original. In the United States, a compilation of facts (a work formed by collecting and assembling data) is protected by copyright only to the extent of the author's originality in the selection, coordination, and arrangement of the facts.

EXAMPLE

Ralph created a neighborhood phone directory for his neighborhood by going door-to-door and acquiring his neighbors' names and phone numbers. The directory's facts (names and phone numbers) are not original. Ralph's selection of facts was not original (he "selected" every household in the neighborhood). His coordination and arrangement of facts (alphabetical order by last name) is routine rather than original. The directory is not protected by copyright.

Facts and databases are discussed in "When You Don't Need a License," chapter 9.

SELECTION AND ARRANGEMENT

In the case *Urantia Foundation v. Maaherra,* the court had to decide whether a book believed by both parties to be the words of celestial beings was copyrightable. The foundation claimed copyright ownership. The defendant, who had distributed a computer disk version of the book without the permission of the foundation, maintained that the book was not copyrightable because no human creativity was involved in creating the book. The court held that even if the book's content originated with a celestial being, there had been sufficient human selection and arrangement of material to satisfy copyright law's "originality" requirement. 114 F3d 955 (9th Cir 1997).

Fixation

According to Section 101 of the Copyright Act, a work is "fixed" when it is made "sufficiently permanent or stable to permit it to be perceived, reproduced, or otherwise communicated for a period of more than transitory duration." It makes no difference what the form, manner, or medium is. An author can "fix" words, for example, by writing them down, typing them on an old-fashioned typewriter, dictating them into a tape recorder, or entering them into a computer. A live television broadcast is "fixed" if it is recorded simultaneously with the transmission.

Uncopyrightable Works

Works prepared by federal government officers and employees as part of their official duties are not protected by copyright. 17 USC § 105. Consequently, federal statutes (the Copyright Act, for example) and regulations are not protected by copyright. This rule does not apply to works created by state government officers and employees.

Titles of works are not copyrightable. However, titles may be protectible under trademark law. See "Titles," chapter 15.

The design of a useful article is protected by copyright only if, and to the extent that, the design "incorporates pictorial, graphic, or sculptural features that can be identified separately from, and are capable of existing independently of, the utilitarian aspects of the article." 17 USC § 101 (definition of "pictorial, graphic, and sculptural works"). For example, while a standard belt buckle design is not protected, a three-dimensional belt-buckle design with a dolphin shape qualifies for limited protection.

Uncopyrightable works and works for which copyright protection has ended are referred to as "public domain" works. See "Public Domain Works," chapter 9.

Procedure for Getting Protection

Copyright protection arises automatically when an original work of authorship is fixed in a tangible medium of expression. 17 USC § 102. Registration with the Copyright Office is optional (but you have to register before you file an infringement suit, if you are a United States citizen or corporation).

The use of copyright notice is optional for works distributed after March 1, 1989. Copyright notice can take any of these three forms:

- © followed by a date and name.

- "Copyright" followed by a date and name.

- "Copr." followed by a date and name.

17 USC § 401.

The benefits of registering a copyright and using copyright notice are discussed in "Copyright Protection," chapter 26. The role of notice for works distributed prior to March 1, 1989, is discussed in "Public Domain Works," chapter 9.

The Exclusive Rights

According to section 106 of the Copyright Act, a copyright owner has five exclusive rights in the copyrighted work:

- **Reproduction Right.** The reproduction right is the right to copy, duplicate, transcribe, or imitate the work in fixed form. Scanning a copyrighted work for use on a Web site is an exercise of the copyright owner's reproduction right.

- **Modification Right.** The modification right (also known as the derivative works right) is the right to modify the work to create a new work. A new work that is based on a preexisting work is known as a "derivative work." Altering a photograph is an exercise of the modification right, as is creating an interactive version of a novel or creating a sequel to a computer game or motion picture.

- **Distribution Right.** The distribution right is the right to distribute copies of the work to the public by sale, rental, lease, or lending. Whether using copyrighted material on the Internet is an exercise of this right is discussed in "When You Need a License," chapter 9.

- **Public Performance Right.** The public performance right is the right to recite, play, dance, act, or show the work at a public place or to transmit it to the public. In the case of a motion picture or other audiovisual work, showing the work's images in sequence is considered "performance." Showing scenes from a copyrighted motion picture in sequence on the Web is an exercise of the public performance right, as is the use of a copyrighted musical composition on the Web.

- **Public Display Right.** The public display right is the right to show a copy of the work directly or by means of a film, slide, or television image at a public place or to transmit it to the public. In the case of a motion picture or other audiovisual work, showing the work's images out of sequence is considered "display." Posting copyrighted material on the Web is an exercise of the public display right.

The exclusive rights are discussed in more detail in "When You Need a License," chapter 9, and "Determining What Rights You Need," chapter 10.

Infringement

Anyone who violates any of the exclusive rights of a copyright owner is an infringer.

EXAMPLE
_____

John scanned Photographer's copyrighted photograph, altered the image by using digital editing software, and used the altered version of the photograph on an e-commerce site. If John used the photograph without Photographer's permission, John infringed Photographer's copyright by violating the reproduction right, the modification right, and the public display right.

A copyright owner can recover actual or, in some cases, statutory damages from an infringer (see "Copyright Protection," chapter 26). The federal district courts have the power to issue injunctions (orders) to prevent or restrain copyright infringement and to order the impoundment and destruction of infringing copies.

There are two essential elements to an infringement case: (a) that the defendant copied from the plaintiff's copyrighted work; and (b) that the copyright was improper appropriation. Copying generally is established by showing that the defendant had access to the plaintiff's work and that the defendant's work is substantially similar to the plaintiff's work.

Most copyright infringement cases are civil cases. However, copyright infringement also can be a criminal offense. According to Section 506 of the Copyright Act, two types of willful copyright infringement are criminal offenses:

- Willful infringement for purposes of commercial advantage or private financial gain.

- Willful infringement by reproducing or distributing copies or phonorecords of copyrighted works having a total retail value of more than $1000 in a 180-day period.

BARTER BOARDS

David LaMacchia, an MIT student, invited users to post commercial software on his bulletin board for exchange with other users. LaMacchia made no money from the exchanges. He was arrested, but the court dismissed the suit because the criminal copyright law in effect at the time of the prosecution applied only to willful infringement for commercial motive or private gain. Congress then amended the law, adding the second violation category discussed in the paragraph immediately above. Prosecutors can use the provision to shut down barter boards through which pirated copies of software and computer games are traded.

The difference between civil and criminal cases is discussed in "Civil and Criminal Cases," in appendix A.

Duration of the Rights

Under current law, the copyright term for works created by individuals is the life of the author plus seventy years. 17 USC § 302(a).

The copyright term for "works made for hire" is ninety-five years from the date of first "publication" (distribution of copies to the general public) or 120 years from the date of creation, whichever expires first. 17 USC § 302(c). Works made for hire are works created by employees for employers and certain types of specially commissioned works. See "The Work Made for Hire Rule," chapter 3, and "Copyright Ownership," chapter 6.

The duration of copyright for older works is discussed in "Public Domain Works," chapter 9.

Limitations on the Exclusive Rights

The copyright owner's exclusive rights are subject to a number of exceptions and limitations that give others the right to make limited use of a copyrighted work. Major exceptions and limitations are outlined in this section. (They are discussed in detail in "When You Don't Need a License," chapter 9).

Ideas

Copyright protects only against the unauthorized taking of a protected work's "expression." It does not extend to the work's ideas, procedures, processes, systems, methods of operation, concepts, principles, or discoveries.

Facts

A work's facts are not protected by copyright, even if the author spent large amounts of time, effort, and money discovering those facts. In the United States, copyright protects originality, not effort or "sweat of the brow."

EXTRACTING FACTS FROM A WEB SITE

In *Ticketmaster Corp. v. Tickets.com, Inc.,* the court held that extracting facts from a Web site is not copyright infringement. "This falls in the same category of taking historical facts from a work of reference and printing them in a different expression," the court stated. 54 USPQ2d 1344 (CD Cal 2000). The court also held that using facts from a Web site is neither an unfair business practice nor unjust enrichment.

Independent Creation

A copyright owner has no recourse against another person who, working independently, creates an exact duplicate of the copyrighted work. The independent creation of a similar work or even an exact duplicate does not violate any of the copyright owner's exclusive rights.

Fair Use

The "fair use" of a copyrighted work, including use for purposes such as criticism, comment, news reporting, teaching, scholarship, or research, is not an infringement of copyright. Copyright owners are, by law, deemed to consent to fair use of their works by others.

The Copyright Act does not define fair use. Instead, whether a use is fair use is determined by balancing these factors (discussed in "When You Don't Need a License," chapter 9):

- The purpose and character of the use.

- The nature of the copyrighted work.

- The amount and substantiality of the portion used in relation to the copyrighted work as a whole.

- The effect of the use on the potential market for, or value of, the copyrighted work.

International Protection

U.S. authors automatically receive copyright protection in all countries that are parties to the Berne Convention for the Protection of Literary and Artistic Works, or parties to the Universal Copyright Convention (UCC). Most countries belong to at least one of these conventions. Members of the two international copyright conventions have agreed to give nationals of member countries the same level of copyright protection they give their own nationals.

EXAMPLE

Publisher, a U.S. company, has discovered that bootleg copies of one of its software products are being sold in England. Because the United Kingdom is a member of the Berne Convention and the UCC, Publisher's work is automatically protected by copyright in England. When Publisher files a copyright infringement action in England against the bootlegger, Publisher will be given the same rights that an English copyright owner would be given.

The copyright laws (and other intellectual property laws) of a number of countries are posted at www.wipo.int/clea.

Works of foreign authors who are nationals of Berne or UCC-member countries automatically receive copyright protection in the U.S., as do works first published in a Berne Convention or UCC country. Unpublished works are subject to copyright protection in the U.S. without regard to the nationality or domicile of the author.

CHAPTER 2

PATENT, TRADEMARK, AND TRADE SECRET LAW

While copyright law is the most important intellectual property law for the Internet, you need to know enough about patent, trademark, and trade secret law to avoid infringing intellectual property rights owned by others and to be able to take advantage of the protection provided by these laws. These three intellectual property laws are discussed in this chapter.

In chapter 26, we discuss ways in which you can use these three laws and copyright law to protect your own material. Ownership of intellectual property is discussed in chapter 3. Choosing product names is covered in chapter 15.

Patent Law

Patent law in the United States is based on a federal statute, the Patent Act. States are prohibited from granting protection similar to that provided by the Patent Act.

Types of Works Protected

Patent law protects inventions (utility patents) and ornamental designs for articles of manufacture (design patents).

Inventions protected by utility patents include any new and useful process, machine, manufacture, or composition of matter. Inventions can be electrical, mechanical, or chemical in nature. Examples of inventions protected by utility patents are a microwave oven, genetically engineered bacteria for cleaning up oil spills, a computerized method of running cash management accounts, and a method for curing rubber.

Internet-related inventions protected by utility patents include communications protocols, data compression techniques, interfaces, networking methods, encryption techniques, interfaces, online payment systems, and information processing and retrieval technologies. In the area of e-commerce, patentable inventions and processes include electronic postage, electronic cash, and e-commerce business methods (discussed later in this chapter).

Examples of manufactured articles protected by design patents are a design for the sole of running shoes, a design for sterling silver tableware, and a design for a water fountain.

Standards

There are strict requirements for granting utility patents and design patents. We'll discuss the requirements in this section.

Design Patents

To qualify for a design patent, a design must be new, original, and ornamental. Design patents are generally not suitable for protecting elements of Internet-related software processes. Design patents are considered rather narrow intellectual property protection because they are limited to the ornamental appearance of an article. Owners of design patents rarely sue to enforce their patents against infringers.

Utility Patents

To qualify for a utility patent, an invention must be new, useful, and "nonobvious."

To meet the novelty requirement, the invention must not have been known or used by others in this country before the applicant invented it, and it also must not have been patented or described in a printed publication in the U.S. or a foreign country before the applicant invented it. The philosophy behind the novelty requirement is that a patent is issued in exchange for the inventor's disclosure to the public of the details of his invention. If the inventor's work is not novel, the inventor is not adding to the public knowledge, so the inventor should not be granted a patent.

Meeting the useful requirement is easy for most inventions. An invention is useful if it can be applied to some beneficial use in society.

To meet the nonobvious requirement, the invention must be sufficiently different from existing technology and knowledge so that, at the time the invention was made, the invention as a whole would not have been obvious to a person having ordinary skill in that field. This requirement makes sure patents are only granted for real advances, not for mere technical tinkering or modifications of existing inventions by skilled technicians.

FIRST TO INVENT OR FIRST TO APPLY?

Who gets the patent if two inventors, working independently of each other, achieve patentable results around the same time? In the United States, the patent goes to the first person who invented the claimed subject matter (even if the first to invent was not the first to file a patent application). Only the U.S. and the Philippines have a first-to-invent system. In other countries, the first person who files a patent application gets the patent, even if he or she is not the first to invent the claimed subject matter.

It is difficult to obtain a utility patent. Even if the invention or process meets the requirements of novelty, utility, and nonobviousness, a patent will not be granted if the invention was patented or described in a printed publication in the U.S. or a foreign country more than one year before the application date, or if the invention was in public use or on sale in the U.S. for more than one year before the application date. This rule is known as the "statutory bar." If you think your technology might be patentable, you should contact a patent attorney before you display or distribute your invention. The one-year grace period following disclosure of the invention is available only in the U.S. In most other countries, the patent application must be filed prior to any public disclosure of the invention.

"PRINTED PUBLICATIONS" ON THE INTERNET

In applying the statutory bar rule, material is considered a "printed publication" if it has been sufficiently accessible to that portion of the public interested in the particular field. Presumably, material made available on the Internet could count as a "printed publication." Contact a patent attorney before publishing information about potentially patentable material on the Web.

Abstract ideas and mental conceptions are not patentable. Discoveries of scientific principles, laws of nature, and natural phenomena are not patentable (although applications of such discoveries are). Mathematical algorithms that have not been reduced to some type of practical application have been held to be unpatentable. However, a claim to a system or method that recites a mathematical algorithm and produces "a useful, concrete and tangible result" may be patentable. *State Street Bank & Trust Co. v. Signature Financial Group*, 149 F3d 1368 (Fed Cir 1998), *cert. denied*, 525 US 1093 (1999). The software process involved in the *State Street Bank* case was used by a computer system to recompute the share prices of a pool of mutual funds after each day's trading activities ended, taking into account the day's gains and losses and expenses attributable to each mutual fund. The final share prices were the "useful, concrete, and tangible result."

Until recently, methods of transacting business were thought not to be patentable. However, in the *State Street Bank* case, the court made it clear that systems or methods which implement business methods are patentable if they meet the requirements of novelty, usefulness, and nonobviousness.

You've probably read about new patents being issued for Internet-related methods of doing business. Here are a few:

■ CyberGold's patent for a method that rewards customers who receive online ads

■ Netcentives' patent for rewarding online purchasers with airline frequent-flyer miles

■ Priceline.com's patent for reverse auctions

■ Open Market's patents related to secure online credit-card payments

■ Amazon.com's patents on "one-click" technology and affiliate programs

Some people think that business methods should not be patentable. In the *State Street Bank* case, the Court of Appeals for the Federal Circuit, which reviews all patent appeals, held that processes which are otherwise patentable subject matter are not rendered unpatentable because they involve business methods. The Supreme Court, by denying *certiorari*, declined to review the position taken by the Court of Appeals. Unless Congress amends the Patent Act, processes involving business methods are patentable. However, they must meet the stringent requirements for patent protection discussed earlier in this section. The Patent and Trademark Office is now subjecting business methods patents to a second-level review.

Procedure for Getting Protection

Patent protection is obtained by demonstrating in an application filed with the U.S. Patent and Trademark Office, www.uspto.gov, that the invention meets the stringent standards for grant of a patent. The patent application process is an expensive, time-consuming process (it generally takes at least two years). Although you can file a patent application yourself, the application process is complex. You should consider using an experienced patent attorney or patent agent (a nonlawyer who has passed the special patent bar exam given by the U.S. Patent and Trademark Office).

If you want to be able to claim "patent pending" status without undertaking the expense and paperwork involved in a regular patent application, consider filing a "provisional patent application" (PPA). A PPA remains in effect for one year. The PPA filing date can be used to prove that the invention described in the PPA document predates other inventions in the field.

Exclusive Rights

A patent owner has the right to exclude others from making, using, selling, offering to sell, or importing the patented invention or design in the United States during the term of the patent. Anyone who makes, uses, sells, offers to sell, or imports a patented invention or design within the United States during the term of the patent without permission from the patent owner is an infringer—even if he or she did not copy the patented invention or design or even know about it.

EXAMPLE

Developer's staff members, working on their own, developed software for manipulating images in multimedia works. Although Developer's staff didn't know it, Inventor has a patent on that method of image manipulation. Developer's use of the software infringes Inventor's patent.

Duration

Under current law (effective June 8, 1995), utility patents are granted for a period of twenty years from the date the patent application was filed.

EXAMPLE

Amazon.com, Inc. was issued a patent on its affiliates program on February 22, 2000. The patent application was filed on June 27, 1997. The patent will expire in June 2017.

Under prior law, patent protection lasted seventeen years from the date the patent was issued. Under the current law, if a patent application is pending for longer than three years, the patent's term can be extended to give the applicant seventeen years to enjoy the patent.

EXAMPLE

Inventor filed a patent application on June 15, 1997. She was granted a patent on December 15, 2000. Her term can be extended so that her patent will not expire until December 2017.

The extension is available only if the delay is not the fault of the applicant.

For utility patents in existence prior to June 8, 1995, the patent term is the greater of seventeen years from the date of issue (the term under prior law) or twenty years from the application filing date. Design patents are granted for a period of fourteen years.

The patent application must contain a written description of the invention and how to make and use the invention in such complete terms as to enable others to make and use it. Once a patent is issued, this information—known as the disclosure—becomes available to the public, as do the patent's "claims" (patentee's defined legal rights). Once the patent on an invention or design has expired, anyone is free to make, use, or sell the invention or design.

The Patent and Trademark Office maintains a free online searchable database of U.S. patents issued since January 1, 1976 at www.uspto.gov/patbib_index.html. IBM has compiled a free searchable database of U.S. patents issued since 1971; it's available at www.ibm.com/patents. Commercial services such as Micropatent (www.micropatent.com) include pre-1971 patents in their databases. Patents may also be searched at Patent and Trademark Depository Libraries located throughout the U.S. Information on the libraries is available at www.uspto.gov.

SAMPLE SPECIFICATION & CLAIM LANGUAGE

The specifications section of Amazon.com's affiliates program starts with this description: "The present invention provides a software system and method for enabling an Internet sales entity . . . to efficiently market and sell goods in cooperation with Web sites or other network sites of respective business partners, referred to herein as "associates." The first claim starts this way: "A method of selling items with the assistance of associates, the method comprising: providing a Web site system that includes a browsable catalog of items and provides services for allowing customers to electronically purchase the items . . ." This patent is Patent 6,029,141, "Internet-based customer referral system."

While most countries publish patent applications, Congress has only recently changed the U.S. Patent Act to allow the Patent and Trademark Office to publish patent applications. Effective November 29, 2000, the Patent and Trademark Office will publish patent applications eighteen months after they are filed, unless the applicant certifies that foreign patent protection is not being sought in a country that requires publication of applications eighteen months after filing. The publication provision does not apply to applications for design patents.

Limitations on Exclusive Rights

There are two major limitations on the patent owner's exclusive rights. They are discussed in this section.

Functionally Equivalent Products

A patent owner can exclude others from making, using, or selling products or using processes that do substantially the same work as the patented invention in substantially the same manner. However, a patent does not protect the patent owner from competition from functionally equivalent products or processes that work in different ways.

> **EXAMPLE**
>
> Microco owns a patent covering a laser printer. While Microco can prevent others from making, using, or selling laser printers that work in substantially the same manner as Microco's printer, it cannot prevent others from making, using, or selling laser printers that operate in a different manner.

Invalidation

The validity of an issued patent is subject to challenge in an infringement proceeding. Defendants in infringement suits usually raise the defense of patent invalidity, asserting that the invention covered by the patent was not novel or nonobvious. It is not unusual for a patent infringement suit to result in a determination that the U.S. Patent and Trademark Office made a mistake in granting the patent.

PATENT VALIDITY

Patent invalidity is certain to be an issue in infringement suits to enforce e-commerce business methods patents. For example, when Amazon.com sued Barnesandnoble.com for infringing Amazon's "One-Click Shopping" patent, Barnesandnoble.com's defenses included patent invalidity. Barnesandnoble.com maintained that One-Click Shopping was not novel or nonobvious—and that the patent examiner who granted the patent to Amazon.com would have realized that had the examiner had all the relevant "prior art" available to him when he reviewed Amazon's patent application.

Avoiding Infringement

New Internet-related and e-commerce patents are being granted in record numbers. If you learn of a patent and are concerned that your operations may infringe it, get advice from a patent attorney.

Consulting a patent attorney is particularly important if your potentially infringing operations are still in the planning stages. Based on the legal advice you receive, you may decide to modify your operations to avoid infringement—or you may decide to get a license from the patent owner. Avoid investing more money or time in your plans until you get legal advice.

If you learn that a patent has recently been granted on a method of doing business you are already using, you may have an "early inventor" defense (also known as a "first inventor" defense). The early inventor defense was added to the Patent Act in late 1999, after the *State Street Bank* case (discussed earlier in this section) was decided. Prior to that decision, business methods were thought not to be patentable. Now thousands of business methods patent applications are being filed. The early inventor defense, applicable only to business methods patents, is a complete defense to infringement for those who meet two requirements:

- Commercially used the subject matter covered in the patent prior to the patentee's patent application date.

- Acting in good faith, "reduced the subject matter to practice" (executed the invention) at least one year before the patentee's application filing date.

"Submarine patents" have long been a concern in fast-moving fields. A submarine patent is one that remains secret until it is issued, by which time competitors and other companies have made substantial investments to use the technology covered by the new patent. There is nothing you can do to eliminate the risk of submarine patents. However, the fact that many patent applications will now be published eighteen months after they are filed helps to reduce the risk.

If you are concerned that someone else is going to apply for a patent on a business method they and you are already using on the Internet, take comfort in the statutory bar mentioned earlier in this section. No patent can be granted on an invention that was in public use or on sale in the U.S. for more than one year prior to the patent application date.

Trademark Law

Trademarks and service marks are words, names, symbols, or devices used by manufacturers of goods and providers of services to identify their goods and services, and to distinguish their goods and services from goods manufactured and sold by others.

EXAMPLE

The trademark *FrontPage* is used by Microsoft Corporation to identify the company's Web development software and to distinguish its software from other vendors' Web development software.

For ease of expression, we will use "trademark" in this book to refer to both trademarks (used on goods) and service marks (used for services).

For trademarks used in commerce, federal trademark protection is available under the federal trademark statute, the Lanham Act. Many states have trademark registration statutes that resemble the Lanham Act, and all states protect unregistered trademarks under the common law (nonstatutory law) of trademarks.

Types of Works Protected

Examples of words used as trademarks are *Kodak* for cameras and *Burger King* for restaurant services. Examples of slogans used as trademarks are *Fly the Friendly Skies of United* for airline services and *Get a Piece of the Rock* for insurance services. Examples of characters used as trademarks are Pillsbury's Dough Boy for baked goods and Aunt Jemima for breakfast foods.

Sounds can be used as trademarks, such as the jingle used by National Public Radio. Product shapes and configurations—for example, the distinctively shaped bottle used for Coca-Cola—can also serve as trademarks.

Standards

Trademark protection is available for words, names, symbols, or devices that are capable of distinguishing the owner's goods or services from the goods or services of others. A trademark that merely describes a class of goods rather than distinguishing the trademark owner's goods from goods provided by others is not protectible.

EXAMPLE

The word "corn flakes" is not protectible as a trademark for cereal because that term describes a type of cereal that is sold by a number of cereal manufacturers rather than distinguishing one cereal manufacturer's goods.

A trademark that resembles a trademark already in use in the U.S. so closely that it is likely to cause confusion or mistake is not protectible. Geographically descriptive marks—"Idaho" for potatoes grown in Idaho—are not protectible trademarks for products that originate in the geographical area (all Idaho potato growers should be able to use "Idaho" in connection with selling their potatoes). Geographically misdescriptive marks that are deceptive are not protectible.

EXAMPLE

Hiromichi Wada, the owner of a Michigan leather goods shop, attempted to federally register the name *New York Ways Gallery* for leather goods. The Patent and Trademark Office refused to register the name because it thought the public would assume Wada's goods were from New York. The Court of Appeals for the Federal Circuit upheld the Patent and Trademark Office's decision. *In re Hiromichi Wada,* 194 F3d 1297 (Fed Cir 1999).

Procedure for Getting Protection

The most effective trademark protection is obtained by filing a trademark registration application in the Patent and Trademark Office, www.uspto.gov. Federal law also protects unregistered trademarks, but such protection is limited to the geographic area in which the mark is actually being used.

Federal Protection

Federal registration is limited to trademarks used in interstate commerce (or intended for use in interstate commerce). Before November 1989, a trademark application could be filed only after the trademark's owner had actually used the trademark in commerce. Under current law, a person who has a "bona fide" intention to use a trademark in commerce may apply to register the trademark.

For federally registered marks, the use of notice of federal registration is optional. A federal registrant may give notice that his or her trademark is registered by displaying with the trademark the words "Registered in U.S. Patent and Trademark Office" or the symbol ®.

State Protection

State trademark protection under common law is obtained simply by adopting a trademark and using it in connection with goods or services. This protection is limited to the geographic area in which the trademark is actually being used.

State statutory protection is obtained by filing an application with the state trademark office. Those relying on state trademark law for protection cannot use the federal trademark registration symbol, but they can use the symbol TM (or, for a service mark, SM).

DOMAIN NAMES AS TRADEMARKS

The mere registration of a domain name does not convey trademark rights. However, if you use your domain name to identify your goods or services—using it in ads for your e-commerce site, for example—it acquires trademark protection. This topic is discussed in "Choosing a Strong Trademark," chapter 15. Domain name registration is discussed in chapter 16.

Exclusive Rights

Trademark law in general, whether federal or state, protects a trademark owner's commercial identity (goodwill, reputation, and investment in advertising) by giving the trademark owner the exclusive right to use the trademark on the type of goods or services for which the owner is using the trademark. Any person who uses a trademark in connection with goods or services in a way that is likely to cause confusion is an infringer. Trademark owners can obtain injunctions against the confusing use of their trademarks by others, and they can collect damages for infringement.

EXAMPLE

Distributed Learning Company is selling a line of interactive training products under the trademark *Personal Tutor*. If Giant Multimedia Company starts selling interactive training products under the name *Personal Tutor*, purchasers may think that Giant's products come from the same source as Distributed Learning's products. Giant is infringing Distributed Learning's trademark.

One of the most important benefits of federal registration of a trademark is the nationwide nature of the rights obtained. For the registrant, federal registration in effect reserves the right to start using the mark in new areas of the U.S.

EXAMPLE

In March 1999, Small Multimedia Company, a California corporation, obtained a federal trademark registration on the trademark *Abra* for computer games. Small Multimedia did not begin using the trademark on computer games in New York until 2000. In September 1999, Giant Company started using *Abra* on computer games in New York. Because Small Multimedia's federal registration gives it a right to use *Abra* throughout the United States that is superior to Giant's right to use *Abra,* Small Multimedia can stop Giant from using *Abra* on computer games in New York—even though Giant started using *Abra* in New York before Small Multimedia did.

Other advantages of federal registration are discussed in "Trademark Protection," chapter 15.

A trademark owner's rights under state trademark law (and the rights of an unregistered trademark owner under federal law) are generally limited to the geographical area in which the owner has used the trademark.

EXAMPLE

(For this example, we changed just one fact from the previous example.) Small Multimedia Company did not get a federal trademark registration. Now Giant's right to use *Abra* on computer games in New York is superior to Small Multimedia's right to use *Abra* on computer games in New York, because Giant was the first to actually use the trademark on computer games in New York.

INTERNET USE

In the last example, what if Small Multimedia Company, the first company to use *Abra* on computer games, sold its games on a Web site? People anywhere in the world could view the Web site. Does that mean that Small Multimedia was using *Abra* throughout the world? We don't know the answer. It is unclear how the above rule would apply when a trademark is protected only under state or common law and is used on the Internet.

Duration

A certificate of federal trademark registration remains in effect for ten years, provided that an affidavit of continued use is filed in the sixth year. A federal registration may be renewed for any number of successive ten-year terms so long as the mark is still in use in commerce. The duration of state registrations varies from state to state. Common law rights endure so long as use of the trademark continues.

Limitations of Exclusive Rights

Trademark law does not give protection against use of the trademark that is unlikely to cause confusion, mistake, or deception among consumers, but dilution laws may provide such broader protection (see "Dilution," chapter 15).

EXAMPLE

Western Software has a federal registration for the use of *Flap* on Web development tool software. If Giant Company starts using *Flap* on its desktop publishing software, Giant may be infringing Western Software's trademarks because consumers may think the desktop publishing software and the Web development tool software come from the same source. If Giant starts using *Flap* on fire extinguishers, though, Giant is probably not infringing Western Software's trademark. Consumers are unlikely to think that the *Flap* software and the *Flap* fire extinguishers come from the same source.

Avoiding Infringement

Tips on how to avoid trademark infringement in naming your products and services are in chapter 15. Tips on how to avoid trademark infringement when choosing domain names are in chapter 16. Rules for using trademarks owned by others are in chapter 24.

Trade Secret Law

A trade secret is information of any type that is valuable to its owner, not generally known, and kept secret by the owner. Even negative information such as research options that have been explored and found to be worthless can be trade secrets.

Trade secrets are protected only under state law. The Uniform Trade Secrets Act, in effect in a number of states, defines trade secrets as "information, including a formula, pattern, compilation, program, device, method, technique, or process that derives independent economic value from not being generally known and not being readily ascertainable and is subject to reasonable efforts to maintain secrecy."

Types of Works Protected

The following types of technical and business information are examples of material that can be protected by trade secret law:

- Customer lists
- Designs
- Instructional methods
- Manufacturing processes
- Document-tracking processes
- Formulas for producing products

Inventions and processes that are not patentable can be protected under trade secret law. Patent applicants generally rely on trade secret law to protect their inventions while the patent applications are pending.

Standards

Six factors are generally used to determine whether material is a trade secret:

- The extent to which the information is known outside the claimant's business.
- The extent to which the information is known by the claimant's employees.
- The extent of measures taken by the claimant to guard the secrecy of the information.
- The value of the information to the claimant and the claimant's competitors.
- The amount of effort or money expended by the claimant in developing the information.
- The ease with which the information could be acquired by others.

Information has value if it gives rise to actual or potential commercial advantage for the owner of the information. Although a trade secret need not be unique in the patent law sense, information that is generally known is not protected under trade secret law.

Procedure for Getting Protection

Trade secret protection attaches automatically when information of value to the owner is kept secret by the owner.

Exclusive Rights

A trade secret owner has the right to keep others from misappropriating and using the trade secret. Sometimes the misappropriation is a result of industrial espionage. Many trade secret case defendants are people who have taken their former employers' trade secrets for use in new businesses, or new employers of such people.

Trade secret protection endures so long as the requirements for protection—generally, value to the owner and secrecy—continue to be met. The protection is lost if the owner fails to take reasonable steps to keep the information secret.

EXAMPLE

After Sam discovered a new method for manipulating images in multimedia works, he demonstrated his new method to a number of other developers at a multimedia conference without requiring the developers to sign nondisclosure agreements. Sam lost his trade secret protection for the image manipulation method because he failed to keep his method secret.

Limitations on Exclusive Rights

Trade secret owners have recourse only against misappropriation. Discovery of protected information through independent research or reverse engineering (taking a product apart to see how it works) is not misappropriation. However, many software license agreements prohibit reverse engineering. This topic is discussed in "When You Don't Need a License," chapter 9.

Federal Criminal Trade Secret Law

The Economic Espionage Act of 1996 (EEA) makes stealing or knowingly buying trade secrets a criminal offense punishable by a fine of up to $250,000, imprisonment of up to fifteen years, or both. The EEA provides higher penalties for stealing or knowingly buying trade secrets for the benefit of a foreign government or agent.

Avoiding Infringement

To avoid infringing trade secrets, you should avoid using valuable confidential business and technical information you acquired while working for a former employer. When you hire someone to perform exactly the same duties he or she used to perform for another company, you run the risk of being sued for trade secret infringement. An individual is allowed to carry general knowledge or skill from one job to the next. Drawing the line between general knowledge or skill and protected trade secrets belonging to the former employer can be difficult. Consider consulting an experienced attorney if you need to make this distinction.

CUSTOMER CONTACTS LIST

Haber worked in sales at North Atlantic Instruments. He left North Atlantic and joined Apex Signal Corporation, where he immediately began calling the customer contacts he had developed and used while working at North Atlantic. North Atlantic sued for trade secret misappropriations and won. The customer contact list was held to be a trade secret belonging to North Atlantic because North Atlantic had taken appropriate steps to keep the information secret. *North Atlantic Instruments v. Haber,* **188 F3d 38 (2d Cir 1999).**

International Protection

To obtain patent, trademark, and trade secret protection in another country, you must comply with that country's requirements for obtaining protection. For these intellectual property rights, there are no international conventions that provide automatic protection for U.S. rights owners. However, the World Intellectual Property Organization has proposed a Patent Law Treaty which will, if adopted, simplify the filing of multi-country patent applications.

Some inventors file patent applications in other countries simultaneously with the U.S. filing. The Paris Convention and the Patent Cooperation Treaty allow an inventor who files a patent application in the U.S. to delay filing in member countries based on the earlier U.S. application date. The European Patent Convention offers a way to file a single patent application for a patent which will be valid in seventeen European countries. The European Community Trademark system provides a centralized procedure for obtaining trademark rights in European Community countries. The Madrid Protocol permits United States trademark owners to obtain trademark rights in a number of countries by filing a single application.

CHAPTER 3

OWNERSHIP OF COPYRIGHTS

This chapter covers the Copyright Act's ownership rules, and, in less detail, the ownership rules for patents, trademarks, and trade secrets. Ownership rules discussed here apply only in the United States. Other countries have their own rules of intellectual property ownership.

The intellectual property ownership rules discussed in this chapter are default rules that apply if the parties—employer and employee, employer and independent contractor, Web developer and client—do not reach their own agreement, in writing, on ownership.

Ownership issues that arise in specific types of relationships are covered in chapters 5, 6, 8, 12, and 13.

Introduction

You need to understand copyright's ownership rules if you acquire, use, or develop Web content. Here's why:

The types of material used for Web site content—music; graphics; text; and video, film, and television show clips—are protected by copyright, as are Web site designs and software. If you want to use copyrighted material belonging to a third party on your Web site, generally you need the permission of the copyright owner, as discussed in chapters 9 and 10. Only the permission of the true owner will protect you from an infringement suit. Getting permission from someone who mistakenly believes he or she is the copyright owner will not protect you.

EXAMPLE

Web Marketing Director saw some photographs she liked on Z Company's Web site. Director contacted Z Company's president and got permission to use the photographs on the Web site owned by Director's company. The photographs were created for Z Company by a freelance photographer. If the copyrights in the photographs are owned by the photographer (likely) and Z Company does not have the right to sublicense the use of the photographs, Z Company cannot authorize Director to use the photographs. Only the photographer can. Getting permission to use the photographs from Z Company will not protect Director if the photographer sues Director for copyright infringement.

If you create Web content or commission freelancers (graphic designers, writers, or photographers, for example) to create Web content, you should give careful consideration to the question who will own the copyright in that content. The exclusive rights of copyright discussed in chapter 1 belong to the copyright owner.

EXAMPLE

Web Entrepreneur commissioned Graphic Designer to create graphics for a Web site. If Web Entrepreneur owns the copyright in the graphics, then Entrepreneur has the exclusive right to reproduce and modify the graphics for use on another Web site. If Graphic Designer owns the copyright, Entrepreneur needs Graphic Designer's permission to reproduce and modify the graphics for use on another Web site.

If you are involved in Web site development, either as a developer or a client, you should give careful consideration to the question of who will own the copyright in Web site designs and program code, for the reason just discussed.

EXAMPLE

Web Developer created a Web site for Client. The Web site includes a shopping cart program. Whether Web Developer can use the shopping cart program in projects for other clients depends on who owns the copyright in the program.

Initial Ownership

Ownership of copyright initially belongs to the author or authors of the work. 17 USC § 201(a).

> **EXAMPLE**
>
> Sarah, a photographer, took a photograph of the Lincoln Memorial. Sarah is the author of the photograph and the initial owner of the copyright in the photograph.

The "author" is generally the individual who created the work, but there is an exception for "works made for hire." This exception is discussed in the next section.

The Work Made For Hire Rule

The "author" of a work made for hire is the employer or hiring party for whom the work was prepared. This default ownership rule is known as the work made for hire rule. Unless the parties have agreed otherwise in a signed written document, the employer or hiring party owns the copyright of a work made for hire. 17 USC § 201(b).

There are actually two branches to the work made for hire rule: one covering works made by employees, and one covering specially commissioned works. 17 USC § 101. We discuss these in this section.

Works Made by Employees

A work created by an employee within the scope of his or her employment is a work made for hire. The employer for whom the work is made is the author of the work for copyright purposes and is the owner of the work's copyright (unless the employee and employer have agreed otherwise).

> **EXAMPLE**
>
> As part of his job, John, an employee of Big Company's training division, created original interactive training materials on e-commerce for Big's marketing staff. Even though John created the training materials, Big is the author for copyright purposes. Big owns the copyright in the training materials (unless John and Big have agreed in a signed contract that John owns the copyright).

The work made for hire rule does not give employers ownership of works made by employees outside the scope of their employment.

EXAMPLE

Darryl, an engineer at Productions, Inc., does nature scene water-colors in his free time. The work made for hire rule does not apply to Darryl's watercolors. If Productions wants ownership of the copy-rights in the watercolors, it must get an assignment (discussed in "As-signments," later in this chapter) from Darryl.

Specially Commissioned Works

The second category of works made for hire is limited to nine types of specially ordered or commissioned works. These are works commissioned for use as:

- A contribution to a collective work.

- Part of a motion picture or other audiovisual work.

- A translation.

- A supplementary work.

- A compilation.

- An instructional text.

- A test or answer material for a test.

- An atlas.

- A sound recording.

For these types of works, if the hiring party and independent contractor creating the work agree in writing, before the contractor begins the project, to designate the work as a work made for hire, the work is a work made for hire. If the parties do not have an agreement to treat the independent contractor's work as a work made for hire, it's not a work made for hire.

EXAMPLE

Game Company hired Don, a software developer, to design the soft-ware for Game Company's new online game (an audiovisual work). Game Company and Don did not agree in writing to consider the software a work made for hire, so the software is not a work made for hire. Don owns the copyright in the software.

Even if the hiring party and independent contractor agree in writing to consider the independent contractor's work a work made for hire, the work is not a work made for hire unless it falls into one of the nine special categories listed in the first paragraph of this subsection.

EXAMPLE

31

ownership
of
copyrights

Sarah commissioned John, a freelance painter, to do an oil painting of Sarah's home. Although Sarah and John agreed in writing that the painting would be considered a work made for hire, the written agreement does not make the painting a work made for hire because the painting is not in one of the nine categories of works that can be specially commissioned works made for hire. If Sarah wants to own the copyright, she needs an assignment (discussed in "Assignments," later in this chapter) from John.

The rules governing ownership of copyrights in works created before January 1, 1978 (the effective date of the Copyright Act of 1976), were different from the rules described in this chapter. The 1909 Copyright Act did not distinguish between employees and independent contractors (works created by both independent contractors and employees were automatically owned by the employer or hiring party unless the parties agreed otherwise). In the case *Community for Creative Nonviolence v. Reid*, 490 US 730 (1989), the U.S. Supreme Court made it clear that the current Copyright Act does distinguish between employees and independent contractors.

The issue in *Reid* was who owned the copyright in a sculpture created by the artist Reid for the Community for Creative Nonviolence (CCNV). The court concluded that the work made for hire rule did not apply for two reasons: Reid was not an employee of CCNV, and the sculpture was not one of the types of works that could be designated a work made for hire by written agreement of the parties.

Foreign Copyright Law

The work made for hire rule discussed in this chapter and in other chapters of this book applies to copyrights in the United States. Other countries have different rules on copyright ownership. Although many countries have rules similar to the first branch of the Copyright Act's rule (works made by employees), the second branch (specially commissioned works) of the U.S. rule does not exist in most countries.

To obtain international copyright ownership for works that fall within the second branch of the Copyright Act's work made for hire rule, parties that commission works should obtain assignments of copyrights (see "Assignments," later in this chapter) from independent contractors. Ownership of independent contractors' works is discussed in "Copyright Ownership," chapter 6.

Joint Authorship and Ownership

According to the Copyright Act, the authors of a joint work jointly own the copyright in the work they create. 17 USC § 201(a). A joint work is defined in Section 101 of the Copyright Act as "a work prepared by two or more authors with the intention that their contributions be merged into inseparable or inter-dependent parts of a unitary whole."

EXAMPLE

Ann and Bruce worked together to create an e-commerce site, with Ann developing the software and user interface and Bruce develop-ing the content. The work is a joint work, and Ann and Bruce jointly own the copyright.

Of course, if Ann and Bruce worked as employees of an employer rather than as individuals, their employer would be the copyright owner, as discussed in "The Work Made for Hire Rule," earlier in this chapter.

You do not become the author of a joint work merely by contributing ideas or supervision to a work. You do so by contributing material that meets the standards for copyright protection (see "Standards," chapter 1).

EXAMPLE

Susan suggested that John write a book on how to beat the stock market, and John did so. Susan is not a joint author of John's book.

JOINT AUTHORSHIP OR NOT?

Corky Ballas, a competitive dancer, asked a music producer to create a compact disk of music appropriate for dance competitions. Ballas made suggestions about concepts and suggested songs for the record-ing. When Ballas and the producer parted company, Ballas claimed to be a joint author of the completed CD. The court held that the pro-ducer was the sole author, because Ballas had contributed only uncopyrightable ideas and concepts to the project. *Ballas v. Tedesco and Ballroom Blitz Music Inc.*, 41 FSupp2d 531 (DNJ 1999).

When the copyright in a work is jointly owned, according to U.S. law, each joint owner can use or license the work (authorize others to use it) with-out the consent of the other owner, provided that the use does not destroy the value of the work and the parties do not have an agreement requiring the con-sent of each owner for use or licensing. A joint owner who licenses a work must share any royalties he or she receives with the other owners.

Many foreign countries (Germany and France, for example) require that all joint owners consent to the grant of a license. Generally, joint ownership is not recommended because of the complications it adds to licensing worldwide rights. In addition, it is unclear what effect the filing of bankruptcy by one joint owner would have on co-owners.

Community Property

In nine states (Arizona, California, Idaho, Louisiana, Nevada, New Mexico, Texas, Washington, and Wisconsin), any property acquired during a marriage is jointly owned by the husband and wife. Whether a copyright in a work created by one spouse during marriage is community property is unclear. In *Marriage of Worth*, a California state court held that the copyrights in several books created by a man during his marriage were jointly owned by the man and his wife. 195 Ca3d 768 (1987). The court's reasoning—that the copyrights were community property because they were the result of one spouse's expenditure of time, effort, and skill during the marriage —could apply to patents, trademarks, and trade secrets as well. However, a federal court in Louisiana recently held that copyrights created by one spouse during a marriage are not community property because treating copyrights as community property would risk damaging the Copyright Act's goals of predictability and certainty as to copyright ownership and national uniformity. *Rodrigue v. Rodrigue*, 55 FSupp2d 534 (ED La 1999).

Assignments

A transfer of the ownership of a copyright is known as an assignment. When a copyright is assigned, the assignee (individual or company to whom it is assigned) becomes the owner of the exclusive rights of copyright in the protected work. (These rights are discussed in "The Exclusive Rights," chapter 1.)

EXAMPLE

Tom, an individual working on his own, created Web development tool software and then assigned the copyright in the software to Software Publisher. After the assignment, Software Publisher has the exclusive right to reproduce and publicly distribute the software. If Tom starts selling the software, he will be infringing the Software Publisher's rights as copyright owner.

The ownership of copyright may be transferred in whole or in part. 17 USC § 201(d). Examples of partial transfers are an assignment of the copyright for a term of ten years (time limitation) and an assignment limited to California (geographic limitation). In addition, the individual exclusive rights (reproduction, modification, and so forth) can be transferred.

Assignments are common in many industries—for example, music composers often assign copyrights in their compositions to music publishers.

An assignment is not valid unless it is in writing and is signed by the owner of the rights conveyed or the owner's authorized agent. 17 USC § 204(a).

IS AN EMAIL A SIGNED WRITING?

So far, only one court has ruled on the question of whether an email satisfies the Copyright Act's "signed writing" requirement. That court held that the email at issue in that case was not "signed." *Ballas v. Tedesco and Ballroom Blitz Music Inc.*, 41 FSupp2d 531 (DNJ 1999). Until this issue is clarified—either through amendment to the Copyright Act or through a general federal electronic records law—don't rely on emails to satisfy the "signed writing" requirement. (A federal electronic records law is likely to be passed by late 2000.)

An assignment can be recorded in the Copyright Office to give others "constructive notice" of the assignment. Constructive notice is a legal term that means you are presumed to know a fact (because it is a matter of public record) even if you have no actual knowledge of the fact. (Constructive notice is discussed in more detail in "Obtaining a License," chapter 10.)

Recording an assignment in the Copyright Office to give constructive notice protects the assignee from future conflicting transfers. An assignment that is recorded properly within one month after its signing prevails over a later assignment. If the assignment is signed outside the U.S., the assignee has two months to record it. 17 USC § 205(d). (The mechanics of recording are discussed in "Obtaining a License," chapter 10.)

EXAMPLE

Songwriter assigned the copyright in her song to Music Publishing Company in Boston on August 1, 1993. On August 15, 1993, Songwriter assigned the copyright in the same song to World Enterprises. So long as Music Publishing recorded its assignment properly in the Copyright Office by September 1, Music Publishing owns the copyright because its assignment prevails over Songwriter's later assignment to World Enterprises.

A properly recorded assignment even prevails over an earlier assignment that was not recorded if the later assignment meets two criteria:

■ The later assignment was taken in good faith and without notice of the earlier assignment.

■ The assignee paid money or something of value for the assignment or made a promise to pay royalties.

EXAMPLE

Author assigned the copyright in his novel to Publishing, Inc. on November 1, 1993. Publishing, Inc. did not record the assignment. On January 15, 1994, Author assigned the copyright in the same novel to Media, Inc. for $10,000. Media, Inc. recorded its assignment in the Copyright Office. So long as Media, Inc. acted in good faith and did not know or have reason to know about Author's 1993 assignment to Publishing, Inc., Media, Inc. owns the copyright. The assignment to Media, Inc. prevails over Author's earlier assignment to Publishing, Inc.

Licenses

A license is a copyright owner's grant of permission to use a copyrighted work in a way that would otherwise be copyright infringement. A copyright owner who grants a license is known as a licensor. A party receiving a license is known as a licensee.

Implied in every license is a promise by the licensor to refrain from suing the licensee for infringement based on activities within the scope of the license.

A copyright license can be exclusive or nonexclusive. An exclusive license is a license that cannot overlap another grant of rights.

EXAMPLE

Author granted Publisher the exclusive right to sell Author's novel in the United States. She granted Movie Developer the exclusive right to create and distribute a movie version of the novel. Both Publisher and Developer have exclusive licenses. There is no overlap between the two licenses.

Under copyright law, an exclusive license is considered a "transfer of copyright ownership." 17 USC § 101. An exclusive license, like an assignment, is not valid unless it is in writing and signed by the owner of the rights conveyed. A nonexclusive license is valid even if it is not in writing.

NO WRITING, NO CASE

During the Cannes Film Festival, New World Entertainment orally agreed to grant Television Espanola the exclusive right to broadcast the television show *Spiderman* in Spain. Written documents were to be prepared by Television Espanola later. When Television Espanola delivered the documents to New World for signing, New World refused to sign, because by then it had granted the broadcast rights for Spain to another party. Television Espanola sued New World for breach of contract. Television Espanola lost the case because oral exclusive copyright licenses are unenforceable. *Radio Television Espanola S.A. v. New World Entertainment, Ltd.,* 183 F3d 922 (9th Cir 1999).

An exclusive license, like an assignment, can be recorded in the Copyright Office to give constructive notice. Recording the exclusive license protects the license against unrecorded earlier transfers of copyright ownership and against later transfers. (See "Assignments," earlier in this chapter.)

Licensing is discussed in detail in chapter 10.

Termination Right

The author of a work other than a work made for hire has the right to terminate any license or assignment granted on or after January 1, 1978 during a five-year period that starts thirty-five years after the grant was made. If the grant involves the right to distribute the work to the public, the termination period begins thirty-five years after distribution begins or forty years after the grant was made, whichever is earlier. 17 USC § 203.

For works published before January 1, 1978, a different rule applies to pre-1978 licenses and assignments: The five-year termination period begins fifty-six years after the work was published. 17 USC § 304(c). For older works in their renewal term in 1998 for which the termination right had expired before 1998, there is an additional five-year termination period beginning at the end of seventy-five years from the date the copyright was originally secured. 17 USC § 304(d). Renewal of copyright, applicable only to pre-1978 works, is discussed in "Public Domain Works," chapter 9.

The termination right cannot be waived in advance. If the author dies before the termination period begins, the termination right can be exercised by the author's widow or widower, children, and grandchildren. If none of these people are alive at the time the termination right can be exercised, the right can be exercised by the author's executor, administrator, personal representative, or trustee.

Owning a Copy of a Work

Copyright law distinguishes the ownership of a copy of a protected work (a print of a photograph, a compact disc, a book, a diskette) from ownership of the intangible copyright rights. The transfer of a copy of a work does not transfer any rights in the copyright. Thus, purchasing a book (a copy of a literary work, in copyright terminology) does not give you permission to make copies of the book and sell those copies.

There are several exceptions to the principle that the transfer of a copy of a work does not transfer copyright rights. We'll discuss the most important ones in the rest of this section.

Displaying a Copy

The owner of a lawfully made copy of a work has the right to display the copy publicly, "either directly or by the projection of no more than one image at a time, to viewers present at the place where the copy is located." 17 USC § 109(c).

Making a Backup Copy

It is not infringement for the owner of a copy of a computer program to make another copy of the program if doing so is necessary to use the program or for archival purposes. 17 USC § 117(a).

Home Audiotaping

No infringement action may be brought against consumers for noncommercial use of digital or analog audio recording devices to make copies of records, tapes, or CDs. 17 USC § 1008.

"First Sale" Doctrine

The owner of a lawfully made copy of a work has the right to resell or otherwise dispose of possession of that copy. This exception to the distribution right is known as the "first sale doctrine." 17 USC § 109(a).

EXAMPLE

Don bought a copy of Publisher's new book on Web design. Don can resell his copy of the book. The first sale doctrine gives him that right.

Sale or License?

The first sale doctrine is only triggered by a sale of a copy of a work, not by a license. Software and database products, whether delivered online or in tangible form, are generally licensed rather than sold. Licenses allow software suppliers to tailor products to specific markets. A multiuser site license, for example, provides different use rights and carries a different price from a single-user license. Software and database suppliers also use licenses to obtain protection for factual information and prohibit reverse engineering. Whether such provisions are binding, given that copyright law does not protect facts and permits reverse engineering, is discussed in "When You Don't Need a License," chapter 9.

SALE OR LICENSE TRANSACTION?

Sometimes the documents used in a transaction use "sale" terminology and "license" terminology, making it unclear whether the transaction is a sale triggering the first sale doctrine or not. In *Adobe Systems Inc. v. One Stop Micro Inc.,* 84 FSupp2d 1086 (ND Cal 2000), Adobe sued a company that had acquired copies of "education versions" (stripped-down, less expensive versions) of Adobe products, removed the "education version" labels, and sold the products to consumers. The defendant claimed that it had a right to distribute the software because it had purchased the copies from educational resellers who had purchased the copies. The reseller agreement used the word "purchase." Other language in the reseller agreement indicated that Adobe was only granting licenses to educational resellers. The court found that the reseller agreement was a license, so the first sale doctrine was not triggered between Adobe and the educational resellers. The court held that the defendant infringed Adobe's copyrights by distributing the products without a license.

For mass-marketed software and databases delivered in tangible form (diskette or CD-ROM), licenses generally take the form of "shrink wrap" agreements contained on or in the product packaging. Some people maintain that shrink wrap agreements do not create binding contracts because they are "contracts of adhesion" (contracts based on "offers" that give the consumer no meaningful choice). They believe that the typical transaction wherein a consumer acquires a copy of mass-market software or database material is a sale, triggering the first sale doctrine.

Some courts agree with this analysis. The Court of Appeals for the Fifth Circuit held that an end-user software license prohibiting reverse engineering was a contract of adhesion. *Vault Corp. v. Quaid Software Ltd.*, 847 F2d 255 (5th Cir 1988). The Court of Appeals for the Third Circuit also held shrink wrap licenses invalid. *Step-Saver Data Systems, Inc. v. Wyse Technology*, 939 F2d 91 (3d Cir 1991). However, more recently, the Seventh Circuit Court of Appeals held that shrink wrap licenses are enforceable unless their terms are objectionable on grounds applicable to contracts in general. *ProCD, Inc. v. Zeidenberg*, 86 F3d 1447 (7th Cir 1996). The court noted that even though the consumer in this case could not review the license terms before concluding the transaction, ProCD's license gave the consumer the right to reject the product if the consumer found the license terms unsatisfactory. Other aspects of the *ProCD* case are discussed in "When You Don't Need a License," chapter 9.

Patents, Trademarks, and Trade Secrets

Patent law does not have a work made for hire rule. Patentable inventions created by employees within the scope of their employment are owned by the employee. However, the employee may have a legal obligation to transfer ownership to the employer under the patent law's "hired to invent" doctrine. This doctrine provides that when an employee is hired to perform research or solve a specific problem, the employer is entitled to get an assignment of a patent received by the employee on the results of the research.

Generally, as a condition of employment, employers require employees to agree to assign their interests in patentable inventions to the employer. The Patent Act implicitly recognizes the validity of such agreements, providing that a patent may be granted to the assignee of the inventor. The Employee Nondisclosure and Assignment Agreement in appendix B (Form 6) includes an assignment clause.

A trademark is owned by the first party to use it in connection with goods or services or the first to apply to federally register it. A trademark can be owned by an individual, company, or any other legal entity. Acquisition of trademark rights is discussed extensively in chapter 16.

An employer or hiring party generally owns trade secrets developed by employees and by independent contractors who are hired to invent.

Ownership of patents, trade secrets, and trademarks, like the ownership of copyrights, can be assigned. As with copyrights, owners of these types of intellectual property frequently grant licenses authorizing others to do things that would otherwise violate the owner's exclusive rights.

CHAPTER 4

CONTRACTS LAW

The purpose of this building block chapter is to provide an overview of the basic principles of contracts law.

In later chapters, we discuss special types of contracts: Web development agreements are discussed in chapter 8, contracts with employees in chapter 5, contracts with independent contractors in chapter 6, licenses in chapter 10 and 21, and contracts for the distribution of Web products in chapter 13. The special legal rules that apply to contracts for the sale of goods are discussed in chapter 18.

What Is a Contract?

A contract is a legally enforceable agreement between two or more parties. The core of most contracts is a set of mutual promises called "consideration." The promises made by the parties define the rights and obligations of the parties.

Contracts are enforceable in the courts. If one party meets its contractual obligations and the other party doesn't ("breaches the contract"), the nonbreaching party is entitled to receive relief through the courts.

EXAMPLE

Web Developer promised to pay Graphic Designer $5,000 for creating certain graphics for Developer's Web site design project. Graphic Designer created the materials and delivered them to Developer, as required in the contract. Developer admits that the materials meet the contract specifications. If Developer does not pay Graphic

Designer, Graphic Designer can go to court and get a judgment against Developer for breach of contract.

Generally, the nonbreaching party's remedy for breach of contract is money damages that will put the nonbreaching party in the position it would have enjoyed if the contract had been performed. Under special circumstances, a court will order the breaching party to perform its contractual obligations.

Because contracts are enforceable, parties who enter into contracts can rely on contracts in structuring their business relationships.

EXAMPLE

Web Marketer entered into a contract with Composer, promising to pay Composer $4,000 for composing a short jingle for use on Marketer's Web site. Shortly after Composer started work on the piece for Marketer—before Marketer paid Composer any money—Composer got an offer from a movie studio to compose all the music for a movie. Composer accepted the movie studio's offer and abandoned Marketer's project. Marketer had to pay another composer $6,000 to do the work that Composer had contracted to do. Marketer can sue Composer and obtain a judgment against Composer for $2,000 (the amount that will result in Marketer's obtaining the music for a net cost of $4,000, the contract price).

In this country and most others, businesses have significant flexibility in setting the terms of their contracts. Contracts are, in a sense, private law created by the agreement of the parties. The rights and obligations of the parties are determined by the contract's terms, subject to limits imposed by relevant statutes.

EXAMPLE

Web Marketer promised to pay Composer $5,000 to create music for Marketer's Web site. Composer created the music and delivered it to Marketer, as required in the contract. Marketer did not pay Composer, so Composer sued Marketer for breach of contract. Marketer's defense was "Composer did what she promised to do, but I never should have agreed to pay her $5,000 for that work. Two thousand dollars is a fair price." The court will enforce Marketer's promise to pay Composer $5,000.

Written Contracts

A deal done on a handshake—"You do X for me, and I'll pay you Y"—is a contract, because it is a legally enforceable agreement involving an exchange of promises. Most contracts are enforceable whether they are oral or written. Nonetheless, you should always have written contracts for all your business relationships.

There are several reasons why written contracts are better than oral contracts:

- The process of writing down the contract's terms and signing the contract forces both parties to think about—and be precise about—the obligations they are undertaking. With an oral contract, it is too easy for both parties to say "yes" and then have second thoughts.

- When the terms of a contract are written down, the parties are likely to create a more complete and thorough agreement than they would by oral agreement. A hastily made oral agreement is likely to have gaps that will have to be resolved later—when the relationship may have deteriorated.

- With an oral contact, the parties may have different recollections of what they agreed on (just as two witnesses to a car accident will disagree over what happened). A written agreement eliminates disputes over who promised what.

- Some types of contracts must be in writing to be enforced. The Copyright Act requires a copyright assignment or exclusive license to be in writing. (See "Assignments" and "Licenses," chapter 3.) State law requirements vary from state to state, but in most states, a contract for the sale of goods for $500 or more must be in writing. (See "Important Provisions of Article Two," chapter 18.)

- If you have to go to court to enforce a contract or get damages, a written contract will mean less dispute about the contract's terms.

Who Can Enter Into a Contract?

Minors and the mentally incompetent lack the legal capacity to enter into contracts. All others are generally assumed to have full power to bind themselves by entering into contracts. In most states, the legal age for entering into contracts is eighteen. The test for mental capacity is whether the party understood the nature and consequences of the transaction in question.

Corporations have the power to enter into contracts. They make contracts through the acts of their agents, officers, and employees. Whether a particular employee has the power to bind the corporation to a contract is determined by an area of law called agency law or corporate law. If you doubt whether an individual with whom you are dealing has authority to enter into a contract with you, insist that the contract be reviewed and signed by the corporation's president.

A corporation has a separate legal existence from its founders, officers, and employees. Generally, the individuals associated with a corporation are not themselves responsible for the corporation's debts or liabilities, including liability for breach of contract.

EXAMPLE

Lisa, a Web developer, entered into a Web development agreement with Start-Up Company. Lisa fulfilled her duties under the agreement, but Start-Up doesn't have the money to pay her. Start-Up's president has plenty of money, and Lisa would like to collect the money from him. She can't, unless the president personally guaranteed Start-Up's obligations.

Offer and Acceptance

A contract is formed when one party (the "offeror") makes an offer that is accepted by the other party (the "offeree"). An offer—a proposal to form a contract—can be as simple as the words, "I'll wash your car for you for $5." An acceptance—the offeree's assent to the terms of the offer—can be as simple as, "You've got a deal." Sometimes acceptance can be shown by conduct rather than by words.

When an offer has been made, no contract is formed until the offeree accepts the offer. When you make an offer, never assume that the offeree will accept the offer. Contractual liability is based on consent.

EXAMPLE

John offered to pay Photographer $500 to use Photographer's photo in John's e-commerce Web site. Photographer said, "Let me think about it." John, assuming that Photographer would accept the offer, used the photo. Photographer then rejected John's offer. Unless fair use applies, John has infringed Photographer's reproduction and public display rights by using the photograph. John should not have assumed that he would be granted a license (a form of contract) by Photographer.

WHEN IS AN ACCEPTANCE EFFECTIVE?

According to the "Mailbox Rule," an acceptance that is mailed is effective when it is deposited in the mail. When is an emailed acceptance effective—when the sender pushes the "send" button, when the email message is available for the recipient to open, or when the recipient opens it? Good question, there is no answer yet.

When you are an offeree, do not assume that an offer will remain open indefinitely. In general, an offeror is free to revoke the offer at any time before acceptance by the offeree. Once the offeror terminates the offer, the offeree no longer has the legal power to accept the offer and form a contract.

EXAMPLE

Animator offered his services to Developer, who said, "I'll get back to you." Developer then contracted with Client to quickly produce a Web-based product involving animation (making the assumption that Animator was still available to do the animation work). Before Developer could tell Animator that he accepted Animator's offer, Animator sent Developer an email that said, "Leaving for Mexico. I'll call when I get back." Developer and Animator did not have a contract. Developer should not have assumed, in entering into the contract with Client, that Animator was still available.

When you are the offeree, do not start contract performance before notifying the offeror of your acceptance. Prior to your acceptance, there is no contract. An offer can be accepted by starting performance if the offer itself invites such acceptance, but this type of offer is rare.

EXAMPLE

Big Company offered to pay Web Developer $20,000 to create an e-commerce Web site for Big Company. Before Developer's president notified Big that Developer accepted the offer, Big sent Developer an email that said, "We've changed our minds. Due to budget cuts at Big Company, we're canceling the project." In the meantime, Developer's staff had begun preliminary work on the project. Developer and Big did not have a contract, so Developer has no legal recourse against Big for loss of the deal or for the costs of the preliminary work.

Until an offer is accepted, the offeror is free—unless it has promised to hold the offer open—to revoke the offer.

EXAMPLE

On June 1, Big Company offered to hire Developer to create an inter-active training work for Big. On June 4 (before acceptance by Developer), Big notified Developer that it was giving the contract to Developer's competitor. Big terminated the offer to Developer. Developer has no legal recourse against Big Company.

If you need time to make up your mind before accepting an offer, get the offeror to give you a written promise to hold the offer open for a few days. That will give you time to decide whether to accept.

Don't reject an offer and then try to accept it. Once an offeree rejects an offer, the offer dies and the offeree's legal power to accept the offer and form a contract terminates.

EXAMPLE

Publisher offered to buy the e-book rights to Author's book for $10,000. Author, hoping for a better offer, said no. Then Author realized that Publisher's offer was the best Author could do. Author called Publisher and said, "I accept your offer." Because the offer was no longer open, Author cannot form a contract by trying to accept the offer.

Except for the simplest deals, it generally takes more than one round of negotiations to form a contract. Often, the offeree responds to the initial offer with a counteroffer. A counteroffer is an offer made by an offeree on the same subject matter as the original offer, but proposing a different bargain than the original offer. A counteroffer, like an outright rejection, terminates the offeree's legal power of acceptance.

EXAMPLE

Publisher offered to buy all electronic rights in Author's book for $10,000. Author responded by saying, "I'll give you an exclusive right to distribute the book online for the next three years for that price." Author's response to the offer was a counteroffer. Author no longer has the legal power to form a contract based on Publisher's offer to purchase the electronic rights in the work.

Forming Contracts Online

There are a number of ways in which contracts are formed online:

- By exchange of emails.

- By merchant acceptance of orders entered on e-commerce Web sites.

- Through online conduct, such as clicking on an "I accept the terms" button.

- Through Electronic Data Interchange (EDI), electronic exchange of purchase orders, and other standardized business documents between computers in a computer-processable format.

As we noted earlier in this chapter, in "Written Contracts," certain contracts must be in writing to be valid. Over half the states have passed laws making electronic records the equal of "hard copy" written records (and a federal law is being considered by Congress). Unfortunately, these laws take three different approaches:

- **The "automatic equivalence" approach** (electronic records are the equivalent of hard copy records).

- **The "by agreement" approach** (electronic records are the equivalent to hard copy records if the parties to the transaction have so agreed).

- **The "digital signature" approach** (electronic records are the equivalent to hard copy records if they are signed with digital signatures using special encryption technology).

Consideration

Consideration, in legal terminology, is what one party to a contract will get from the other party in return for performing contract obligations.

EXAMPLE

Web Developer promised to pay Artist $500 if Artist would let Developer use one of Artist's drawings in Developer's new project. The consideration for Developer's promise to pay Artist $500 is Artist's promise to let Developer use the drawing. The consideration for Artist's promise to let Developer use the drawing is Developer's promise to pay Artist $500.

According to traditional legal doctrine, if one party makes a promise and the other party offers nothing in exchange for that promise, the promise is unenforceable. Such a promise is known as a "gratuitous promise." Gratuitous promises are said to be "unenforceable for lack of consideration."

EXAMPLE

John told Sam, "When I buy a new car, I'll give you my truck." John bought a new car but did not give Sam the truck. According to traditional legal doctrine, John's promise to give Sam the truck is an unenforceable gratuitous promise. Sam gave nothing to John in exchange for John's promise to give Sam the truck.

In some states, a gratuitous promise can be enforced if the party to whom the promise was made relied on the promise. Other states no longer require consideration for certain types of promises.

Lack of consideration is rarely a problem for promises made in the context of business relationships. In most business contracts, there is consideration for both parties ("mutual consideration," in legal terminology).

The lack of consideration problem can arise in the context of amendments to contracts, however. Also, in some states, a promise to hold an offer open (see "Offer and Acceptance," earlier in this chapter) is unenforceable unless the offeree gives the offeror consideration (pays the offeror money) to keep the offer open.

A special application of the problem of lack of consideration in contracts with employees is discussed in "Using the Employment Agreement," chapter 5.

Typical Contract Provisions

Many contracts include special types of provisions. We'll discuss these common types of provisions in the next subsections.

Duties and Obligations

The duties and obligations section of a contract is a detailed description of the duties and obligations of the parties and the deadlines for performance. If one party's obligation is to create a Web site design or online product or software or content for a Web site design or online product, detailed specifications should be stated.

Warranties and Indemnities

A warranty is a legal promise that certain facts are true. Typical warranties in contracts concern such matters as ownership of the contract's subject matter (for example, copyrights) and the right to sell or assign the subject matter. In Web development agreements and content licenses, warranties of ownership of intellectual property rights and noninfringement of third parties' intellectual property rights are common. For contracts involving the sale of goods, certain warranties are implied under state law unless specifically disclaimed by the parties (see "Important Provisions of Article Two," chapter 18). A warranty provision is usually accompanied by an indemnity in which the warranting party promises that if the warranty is breached, the warranting party will pay the other party's costs arising from the breach.

Termination Clauses

These clauses ensure that either or both parties have the right to terminate the contract under certain circumstances. Generally, termination clauses describe breach of contract events that trigger the right to terminate the contract (for example, nonpayment of royalties). Termination clauses also describe the methods of giving notice of exercise of the termination right, and whether the breaching party must be given an opportunity to cure the breach before the other party can terminate the contract.

Remedy Clauses

These clauses state what rights the nonbreaching party has if the other party breaches the contract. In contracts for the sale of goods, remedy clauses are usually designed to limit the seller's liability for damages (see "Important Provisions of Article Two," chapter 18).

Arbitration Clauses

An arbitration clause states that disputes arising under the contract must be settled through arbitration rather than through court litigation. Such clauses generally include the name of the organization that will conduct the arbitration (the American Arbitration Association, for example), the city in which the arbitration will be held, and the method for selecting arbitrators. Arbitration is discussed in "Arbitration," appendix A.

Merger Clauses

Merger clauses state that the written document contains the entire understanding of the parties. The purpose of merger clauses is to ensure that evidence outside the written document will not be admissible in court to contradict or supplement the terms of the written agreement. In complex contracts, the parties often go through several rounds of negotiations before they reach their final agreement. When a contract contains a merger clause, the final outcome of all previous discussions and drafts is considered to be "merged" into the written document.

EXAMPLE

Sam created a Web site design for Harry pursuant to a written development agreement containing a merger clause. When Harry received the beta version of the Web site design, he was unhappy because the design did not include a feature for accepting email inquiries from site users. Nothing in the development agreement or specifications mentions this feature, but Harry claims that he and Sam discussed such a feature. Because the agreement has a merger clause, contracts law provides that the written document contains the entire under-standing of the parties. Even if Sam and Harry did discuss the additional feature, evidence of that discussion would not be admissible in court. Sam does not have to add the feature.

Tips for Contracts

The contract formation process varies widely, from contracts formed quickly in face-to-face meetings to contracts formed after teams of attorneys have spent months in negotiations. Here are some general tips for all types of contracts:

■ **Write it down.** All contracts should take the form of a written document signed by both parties. You do not have to hire an attorney to create a written contract. If you reach an agreement over the phone or in a meeting, write the agreement as soon as possible and have the other party sign the written memorandum. If you are making a written offer, you may want to make your offer in the form of a letter, with a space at the end for the offeree to indicate acceptance by signing.

■ **Make sure you are comfortable with your obligations.** If a term—for example, a deadline—makes you uneasy, make a counteroffer that substitutes a term with which you are more comfortable. Do not assume that the other party will excuse you from strict compliance and do not rely on the other party's oral assurances that it will not insist on strict compliance.

■ **Remember Murphy's Law.** Before you sign a contract, consider what could go wrong or what could make performance of your obligations difficult or expensive. If the actual performance is more difficult or expensive than you anticipated, that is not a valid excuse for not performing. Enter into a contract only if you believe that you can meet your obligations.

■ **Don't leave anything out.** Accurately cover all aspects of your understanding with the other party. If the other party wrote the agreement based on an oral understanding reached earlier, make certain that the written terms match the terms of your oral agreement. Don't leave points out of the written document, even if the other party says, "We don't need to put that in writing."

■ **Cover all options.** Cover all options, consequences, and possibilities. You should not fail to address an issue because it is sensitive. Deal with sensitive issues during negotiations. Make sure that your contract includes a merger clause (see "Typical Contracts Provisions," earlier in this chapter) to avoid disputes about whether proposals made during negotiations but not included in the final written agreement are part of your contract.

- **Don't use unclear language or try to sound like a lawyer.** If you don't understand exactly what the other party is expecting you to do, don't try to camouflage the lack of understanding by using vague language. Vague language leads to misunderstandings, disputes, and lawsuits. Use simple language that accurately expresses your agreement with the other party. Don't try to sound like a lawyer, and don't complicate things unnecessarily.

- **Define any ambiguous terms.** There's a classic contracts case in which one party contracted to sell chickens to the other party. The seller thought "chicken" meant chicken of any age, including old and tough chickens. The buyer assumed "chicken" meant tender young chickens suitable for frying. The seller shipped old chickens, and the buyer screamed "breach." To avoid such misunderstandings, define any terms that may be ambiguous.

- **Be careful using "terms of art."** Terms of art are words with specific meaning in the law. "Assignment," for example, has a number of meanings in the English language. In intellectual property law, assignment means a transfer of ownership of intellectual property (see "Assignments," chapter 3). Use assignment in your contracts when you mean transfer of ownership of intellectual property. Don't use the word in its other meanings or you will create confusion. A number of terms of art are defined throughout this book.

- **Use terms consistently.** When you write contracts, you are creating your own law. Legal writing is not creative writing. Don't use "royalty" in one paragraph, "license fee" in a second paragraph, and "use fee" in a third paragraph. Pick one term and stay with it throughout the contract.

Battle of the Forms

In the business world, contracts are often created based on an exchange of forms. The offeror sends a proposal to the offeree, and the offeree accepts by sending back a purchase order form. While the purchase order normally contains a number of terms that match the proposal's terms (price and delivery date, for example), it will generally include additional or contradictory terms as well.

The legal rules for determining what terms are included in a contract created this way are complex (attorneys call the process the "battle of the forms").

These rules are discussed in "Important Provisions of Article Two," chapter 18. To avoid the battle of the forms, don't create a contract with a client by exchanging documents containing inconsistent terms. Make every effort to get the client to sign your proposal or negotiate a separate contract. If the client must use a purchase order, read it carefully, including its fine print, as soon as you receive it. If the purchase order form contains terms that are unacceptable to you, notify the client of your objection as soon as possible.

CHAPTER 5

EMPLOYEES

If you have employees, you should take proper steps to ensure that you own your employees' contributions to your Web sites or Web products. This chapter focuses on practical applications of the Copyright Act's work made for hire rule, on the limitations of the rule, and on strategies for overcoming those limitations.

Monitoring employee email is discussed in chapter 23. Union issues are addressed in chapter 22. Other employment issues—for example, employment law and labor law issues—are beyond the scope of this book.

Works Made by Employees

According to the Copyright Act's work made for hire rule, an employer is the "author" and copyright owner of a work made for hire unless the parties agree otherwise. A work made for hire is a work created by an employee within the scope of his or her employment. Certain types of specially commissioned works can also be works made for hire, as discussed in "The Work Made for Hire Rule," chapter 3, and in "Copyright Ownership," chapter 6.

The work made for hire rule reverses the Copyright Act's general rule on copyright ownership, which states that the individual who creates a work owns the copyright in that work. This rule is discussed in "Initial Ownership," chapter 3.

The Copyright Act's general ownership rule and the work made for hire rule apply only in the United States. Other countries have their own copyright ownership rules. Most have something similar to the "employee branch" of the Copyright Act's work made for hire rule.

The work made for hire rule applies only to works created by employees within the scope of their employment. It does not apply to works created by employees on their own, nor does it apply to works created by independent contractors for hiring parties. (See "The Work Made for Hire Rule," chapter 3.)

Who Is an Employee?

The Copyright Act does not define the term "employee." The Supreme Court has held that thirteen factors must be considered to determine whether a worker is an employee or an independent contractor. No one factor is determinative. The factors are:

- Whether the hiring party had a right to control the manner and means by which the product is accomplished.

- The level of skill required.

- Whether the instruments and tools used were provided by the hiring party or the hired party.

- Whether the hired party worked at his or her place of business or the hiring party's place of business.

- The duration of the relationship between the two parties.

- Whether the hiring party had the right to assign additional projects to the hired party.

- The extent of the hired party's discretion over when and how long to work.

- The method of payment.

- Whether the hired party had a role in hiring and paying assistants.

- Whether the work was part of the regular business of the hiring party.

- Whether the hiring party was in business at all.

- Whether employee benefits were provided by the hiring party for the hired party.

- How the hiring party treated the hired party for tax purposes.

These factors are from the *Community for Creative Nonviolence* case discussed in "The Work Made for Hire Rule," chapter 3.

Whether your employee creates a tiny amount of content or code for your project or handles the entire project, as the employer, you own the copyright in the employee's work so long as the employee's work is done within the scope of employment. An employee—although the actual human author—is not considered the author of a work made for hire for copyright purposes. Of course, you and your employee can agree that the employee will own the copyright, as discussed in "Giving Ownership to an Employee," later in this chapter.

EXAMPLE

Writer, employed by Developer to write text for online training products, wrote all the text for Developer's new product, *Hiring Smart*, during work during normal working hours as part of Writer's job. The text is a work made for hire. The copyright law considers Developer the author of Writer's text. Unless Writer and Developer have agreed otherwise, Developer owns the copyright in the text.

Because you, the employer, are deemed the author and copyright owner of works made for hire, you can use works made for hire without obtaining permission from the employees who created them. Any employee who exercises the copyright owner's exclusive rights in a work made for hire infringes the employer's copyright.

EXAMPLE

Writer in the previous example quit working for Developer and formed his own company. Writer has informed Developer that Developer no longer has Writer's permission to use the text created by Writer. In his first project for the new company, Writer uses a modified version of the text Writer had written for *Hiring Smart*. Because Developer owns the copyright in the text, Developer does not need Writer's permission to continue to use the text. Writer's modification and use of the text in Writer's own project infringes Developer's copyright.

The work made for hire rule applies whether the employer is an individual, partnership, or corporation. For corporate employers, the rule applies to works created by officers and managers as well as to works created by rank and file employees.

EXAMPLE

John, the cofounder and president of ABC Multimedia Company, a California corporation, created the retail kiosk work, *Wine Finder*, within the scope of his employment with ABC. The copyright in *Wine Finder* belongs to ABC Multimedia, not to John. Although John may think of ABC as his company, the corporation is a separate legal entity. If John has a falling out with his cofounder and leaves ABC, ownership of the copyright in *Wine Finder* remains with ABC.

Using the Employment Agreement

Don't rely solely on the Copyright Act's work made for hire rule as a means of obtaining ownership of works made by your employees. Supplement the work made for hire rule by getting all employees to sign an "Employee Nondisclosure and Assignment Agreement" (Form 6 in appendix B). In the rest of this chapter, we'll refer to this agreement as the Employment Agreement.

The Employment Agreement protects you against employee claims that works were created outside the scope of an employee's employment. It gives the employer an assignment of intellectual property rights in:

- Works conceived or developed during the period of the employment.

- Works that relate at the time of conception or development to the employer's business or research.

- Works that were developed on the employer's time or with the use of its equipment, supplies, facilities, or trade secret information.

- Works that resulted from work performed for the employer.

Limitations on the Work Made for Hire Rule

There are four limitations on the work made for hire rule that make it prudent for you to use the Employment Agreement with all employees as a backup to the work made for hire rule.

International Ownership

In other countries, ownership of employee-made works will be determined by applying local law rather than U.S. law. Although many countries have rules similar to the work made for hire rule, some do not. The assignment provision of the Employment Agreement (see Article 3 of Form 6 in appendix B) is designed to give you ownership rights in employee-made works that will be recognized throughout the world.

Works Outside the Scope of Employment

The rule does not give employers ownership of works created by employees outside the scope of their employment. In start-up companies and new industries, job descriptions are sometimes vague or nonexistent, and employees frequently wear many hats or take on responsibilities beyond those contemplated at hiring time. These factors could provide a basis for an employee's claim that you, the employer, do not own the copyright in a particular work because the work was created outside the scope of the employee's employment.

EXAMPLE

Start-Up Company hired Sue to do graphic design work. In her free time, Sue began to assist the company's in-house Web designer, eventually taking over many of the Web designer's duties. Web design work done by Sue could be deemed outside the scope of Sue's employment. That would mean that Sue—not Start-Up—owns the copyrights in Sue's Web design work.

Employee or Independent Contractor?

The rule applies only to works created by employees, not to works created by independent contractors. It is sometimes difficult to tell, using the factors discussed in "Who is an Employee?," earlier in this chapter, whether a worker is an employee or an independent contractor.

EXAMPLE

Media Company hired Mark, an animator, to do the animation work for Media's new computer game. Three factors in Mark's relationship with Media indicate that Mark is an independent contractor: Mark worked at home, Media had no right to assign him more work, and Media did not give him employee benefits. However, three factors indicate that Mark is an employee of Media: Media provided the tools for the job, Media provided detailed instructions for the work, and Media required Mark to be available for meetings from 9 a.m. to 6 p.m., Monday through Friday. In this situation, it is difficult to tell whether Mark is an independent contractor or Media's employee.

Should one of your employees someday maintain that he or she worked for you as an independent contractor rather than as an employee, and that therefore you can't rely on the work made for hire rule for ownership of copyrights in works he or she created, you can say, "It doesn't matter whether you were an employee or an independent contractor. You assigned me those copyrights when you signed the Employment Agreement."

Patents, Trademarks, and Trade Secrets

The work made for hire rule does not apply to patents, trademarks, trade secrets, or other forms of intellectual property. The assignment provision of the Employment Agreement (Article 3 of Form 6, appendix B) gives you, the employer, ownership of these other forms of intellectual property. That means you don't have to worry about these other laws' ownership rules for works created by your employees.

Provisions of the Employment Agreement

The Employment Agreement contains two important provisions:

The Confidentiality Provision

The confidentiality provision of the Employment Agreement (Article 2 of Form 6) is a necessary part of your trade secrets protection program. (See "Trade Secret Protection," chapter 26.) "Confidential information" is defined as any information not generally known in the relevant trade or industry that is either obtained from the employer, or learned or developed by the employee in the scope of his or her employment.

The Assignment Provision

The assignment provision of the Employment Agreement (Article 3 in Form 6) is broad enough to give you ownership of trade secrets, trademarks, and patent rights arising out of an employee's work for you. The "power of attorney" aspect of the Agreement (Section 7.2) gives you the authority to execute and file copyright assignment documents on behalf of the employee to secure and record your ownership rights in intellectual property created by the employee. The power of attorney does not give you authority to act for the employee in other ways.

If you are located in California, you should be aware of Section 2870 of the California Labor Code. It states that any employment agreement provision that requires an employee to assign to the employer any inventions the employee developed entirely on his or her own time without using the employer's equipment, supplies, facilities, or trade secret information is unenforceable and against public policy. The statute makes an exception for inventions that relate to the employer's business, research, or development, or that result from work performed by the employee for the employer. The Employment Agreement's assignment provision does not give you ownership of inventions that are non-assignable under Section 2870. (See the "Limited Exclusion Notification" at the end of Form 6.)

List of Employee Inventions

The Employment Agreement does not give you ownership of intellectual property already owned by an employee when he or she started work for you (see Section 3.2(b) in Form 6). If the employee owns copyrights or other intellectual property at the time the employment begins, it should be listed in Exhibit A to the agreement, "Prior Work Products." If you want to use listed inventions, you will have to negotiate with the employee for a separate license or an assignment (see "Assignments" and "Licenses," chapter 3, and "Obtaining Licenses," chapter 10).

When Employees Should Sign

Each employee should sign a copy of the Employment Agreement before he or she begins work or on the first day of work. That way, the job will be the consideration that you give the employee in exchange for the employee's signing the Employment Agreement. An Employment Agreement that is signed later may be unenforceable for lack of consideration, although in some states, continued employment may count as consideration for "at will" employees (those without employment contracts). Consideration and the problem of lack of consideration are discussed in "Consideration," chapter 4.

Delayed Signing

Getting an Employment Agreement signed by an employee after the employee has started work is better than not getting the agreement signed at all. It is a good idea to offer some consideration—money or a promotion—to a late signer in order to avoid a "lack of consideration" defense (see "Consideration," chapter 4). The Employment Agreement, in that case, should state what consideration you gave the employee in exchange for the employee's signing the agreement.

If you are concerned that the work done by a former employee was not covered by the work made for hire rule because it might have been done outside the scope of employment, or because the individual could have been an independent contractor rather than an employee, consider asking the individual for an assignment. (See Forms 9 and 10 in appendix B.) If he or she agrees to execute an assignment, provide some consideration for the assignment. Asking for an assignment, of course, will alert the individual to the fact that you think there may be some defect in your title to the work. The former employee may refuse to give you the assignment.

Independent Contractors

Do not use the Employment Agreement with individuals who work as independent contractors. Instead, use the Content Development and Tranfer Agreement (Form 7 in appendix B) or the Independent Contractor Agreement (Form 14 in appendix B), discussed in "Copyright Ownership," chapter 6.

Determining whether an individual is an employee or an independent contractor can be complex (see "Who is an Employee?," earlier in this chapter). You should consider consulting an experienced attorney in close cases. As a practical matter, it will probably be difficult for you to convince a court that an individual whom you did not treat as an employee for tax or employment-benefit purposes should be treated as an employee for copyright ownership purposes.

Giving Ownership to an Employee

If you want to give a key employee ownership of a work created within the scope of employment, it is easy to do so. You and the employee simply have to sign a written agreement stating that the employee owns all copyright rights in the work. An oral agreement is not sufficient to give an employee ownership of works made for hire.

If you sign an agreement giving copyright ownership in a work to an employee, you as the employer will still be considered the author of the work for copyright purposes, but the employee will be the copyright owner. If you give an employee copyright ownership, you should consider having the employee grant you an irrevocable, nonexclusive, royalty-free, worldwide license to use the work and to modify it for use in future projects and different media. License provisions are discussed in "Obtaining Licenses," chapter 10.

Joint Ownership

An employee is not a joint owner of a work made for hire unless the employer assigns an ownership interest to the employee. An employee's contributions to a work made for hire do not make the employee a joint author or a joint copyright owner.

EXAMPLE

Dan hired Janet to help develop a Web site, *Restaurant Guide.* Janet helped Dan with all aspects of the development of the Web site. If Janet is Dan's employee and Janet's contributions to *Restaurant Guide* are made within the scope of Janet's employment, Dan, as the employer, owns the entire copyright in *Restaurant Guide.*

Rights of Former Employers

Respect the intellectual property rights of your employees' former employers. If one of your employees created a copyrighted work within the scope of employment with a former employer, the former employer owns the copyright (unless the employee and former employer agreed otherwise). Trade secrets developed for a former employer are also normally the property of the former employer. Avoiding trade secret infringement in hiring is discussed in "Trade Secrets," chapter 2.

While employees are free to reuse generally known ideas that they used for a former employer and to draw on their general knowledge and job skills, do not permit your employees to use copyrighted material or trade secrets belonging to former employers without getting licenses.

CHAPTER 6

CONTRACTORS AND CONSULTANTS

Most freelancers and consultants are considered independent contractors for copyright law purposes. According to copyright law, when an independent contractor creates a work for a hiring party, the copyright is owned by the independent contractor unless the hiring party takes steps to secure ownership.

This chapter deals with legal issues arising out of the use of independent contractors, including the steps that you should take to get ownership of copyrights in works created by independent contractors such as graphic artists, writers, content specialists, and software designers.

Who Is an Independent Contractor?

The Copyright Act does not define "independent contractor" or "employee." Instead, according to the Supreme Court, whether a worker is an employee or an independent contractor must be determined by weighing thirteen factors. (These are the same thirteen factors listed in "Who is an Employee?," chapter 5.)

No one factor is determinative. The factors are as follows:

- Whether the hiring party had a right to control the manner and means by which the product is accomplished.

- The level of skill required.

- Whether the instruments and tools used were provided by the hiring party or the hired party.

- Whether the hired party worked at his or her place of business or at the hiring party's place of business.

- The duration of the relationship between the two parties.

- Whether the hiring party had the right to assign additional projects to the hired party.

- The extent of the hired party's discretion over when and how long to work.

- The method of payment.

- Whether the hired party had a role in hiring and paying assistants.

- Whether the work was part of the regular business of the hiring party.

- Whether the hiring party was in business at all.

- Whether employee benefits were provided by the hiring party for the hired party.

- How the hiring party treated the hired party for tax purposes.

Much Web development and content creation work is done by freelance professionals who work on a project basis. A worker who is hired on a project basis—whether for a lump-sum fee or at an hourly rate—is probably an independent contractor rather than an employee, especially if the worker provides his or her own workplace and tools, and works without day-to-day supervision. Partnerships and corporations can also be hired on an independent contractor basis.

Unless you have good reason to believe (based on the thirteen-factor test) that a particular worker hired on a project basis is an employee, you should assume that such a worker is an independent contractor. As a practical matter, it will probably be difficult for you to convince a court that an individual whom you did not treat as an employee for tax or employment-benefit purposes should be treated as an employee for copyright ownership purposes.

Copyright Ownership

When a hiring party and an independent contractor fail to address the issue of ownership of copyrights in works created by the independent contractor, the copyrights are owned by the independent contractor. This "default rule" is the opposite of the default rule for works created by employees (discussed in "The Work Made for Hire Rule," chapter 3, and in "Works Made by Employees," chapter 5).

You should try to obtain ownership of copyrights in all works created for you by independent contractors. There are two ways to obtain ownership:

- **Assignment.** For all types of works created for you by independent contractors, you can obtain ownership of copyrights by including an assignment provision in your contract with the independent contractor.

- **Work made for hire agreement.** For contributions to audiovisual works and eight other types of works (listed in "Work Made for Hire Agreements," later in this chapter), you can obtain ownership of copyrights by including a work made for hire agreement in your contract with the independent contractor. This approach makes use of the second branch (specially commissioned works) of the Copyright Act's work made for hire rule (see "The Work Made for Hire Rule," chapter 3).

These two options for obtaining ownership are discussed in the next two subsections, "Assignments" and "Work Made for Hire Agreements." Unless you use one of these two options, the copyrights in works created for you by independent contractors will be owned by the contractors—even though you ordered and paid for the work.

EXAMPLE

Developer hired Software Design House on a project basis to create the software engine for Developer's new computer game. Developer did not get Software Design House to sign a work made for hire agreement, nor did it get an assignment of the copyright in the software from Software Design House. Software Design House owns the copyright in the software that it created for Developer's computer game.

Assignments

If you get an assignment of copyright from an independent contractor who creates material for you, you will own the copyright in the contractor's work. (See "Assignments," chapter 3.)

The independent contractors who give you assignments will have the right to terminate the assignments in thirty-five years (see "Termination Right," chapter 3). There is nothing you can do about this situation.

For an example of an assignment provision that you can use in contracts with independent contractors, see Section 5.2 of the Content Development and Transfer Agreement (Form 7 in appendix B) and Section 4.4 of the more general Independent Contractor Agreement (Form 14 in appendix B). These assignment provisions include a power of attorney. (Power of attorney provisions are discussed in "Using the Employment Agreement," chapter 5.) Other aspects of independent contractor agreements are discussed in "Contracts With Independent Contractors," later in this chapter.

If you are in a community property state, you may want to get the spouses of married independent contractors to sign quitclaims (Form 12 in appendix B). The reason is given in "Community Property," chapter 3.

Work Made for Hire Agreements

For certain types of works, you can obtain ownership of works created by independent contractors by using a work made for hire agreement (Form 15 in appendix B). This method of obtaining ownership makes use of the second branch of the Copyright Act's work made for hire rule (discussed in "The Work Made for Hire Rule," chapter 3).

Both you and the independent contractor must sign the work made for hire agreement in order to designate the contractor's works as made for hire.

Limitations

If you are going to use a work made for hire agreement rather than get an assignment, make sure you understand the limitations of work made for hire agreements.

Types of Works

A work made for hire agreement is only effective for nine types of specially commissioned works:

- Contributions to collective works.

- Part of a motion picture or other audiovisual work (many multimedia works are audiovisual works).

- Translations.

- Supplementary works (works prepared as adjuncts to other works).

- Compilations.

- Instructional texts.

- Tests or answer material for tests.

- Atlases.

- Sound recordings.

These are the same nine types of works listed in "The Work Made for Hire Rule," chapter 3 (in the discussion of the specially commissioned works branch of the rule).

SOUND RECORDINGS

An amendment to the Copyright Act signed into law on November 29, 1999 added sound recordings to the list of types of specially commissioned works for which a work made for hire agreement is effective. Congress is currently considering another amendment to *remove* sound recordings from the list. Right now, a work made for hire agreement is effective for sound recordings created on or after November 29, 1999. For sound recordings created before November 29, 1999, a work made for hire agreement is effective for a contribution to a sound recording only if the contribution is a contribution to a collective work or the sound recording is a compilation.

While some books of legal forms—particularly older ones—give the impression that you can make any type of specially commissioned work a work made for hire by getting a work made for hire agreement from the independent contractor, that is not true.

EXAMPLE

John hired Writer, a freelancer, to write Publisher's biography. John got Writer to sign an agreement stating that the work was to be considered a work made for hire. The agreement was worthless. Biography is not one of the types of specially commissioned works that can become a work made for hire based on agreement of the parties. Unless John got an assignment from Writer, Writer owns the copyright in the biography.

Unsolicited Works

You can't use a work made for hire agreement to obtain ownership rights in works that "came in over the transom"—that is, unsolicited work. To obtain ownership rights in works that you did not commission, you need an assignment.

Foreign Rights

A work made for hire agreement probably won't get you foreign rights in the commissioned works because the work made for hire rules of most countries do not have anything comparable to the specially commissioned works branch of the Copyright Act's work made for hire rule. To protect your ownership abroad, obtain assignments from independent contractors.

Timing

Several courts have held that a work made for hire agreement for a specially commissioned work is valid only if the agreement is signed before the work is begun. You should make every effort to get your independent contractors to sign work made for hire agreements before they start work on your projects.

If you discover that an independent contractor has started work without signing the work made for hire agreement, you should try to get the contractor to sign an assignment (Forms 8 and 9 in appendix B) rather than using a work made for hire agreement.

If the contractor refuses to give you an assignment, try to get a broad written license from the contractor. If the contractor refuses to grant a written license, you will have to rely on an implied license (discussed in "Implied Licenses," later in this chapter).

You can claim copyright for a Web site or a Web product as a whole even though an independent contractor owns the copyright in a component (see "Copyright Protection," chapter 26).

California Labor Code

A provision of the California Labor Code states that a person who commissions a work made for hire is the employer of the hired party for purposes of worker's compensation, unemployment insurance, and unemployment disability insurance laws. No one is certain exactly what the provision means. If you are located in California, you may want to acquire ownership of copyrights in works made by independent contractors by assignment rather than using work made for hire agreements.

Implied Licenses

If you order and pay for a work created by an independent contractor and fail to get an assignment or a work made for hire agreement, you may have an implied license to use the contractor's work as intended by you and the contractor. An implied license to use the work is much less valuable than owning the copyright in the work.

If you own a work created by a independent contractor, you can exercise all of the copyright owner's exclusive rights in the work—in other words, you can make copies of the work, modify the work, distribute the work, and publicly perform and display the work (see "The Exclusive Rights," chapter 1). If you merely have an implied license to use the work, you can only do those things that are within the scope of the license (and you and the contractor may not agree on the scope of the license).

EXAMPLE

67

contractors
and
consultants

Developer hired Graphic Designer on a freelance basis to create graphics for a client's Web site. The graphics are so good that Developer would like to modify them for use in other clients' Web sites. If Developer owns the copyright in the graphics, Developer can modify and reuse them. If Developer just has an implied license to use the graphics, the implied license probably only authorizes Developer to use the graphics in the original client's project.

License scope is discussed in more detail in "Determining What Rights You Need," chapter 10.

Contracts with Independent Contractors

You should have written contracts with all of your independent contractors for the reasons stated in "Written Contracts," Chapter 4.

Contract Provisions

The contract with an independent contractor should include, in addition to an assignment or a work made for hire agreement (see "Copyright Ownership," earlier in this chapter), the following provisions:

- Deliverables or services, described as specifically as possible.

- Deadlines.

- Payment and payment schedules.

- Responsibility for expenses.

Services of Individuals

If you enter into a contract with a corporation and expect to get the services of particular individuals employed by the corporation, your contract should state that the work can be done only by the named individuals. Otherwise, the corporation will be free to use any of its employees to do the job.

Warranties

You should get warranties and an indemnity from each independent contractor. For examples, see Sections 7 and 8 of the Content Development and Transfer Agreement (Form 7 in appendix B) and Sections 4.6 and 4.8 of the Independent Contractor Agreement (Form 14).

Warranty and indemnity provisions are designed to give you legal recourse against a contractor who uses works belonging to others. If a contractor gives you material that infringes a third party's copyright, incorporating that material into your project will make you liable for infringement of the third party's copyright.

EXAMPLE

Developer hired Graphic Artist to create original graphics for Developer's Web site, *Downtown Tonight.* Graphic Artist took some designs from another Web site and delivered them to Developer to fulfill her contract with Developer. When Developer incorporated the designs into *Downtown Tonight,* Developer infringed the copyright owner's rights.

Warranty provisions are discussed in more detail in the section "The Contract," chapter 8.

Of course, these provisions are not worth much if the contractor does not have the resources to pay the damages. You may want to consider obtaining insurance to cover that risk.

Nondisclosure Provisions

The contract should contain a nondisclosure provision. Such provisions are part of a trade secrets protection program (see "Trade Secret Protection," chapter 26). For examples, see Section 4.2 of the Content Development and Transfer Agreement and Section 4.2 of the Independent Contractor Agreement (Forms 7 and 14 in appendix B).

Miscellaneous Issues

If you will be using an independent contractor's name, voice, image, or face, your contract should include a release authorizing that use to avoid violations of the laws of publicity and privacy (see Chapter 7).

If you will be hiring independent contractors (actors, musicians, directors, or screenwriters) who belong to entertainment industry unions, read about union issues in chapter 22.

Standard Agreements

Independent contractors in many fields have professional associations that have developed and distributed standard agreements. The Graphic Artists Guild, for example, has standard contracts for use by graphic designers and illustrators with clients.

If a contractor insists on using a standard form, read the form carefully, particularly the ownership of rights provision, and be prepared to negotiate over deleting unacceptable provisions and adding your own provisions.

Employment Law Risks

If federal or state authorities conclude that an individual that you have treated as an independent contractor is an employee, you could have a number of problems. They could include:

- Federal tax liability for failure to withhold payroll taxes for the individual.

- Liability for worker's compensation awards paid to the individual.

- Liability for violation of state and federal wage and hours laws.

- Liability for violation of wrongful discharge laws.

You should be aware that the distinction between employees and independent contractors has importance in areas of the law other than copyright law. An individual who is an independent contractor for copyright law purposes may not be an independent contractor for employment law purposes.

CHAPTER 7

THE LAWS OF DEFAMATION, PUBLICITY, AND PRIVACY

The law of defamation protects individuals against the dissemination of falsehoods injurious to their reputation. In this chapter, we will explain the basic legal principles of defamation so that you can recognize the kind of material that might be defamatory.

You must make certain that you don't violate rights of publicity and privacy of individuals whose names or images you use on your Web site or in Web products. We will explain these rights and how you can avoid violating them by getting releases. Web site privacy policies are covered in chapter 17. Employer monitoring of employee email and Internet use is covered in chapter 23.

Defamation

The law of defamation (also known as libel and slander) protects an individual against the dissemination of falsehoods about the individual. Defamation is defined as a false statement about a person, communicated to at least one other person, that injures the defamed person's reputation or subjects the defamed person to hatred, contempt, or ridicule.

To recover damages for defamation, a plaintiff must prove that the statement was false and:

■ Was communicated to others.

■ Was reasonably understood as referring to the plaintiff.

■ Injured the plaintiff.

Injury can consist of monetary losses, damage to reputation, or mental anguish. A public figure or official must prove that the publisher or broadcaster made the statement either knowing it was false or entertaining serious doubts about its truth. A private individual only has to prove that the publisher or broadcaster acted negligently in failing to ascertain that the statement was false. The higher burden for public figures and officials flows from the First Amendment.

Here are some tips for avoiding libel:

■ **Original text:** If you plan to use any statements that could injure someone's reputation, make certain you can prove that the statements are true. There is often a big difference between "knowing" that something is true and being able to prove that it is true. Journalists are taught to be particularly careful about statements concerning arrests and convictions and statements concerning professionals' qualifications and ethics.

■ **Licensed text:** If licensed materials include potentially defamatory material, don't use the material. If you use it, even though the material didn't originate with you, you could have liability for defamation.

■ **Photographs:** With digital editing software, it's easy to edit and merge photographs. Avoid using an edited image that falsely associates an individual with controversial or unsavory events, places, or people. Using an altered image that puts a person in a "false light"—for example, a photograph created by merging a photograph of an elected official with a photograph of a Mafia figure—will expose you to liability for defamation.

■ **Quotations:** Many people believe that one who merely quotes what someone else said has no liability for defamation. This is not generally true (although some states have limited exceptions for the news media). Don't quote a statement made by someone else if that statement could harm someone's reputation unless you know the statement is true.

■ **Opinion:** Many people think that you can escape liability for defamation by couching a statement as your opinion. This is not true. For example, publishing the statement, "In my opinion, our senator has run up thousands of dollars in gambling debts" is defamatory if it is untrue. Don't use a statement of opinion that might harm an individual or corporation's reputation unless you have a factual basis for the opinion.

- **Statements about Corporations:** Corporations can recover damages for defamation. Many executives are zealous about protecting their corporation's reputation. If you make statements that might damage a corporation's reputation, make sure the statements are true.

Whether Internet service providers (ISPs) and bulletin board operators are liable for defamatory statements posted by system users is discussed in "Liability for Other Wrongs," chapter 25.

ANTI-COMPANY SITES

A number of angry former and current employees have set up Web sites criticizing their employers. If these sites publish defamatory statements about the target company, legal action may be appropriate. However, in the United States, mere griping is probably protected as free speech.

The Right of Publicity

Over half the states in the United States recognize that individuals have a right of publicity. The right of publicity gives an individual a legal claim against one who uses the individual's name, face, image, or voice for commercial benefit without obtaining permission. The states recognizing the right are Alabama, California, Connecticut, Florida, Georgia, Hawaii, Illinois, Indiana, Kentucky, Massachusetts, Michigan, Minnesota, Missouri, Nebraska, Nevada, New Jersey, New York, Ohio, Oklahoma, Pennsylvania, Rhode Island, Tennessee, Texas, Utah, Virginia, Washington, and Wisconsin.

EXAMPLE

Photographer took a photo of Clint Eastwood standing on a street corner in Carmel. He licensed the use of the photo to Ad Agency, which used the photo in a client's magazine ad. Unless Eastwood gave permission for the use of his image in the ad, the use of the image violated Eastwood's right of publicity (even though Ad Agency had the copyright owner's permission to use the photo).

Remedies for misappropriation of the right of publicity include injunctions against continued use of the misappropriated name, face, image, or voice, and damages based on the fair market value of the use or the profits earned by the misappropriating party.

In recent years, courts have expanded the right of publicity by giving a broad interpretation to the question of whether an individual's "image" has been taken. For example, the use of the slogan "Here's Johnny" by a portable toilet provider was held to violate Johnny Carson's right of publicity. *Carson v. Here's Johnny Portable Toilets, Inc.*, 698 F2d 831 (6th Cir 1983). An ad showing a robot game hostess in a blonde wig and evening gown was held to violate Vanna White's "identity." *White v. Samsung Electronics America, Inc.*, 971 F2d 1395 (9th Cir 1992), *cert. denied*, 508 US 951 (1993).

DIGITAL EDITING AND PUBLICITY

Los Angeles Magazine published a computer-generated photograph of actor Dustin Hoffman superimposed over the body of a female model. The magazine did not seek Hoffman's permission. He won a $3 million judgment against the magazine in a right of publicity lawsuit. *Hoffman v. Capital Cities/ABC, Inc.*, 33 FSupp2d 867 (CDCal 1999).

The right of publicity cannot be used to stifle comment on the lives of public persons (Howard Hughes, Marilyn Monroe) or on the lives of nonpublic persons who are connected to someone famous (the widow of Ernest Hemingway, the children of Julius and Ethel Rosenberg). Newspapers and news magazines have a "fair use" privilege to publish names or images in connection with reporting a newsworthy event. Such use is known as "media use." The media use exception has been held to apply to nonprint media such as motion pictures.

One line of cases holds that a publication may use an individual's name or likeness so long as that person is used to illustrate a point stemming from a documentary or an article on a subject of general or public interest. Another line holds that the media are permitted to use photographs of individuals in an article about social issues even though the actual subjects of the photos have only a minimal connection with the article's subject.

The law of publicity varies from state to state. How these laws apply to Web use is unclear. In the world of print publications, the common sense approach to determining whether you need permission to use an individual's name or image is to ask whether the name or image will be used to help sell products or services. If the answer is "yes," the general rule is that permission should be obtained. On the Web, the distinction between selling and reporting is blurred. Many Web sites do both.

EXAMPLE

Giant Company used Famous Actor's photograph on its "information only" Web site. No products are sold from the site. The site just gives information about Giant and its products and information on topics of interest to Giant's typical customer. Has Giant used Famous Actor's photograph to sell its products? We don't know the answer.

The use of an individual's image without permission in a banner ad would probably be misappropriation in many of the states recognizing a right of publicity. Any advertising-like use of an individual's name or image on an e-commerce site is probably misappropriation. In fact, any use by a for-profit company on its Web site (as in the example immediately above) might be considered use for commercial benefit.

You should avoid trying to determine which states' laws you need to worry about. Instead, you should obtain releases from any person whose name, face, image, or voice is recognizable in material you use on the Web unless it is clear that your use is noncommercial or falls in the media use area. A release form is included in appendix B (Form 10).

Experienced performers and models are accustomed to signing these releases. If a person won't sign a release, don't use his or her name, face, image, or voice in your Web site or online products. If you are using a client's employees as actors, models, or narrators, make sure the employees sign releases. If you are using your own employees, make sure they sign releases.

Photographs and Film Clips

If you want to use a photograph of a living person, get the person to sign a statement authorizing you to use his or her face or image as shown in the photograph. You also need a license authorizing you to use the photograph, unless you own the copyright in it. (See "When You Need a License," chapter 9).

Some photographers routinely obtain releases, but don't assume that this is the case. Even if the photographer did obtain a release, the release may not be broad enough to cover your use of the photograph. If you will be obtaining photographs from a stock photo agency, (discussed in "Licensing Photographs and Still Images," chapter 11), tell the agency at the outset that you will need model releases so the agency will only send you photos for which releases are available.

If you want to use a clip from a film or television show, you should obtain releases from all performers shown or heard in the clip. Motion picture producers often require performers to sign releases authorizing the use of the actors' name, face, voice, or image in clips, but the scope of such releases may be too narrow to cover your use (they may cover only the use of clips for publicizing the movie). If the performers shown or heard in the clip belong to the Screen Actor's Guild (SAG) or American Federation of Television and Radio Artists (AFTRA), you cannot use the clip without getting their consent (see "Reuse Provisions," chapter 22).

To make the clearance process easier, you may want to eliminate certain individuals from the clip. You'll need the consent of the clip's copyright owner to modify it (see "Determining What Rights You Need," chapter 10). For example, one multimedia developer wanted to use a television clip of an interview between Isaac Asimov and Jane Pauley. Rather than negotiate with Pauley, the developer eliminated Pauley's image and voice from the clip.

Sound Recordings

If you want to use an excerpt from a sound recording, get the consent of anyone whose voice is heard in it. In addition, you should get copyright licenses from the musical composition's copyright owner and the master recording copyright owner (see "Licensing Music for the Internet," Chapter 21), and comply with AFTRA and American Federation of Musicians reuse requirements (see "Reuse Provisions," chapter 22).

Deceased Individuals

In some states, an individual's right of publicity terminates when the individual dies. In other states, the right passes to the heirs of the deceased original owner. In California, Oklahoma, and Texas, the right passes on to the heirs only if the person's likeness has acquired some commercial value at the time of death. In Kentucky, the right is passed on to heirs for public figures only.

The right of publicity lasts fifty years in several states, seventy years in California, and up to one hundred years in Oklahoma. In Tennessee, the right lasts as long as it is continuously exploited by the heirs (Elvis lived there).

DIGITAL RESURRECTION

Digital technology can be used to extract the image of a celebrity from film footage and insert the celebrity's image into a current commercial. Fred Astaire appeared in an ad for Dirt Devil, and Elvis appeared in an ad for Pizza Hut. The right of publicity must be considered when using digital images in this manner. You may need permission from the deceased celebrity's heir or estate.

The Right of Privacy

Most states in the United States recognize that individuals have a right of privacy. The right of privacy gives an individual a legal claim against someone who intrudes on the individual's physical solitude or seclusion, and against those who publicly disclose private facts. Remedies for invasion of privacy include injunctions against continued intrusion and damages for mental distress.

The right of privacy cannot be used to prohibit publication of a matter of public or general interest—whether as news or as entertainment. Instead, this right protects the privacy of private life. Liability exists only if the defendant's

conduct was such that the defendant should have realized that it would be offensive to persons of ordinary sensibilities.

INVASION OR NOT?

An unauthorized photograph of the Gills, in an "affectionate pose,"
was published in two magazines to illustrate an article on love. The
Gills sued the publisher for invasion of privacy. The court found that
their privacy was not wrongfully invaded because the Gills had "voluntarily exposed themselves to public gaze" by sitting in a public area.
The court hinted that it would have ruled the other way had the photo
been used for advertising purposes. *Gill v. Hearst Publishing Co.*, 40
Cal2d 224 (1953).

A truthful statement is not defamatory, but a truthful statement that discloses private facts about an individual in an objectionable manner may violate
the individual's right of privacy.

EXAMPLE

Web Journalist discovered that Sue was abused as a child and reported that fact without Sue's permission in a story on child abuse.
Journalist's statement about Sue is not defamatory, because the statement was true, but Journalist may have violated Sue's right of privacy
by publishing the statement.

Permits

If you are going to shoot photographs or video on public property, get a permit from the appropriate government authority (usually a local or state film
commission).

If you are going to shoot on private property, get a location release from
the property owner that authorizes you to enter and use the premises for shooting and to show the premises in your work. A location release is included in
Appendix B (Form 11).

If your shots of public or private places will prominently show a work that
is protected by copyright—a sculpture, for example—you should obtain a license from the copyright owner authorizing you to use the image. Because
ownership of the copyright in a work is distinct from ownership of a copy (see
"Owning a Copy of a Work," chapter 3), the owner of the copy of the work that
you film or photograph is probably not the owner of the copyright in that
work.

EXAMPLE

Mr. Rich has given Developer permission to create an "online art gallery" showing Mr. Rich's private art collection. Unless Mr. Rich owns the copyrights in the paintings in the collection, Mr. Rich cannot authorize Developer to use images of the paintings in an online gallery. If Mr. Rich did not get copyright assignments from the artists who created the paintings, Developer should get permission to use the images of the paintings from the artists (or those to whom the artists assigned the copyrights).

For other copyrighted items that will be shown in photos or video footage, the general rule on getting permission is that you should get permission if the item will be prominently featured or will be a prominent part of the story. If you get items from a prop house, do not assume that the prop house has the right to authorize you to use images of the items on the Web.

PROP CLEARANCE

Some courts have held that showing a copyrighted item in a motion picture or television show is fair use. Briefly showing a copyrighted baby crib mobile in a motion picture without permission was held to be fair use in *Amsinck v. Columbia Pictures Industries, Inc.*, 862 FSupp 1044 (SDNY 1994). However, other cases have ruled that showing copyrighted prop items was not fair use. In *Ringgold v. Black Entertainment Television, Inc.*, the court concluded that the use of a poster of art work, fleetingly glimpsed as part of a room's décor in a sitcom, was not fair use. 126 F3d 70 (2d Cir 1997). We recommend that you follow the rules for prop clearance discussed here.

Many copyright owners will be happy to give you permission without any charge. In the entertainment industry, product manufacturers often pay product placement fees to have their products prominently shown in a motion picture or television series.

PRODUCT PLACEMENT OFFER

The director of advertising public relations for Timex was approached by a promotions company representing a well-known novelist. The promotions company offered to put a Timex-brand watch in the novelist's next book, movie, and online game if Timex would pay a product placement fee of $1.3 million dollars. Timex declined the offer.

CHAPTER 8

WEB DEVELOPMENT AGREEMENTS

This chapter discusses the legal issues in Web site development agreements. It contains tips for both parties—Web site developer and client—on how to handle these issues in order to avoid legal problems later.

Publishing and distribution agreements for Web products are discussed in chapter 13.

Proposals and Bids

Web site development generally is a multistage development process. First, the developer creates the Web site design. Next, the developer creates the beta (working) version of the Web site, tests it, and delivers it to the client for testing. Finally, the developer creates the final version and delivers it to the client for testing. Although many Web sites involve only text and graphics, more complex Web sites may include software or "scripts."

Web development proposals should be written. Oral proposals are rarely complete. It is difficult in a phone conversation or face-to-face meeting to remember everything that should be covered in a Web development proposal.

In the rest of this section, we give tips on handling proposals and bids for Web sites.

Tips for Clients

The developer needs to understand what features you want in your Web site in order to create a proposal. If you don't know what you want, you should spend some time on the Internet reviewing existing sites. Look at other sites designed by the developer, talk to Web site owners about what has worked for them, and read up on Web marketing (or hire a Web marketing consultant).

At the end of this chapter, you'll find an article, "Anatomy of an RFP," which explains how to create a good request for proposal (RFP) for Web design services. This article was originally published in *iDecisionMaker* (www.iDecisionMaker.com) and is used here with permission.

Tips for Developers

Don't spend a lot of time and effort on a proposal for a potential client without making sure that the client is seriously considering the project and has the ability to pay for the project. Even then, not every proposal will result in a contract.

If you know you will have to spend several hours meeting with a potential client to determine what the client needs before you can even prepare your proposal, try to get the client to agree to pay you for that time at an hourly consulting rate.

EXAMPLE

Sue, a Web developer, spent many hours meeting with Toy Company's marketing staff before she created a detailed proposal for an e-commerce Web site for the company. Toy Company considered Sue's proposal but decided against it. Sue cannot charge Toy Company for the time she spent on the proposal unless Toy Company had agreed to pay for that time.

Make certain that the person with whom you are dealing has the authority to approve the project. It that person does not have the authority, find out as soon as possible whether the person with authority is really interested in doing the project.

Don't start on a project until the client has signed a written contract. Your proposal to a client is an offer. Until your client accepts the offer, there is no contract. (See "Offer and Acceptance," chapter 4.)

Some companies send RFPs to several developers. Responding to an RFP takes considerable time and effort. If you respond with a bid but do not get a contract, you will have no legal basis for getting reimbursement for the time you spend preparing your response.

Any proposal that you send to a potential client is protected by copyright. However, copyright protection does not cover the ideas used in the proposal.

(This topic is discussed in "Limitations on the Exclusive Rights," chapter 1, and in "When You Don't Need a License," chapter 9.) If the recipient of a proposal photocopies the proposal, that's copyright infringement. If the recipient hires another developer to create a Web site based on the ideas used in the proposal, that's not copyright infringement. You may be able to get some protection for a proposal containing novel ideas by getting your client to sign a nondisclosure agreement (Form 1, appendix B). These agreements are discussed in "Trade Secret Protection," chapter 26.

If you make an oral proposal and it is accepted, you still should have the client sign a written contract. If the written contract contains terms that you did not mention in your oral proposal, the client may think that you are trying to change the deal.

Some Web developers have a standard proposal format that they use with all clients. This saves time and eliminates the possibility that a key provision will be left out of a particular proposal. In both the formal proposal and the contract, be as specific as possible about what you are to create for the client. Vagueness in the proposal and in the contract can camouflage misunderstanding that will come to light later, when you deliver the material to the client for testing.

If your bid is accepted, you will be bound by the price and terms of your bid. If you discover that you made a mistake in calculating your price, you probably will still have to absorb the added cost yourself.

EXAMPLE

Web Developer agreed to create a Web site design for Client for $15,000. When Developer was calculating her out-of-pocket costs for the project, she forgot to include the cost of content licenses (Developer's responsibility, according to the proposal and contract). Developer will have to absorb the license fees, reducing her profit on the project.

Key Provisions in the Agreement

An agreement between a Web developer and a client should always take the form of a written contract signed by both parties (see "Written Contracts," chapter 4). If the developer's written proposal to a client is complete, a contract can be formed by having the client sign the proposal to indicate acceptance. Developers may want to finish proposals with acceptance instructions, such as, "If you wish to accept this proposal and form a contract on the terms stated in this proposal, please sign below and return this proposal to me."

It's permissible for the developer and client to make handwritten changes to the proposal or mark provisions out. However, both parties should initial any changes or deletions to avoid disputes later.

The balance of this section discusses the issues that should be covered in a Web development agreement, with tips for clients and developers. A sample Web development agreement is in appendix B (Form 2).

Specifications

A Web site development agreement should include detailed technical and design specifications. The specifications define the scope of the developer's obligations, and they should be as specific as possible.

Detailed specifications serve two purposes: First, the process of creating them helps avoid misunderstandings about the responsibilities of the developer and the client. Second, if there is a dispute later about whether the developer has performed the contractual obligations, the specifications will establish the scope of those obligations.

Licenses

The developer and client should discuss the range of content options before entering into a contract. Typically, the client provides certain content (referred to as "Client Content" in Form 2), and other content is licensed from third parties.

The agreement should state which party will obtain licenses to use third-party content and which party will be responsible for paying license fees. This information goes in Section 5.7. It should also state which party will be responsible for obtaining and paying for licenses to use Web site development software (referred to as "Developer Tools"). In Form 2, the developer is responsible for these licenses (Section 5.8).

If third-party software will be used in operating the site—payment software for e-commerce transactions, for example—the agreement should state which party will obtain and pay for licenses to use that software. This information goes in Section 5.9.

Licensing costs for obtaining permission to use content owned by third parties can be substantial (the licensing process is described in chapter 10). It may be possible to obtain suitable material relatively inexpensively from stock houses and media libraries (see "Stock Houses and Libraries," chapter 10). A list of stock houses and media libraries appears in appendix D.

Tips for Clients

You need to determine whether you own or have the right to use all the material included in client content. This topic is discussed in "Using Works You Own," chapter 9. If client content includes material owned by third parties, you may need to get licenses to use the material on a Web site. Don't assume that you have a right to use third-party content just because you've used it in the past. The prior use may have been unauthorized—or it may have been authorized based on a limited license grant.

EXAMPLE
_____

Z Company wants Web developer to use a photograph that appeared on a Z Company marketing brochure two years ago. Photographer—the copyright owner—gave Z Company a license to use the photograph in the brochure, but only for one year. The old license does not give Z Company the right to use the photograph on its Web site.

Tips for Developers

If the client is expecting you to use expensive content—a famous photograph, for example—and you are responsible for licensing third-party content, you should raise your price or get the client to reimburse you for the costly license fees and the cost of personnel time for negotiating licenses. Be careful not to commit yourself to obtaining rights in specific works, because those works may not be available for licensing. If the client requests specific works, make sure that you have the right to substitute different works if the requested works are not available.

Ownership

One of the most important issues to address in the contract is who will own the copyright and other intellectual property rights in the Web site. By addressing this issue in the written agreement, you will eliminate future legal disputes over ownership. The client does not obtain ownership of the copyright in the Web site by paying for its development. (Ownership of works created by independent contractors is discussed in chapter 6.)

The approach taken in Form 2 is that the client gets ownership of the Web site content (including images, user interface, and software) and documentation and all intellectual property rights (Section 5.1). Change this provision if the developer is to retain ownership. One approach to ownership is for the client to own the project as a whole, while the developer retains ownership of certain components. To use this approach, list the components for which the developer is to retain ownership in Section 5.3. For any components owned by the developer, Form 2 provides that the developer grants the client a license to use the components (see the last sentence in Section 5.3).

Tips for Clients

Generally, you should try to obtain ownership of all material created for you by the developer. If you do so, you will then have all the copyright owner's exclusive rights in the material—including the right to modify it for use in later projects and different media—as well as any other applicable intellectual property rights such as patent and trade secret rights.

However, the developer may resist giving you outright ownership. If the developer is to retain copyright ownership of all or part of the Web site material, you should make certain that the agreement gives you the right to use and modify the material owned by the developer in every way and every media that you believe will be necessary, both now and in the future, amending the last sentence of Section 5.3 if necessary.

If you are to own the copyright, the contract should provide for an assignment of those rights to you (Section 5.2). You also want the developer to sign a separate "short form" copyright assignment (Form 9 in appendix B) for recording your assignment with the Copyright Office. (Recordation of copyright assignments is discussed in "Assignments," chapter 3.) The power of attorney clause (Section 5.4) authorizes you to execute and file assignment documents if you are unable to obtain the developer's signature on applications for copyrights, patents, and other rights.

Getting an assignment of the copyright from the developer does not give you ownership of content or components owned by third parties. The developer cannot assign rights that he or she does not own.

EXAMPLE

Developer created online training materials for Big Company and assigned the copyright in the materials to Big. The materials contained an excerpt of a song written by Joe Composer. (Developer obtained a license to use the song in the training materials.) Since Developer did not own the copyright in Joe's song, Developer's assignment of its copyright in the materials to Big did not give Big ownership of the copyright in Joe's song.

Tips for Developers

If you agree to assign the copyright in the material you create to the client, you will not be able to use that material in other projects, nor will you be able to modify it for other projects. Once you assign the copyright, the client will have the copyright owner's exclusive rights.

EXAMPLE

Developer created an online game that used a software engine for manipulating game images. Developer assigned the copyright in the game to Big Company. If Developer uses the software engine in a new online game without getting a license from Big, Developer will be infringing Big's copyright.

If you are creating material to fill a client's special needs, you may not object to giving the client ownership of the copyright (particularly if the client is willing to pay a higher fee for an assignment of all rights). You may, however, want to retain copyright ownership of some components—for example, a software engine, certain graphics, or a "shopping cart" program for online sales transactions. (You can use Section 5.3 of Form 2 to do that.) Unless you retain copyright ownership of the components or get a license from your client to reuse them, your use of the components in future projects will infringe the client's copyright.

If the copyright is to be owned by the client, you may want to include a clause in the contract authorizing you to make demonstration copies of the work to show to future clients. Such demonstrations are public performances of the work. This topic is discussed in "When You Need a License," chapter 9.

Warranties

Web development agreements generally contain a performance warranty by the developer and intellectual property warranties by the developer and the client.

In Form 2, the developer's performance warranty is that the Web site will be of high quality, will be free of defects in material and workmanship in all material respects, and will conform in all respects to the functional and other descriptions contained in the specifications (Section 4.1). Other possible performance warranties are that the Web site will operate with named Web browsers or a warranty that it will operate error-free for a stated period of time.

Intellectual property warranties and indemnities protect one party against the possibility that the other party has provided material owned by a third party. If the developer uses content or software owned by others without permission or violates other third-party rights, the client will be liable for infringement for using the material on its Web site (even though innocent of intent to infringe).

EXAMPLE

Developer created a Web site called *Cheese Expert* for client Online Gourmet. *Cheese Expert* contains pictures of Minnie Mouse and Mickey Mouse. Developer did not obtain permission from The Walt Disney Company to use the images of Minnie and Mickey. Online Gourmet's operation of the *Cheese Expert* Web site infringes Disney's copyright rights and possibly its trademark rights as well, unless the use is fair use. (See "Characters," chapter 11.)

If the client provides—as part of its client content—material that belongs to third parties, without getting permission to use the material in the project, the developer will be liable for infringement for using the material (even though innocent of intent to infringe).

EXAMPLE

Online Gourmet (from the previous example) gave Developer text on varieties of soft cheese to use on the Web site. The text is from an article that was published in a food services industry magazine. Online Gourmet did not get the copyright owner's permission to use the text, but Developer didn't know that. Developer scanned the text and added new subheadings, then used the text on the *Cheese Expert* site. Developer's use of the article infringes the copyright owner's rights.

Intellectual property warranties do not protect the party receiving the warranty from being sued by a copyright owner. In the examples just given, Online Gourmet can be sued by Disney whether or not Developer warranted that all material used in the Web site was noninfringing. Developer can be sued by the text's copyright owner, whether or not Online Gourmet warranted that the use of its client content was noninfringing. Warranties and indemnifications permit the protected party (Online Gourmet in the first example, Developer in the second example) to collect from the warranting party the costs of infringement suits brought against them. Costs could include a money judgment and attorneys' fees.

There are three levels of intellectual property warranties:

- **The "absolute" warranty**. "The work does not and will not infringe any third-party intellectual property rights." (This is the approach taken in Section 8.1 of Form 2.)

- **The "know or should know" warranty**. "To the best of my knowledge, the work does not and will not infringe any third-party intellectual property rights."

- **The "actual knowledge" warranty**. "To my actual knowledge, the work does not and will not infringe any third-party intellectual property rights."

Tips for Clients

You should try to get absolute intellectual property warranties and an indemnification from the developer. Section 8.1 contains other developer warranties that supplement the intellectual property warranties.

The warranty in Section 8.1(e)—that the Web site was created solely by the developer, the developer's full-time employees acting within the scope of the employment, or independent contractors who assigned their rights to the developer—is designed to assure you that the developer owned from the outset or acquired all copyrights in the material. (See chapters 5 and 6 for discussions of ownership of works created by employees and independent contractors.) If the developer does not own the copyrights, the developer cannot assign them to you (and your use of the material may infringe the rights of the true owners). Section 8.1(f) ("Developer is the owner") supplements the Section 8.1(e) warranty and adds a warranty that the material is not subject to liens or security interests.

Tips for Developers
Some developers try to negotiate for the know or should know intellectual property warranty or actual knowledge warranty rather than the unlimited absolute warranty. Here's why: Although you should do everything possible to ensure that work does not infringe the intellectual property rights of third parties, it can be difficult to be certain that a work composed of many components does not infringe. For example:

- The employee who created the software code for a Web site may have reused software code that is owned by a former employer. (See "Rights of Former Employers," chapter 5.)

- An independent contractor hired to create a component may have copied someone else's work.

- A content owner who granted a license to use his music throughout the world may turn out to not be the owner of the copyright in the music in all countries.

Patents are a particular problem: If you give a warranty that the work does not infringe any patents, you may later be held liable for infringing a patent that had not yet been issued when you did the work. Some developers will warrant only that, to the best of their knowledge, the work does not infringe any patents in effect on the date the finished product is delivered to the client. Another way to limit warranty exposure is to put a "ceiling" on your liability—limiting it, for example, to your total compensation for the development of the Web site.

Other Important Provisions

In this section, we discuss other important provisions of a Web development agreement.

Deliverables

Typical deliverables are the Web site design, beta version (test version), and final version with source material. For Form 2, the deliverables are to be stated in Schedule B (which also contains delivery dates and payment dates). Other deliverables can be added—for example, an alpha version (first version).

Delivery Schedule

The contract should state when the developer must deliver "deliverables" and the finished project to the client. This information goes on Schedule B.

Developers: Make certain that the deadlines are realistic. Serious delay on your part can be grounds for termination by the client—especially if the contract states that "time is of the essence" for performance of contract obligations. If the client is entitled to terminate the contract because of your failure to deliver the project on time, you may have to absorb the costs that went into the project before the termination. Normally, the client will have no obligation to reimburse you for those costs.

Payments

Web development agreements often provide for several payments over the course of the development process. Typically, a first payment is due when the contract is signed. If the developer will have substantial start-up costs for the project, this first payment will probably be a significant percentage of the project's total cost. The next payment is due when the completed Web site design is accepted by the client. Additional payments are due when the client accepts the beta version of the Web site and the final version. This is the approach taken on Schedule B of Form 2.

Sometimes the agreement provides that the developer will receive a bonus for completing the entire project by a certain date. Schedule B includes a "bonus payment" provision.

Payment does not have to be money. Some Web developers are entering into profit-sharing agreements with clients, taking a small percentage of the Web site's ad or e-commerce revenues as all or partial compensation for the Web development work. Other Web developers are taking their compensation in the form of stock in the client company.

Testing and Acceptance

A Web development agreement should include a "testing and acceptance clause" stating the number of days the client has to test and accept or reject the developer's work. Such clauses generally provide that if the client has not given notice of rejection within the stated time period, the work will be deemed to be accepted—meaning that it will then be late for the client to say, "I won't accept this. Do it again." In Form 2, the testing and acceptance clause is Section 3.

Credit Clause

A "credit" clause specifies the form a developer's credit will take. Credits usually consist of the developer's logo and a few lines of text, with a link to the developer's own resume Web site. Three possibilities are: a footer credit, in which the credit runs at the bottom of each Web page; a banner credit, in which the credit is displayed on a banner on one or more pages of the site; and an acknowledgments page credit in which the credit appears only on a single page. In Form 2, the credit format is to be stated on Schedule E.

Corrections and Support

Many development contracts provide that the developer will make changes to correct performance errors for free during a warranty period and provide stated support services during the warranty period (Sections 4.1 and 4.2 of Form 2). The developer may also agree to provide maintenance services for an additional fee after the warranty period ends (Section 4.3).

Termination

Termination clauses provide that either or both parties have the right to terminate the contract under certain circumstances. Generally, termination clauses describe breach of contract events that trigger the right to terminate the contract—for example, the developer's failure to deliver an acceptable beta version or final version within the time specified in the contract. Form 2's termination clause is in Section 9. Section 9.1 states that in the event of termination for cause by the client (for breach by the developer), the client has the right to require the developer to deliver the work-in-progress to the client. The developer may keep any milestone payments that have been paid or are due, as payment for the material completed as of the time of termination. In the event of termination for cause by the developer (for breach by the client), the developer owns the work-in-progress.

Some contracts also provide that one or both parties may terminate the contract for convenience, upon notice to the other party and payment of a cancellation fee. Form 2 contains such a clause (Section 9.2). A termination for convenience clause allows one party to terminate the contract without proving that the other party has breached its contractual obligations.

Nondisclosure Agreement

If the client will be giving the developer access to proprietary or confidential information or trade secrets, the agreement should include confidentiality provisions (Section 7). Confidentiality provisions are discussed in "Trade Secrets," chapter 26.

Anatomy of an RFP

By Anna Talerico
Copyright 1999, 2000 by iDecisionMaker

A recent study confirmed what Web site producers have known all along—companies that don't have a well-defined planning and evaluation process for purchasing web services end up being less satisfied than companies that do. In a nutshell, if you don't plan, you'll probably experience a lot of disappointment along the way.

Despite what David Siegel says, putting together a request for proposal is one of the most important first steps you can take towards a well-managed Web project. A thorough RFP, sent to the right Web development shops, can mean the difference between a site that meets and exceeds your expectations and one that falls radically short. Unless your idea of a great site is one that is 60 percent over budget, sixty days late, and 60 percent less effective than you thought it would be in the end, use a good RFP.

Anyone who has ever evaluated Web proposals can appreciate the order that an RFP can bring to the otherwise chaotic process. You ask for a quote on the same type of site from four different Web shops and get back wildly varying prices and solutions. One firm can build your site in thirty days for $3,000 using an off-the-shelf software package. Oh yeah, the firm will throw in free hosting for a year if you sign the contract today. The second firm wants $100,000. It needs six months to create your site and $2,000 a month to host the site. This firm's proposal doesn't mention anything about the software the firm will use to build the site. The third firm will build it in Cold Fusion for $50,000 and two months of development time, but its proposal doesn't mention anything about hosting. And the fourth firm didn't respond to your request for a quote because it went out of business before it could finish writing the proposal.

Web shops are not exactly known for their good business practices. (Some are known for their unruly, unpredictable behavior, however.) Despite those realities, and if your company is like most doing something on the Web, you still don't have a defined process for evaluating and purchasing Web services. You may even have gotten burned a few times by the Web site factory down the street. Standard operating procedure is to meet with a few different people, tell them what you want to have on your site and wait for the proposals to come back. What a mess. In this scenario, you have no way of comparing apples to apples. And, unless you are an Internet veteran who knows what to look for, you are totally at the mercy of the Web shops to include all the necessary information in their proposals.

That's where the RFP comes in. As the first step in the client/agency relationship, the RFP puts you in charge. Use the RFP as it was intended—as a tool to help you ensure that the proposals you get include all of the information necessary for you to make an informed decision.

But what you will get back will only be as good as what you put out there. I remember an RFP with the question "How much does it cost to build a Web store?" Hmm. I wanted to respond with, "How much does it cost to build a house?" but tact got the better of me. If you send out an RFP with vague questions, no direction, and little information about your company's needs, you might as well not send one out at all. An RFP should state what your objectives are, what your Web site functionality and content needs are, and when the site needs to be delivered.

An RFP is really useful when you are building a site from the ground up. But it is also appropriate when you are making substantial additions or modifications to an existing site. And there is no reason you shouldn't use an RFP if you are looking to hire an interactive agency of record. So whether you are about to undertake a single project, or you are in the midst of writing your Web marketing plan for the next twelve months, it is time to put together an RFP. By taking the time to plan in advance, you can take control of your web projects and get the results you need.

What Makes for a Good RFP?

It's pretty simple. Just be as specific as you can be about what you want. For different companies that means different things. You may not have any idea what your site content should be, or what the technical requirements will be. But if you do—make sure you put them in your RFP. Crafting a good Web RFP is a delicate balance of providing enough information so that the candidates can respond with a complete proposal and a firm price, but allowing enough room for them to bring their expertise to the table. Let them show you their stuff-after all, they are the experts.

Before you write your RFP, decide within your organization who is going to be on the Web decision making team. Make sure that any specific information they need to evaluate the proposals is included in the RFP so that you don't have a million rounds of additional questions after the responses come back. Once you've gathered together all of your criteria, it's time to put it together. Here's a list of the basic information you want to include in your RFP:

Company and Industry Background
Provide background information on your company and your industry. List the number of employees you have as well as offices and locations. If possible,

include brochures and product sheets. Prepare a list of competitors (include Web site addresses) and define your place in the market.

Objectives

Define what end-result(s) you would like to accomplish with your Web site project. Do you want to educate the market on your products and/or services? Do you need an interactive tool that will help generate qualified leads? Are you going to sell products from your site using an e-commerce solution? Write down what you want to achieve from your Web site.

Scope

Describe what you need the firm to do for you. If you are hiring a firm to do it all, then you might say something to the effect of, "The scope of this project will be to produce our Web site from concept to completion. We require a firm that can handle the tasks of organization and site planning as well as interface design, all aspects of production, ongoing maintenance, marketing and hosting." Otherwise, list the exact role the firm will play in the project. For example, do you need the firm to write all of the Web site copy from scratch, or will you be providing the firm with copy to edit and place into its design? Do you have an internal development team that will roll out the Web site technologies, or do you need the firm to author that as well?

Site Requirements

Cut loose and be as specific as possible about what you want your site to do and how you want the site to do it. You can't include enough information here. Do you want your Web firm to build you a store? Just a few of the things the firm will need to know are what types of products you will sell, how many products, how often the products change, if the products have accessories, if they ever go on sale, how you will fulfill orders, if you have an existing inventory or accounting system that will need to be integrated with the site, if you have an Internet merchant account, and on and on.

In addition to descriptions of high-level functionality, include performance requirements as well. If you want your site to be compatible with certain browsers or want your pages to load within a certain number of seconds, make sure you include that information in this section.

Don't be afraid to list too much. One word of caution, however: It's possible that your site requirements might conflict with your objectives. Consider including a brief statement at the bottom of this section that indicates your willingness to listen to reasons why you should modify your requirements.

Maintenance Considerations

Whether you'll be maintaining the site, or hiring the firm to do so, it's important for you to know what type of site you are buying. Will the firm build your site in Cold Fusion, ASP, or JSP? Will the firm be creating the pages with a page editor like Dreamweaver or FrontPage? Will it use programming languages such as C++ or Perl to create custom solutions? Use this section to ask two simple questions: What software and programming languages will the firm use to build the site? And what will be required to maintain it?

If you plan on maintaining the site in-house, you will need to know what experience and skills your staff will require. Also, use this section to tell the candidates what your maintenance plans are. Will you be hiring the firm to make changes and updates on a regular basis, or will the firm be handing the site keys over to your staff? Ask if your staff will need to be trained and make sure the firm includes the fee for any necessary training in their bid.

Hosting Requirements

Ask for the hosting requirements of the site. If you have any preferences or requirements of your own, say so here. Ask the firm to describe its hosting capability and services. If the firm that builds the site will host it, the firm should provide you with a hosting price, or at least a price range. The firm you select may not offer hosting, in which case you will need for the firm to provide assistance with the selection of a suitable hosting provider. Make sure you get all of the hosting information up front-the last thing you need is to be stuck with a site that no one will host.

Technical Considerations

This is important if you have an existing site that you need modified or expanded. The firm tackling that type of project needs to know how the site was built, its platform, what software the site is using, etc. If you don't have the answers to these questions, then go back to the firm that originally built the site and find out.

Additional Items

You'll probably have some very specific concerns that you'll want addressed and this is the place to do it. Use these questions and statements as a way to "pre-screen" whether or not the company will be a good fit with yours. You may ask that a sample project contract be included with the proposal. Or you may ask for the background and experience of the staff. Perhaps you are concerned about the security of the site while it is under development. Go crazy and ask whatever you need in order to be comfortable with the candidates.

It may go without saying, but don't forget to include the basics. Put your company name, address, and Web site along with the RFP contact name, address, and phone number somewhere on your document. You also want to make sure the due date is clearly stated somewhere. Include a little information on how you want the proposals submitted (hard copy or email?). An often over-looked detail is the period of time during which you are willing to take questions. Most of the shops to which you send your RFP will have a few questions. In order to control the amount of time you spend reviewing the project with the candidates, you may want to limit the question/answer period to just a few days.

The outline above should be enough to get you started on your RFP. Log on to iDecisionMaker.com for some great RFP tips and Microsoft® Word® templates that you can use to help you build your next RFP.

The RFP Is Just the First Step

Whether you know a lot about the Internet or just enough to get around, preparing an RFP will start your Web project on the right foot. If you set a reasonable deadline for submission (two weeks minimum), the firms should have plenty of time to prepare proposals that include all of the information you need to make an informed choice. A note on timeliness—if a firm can't submit their proposal on time, how can they possibly finish your site on time? If someone asks for an extension, take that as a warning and cross them off your list.

Even though you will be comparing apples to apples—not all apples are created equal. Once you have reviewed all of the proposals, you'll find that some are better than others. That's when it is time to have meetings and to see if the chemistry is right. Do you like them? More importantly, do you think you can work with them on an extended project? If you think that you have finally found the right firm, sign a letter of intent, get the contract signed, and get started! The Internet waits for no one, and time is ticking.

CHAPTER 9

USING PREEXISTING WORKS

Found some great content for your Web site or Web product? Chances are that it's protected by copyright. Here's why:

■ Copyright protection is available for text, art, graphics, photos, and music (both compositions and sound recordings) and is easy to obtain. See "Types of Works Protected by Copyright," chapter 1.

■ Copyright protection lasts a long time. Under current U.S. law, the copyright term for a work created by an individual is the life of the author plus seventy years. See "Duration of the Rights," chapter 1.

Every time you use a copyrighted work owned by a third party, you must determine whether it is necessary to obtain a license from the owner. For most uses, a license should be obtained.

In this chapter, we will discuss:

■ When you do and don't need a license to use a copyrighted work.

■ When you do and don't need a license to use material you find on the Internet.

■ The use of public domain works.

■ The use of works that you own.

Special aspects of distance learning and educational use are covered in chapter 27.

When You Need a License

You need a license to use a third party's copyrighted work if your intended use of the work would, without a license, infringe any of the copyright owner's exclusive rights (discussed in "The Exclusive Rights," chapter 1). Using material on the Internet requires the exercise of at least two of the copyright owner's exclusive rights: the reproduction right and the public display or performance right.

The Reproduction Right

The first right involved in using material on the Internet is the reproduction right. You must reproduce the work to upload it to a server. Transmitting the work over networks requires multiple reproductions, and the computers of those who access your Web site must make temporary random access memory copies.

The Public Display or Performance Right

Using material on the Web is also an exercise of the public display or performance right. According to the Copyright Act, a work is displayed or performed "publicly" if it is transmitted to a place where a substantial number of persons outside of a normal circle of family and friends is gathered, whether the individuals receiving the performance or display receive it in the same place at the same time or in separate places at different times. (All of the definitions used in this section are from Section 101 of the Copyright Act, 17 USC § 101.)

To "display" a work means to show a copy of it. Posting text, graphics, and photographs on the Web is public display. Posted works are "shown" to members of the public (Web users).

To "perform" a work means to "recite, render, play, dance, or act it, either directly or by means of any device or process." Providing a recitation of a poem or literary or dramatic work on the Web is public performance of the work. Using motion picture (or other audiovisual) images in sequence or with audible sound is public performance. (By definition, showing individual images of a motion picture nonsequentially is public display.) Providing a music clip for Web site users to hear, a music video, or a Webcast of a concert is public performance.

Thus, using copyrighted material on the Internet is an exercise of at least two of the copyright owner's rights: the reproduction right and the public display or public performance right. Using copyrighted material owned by others on the Internet requires a license unless "fair use" or one of the other exceptions to the owner's rights applies. (Exceptions are discussed in "When You Don't Need a License," later in this chapter.)

DISTRIBUTION RIGHT?

A few courts have held that using copyrighted material on the Internet without the copyright owner's permission infringes the distribution right. Certainly posting material is "distribution" in the normal meaning of the word (getting the material to others). However, it may not be "distribution" according to the Copyright Act. Here's why: The Copyright Act gives copyright owners the right to distribute "copies" of the work to the public. "Copies" are defined as "material objects . . . in which a work is fixed." When work is posted on the Web, the party posting it is not providing material objects in which the work is fixed (but simply making the material available for users to view). Just to be on the safe side, the content licenses in appendix B include a license of the distribution right.

Myths

There are a number of myths concerning the necessity of getting a license. Don't make the mistake of believing them:

Myth #1: "Everything on the Web is in the public domain."
A lot of public domain material is available on the Web—federal government reports and uncopyrightable factual information, for example. However, much of the material that is on the Web is protected by copyright. (Copyright basics are discussed in chapter 1.)

Myth #2: "If I find something on the Web, it's okay to copy and use it without getting permission."
While you are free to copy public domain material that you find on the Web, generally you should not copy copyrighted material without getting permission from the copyright owner— whether you find the material on the Web or in a more traditional medium such as a book, music CD, or software disk.

Myth #3: "Anyone who puts material on the Web wants people to use that material, so I can do anything I want with material I find on the Web."
Individuals and organizations put material on the Web to make it accessible to others. They do not give up their copyright rights by putting material on the Web.

***Myth #4: "It's okay to use copyrighted material belonging to others on my
Web site so long as I don't charge people anything to view my Web site."***
Unless your use of the copyrighted work is fair use (see "Fair Use," later in this
chapter), you need a license to copy and use the work in your Web site even if
you won't be charging people to view your Web site.

***Myth #5: "My Web site will be a wonderful showcase for the copyright
owner's material, so I'm sure the owner will not object to my use of the
material."***
Don't assume that a copyright owner will be happy to have you use his or her
work. The owner may, for example, be concerned that the reproduction quality of your Web site will not do the work justice. Or the owner may be concerned that your use of the material on your Web site will make it easy for
others to make their own unauthorized copies of the material. Even if the owner
is willing to let you use the work, the owner may want to charge you a license
fee. Content owners see the Web as a new licensing market.

***Myth #6: "I don't need a license because I'm using only a small amount of
the copyrighted work."***
It is true that de minimis copying (copying a small amount) is not copyright
infringement. Unfortunately, it is rarely possible to tell where de minimus copying ends and copyright infringement begins. There are no clear delineations.

Copying a small amount of a copyrighted work is infringement if what is
copied is a qualitatively substantial portion of the copied work. In one case, a
magazine article that used three hundred words from a 200,000-word autobiography written by President Gerald Ford was found to infringe the copyright
on the autobiography. Even though the copied material was only a small part
of the autobiography, the copied portions were among the most powerful passages in the autobiography. *Harper & Row, Publishers, Inc. v. Nation Enterprises*,
471 US 539 (1985).

Copying any part of a copyrighted work is risky. If what you copy is truly a
tiny and nonmemorable part of the work, you may get away with it (the work's
owner may not be able to tell that your work incorporates an excerpt from the
owner's work). However, you run the risk of having to defend your use in expensive litigation. If what you are copying is tiny, but recognizable as coming
from the protected work, it is better to get a license (unless fair use or one of
the other exceptions discussed in "When You Don't Need a License," later in
this chapter, applies). You cannot escape liability for infringement by showing
how much of the protected work you did not take.

***Myth #7: "The copyright owner will never know I used the material on the
Web."***
When you use someone else's material on the Web, others can see what you've

done. This situation is different from copying copyrighted material for private use (photocopying a magazine article or duplicating a software diskette). Some content owners are now using Web crawlers and other technology to locate unauthorized use of their material.

Myth #8: "I paid for the compact disc (audiotape, videotape, book, article, photographic print) that I'm going to copy, so I already have the permission I need."

Copyright law distinguishes between ownership of the copyright in a work and ownership of a copy of the work. Purchasing a copy of a work (a compact disc, audiotape, videotape, book, article, or photographic print) does not give you permission to exercise the exclusive rights of copyright. (See "Owning a Copy of a Work," chapter 3.)

Myth #9: "I didn't know I needed a license. Because my infringement was innocent rather than intentional, I'm not liable for infringement damages."

Lack of intent to infringe is not a defense to infringement—nor is ignorance of the copyright law.

In one case involving innocent infringement, a federal appellate court refused to dismiss a case brought against the Sara Lee Corporation for unauthorized distribution of books by Sara Lee. Sara Lee thought it was getting its copies of the book from an authorized distributor. Between the copyright owner and an innocent infringer, the court reasoned, the innocent infringer rather than the copyright owner should suffer. *Pinkham v. Sara Lee Corp.*, 983 F2d 824 (8th Cir 1992).

Myth #10: "I don't need a license because the project in which I'm going to use the copyrighted material will only be used on my company's intranet, not on the Web."

Using the material on the company intranet will require reproduction of the material. And use on the company intranet is public display or performance, not nonpublic display or performance. (See the definition of "public," at the beginning of this section.)

Myth #11: "I'm only going to use the material on my personal home page, so I don't need a license."

The Copyright Act does not permit copying, performance, or display for "private use" other than under the fair use doctrine. Whether using material on a personal home page is fair use is unclear (there are no cases).

Myth #12: "I don't need a license to use copyrighted material in a Web site for a nonprofit group."

Copying for educational or public service use may or may not be fair use. Type of use is one of the factors that determines whether a use is fair or unfair. Other factors must be considered. (Fair use is discussed in "When You Don't Need a License," later in this chapter.)

Myth #13: "The work I want to use doesn't have a copyright notice on it, so it's not copyrighted. I'm free to use it."

For works published on or after March 1, 1989, the use of copyright notice is optional. The fact that a work doesn't have a copyright notice doesn't mean that the work is not protected by copyright. Unless you have good reason to believe a work is in the public domain (see "Public Domain Works," later in this chapter), assume that it is protected by copyright.

Myth #14: "Since I'm planning to give credit to all authors whose works I copy, I don't need to get licenses."

If you give credit to a work's author, you are not a plagiarist (you are not pretending that you authored the copied work). However, attribution is not a defense to copyright infringement. As a practical matter, attribution will increase your risk of getting caught if the owner uses a Web crawler to search out unauthorized use of material.

Myth #15: "I don't need a license because I'm going to alter the work I copy."

You cannot escape liability for copyright infringement by altering or modifying the work you copy. You can use a copyrighted work's unprotected elements, as discussed in "When You Don't Need a License," later in this chapter, but if you copy and modify protected elements of a copyrighted work, you will be infringing the copyright owner's modification right (in addition to the reproduction and display or performance rights). You may also be infringing the owner's moral rights or rights under the Visual Artists Rights Act (discussed in "Moral Rights" and "The Visual Artists Rights Act," chapter 10).

Myth #16: "If I paraphrase the author's words rather than use the author's words verbatim, I won't need a license."

Paraphrasing can be copyright infringement. Infringement is not limited to word-for-word copying. If the paraphrased version of a protected work copies the work's protected "expression"—which is more than the words alone—the paraphrased version infringes the copyright on the original work.

Myth #17: "Rather than just scanning in the copyrighted cartoon character I want to use, I'll hire an illustrator to create my own version of the cartoon character. That way, I won't need a license."

Using an illustrator's version of a character is copyright infringement if the illustrator copied the protected character. If you tell the illustrator, "Draw me a character that looks like Garfield," the illustrator's character will be a copy of

Garfield (assuming the illustrator is competent). If you can't afford a merchandise license (see "Characters," chapter 11) to use a protected character—or the owner will not grant you a license—create your own original characters.

Myth #18: "We've used this song (photo, design, and so on) in our productions in the past, so we don't need to get a license to use the work now."
Don't assume that past use was licensed use. Even if the past use was licensed, the license may not cover your use now because the license may have authorized one-time use only, or may have been limited in duration, or there may have been other restrictions. This topic is discussed in "Works You've Used Before," later in this chapter.

Myth #19: "The author of the work that I want to use lives in England, so the work is not protected by copyright in the United States."
Do not assume that a work lacks copyright protection in the United States because its author is a foreigner. Foreign authors who live in countries that belong to the Berne Convention or the Universal Copyright Convention automatically obtain copyright protection here. (See "International Protection," chapter 1.) Most major countries are members of at least one of these conventions.

When You Don't Need a License

There are several situations in which you can use a copyrighted work without getting a license. We'll discuss them in this section.

Fair Use

You don't need a license to use a copyrighted work if your use is "fair use." The fair use exception to the copyright owner's rights was created to allow limited use of copyrighted material for purposes such as criticism, comment, news reporting, teaching, scholarship, and research. Examples of fair use are quoting passages from a book in a book review; summarizing an article, with brief quotations, for a news report; and copying a small part of a work to give to students to illustrate a lesson.

Unfortunately, it is difficult to tell whether a particular use of a work is fair or unfair. Determinations are made on a case-by-case basis by considering four factors:

- **Purpose and character of use.** The courts are most likely to find fair use where the use is "transformative" and for educational or other noncommercial purposes. The use of a copyrighted work to create a new work is transformative if the new work adds some additional element or has a different character or serves a different purpose. Nontransformative use-where the new work merely serves the same objectives as the original work, or supersedes it-is less likely to be fair use.

■ **Nature of the copyrighted work.** The courts are most likely to find fair use where the copied work is a factual work or a work that has already been distributed. They are least likely to find fair use where the copied work is creative or fictional, or the work has never before been published.

■ **Amount and substantiality of portion used.** The courts are most likely to find fair use where what is used is a tiny amount of the protected work. They are least likely to find fair use where much of the protected work is used. If what is used is small in amount but substantial in terms of importance—the heart of the copied work—a finding of fair use is unlikely.

■ **Effect on the potential market for, or value of, the protected work.** The courts are most likely to find fair use where the new work is not a substitute for the copyrighted work. They are least likely to find fair use where the new work is a complete substitute for the copyrighted work. The Copyright Office has observed that it seems likely that courts, when analyzing this factor, will consider the special nature of the Web: Because online material can be easily copied and distributed downstream, even an isolated unauthorized use of copyrighted material may expose the work to many additional unauthorized uses, resulting in a significant impact on the market for the work.

Practical Advice

So far, there's been quite a bit of discussion by commentators on what sorts of Internet uses should be fair use. (For example, some people think that any noncommercial use of copyrighted material on the Web should be fair use.) However, there aren't many cases. In the rest of this section, we give some practical advice on relying on fair use.

If you are creating a Web site or Web product for a charitable organization or public service group—for example, a Web site for the local United Way organization, or Web training materials on how to perform CPR for the American Red Cross—it is possible that you can justify copying small amounts of material as fair use. Even then, you may prefer to get a license (to avoid the possibility of having to defend an infringement suit on fair use grounds). Maybe you can get the copyright owners whose works you use to waive the licensing fee to help a good cause.

NONPROFIT USE AS INFRINGEMENT

The Webmaster for the National Association of Fire Equipment Distributors (NAFED) placed copyrighted clip art images of firefighters on NAFED's Web site, for downloading by site users. The copyright owner sued, and NAFED maintained that the use was fair use because NAFED is a nonprofit association and did not charge users for the images. The court held that NAFED's use was commercial use because using the images helped NAFED promote the organization and raised Web site advertising revenues. The use was not fair use. *Marobie-FL v. National Assoc. of Fire Distributors,* 983 FSupp 1167 (ND III 1997).

If your project is commercial—an e-commerce Web site or Web products that will be licensed or sold—it will be hard to succeed on a fair use defense. It seems likely that even an "information only" Web site for a for-profit company (one that doesn't process orders) will be viewed as "commercial." The use of material on a corporate intranet or in in-house training materials is also likely to be considered commercial use. See "Fair Use," chapter 27.

If your use of copyrighted material serves traditional fair use purposes-criticism, comment, news reporting, teaching, scholarship, and research—you have a better chance of falling within the bounds of fair use than you do if your use is for other purposes. Compare these two examples:

- **Example 1:** The most recent issue of the print magazine *For the Web* featured a long article evaluating new Web design software. John criticized the magazine article on his Web site, claiming that the product ranking criteria used in the article were flawed. To illustrate his points, he quoted several sentences from the article. This use of article excerpts is likely to be fair use.

- **Example 2:** John scanned the entire article described in Example 1, as soon as it was published, and posted it without comment on his Web site so that other people wouldn't have to buy copies of the magazine. This use of the article is not likely to be fair use. John has created a substitute for the copyrighted work.

Don't assume that other countries' laws permit the use of copyrighted material for purposes considered to be fair use in this country. In the United Kingdom, for example, the "fair dealing" exception to copyright owners' rights is much more limited than our "fair use."

TRANSFORMATIVE USE

Don't make the mistake of thinking that making print material available online for comment is transformative use. In *Los Angeles Times v. Free Republic*, the defendant claimed that its posting of newspaper articles was transformative because Web site visitors could add comments following each article. The court held that the use of the articles was not fair use. 54 USPQ2d 1453 (CD Cal 2000).

Parody

Copying a copyrighted work for purposes of parodying or satirizing the protected work may be fair use. Parody is considered fair use if the parody does not replace the copyrighted work in the marketplace, and if no more of the copyrighted work is used than is necessary.

In 1994, the Supreme Court decided a case in which a music publisher was suing a rap group for creating a parody of the publisher's song, "Oh, Pretty Woman." The Court held that the group's parody of the song could be fair use even though the group's use was for "a blatantly commercial purpose," because parody "can provide social benefit, by shedding light on an earlier work, and in the process, creating a new one. *Campbell v. Acuff-Rose Music, Inc.*, 510 US 569 (1994).

For a parody to qualify as fair use of a protected work, the copied work must be the object of the parody.

EXAMPLE

The use of a purple-costumed "Barney" look-alike dinosaur in an act performed at sporting events was held to be fair use, because it parodied a number of characteristics of the well-known television character, including its "naïve, sappy, and corny personality." *Lyons Partnership v. Giannoulas,* 14 FSupp2d 947 (NDTex 1998).

Using content from the protected work to parody a different work or topic doesn't count.

EXAMPLE

A book about the O.J. Simpson murder trial, *The Cat NOT in the Hat! A Parody by Dr. Juice,* was held not to qualify for a parody defense. *The Cat NOT in the Hat* didn't parody the well-known Dr. Seuss book; it made fun of the Simpson trial. *Dr. Seuss Enterprises L.P. v. Penguin Books USA, Inc.,* 109 F3d 1394 (9th Cir 1997).

Reverse Engineering of Software

In *Sega Enterprises v. Accolade*, a federal appellate court held that copying software for reverse engineering purposes is fair use if the copying is necessary to understand the ideas and processes used in a copyrighted work. (Reverse engineering is taking a product apart to see how it works.) The copying must not exceed what is necessary to understand the unprotected elements of the copied work. 977 F2d 1510 (9th Cir 1992).

An important element of the *Sega* decision was that the Accolade game software did not compete with the copied Sega software. The issue of copying for reverse-engineering purposes to create a competitive product was not addressed in that case. However, a later case, *Sony Computer Entertainment v. Connectix Corp.*, 203 F3d 596 (9th Cir 2000) held that intermediate copying for purposes of reverse engineering a product to develop a competing product is fair use. In the *Sony* case, the defendant's engineers made intermediate copies of the Sony PlayStation's BIOS (basic input-output system) in order to develop a software product that emulated the PlayStation (permitting users to play games designed for the PlayStation without having to buy a PlayStation game console). The final version of the defendant's product did not contain any of Sony's software.

License Prohibitions

Most software is licensed rather than sold, and many licenses contain provisions prohibiting reverse engineering. With such provisions, software suppliers are attempting to use contracts law to impose a restriction not contained in the copyright law. Some people feel that these provisions are unenforceable because the Copyright Act preempts state laws such as contracts law and because the shrink wrap licenses containing such provisions do not form binding contracts. One Court of Appeals has held that a shrink wrap term prohibiting reverse engineering was unenforceable. (See "Owning a Copy," chapter 3.) However, other courts are likely to uphold such provisions, particularly in transactions in which the licensee had an opportunity to review the term before completing the transaction. (See "Clickwraps," chapter 18.) A proposed new uniform state law would, if adopted, make the prohibition against reverse engineering binding. See "UCITA," chapter 18.

Home Videotaping

In the 1980s, in the so-called "Betamax" case filed against Sony by several motion picture studios, the Supreme Court found that home videotaping of television programs with VCRs is noninfringing fair use. The Court's decision was based on the four-factor analysis discussed in "Fair Use," earlier in this chapter. The Supreme Court emphasized that a study showed that most home VCR users taped television programs for noncommercial, time-shifting purposes (so they could watch the copied programs at a more convenient time). *Sony Corp. v. Universal City Studios, Inc.*, 464 US 417 (1984).

The Betamax case does not say that all videotaping of television programs is fair use. Don't rely on the case to justify using clips from programs you've recorded with your VCR on your Web site or in Web products.

Copying Facts

You don't need a license to copy facts from a protected work. The copyright on a work does not extend to the work's facts. This is because copyright protection is limited to original works of authorship (see "Standards," chapter 1), and no one can claim originality or authorship for facts. You are free to copy facts from a copyrighted work.

EXAMPLE

Susan spent months and thousands of dollars researching President Kennedy's assassination. She discovered a number of never-before-known facts about Lee Harvey Oswald. She reported her discoveries in a book. The copyright on Susan's book does not protect the facts that Susan discovered.

BEST-SELLER LIST

The New York Times threatened to sue Amazon.com for posting data from the newspaper's best-seller list on the Amazon.com Web site. *The New York Times*—realizing, no doubt, that it not could prevent Amazon.com from using the factual information—worked out an agreement with Amazon.com under which Amazon may use the list in alphabetical order after *The New York Times* publishes it.

Use Caution

If you plan to rely on this principle, make certain that what you want to use is facts—not estimates or predictions. See "Facts or Estimates," in this section. Be cautious about how you extract facts from copyrighted material. If you copy expression as well as facts, you will have exercised the copyright owner's rights in the protected expression. Scanning a factual article such as a news article and posting the article on your Web site is not just copying facts, it's copying the expression in the writer's words, structure, and organization.

Even posting an abstract or summary of an article can be infringement. In one case, the court held that a company that wrote and published abstracts of newspaper articles infringed the copyrights on the articles because the abstracts followed the same chronological and substantive groupings of facts and resulted in the same conclusions. *Nihon Keizai Shimbun, Inc. v. Comline Business Data, Inc.*, 166 F3d 65 (2d Cir 1999).

FACTS OR ESTIMATES

Kenneth Kapes, a coin dealer, maintained a Web page showing retail prices of many coins. He obtained the price data from CDN Inc.'s wholesale lists. CDN sued Kapes for copyright infringement, and Kapes defended on the grounds that the coin prices were uncopyrightable facts. The court found that the prices were not facts, but estimates of value based on CDN's expertise. CDN testified that it determined prices for individual coins after sifting through relevant literature, keeping track of the economy and exchange rates, determining what was important, and weighing all the factors that could affect wholesale "bid" and "ask" prices. Had CDN merely discovered and reported existing facts, the outcome would have been different. *CDN Inc. v. Kapes,* 197 F3d 1256 (9th Cir 1999).

"Hot News"

While facts are not protected by copyright, using "hot news" gathered by a competitor may be wrongful misappropriation. In *International News Service v. Associated Press*, Associated Press sued to enjoin INS from taking and selling news about World War I battles, gathered at the front by AP journalists. INS took the facts from AP postings on public bulletin boards and from early editions of newspapers published by AP members. The Supreme Court held that even though facts are not protected by copyright, hot news misappropriation is actionable if the plaintiff had compiled information at some cost or expense; the information had significant commercial value while it was fresh; the defendant took the news generated by the plaintiff for its own commercial purposes, without engaging in its own newsgathering; and the parties were in competition with one another. 248 US 215 (1918).

The National Basketball Association used the hot news misappropriation theory in a suit against sports score reporting services to try to stop the defendants from providing "almost real time" scores from basketball games through pager services and on America Online. The court found that the defendants had not engaged in unlawful misappropriations because the NBA had failed to show any adverse competitive effect from the defendants' service on the market for live attendance or licensing live broadcasts of games. It also stated that the NBA failed to show free-riding because the defendants collected the information themselves by having reporters watch games on television or listen to them on the radio rather than taking the information from competitive NBA data networks or pages. *National Basketball Association v. Motorola*, 105 F3d 841 (2d Cir 1997).

Databases and Research Reports

Databases are compilations of facts (works formed by collecting and assembling data). A compilation of facts is protected by copyright only to the extent of the author's originality in the selection, coordination, and arrangement of facts. The Supreme Court has held that a typical telephone directory lacks sufficient originality to be copyrightable. *Feist Publications, Inc. v. Rural Telephone Service Co.*, 499 US 340 (1991). Here's why: Every "listed" number is included, so there is no originality in the selection of material. Coordination and arrangement—alphabetical order by last name—are routine rather than original.

Some compilations have sufficient originality in selection, coordination, or arrangement of their material to be protected by copyright. You are free to use the facts from such databases. However, if you reproduce or display the whole database, you will be copying the protected elements (selection, coordination, arrangement) and infringing the copyright on the compilation.

Databases and research reports are often licensed rather than sold, and the licenses generally contain restrictions on use—for example, a prohibition against commercial use of the data or against use on a Web site, or a limitation to educational use. With these restrictions, the content owners are trying to use contracts law to get protection for facts. Some experts think that such restrictions are void because the federal copyright law preempts contracts law in this area. The case mentioned below in "Database Copying" is one of the few cases to address this topic.

DATABASE COPYING

ProCD compiled information from more than three thousand telephone directories into a computer database and sold the database on CD-ROM discs. Matthew Zeidenberg bought a copy, copied the uncopyrightable database, and made the database available for a fee over the Web. ProCD sued, claiming that Zeidenberg had violated the shrink wrap license printed on the ProCD box, which limited use of the database to personal use. Zeidenberg maintained that the shrink wrap license was unenforceable because facts cannot protected by copyright. The court held that the license was an enforceable contract between Zeidenberg and ProCD. *ProCD, Inc. v. Zeidenberg*, 86 F3d 1447 (7th Cir 1996). Another aspect of this case is discussed in "Owning a Copy," chapter 3.

Proposed legislation that would give legal protection to databases—not under copyright law, but in a separate law—is pending in Congress. Several other countries already provide legal protection for databases.

Copying Ideas

You don't need a license to copy the ideas used in a copyrighted work. Copyright does not protect a work's ideas, processes, or systems. Under copyright law, you are free to copy these elements.

EXAMPLE

John's copyrighted book explains a new system of bookkeeping created by John. While John's copyright protects his expression in the book (his description of the bookkeeping system), it does not protect the system itself or the ideas that make up the system. Others are free to study John's book, figure out and use the bookkeeping system, and even write their own books describing the system.

Unfortunately, the line between ideas and "expression" is difficult even for experienced attorneys to draw. Only a few generalizations are possible:

■ A work's theme or purpose—for example, training telemarketers or helping consumers pick wine—is an unprotected idea.

■ Stock characters and situations are unprotected ideas. Examples of stock characters are the jealous boyfriend, proud grandparents, and starving artist. Examples of stock situations are the conflict between a parent and a teenaged child and the rivalry between two siblings. So-called "distinctively delineated" characters, such as Tarzan, E.T., and Indiana Jones, are protected by copyright and possibly by trademark as well (see "Characters," chapter 11).

■ A novel's detailed plot is protected expression, even though stock situations within the plot are not protected.

If there is only one way to express an idea (or only a limited number of ways), you can copy the expression as well as the idea. For example, one case permitted the copying of a set of game rules because there were only a limited number of ways to express rules for that type of game. Because this concept, called the "merger" principle, is complex, you should consult an experienced copyright attorney before you rely on it.

Is it okay to copy the layout or template of an existing Web page? (Some Web design books say it is.) In terms of copyright law, the principle is easy: You are free to copy the ideas, processes, or systems used in the existing Web page, but you cannot copy the page's expression.

EXAMPLE

Recycling Company's competitor, MoCo, has a Web site that consists of four components—information about MoCo, information about MoCo's services, statistics about the growing popularity of recycling in the U.S., and a request form that users can email in to get more information on the company's services. Recycling Company is free to put together its own Web site with company information, service information, statistics, and an email request form.

How much further Recycling Company can go is unclear, because it's difficult to draw the line between ideas and expression. In a few years, we may have answers to such questions as "Is it okay to copy a feature (such as a scrollable message board) used in other Web sites if I write my own code?" This topic is the twenty-first century equivalent of the "look and feel" software user interface copyright cases of the 1980s.

If you plan on using the ideas or approach used in an existing Web site or Web product, don't forget about patent rights. If what you want to use is covered by a patent, you will need a license from the patent owner. See "Patent Law," chapter 2.

Using Material from the Web

Much of the material that is on the Internet is copyrighted. If you find material on the Internet that you want to use in your own project—on a Web site, in a Web product, or in some other medium such as a print newsletter or a corporate presentation—don't make the mistake of assuming that you are free to use the material. If the material is in the public domain, you do not need permission. If it is copyrighted, unless fair use or some other exception to the copyright owner's rights apply, you need permission. Posting copyrighted material on the Web is not a waiver of copyright or an open invitation use the material.

EXAMPLE

Sally has been asked to give a presentation to her company's management on technologies for online learning. She went on the Internet and found an article reviewing the latest technologies. Unless fair use applies (unlikely, because Sally works for a for-profit company), Sally should get permission from the copyright owner before posting the article on the company intranet for others in the company to see or making copies of the article to distribute at her presentation. She can use facts or ideas from the review without getting permission.

Limited Permission Grants

In a number of documents that are available on the Web, you'll see a statement that it's permissible to copy the document for certain purposes. Here are three examples:

- "This article may be copied in its entirety for personal or educational use. The copy should include a License Notice at the beginning and at the end. It may not be modified without the written permission of the authors."

- "Permission is granted to freely copy this document in electronic form, or to print for personal use."

- "All the text and pictures on this Web server are copyrighted. You may use the pictures for any noncommercial purpose if you attribute the source."

Authors place these "limited permission grants" on their documents because they want the documents to be shared and used for certain purposes (and they don't want to be bothered with requests for permission for such uses). Don't confuse a limited permission grant with a waiver of copyright. A limited permission grant is just a license to use the work in ways stated in the limited permission grant—and only in those ways. (Licenses are discussed in chapters 3 and 10.)

Limited permission grants generally appear on a Web site's Terms of Use. See "Terms of Use," chapter 12.

Uses Not Covered

If you want to use a document or image in a way that is not authorized in the Terms of Use, contact the copyright owner and get permission. If you don't, you will be infringing the copyright on the work.

EXAMPLE

Developer found some images she liked on a Web page. The Web page stated, "You may use these images for any noncommercial purpose if you attribute the source." If Developer uses those images in a commercial CD-ROM product without getting permission from the owner, she will be infringing the copyrights on the images. Developer should go through the normal licensing process if she wants to use those images in her commercial product.

Don't assume that a copyright owner who has given a limited permission grant will be happy to have you use the work for purposes beyond those stated in the grant. If you want to use a work in a way not covered by the grant, follow the procedure that you would use with copyrighted works from traditional media: Get permission before you use the work. Once you have stepped outside the bounds of the grant, you are on dangerous ground unless your use is fair use.

Be cautious about concluding that the use you want to make of the work is within the scope of a limited permission grant. If there's any doubt about whether the grant covers your planned use, contact the copyright owner to discuss your plans and get written permission giving you the right to use the material in your project (see "Determining What Rights You Need," chapter 10). If you assume the grant covers your use and you use the work, the copyright owner may disagree and sue you.

EXAMPLE

Developer found a short geography quiz on a Web site for educators. The Web site Terms of Use stated that material from the site could be copied and used for educational purposes. Developer, relying on the limited permission grant, used the quiz on a subscription-based edutainment site for children. The copyright owner could sue Developer for copyright infringement, claiming that Developer's use of the quiz was commercial use rather than educational use.

In the above example, if the copyright owner sues, it is possible that the developer ultimately will win the lawsuit. However, it would have been wiser for the developer to have contacted the copyright owner and requested, for a reasonable fee, permission to use the quiz. If the owner refused to give permission or the fee was too high, the developer then could have substituted other material and avoided litigation.

Who Is the Owner?

If you want to use material put on the Web by someone other than the copyright owner, but with the owner's permission, you need permission from the owner, not from the poster.

EXAMPLE

Online Bookseller got Author's permission to post a chapter from Author's new book on insects on Online Bookseller's Web site. Science Online wants to use the chapter on its site. Science Online needs permission from the copyright owner (probably Author or Author's publisher, if Author assigned the copyright to Author's publisher).

Getting permission to use material you find on the Internet is complicated by the fact that some people post copyrighted material they do not own or have permission to use. If someone has posted copyrighted material in violation of the copyright owner's exclusive rights, getting the poster's permission to use the copyrighted material will do you no good. You need the owner's permission.

EXAMPLE

John, a fan of the cartoon strip "Peanuts," used a picture of Snoopy on his Web site without getting permission from the copyright owner. Developer downloaded the picture and used it in her CD-ROM product, with John's permission. Getting permission from John is worthless, since John does not own the copyright (and is himself probably an infringer of the owner's exclusive rights).

Do not assume that the person who posted the document is the owner. Ask questions: Who created the document? What is its origin? If there's any doubt about whether the person who put the document up is the owner, don't use the document. It is always a good idea to ask for warranties of ownership and noninfringement (discussed in "Obtaining a License," chapter 10).

Finally, when getting permission, be wary of people who mistakenly think they own the rights in material they have commissioned in the past.

EXAMPLE

Developer saw some photographs she liked on Z Company's Web Site. Developer contacted Z Company's president and got permission to use the photographs on Developer's Web site. If the copyrights in the photographs are owned by the photographer who took them (likely, if the photographer was a freelancer), Z Company cannot authorize Developer to use the photographs. Only the photographer can.

Copyright ownership rules are discussed in chapter 3. Ownership of works created by independent contractors is discussed in "Copyright Ownership," chapter 6.

Implied Licenses

Copyright law recognizes that permission to use copyrighted material can be implied from a copyright owner's conduct or from custom. Here are three examples of how the doctrine of implied license applies in cyberspace:

1. When you want to access a document a copyright owner has placed on a Web server, your computer will have to make a temporary copy of the document in its random access memory (RAM). Most copyright experts believe that the copyright owner, by posting the document, has implicitly given you permission to make that temporary copy.

2. When the user of an online service provider sends a message to a public message board, many copyright attorneys believe that the author of the message implicitly gives the online service provider permission to display the message.

3. Some people, when replying to an email message or a message board message, repeat the message (or part of it). Most copyright experts believe that the message's author implicitly gives others permission to copy the message for the purpose of replying to it. (Copying for the purpose of reply could also be fair use.)

The doctrine of implied license is a narrowly applied "gap filler" that's used when implied permission makes sense—based on circumstances (Examples 1 and 2), or on custom (Example 3). At the present, people familiar with Internet usage have different opinions about the scope of the implied license that arises from posting material on the Internet. For example, some people think that posting a document gives an implied license to Internet users to print out a "hard" copy of the document (in addition to making a temporary copy in the computer's RAM). Others would say the implied license is limited to permission to make a temporary copy in the computer's RAM.

Be cautious about relying on an implied license while Internet custom and fair use rules are still developing. Don't try to stretch the implied license doctrine—for example, relying on the doctrine to justify printing out several hundred messages from a message board and selling them as a compilation of views on the topic.

Public Domain Works

You don't need a license to use a public domain work. Public domain works—works not protected by copyright—can be used by anyone. Because these works are not copyrighted, no one can claim the exclusive rights of copyright for such works.

The rules regarding what works are in the public domain vary from country to country. A work in the public domain in the United States may be protected by copyright in Canada or other countries.

There are several ways in which works fall into the public domain in the United States:

- **Expiration of the copyright.** All works first published before January 1, 1923, are in the public domain in the United States because their copyrights have expired. No new works will enter the public domain in the U.S. through expiration of copyright until January 1, 2019. We discussed the copyright term for works created on or after January 1, 1978, in "Duration of the Rights," chapter 1. Different copyright term rules apply to works that were published prior to that date. If you are interested in the details of copyright terms for older works, see "Copyright Expiration" in this section.

■ **Failure of the copyright owner to renew the copyright.** Under the 1909 Copyright Act, copyright protection lasted twenty-eight years. A copyright owner could obtain an additional term, known as a "renewal term," by filing an application to renew in the twenty-eighth year. The Copyright Renewal Amendment of 1992 eliminated the requirement of filing a renewal application for works published between 1964 and 1977, inclusive. Renewal is not required for works created after 1977. However, before 1992, a number of works entered the public domain because the copyright owner failed to file a renewal application.

■ **Failure to use copyright notice of publicly distributed copies of a work (for works published before March 1, 1989).** Under prior law, the distribution of copies without copyright notice resulted in the forfeiture of copyright protection. For works distributed before January 1, 1978, forfeiture was automatic. For works distributed between January 1, 1978 and March 1, 1989, notice was required, but failure to use notice did not necessarily result in forfeiture of copyright protection. Parts of the UNIX operating system software are in the public domain because copies were publicly distributed without notice. The use of copyright notice is now optional, as we explained in "Procedure for Getting Protection," chapter 1.

LONG WAIT

No new works will enter the public domain in the United States through expiration of copyright until January 1, 2019. That's because Congress, in the 1998 Sony Bono Copyright Term Extension Act, extended the term of copyright by twenty years—applying the extension to *all works still protected by copyright in 1998*. Copyrights which had already expired in 1998—works published before January 1, 1923—were not affected by the act and are in the public domain in the United States.

Copyright Expiration

Under current U.S. copyright law, determining when a work's copyright has expired is simple. For a work created by an individual, the copyright expires seventy years after the death of the author. (There's a different rule for works made for hire, as we discussed in "Duration of the Rights," chapter 1.)

For works published before January 1, 1978, the effective date of the current copyright law, the rules are different. As we mentioned in "Long Wait" in this section, the Sonny Bono Copyright Term Extension Act extended the term of copyright by twenty years for all copyrights still in existence in 1998. A copyright that was in existence before January 1, 1978 and still in existence in October 1998 now has a term of 95 years. Thus, the copyright on a work first published in 1923, if renewed, will expire at the end of the day on December 31, 2018. (All copyright terms run to the end of the calendar year in which they expire.) A copyright on a work first published in 1924, if renewed, will expire on December 31, 2019.

There are special rules for works created before January 1, 1978 but unpublished: Copyright in such works lasts for the life of the author plus seventy years (or, for a work made for hire, the term stated in "Duration of the Rights," chapter 1). However, in no case will such copyrights expire before December 31, 2002. If these works are published before December 31, 2002, they will be protected until at least December 31, 2047.

Restored Foreign Copyrights

In the 1990s, Congress passed two laws which had the effect of restoring U.S. copyright protection for certain types of foreign works. For works whose copyrights are restored under either of these provisions, the duration of copyright is the same as it would have been had the work never entered the public domain in the U.S. The two provisions are discussed in this section.

NAFTA Legislation

First came the restoration of copyright for 345 movies from Mexico and Canada that had fallen into the public domain here because they were published without notice between 1978 and March 1, 1989. The legislation was part of the North American Free Trade Agreements (NAFTA) with Mexico and Canada.

GATT Legislation

The second piece of copyright restoration legislation, Section 104A of the Copyright Act, restored the U.S. copyrights for certain foreign works that entered the public domain in the U.S. because the copyright owner failed to comply with formalities once imposed by U.S. law (renewal, notice, or the former law's domestic manufacturing requirements). Section 104A also restores the U.S. copyright for certain foreign sound recordings and works first published in a country with which the U.S. did not have a copyright treaty.

Section 104A applies only to foreign works from countries that are members of the Berne Convention or the World Trade Organization, and only if the work was still protected by copyright in the "source country" on January 1, 1996. The law was part of the Agreement on Trade-Related Aspects of Intellectual Property Rights (TRIPS), an annex to the international treaty, General

Agreement on Tariffs and Trade (GATT). It contains provisions designed to protect the interests of those who used "restored copyright" works prior to January 1, 1996. A list of copyright owners who have filed notices of intent to enforce restored copyrights can be found at www.loc.gov/copyright/gatt.html.

Finding Public Domain Works

The Copyright Office does not maintain a list of public domain works, nor does it publish annual lists of copyrights that will expire at the end of the year. You have to find these works yourself.

If the copyright notice on a work is for a year prior to January 1, 1923, the work is in the public domain. It will be harder to determine expiration dates for works covered by the current Copyright Act: Except for works made for hire, the duration of copyright is seventy years beyond the life of the author rather than a set number of years.

If you are interested in using a work to which the 1909 Copyright Act's renewal requirement applies, you can order a Copyright Office renewal search to find out whether the copyright was renewed. (There is a fee. Searches are discussed in "Determining Who Owns the Copyright," chapter 10.) The provisions on renewal are complex, and you should get an experienced attorney or rights clearance agent to help you determine how those rules apply to a particular work.

FAILURE TO RENEW

The motion picture *The Little Shop of Horrors* went into the public domain at the end of 1988 because the copyright on the motion picture was not renewed. The John Wayne film *McClintock* went into the public domain at the end of 1991 because its copyright was not renewed. (However, permissions may still be required to use clips from these films, for reasons stated in "Complications," later in this section, and in "Licensing Film and Television Clips," chapter 11.)

Unless you know that a work was distributed without copyright notice, you will only learn about it if the issue has been raised in a reported court decision.

The Copyright Office does not keep copies of works whose registrations have expired. Some content providers sell copies of public domain works, such as WPA photographs (see appendix D). The Library of Congress has copies of some of these works. We've included resource information to help you locate public domain material in "Licensing Photos and Still Images," chapter 11, and "Public Domain Music," chapter 21.

Complications

Derivative works (works based on preexisting works) are often created from public domain works. New material in a derivative work is protected by copyright. For example, in the case *Brown v. McCormick*, 23 FSupp2d 594 (D Md 1998), a quilt based on public domain quilts in the Smithsonian Museum was held sufficiently original to be protected by copyright.

You cannot copy the new material in a new version of a public domain work unless you obtain a license from the owner of the copyright in the derivative work, but you can use the elements that came from the public domain work.

EXAMPLE

The movie *Coast* is based on a public domain novel. If Web Developer wants to use a clip from the movie, Developer must get a license from the owner of the copyright in the movie. Developer is free to use an excerpt from the underlying novel.

COPYING A COPY

The general rule is that it's okay to copy a public domain work, but copying a modern-day copy of a public domain work may be infringement. For example, according to copyright law, anyone is free to photograph the painting *The Last Supper*, but if you scan a postcard showing the painting, that may be copyright infringement. The important question is whether the copy—the postcard's photograph of the painting—has sufficient originality to qualify for copyright protection. This issue was raised in the case *Bridgeman Art Library, Ltd. v. Corel Corp.* Bridgeman claimed that Corel had copied images from Bridgeman's CD-ROMs of artwork photos and used the copied images in its own CD-ROM products. The court held that Bridgeman's photos—"slavish copies" of public domain works of art—were the product of skill and effort, but they were not original. As the court noted, the point of the exercise was to reproduce the underlying work "with absolute fidelity." Because Bridgeman's copies were not original, they were not copyrighted, and Corel was free to copy them. 36 FSupp2d 191 (SD NY 1999).

Sometimes the derivative work is in the public domain because the owner didn't renew the copyright, but the underlying work is still protected by copyright.

EXAMPLE

The movie *Dream* is based on a novel of the same name. Both the movie and the novel are pre-1978 works to which the 1909 Copyright Act's renewal requirement applied. The owner of the copyright in the novel filed a renewal application at the appropriate time in 1980, but the owner of the motion picture copyright did not renew its copyright. The underlying work, the novel, is protected by copyright. The derivative work, the movie, is not protected.

If the underlying work is protected but the derivative work is not, and you want to use an excerpt of the derivative work, you will generally need permission from the underlying work's copyright owner. This topic is discussed in "Determining Who Owns the Copyright," chapter 10.

If a public domain work incorporates another work, the incorporated work may still be protected by copyright. If the incorporated work is protected by copyright, you must get a license from the owner of that copyright if you want to use an excerpt of the public domain work that incorporates the protected work.

EXAMPLE

The movie *Mountains* is in the public domain because the renewal requirement applies to the movie and the copyright owner did not renew the copyright. *Mountains* contains a song that is still protected by copyright. If Developer wants to use a clip of *Mountains* that contains the song, Developer needs a license from the owner of the copyright in the song.

Using Works You Own

You can use works that you own without worrying about obtaining licenses.

Existing Works

If you own the copyrights in all preexisting works that you will be using, you don't need to obtain licenses.

If you are an employer, you own the copyrights in the United States in works created for you by employees acting within the scope of their employment. (See "The Work Made for Hire Rule," chapter 3, and "Works Made by Employees," chapter 5.) You may not own those rights in other countries. You do not own even the U.S. rights in works created for you by independent contractors unless you obtained assignments from them or the works had the status of "specially commissioned works made for hire." (See "Copyright Ownership," chapter 6.)

If you created a work for a past employer within the scope of your employment, you do not own the copyright in that work. (See "The Work Made for Hire Rule," chapter 3.) You cannot use the work without obtaining a license.

If you created the work as an independent contractor, you own the copyright unless you assigned the copyright to the hiring party or you signed a valid work made for hire agreement. (See "Copyright Ownership," chapter 6.)

New Works

You can avoid obtaining licenses to use third-party content if you create your own content. If works will be created by employees or independent contractors, be sure you follow the strategies described in earlier chapters to ensure that you obtain copyright ownership in the United States and throughout the world. (These strategies are described in the "Using the Employment Agreement," chapter 5, and in "Copyright Ownership," chapter 6.) As we explained in those chapters, you should use Form 6 from appendix B with employees and Form 7 or Form 14 with independent contractors.

Special rules apply if you plan to modify a "work of visual art" even if you own the work. A work of visual art, for copyright purposes, is a limited edition painting, drawing, print, sculpture, or a photograph produced for exhibition purposes. The rules apply if the work was created by an artist after the effective date of the Visual Artists Rights Act of 1990. (This law is discussed in chapter 10.) Moral rights may also apply to modifications. See "Moral Rights," chapter 10.

Works You've Used Before

Don't assume that you own a work or have a right to use it on the Internet just because you've used it before. The prior use may have been unauthorized—or it may have been authorized based only on a limited license grant. Check your documentation for the earlier use. If you don't have any documentation, check with the owner of the work.

THE *TASINI* CASE

In the early 1990s, Jonathan Tasini and other freelance writers licensed their articles to newspaper and magazine publishers such as *The New York Times, Newsday,* and *Time Inc.* for one-time "first publication" use in print publications. When their articles were later used in electronic databases without their permission, they sued the publishers and the database companies. The publishers maintained that they had the right to include the articles in the databases because the databases were revisions of the "collective works" (magazine or newspaper issues) in which the articles were originally published. (An obscure provision of the Copyright Act, Section 201(c), gives the owner of the copyright in a collective work the right to reproduce and distribute contributions to the collective work in a revision or later issue of the collective work.) The federal district court agreed with the publishers. The Court of Appeals, however, reversed, holding for the plaintiffs. *Tasini v. The New York Times Co.,* 206 F3d 161 (1999). The Court of Appeals ruled that the database republication of the articles was not a "revision" of the original collective work. The publishers may have infringed the writers' copyrights by using the articles in the databases. (The case is still pending, and the publishers have raised several other defenses.)

CHAPTER 10

CLEARING RIGHTS AND OBTAINING LICENSES

Most of this chapter is devoted to the licensing process and its three steps:

1. Determining who owns the copyrights in the works you want to use.

2. Determining what rights you need.

3. Obtaining licenses from the copyright owners.

At the end of this chapter, we'll discuss:

■ How to use a rights clearance agency, licensing agents, stock houses, and media libraries to avoid many of the difficulties involved in licensing.

■ Copyright assignments, an alternative to licensing.

■ The Visual Artists Rights Act and "moral rights," which impose restrictions on modifying certain types of works.

The industries that generate the types of works that you are likely to want to license are described in chapter 11. Music licensing is discussed in chapter 21.

Determining Who Owns the Copyright

The first step in the licensing process is determining who owns the copyright in the work you want to use.

If the work you want to use contains a copyright notice (many works do, although use of copyright notice is now optional), the name on the notice is your starting point. It is the name of the copyright owner at the time your copy of the work was published—but not necessarily the work's creator or the current copyright owner.

The copyright owner named in the notice may have assigned the copyright to someone else after your copy was published. (Assignments are discussed in "Assignments," chapter 3.) You need to trace the work's "chain of title" (just like in real estate) to find the current owner, because your license must come from the current copyright owner.

EXAMPLE

John, a freelance writer, assigned the copyright in his article on adventure travel to Mega Books, Inc. If Adventure Travel, Inc. wants to use John's article on its Web site, Adventure must get permission from Mega Books, not from John.

The rest of this section tells you how to check a work's chain of title and how to find the party who has authority to grant you a license to use a work.

Is the Work Registered?

The chain of title for a registered work can be checked by obtaining an "assignment search" of the Copyright Office's files (discussed in "Checking the Chain of Title," later in this section).

There are five ways to find out whether a work's copyright has been registered:

- Check the Copyright Office's online databases, which are described at www.loc.gov/copyright/guide.html. Only works registered after January 1, 1978, are included in these databases.

- Check the *Catalog of Copyright Entries*, which lists registered works by title. This catalog is published by the Copyright Office. It was discontinued in 1982, but you may find it useful when researching older works. Some libraries have copies of the catalog. The catalog divides works into eight categories (literary works, performing arts, motion pictures and filmstrips, sound recordings, serials and periodicals, visual arts, maps, and renewals).

■ Order a Copyright Office registration search from the Copyright Office's Reference and Bibliography Section by filling out a copy of a Search Request Form and sending it to the Copyright Office. The form is available online as part of Information Circular 22. (Click on "Information Circulars" on the Copyright Office's home page, www.loc.gov/copyright, for an index of the circulars.) You have to print it out and mail it or fax it to the Copyright Office. Check the "Registration" box at the top and provide as much of the requested information on the work as you can. The Copyright Office will charge you $65 per hour for a search.

■ Hire a copyright search firm to conduct a Copyright Office registration search for you. A list of search firms appears in appendix C. Using a search firm will cost more than a Copyright Office search done by the Copyright Office Reference and Bibliography Section staff, but you will get the results faster.

■ Do a Copyright Office search yourself, if you live in the Washington, D.C. area, using microfilm and automated registration records in the Copyright Office.

Checking the Chain of Title

How you check a work's chain of title depends on whether the copyright has been registered or not.

Registered Copyrights

If the copyright in the work has been registered with the Copyright Office, you trace the work's chain of title by obtaining a Copyright Office assignment search. The Copyright Act permits assignees to record their assignments with the Copyright Office to give others constructive notice of the assignment, just as purchasers of real estate do in recording their purchases in county records. (Recording assignments is discussed in "Assignments," chapter 3). A Copyright Office assignment search will reveal whether any assignments of the work's copyright have been recorded.

An assignment search, like a registration search, can be obtained by filling out a Search Request Form (check the "Assignment" box on the form) and sending it to the Copyright Office's Reference and Bibliography Section; by hiring a copyright search firm; or by checking the Copyright Office's files yourself. (The online databases mentioned earlier in this section contain information on assignments.) These options are described in "Is the Work Registered?," earlier in this section.

If the work was published before January 1, 1978, you may want to request a renewal search as well as an assignment search, to see if the copyright was renewed. (See "Public Domain Works," chapter 9.) If there was no copyright renewal, the work may be in the public domain. The Copyright Renewal Act of 1992 automatically extended the term of copyright for copyrights secured between January 1, 1964 and December 31, 1977, making renewal registration optional for such copyrights.

The *Catalog of Copyright Entries* does not include entries of assignments, so it cannot be used to check the chain of title. However, it does contain information on renewals.

An assignment search will only reveal assignments of registered copyrights that have been recorded in the Copyright Office. It will not reveal recent assignments that have not yet been cataloged.

Unregistered Copyrights

If the copyright has not been registered, a Copyright Office search will not help you. The only way to check the chain of title for an unregistered work is to contact the copyright owner named in the copyright notice and ask whether the copyright has been assigned.

Secret Assignments

If you obtain a license from the person or company that you think is the current copyright owner (because that's what the Copyright Office's assignment records indicate) and later learn that your assignor had actually assigned the copyright to someone else before giving you a license, your license will still be valid if it meets three criteria:

- You didn't know of the unrecorded assignment at the time you entered into the license agreement.

- The license is nonexclusive. (An exclusive license is one that does not overlap another grant of rights. See "Licenses," chapter 3.)

- The license is in writing.

According to the Copyright Act, a nonexclusive written license prevails over a conflicting earlier copyright assignment if the license was taken in good faith before the copyright assignment was recorded, and without notice of the copyright assignment. 17 USC § 205(e).

EXAMPLE

According to the Copyright Office's records, songwriter Ben assigned the copyright in Ben's song, "Foggy Day," to Rotten Music in 1988. In January 2000, Rotten assigned the copyright in "Foggy Day" to First State Bank. First State Bank did not record its assignment. In June 2000, Rotten gave Web Developer a written nonexclusive license to use "Foggy Day" in an online tour of the city of San Francisco. (Rotten didn't tell Developer it had assigned the copyright to First State Bank, and Developer had no reason to know about the assignment.) Developer's license from Rotten is valid because it is in writing and nonexclusive and because Developer got it in good faith and without notice of Rotten's assignment to First State Bank. First State Bank should have protected its interests by recording its assignment. (Recording is discussed in "Assignments," chapter 3.)

If your license is exclusive, you have to record it in the Copyright Office to obtain protection against a conflicting earlier transfer. (See "Obtaining a License," later in this chapter).

Later Assignments

If you get a license from the copyright owner and the copyright owner later assigns the copyright to someone else, the new owner cannot revoke your license if it is nonexclusive and in writing. A nonexclusive, written license prevails over a later assignment.

EXAMPLE

On May 1, Author granted Adventure Travel, Inc. a written, nonexclusive license to use excerpts from Author's book on Adventure Travel's Web site. The next month, Author assigned the copyright in the book to Electronic Publisher. Electronic Publisher cannot require Adventure Travel to get a new license from Electronic Publisher.

Multiple Assignments

If the copyright has been assigned several times, you need to get your license from the current owner of the copyright—the most recent assignee.

EXAMPLE

Composer assigned the copyright in her song to Small Music, which recorded the assignment. Small Music later assigned the copyright to Big Music, which recorded the assignment. If Web Developer wants to use the song written by Composer, Developer should get a license from Big Music.

Existing Licenses

Both exclusive licenses and nonexclusive licenses can be recorded in the Copyright Office. (Details of recording are discussed in "Obtaining a License," later in this chapter.) Your Copyright Office search report will tell you what kind of existing exclusive licenses there are on a work. Most nonexclusive licensees do not record their licenses.

Unless you want an exclusive license, you don't need to worry about non-exclusive licenses. An existing nonexclusive licensee has no grounds for complaint if you are granted permission to use the same work on a nonexclusive basis.

Exclusive licenses are a potential problem, though. A copyright owner cannot give you a license that conflicts with an existing exclusive license.

EXAMPLE

Joan wants to use excerpts of Publisher's reference book in an online encyclopedia. Publisher has already granted Massive Multimedia an exclusive license to use the reference book on the Internet. Publisher cannot give Joan an exclusive or nonexclusive license to use the reference book.

According to U.S. copyright law, an exclusive licensee can grant sublicenses unless the license agreement states otherwise (an exclusive licensee is considered an "owner" of an interest in copyright). In the previous example, Developer should find out whether Massive Multimedia has the right to sublicense. If it does, Developer should ask Massive for a nonexclusive license to use excerpts of the reference book.

Finding the Owner

If you have obtained a Copyright Office search for the work you want to use, the search report will give you the copyright owner's address.

If the work is unregistered and a Copyright Office search is not possible, the work's copyright notice page may give the copyright owner's address. For books, the publisher may act as the author's licensing agent, even if the publisher does not own the copyright (or at least the publisher may be able to contact the author for you). For motion pictures, the film archives at University of California–Los Angeles, the University of Southern California, and the Academy of Motion Picture Arts and Sciences in Los Angeles may help.

CAN'T FIND THE OWNER?

In Canada, when someone wants a license to use a published work whose owner cannot be found, they can apply to the Copyright Board (a government body) for a compulsory license to use the work. We don't have a similar law in the U.S., but the Copyright Office recently recommended that Congress consider providing for compulsory licensing of such "orphan works."

Jointly Owned Works

For jointly owned works, a single co-owner can give you a nonexclusive license to use the work in the United States unless the co-owners have a contract requiring the consent of all co-owners (see "Joint Authorship and Ownership," chapter 3). It's safer to contact all co-owners.

Complications

Determining who owns the copyright in the work you want to use can be complicated by a number of factors. We discuss four such factors in this subsection.

Copyrighted Components

If the work you want to use incorporates several different copyrightable works, you may need more than one license.

> **EXAMPLE**
>
> Online Training Company wants to use a film clip in a new training product. The film clip contains part of a song. The film's copyright owner does not own the copyright in the song (the film's producer got a nonexclusive license to use the song in the movie). Online Training needs to obtain two licenses—one from the owner of the film copyright and one from the owner of the music copyright. The owner of the film copyright cannot authorize Online Training to use the music component of the film clip.

If you only want to use a separately owned component of a larger work, you do not need to get a license from the owner of the copyright in the larger work.

> **EXAMPLE**
>
> Web Developer wants to use a photograph that was used in a brochure produced by Graphic Artist. The photograph was created by Photographer, who gave Graphic Artist a nonexclusive license to use it in the brochure. Developer does not need to get a license from Graphic Artist. She does need to get a license from Photographer.

Derivative Works

If the work you want to use is a derivative work (a work based on a preexisting work) created and owned by someone other than the owner of the underlying work, you will probably need a license from the owner of the underlying work as well as a license from the owner of the derivative work.

EXAMPLE

Game Developer wants to create an online version of Gameco's popular CD-ROM game. The Gameco game is based on a popular action film. (The film's copyright owner granted Gameco a license to create a CD-ROM product using the plot and characters from the film.) Game Developer needs licenses from both Gameco and the film's copyright owner.

If the excerpt from the derivative work that you want to use was created entirely by the creator of the derivative work and is not based on the underlying work, you do not need a license to use the underlying work.

Split Rights

Copyright rights for certain types of work—books and music, for example— are often split among several parties through the grant of a number of exclusive licenses. If the copyright owner has split the rights geographically, you will have to get licenses from all the exclusive licensees to obtain worldwide rights.

In some industries, rights are split among several owners by market segment or medium as well as geographically.

EXAMPLE

Author granted Book Publisher an exclusive license to publish Author's novel in print form and to license the novel to others for book club and condensed-book print publication. Author granted Producer the exclusive right to make a motion picture version of the novel. Author retained all other rights in the novel. The copyright rights in the novel have been split by market segment and medium.

If your Copyright Office search reveals that the rights in a work have been split among several owners, you need to get a license from the assignee or exclusive licensee who owns the particular rights that you need.

EXAMPLE

Marketing Company wants to use excerpts of Author's book on its e-commerce site. Author granted Book Publisher an exclusive license to publish Author's book in print form, retaining all other rights. Marketing Company needs to obtain a license from Author (but Marketing Company should carefully review the preexisting license's grant of rights language).

If the rights have been split, it can be difficult to determine which assignee or licensee owns the rights you need.

EXAMPLE

131

clearing
rights and
obtaining
licenses

Web Developer wants to use an excerpt from Author's book in an online multimedia encyclopedia. The Copyright Office search shows that Author granted Movieco "all audiovisual rights" in Author's book. Author retained all other rights. Although Developer's multimedia work is an audiovisual work as defined by the Copyright Act (see "Types of Works Protected by Copyright," chapter 1), it is unclear whether the term "audiovisual rights" as used in Author's grant to Movieco gives Movieco the right to grant licenses for use of the book in Web products. To be safe, Developer may have to obtain licenses from both Author and Movieco.

This topic is also discussed in "Electronic Publishing," chapter 12, which covers licensing issues of interest to content owners and publishers.

Electronic Rights

If material you want to use was previously published in print publications, don't assume that the publisher of the print publication in which the material originally appeared can grant you a license to use the material on the Internet. A one-time use print license that does not explicitly include electronic rights does not include the right to use the material on the Internet. This issue was decided in the *Tasini* case, discussed in "Works You've Used in the Past," chapter 9. This topic is also covered in "Electronic Publishing," chapter 12.

In more recent licenses, publishers may have electronic rights. Even for older licenses, some publishers have managed to amend their original agreements with writers and photographers to acquire electronic rights.

Determining What Rights You Need

The second step in the licensing process is determining what rights you need to license from the copyright owner.

Scope of the License

To shield you from an infringement suit, your license must authorize every type of use that you will be making of the licensed work. Consequently, you need to determine how you will be using the work and what rights you need before you seek your license. A license is no protection for uses not authorized in the license.

EXAMPLE

Bay Area Products obtained a license to use Photographer's photograph of the Golden Gate Bridge in Bay Area's Web site. Although the license did not authorize Bay Area to alter the photograph, Bay Area's Web designer eliminated the cars and pedestrians shown in Photographer's photo and created an uncluttered image of the bridge. If Photographer sued Bay Area Products for unauthorized exercise of the modification right, Bay Area's license would be no defense.

Using a licensed work in ways not authorized in the license may be material breach of the license agreement. If it is, the licensor can terminate the license. (Breach of contract is discussed in "What is a Contract?," chapter 4.) In the previous example, the alteration of the photograph is probably a material breach of the license agreement. If Photographer terminates the license, Bay Area Products will no longer have even the right granted to it in the license (the right to use the original photograph in the Web site).

GOING BEYOND THE RIGHTS GRANTED

Mendler, a photographer, granted Winterland Productions a license to use Mendler's photos of the America's Cup yacht race as models for illustrations to be used on T-shirts. The license did not authorize Winterland to use reproductions of the photographs on shirts, but it permitted Winterland to scan the photos and alter them to create an illustration. Winterland used the scanned images with only minor alterations, and Mendler sued for infringement. The court held that Winterland's use of the scanned images was photographic reproduction, which was unauthorized use exceeding the terms of the license. *Mendler v. Winterland Productions, Ltd.,* 207 F3d 1119 (9th Cir 2000).

If you want the right to use the licensed work in more than one project, the license must explicitly give you that right.

EXAMPLE

Web Developer obtained a license to use a five-second clip of Movieco's movie in Developer's virtual tour site, *City Tour.* Developer later used the same film clip in another work, *Downtown.* Developer's second use of the film clip is copyright infringement.

If you want to use the licensed work in merchandise such as T-shirts and coffee mugs as well as on the Web, you need "merchandising rights." Merchandise licenses are discussed in "Characters," chapter 11.

MERCHANDISING RIGHTS

Patricia McCormick, the technical consultant to the production company that made the movie *How to Make an American Quilt,* asked Barbara Brown to design a quilt pattern for use in the movie. Brown, an attorney, retained the copyright in her design. Universal Studios, which released the movie, featured Brown's quilt design in movie-related merchandise, and Brown sued. Universal didn't have a leg to stand on. It didn't dispute that the merchandise use was unauthorized copying of the quilt design. *Brown v. McCormick,* 23 FSupp2d 594 (D Md 1998).

Disclosure

Before you are quoted a license fee, you will need to disclose to the copyright owner (or the rights clearance agency) all uses you are planning to make of the work, and provide detailed information about your planned use of the work. Copyright owners use this information in determining the license fee.

What Rights?

You may need permission to exercise some or all of the copyright owner's exclusive rights. (These are defined in "The Exclusive Rights," chapter 1.) For all Web or online publishing projects, you should get the right to reproduce, distribute, and publicly display or perform the licensed work. This topic is discussed in "When You Need a License," chapter 9. If you plan to alter or modify the licensed work, you also need permission to exercise the modification right.

For a CD-ROM product, whether you need permission for public performance and public display depends on how your product will be used. You don't need such a license if your work will be used only by consumers in their own homes. You do need these rights if the work will be used in one of the following three ways:

- If it will be shown at a place open to the public.

- If it will be shown at a place where a substantial number of persons outside a normal circle of family and social acquaintances gathers.

- If it will be transmitted to the public or to a public place by means of a device or process, whether the audience is in the same place or in separate places.

Products that will be used at information kiosks in places such as convention centers, train stations, and tourist attractions will be publicly performed and displayed because they will be shown at a place open to the public. Products used for corporate training or presentations will be publicly performed and displayed because—whether they are online or CD-ROM products—they will be shown at a place where a substantial number of persons outside a normal circle of family and friends gathers. Products that will be transmitted to guest rooms in hotels will be publicly performed and displayed because they are transmitted to the public by means of a device.

Computer games distributed for home use do not require a public performance or display license, but those delivered online and those used in arcades do.

Obtaining a License

The third step in the licensing process is obtaining a license from the copyright owner. Two sample content licenses are included in appendix B, one for licensing text (Form 3), and one for licensing photos or video footage (Form 4). These forms assume that material is being licensed for nonexclusive use and that the material is already in existence. The copyright owner is referred to as the "licensor," and the party receiving permission to use the material is referred to as the "licensee."

In the rest of this section, "you" refers to the licensee. In chapter 12 (where we give the licensor's viewpoint on licensing), "you" refers to the licensor.

Terms

The license terms should cover the following points:

- What is being licensed? This information goes in Section 1 in Forms 3 and 4. It is referred to elsewhere in the license as the "Work." To avoid later disputes, be as specific as possible—identifying what is being licensed, for example, as "the text of chapter 8 of the first edition of the book *Internet Law and Business Handbook*, or "the photograph called *View of San Francisco from the Bay Bridge*." For text and photo licenses, attach a photocopy of the text or the photographs to the license agreement if possible. If the copyright for the material has been registered with the Copyright Office, you may identify the licensed work by the title and registration number. If excerpts of a work are being licensed—rather than the whole thing—the agreement should make that clear.

- In what projects or products will you be permitted to use the Work? This information goes in Section 2 and is referred to elsewhere in the license as the "Project." For example, are you obtaining the right to use the material on your Web site or on your company's intranet? In an online encyclopedia? In marketing material of any sort, including print media material? On merchandise such as T-shirts or coffee mugs? Be specific in filling out Section 2—for example, "the Web site operated by or for Licensee at the URL www._____.com and marketing material in any media relating to such Web site."

- What rights are being granted? This point is covered in Section 3 of Forms 3 and 4. Section 3 provides for a broad grant of rights. However, you made need additional rights. If you intend to use licensed text as a "voice-over" in a computer game, you will need a public performance right. If you plan to modify the licensed material more than Section 3 permits, change Section 3 to give you the enlarged modification right.

- If the Project includes a Web site, Section 3 gives the licensee the right to permit end users of the Web site to download one copy of the text for personal, noncommercial use. If the Project includes an internal network (intranet), Section 3 gives you the right to copy the text for your internal business purposes.

- Is the license exclusive or nonexclusive? Modify Section 3 if the license is to be exclusive.

- Will Licensor get a credit? If so, how will it read? This information goes in Section 4. Options for credit placement are discussed in "Other Important Provisions," chapter 8.

- What is the license fee (Section 5)? The license fee could be a single one-time fee, an annual fee for each year you use the licensed work, or a percentage of your Web site's or Web product's revenues. The license fee does not have to be money. It could be products or services, publicity, or just a credit.

- What is the term (duration) of the license (Section 6)? It can be perpetual or limited in duration.

- What warranties is the licensor giving (Section 7)? You should try to get warranties and an indemnity from the licensor to ensure that the licensor has sufficient rights to grant you rights. Sections 7 and 8 are typical warranty and indemnity provisions. These provisions are designed to give you legal recourse against a licensor who licenses you material that infringes the legal rights of third parties, or one who has already licensed the material on an exclusive basis to someone else. If a licensor provides you with material that infringes a third party's copyright, the use of that material in your Web site, intranet, or online products will make you liable for infringement of the third party's copyright even if you were not aware of the infringement. This topic is discussed in "Key Provisions in the Agreement," chapter 8.

It's possible that you will not be able to obtain these warranties and indemnities, or that the licensor will only give you limited versions. In that case, you must decide if using the work is worth the legal risk involved.

LICENSE WARRANTIES

The text and photograph licenses in appendix B (Forms 3 and 4) include a warranty that use of the licensed material will not violate the rights of any individuals. If you use licensed material that infringes third-party rights, this warranty will not protect you from being found liable to the individual whose rights are infringed by your use of the material. It does, however, give you a legal right, in conjunction with the license's indemnification provision, to require the licensor to reimburse you for any judgment entered against you.

Formalities

There are certain formalities to attend to in getting a license. They are different for exclusive licenses and nonexclusive licenses.

Exclusive Licenses

Exclusive copyright licenses must be signed and be in writing to be valid. It is a good idea to get exclusive copyright licenses notarized. Notarization is legal evidence of the signing of the license. 17 USC § 204.

GET IT IN WRITING

Fortune published an article by David McClintick on how Giancarlo Paretti obtained financing for his takeover of MGM. *Fortune* (owner of the copyright) sold motion picture rights to the article to Hallmark Entertainment. However, a Hollywood producer claimed he had been granted the motion picture rights in an oral agreement with the magazine and McClintick. *Fortune* sued the producer, seeking a declaratory judgment that the producer had not been granted the rights, and the producer countersued *Fortune* claiming breach of contract. The court ruled for *Fortune*. Because the Copyright Act requires exclusive licenses and assignments to be in writing, the producer did not have a claim for breach of contract. *Time, Inc. v. Kastner,* 972 FSupp 236 (SDNY 1997).

If you are obtaining an exclusive license, record it in the Copyright Office. If you record it "in the manner required to give constructive notice," your license will take priority over a conflicting assignment or exclusive license, as explained in "Licenses," chapter 3.

There is no official Copyright Office form for recording assignments or licenses, so you have to create your own document. You can record the license itself, but most people make up a "short form" license for recording. (You can modify Form 9 in appendix B.) The Copyright Office has a Document Cover Sheet you should use for submitting the document for recording. The Document Cover Sheet is available for printing online from the Copyright Office's Web site at www.loc.gov/copyright/forms/formdoc.pdf.

To record "in the manner required to give constructive notice," your recorded document must give the title or copyright registration number of the work being licensed. 17 USC § 205(c). If the copyright in that work has not been registered with the Copyright Office, recording your license will not give constructive notice. If the copyright of the work you are licensing has not been registered, insist that the licensor register the copyright by sending a completed registration application to the Copyright Office (see "Copyright Protection," chapter 26).

Nonexclusive Licenses

Oral nonexclusive licenses can be enforced—if you can prove their existence. However, you should always get a written license so that you will have proof of the license and its terms. Getting the license in writing will give you protection against conflicting earlier and later transfers, as discussed in "Determining Who Owns the Copyright," earlier in this chapter.

You can, if you wish, get a nonexclusive license notarized and record it in the Copyright Office. The Copyright Act doesn't say that there is any advantage to doing these things for nonexclusive licenses.

Termination Right

The author of a work other than a work made for hire has the right to terminate licenses or assignments at certain times, as explained in "Termination Rights," chapter 3. The termination right is likely to be of importance only for a small percentage of Web content licenses. For such licenses, the effect of the termination right will be mitigated by the termination right's derivative works exception, which states that "a derivative work prepared under authority of the grant before its termination may continue to be utilized under the terms of the grant after termination."

EXAMPLE

In 2000, Virtual Anatomy, Inc. got a perpetual license to use Photographer's photographs in Developer's "virtual lab" products, *The Heart* and *The Lungs.* Virtual Anatomy created *The Heart* but did not get around to creating *The Lungs.* If Photographer or Photographer's heirs exercise the termination right and terminate Virtual Anatomy's license, Virtual Anatomy can continue to use the photograph in *The Heart* but it cannot use the photograph in *The Lungs* or in a new version of *The Heart.*

Possible Licensor's Title Defect

If your license is for a work first distributed to the public between 1972 and 1977, and if the licensed work was not a work made for hire when created, and if your licensor is someone other than the original copyright owner, your licensor's title to the work has a potential defect. This defect arises from the renewal provisions of the 1909 Copyright Act that were carried forward in "transition" provisions of the 1976 Copyright Act. The Supreme Court has interpreted those provisions as giving the heirs of a copyright owner the right to terminate an assignee's or licensee's right to use the licensed work beyond the original twenty-eight-year copyright term. (The case is discussed in "The *Rear Window* Problem," in this section).

EXAMPLE

In 1993, Publisher granted Developer a license to use an excerpt from a book written by Author, an individual. The book was first published in 1972. Publisher was assigned the copyright and the renewal term rights by Author in 1978. Author died in 1980, long before the renewal period would start (in the twenty-eighth year, 2000). Author left a widow and one child. If Author's widow and child apply in 2000 to register a claim to the renewal term, they will be able to terminate Publisher's assignment. That will take away Publisher's right to license the book for the remainder of the copyright term (2001 through 2067) and the basis for Developer's right to use the book. If Developer wants to use the excerpt of the book beyond December 31, 2000—even in a product that Developer created before that date—Developer must obtain a new license from Author's widow and child.

This defect exists only for works published before January 1, 1978 that are not works made for hire as defined under the 1909 Copyright Act. The 1909 Copyright Act applied a broader definition of the term than the present Copyright Act does. (See "The Work Made for Hire Rule," chapter 3.) Because the right to cut off licenses and assignments applies only to the author's heirs and not to the author, evaluating the risk means guessing whether the author is likely to die prior to the beginning of the renewal period (the twenty-eighth year of the original term).

If you are considering licensing a work that was first distributed between 1972 and 1977 (inclusive), you should be aware of the potential defect in the licensor's title. As each calendar year ends, works published twenty-eight years earlier, by authors still living, become free of this risk. In 2000, the risk exists for works first published between 1972 and 1977 (inclusive). In 2001, the risk exists for works first published between 1973 and 1977. In 2002, the risk exists for works first published between 1974 and 1977. This risk does not exist for works published after 1977 because the copyright term for those works is determined by the current Copyright Act, which does not require renewal.

If you must license a work for which this risk exists, be aware that you may have to obtain a new license from the author's heirs. While you could get a backup license from the author's spouse and children now to protect you from the risk of having your license terminated in the future, this strategy is not foolproof. The spouse and children could predecease the author. Then the right to claim the renewal term would pass to those designated in the author's will (or the author could change spouses before dying).

THE *REAR WINDOW* PROBLEM

Copyright attorneys call the title defect for works distributed between 1972 and 1977 the *Rear Window* problem because the Hitchcock movie of that name was the focus of the Supreme Court case that gave rise to the problem. The movie *Rear Window* was based on a short story by Cornell Woolrich. While Woolrich was alive, he gave a motion picture studio the right to make a movie version of his story. Woolrich also promised to obtain the copyright renewal term for the story and grant renewal term rights to the studio. However, Woolrich died before renewal time came. He left no spouse or children, so renewal rights went to his estate. His executor assigned the renewal rights to a Mr. Abend. The Court held that the owner of the movie could continue to use the story in the already-made movie after the original term of copyright expired only if Mr. Abend consented. *Stewart v. Abend,* 495 US 207 (1990).

Rights Clearance Agencies

To obtain the licenses that you need, you may want to use a rights clearance agency. These agencies are also known as rights and permissions agencies and copyright clearance agencies. There is a list of such agencies in appendix C.

A rights clearance agency will find out who owns the rights you need and negotiate licenses for you. (You should still read the earlier sections of this chapter and become familiar with licensing issues so that you'll understand the process.) Because these agencies perform rights clearance and licensing as their business, they can probably obtain licenses for you in far less time than it would take you to obtain them yourself.

Most rights clearance agencies charge by the hour. An initial consultation is generally free (but you should ask). You should first determine whether the works you want to use are likely to be available (and for what fee) and whether the agent can suggest alternatives to unavailable or expensive material. Sometimes an agent can give you ideas if you need suggestions for works you might license and use.

These agencies frequently handle right of publicity releases for photographs of celebrities (see "Right of Publicity," chapter 7) as well as copyright licensing.

Licensing Agents

Some content owners have authorized licensing agents to handle licensing requests for the owners' material. Licensing agents are also referred to as "licensing collectives." Several agencies handle various types of music licenses. (These are discussed in "Licensing Music for the Internet," chapter 21.) The Copyright Clearance Center handles licensing for a number of book and periodical publishers and image owners.

A number of content owners are moving toward online rights management. Some handle their own licensing through Web licensing centers. Others have authorized companies operating online licensing "aggregator" sites to act as their licensing agents. (Aggregator sites offer content owned by more than one publisher.) We have included contact information on some of the aggregator online licensing sites.

Stock Houses and Libraries

You can obtain film and video clips, photographs, illustrations, music, and sound effects from stock houses and from music and media libraries. A list of stock houses and media libraries appears in appendix D. A number of these organizations display samples of their material on their Web sites.

Stock houses and libraries frequently own the copyrights in works that they license (or they provide material that is in the public domain, such as WPA photographs). They will, for a separate fee, do research for you to help you find suitable material (or you can hire your own content specialist).

As with other content licenses, you should make sure that licenses issued to you by stock houses or libraries cover all of the rights needed for your intended uses of the licensed works (see the "Determining What Rights You Need," earlier in this chapter).

Copyright Assignment

If you find a work that is owned by a single owner and is suitable for your repeated use, a copyright assignment may be preferable to a license. With a copyright assignment, you will be able to modify the work and use it in many projects (subject to Visual Artists Rights Act and moral rights limitations, discussed later in this chapter). Because an assignment gives you all of the copyright owner's exclusive rights in the work (see "Assignments," chapter 3), you won't have to predict in advance what rights you will later need.

If you get an assignment, the assignor will have the right to terminate the assignment later, as discussed in "Termination Right," chapter 3. However, you will still be able to use the assigned work in products prepared before termination. (See the discussion of the termination right in "Obtaining a License," earlier in this chapter.)

To be valid, a copyright assignment must be in writing and be signed by the copyright owner. You should obtain warranties of title and noninfringement and an indemnity from the assignor, as discussed in "Obtaining a License," earlier in this chapter.

Within one month of the execution date, you should record a notarized, short-form assignment (Form 9 in Appendix B) in the Copyright Office "in the manner required to give constructive notice" (see the discussion of this phrase in "Obtaining a License," earlier in this chapter). Use the Document Cover Sheet referred to in the discussion of formalities for exclusive licenses, in "Obtaining a License," earlier in this chapter. Recording the assignment will protect it against conflicting assignments (see "Assignments," chapter 3).

The Visual Artists Rights Act

If you are planning on modifying a third-party work, you should consider whether modification will violate the author's rights under the Visual Artists Rights Act (VARA).

VARA Rights

VARA gives the owner of a "work of visual art," created on or after June 1, 1991, the right to claim authorship of the work and the right to prevent four things:

- Any intentional distortion, mutilation, or other modification of the work that would be prejudicial to the artist's honor or reputation.

- Destruction of a work of recognized stature.

- Use of the artist's name as the author of a work that the author did not create.

■ Use of the artist's name as the author of a work that has been modified in such a way as to be prejudicial to the artist's honor or reputation.

VARA CASE

The city of Indianapolis destroyed artist Jan Randolph Martin's sculpture, "Symphony #1." Martin sued the city under VARA and was awarded $20,000 in statutory damages and $131,253 in attorney's fees. *Martin v. City of Indianapolis,* 192 F3d 608 (7th Cir 1999).

Altering a photograph of a work of visual art for use on the Web would not be considered a distortion or mutilation of the work of visual art. However, posting the photograph with the artist's name could be a violation of the third or fourth right.

Artists who created works of visual art before June 1, 1991, also have VARA rights if the artist did not transfer the copyright in the work before that date.

Definition of Works of Visual Art

According to VARA, works of visual art are limited to the following categories of works (in single copy form or as signed and numbered limited editions of no more than two hundred copies):

■ Paintings.

■ Drawings.

■ Prints.

■ Sculptures.

■ Photographs produced for exhibition purposes.

Excluded Works

Works made for hire are not works of visual art, nor are the following types of works:

■ Posters.

■ Maps, globes, and charts.

■ Technical drawings.

■ Diagrams.

- Models.
- Works of applied art.
- Motion pictures and other audiovisual works.
- Books, magazines, newspapers, and periodicals.
- Databases.
- Electronic information services and electronic publications.
- Merchandising items.
- Advertising material and packaging material.

Duration of Rights

The artist who creates a work that is protected under VARA owns the VARA rights in the work even if he or she has assigned the copyright in the work to someone else. The VARA rights endure for the artist's lifetime. If the work was created prior to June 1991, and is covered by VARA because the artist retained the copyright, the VARA rights endure for the life of the artist plus fifty years.

Waiver

The VARA rights cannot be transferred, but they can be waived through a written document signed by the artist. If you intend to use a work of visual art in your project in a way that might violate the author's VARA rights, you should obtain a waiver of those rights. This advice applies even if you own the copyright in the work or have obtained a license from the current copyright owner to use the work of visual art.

Moral Rights

Most other countries have long recognized moral rights for many types of copyrightable works, not just for works of visual art. Moral rights include the rights of paternity, integrity, and repudiation.

The right of paternity (also called attribution) is the right to claim authorship of a work and to be recognized as the work's creator. This right allows an artist to insist that his or her name continue to be associated with a work even after the artist has parted with the copyright, and—in the case of unique works of visual art—the tangible work of art (such as a sculpture). The right of integrity is the right to prevent any destruction, mutilation, or alteration of the work. The right of repudiation is the right to disavow works improperly attributed or altered without approval.

A MORAL RIGHTS CASE

An appellate court in France held that the colorization of the film *Asphalt Jungle* violated the moral rights of the film's director and screenwriter.

Several states—New York and California, for example—have statutes that give limited moral rights to certain types of artistic works. In addition, artists sometimes include moral rights provisions in contracts and assignments with parties who buy their works. Entertainment industry collective bargaining agreements provide rights similar to moral rights (see "Reuse Provisions," chapter 22).

CHAPTER 11

LICENSING CONTENT: INDUSTRY BY INDUSTRY

Web content is drawn from several different industries. Each of the industries from which content is drawn has its own licensing issues. Those issues are described in this chapter. Checklists for clearing different types of content are at the end of the chapter.

Music licensing is discussed in chapter 21. The fundamentals of copyright clearance (applicable to all types of copyrightable works) are discussed in chapters 9 and 10.

General Advice

The most important lesson in clearing material is to begin early. If you don't, you may find yourself unable to use material simply because you have not allowed enough time to get the licenses, releases, and permissions you need. Consider using an attorney or a rights clearance agency (discussed in Chapter 10) if you have complex clearance issues.

To be successful in clearing rights, follow these five rules:

- **Identify your needs early.** Doing this is critical, because licensing is a slow process. You may find that some of the material you want to use is not available, and you may encounter unexpected delays. For example, in a clearance project undertaken by one of the coauthors of this book, the owner of one of the works had declared bankruptcy several years before the clearance was being done. It took two months just to identify the new owner.

- **Budget realistically for the cost of clearance.** Clearing rights can be expensive, both in license fees and professional fees for attorneys or clearance agents. The costs will depend on the nature of the works you want to use and the rights you want. The shorter the period you have for clearing rights, the more expensive rights clearance will be (because you will have no time to negotiate or to substitute cheaper alternatives).

- **Always have an alternative.** Don't plan your project around content owned by a third party unless you are confident that you can obtain the necessary rights. The rights may have been licensed already, or they may not be available at a reasonable price. For example, the owners of the copyright in the official anthem for one state wanted $10,000 to grant permission for use of the anthem in a CD-ROM atlas of the U.S. The fee was simply too much, and the developer did not include the anthem.

- **Be prepared for the unexpected.** Be creative in clearing rights. The content owner may be willing to settle for nonmonetary compensation (such as a credit and a link to the owner's site). In one case, performers were persuaded to accept donations to a designated charity in lieu of the modest amount the developer could have afforded to pay them.

- **Be frank.** Be prepared to be open about the nature of the project and the rights you will need in your first contact. Although you may consider your project to be confidential, you must be prepared to share your plans with the content owner in order to persuade the content owner to grant you a license.

Licensing Text

The primary concern in clearing text is copyright. The first question to ask in clearing text is whether the text is still protected by copyright (see "Public Domain Works," chapter 9). Because the Internet is global in nature, you will need to be concerned about foreign copyright laws as well as United States copyright laws. Determining whether a work is in the public domain can be complicated. We recommend that you consult an attorney familiar with U.S. and international copyright law if you think works you want to use are in the public domain.

If the text is based on another work, such as a play or a movie, you may need to get permission from the owner of the other work as well as the copyright owner of the text. (See "Determining Who Owns the Copyright," chapter 10.) Parts of the text or supplementary materials accompanying the text, such as illustrations and charts, may not be owned by the owner of the copyright in the text. Characters used in the text may be owned by someone else (and used by the text's author under a license). See "Characters," later in this chapter. For books, reading the acknowledgments and credits carefully will help you identify separately owned material. For example, the "acknowledgments" page of this book indicates that several chapters were written by people other than the book's authors.

Clearance Steps

If the text you want to use is protected by copyright, you should do the following things to clear it:

- **Identify what you want to license.** The license could include the storyline, characters, and setting—or just certain lines of text.

- **Identify the rights you need.** If you are simply using part or all of the text without altering the text (for example, using it in an online encyclopedia), you may only need reproduction, display, and distribution rights. However, if the text will be used in a "voice-over" (as spoken works), you may need "spoken-word" rights. If you intend to use the text as the basis for an entirely new work, such as a game based on a book, you will need the modification right.

- **Determine whether you need sublicensing rights.** You need sublicensing rights if you plan to authorize another party to exercise the rights granted to you in the license. For example, if you want to be able to authorize your site's users to download or print the licensed text, the license must give you that right (as the Form 3 text license in appendix B does).

- **Determine whether you need subsidiary rights.** Examples of subsidiary rights are the right to use the author's name, image, and biography in your marketing materials and packaging; the right to make sequels or a television show using the licensed text; and the right to use the licensed text in toys, T-shirts, and other merchandise.

- **Define the "product" in which you will be using the licensed work.** This topic is discussed in "Obtaining a License," chapter 10.

- **Determine whether the text defames or invades the right of privacy or publicity of any actual individuals.** These topics are discussed in chapter 7. Using fictional characters can defame actual individuals if the characters are recognizable as the actual individuals on which the characters are based. You could seek to obtain a release from the individual, but such a release in these circumstances is not likely to be granted. The most common solution is to obtain strong "representations and warranties" and an indemnity from the licensor (see Sections 7 and 8 in Form 3). The alternative is to review the material yourself with your legal counsel to ensure that you are comfortable with any potential legal risks.

■ **Determine whether your use of the material requires any trademark licenses.** Trademarks are discussed in chapters 2 and 15, and in "Using Third-Party Trademarks," chapter 24. Characters are protected by both copyright and trademark law. See "Characters," later in this chapter. The title of a book or an article is generally not protectible by trademark unless it is part of a series or is famous on its own. (See "Titles," chapter 24.) Generally the use of a trademark in text—for example a "Honda car" or a "Nestle chocolate bar"—is not a violation of trademark rights so long as it does not appear to create an association with the trademark owner. This type of trademark use is called "collateral use" because its purpose is to identify the particular product, not to identify the source of the product.

■ **Determine whether your use of the material violates the author's moral rights, discussed in "Moral Rights," chapter 10.** You may need to obtain a waiver of these rights.

A checklist for text licensing appears at the end of this chapter.

UNCERTAIN RIGHTS

For text and photographs that predate the Digital Age, publishers may be uncertain about whether they own digital rights. Following the *Tasini* decision discussed in "Works You've Used Before," chapter 9, many publishers have become cautious about granting licenses for digital uses if the rights situation is not clear.

Locating Owners

Identifying rights owners for text can be difficult. Understanding common industry practices will help you figure out where to start.

Books

The book publishing industry has two general categories of books—trade and nontrade.

Trade Books

The term "trade books" means books of general interest (fiction, nonfiction, and poetry). Trade books generally are written by authors who are not employees of publishing companies. The individual author either assigns his or her entire copyright to the publisher or grants the publisher rights that fall short of total assignment—for example, "the right to publish in book form."

In the past, the "all rights" assignment (assignment of the entire copyright) was common, so the publisher was the copyright owner. The current trend is for writers to try to retain rights for licensing to other parties. Whether new media rights should remain with the writer or go to the book publisher is currently the subject of spirited debate. Nonetheless, if you want permission to use part of a book, the permissions department of the book's publisher is a good place to start. Even if the publisher doesn't own the copyright, the publisher may be the owner's licensing agent. If not, the permissions department should be able to put you in contact with the copyright owner or the owner's agent.

You should request Copyright Office registration and assignment searches to confirm what the permissions department tells you about ownership of rights. Copyright Office searches are discussed in "Determining Who Owns the Copyright," chapter 10.

In book publishing, split rights situations are common, with either the author or the publisher splitting subsidiary rights among a number of exclusive licensees. For example, clearing three pages of text for IBM's Columbus CD-ROM title required getting permission from seven rights owners (four in the U.S. and three in Europe).

The current trend is to negotiate and grant exclusive licenses by market or media segment. Some common rights categories are the first publication right, the reprint right, the audiocassette right, the audiovisual or motion picture right, and the electronic version right. If the rights are split up, it may be difficult to tell who has the authority to grant you a license.

Nontrade Books

Nontrade books—reference and educational books—usually are written by the publisher's employees and are works made for hire. If you want to use excerpts from a nontrade book, you should contact the publisher. However, if the publisher already has granted exclusive licenses, it may be difficult to determine whether the publisher or one of its licensees has the authority to issue you a license.

Newspapers, Magazines, and Journals

If you wish to use factual material from newspapers, magazines, and journals, review it to make sure that you need a license. You do not need a license to use facts. A work's copyright does not cover its facts. The reason is discussed in "When You Don't Need a License," chapter 10.

Newspapers

Many newspaper articles are works made for hire written by newspaper employees. However, the writer may not be an employee of the newspaper in which you read the article. Many newspapers are now licensing articles from major newspapers such as *The New York Times* or the *Washington Post*.

Special features are often specially commissioned works made for hire. However, they may also be works created by independent contractors (freelance writers), and licensed to the publisher for one-time use only (as in the *Tasini* case, discussed in "Works You've Used Before," chapter 9). Copyrights in syndicated columns ("Dear Abby," for example) are generally owned by the syndicator.

Magazines

Many magazine articles are written by employees or by freelancers as specially commissioned works made for hire. Some articles are written by freelancers who retain their copyrights, as in the *Tasini* case.

The copyright on an issue of a magazine does not cover preexisting material used in the magazine unless the preexisting material has been assigned to the publisher or is a work made for hire.

In the past, many magazines obtained from freelance authors only one-time publication rights or North American serial rights (that is, the exclusive right to publish the article in newspapers, magazines, and other serials in North America for the copyright term). The freelance author retained all other rights. Now, an increasing number of magazines require that a freelance author assign all rights to the magazine.

Journals

Articles in technical and scholarly journals are written primarily by freelancers. Many are written as specially commissioned works made for hire. Other articles are written by freelancers and licensed or assigned to the journal.

Other Resources

If you are having trouble locating the author of an article, you may be able to get information from one of the writers' organizations, such as the National

Writers Union, the Writers Guild of America, Authors Guild, and the American Society of Journalists and Authors. Three organizations—the Authors Guild, American Society of Journalists and Authors, and the Association of Author's Representatives—have created the Author's Registry, which provides contacts for authors and their representatives. Information on how to contact these organizations is in appendix E.

R.R. Bowker publishes a number of books about the publishing industry that may be helpful in locating authors or their representatives. The most useful of these works for clearance purposes is *Literary Market Place*.

licensing
content

Licensing Photographs and Still Images

The primary concern in clearing photographs and still images is copyright. As with text, the first question to ask in clearing photographs and still images is whether they are still protected by copyright.

A photograph may contain images of other copyrightable works, such as sculptures or paintings, which are separately owned and need to be separately cleared.

Some photographers may be reluctant to grant you a license to use their photographs online. This may be because they are concerned that the digitized version that you create will be redistributed to others and that you and others will alter the image without permission. Once a photograph has been digitized, it can easily be copied, distributed, and altered.

PHOTOGRAPHER'S PERSPECTIVE

If you are a photographer who is interested in establishing a successful stock photography business on the Internet, you should read Rohn Engh's book, *sellphotos.com*, published by Writer's Digest Books.

If you are negotiating with a graphic artist or illustrator for permission to use his or her work, he or she probably will want to know how you plan to use the work. You should be prepared to discuss your potential use in detail, because many graphic designers are concerned about how their works will look when incorporated into larger works. For example, the Graphic Arts Guild standard contract states that "any electronic alteration of original art (color shift, mirroring, flopping, combination cut and paste, deletion) is prohibited without the express permission of the artist."

PUBLIC DOMAIN PHOTOS

A number of federal government Web sites contain public domain photos—for example, the United States Air Force site (www.af.mil); the United States Army site (www.army.mil); and the National Archives and Records Administration (NARA) site (www.nara.gov). Not all photos posted on federal government sites are in the public domain, so check for copyright restrictions. For example, the NARA site states, "Please note that a few images on our site have been obtained from other organizations and that these are always credited. Permission to use these photographs should be obtained directly from those organizations."

Clearance Steps

If the photograph or still image is protected by copyright, you need to identify the rights you will need. If you are simply including part or all of the photograph or still image without alteration, you may only need reproduction, display, and distribution rights. If you intend to alter the photograph, you will need the modification right. If you are using the photograph or still image online, you also may need the right to publicly display the photograph in your work.

Review photographs and still images carefully to make sure they do not defame individuals who are shown. A book publisher who inserted an image of a model into a photo of an older man holding a "dirty book" was found liable for defamation (discussed in chapter 7).

Using a photograph that shows a recognizable individual or individual's home could violate the individual's rights of privacy and publicity. If the photographer did not obtain a broad release (discussed in "The Right of Publicity," chapter 7) and it is not possible for you get a release, the most common approach is to obtain strong "representations and warranties," backed by an indemnity, from the licensor that the photograph does not invade any individual's rights of publicity or privacy or defame anyone. (See Sections 7 and 8 in Form 4.)

If you plan to alter a work of visual art, you should read "The Visual Artists Rights Act," chapter 10, and you should get any necessary waivers from the artist who created the work. The act defines a work of visual art as a limited-edition painting, drawing, print, sculpture, or photograph produced for exhibition purposes. Works made for hire are excluded from the definition. You also may need waivers of moral rights (discussed in "Moral Rights," chapter 10).

You may need permission to use photographs or images of actual goods bearing trademarks. This topic is discussed in "Using Third-Party Trademarks," chapter 24. Characters shown in photographs and images may be protected by trademark law and copyright law. See "Characters," later in this chapter.

For the other steps in clearing photographs and images, see "Clearance Steps" in the "Licensing Text" section of this chapter.

Locating Owners

Identifying the owners of photographs and still images can be one of the most difficult clearance tasks. Common industry practices are described in this section.

Photographs

Copyrights in photographs made by employees—a newspaper photographer or an employee of a corporation's communications department, for example— are owned by the employer.

Many photographers work as independent contractors. Copyrights in photographs created by a photographer for a client ("on assignment") are owned by the photographer unless the client got an assignment of the copyright (unusual) or the photograph was made as a specially commissioned work made for hire. (This topic is discussed in "Copyright Ownership," chapter 6.)

Determining who owns the copyright in a photograph made by a freelance photographer can be difficult. If the photograph was created by a freelance photographer for a client and the copyright is not registered, the only way to determine who owns the copyright is to ask the photographer or the client. Either or both of these parties may have misconceptions about the rules of copyright ownership or the application of the rules to the particular photograph. For example:

- The client may think that because it has a print of the photograph, it owns the copyright and has the right to authorize use of the photograph. This ignores the distinction copyright law makes between ownership of a copy and ownership of copyright rights (discussed in "Owning a Copy of a Work," chapter 3).

- The client may think that because it ordered and paid for making the photograph, it owns the copyright. This ignores the ownership rules for works created by independent contractors (discussed in "Copyright Ownership," chapter 6).

- The photographer may not remember giving an assignment or signing a work made for hire agreement, or may not understand the legal significance of those agreements.

The problem of determining copyright ownership for photographs is further complicated because photographs are often incorporated in other works— ads, brochures, and magazine articles, for example. Frequently, the only copyright notice in these works is the one for the owner of the copyright in the larger work. To determine who owns the copyright in the photograph, you have to contact the owner of the copyright in the larger work.

If you have a copy of the book or magazine in which the photograph appeared, it may include the name of the photographer. If not, you can call the publication to try and identify him or her. Generally, a search of the Copyright Office will be of limited value because of the difficulty of identifying the photograph. You may be able to locate the photographer by contacting stock agencies or by contacting the Picture Agency Council of America (the trade association of photo stock agencies). Many professional photographers have Web sites.

You can avoid ownership questions by using stock photography from stock houses or media libraries, discussed in "Stock Houses and Libraries," chapter 10. Some of these companies offer image catalogs online.

Graphics and Illustrations

Graphics and illustrations created by employees—for example, a magazine cover by an employee of a magazine publisher—are owned by the employer as works made for hire.

If the graphics or illustrations appear in a work created for another party, the other party may own the copyright.

EXAMPLE

Ed, an employee of Ad Agency, created an ad for Client. The copyright in the ad belongs to Client if Client got an assignment of the copyright. Otherwise, Ad Agency owns the copyright.

In the United States, much of the graphic design and illustration work is done by independent contractors. Designs and illustrations made by independent contractors may be owned by the hiring parties through assignment or as specially created works made for hire. However, the standard contracts put out by the graphic arts trade associations generally provide that the artist owns the copyright.

Clip Art and Development Tools

In your projects, you generally can use clip art and stock content from Web and multimedia development tool software without obtaining content licenses. However, you should carefully review the written material distributed with these works. In many cases, the material comes with express or implied licenses that restrict use of the collection. Some of these licenses provide only limited permission to use the product—for example, use for noncommercial purposes. Public display rights, which are necessary for Web use, may not be included.

The packaging for these products can be deceptive. You may have to read the "read me" file to determine what uses are authorized.

Fine Art

As with photographs, the ownership of copyrights in works of fine art is subject to significant confusion. Owners of a copy of the work—a painting or a sculpture, for example—often think they own the copyright in the work. However, under current law, unless they employed the artist or obtained an assignment of the copyright from the artist, they don't. One who acquires a copy of a work (the tangible item, such as a statue or painting) does not automatically acquire the copyright. This topic is discussed in "Owning a Copy," chapter 3.

If you want to use an image of a work of fine art and the owner of the tangible item doesn't own the copyright, you should find the artist and obtain a license from the artist. (This topic is discussed in "Permits," chapter 7.)

Licensing Film and Television Clips

Motion pictures and television series, miniseries, and documentaries are protected by copyright law as audiovisual works. To lawfully use a film or television clip, depending on the situation, you may have to obtain licenses or releases from a number of parties:

- The owner of the copyright in the underlying work (novel, short story, play) on which the work you want to use is based.

- The owner of the copyright in the motion picture, television series, or documentary you want to use.

- The performers (and possibly other contributors).

You also will have to pay applicable union reuse fees. If the film clip contains music or choreography, you also may have to obtain separate licenses for those.

The Underlying Work's Copyright

Many movies, television series, and miniseries are derivative works based on original plays, short stories, or novels. If you want to use a clip from a movie that was based on a play, short story, or novel, you should obtain Copyright Office registration and assignment searches to find out who owns the copyright in the underlying work, if it is not in the public domain. Unless the studio acquired all rights in the underlying work or a very broad license, you may need a license from the owner of the underlying work.

The Desired Work's Copyright

You should request Copyright Office registration and assignment searches to find out who owns the copyright in the motion picture, television series, miniseries, or documentary. In recent years, many studios have assigned the copyrights in their entire libraries of copyrighted motion pictures, so you cannot assume that the company named in the copyright notice is the current owner of the copyright.

The licensing of motion picture clips—particular a clip from a major motion picture—may be particularly difficult. Studios are sometimes reluctant to license a portion of the work because they are concerned that doing so would cheapen the work as a whole and damage the market for the work. Also, a studio may consider clip licensing more trouble than it's worth, given the complicated multiple permission and release requirements that may apply.

Most prime-time television series and documentaries are not owned by the television networks that broadcast these programs. They are licensed by the networks from independent producers. However, networks sometimes acquire audiovisual rights in series or documentaries. This situation may change as the rules regulating network ownership change.

Performers and Contributors

Find out whether those who worked on the movie, television series, miniseries, or documentary—writer, writer-producer, director, and performers—have an ownership interest in the copyright. In the United States, generally they do not, because their contributions are works made for hire, and the "author" and copyright owner is the production company. However, in many European countries, a motion picture's director, screenwriter, and music composer are all considered the authors of the work.

The Writer

The script is usually a specially commissioned work made for hire owned by the studio. Sometimes, though, an original script created by a writer "on spec" (without a contract) is used. In that situation, the studio usually gets an assignment of the screenplay copyright and registers the assignment in the Copyright Office.

However, if the script was subject to the Writers Guild's Basic Agreement, the writer may have retained certain rights. Thus, either the producer or the writer may own the rights you need. See "Reuse Provisions," chapter 22.

The Director

Contracts between motion picture studios and directors generally provide that the director's contribution to a motion picture is a work made for hire that belongs to the studio. However, directors sometimes include in these contracts a clause requiring that the director's consent be obtained if the work is to be altered. Under the Directors Guild Basic Agreement, a director must be consulted if a theatrical motion picture is edited for certain other uses. See "Reuse Provisions," chapter 22.

Performers

Contracts between studios and performers generally provide that a performer's contribution is a work made for hire owned by the producer, so you probably don't need to get copyright licenses from performers shown in the clip (although you do need a license from the clip's copyright owner).

You probably will need to obtain releases from all performers shown or heard in the clip, if the studio didn't get broad releases from them. If the performers belong to the Screen Actors Guild (SAG) or the American Federation of Television and Radio Artists (AFTRA), in most instances union rules require that performers' consent be obtained and that reuse fees be negotiated or paid before a clip containing photography or sound track of the performer is used in another work. A reuse fee is generally charged for such consent. See "Reuse Provisions," chapter 22.

Union Reuse Fees

Directors, actors, and screenwriters generally belong to unions. The unions have collective bargaining agreements with studios requiring the payment of reuse fees when a film or film excerpt is used in a medium other than the medium for which the film originally was intended. If you use a film clip in a project, the current owner of the motion picture copyright will have to pay those reuse fees (and will add the fees to the cost of your license). Union reuse fees are discussed in "Reuse Provisions," chapter 22.

Music or Choreography

If the clip contains music or choreography, you may have to obtain a separate license authorizing you to use it. If the music or choreography was created and recorded as a work made for hire for the studio, the owner of the clip's copyright owns the rights to the music or choreography and can authorize you to use the music. However, if the music or choreography was not created as a work made for hire and is still protected by copyright, the clip's copyright owner usually will not have authority to grant you a license to use the music or choreography as contained in the clip. In that case, obtain Copyright Office registration and assignment searches to determine who owns the music or choreography copyright. (Copyright Office searches are discussed in "Determining Who Owns the Copyright," chapter 10).

If the music was recorded from a record company's "master recording," you also may need a separate license from the owner of the master recording copyright. Music licensing is discussed in chapter 21.

Clearance Steps

As with text and photographs, the first step in clearing motion picture and television clips is to find out whether the motion picture, television series, miniseries, or documentary (and any incorporated other copyrightable works) are protected by copyright. Even if the motion picture is in the public domain, incorporated works such as musical compositions could still be protected—as could the work on which the motion picture was based. You also must consider whether you need releases from performers and contributors and whether you need to pay union reuse fees, as described earlier in this section.

If you are simply including part or all of the clip without alteration, you may only need reproduction, public performance, and distribution rights. If you intend to alter the clip, you will need the modification right. To modify the work, you may need a waiver of moral rights, discussed in "Moral Rights," chapter 10, or permission from the director.

CHARACTER INSERTION

With digital technology, it is possible to insert a performance by a living actor into an old film. For example, one episode of the sitcom *Suddenly Susan* used a scene from the 1938 film *Robin Hood,* with *Suddenly Susan* star Brooke Shields added to the *Robin Hood* scene. Alteration of film clips requires the permission of the copyright owner and possibly the permission of the film's director.

Review the clip carefully to determine if there are defamation and right of publicity and privacy concerns for any recognizable individuals shown in the clip. These topics are discussed in chapter 7. If the studio or producer obtained permits and releases, review those to determine if they will protect you. If the clip shows copyrighted or trademarked products, read "Permits," chapter 7, and "Using Third-Party Trademarks," chapter 24.

It probably will be difficult to obtain rights to use stills or characters from a motion picture clip in other products such as toys and T-shirts, because most studios have active merchandising programs. (See "Characters," later in this chapter.)

The other steps involved in clearing film and television are discussed in the "Clearing the Rights" section of "Licensing Text," earlier in this chapter.

Locating Owners

The credits on a motion picture or television program are your starting point. Unfortunately, older films were not as careful about giving credit, so you need to be particularly careful in relying on credits in such films. Motion picture copyrights are frequently registered with the Copyright Office, so a registration search may be helpful. Contacting the studio or production company may also be helpful. SAG and AFTRA will be able to assist you in locating performers or their agents. (Contact information for these organizations is in appendix E.)

Additional information is available in various film libraries. The largest such library on the West Coast is at the University of California at Los Angeles (UCLA). The UCLA Archive publishes *Collection Profiles* and *Study Guides* describing its holdings.

Media Libraries

Many of the difficulties in licensing movies can be avoided by using video clips from media libraries. Media libraries generally own the copyrights in their videos. However, they may not have cleared union reuse fees or the publicity rights of the individuals appearing in the video, and they may not be able to grant you all the rights you need for your intended use of the clip.

If you are obtaining video clips from an independent producer or a video library, make certain that the producer obtained the releases required under the law of publicity. If you will be using a video clip that contains copyrighted music or choreography owned by someone other than the producer, get separate licenses to use the music or choreography. Even if you have good reason to believe that a producer has the right to grant you a license to use the music or choreography, your use will infringe the music or choreography copyright if the producer does not have that right. If the clip shows copyrighted objects—sculptures or paintings, for example—you may also need a license to use the images of those objects.

Other steps for clearing video footage are discussed in "Clearance Steps," in the "Text Licensing" section of this chapter.

Characters

If you want to use a character from a novel, game, motion picture, television series, fiction series, or cartoon strip, you may need to obtain a "merchandise license" from the owner of the character. So-called "distinctively delineated" characters are protected under both copyright law and trademark law. Copyright law protects the character's appearance or fictional character delineation, while trademark law protects the owner's right to use the character in connection with goods or services.

EXAMPLE

Toy Company's marketing director wants to use an image of the "Pea-nuts" character Snoopy on the company's Web site. Using the image without obtaining a merchandise license is probably infringement of the owner's copyright and trademark rights.

A typical merchandise license authorizes the licensee to use the licensed character or title in artwork preapproved by the licensor in connection with the manufacture, sale, and distribution of specified products.

The copyright on a character is not necessarily owned by the copyright owner for the work in which the character appears, because characters them-selves are protectible under copyright law. When the same character appears in a series of books written by different authors, the character may be separately owned (and the use of the character licensed to the authors of the books). Sepa-rate ownership of a character also occurs when a character that appeared in a work in one medium—a film, for example—is later used in another type of work, such as a computer game.

If you want to use a character from a novel, first review the credits page to determine if the character is separately owned. If you are trying to clear char-acters, you may want to search the Copyright Office records for the character alone as well as for the work in which the character appears. You may also want to perform a search in the U.S. Patent and Trademark Office to determine if the character is registered as a trademark. The trademark registration will in-clude the name and address of the owner of the trademark.

If you are trying to clear cartoon characters, you also should consider con-sulting the Screen Cartoonists Union, Local 839 of the International Alliance of Theatrical State Employees (IATSE).

USING CHARACTERS

American Honda Motor Company aired a television commercial fea-turing a young, well-dressed couple in a Honda automobile being chased by a high-tech helicopter. The ad agency that created the com-mercial had called the project "James Bob" and requested talent agents to provide "James Bond"-type characters for the commercial. MGM, the owner of the copyrights to sixteen James Bond films, sued, and the court granted MGM a preliminary injunction against Honda's further use of the commercial. *Metro-Goldwyn-Mayer v. American Honda Mo-tor Co.*, 900 FSupp 1287 (CD Cal 1995).

Games

If you want to create a sequel to a computer game or additional play levels for a computer game, you need a license from the game's copyright owner. The sequel or additional play levels will be a derivative work based on the original game. "Tip books" are generally derivative works requiring licenses as well. Sequel rights are discussed in "Key Issues in Web Product License Agreements," chapter 13.

NEW PLAY LEVELS

FormGen made and owned the copyright to the popular computer game *Duke Nukem 3D*. Micro Star downloaded three hundred user-created additional levels of the game and stamped them into a CD, which it sold as *Nuke It*, in a box decorated with screen shots from *Duke Nukem 3D*. In litigation, Micro Star claimed that *Nuke It* could not be a derivative work based on FormGen's game because *Nuke It* did not contain any art files from *Duke Nukem 3D*. The court disagreed, holding that FormGen had a copyright in the Duke Nukem story as well as in the art files. The court held that the stories told in *Nuke It* were sequels to the Duke Nukem story, and the copyright owner has the right to create sequels. *Micro Star v. FormGen Inc.,* 154 F3d 1007 (9th Cir 1998).

Software

If you are using software that is owned by a third party, you should obtain a license from the copyright owner. If your software is developed for you by a software consultant or Web developer, you should obtain a copyright assignment or license from the consultant or developer.

Checklist for Licensing Text, Photographs, and Still Images

1. Is the material you want to use protected by copyright?

2. Does the material include or show other copyrightable works that require separate clearance, or is it based on another copyrightable work?

3. What elements do you want to license from the copyrighted material?

4. What rights do you need?

5. What geographical areas do you want to cover in your license?

6. Who owns the rights you need in those geographical areas?

7. Do you need sublicensing rights or subsidiary rights?

8. How do you define your product?

9. Does the material include or refer to recognizable individuals or their homes (requiring defamation and privacy/publicity clearance)?

10. Do you need trademark licenses?

11. Do you need waivers of moral rights or Visual Artists Rights Act rights?

Checklist for Licensing Motion Picture, Television, and Video Clips

1. Is the clip protected by copyright?

2. Is the clip based on another work, such as a film based on a book?

3. If the clip contains music, is the music of the soundtrack owned by a different company?

4. If the clip contains music, is the performance of the music in the soundtrack (the sound recording) owned by a different company?

5. Does the clip include dancing? If so, who owns the copyright in the choreography?

6. Does the clip include voice-over? If so, who owns the copyright in the voice-over?

7. Does the clip include animation or other special effects?

8. Does the clip include other copyrightable or trademarked works such as a toy or sculpture that you also will need to clear?

9. What rights do you need?

10. What geographical areas do you want to cover?

11. Who owns the rights you need in those geographical areas?

12. Do you need sublicensing rights or subsidiary rights?

13. How will you define your product?

14. Does the clip include recognizable actors whose rights of publicity need to be cleared?

15. Does the clip include acting by "doubles" or stunt actors whose performance needs to be cleared?

16. What union reuse fees need to be paid? What permissions need to be obtained?

17. Does the clip include recognizable homes or locations which need to be cleared?

18. Does the clip violate the privacy rights of any individual?

19. Are there third-party contract rights that need to be waived (from the writer or director, for example)?

20. Do you need a waiver of moral rights of the producer or director?

CHAPTER 12

CONTENT OWNER AND PUBLISHER ISSUES

This chapter covers legal and business issues of interest to content owners and publishers. We'll discuss:

- The new opportunities the Internet presents for content owners and publishers.

- Technological approaches to protecting your material.

- The importance of taking inventory of your content to determine whether you have electronic publishing rights.

- Web license agreements from the content owner's perspective. (In "Obtaining a License," chapter 10, we discuss Web license agreements from the licensee's perspective.)

- Web site Terms of Use documents, which state the conditions under which a user may access the Web site and use the Web site's content. (This topic is of interest to anyone who has a Web site, not just to traditional publishers.)

In this chapter, the word "you" refers to the content owner or publisher.

New Opportunities

As you probably know, the Internet and electronic publishing provide a number of new opportunities for content owners and publishers. These new opportunities include using the Web to market print products, to deliver content, and to license content for use on other Web sites and in online products and e-books.

Web Marketing

Many publishers and content owners are using Web sites to market their material. Book and magazine publishers have set up Web sites to provide information on their publications, with sample chapters and tables of contents. A number of image owners provide online catalogs of their material (examples are listed in appendix D). Record companies provide free samples of their new releases online through music clips.

Many publisher and content owner sites are e-commerce sites: Those who want to purchase print material can purchase material on the site, for delivery off-line (by U.S. mail or a package delivery service).

Content Delivery

Some publishers and content owners are providing the actual content of their products online for viewing or downloading. Some of the online publishing sites are fee-based or subscription-based. Others are free. Some of the free sites get revenue from advertising.

Publishing online saves printing and distribution costs. End users like online availability because they get instant access to the material they want (no waiting for the U.S. mail or delivery service to deliver it).

Some content owners and publishers are using "aggregator" sites to make their material available online. For example, a number of different content owners' material is available for download from Fatbrain.com. Material of interest only to a small market can be offered online through aggregator sites. The legal relationship between a content owner and an aggregator is based on a license from the content owner. In the license, the content owner authorizes the aggregator to include the content owner's material in a database and supply it to end users.

Many publishers and content owners are making available online material previously published in print form. For example, many newspapers and magazines make articles from past issues available online. End users can get instant access to material they once had to go to a library's periodical room to view on microfilm or microfiche. The publisher can get additional revenue from use of previously published material. In some cases, material is provided for free, to entice Web users to order subscriptions.

Web Licenses

Publishers are licensing their material for use on Web sites and in Web products. The Web has created new markets for publishers' content. Content is needed for corporate Web sites and intranets, online games and entertainment sites, and distance learning materials.

Online licensing—also known as online rights management—is in its infancy. Already, some licensing agents have set up licensing sites (see "Licensing Agents," chapter 10). Offering online licensing makes it easy for those wanting to license your material to locate it and obtain licenses.

SUCCESS IN ELECTRONIC PUBLISHING

To be successful in the new world of electronic publishing, publishers and content owners need to:

- Inventory what rights you have in existing works. This topic is discussed in "Online Publishing."

- Develop standard terms and new pricing models for electronic licensing.

- Keep track of new developments, both legal and technical. The *Tasini* case, discussed in "Electronic Publishing," is the example of such a legal development. Copy protection devices are an example of a technical development.

Protecting Your Material

There is a downside to making your material available online: Digital copies are perfect copies, and the Internet makes it easy to distribute a large number of perfect copies of digitized material. In this section, we'll discuss access control technology and copy protection devices.

Access Control Technology

Access controls limit who can view material on the Web. They include firewalls, password protection, IP address recognition systems, and encryption.

Firewalls are created by a server, to protect material located on an intranet from those not authorized to use the intranet.

EXAMPLE

Publisher authorized Big Company to use chapters from Publisher's technical manuals on Big's intranet. A firewall could be used to restrict access of the material to authorized intranet users (such as Big's employees and contractors).

Password protection systems require those wishing to access the material to type in a password. Many fee-based online journals rely on passwords to limit access to those who have paid the fees. On some Web sites, a summary of the material is free. Downloading the actual article requires a password or credit card charge authorization.

IP address recognition systems restrict access to computers that have specific IP addresses or domain names. Encryption technology restricts access to those possessing the authorized decryption key. It "codes" information from a sender into unreadable form. Only an authorized receiver who holds the key to decode the information can access it.

Copy Protection Devices

Technologies that control access cannot control what is done with a work once it has been accessed. Once a user has accessed material, copy protection devices are used to control what uses the user can make of the material (printing, downloading, or electronic distribution). For example, "digital container" technologies encode a digital work and wrap it in a proprietary file format that can be opened only by software that reads and abides by the usage rules contained in the file. If the work is disseminated downstream, the file format goes with it, and the work cannot be accessed by anyone who does not have the proper viewer and authorization.

Electronic Publishing

If you are making a transition from print publishing to electronic publishing or want to take advantage of the new licensing opportunities presented by the Web and electronic publishing, you must determine whether you have electronic publishing rights in your content.

INVENTORIES NEEDED

"Relatively few content producers in any media have made the necessary investment over time to build complete and accurate, and detailed information on what they own and/or what rights they may have."—Isabella Hinds, *Marketplace for Licensing in Digital Distance Education* (included with the U.S. Copyright Office's *Report on Copyright and Digital Distance Education*).

For material in which you own the copyright, you do have the right of online use. However, don't assume you own the copyright in material simply because you paid for its creation. You own material created by your employees within the scope of employment. You do not own material created by independent contractors unless you obtained an assignment of copyright or the material was created as work made for hire. Copyright ownership is discussed in chapters 3, 5, and 6.

Material You Do Not Own

For material you do not own, whether you have the right to use material in electronic form and to sublicense others to use it in electronic form is determined by your publishing contract or license to use the material. Don't assume that you have the right to use previously published articles online.

Whether an existing license gives you the right to use or distribute material in electronic form may not be clear.

EXAMPLE

In the 1950s, Composer granted Film Company the right to use Composer's musical composition "Summer" in the motion picture *Summer Dreams*. The license grants Film Company the right to "exhibit, distribute, exploit, market, and perform" the composition in the motion picture. Film Company wants to create an "interactive online film" version of *Summer Dreams*. It is unclear if the license permits Film Company to use the song in the online version. Composer (or Composer's heirs or assignee) may argue that interactive online films didn't exist when the license was granted, and, therefore, the license could not possibly authorize Film Company to use the song in an interactive online film.

Courts have taken different approaches to this old license/new technology problem. One approach holds that any uses which reasonably fall within the medium described by the license are included in the license grant. This approach was used by the court in the case *Bartsch v. MGM*, 391 F2d 150 (2d Cir 1968). The issue in that case was whether a 1930 license to "copyright, vend, license and exhibit" a motion picture photoplay throughout the world gave the licensee a right to use the material on television. The other approach holds that only uses that are within the unambiguous core meaning of the original grant are included. This approach was used in *Rey v. Lafferty*, 990 F2d 1379 (1st Cir 1993), described in "Old License, New Media," below.

To resolve uncertainties as to whether an old license grants a right to use the licensed material in a new medium, the courts have considered evidence of the intent and expectations of the parties, the actual language of the license, and industry practice. If a license states that the licensee may exercise the granted rights "by any means or methods now or hereafter known" (a "future technology" clause), it is more likely that a court would determine that the license grant includes electronic publishing rights. If you are uncertain as to whether your licenses include electronic publishing rights, consult an experienced copy-right attorney. If you do not have electronic rights for content you would like to exploit in electronic form, perhaps you can amend your contract or license with the content owner to obtain electronic rights.

OLD LICENSE, NEW MEDIA

In the 1940s, Margaret Rey wrote seven books about the adventures of Curious George, a monkey. In the 1970s, she granted an invest-ment firm the right to produce 104 episodes of *Curious George* for television viewing. In the early 1990s, the investment firm wanted to distribute the episodes on videocassette. The court held that the li-cense did not give the investment firm the right to distribute the tele-vision shows in videocassette form. *Rey v. Lafferty,* 990 F2d 1379 (1st Cir 1993).

Electronic Databases

Don't assume that you have the right to include your previously published content in electronic databases. If you obtained only one-time publication rights for articles, you do not have the right to use the articles in databases. This point was established in the *Tasini* case, discussed in "Works You've Used Be-fore," chapter 10. However, you may be able to obtain database rights from the content owner.

Out-of-Print Clauses

Many book publishing contracts include out-of-print clauses stating that any rights granted to the publisher in the contract revert to the author once the book is out of print. The publisher no longer owns the rights and can no longer exploit them. The general definition of out-of-print is that a book is out-of-print if it is no longer available in stock in the publisher's or distributors' warehouse.

You do not have the right to publish material electronically if your license to use the material has an out-of-print clause and the material is out-of-print according to the contract's definition of out-of-print. All copyright rights now belong to the author.

New Acquisitions

If you want the right to publish material online or license it to others for online use, negotiate for broad electronics rights clauses in your new publishing agree-ments and licenses. You may not always be able to obtain electronic rights. Many authors and other content developers want to retain electronic rights.

Granting Licenses

In this section, we'll discuss Web content licensing issues of concern to licensors. (The licensee viewpoint is given in "Obtaining a License," chapter 10.) Two sample content licenses are included in appendix B, one for licensing text (Form 3) and one for licensing photos or video footage (Form 4). We'll refer to these form licenses in this section.

These forms assume that material is being licensed for nonexclusive use and that the material is already in existence. The copyright owner is referred to as the "licensor," and the party receiving permission to use material is referred to as the "licensee." In the rest of this section, "you" refers to the licensor.

Terms

The license terms should cover the following points:

- What is being licensed? This information goes in Section 1 in Forms 3 and 4. It is referred to elsewhere in the license as the "Work." To avoid later disputes, be as specific as possible—identifying what is being licensed, for example, as "the text of chapter 8 of the first edition of the book *Internet Law and Business Handbook*, or "the photograph called *View of San Francisco from the Bay Bridge*." For text and photo licenses, attach a photocopy of the text or the photographs to the license agreement if possible. If the copyright for the material has been registered with the Copyright Office, you may identify the licensed work by the title and registration number. If excerpts of a work—rather than the whole thing—are being licensed, the agreement should make that clear.

- In what projects or products are you permitting the licensee to use the Work? This information goes in Section 2 and is referred to elsewhere in the license as the "Project." Get the licensee to be specific about how the licensee plans to use your material. You may not want your material used in a licensee's project, or you may not want to be associated with a licensee's products or services. If the licensee wants to define the Project broadly, remember that a license to use material in multiple projects or in a broadly defined, open-ended project should generally cost more than a license to use material in a single, narrowly defined project. Make sure that the definition of the Project is not ambiguous. If the licensee fills out the Project section and you don't understand the licensee's terminology, get help. Don't sign a license without understanding what uses you are authorizing the licensee to make of your content.

- What rights are being granted? This point is covered in Section 3 of

Forms 3 and 4. Section 3 provides for a broad grant of rights. This grant may be broader than the rights you are willing to grant. If so, you need to modify this provision. For example, you may not want to grant the licensee the right to modify your material (or you may want the right to approve modifications). If the licensee wants a broad exclusive license, consider that you will be giving up the right to license the material to others, and charge a higher fee. Perhaps the licensee will be content with a short-duration exclusive license or with a narrow exclusive license—for example, the exclusive right to use the material for Web-based marketing directed at physicians.

■ What use rights can the licensee give its Web site users? Section 3 states that if the Project includes a Web site, end users of the Web site may be permitted by the licensee to download your material for their own use. You should make certain that the license authorizes user downloading only for Web site users' personal, noncommercial use, as Section 3 provides. That way, you can obtain additional license revenue from site users who want to use the material for commercial purposes.

■ When do the licensee's use rights begin? For a text license, if you sell your material on a subscription basis, you may want to state in the license that the licensee's use rights do not begin until several weeks after your publication date (to avoid having the electronic version compete with your print version).

■ Is the license exclusive or nonexclusive? Modify Section 3 if the license is to be exclusive.

■ Will you get a credit? If so, how will it read? This information goes in Section 4. A credit will make it easy for others who want to license your text to contact you. If you have a Web site, ask that the credit include a link to your Web site. Options for credit placement are discussed in "Other Important Provisions," chapter 8.

■ What is the license fee (Section 5)? It could be a single one-time fee, an annual fee for each year the licensee uses the Work, or a percentage of the licensee's Web site or Web product revenues. The license fee does not have to be money. It could be products or services, publicity, or just a credit.

■ What is the term (duration) of the license (Section 6)? It can be perpetual or limited in duration.

■ What warranties are you giving? Sections 7 and 8 are typical warranty and indemnity provisions. Licensees have good reason for asking for warranties and indemnities: If the licensed material infringes any third-party copyrights, the licensee will also infringe those rights by using the material (even though innocent of intent to infringe). The intellectual property warranty in Section 7 is an absolute warranty. You may want to substitute less stringent warranties, as discussed in "Key Provisions in the Agreement, " chapter 8. Or you could try to negotiate for a dollar limit for your exposure on the indemnity—for example, no more than the license fee.

■ Do you need to delete the warranty concerning publicity and privacy rights? Section 7 includes a warranty that use of the licensed material will not violate the rights of publicity or privacy of any individual (Section 7(c)). For a photo or video license, if your material shows recognizable individuals and you do not have releases, delete the provision and make it clear that the licensee has the responsibility to obtain necessary releases.

Formalities

License formalities are discussed in "Obtaining a License," chapter 10.

Terms of Use

A Web site's Terms of Use document is the site owner's statement of the conditions under which the user may access the Web site. Web site Terms of Use documents are used to remind site users that site content is protected by copyright, to tell them what uses they may make of the site's content, and to protect the site owner from liability for inaccurate information. We discuss Terms of Use provisions briefly in this section. For more information and a sample Terms of Use document, consult our book *Internet Legal Forms for Business*. A case raising the question whether terms of use are binding on site users is discussed in "Linking," Chapter 20.

Copyright Information

Most Web site Terms of Use documents begin with information about the copyright status of the site's material. Posting material on the Web is not an abandonment of copyright. However, some people mistakenly believe that all material on the Web is copyright-free. For that reason, a Web site Terms of Use page will usually include a statement that the contents of the Web site are protected by copyright under both United States and foreign laws. Web site owners should also use copyright notice (discussed in "Copyright Notice and Warnings," chapter 26) on the site to remind site users that site content is copyrighted material.

Many Web site owners are willing to allow site users to print or download the site's material for certain purposes without requesting permission. These "limited permission grants" usually appear in the Terms of Use. A limited permission grant is actually a license to use the Web site's materials. If you want to grant users of your site permission to download or print the site's material, be careful: If your Web site contains material owned by others, which you've licensed, your license controls the extent to which you can lawfully authorize site users to use the licensed material.

EXAMPLE

High Tech Company's Web site contains graphics created and owned by Graphic Artist. If High Tech's license from Graphic Artist does not give High Tech the right to permit user downloading of the graphics, the High Tech site's Terms of Use should not authorize user downloading of the graphics.

Many licenses to use content on the Web authorize the licensee to permit site users to download the licensed material for personal, noncommercial purposes. If your current content licenses do not contain such a provision, you may want to try to obtain such a provision in future content licenses.

Many Web sites permit users to communicate with the Web site operator. If your Web site provides this function and you want to be able to use the user submissions in the future, your Terms of Use should give you the right to use the submissions. Under copyright law's ownership rules (discussed in chapter 1, Copyright Law Basics), the copyright in material created by a site user belongs to the user (or the user's employer, if the user's communication is within the scope of the user's employment).

EXAMPLE

Jungle Company's Web site permits site users to submit product reviews for products sold on the Web site. Sue submitted a review of a Jungle product. Sue is the copyright owner of the review. If Jungle wants to post Sue's product review on its Web site, it needs a license from Sue.

(How to avoid liability for infringing and defamatory user submissions is discussed in chapter 25).

Inaccurate Information

If information on your Web site is inaccurate and a site user detrimentally relied on the information, it is possible that you could be liable to the user for damages. Many Terms of Use pages include a provision warning site users that the Web site may contain inaccurate information and users should not rely on the site's information.

CHAPTER 13

WEB PRODUCT DISTRIBUTION AGREEMENTS

In this chapter, we will discuss the special business and legal issues involved in publishing and distribution agreements for Web-based products such as on-line games and distance learning materials. The issues discussed here also apply to CD-ROM products.

When one party develops a Web product and another company distributes it, the developer grants either an assignment or license to the company that will distribute the product. We will discuss those two options in the first section of this chapter. We'll refer to the company handling distribution as the "publisher."

In the second section, we will review key license agreement issues and offer negotiating tips for developers and publishers. In the developer tips sections, "you" refers to the developer. In the publisher tips sections, "you" refers to the publisher. The final section discusses additional publisher concerns.

Assignment or License?

One of the key issues is whether the developer will assign all rights in the product to the publisher or just grant the publisher a license to distribute the product. An assignment is a transfer of ownership. A license is a grant of permission to use the work in ways that would otherwise be infringement. See "Assignments" and "Licenses," chapter 3.

Assigning the Rights

The assignment of all rights in the product by the developer to the "publishing" company is quite common in the film and book publishing industries. This assignment may have certain exceptions (in the book publishing industry, for example, movie and television rights are often retained by the author). Such assignments are also common in the multimedia CD-ROM industry for single or narrow-use applications.

For a mass market product in which the developer assigns all rights, the developer's compensation generally takes the form of an advance and royalties. Advances are the initial payment that the developer receives from the publisher before distribution of the product. Royalties are paid during distribution. The amount of the royalties will depend on the nature of the product, the market, and the developer's involvement in the product's development. For example, the royalties for an original online or CD-ROM product may be quite different than the royalties on clothing or other merchandise articles. (For CD-ROM titles, royalties for merchandise articles are generally one quarter to one half the royalty for the original product.)

Developer Tips

If you, the developer, assign all rights in your product to the publisher, you will not be able to port the work to a different platform (such as a game console) or reuse either the product or its component parts in another project. The copyright owner's exclusive rights will belong to the publisher. (Reuse of material protected by assigned copyrights is discussed in more detail in "Key Provisions in the Agreement," chapter 8.) Component parts include the underlying software, the storyline or text, the characters, the user interface, preproduction materials such as scripts and storyboards, sound effects, music, and the source art (which can include photographs; two-dimensional, hand-drawn art; three-dimensional rendered images; and video).

If you wish to use those components in other products, you must obtain a "license back" from the publisher. As a licensee, you will need to address many of the same issues (such as scope of the rights) as a publisher who is a licensee. However, some issues that apply to the publisher, such as warranties regarding performance, would not be relevant to you because you created the product and are familiar with its performance.

Another option, if you wish to use a component in other projects, is to retain ownership of the component, granting the publisher a nonexclusive perpetual right to use the component. This arrangement, known as a "technology trade" or "technology transfer," is becoming common for development engines because of the huge time and manpower investment required to create these engines.

Publisher Tips

For you, the publisher, the advantage of an assignment is that it provides you with all rights in the product, and it does not require you to predict which rights will be most valuable in the future. For a game product, even a general assignment should state clearly whether it includes an assignment of rights in the characters and settings in the product. Characters and settings could have significant value in sequels and other media.

Licenses

There are two kinds of licenses: exclusive and nonexclusive (these terms are defined in "Licenses," chapter 3). In most publishing contracts, the publisher will want exclusivity. Exclusivity ensures the publisher that money spent on promotion will result in revenues to the publisher and not to a second "free riding" publisher.

Developer Tips

If you license the rights in your product instead of assigning the rights, you must carefully define the scope of the license. You should expect that the publisher will wish to obtain the broadest possible grant of rights to avoid uncertainties about product distribution. The most important issues that will arise in the license form of publishing agreements are discussed in "Key Issues in License Agreements," later in this chapter.

You may wish to limit the exclusivity to the markets in which the publisher is best able to exploit the product.

EXAMPLE

Developer developed an interactive history of the Korean War. She granted an exclusive license to distribute the work in CD-ROM and diskette form to Book Publisher. However, she granted the exclusive rights to create a television documentary to Television Producer because Television Producer had more experience in the television industry.

In exclusive agreements, make sure that the publisher has a strong incentive to distribute the product. If the publisher changes its corporate strategy or simply fails to market your product, your expected revenues (which are generally based on royalties arising from sales) will be lower than you expected. Such incentives can take a variety of forms: legal obligations (with rights reverting to you, if the publisher fails to meet the obligations) or minimum payments, for example.

The legal obligation to exploit a product traditionally requires one of four types of effort from the publisher:

- Best efforts.

- Reasonable commercial efforts.

- Efforts in comparison to other types of products.

- More detailed effort requirements (such as advertising budgets).

One problem with this legal obligation to exploit is that most publishers will not agree to employ best efforts because the legal standard for best efforts is so high that it is difficult to meet. Unfortunately, the reasonable commercial efforts standard is less precise and could be difficult to enforce. The latter two forms of effort may require difficult predictions about what amount of advertising and other promotion efforts are appropriate.

Rather than rely solely on such legal standards, you should ensure that the publisher has a clear economic incentive to exploit your product. This can take the form of a large advance to you, minimum royalties, or a combination of the two.

In exclusive agreements, you also should be alert to the remedies for the lack of performance by the publisher. If your only remedy for any failure of performance by the publisher is to terminate the publisher, you may face a difficult choice. Termination will probably be costly for you because you must find a new publisher and restart an advertising campaign. A new publisher may be reluctant to take on a product that it believes has "failed."

Publisher Tips

If you do not have the negotiating leverage to obtain an assignment, you will have to be satisfied with a license. In that case, you should ensure that you get a right of first refusal to exploit the product in forms other than the "core" product form (Web product, CD-ROM, or diskette). The most common noncore product rights are:

- Right to port to other platforms and media.

- Right to localize for other languages.

- Right to develop publisher-originated sequels.

- Right to distribute developer-originated sequels

- Right to complete an unfinished work.

- Merchandising and ancillary rights.

These noncore product rights are discussed later in this chapter.

Key Issues in Web Product License Agreements

The key issues for license agreements are platforms, types of media, ancillary rights, sequel rights, advances, and royalties. These issues may also be important for "license back" of rights in components to the developer (if the developer has assigned all rights to the publisher).

Platforms and Media

The publishing agreement should clearly state the platform or platforms and media for which the developer is granting rights to the publisher. Some products may be exploited on a variety of platforms—home video console systems such as Sony PlayStation, handheld systems such as GameBoy, and arcade systems. Some products may be exploited in a variety of media—on the Web and other computer networks, CD-ROMs, diskettes, and cartridges. It may also be appropriate to consider distribution via cable or telephone lines and use on interactive television.

Developer Tips

You should be confident that the publisher has the ability to exploit your product on all of the platforms granted in the license. The publisher will want the broadest possible rights to maximize the return on its investment in the product. One common solution is to give the publisher the right to exploit the rights on certain platforms, with a "right of first refusal" to exploit the work on other platforms. A right of first refusal is a right to match a proposed offer or an actual offer from a third party. You can then exploit your product on other platforms if the publisher chooses not to do so.

If your contract with a publisher includes a right of first refusal for the publisher, make certain that it contains a time limit—for example, ten days from the date the publisher is notified of the offer. Also, make certain that the provision requires the publisher to match all terms of the other offer—for example, minimum royalties, marketing commitments, and revision rights—and not just the compensation term.

Another possibility is to grant the publisher broad platform rights, but to have specific platform rights revert to you if the publisher does not exploit them by a stated date. A weaker form of the right of first refusal is the "right of first negotiation," which requires you to negotiate in good faith with a publisher for a limited time period.

Publisher Tips

If you are getting a right of first refusal for different platforms or media, try to establish the terms upon which you will be able to distribute such new versions (generally, the publisher will prefer the same terms as those for the original version). This approach saves you from having to conduct a separate negotiation for each new version.

Consider whether the developer should be permitted to make modifications for platforms with which the developer is not familiar. In other words, do you wish to subsidize the developer's learning to create a product for a new platform? The publisher also should establish what materials-such as source code, graphics files, and camera-ready art-the developer will provide if the publisher (or the publisher's contractor) creates the modifications. Access to the developer's materials could substantially reduce the cost of creating these new versions.

Ancillary Rights

The product may have the potential for significant revenue from "ancillary" rights. Ancillary rights are those to exploit the storyline, characters, or settings in other media, such as books, television, merchandising, and films. For example, the sale of "hint books" for video games can be lucrative.

Many Hollywood films now make more from merchandising the characters in their films than they make from the actual box office receipts. For example, the original *Batman* movie grossed approximately $400 million worldwide from performance in movie theaters, but earned more than $500 million through merchandising sales of clothing, toys, games, and videocassettes.

Sequel Rights

If the product is one that lends itself to sequels, sequel rights are important to the developer and the publisher. Many game programs, because of the characters in their games, present rich opportunities for sequels. For example, Brøderbund has been successful in exploiting sequels of Carmen Sandiego. (In fact, Brøderbund once expressly stated that its corporate strategy was to "develop products that may be expanded into families of related sequel or complementary products that achieve sustained consumer appeal and brand name recognition"). In the film industry, the *Star Wars* series has been a huge success.

Developer Tips

You must decide if you wish to grant sequel rights to the publisher and what the terms will be. You may decide to use the terms of the original license agreement for the sequel, or you can provide for a separate negotiation at the time the sequels are ready for development. A common solution is to give the publisher a right of first refusal to distribute sequels. This compromise is advantageous for both parties because the publisher is already familiar with the original work and its marketing, and you avoid the expense of working with a new publisher. At the same time, you can feel comfortable that the right of first refusal ensures that you will receive market value for your sequel.

If you grant sequel rights, pay careful attention to the definition of the scope of sequel rights. Is a sequel a product that includes the use of a single character, or must it include the entire ensemble of characters in the original product? The contract provision on sequel rights should also deal with the publisher's rights to propose sequels, and the terms for the creation and distribution of such sequels by the publisher.

This issue takes a different form when you have assigned all of your rights to the publisher. In that structure, the publisher has the right to create sequels because one of the rights that you assigned is the modification right (see "The Exclusive Rights," chapter 1). You then need to include contract provisions to give you the right to participate in creating and distributing sequels.

Publisher Tips

The ability to market a series instead of a single product can substantially increase the return for the publisher. Consequently, the right to distribute sequels is critical.

The publisher should establish the terms on which such sequel rights will be made available in as much detail as possible. If the publisher cannot obtain an absolute right to distribute sequels, a right of first refusal is the next best alternative, preferably based upon the same terms as those for distribution of the initial product. The disadvantage of the right of first refusal is that it simply creates an "auction" with third parties, a situation that may not recognize the publisher's contribution to the value of the original product.

The publisher should try to get the following minimum information from the developer to decide whether to exercise its right of first refusal to distribute a sequel:

- A written proposal (including a budget) from the developer to create the sequel.

- The royalty percentage for the sequel (if not already established).

- The advances (if not already established).

- Other appropriate distribution terms.

If the publisher decides not to exercise the right of first refusal on a proposal, the developer should be allowed to offer rights in the sequel on the same terms to a third party for a limited period of time—typically from thirty to 120 days. If this time period is not limited, the publisher takes the risk that over time the initial product will become more successful and the original terms for the sequel will become more attractive. To ensure that the publisher and third parties compete on an equal basis for the sequel rights, the term during which the developer can offer such terms should be limited.

As an alternative, the publisher should try to include a "right of last look." This right gives the publisher a final opportunity to obtain rights in the sequel if the developer is about to enter into an agreement with a third party. A right of last look generally offers the publisher the opportunity to obtain the rights on the same terms as the third party. It is usually of short duration (three or fewer business days).

The publisher should also try to ensure that it has the right to develop sequels based on its own ideas. For example, the developer may decide not to create any further sequels, for reasons not based on the economic success of the original product. The publisher may believe that a sequel would be successful, and the publisher should have the right to invest in such a sequel. To avoid conflict with the developer, the publisher should consider offering the developer the right of first refusal to create that sequel based on the publisher's ideas. However, if the developer does not exercise that right, the publisher should be able to make the sequel. Naturally, the royalties paid to the developer for a sequel based on the publisher's ideas should be less than those for the original product.

Advances

Advances can be paid in a lump-sum payment or a series of payments tied to milestones in the development of a product. Advances are determined in a variety of ways: They can be arbitrary amounts set to encourage the publisher to exploit the product, or they can be tied to the expense of developing a particular product. These expenses can include traditional costs, such as employee and independent contractor salaries, and third-party license fees. They can also include less traditional expenses such as the premiums for "errors and omission" insurance or the purchase of needed equipment.

EXAMPLE

Developer is a small company that is negotiating its first transaction with Publisher. Publisher is willing to pay Developer an advance to cover the expenses of developing the product. However, Developer needs a powerful new computer and a scanner to create the new product. Publisher may be willing to increase the size of the advance to permit Developer to purchase or lease the necessary equipment.

Developer Tips

One of the most important issues for the developer is whether the advances are refundable or nonrefundable. Refundable means you may have to repay the advances to the publisher for certain defined reasons. It may be appropriate to repay the advances if you are unsuccessful in creating the product for certain reasons under your control, such as loss of employees or accepting additional work. However, a requirement to refund the advances if your product is not successful in the marketplace is unreasonable. Such a requirement would mean that you would lose both the money and the time that you spent in developing the product.

Frequently, advances are nonrefundable, but recoupable from the royalties due to you. Recoupment can take many forms. The most common form requires withholding of all your royalties until all of the advances from the publisher have been repaid. The potential problem with this is that you will not have any cash flow from royalties after the delivery of the product until *all* of the advances are repaid. Depending on the amount of the advances, this repayment could take months or even years. One compromise is to permit recoupment of a designated percentage of your royalties so that the publisher receives repayment of advances (although more slowly than under the prior structure) and you receive revenue immediately from the distribution of the product.

EXAMPLE

Publisher paid Developer a $200,000 advance, which is recoupable from a 10 percent royalty on net revenues from the sale of the product. The royalties due to Developer were $50,000 in the first quarter, $70,000 in the second quarter, $100,000 in the third quarter, $120,000 in the fourth quarter, and $170,000 in the fifth quarter. If all advances are recouped from royalties before any payment of royalties to Developer, Publisher will be repaid its advances by the third quarter. Developer will not be paid royalties until the third quarter. The first payment will be $20,000. If the Publisher agrees that recoupment will be limited to 50 percent of the royalties due to Developer, Developer will receive payments of $25,000 in the first quarter, $35,000 in the second quarter, $50,000 in the third quarter, $60,000 in the fourth quarter, and $140,000 in the fifth quarter. Publisher will not be repaid until the fifth quarter (instead of in the third quarter).

When you are contemplating a distribution agreement for a series of products, the issue of cross-recoupment frequently arises. Cross-recoupment is the right of the publisher to obtain repayment of advances on one product from royalties for another product. Cross-recoupment permits the publisher to spread its risk among several products, some of which may be less successful than others. This request is generally reasonable, because it permits the parties to share the risks and rewards more equally.

Publisher Tips

In most cases, advances will be recouped against royalties. The procedure for recoupment of advances requires a careful balance of developer and publisher concerns. You will want your advance repaid as rapidly as possible, a goal best achieved by withholding all of the royalty payments due to the developer until the advance is repaid. However, you should recognize the potential problem this may create for the developer. Many developers are thinly capitalized and may depend on the revenue from the product being distributed while they work on other projects. By simply decreasing the percentage of the royalty payments used to recoup the advance from 100 percent to a lower percentage, you can ensure that the developer continues to have a revenue stream. If the agreement includes the right to distribute multiple products from the same developer, you should ensure that you can cross-recoup your advances (recoup advances for one product against another product).

Royalties

Royalties can take many forms. In fact, they represent one of the most flexible means of allocating a financial return between the parties. The balance of this section will discuss the most common issues that arise in determining royalties.

Although many developers focus on what percentage they will get of the royalty base, the definition of the royalty base is the more important issue. The initial question in this definition is whether royalties will be paid on gross or net revenues. Gross revenues are all revenues received from the distribution of the product, without any deductions. The problem with the use of gross revenues is that they don't reflect the profits of the publisher. The publisher is likely to be conservative in setting royalties based on gross revenues because of uncertainties about what the actual profit will be. This problem can be particularly acute if the product includes significant amounts of third-party content for which the publisher is responsible for paying license fees. (See "Obtaining a License," chapter 10.) In this situation, the publisher may have great difficulty in estimating its profits on the product in advance.

Developer Tips

The advantage to you of royalties paid on gross revenues is that gross revenues are relatively easy to calculate. Unlike net profits, gross revenues are much less subject to manipulation. The dispute between Art Buchwald and a major movie studio described in "Net Profits" illustrates the manipulation problem.

NET PROFITS

Art Buchwald contributed a brief story idea to the studio for an initial $10,000 payment. He was to get a fixed fee and a share in the net profits if the idea was used in a film. Eventually, the idea was used for the Eddie Murphy movie, *Coming to America*. The studio denied that the idea was the basis for the movie, but a judge disagreed. The studio then stated that though the movie grossed more than $350 million worldwide, the movie had a deficit of $18 million under the net profits definition. Buchwald challenged the studio over its calculation of net profits. The trial revealed many examples of the studio marking up the costs of services it provided to cover its overhead and make further profits. For example, the deductions included a 10 percent advertising overhead that was not related to actual costs, and a 15 percent overhead charge that was found not even "remotely" to correspond to actual costs. In fact, the judge described a 15 percent overhead charge on an operational allowance for Eddie Murphy Productions as "charging overhead on overhead."

If properly defined, the net profits royalty base poses little risk to the developer. The use of net revenues may actually mean a greater return to you: The publisher may be willing to pay a higher percentage of the net revenue. The critical issue is the list of what items are deducted from gross revenues to calculate net revenue. The most common deductions are:

- Sales and use taxes.
- Shipping charges.
- Shipping insurance.
- Returns.
- Discounts (including cooperative advertising).
- Costs of manufacturing.

For products that will have significant international sales, net revenues may also include a deduction for royalty payments that cannot be brought back into the United States because of currency control or similar laws of foreign countries. (Some countries do not permit revenues earned in that country to be converted into dollars and transferred out of the country.)

You should review the components of net revenue carefully for deductions that are controlled by affiliates or subsidiaries of the publisher. These types of deductions may not reflect the market costs of the goods or services being provided.

To reflect the true price of your product, the price used to calculate gross revenues or net revenues should be fixed in a market transaction. Avoid having this price based on sales by the publisher to its related companies, such as sales subsidiaries, because that price may be quite different from market price due to taxes and other concerns.

The requirement of minimum royalty payments is one of the most effective devices to ensure that the publisher remains committed to exploiting the product. It sets clear expectations between you and the publisher. Generally, such minimums are set on a calendar-year basis. The amount varies depending on the price of the product and the sales expectations. On the other hand, you and the publisher may have different expectations for the product and it may be difficult to agree on an amount acceptable to both parties. Annual minimums are rarely used in nonexclusive licenses.

Publisher Tips

Make sure the method of calculating royalties is clearly defined. You should try to establish in advance the reduction in royalties for derivative products that you develop on your own or on products you must complete. Obviously, the royalty for such products should be less than the royalties for those products that the developer has successfully completed. This point also applies to publisher-created ported versions, foreign language versions, and sequels.

Warranties

A warranty is simply a legal promise that certain facts are true. Most publishing agreements include a warranty section in which the developer warrants certain facts. Warranties are discussed in "Key Provisions in the Agreement," chapter 8.

Credits

The agreement should state what form the developer's credit should take and where the credit should be placed.

Remedies

Remedies are the relief for the failure ("breach") of a party's obligations under the distribution agreement. (Breach of contract is discussed in "What Is a Contract?," chapter 4.)

Developer Tips

Termination of the agreement is a "blunt" remedy. It may not be an effective remedy for many lesser breaches of obligations under the agreement. If you terminate the agreement, you must then find a new publisher and start the advertising and distribution process once again.

You should consider what type of "intermediate" remedies should be available to you for a less than complete failure on the part of the publisher. For example, if the publisher is successfully distributing your product in the United States but not in Europe, you will have a difficult decision if your choices are limited to taking no action or terminating the entire agreement. Instead, you should consider an intermediate remedy that permits termination in the countries in which the publisher is not performing successfully. Intermediate remedies should be put in place at the time the agreement is drafted.

You also should be aware of remedies that may be imposed on you for the breach of your obligations. One of the most common and most important remedies is an indemnity of the publisher for infringements of third-party intellectual property rights. The costs of defending and paying damages in an infringement case could far exceed the revenues you receive under the agreement. The most efficient way of avoiding this liability is to properly clear any third-party content before using it (see chapters 9 and 10).

You may wish to try to limit your liability for damages under this indemnity obligation. For example, you could ask to limit your liability under the agreement to the amount of your royalties. However, the publisher may be reluctant to permit such a limit. This is because the publisher's liability is likely to be significantly greater than the sum of all of the royalties paid to you. (The publisher's liability will be based on its profits, not royalty payments to you.) One potential compromise is to set a large amount based on the predicted sales or obtain insurance against this risk. Unfortunately, at the current time, it is difficult to obtain insurance for this type of risk. The issue of limiting your liability for infringement of third-party intellectual property rights may be one of the most contentious ones in your negotiations with the publisher.

Additional Publisher Issues

In this section, we address additional issues of importance to publishers.

Right to Complete

Many developers are thinly capitalized organizations that may not be able to complete a project if a key developer leaves. Consequently, the publisher should ensure that it has the right to complete a product if the developer is unsuccessful. Completion rights should also apply to ported versions, foreign language versions, and sequels whose development was begun by the developer. If the publisher does not have an assignment of rights in the product or the explicit right to modify the product, the publisher will not have the rights to complete a product. At the same time, the developer may not have the resources to repay any advances. Thus, the publisher will be left with an unfinished product and an unrecoverable advance.

Due Diligence

Due diligence is the shorthand term for the investigation of facts and legal issues undertaken by lawyers (or others) as part of a business transaction. In distribution agreements, the most important part of the publisher's due diligence is ensuring that the developer has properly done two things:

- Cleared any rights to third-party content used in the product. (See chapters 9 and 10.)

- Obtained the necessary assignments from the individuals who helped to create the product. (See chapters 5 and 6.)

The publisher will be liable for infringement if it distributes a product that includes third-party material without appropriate permission. Ignorance or warranties from the developer are not a defense to copyright infringement by the publisher. The publisher will have a substantially greater liability for mistakes on these issues than the developer. Damages awards to third parties will be calculated on the publisher's profits, not on those of the developer (or the royalties paid by publisher to developer). Damages are discussed in "Copyright Protection," chapter 26.

EXAMPLE

Developer used a video clip from the film *The Terminator* in a product on sales training without clearing the rights to use the clip. Publisher got a warranty from Developer of ownership of all rights in the product and a warranty of noninfringement of third-party rights in the distribution agreement. The Publisher distributed the product to retail stores. The film's copyright owner will probably sue both Developer and Publisher. Even though Publisher got a warranty that the product did not infringe third-party rights, both parties will be liable for copyright infringement because Developer failed to get a license to use the clip.

Although the publisher can obtain warranties from the developer that no intellectual property infringement problems exist, warranties will not protect the publisher against embarrassment and business problems arising from the unauthorized use of third-party materials. The publisher also may find that the developer does not have the resources to reimburse the publisher for damages paid to such a third party, despite having a legal obligation to do so.

To avoid "buying" a lawsuit, the publisher or its attorney should understand how the product was developed, review third-party content licenses, and review the developer's agreements with its employees and independent contractors. (License terms are discussed in "Obtaining a License," chapter 10.) It is much cheaper to discover and resolve problems before beginning distribution of the product.

EXAMPLE

Publisher performed due diligence on a virtual golf game it wanted to distribute online. Publisher reviewed the assignment agreements with the individuals who created the game and the golf celebrity who licensed his name to be used on it. Publisher discovered that several of the individuals involved in the development of the game were not full-time employees of Developer at the time they worked on the game and they had not executed assignment agreements. The golf celebrity had licensed his name only for a year. Before licensing the product, the Publisher should ensure that the individuals have executed appropriate assignment agreements. Publisher may also wish to extend the term of the celebrity license and broaden its scope.

Bankruptcy

If the publisher has received and recorded an assignment of all rights in the intellectual property of a product, then it is relatively well-protected against the consequences of the developer's bankruptcy. (See "Assignments," chapter 3, and "Copyright Assignments," chapter 10.) However, a problem could arise in identifying the materials (source code, graphics files, and so forth) to which the publisher has rights if the developer is also simultaneously creating other products when bankruptcy occurs. To avoid this problem, the publisher should consider an escrow arrangement in which all materials are deposited on a regular basis with a third-party escrow agent.

Bankruptcy of a developer poses potentially serious problems for the publisher if the publisher has a license rather than an assignment. Generally, a United States bankruptcy court can terminate a license agreement if it is considered to be "executory"— one in which both parties have continuing obligations. The license agreements described in this chapter would be considered executory. For example, the publisher's obligation to pay royalties and the developer's indemnity of the publisher for intellectual property infringement are sufficient continuing obligations to make the license agreement executory. If the trustee in bankruptcy determines that the license is "burdensome" on the bankrupt company, the trustee can terminate the license and make the licensee (in this case, the publisher) an unsecured creditor with no further rights under the agreement and only a claim for damages. An unsecured creditor generally is paid only a small percentage of the amount of its claim.

In addition, the trustee can then relicense the product to a third party. In the United States, this problem was partially solved by amendment to the

Bankruptcy Code in 1988. This amendment (found in 11 USC § 365(n)) provides that a licensee can retain its right under a license agreement so long as it continues to pay royalties and waives the right to future performance from the bankrupt party (for example, correction of errors) and certain other rights.

Unfortunately, this amendment solves only part of the problems for a publisher. Three other problems exist:

1. This amendment applies only to intellectual property rights arising under United States law. Thus, if the agreement includes the right to distribute the product outside of the United States, such rights would be subject to bankruptcy laws of each foreign country.

2. The amendment does not apply to trademark and service mark licenses. At the request of the United States Trademark Association (now the International Trademark Association), trademarks were excluded from this provision. Thus, the trustee in bankruptcy is still able to terminate a trademark license if the trustee can convince the bankruptcy court that the license is burdensome.

3. The amendment may not apply to exclusive copyright licenses in the United States. Such licenses are a "transfer of interest in copyright" and not a mere license. (See "Licenses," chapter 3.) The most effective way of protecting an exclusive copyright license is to register the copyright and record the existence of the exclusive license against the registration. (See "Assignments," chapter 3.) Once such a transfer is recorded, it will give constructive notice of the transfer and prevent future assignees or licensees from obtaining superior rights. Although the effect of a bankruptcy on an exclusive copyright license is not clear at the present time, an exclusive copyright license that is properly recorded should survive bankruptcy.

The solution to the problem of possible developer bankruptcy is difficult and will vary depending on the nature of the rights granted and your negotiating leverage. You should contact your legal counsel for advice on how to deal with this problem.

Right to Sue Infringers

Once the publisher has paid for the right to distribute the product, it should be able to stop third-party infringers or require the developer to do so by requiring that the developer sue third parties to stop the sale of infringing products. The right to sue "offensively" generally belongs to the owner of the copyright (or trademark). Thus, unless the publisher has received an assignment of all rights in the product, this right to sue will reside with the developer. An important exception to this rule in the United States permits an exclusive copyright licensee to sue third parties for infringement. However, the right of an exclusive licensee to sue varies depending on the country and the type of intellectual property (patent, trade secret, copyright, or trademark). Consequently, the publisher should deal with this issue expressly in the distribution agreement.

Another problem in the right to sue third parties for infringement arises for components of the product that the developer does not own, such as photographs or characters. If the developer has only licensed such rights and those licenses are nonexclusive, then the developer will not have the right to sue for infringement of rights in those components. Unless the developer obtained the right to sue for infringement of components in its license agreements, the developer will have only the right to sue third parties for copying of the "whole work," not for copying of components. (These rights under trademark law are a little different because they are based on "confusing similarity," discussed in "Scope of Trademark Rights," chapter 15.)

EXAMPLE

Developer has nonexclusively licensed a photograph of Marilyn Monroe for her celebrity trivia game. She used the photograph prominently on the front package of her game. A competitor with a similar game used the same photograph on the front of the package of his game. Developer will not be able to sue her competitor for copyright infringement without the permission of the copyright owner of the photograph because she only has a nonexclusive license.

Generally, the agreement should state whether the publisher or the developer has the first right to sue a third party for infringement. If that party decides not to bring suit within a limited time period, the other party should have the right to bring the suit. The agreement should also provide that the party not bringing the suit will assist the other party. Finally, the agreement should allocate the division of any damages received from such a lawsuit. The failure to do so can lead to litigation between the developer and the publisher. One common solution provides that the damages, after deductions for the expense of the lawsuit (including attorney's fees), should be split in some fixed percentage between the parties.

If the developer retains ownership of the intellectual property in the product, the developer may wish to have authority to approve any lawsuit settlements to avoid settlements that would adversely affect its rights. If the developer refuses to approve the settlement, the developer should have the obligation to take over the litigation and pay the publisher for the amount spent in the litigation. Otherwise, the developer could block settlement of the lawsuit and force the publisher to continue the lawsuit without bearing any expense itself.

CHAPTER 14

BUSINESS MODELS FOR THE INTERNET AND NEW MEDIA

By Gail L. Grant
GLG Consulting
grant@glgc.com

Overview

The purpose of this report is to examine the impact of the Internet on business models and review the different types of business models that are used by companies employing the Internet for sales. The report starts with a brief background of how Internet commerce got to the point that it could impact the way people do business. The paper moves on to define the term business model and the points of contact between the Internet and the classical models. The different impact points and the resulting business models are explored, giving examples of companies and/or industries using those models.

This article is excerpted from a CommerceNet research report, entitled "Internet Business Models, which is approximately twice the length of this article and three update reports published in 1998 and 1999. Contact CommerceNet at elizabeth@commerce.net to inquire about purchasing these reports.

I. Industry Background and Evolution

Before we look at Internet business models, it is useful to understand how we got to this point. Many people have not internalized just how rapidly the Internet has become a part of our lives. Part of the reason for the changing models is the rapidity of that growth and the potential it holds for businesses. The Internet has gone from the domain of academics and researchers in its early days to a part of many people's daily lives. Its growth has been incredible, doubling in the number of computers connected every eighteen months and doubling in the number of users every twelve months, until recently when growth has slowed somewhat. There are more computers on the Internet today in the Faeroe Islands—a small group of islands between Iceland and Norway with a total population around 40,000—than there were on the whole Internet in 1982. As of October 1999, estimates for the number of computers connected to the Internet ranges from over 56 million (Network Wizards, http://www.nw.com) to over 64 million computers (C. Huitema, Bellcore, http://www.netsizer.com). NUA (http://www.nua.ie) estimates the number of users at 201 million as of November 1999. It isn't just the number of users that is growing: the amount of commerce over the Internet is growing faster than the number of users or systems connected, with growth rates ranging from twofold to tenfold increases per year.

The reasons for this growth are **accessibility, information,** and **reach**. Before 1993, the applications used on the Internet, with the exception of email, were too confusing to use for most people. This hampered the accessibility for nontechnical people. As user-friendly applications became available, more people and companies started using the Internet. For the past five years, these three aspects have been fueling each other: as the number of people and companies connected to the Internet grew, new, user-friendly applications have appeared and more and more information has been made available online.

There are a few key milestones in Internet commerce: 1989, 1991, and 1993. Without all of these milestones, Internet commerce was not possible, or at least highly unlikely. There really wasn't *any* Internet commerce before 1994. Less than 5 percent of the people using the Internet today were using it five years ago and less than 0.1 percent were using it ten years ago. Even though these milestones occurred before Internet commerce began, without these events, the applications, information, and reach would never have spiraled upward, to create a major business channel without these events. Let's take a look at these pivotal events.

- 1989: Tim Berners-Lee invented the Web

- 1991: First Web browser and NSF/DARPA remove commercial use restrictions

- 1993: Mosaic released by NCSA

These are the milestones that opened the door to Internet commerce. Without Tim Berners-Lee's idea of the World Wide Web, there would have been no Web browsers to make it easy to use the Internet. Without the change in policy, commerce would have been impossible. Without the first browser introduced, showing it could be done, NCSA would have never introduced Mosaic and the NCSA Web server. Without Mosaic, companies could not have experimented with using the Web without spending money, which would have greatly lengthened the amount of time it took for the Internet to grow so dramatically. And without the Internet, public key infrastructure products would still be relegated to the realm of research and government. The ramifications of all these changes began to be forecasted in early 1995.

195

business
models for
the internet
and new
media

Enter Commerce

In April of 1995, Forrester Research shocked the world by predicting that the Internet economy—commerce, access, services, software, and hardware—would reach $10 billion dollars by the year 2000. This was a very aggressive and, to some, unbelievable number. At that point in history, the number of commercial systems on the Internet had just surpassed the number of educational / research systems and the majority of companies still didn't have Web sites. The legion of Internet startups was just forming. Less than a year later, Forrester upped the figure to $30B and then to $200B, still talking about the Internet economy and $92B for Internet commerce.

An important barrier was crossed with the 1995 Forrester prediction: the association of the Internet with the generation of billions of dollars in revenue. This prediction made other firms reassess their views. Forrester was followed by predictions from IDC and Price Waterhouse, also pegging Internet commerce revenues at over $100B by the year 2000. Although some companies, such as Jupiter Communications and Simba/Cowles, had more stately predictions, the trend started heading up.

The next big word for the Internet was the "t" word: trillion. ActivMedia was the first research firm to predict that the Internet would reach $1.2 trillion by the year 2001. Now, the "t" word has become commonplace: IDC Research now pegs Internet commerce at $1 trillion by 2003, joining the analysts using the "t" word. Forrester Research now sets the global market at between USD1.4 trillion and $3.2 trillion by 2003. Current predictions for the top three firms that make predictions are charted below. Note that Forrester now quotes a range, rather than a set figure. That is reflected by two sets of bars for them, one with the low figure and the second set with the high forecast.

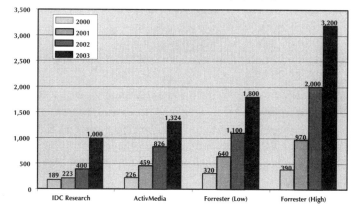

These figures bode well for the future of the Internet as a major component of companies' business models.

II. Internet Commerce Today

To bring these forecasts into context, let's look at what has already happened.
Some people find these numbers high, others think they are low. Perhaps a
more useful guide is the numbers which have been reported for the past few
years. Although the experts don't agree exactly how much, Internet commerce
has been growing steadily. Just about all the research companies, regardless of
the numbers quoted, believe that commerce on the Internet is at least doubling
every year. Here are the reported figures for 1996–1998:

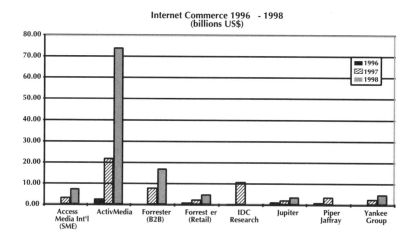

ActivMedia once again takes the high spot, with other firms making more
modest assessments. Initial figures for 1999 put commerce figures between

197

business
models for
the internet
and new
media

$10B and $95B and all the experts are remarking on the tremendous growth in online sales. As you can see, although there are some similarities of the figures, the research firms don't agree on even what has already been sold over the Internet. One explanation for this is the differences in what is being counted. These decisions aren't that easy to make. Some things are hard to position: do you include in revenue figures stock trades or just commissions? Foreign Exchange? Currency Management Corporation alone transacted $20 billion (USD) in currency trades in 1997, so obviously, this isn't being counted in most of the forecasts, nor is online trading or Financial EDI going over the Internet.

It is important to keep this all in the context of the overall market, where billions of dollars is just a drop in the bucket. The Organization for Economic and Cooperative Development (OECD) pointed out that 1997 figures account of only half of one percent of all retail sales in G7 countries and even the rosy trillion-dollar forecast would only account for 15 percent of total sales. Even if the figures are small, Internet commerce is growing rapidly. Price Waterhouse predicts that business-to-business Internet commerce will double every three to four months (up from every six months last year) and most firms peg CAGR at over 100 percent for the next five years. There are also substantial barriers outside the USA. In Europe, higher telephone charges, the language barrier, and disparate tax levels impede progress and in Asia, the average consumer cannot afford a computer. Even in the USA, only about 30 percent of the population is online, according to the CommerceNet/Nielsen survey. The story for corporations is different.

Corporate Internet Growth

Despite the barriers, corporations are getting online in unprecedented numbers, which bodes well for business-to-business sales. According to IDC, 75 percent of top Asian companies—more than double the 1997 number—have Web sites and 81 percent of U.S. companies with more than 100 employees. Durlacher Research Ltd stated that 94 percent of the U.K. companies surveyed had Internet access. A MORI study stated that 60 percent of European corporations are online and that half the remainder plan to go online this year.

For the Small to Medium Enterprise (SME), the Internet penetration is lower. Although the majority of SMEs have access to the Internet, current estimates for SMEs with Web sites range from a low of 9 percent (IDC) to 24 percent (IBM) to a high of 37 percent (CyberDialogue/findsvp). The Internet has now grown to the point that many companies are changing the ways they do business in order to take advantage of the Internet. For some companies, the changes are minor, but other companies have rewritten the way they do business from the ground up.

These continually escalating numbers act as an impetus to small businesses, encouraging them to use the Internet. It also can act as a wake-up call to large traditional firms, warning them of the expanding trend to Internet usage. Although the majority of large firms in the USA now have some form of Internet business, there are still holdouts that are likely to suffer for their lack in the near future. These predictions are just the first of the wave. The second part is several recent reports on the Internet and its benefits.

U.S. Department of Commerce Report

If you haven't read the June 1999 report *The Emerging Digital Economy II*, you should. It can be found at http://www.ecommerce.gov/ede/ for the online HTML version or the PDF version can be downloaded from http://www.ecommerce.gov/ede/ede2.pdf. The report states that the "digital economy" can be credited with *one-third* of the nation's real economic growth between 1995 and 1998. It also predicts that by 2006, almost half the workforce will be employed by industries that are either producers or heavy users of information technology products. The report contains some interesting predictions and is surprisingly up-to-date for a government report.

Beyond the report mentioned above, the Department of Commerce has promised to publish more data related to e-commerce, primarily through two initiatives. The Census Bureau has launched an initiative to deliver official measurements of e-commerce in the USA. By late 2000 or early 2001, the Census Bureau will release the first official e-commerce revenue figures, covering online retail trade for 1998 and 1999. The Bureau of Economic Analysis (BEA) also plans to develop new measures reflecting e-commerce and to take account of the effects of the digital economy on overall economic activity. This additional reporting will add impetus to Internet migrations.

The U.S. government continues to support the Internet as a strategic element in the growth of the economy. Federal Reserve Chairman Alan Greenspan has repeatedly credited "technology" and the Internet with a role in the impressive economic growth in the USA. This governmental support has added confidence in the Internet as a business tool, especially in the business-to-business sector.

University of Texas/Cisco Report

Another June 1999 report came from the University of Texas, sponsored by Cisco Systems. The findings from this report were based on interviews with over 3,000 U.S. companies, all of which generated some portion of their revenues from Internet products and/or services. The report pegged the U.S. Internet economy at $301 billion in 1998. This nets to a CAGR of 175.4 percent over 1997. The Internet economy was also credited the Internet with creating jobs for 1.2 million people in 1998. This amount is over 40 percent of *all* the new jobs created in the U.S. during 1998. The survey also found that Internet workers were 65 percent more productive than their non-Internet counterparts.

199

business
models for
the internet
and new
media

An interesting characteristic of the report is that it attempted to quantify the size of the Internet economy by relating it to the real world. Based on this comparison, the Internet economy would rank among the top 20 countries (18th after Switzerland and ahead of Argentina) in size. Comparing the Internet to other business sectors, in just five years its $301 billion figure has put the Internet ahead of veteran sectors like energy ($223B) and right behind automotive ($350B). Internet workers also produce more revenue: the average revenue per Internet economy worker was quoted as approximately $250,000, which is 65 percent higher than other industries. Note that only slightly over $100B of the Internet economy number quoted above was actual Internet sales. The rest was infrastructure and application layers.

There was a very insightful conclusion from the UT/Cisco report that relates intimately to Internet business models. This study found that the Internet isn't causing disintermediation, on the contrary, it is *spawning new forms of intermediation*:

While it is intuitive to think of "disintermediation" in an electronic world, this study provides evidence that Internet intermediaries are already playing an important role in shaping the Internet economy. These intermediaries generated and estimated $58 billion in 1998, nearly a third of the total revenues for Internet commerce and intermediary based transactions. It is also important to note that only commissions (which typically account for less than 10 percent of the value of a transaction) were counted as revenues for intermediaries like online travel agents and auction houses. In other words, the total business associated with intermediaries were much bigger than the $58 billion figure.

The ease of using the Internet to sell is spawning new businesses of all types, especially in the area of intermediaries. Although the Internet threatens many traditional resellers, it has also opened new opportunities for those who add value to the purchase through aggregation, additional services, ease of use, and integration with other products and services. In the early days, most of these mediated sales were either from old companies using the Internet as a new way to reach customers or new Internet companies formed specifically for Internet sales. This continues to expand and is one of the areas that should be watched closely. Portals, aggregators, sellers of books/CDs, and many of the top Web sites act as intermediaries. But there is also a downside to this phenomenon: this growth of intermediaries is causing problems for those who have traditionally had a "lock" on mediation, such as the stock exchanges, non-Internet travel agents, and other small businesses who sell other companies' products.

Giga Information Group Report

In early August 1999, Giga released a report on the savings that accrue from conducting business online. They estimate that businesses saved $17.6 billion in 1998, with the majority of that figure ($15.2B) enjoyed by U.S. firms. The firm estimates that business usage of the Internet will save companies $1.25 trillion globally by 2002. Cost savings generally result in higher profit, rather than increased revenues. Giga estimates that U.S. business alone will enjoy increases in profits of between $360 billion and $480 billion from Internet-based cost savings alone. In addition to the savings from selling online, Giga sees six areas where companies will benefit from Internet usage:

- **Order management for distributors and resellers:** the use of Web sites to submit orders, check pricing/order status, and ask questions. This service will also lower the costs for the distributors and resellers.

- **Sell-side distribution:** using the Web to more efficiently distribute marketing messages, sales information, and training to field employees.

- **Procurement/supply chain management:** the use of intranets and extranets to facilitate orders and procurement.

- **Routine employee transactions**: facilitation of processes such as benefits enrollment, job postings, and promotions, plus mundane business processes like travel arrangements and expense reports.

- **Marketing**: using the Internet to promote the company and its products—the Internet is a powerful tool to effectively communicate a company's position.

- **Customer service**: Companies can use the Internet to build customer relationships.

Before we look at the changing business models, it is important to define the term.

III. What Is a Business Model?

There are several different ways of defining "business model," but for the purposes of this report, the definition is *the approach a company takes to making money.* The approach or system enables a company to grow and make money on a sustainable basis. This articulation of a business model is derived from a presentation by Darlene Mann of Onset Ventures to the Bay Area Internet Users group. The presentation can be viewed at: http://www.baiug.org/speakers/onset/. A business model includes:

1. **Markets/Customers**—who is the customer and who is the competition

2. **Products/Services**—what a company sells

3. Channels of Distribution—how the products/services are sold and delivered

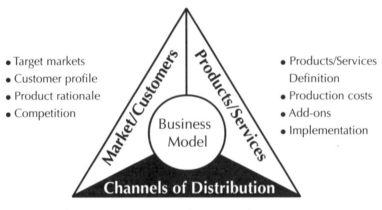

- Target markets
- Customer profile
- Product rationale
- Competition

Market/Customers

Products/Services

Business Model

- Products/Services Definition
- Production costs
- Add-ons
- Implementation

Channels of Distribution

Strategies and processes for:
- Marketing
- Sales
- Distribution

Markets/Customers articulates which markets a company is targeting; **who** is the customers and why they need this product—as well as competition and funding requirements are a part of this segment. Products/Services defines **what** products and services will be sold, how much they cost to produce, pricing, and additional products/services that can be offered to the customer. It also includes how they are implemented: whether they are produced in-house, acquired elsewhere, or a combination of development and integration. Channels of Distribution articulates the strategies and processes for marketing, sales, and distribution: **how** the offerings will be marketed, whether sales will be direct or through channels, who are a company's partners, and how the product/service is delivered to the customer. A business model touches every facet of corporate life, but the *focus* of the business model is the about how a company makes money in a sustainable manner. The discussion below will focus on corporate changes that are primarily revenue-based. For each of the three aspects of a business model—customers/markets, products/services and channels—we will first look at an overview of the changes in this area and examples of usage. After all the potential changes have been examined, we'll look at the issues for each aspect and with Internet commerce in general.

IV. Customers/Markets

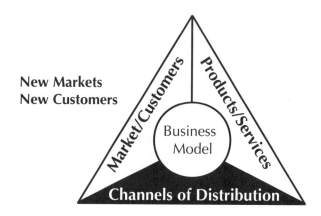

**New Markets
New Customers**

The impacts of the Internet in this area of the business model are both customers and markets. These changes can expand the potential for revenue, altering a company's business model, extending the potential customer base. Who is considered to be a customer or prospect can be radically changed by the Internet. Since the Internet is global, it is just as easy to click on a link that is on a computer that is down the hall as it is to click on a link thousands of miles away. This global nature opens up new customer and market possibilities for companies both large and small. It enables even small companies to contemplate selling to foreign markets. For large companies, the markets' impact tends to be less, but the Internet offers a new way to reach more customers.

There can also be a change to the type of customer that is targeted. This is more common for large companies than small. Many services which corporations offered only to their largest customers can now be offered over the Internet to a much wider clientele, due to the efficiencies of the Internet as a service delivery mechanism. The Internet expands who a company can consider to be a customer both geographically and economically. The other impact to the market is the change in the nature of competition. Due to the low costs of setting up an Internet site, it is possible for a small organization to compete successfully with organizations many times their size.

Generally, changes to customers and markets are enabled through changes to at least channels and sometimes also in the products/services offered. A virtual prerequisite to expanding customers/markets is to also change the channels of distribution to include Internet sales, although sometimes the sales efforts are minimal. There are many examples of companies that have online catalogs, but require the customer to call to place an order.

Classically, markets are either defined as geographic markets, such as Japan, the USA, Germany, etc., or as vertical (textiles, electronics, etc.) or horizontal markets (desktop publishing, help desk applications, etc.). Customers are typically defined by profile: company size, the person in the company which would purchase a certain product and the divisions within a company that would most be interested in a product. With the advent of the Internet, there has been a subtle change, a new evolution of the term "market." Some companies are now defining their target market as the online population.

203

business
models for
the internet
and new
media

V. New Products and Services

This business model area is where the most innovation possible but it is unfortunately the one least commonly changed, except among new Internet startups. The capabilities of the Web and usage patterns often drive the business model changes in this arena. Changes to the products and services component of the business model can be seen in different products than those sold through traditional channels, new services that would not be possible except on the Internet, and new pricing models. These changes are often related: a company may start offering an online library of product-specific books on its Web site and create a new revenue source through the commissions Amazon.com pays its affiliates. How a product is acquired or created or produced for sale can also change the model, due to the difference in cost. But this area also includes the most basic fiscal component of a business model: how a company makes money.

Traditionally, companies have sold products or services, but the Internet changes what it is possible. Now, the line between products and services has blurred and some new categories have emerged which are part product and part service. These product-services tend to combine programmatic interfaces—like the ability to search—with pay-per-view pricing for the product. Some companies are selling their own products, but many—such as http://www.newspage.com from NewsEdge, http://www.news.com from c|net—simply aggregate news or other information/services from other sources.

There is an interesting difference between these two companies: although they have similar offerings, the c|net offering is free and the NewsEdge product charges for access to most articles. The difference is in what they each "sell." This brings us to pricing and revenue models. Some of the new revenue models include audience access, percentage sales, subscription, and fees. C I net "sells" audience access and NewsEdge sells audience access, subscriptions, and pay-per-view.

Although percentage sales, subscription, and fees are common in the real world, with numerous analogs, there isn't a good counterpart in the real world to audience access or pay-per-view of documents. There is a whole new class of company selling audience access as their primary or secondary product-service. These companies are generally called portals, since they are often the first page a user sees, their starting point to find what they want on the Web. These companies continue to evolve, but they have created an interesting new product-service mix and a new business model that may have dramatic effects in the future.

Different Products

There are three ways companies change their product mix when selling over the Internet:

1. **Internet-specific offerings**—selling products not sold elsewhere or in a different form than the traditional product, sometimes as a subset of the traditional product

2. **Complementary reselling**—offering new products that group logically, but are manufactured by another firm

3. **Rewarded pass-through**—pointing a buyer at a product sold by another firm and receiving an commission or a bounty for doing so

These three can be characterized by the degree of involvement in the product and cost of producing the product. Internet-specific offerings are created by the corporation and sold online directly and/or through partners. Complementary reselling still has the corporation doing the sale, but the product is not their own. The Internet has also added a new twist, where the corporation doesn't even complete the sale; they simply pass the sale through to the product's seller for completion. These product changes can have an impact on revenue in two ways: increased gross and/or decreased costs.

Many new products-services tend to be delivered online and often have a higher cost associated with developing them, compared to re-worked existing offerings, although the long term costs of delivery are usually lower after development costs have been recouped. The most common savings are cost of sales. Since the sale takes place on the Internet, there is less cost associated with the sale, compared to either tele-sales or direct sales. Both complementary re-sale and rewarded pass-through require less involvement by the corporation than in-house products. The highest costs are for new products that are developed in-house.

205

business
models for
the internet
and new
media

New Services

The Internet provides the infrastructure that allows companies to offer new services that were not possible before or were only available via telephone or high-priced private networks. Because the new services don't have to pay for the infrastructure, they can be offered for a lower price and still make a profit. The oldest Internet service is the infrastructure itself: Internet access. The most dramatic new services are financial: both stock and foreign exchange trading.

Although the original Internet was funded by the U.S. government, that is no longer the case. Internet infrastructure is provided primarily by Internet Service Providers (ISPs), who sell Web site hosting, corporate Internet connections, and individual Internet accounts. This was the first service the Internet made possible and among the first group of companies to benefit from the Internet explosion. Although there are thousands of ISPs around the world, there has been a consolidation of the top ISPs into a small group of dominant players.

One new type of service that uses the Internet infrastructure is Internet telephony. This means that a conversation takes place between two people travels over the Internet instead of over long-distance carrier lines. In some instances, the entire call is done using computers, but services are popping up which use Internet points of presence to transfer the call from the local phone loop through the Internet to a point of presence close to the call destination. An SRI Consulting study predicts that Internet telephony will capture 5 percent of all long-distance calls worldwide by the year 2002 and that the Internet telephony, including services, hardware, and software, will grow to $9 billion by 2003.

New Pricing/Revenue Models

Other than traditional product and service revenue models, there are four new revenue elements that are used in the revenue mix:

1. **Audience access**—rates similar to traditional advertising, for ads on popular Web sites, as well as entry points to services

2. **Percentage sales**—similar to commissions for resellers, but generally smaller amounts

3. **Subscription**—similar to magazine subscriptions, but also including databases and online application access

4. **Fees**—transaction, pay-per-view, pay-per-play, rentals, and bounties

Audience access refers primarily to high-traffic Web sites and the sites that are called portals: Yahoo!, NBC-Snap, Microsoft Network, AOL, etc. which sell the rights to put a product or service before the portal's users. This can take a number of forms: advertising banners, special placement in directory categories, service agreements, spotlights, and premium placement on search results. Portals also make money in other ways, but advertising is the primary one in most cases. Internet advertising is a growing industry: the Internet Advertising Bureau put the 1997 total for online advertising revenue at $907 million, more than three times the 1996 figure. Veronis, Suhler & Associates forecasts online advertising will reach $6.5 billion dollars by 2002, eMarketer says $8 billion by 2002, and Forrester pegs it at $15 billion by 2003. Audience access has also given rise to a whole new twist to the ratings industry: Internet usage ratings. These companies make money by counting how many people are using a particular portal or Web site.

Percentage sales generate revenue like most resellers: through purchasing a product at wholesale or discount and selling it at retail prices. A new twist has also been added to this model: sometimes the "reseller" doesn't even buy or ship the product! The classic example of this was the Internet Shopping Network, which sold computer-related products online and forwarded the order on to the manufacturer. They recently sold their customer base to another computer superstore, CyberPost, and now focus exclusively on First Auction. Percentage sales are also sometimes used as a part of the revenue mix for providing commerce services, like automated Internet credit card processing.

Subscription sales are most common for publications and sites that offer news and information. While periodical publishers are the most common users, there is a growing number of sites which use subscription for database access. A good example of this is Hoover's profiles (http://www.hoovers.com). A user buys monthly or annual access to the regularly updated Hoover database of company profiles for thousands of companies, both public and private. Hoover's allows anyone to access "company capsules" or small abstracts of the information available to members, but only subscribers can view all of the information in the profiles.

Fee revenues come in five flavors: transaction, pay-per-view, pay-per-play, rentals, and bounties. Pay-per-view is most common with publications and is used for paid viewing of articles and reports. Transaction fees are often charged by commerce service providers for each transaction processed. There has been much talk about pay-per-view movies, but the size of movies is still too large for this to be practical for most Internet users. Pay-per-play is used by game sites to allow users to play a particular game. Rentals are generally the rental of software. A company uses an application online that is running on someone else's system and pays a rental fee for its usage. Interliant, an ISP in Texas, recently launched a Web site for software rental. They currently only rent five applications, but they hope to expand that to fifty by year's end. Bounties are the model used by Jumbo, Inc. and the Jumbo Download Network (http://www.jumbo.com). This company makes money from a fee charged the software's owner for each download initiated. Another use of fees is for selling items through Internet auctions.

Internet auctions are the latest hot trend in Internet business models. There are two different models for how these companies make money: percentage sales/fees and classic resellers. Both First Auction and eBay make money from fees from the seller and a percentage of the sale. ONSALE and uBid have more of a reseller model. These companies are doing well: eBay Inc. has 850,000 registered users and has taken more than 80 million bids on 21 million items in the past three years. Sotheby's has also entered the online auction market, as well as specialty auction houses like http://naturalhistoryauction.com, which deals in minerals, fossils, dinosauria, and meteorites, and http://littlegarage.com, which puts potential auto sellers in contact with would-be-buyers. The Internet Shopping Network's change of focus from online superstore to Internet auctioneer is also evidence of this growing trend.

VI. Channels of Distribution

New Sales Channel
Distribution Alternatives

The two primary impacts of the Internet on channels are in the areas of sales and distribution. One of the Internet characteristics that drives these opportunities is the reach of the Internet. There are very few countries in the world without Internet connectivity, and corporations are going online in steadily increasing numbers. The second is the capabilities of the Web. Using the Web, a customer can find the product they want on the Internet, fill out an invoice, and pay for the purchase online, without human intervention. The Web is particularly well suited to presenting complex configurations and options, research, and instantaneous 7x24 shopping.

For some new companies and a few old ones, the change is not just a new potential sales channel, but often the *only* sales channel. Amazon.com has over three million customers who buy books online. It has no physical store where customers can come in to browse and none of the costs associated with a physical presence, or brick and mortar, as it is called in the banking industry. These lower physical plant costs do not necessarily mean lower overall costs, as will be discussed later.

The Internet as a New Sales Channel

Changing the channels of distribution to include the Internet is not only the most common business model change, but also the easiest to understand. A company simply sells its products and services online. There has been a great deal of debate over exactly what constitutes an Internet sale. Some purists maintain that unless the entire transaction is completed on the Internet, including configuration and payment, it isn't really an Internet sale. Others claim that because the Internet was the source of a sale, it doesn't really matter whether the actual payment is taken online. The most liberal view sees the customer making the decision to buy the critical factor, whether the order and payment are taken online or not. For the purposes of Internet business models, any purchase "won" via the Internet changes the **how** of business models or the channels a company uses for sales, whether or not the transaction was completed on the Internet, even if the order is taken over the telephone.

There is a number of facets to using the Internet as a new sales channel, from getting an online decision to purchase from a customer to complete online sales including delivery of the purchase. Between these two extremes are the taking of orders and online payment, plus online delivery in some instances. Generally, this is an evolution of usage, with companies moving to the more advanced stages as success and strategy dictates. These stages can be characterized in the following manner:

Decision Order Payment Delivery Primary Channel

Conservative   Aggressive

For the first three stages, there is a logical progression. The ability for a customer to decide to purchase online is the most conservative change to a business model. Many companies start at this point. In terms of implementation, this means that the company puts up a Web site that allows the customer to browse the products it offers and perhaps even configure them and get pricing. Once the customer has completed their configuration or browsing, commitment to the purchase takes place either over the telephone or at a physical store or site. The next logical step is to allow the customer to commit online by placing their order. Here, companies include the ability for a customer to actually place an order online via their Web site. The next step up the scale is online payment. Not only does the customer decide and order online, but they also pay online. After completing the order, a customer then provides credit or debit card information to complete the transaction.

Online delivery is the next logical step, if it is possible and practical. This step, when taken, is usually concurrent with online payment, since merchants do not want to deliver goods without payment for those goods. In this case, the customer finds what they want to purchase, fills out an order form, provides a card to pay for the purchase, and then downloads the purchased item to their computer or are given access to a restricted Web site. In the case of tangible goods, online delivery is impossible, since a piece of hardware cannot be routed through the Internet to the customer. Up to this point, the steps have generally been logical, with each building on the previous step. The logical progression ceases with the most aggressive version of the Internet as a sales channel: the Internet as the *only* or primary sales channel. These sites may or may not employ all the facets of Internet sales. Some don't even go beyond online decision, as discussed below, but other companies are actually betting their business on Internet sales.

There tends to be increasing expenses for implementation as you move up the steps, and this can often influence just how far a company goes in online sales. Although there is also usually an increase in implementation costs, often these costs are made up in operational savings, making the changes worthwhile. These changes all influence the business model. Let's look at each of these and who is using them.

The industries that most commonly provide for online decision are the automotive, financial services (especially credit card applications, loans, and some mutual funds) and insurance industries. This is also the common entry point in any industry for companies simply wanting to "try out" online sales. Some companies choose this facet, not as the entry point, but also as the end point of Internet sales. There may be compelling reasons for not completing the commitment online. In the case of a credit card application or loan, there are signatures which are required to make the transaction binding. With a car, the customer may make the decision online, but the classical method of distribution for this industry is a dealership, so the customer must be directed to the dealership to complete the purchase. Some mutual fund companies have decided that they are uncomfortable with online orders, due to the SEC's disclosure requirements. Regardless of the reason, these companies are changing their business models to include the Internet as a new sales channel.

The taking of orders over the Internet is growing rapidly, but most companies don't stop with just taking the order online; they also now take payment or payment instructions online. Companies are finding that the ability for a customer to make a commitment to purchase online increases the likelihood of a sale and decreases the personnel required to make a sale. Although most companies are moving to online payment, online orders without payment are very common in the the financial services industry, business-to-business with new customers, and some high end software vendors. The choice between online orders and online payment is often decided due to high product prices or non-card payment methods. Some companies don't offer online payment because the methods that their customers use to pay are not readily implemented and/or implement-able online, except with EDI. Although electronic check solutions are growing, they are still in their infancy. There is also the question of handling new customers online, where there is not an established relationship, making it risky for a company to simply invoice an unknown company.

Online payment is typically implemented by sites that sell to consumers and/or sell items usually purchased using credit cards. These sites tend to have a higher volume of transactions, making online payment more important to their Internet sales efforts. Good examples of online payment are all the early entries—books, music, computer hardware, and software—as well as most EDI solutions. Most companies that target the Internet market also take online payment, regardless of industry, but these will be discussed below in the primary channel section.

Some companies go even farther than online sales to actually delivering their product or service over the Internet. Online delivery is much less common, since only a minority of products and services can actually be delivered via the Internet. The most common products for complete Internet sales and delivery are software, software licenses, and information, such as newspapers, research reports, presentations. The most popular online services are trading, database searches, customer service, online application software use, training, and Internet telephony. Unfortunately, although software products could be downloaded over the Net, most are too large to be able to make this practical for the modem-connected user. The ability to complete the entire transaction online has tremendous cost benefits. Although many companies sell online, the delivery of the goods must be handled by a human being (usually) or robotic system (rarely). This is far more expensive than allowing a computer system to handle the delivery of the product or service. Online delivery also changes the markets that a company can pursue and the cost savings are not just for the seller, but also the buyer.

Characteristics of Internet Companies

Companies who use the Internet as their primary market and Internet sales as their primary revenue generator are still the exception to the rule, although that is changing. These companies share some characteristics in common that should be remembered. The first characteristic is that the companies are either new companies, founded specifically to take advantage of the Internet or are closely related to the Internet and its usage. It is important to remember that the company who tries to become an Internet market company with products for a customer base that is not predominantly online will probably fail. These companies have done their homework and know what their market wants. The early companies that went into the music business online knew that the current demographic mean (at that time young male college students) bought lots of music CDs, increasing their likelihood of success. In fact, Egghead Computer closed its eighty stores in the spring of 1998, planning to move its entire business to the Web. Egghead Software decided that a large enough portion of their customer base was online to allow them to close their physical stores and look to the Internet as their primary sales channel. Egghead's experiment with online as a primary channel resulted in its merger with OnSale.com, raising the question of whether this is success or failure.

The second characteristic of these companies is flexibility, the capability to be either proactive or reactive, depending on the situation. This is critical in the fast-paced Internet market, where six months from now the market could have substantially changed to a new demographic mix. Internet Shopping Network was flexible enough to move into the auction business, when they thought the time warranted the move. Cisco was able to change the way they did business because they recognized that the Internet offered tremendous potential for them, given that their products are primarily network products, most of which are used on the Internet. This flexibility can have huge payoffs.

The final characteristic of Internet market companies is that they must be well-funded. A quick look at the results of most of these companies will show that only a handful are profitable yet and most are probably years from profitability. Yet the market has placed extraordinarily high valuations on many of these companies. This has two impacts: the companies tend to have large amounts of capital available for acquisitions and mergers, as well as having the funds necessary to build brand awareness. Even with the cost savings the Internet provides, building brand recognition is costly. Some of these companies also have problems with the traditional side of their business, such as delivery of goods and this causes additional expense, as will be discussed below in the Viability section.

VII. Issues

Up to this point, all the discussion has been on the positive side of the business model changes that the Internet offers. But all the changes are not positive. There are issues with virtually every area of change. The issues have not been discussed in the individual sections because they often overlap between markets, offerings, and channels. The issues of Internet business models can be broadly grouped into channel conflict, market conflict, legal issues, technology issues, and profitability.

Channel conflict effects both the markets and customers, as well as how the product is sold. This is generally a clash of old vs. new and the challenge is to be able to get from the old to the new without going out of business. Market conflict is most common among large companies who may have different prices for different markets, making online sales a challenge. Legal issues include the legality of the sale of a product, taxes and export fees, distribution rights, jurisdiction, and licensing. Technology issues vary, depending on the type of products being sold and the type of customer who buys them. They can range from the operational issues with maintaining a real-time service to the challenge of implementing online sales without the necessary in-house expertise. The final issue is whether any of these changes or new business models are viable in the long run.

VIII. Viability

For large companies selling online, Internet sales are generally successful and improve revenues and profitability, but the jury is still out on the aggressive new business models of the Internet market companies. The Icegroup (http://www.icegroup.com) analyzed the second quarter 1998 results of Amazon.com and found that Amazon.com would have to generate $1 billion in sales to just break even. The average order cost them $40.81 to process, but the average order value was only $35.59, meaning that they lost approximately $5.22 for every order processed. So where is the supposed improved cost structure of Internet sales? Obviously, Amazon.com needs to reduce the costs of processing an order in order to be profitable anytime soon. To complicate matters, although the management recognizes the issue and has been hiring experts in the industry to help lower these costs, one company has protested: Wal-Mart. A key to Wal-Mart's success has been a proprietary logistics and information system developed over many years that enables Wal-Mart to respond quickly to needs in a particular store. The suit claims that Amazon.com intentionally hired individuals from Wal-Mart to gain information about this system, thereby violating the Arkansas Trade Secrets Act.

The portals have been a successful business model to date, with Yahoo! posting impressive gains and very respectable net revenues. The question here is not whether the concept of portals can be profitable, but whether the large firms with better name recognition will overtake these new players and supplant them. The use of portals is expected to explode over the coming years and Gartner has identified five clear leaders by 2000 as Yahoo!, Disney-Infoseek, NBC-Snap, Netscape's Netcenter and Liberty Media. This leaves out several players that should not be discounted. Microsoft has made extensive investments in developing a portal of its own and AOL is currently ranked highest among home users. Other media giants could also step into this market, although Time-Warner's initial effort have not been successful.

The most interesting new model is that of Internet auctions. There is an appeal to both businesses and consumers in being able to bid on items to get a bargain. Since many of the auction sites deal with surplus and refurbished goods, this new channel also has appeal to the firms that want to reduce inventory and get older products off their balance sheet. Egghead is also engaging in auctions and many firms are likely to jump on this bandwagon. One of the big questions of profitability for any of the Internet market firms is market saturation: how many portals or auctioneers or brokerage firms can be successful? Only time will tell.

IX. Future Models

Although a few interesting new models, like auctions and portals, have emerged, very few business models take full advantage of the capabilities of the Web and the reach of the Internet. Future models are likely to better incorporate the seamless integration of the Web, creating virtual corporations and partnerships between possibly unlikely companies. The MetalExchange is just the start of the types of industry-specific sites that could be seen in the future.

Another popular model in the future may be along the lines of the aggregator, where a company makes money from linking related services tightly together. An example of this might be a real estate purchase, where the title search, assessment, inspections, mortgage services would appear on a site that included moving services, painters and other related products and services. It may even be possible that these sites will offer turn-key solutions, with package pricing for procuring a mortgage, getting a house inspected, the title search, and some small amount of painting/repair.

Future models will make strong use of partnerships, seeking out partners that have what a company needs and trading items of equal value to the partner in exchange. Some partnerships will be trades of this sort, while others may involve cooperative cross-selling, sponsored Web sites, exclusivity, or advertising agreements. A recent buzzword is communities of commerce (CoC), which may also point a direction for the future. There are two definitions of CoC's: a group of vendors in a value chain, like the real estate example above, and online versions of physical communities.

X. Summary

It is certain that more services and new products not yet envisioned will emerge in the future, but despite all these new models, most companies are not new. They must deal with their existing models and migration to new models or subtle changes, as conditions and opportunity dictate. The task of a new company is in some ways much easier, because they lack the shackles of existing products, procedures, and sales channels that the mature company has built up over the years. In other ways, the task for the mature company is easier, since selling online is generally just an expansion, not the sole focus of the business. New or old, most companies can benefit from the one or more of the changes mentioned above.

ASPECT	BUSINESS MODEL CHANGE	REVENUE IMPACT
Markets/Customers	More markets/customers	More sales
Products/Services	Different products, new services	More revenue sources, diversification
Products/Services	New pricing/revenue models	Change in costs, new potentials for revenue
Channels of Sale	New sales channel	Decreased cost of sales, service
Channels of Sale	New distribution methods	Decreased operational costs

Small companies can expand their markets, and large companies can gain more customers and therefore more sales. Adding different products and new services changes a company's cost structure and opens new potential revenue sources, diversifying the company's sources of revenue. New pricing/revenue models change both the amount of revenue per sale, as well as the costs and adds new potential for revenue. Adding the Internet as a new sales channel can help to reach more customers, but also decrease costs of both sales and service. Delivering goods online can decrease operational costs. Both of these channel changes improve profitability.

The new Internet business models are portals, Internet auctioneers, and other companies that target the Internet as their primary market. Portals, auctioneers, and aggregators have the most interesting revenue models, but the moving of traditional businesses online, like financial services, publishing, and travel, can be highly successful with their alternate business models. As mentioned before, there is a dependence of all other changes on a change in the channels strategy because without Internet sales, the business model changes aren't really Internet sales. The purpose of all the changes is to enable a company to more successfully make money in a sustainable manner. The dependence between the areas can be visualized as a triangle:

215

business
models for
the internet
and new
media

From this paper, one thing has clearly emerged: the key to Internet-related business model changes of any sort is selling online. Until a company sells online in some manner, all the other changes are impossible. With online selling—the opportunity of offering new products and services, of experimenting with different revenue models and the possibility of expanding to new markets while reducing costs—opens new possibilities for companies large and small. As with any business model change, only time will show which changes are most effective.

CHAPTER 15

CHOOSING NAMES FOR YOUR PRODUCTS

Trademarks and service marks are words, names, symbols, or devices used by manufacturers of goods and providers of services to identify their goods and services, and to distinguish their goods and services from goods manufactured and sold by others. (For simplicity, the word trademark will serve as a short-hand term in this book for both trademarks and service marks.)

Trademarks can be among your most valuable assets, whether you are involved in e-commerce or a traditional "bricks and mortar" business. The value of the *Coca-Cola* trademark has been estimated to be in the billions of dollars.

This chapter covers two main topics:

■ Choosing a strong trademark for your products or services that will qualify for the broadest trademark protection.

■ Clearing a trademark (choosing a trademark that does not infringe another company's trademark or trade name).

We'll also discuss the standards for determining "confusing similarity" between trademarks, the treatment of titles under trademark law, dilution law, and international trademark protection.

The basics of trademark law are covered "Trademark Law," chapter 2. Conflicts between trademarks and domain names are covered in chapter 16. Rules for using third-party trademarks are covered in chapter 24. The steps that you must take to protect your trademark rights are discussed in "Trademark Protection," chapter 26.

Choosing a Strong Trademark

Trademarks can be words, symbols, slogans, or devices. They take many forms:

Type of Trademark

Word: *Apple* for computers, *Coca-Cola* for soft drinks.

Design: The Prudential's rock for insurance services, Apple's multicolor bitten apple for computers.

Phrase: *Fly the Friendly Skies* for airline services, *The Weiner the World Awaited* for meat.

Shape: The pinched scotch bottle for whiskey, the Coca-Cola bottle shape for soft drinks.

Sound: The roar of the MGM lion for films, the Star Wars theme music for films and videotapes.

Such words, symbols, and devices can be grouped into four categories depending on their ability to serve as a trademark: generic, descriptive, suggestive, and arbitrary or fanciful. We'll discuss these four categories in this section. Because arbitrary or fanciful terms receive the strongest protection under trademark law, you should choose a trademark that is arbitrary or fanciful.

Generic Terms

A generic term can never function as a trademark because it is a commonly used name of a particular type of good or type of product. Examples of generic terms are *386* for microprocessors and *Softsoap* for hand soap.

Do not choose a generic term for your trademark. Such a term will not qualify for trademark protection.

EXAMPLE

Developer chose the trademark *Web Page Design Software* for its software. This trademark is generic for this type of software and Developer will not be able to prevent a competitor from using *Web Page Design Software* for the competitor's own product.

"YOU HAVE MAIL"

America Online, Inc. filed a lawsuit against AT&T to prevent AT&T from using the phrase, *You Have Mail,* in connection with AT&T's email service. The court held that AT&T was free to use the phrase, because the phrase is generic. *America Online, Inc. v. AT&T Corp.,* 64 FSupp2d 549 (ED Va 1999).

Descriptive Terms

A descriptive term is one that directly describes the characteristics, functions, or qualities of a product. Examples are *Five Minute* for fast-drying glue, *After Tan* for lotion to be used after sunbathing, and *Food and Beverage Online* for a Web site that provides news and information for the food and beverage industries. Surnames—for example, *McDonald's* and *Dupont*—are also considered descriptive.

Although descriptive words or symbols may serve as trademarks, they qualify for trademark protection only if they have "secondary meaning." Secondary meaning is a term in trademark law that means that the public already associates the trademark with the goods of a particular company.

EXAMPLE

A federal appellate court found that the word *Fish-fri* was descriptive when used on fish-coating mixes. Because the trademark had acquired secondary meaning in the geographical area in which it was used, the court found that the trademark was protectible as a trademark. *Zatarains, Inc. v. Oak Grove Smokehouse, Inc.,* 698 F2d 786 (5th Cir 1983).

Secondary meaning is achieved through advertising and sales. Market surveys are frequently used to prove secondary meaning. In the *Fish-fri* case, the trademark owner used a market survey that showed that 23 percent of shoppers surveyed identified *Fish-fri* as a product on the market for use in frying fish.

The problem with choosing a descriptive term as your trademark is that until secondary meaning is established, any competitor could adopt the same descriptive term for similar goods. You would not be able to prevent the competitor from using the term on his or her goods.

EXAMPLE

Developer picked *PC Gallery* as its trademark for its CD-ROM multimedia software product. This product is a series of pictures of famous paintings with commentary. However, Developer did not have much money and only sold one hundred copies of its program over several years. Two years later, Big Company started offering its own collection of paintings under the trademark *PC Gallery*. Big is probably not infringing the rights of Developer because *PC Gallery* is descriptive and Developer has not sold sufficient copies of his program to create secondary meaning in the trademark.

Three varieties of descriptive terms and symbols present particular problems:

- **Laudatory terms.** Terms that are laudatory in general (rather than laudatory about a particular product) are generally not protectible as trademarks until you obtain secondary meaning because such terms need to be used by other companies. Examples are *Best* and *Blue Ribbon*.

- **Geographically descriptive terms.** If a geographic area is well known for a particular type of product, the area's name is not protectible as a trademark for that type of product. All sellers of that type of product should be able to use that term. Examples are *New England* for clam chowder and *Cambridge Digital* for computers (Cambridge is the home of a number of computer companies whose products are digital in nature).

- **Common symbols.** Marks that include commonly used designs and symbols—triangles and squares, for example—will require proof of secondary meaning unless the design is unique.

Suggestive Terms

A suggestive term infers something about the qualities, functions, or characteristics of the goods without directly describing them. Such terms are protectible under trademark law *without* the necessity of proving secondary meaning. (Secondary meaning is discussed in "Descriptive Terms," earlier in this chapter.) Examples of suggestive trademarks are *Rapid Shave* for shaving cream and *7-11* for convenience store services.

The distinction between suggestive and descriptive trademarks is one of the most important ones in trademark law, but it also is difficult to draw. If a term requires imagination or thought to reach a conclusion as to the nature of the goods or services—for example, *7-11* for convenience store services—it is considered suggestive rather than descriptive.

SUGGESTIVE OR DESCRIPTIVE

A real estate referral services firm chose *Home-Market.com* as its common law trademark and domain name. The firm sued to stop a Web developer from using *Home-Market.net* as a trademark and domain name for its business, which designed Web sites for real estate agents. The plaintiff claimed that *Home-Market.com* was suggestive for the services it offered, but the court found it to be descriptive. Because the plaintiff could not prove secondary meaning, it lost the case. *Shade's Landing, Inc. v. Williams,* 76 FSupp2d 983 (D Minn 1999).

Arbitrary and Fanciful Terms

An arbitrary term is a commonly used word that is applied to a product or service with which that term is not normally associated. An example is the word *Apple* for computers. (The term would be generic if used for the fruit.)

A fanciful term is a coined or created word or symbol. *Kodak* for film is an example of a coined term.

If you choose an arbitrary or fanciful term as the trademark for your product, you will receive the broadest possible trademark protection. Because an arbitrary or fanciful term has no relationship to the products or services to which it is applied (unlike generic and descriptive terms), other companies do not need to use such a term on their products. Like suggestive terms, these terms are protectible without proof of secondary meaning, and you receive rights in such trademarks immediately upon use or upon filing a federal intent-to-use application.

Domain Names as Trademarks

A domain name can be used as a trademark. The Patent and Trademark Office will register domain names that are used as trademarks and meet requirements for registration as trademarks.

Obtaining a domain name registration for a name (discussed in chapter 16) does not automatically give the domain name registrant trademark rights in the name. Only domain names that are capable of distinguishing the owner's goods or services from the goods or services of others qualify for trademark protection. Generic domain names such as *aspirin.com* and *petstore.com* do not qualify for trademark protection. Descriptive domain names—PC *Gallery.com*, for example—cannot be protected as trademarks until they acquire secondary meaning.

The use of trademark law to resolve domain name disputes is discussed in "Domain Name Registration," chapter 16. Laws protecting trademark owners against those who register domain names that are identical to or confusingly similar to the owners' trademarks are discussed in "Cybersquatting," chapter 16.

Clearing a Trademark

Trademark rights in the United States arise in three different ways: under common law, through state registration, and through federal registration. The three methods of obtaining trademark protection are discussed in "Trademark Law," chapter 2.

No matter which method of trademark protection you choose, before adopting a trademark, you should ensure that it is available. Clearance of trademarks is a complex but necessary process. It is much cheaper to ensure that the trademark is available before adopting it than to try to purchase the rights of third parties once the trademark is in use and you have invested in packaging, advertising, and domain name registration.

AMAZON BOOKSTORE COOPERATIVE

Amazon Bookstore Cooperative was in business in Minneapolis before Amazon.com set up shop on the Web. (It is not clear whether Amazon.com knew about Amazon Bookstore Cooperative when Amazon.com chose its name.) The cooperative had a right to challenge the online store's use of *Amazon* in the book business. After all, Amazon.com's Web site is accessible from Minneapolis. Book purchasers in Minneapolis might assume the Amazon.com Web site was operated by the local bookstore cooperative. However, Amazon Bookstore Cooperative and Amazon.com reached an agreement: Amazon Bookstore Cooperative assigned all rights in the trademark *Amazon* to Amazon.com, with Amazon.com licensing limited rights to use the name back to Amazon Bookstore Cooperative.

Generally, a trademark is cleared in two steps: a federal registrations search, then a state and common law search.

Federal Registrations Search

The purpose of the federal search is to determine if there are any federally registered trademarks that are "confusingly similar" to the trademark that you want to adopt. If you adopt a trademark that is confusingly similar to an existing trademark, the owner of the existing trademark will be able to prevent your use and registration of the trademark. The determination of whether a trademark is confusingly similar to an existing trademark is based on an eight-factor test that is discussed in "Scope of Trademark Rights," later in this chapter.

The Patent and Trademark Office's trademark database, "TESS" (Trademark Electronic Search System), is available online at the PTO's Web site, www.uspto.gov (click on "Searchable Databases"). The Web database does not include new trademark applications that were filed during the last two to four months. For recent applications, you can search X-Search, the PTO's internal trademark database, for a fee at the PTO's Trademark Search Library in Arlington, Virginia, or at Partnership Patent and Trademark Search Libraries in Sunnyvale, California; Detroit; and Houston. Trademark search firms, listed in appendix C, will do a search for you for a fee.

The federal registrations search does not indicate whether a term is available for your adoption, only that it is not available (because the term is confusingly similar to a federally registered trademark that is still in use). If the search shows a confusingly similar trademark, you should check to see if the trademark is still in use. If the company has ceased using the trademark for more than two years and does not intend to use the trademark again, the trademark may be available for your use despite the federal registration. However, you may have to purchase or "cancel" the trademark (an administrative procedure done through the U.S. Patent and Trademark Office) in order to register your trademark.

Even if the search is "clear," just because someone has not federally registered a trademark does not mean that the trademark (or a similar trademark) is available. Your proposed trademark or a similar one may be in use for similar goods by another company that has superior rights based on common law (the other party may also have rights based on a state trademark registration).

Although you can perform a preliminary review of a trademark search report yourself, you should consider having an experienced trademark attorney review the search report because trademark law includes a number of obscure rules that make it difficult to interpret a search report. For example, according to the doctrine of "foreign equivalents," all foreign words must be translated into English and then compared with existing trademarks.

EXAMPLE

WebDev, Inc. owns a federal trademark registration for the trademark *Vert* for Web development tool products. The word *vert* is French for "green." WebDev can prevent another company from using *Green* for Web development tool products. Although *Vert* and *Green* are very different in appearance and sound, according to the doctrine of foreign equivalents, *Vert* and *Green* are considered the same word.

State and Common Law Search

The second step is to search for state trademark registrations and common law uses. The common law search will review both trademark use (use on products) and trade name (use for company names). The earlier user of a word or device for a trade name (for example, WebDev, Inc. is a trade name) can prevent the use of a similar word or device as a trademark for similar goods or services. A trademark search firm can do this search for you (see appendix C). However, these firms do not interpret the results for you. For that, you need a trademark attorney.

The state and common law search generally will produce many more potential problems than the federal registrations search. However, you may discover that many of the trademarks listed in the search report are no longer in use (or the companies that own them are out of business).

A trademark search firm will generally take seven to ten days to provide you with a complete state and common law search report, although you can pay more to get the search completed faster. Clearance at the state and common law level can take several weeks as you try to gather information on the current use of the trademarks shown in your search report. You should consider using an experienced trademark attorney to interpret the search report.

Domain Name Search

If you are planning on using your chosen trademark as a domain name, you also need to check to see if the name is available for domain name registration. Altavista is said to have paid $3.5 million to buy "Altavista.com" from the registrant. Domain name registration is discussed in chapter 16.

Even if you are not planning on using the trademark as your domain name, it is a good idea to check domain name registrations to see if the name has been registered. As we discussed earlier in this chapter, domain names can be used as trademarks.

Titles

Treatment of titles is a special issue in trademark law. The title of a film or book is generally not protectible under trademark law unless it is part of a series or has obtained secondary meaning through extensive use. For example, *Star Wars* is protectible as a trademark because it is part of a series of films. *Gone With the Wind* is protectible because the film has achieved great fame.

This special rule has not yet been applied to game or software product titles or Web site titles, but it might be applied in the future. If it is, it will make obtaining trademark rights for single products (as opposed to a series) much more difficult.

Scope of Trademark Rights

Trademark law does not give protection against use of a trademark that is unlikely to cause confusion, mistake, or deception among consumers (but dilution laws, discussed in "Dilution," later in this chapter, may provide protection).

EXAMPLE

Western Software has a federal registration for the use of *Flap* on Web development tool software. If Giant Company starts using *Flap* on desktop publishing software, Giant may be infringing Western Software's trademarks because consumers may think the desktop publishing software and the Web development tool software come from the same source. If Giant starts using *Flap* on fire extinguishers, though, Giant is probably not infringing Western's trademark. Consumers are unlikely to think that the *Flap* software and the *Flap* fire extinguishers come from the same source.

A senior party of a trademark is the first person or company to use the trademark or file a federal "intent-to-use" application to register the trademark. A junior party is the second (or later) person or company to use the trademark or file a federal intent-to-use application to register the trademark. (Intent-to-use applications are discussed in "Trademark Law," chapter 3.) A senior party can prevent a junior party from using the trademark without proving that consumers are actually confused by the junior party's use of the trademark. The senior party need only show that a "likelihood" of confusion exists.

Determining Confusing Similarity

The test for determining whether two trademarks are confusingly similar varies in minor ways in different parts of the country. The test includes multiple factors, but eight of the most common factors are described in the next sections. (This test is used in the Ninth Circuit, which interprets the law in the states of Washington, Oregon, California, Arizona, New Mexico and Idaho.)

The analysis of the potential for confusion is one of the most difficult areas in trademark law. Once again, this is one area where it is advisable to obtain the advice of an experienced trademark attorney who is familiar with the court decisions in this area.

Trademark Strength

Descriptive trademarks generally have the narrowest scope of protection, because other companies need to use these terms on their goods. Suggestive trademarks have a narrower scope of protection than either arbitrary or fanciful trademarks. Arbitrary and fanciful trademarks receive the broadest protection, because other companies do not need to use such trademarks. (The categories of trademarks are described in "Choosing a Strong Trademark," earlier in this chapter.)

A trademark may be strong despite its category because of its use in advertising and sales. For example, *McDonald's* is a descriptive trademark, and thus normally would be weaker than other types of marks. However, its extensive use in advertising and high visibility have made it one of the strongest trademarks in the United States.

"INITIAL INTEREST" CONFUSION

One court has recently expressed concern about "initial interest confusion." If Company A uses Company B's trademark as a domain name, consumers may think that Company A's Web site is Company B's Web site. Web users searching for Company B's site may go to Company A's site. Even if Company A posts a notice on its Web site that it is not affiliated with Company B, consumers will have been initially confused. When Company A and Company B are in the same business, "initial interest" confusion may be trademark infringement. (This was essentially the situation in the *Brookfield* case, discussed in "Using Third-Party Trademarks," chapter 24.) In a later case, the Court of Appeals for the Ninth Circuit indicated that initial interest confusion may exist even when the domain name owner and the trademark owner are in different businesses. *Interstellar Starship Services, Ltd. v. Epix Inc.*, 184 F3d 1107 (9th Cir 1999). However, in another case, a federal district court found that dissimilarity of goods and services resolved the initial interest confusion question. In that case, The Network Network, a training provider for information technology professionals, had the domain name registration for "tnn.com." CBS owned the registered service mark for *TNN* (which stands for The Nashville Network). The court noted that the services of The Nashville Network and The Network Network were not related, making a likelihood of confusion analysis unlikely. "Unlikely indeed is the hapless Internet searcher who, unable to find information on the schedule of [upcoming Nashville Network broadcasts], decides to give up and purchase a computer network maintenance seminar instead." __ FSupp2d __ (CD Cal 2000).

Difference Between the Goods

Even if two trademarks are identical, there is no confusing similarity (and, thus, no infringement) if the goods are sufficiently different.

EXAMPLE

The use of *Pomegranate* for earth movers would not prevent the use of *Pomegranate* for a Web page design software. If *Pomegranate* was first used for graphic design software, though, its use by another software publisher for Web page design software would infringe the rights of the earlier user.

The goods on which similar trademarks are used need not be "competitive" for there to be confusing similarity (and, thus, trademark infringement). Confusing similarity also extends protection against confusion of "association or sponsorship."

EXAMPLE

Although clothing is not competitive with films, the owner of the *Star Wars* trademark can prevent the use of *Star Wars* on clothing by Fashion House, Inc. Such use is likely to lead to confusion of association or sponsorship because film companies frequently sell clothing based on movie titles.

Similarity of the Marks

Similarity can be one of the most important factors in determining the potential for confusion. Whether two trademarks are similar is determined by comparing the sight, sound, and meaning of the two trademarks.

In reviewing two trademarks for similarity, you must carefully analyze the common elements of the two. The use of a common suffix such as "tronics" does not make the two marks similar.

You must also consider the visual appearance of the two trademarks. For example, *Rain Barrel* and *Rain Fresh*, although different in immediate appearance, have a similar commercial impression.

If two trademarks are "sound alikes," the fact that the products are sold primarily by phone will increase the chance for confusion and the possibility of infringement. In determining whether the trademarks are sound alikes, you should consider the number of syllables, the stress pattern, the accent, and possible mispronunciations. For example, *Dramamine* and *Bonamine* were found to be confusingly similar. The key issue is the commercial impression produced by the mark.

".COM" AND SIMILARITY

Adding ".com" to a mark that someone else is already using does not create a new mark that's dissimilar to the preexisting mark. For example, in one lawsuit, the defendant's domain name *cardservice.com* was held to exactly duplicate the plaintiff's *Cardservice* mark. *Cardservice International, Inc. v. McGee,* 950 FSupp 737 (ED Va 1997).

Evidence of Actual Confusion

If there is evidence of actual confusion, it will frequently be the critical evidence against the junior party. It is difficult to overcome evidence of actual confusion.

Marketing Channels

If one product is sold only at wholesale and the other only at retail, the likelihood of confusion may be substantially reduced. Similarly, if one product is sold directly to the consumer while the other one is sold through distributors, the likelihood of confusion may be low.

Degree of Care Exercised by Purchasers

There is an assumption that a purchaser will exercise greater care in choosing a more expensive product than in choosing an inexpensive product. Consequently, a trademark used on products that are purchased casually, at a low price, is more likely to be found to infringe a similar trademark than the same trademark used on expensive products would be.

EXAMPLE

If Developer adopts the trademark *Apiware* for his $15 computer game, he is likely to be found to infringe Publisher's rights in *Apillaware* for another $15 computer game. However, if Developer's and Publisher's products are both $10,000 Web development software, Developer's use of *Apiware* might not infringe Publisher's rights in *Apillaware*.

Defendant's Intentions

If the junior party adopted the trademark with the intent of emulating the senior party's trademark, this factor will weigh against the junior party. Although it is permissible to emulate another party's trademark, you take an additional risk in doing so because the courts are more willing to protect the senior party.

Likelihood of Expansion

The last factor that must be considered in determining whether two trademarks are confusingly similar is whether the senior party is likely to expand its use of the trademark to the products on which the junior party is using the mark. Thus, you must analyze not only the current business of the senior party, but also its potential for expansion into other product areas.

> **EXAMPLE**
>
> Developer has adopted the trademark *Attiware* for its car game software for young children. If Clothing Company adopts *Attiware* for car toys, it might be an infringement of Developer's rights because many game software companies also sell toys based on their games.

SIMILARITY ON THE WEB

According to the Ninth Circuit Court of Appeals, in the context of the Web, three of the eight factors discussed above are more important than others—the similarity of the marks, the difference between the goods or services, and the marketing channels. *Goto.com, Inc. v. The Walt Disney Company,* 202 F3d 1199 (9th Cir 2000). Goto.com maintained that Disney's logo was confusingly similar to the *Goto.com* mark. According to the Ninth Circuit, the logos were "glaringly similar." As to the difference between the parties' goods, the court noted that even Web services that are not identical are capable of confusing the public because many Web sites "coordinate a bevy of distinct services under a common banner." Addressing the marketing channels factor, the court stated that the Web is particularly susceptible to a likelihood of confusion because it allows for competing marks to be encountered at the same time, on the same screen. The federal district court had granted a preliminary injunction against Disney's use of the Disney logo, and the Ninth Circuit affirmed.

Dilution

Although most trademark rights are based on likelihood of confusion, certain trademarks may qualify for more extensive protection under a theory called "dilution." Dilution is a separate legal theory that exists under federal law and the laws of many states. Dilution laws give owners of strong trademarks the right to prevent a similar mark from being used on completely different products or services.

> **EXAMPLE**
>
> The *Mercedes* trademark is one of the best known trademarks in the world. If Developer adopts *Mercedes* as the title of its game software program, the Mercedes-Benz Company would probably be able to prevent such use under federal and state dilution laws even though Mercedes-Benz does not distribute game software and is unlikely to start distributing such software.

Dilution laws are meant to address the strong trademark owner's concern that other companies will try to obtain a "free ride" on the trademark's established reputation in fields other than the field in which the owner is using the mark. In the last example, Developer is trying to use the fame of the *Mercedes* trademark to sell its game. Such free riders may weaken the distinctiveness of the trademark and damage the reputation of the owner of the original mark.

The Federal Trademark Dilution Act protects famous marks (whether registered or not) from dilution to the distinctive quality of the mark. Whether a mark is famous is determined by considering eight factors, including the degree of distinctiveness of the mark, the duration and extent of its use, and the degree of recognition of the mark.

International Trademark Protection

Trademark protection outside the United States varies from country to country. Some countries, such as Japan and Germany, provide virtually no protection for unregistered trademarks. In those countries, only the most famous trademarks, such as *Coca-Cola* and *Mercedes*, will be protected without registration.

Other countries may have a different view of what is confusingly similar. Foreign trademark laws frequently provide broader protection for trademarks in the computer industry than is provided in the United States. You should be aware that registration in the United States will not protect your rights in foreign countries. In fact, in some countries, trademark pirates make a living by registering trademarks of foreign companies and selling them back to the foreign company when it starts to do business in that country.

If you will be selling your product outside the United States, consider registering your trademarks in the countries that are most important to your business. You also should consider registering your trademarks in the countries known for trademark piracy. International trademark registration can be quite expensive. You should analyze the risks and rewards carefully.

CHAPTER 16

DOMAIN NAMES

A domain name is the way that people can identify and find you and your company on the Internet. You don't have to get a domain name—people can reach you on the Web by using your Internet Protocol (IP) address (a string of eight characters). However, domain names are easier for people to remember than a string of numbers. To have an effective online presence and use the Web for marketing, you must choose and register a domain name. This chapter covers domain name registration, selection, and transfers.

We'll also discuss remedies trademark owners can use against cybersquatters. In the past few years, there have been many reports of people registering well-known trademarks and company names in hopes of forcing the trademark owner to buy the domain name, or to prevent the trademark owner from getting the domain name. These practices are known as "cybersquatting."

Domain Name Registration

A domain name is a street address on the Internet. Here are two examples:

"aol.com" (the domain name for America Online)

"laderapress.com" (the domain name for the publisher of this book)

The suffix ".com" is a global top-level domain (gTLD). The other gTLDs are ".net," ".org," and ".int." Additional gTLDs may be available before the end of 2000.

The suffix ".com" was originally intended to be used by commercial entities, ".net" by network providers, and ".int" by organizations established by international treaties and databases. However, this plan has not been enforced. An applicant for a domain name with a ".com," ".net," or ".org" suffix is not required to prove that it belongs to the class for which the suffix was intended.

In the United States, three additional gTLDs are available for certain types of organizations—".gov " for federal government offices, ".edu " for educational institutions, and ".mil" for military organizations. Geographic suffixes are also available. These correspond to the internationally recognized country abbreviations—for example, ".uk" and ".fr " for the United Kingdom and France.

In a domain name, the name or initials to the left of the suffix identify the host computer (for example, America Online in aol.com and Ladera Press in laderapress.com). For email address purposes, a third name can be added to the domain name to identify an individual—for example, smith@abcxyz.com.

Domain Name Registrars

From 1993 until June 1999, Network Solutions, Inc. (NSI) handled all domain name registrations in the United States in the ".com," ".net," and ".org" gTLDs, pursuant to a Cooperative Agreement with the United States Government. Now, however, a number of additional companies are offering domain name registration services. NSI still maintains the database of domain names and their registrants, known as the "WHOIS" database, for these gTLDs, but all other registrars have access to the database.

New registrars for the ".com," ".net," and ".org" domains are accredited by the Internet Corporation for Assigned Names and Numbers (ICANN). ICANN (www.icann.org) is a global nonprofit corporation created to oversee the Internet's core technical management functions, including IP address space allocation, Protocol parameter assignment, domain name system management, creation of new gTLDs, and root server system management. Any company that meets ICANN's standards for accreditation and has signed an accreditation agreement with ICANN may now offer domain name registration services.

The ICANN site provides an up-to-date list of accredited and operational registrars in the ".com," ".net," and ".org" gTLDs at www.icann.org/registrars/accredited-list.html (the page has links to the various registrars' registration Web sites). For information on registrars for the geographic domains, go to www.iana.org/cctld.html.

The Registration Process

Before you register a domain name, you must obtain an IP address from your Internet service provider (ISP). A searchable list of ISPs is available online at http://thelist.iworld.com.

In the past, many businesses had their ISPs handle registration for them. If your ISP is registering your domain name for you, make certain that you—not the ISP—are listed as the owner. After all, you may want to change ISPs in the future, and you should be able to do so without getting a new domain name. The domain name you use is an important part of your identity in the online world. (If the domain name you are using is currently owned by your ISP, you need a domain name transfer, discussed at the end of this section.)

You can register your domain name yourself. Each operational registrar has set up a registration Web site. To determine whether a particular domain name is available for registration, choose a registrar from ICANN's list of approved and operational registrars. Go to your chosen registrar's domain name registration site and follow the simple instructions for finding out whether the name you want is available.

EXAMPLE

Sue, a florist, wanted to know whether "flowers.com" is available for registration. She visited the Web site for one domain name registrar, www.register.com, and inquired whether the name was available for registration (by typing "flowers" into the "Check It" blank and checking "com" in the list of suffixes). She learned that "flowers.com" is taken.

The basic domain name registration rule is "first come, first served"—if you apply to register a name and it has not been registered as a domain name in the gTLD for which you want the name, you'll generally get the name. However, you can lose your right to the domain name— even after you have started using it in your business—to someone with superior trademark rights in the name.

That's exactly what happened in the case *Brookfield Communications, Inc. v. West Coast Entertainment Corporation*, 174 F3d 1036 (9th Cir 1999). In 1993, Brookfield started using the trademark MovieBuff. West Coast registered moviebuff.com as a domain name in 1996. Both companies provided searchable databases containing entertainment industry information. When Brookfield learned that West Coast intended to launch a Web site at moviebuff.com, Brookfield sued West Coast for trademark infringement, claiming that West Coast's use of the domain name was likely to cause consumer confusion and, therefore, violated the federal trademark statute. (Trademark protection is discussed in "Trademark Law," chapter 2, and in chapter 15.)

The federal Court of Appeals for the Ninth Circuit granted Brookfield a preliminary injunction prohibiting West Coast from using the domain name moviebuff.com. The court stated that "[r]egistration of a domain name for a Web site does not trump long-established principles of trademark law. When a firm uses a competitor's trademark in the domain name of its Web site, users are likely to be confused as to its source or sponsorship."

(Another aspect of this case, West Coast's metatag use of moviebuff, is discussed in "Using Third-Party Trademarks," chapter 24.)

Choosing a Domain Name

Avoid registering a name as a domain name if you know that someone else is using the name as a trademark for the type of goods or services you will be providing or related goods or services.

EXAMPLE

Major Company has a federal trademark registration for *Juto*. It uses *Juto* on children's clothing and has spent a lot of advertising dollars creating the *Juto* brand. Sue wants to use juto.com as the domain name for her toy e-commerce site. The name is available for domain name registration. Sue should not choose juto.com as her domain name. She can get the domain name registration, but Major Co. may sue her for trademark infringement when she begins using the name on her e-commerce site. Although children's clothing and toys are not exactly the same line of business, they are related. Major Co. may convince a court that consumers who visit juto.com will think that the Web site is operated by Major Company.

Ideally, you should have a trademark attorney conduct a full trademark search on the name you want to use as a domain name, to determine whether the name is in use as a trademark. (Trademark searches are discussed in "Clearing a Trademark, "chapter 15.)

If the name you want is in use as a trademark, the trademark owner may object to your use of the name as a domain name even if your business is different from the trademark owner's business. The trademark owner may believe that your use of the domain name will cause Web users to think that your Web site is the trademark owner's Web site. This type of consumer confusion is known as "initial interest confusion." It is discussed in "Scope of Trademark Rights," chapter 15.

The trademark owner could also maintain that your use of the domain name will dilute the value of the trademark.

EXAMPLE

Hasbro, Inc., the owner of the federally registered trademark *Clue* for a mystery board game, sued Clue Computing under the Federal Trademark Dilution Act law for registering and using clue.com as a domain name. Hasbro claimed that Clue Computing's use of the domain name diluted its trademark. Hasbro ultimately lost the case because the court found that Hasbro had not proved the *Clue* mark to be famous, a requirement for federal antidilution protection. *Hasbro, Inc. v. Clue Computing*, 66 FSupp2d 117 (D Mass 1999). The federal antidilution law is discussed in "Dilution," chapter 15.)

Most companies choose a domain name that is readily associated with the company's name—an acronym or shortened version of the name, for example, such as "aol" for America Online. However, the fact that you have incorporated under a name does not automatically give you the right to get a domain name registration for that name—nor does the fact that you have been using the name. Someone else may already have registered the name as a domain name or may be using the name as a trademark.

EXAMPLE

Delta Airlines uses the name *Delta* for airline services. Delta Faucet Company uses *Delta* for faucets. Delta Financial Corporation uses *Delta* for financial services. The three companies can all use *Delta* without causing consumer confusion, because they are in different markets. However, there can only be one delta.com, because a domain name must be unique. That domain name belongs to Delta Financial Corporation.

If you know that you and another company have the same name or are using the same word as a trademark (legitimately, in different areas of business), consider using a variation of the word as your domain name.

EXAMPLE

Delta Airlines uses delta-air.com as its domain name. Delta Faucet Company uses deltafaucet.com.

If you have not yet registered the domain name corresponding to your company name and your most important trademarks, consider doing so. You also may want to consider registering more than one domain name for your business. (Then, if a dispute arises on one name, you'll have a backup name ready to use.)

You also may want to obtain a federal trademark registration on your domain name. Trademark registration and rights are discussed in "Trademark Law," chapter 2, and in chapter 15.

IMPORTANCE OF DOMAIN NAMES

Before America Online Inc. announced that it would acquire Time Warner Inc., it registered at least twenty-one domain names that might be useful to the new company, including AOLTime.com, AmericaOnlineTimeWarner.com, and AOLTW.com. According to Cheryl Regan, a spokesperson for Network Solutions, Inc., registering domains is important in planning mergers. "It's important to your identity—as much as your printed materials," she said.

Domain Name Transfers

Domain name registrations are transferable. There are several reasons for domain name transfers—to carry out a corporate acquisition or merger, to resolve a domain name dispute, or to get ownership out of the name of an ISP and into the name of the actual user. Some companies have purchased domain names from their original registrants for large sums of money—$7.5 million for Business.com and $3 million each for Loans.com and Wine.com.

For information on the mechanics of the transfer, visit the Web site of the current domain name registrar for the domain name (NSI, for example).

Cybersquatting

In this section, we'll discuss two remedies for cybersquatting: a federal law called the Anticybersquatting Consumer Protection Act and ICANN's Uniform Domain Name Dispute Resolution Policy.

Anticybersquatting Consumer Protection Act

Until late 1999, there was no U.S. law specifically targeting cybersquatting. Instead, trademark owners sued cybersquatters under trademark law or dilution law to get court orders canceling or transferring cybersquatters' domain name registrations.

EXAMPLE

The Archdiocese of St. Louis owned the common law trademark Papal Visit 1999. When Internet Entertainment Group (IEG) used papalvisit.com as the domain name for an adult Web site, the archdiocese sued IEG for trademark dilution and obtained a preliminary injunction against IEG's use of the domain name.

In November 1999, a new U.S. law, the Anticybersquatting Consumer Protection Act (ACPA), became effective. ACPA states that a person who registers, "traffics in," or uses a domain name that is identical to or confusingly similar to a distinctive mark with "bad faith intent" to profit is liable in a civil action to the owner of the mark. (For famous marks, liability exists if the domain name is identical or confusingly similar to or even dilutive of the mark.) "Trafficking in" domain names includes selling, purchasing, loaning, pledging, and licensing domain names.

The law protects common law and state-registered trademarks as well as federally registered trademarks. The law gives courts the power to order cancellation or transfer of the domain name registration and to award actual money damages and profits or statutory damages up to $100,000 to a successful plaintiff.

Bad Faith

In determining whether a domain name registrant has bad faith intent, courts may consider nine factors:

1. Whether the registrant has trademark or other intellectual property rights in the domain name).

2. Whether the domain name is actually the registrant's name.

3. Whether the registrant has used the domain name in connection with a bona fide offering of goods or services.

4. Whether the registrant is making bona fide noncommercial or fair use of the mark in a site accessible under the domain name (trademark fair use is discussed in "Using Third Party Trademarks," chapter 24).

5. Whether the registrant intended to divert consumers away from the mark owner's Web site to the registrant's site.

6. Whether the registrant has offered to sell the domain name to the mark owner without having used it in the bona fide offering of goods or services.

7. Whether the registrant gave misleading false contact information when applying for the domain name or failed to maintain accurate contact information.

8. Whether the registrant has multiple registrations of domain names identical or similar to marks owned by others.

9. The extent to which the mark is distinctive and famous.

These factors are designed to balance the property interests of trademark owners with the interests of others who seek to make legitimate, lawful uses of those trademarks. Courts may consider additional factors as well.

The first four factors, if present, would tend to weigh against a finding of bad faith intent to profit. For example, the first factor recognizes that several companies can lawfully use the same name as a trademark so long as they are in different businesses, making consumer confusion unlikely (as we discussed earlier in the *Delta* example). Factors five through eight would tend to weigh toward a finding of bad faith. The ninth factor suggests that the more famous or distinctive the mark, the more likely is a finding of bad faith.

AN ACPA CASE

In *Bargain Bid v. Ubid*, 2000 US Dist LEXIS 3021 (ED NY 2000), the plaintiff—operator of the bargainbid.com Web auction site for computers—alleged that one of Ubid's affiliates had registered the domain name barginbid.com with the intent to divert customers from the bargainbid.com site to Ubid's site. (The barginbid.com site contained a link to the Ubid site.) Using ACPA, Bargain Bid obtained a preliminary injunction against Ubid and the affiliate, enjoining them from using Bargain Bid or barginbid.

Personal Names

ACPA also protects personal names, imposing liability on one who registers the name of a living person as a domain name, without that person's consent, intending to profit from that person's name by selling the domain name to that person or anyone else. Remedies include injunctions for forfeiture, cancellation, or transfer of the domain name and an award of attorney's fees and costs. The "personal names" provision applies only to domain names that were registered on or after November 29, 1999 (the effective date of ACPA). Actor Brad Pitt used this provision in his suit against the Finnish registrants of bradpitt.net.

In Rem Actions

ACPA allows a trademark owner to bring an action against the domain name itself if the domain name registrant is not subject to personal jurisdiction or has provided false contact information and cannot be found through the exercise of due diligence. These actions are called *in rem* ("against the property") actions. Money damages are not available in an *in rem* action—just an injunction ordering the forfeiture, cancellation, or transfer of the domain name.

ICANN Uniform Domain Name Dispute Resolution Policy

ICANN's Uniform Domain Name Dispute Resolution Policy (UDRP) provides another way for trademark owners to deal with cybersquatters—filing a complaint under the UDRP. The UDRP states that ICANN will transfer or cancel a domain name that has been registered and is being used in bad faith.

No other remedy (such as damages) is available to the trademark owner in an ICANN proceeding.

The UDRP applies to all domain names in the ".com," " .net," and ".org" gTLDs. It is incorporated by reference into every new domain name registration agreement and every domain name renewal agreement. It applies to some geographical TLDs as well.

Procedure

The determination whether a domain name has been registered and is being used in bad faith is made by a neutral arbitrator (or arbitrators) known as an Administrative Panel. ICANN itself does not take part in the determination. ICANN has authorized a number of alternative dispute organizations (called Providers) to provide arbitrators for Administrative Panels. (The list can be found at www.icann.org/udrp/approved-providers.htm.)

A UDRP proceeding begins when a trademark owner files a complaint with one of the approved Providers stating that a domain name registrant's domain name is identical to or confusingly similar to a trademark or service mark in which the complainant has rights; the registrant has no rights or legitimate interest in the domain name; and the domain name has been registered and is being used in bad faith. Each Provider's Web site gives information on how to file a complaint. The domain name registrant (respondent) has twenty days from the date of the commencement of the proceeding to submit its response. Participation by the registrant is mandatory.

The Administrative Panel normally makes its decisions based on statements and documents submitted in accordance with the Policy and Rules for the Policy. No in-person hearing, teleconference, videoconference, or Web conference is held. The Administrative Panel can decide the matter in accordance with any rules and principles of law that it deems appropriate. It is free to choose from whatever legal system or systems it deems appropriate. Decisions can be appealed to courts.

Bad Faith

The UDRP states that the following actions are considered evidence of bad faith registration and use:

- Registering a domain name primarily for the purpose of selling it.

- Registering a domain name primarily for the purpose of preventing the trademark owner from getting it.

- Registering a domain name primarily for the purpose of disrupting a competitor's business.

■ Using a domain name in an intentional attempt to attract users to a Web site, for commercial gain, by creating a likelihood of confusion with the complaining party's mark as to source, sponsorship, or endorsement.

The Policy states three factors that will establish that the domain name registrant has rights to or legitimate interests in the domain name:

■ The registrant has used (or is preparing to use) the domain name in connection with a bona fide offer of goods or services prior to receipt of notice of the dispute.

■ The registrant has been commonly known by the domain name.

■ The registrant is making a legitimate noncommercial or fair use of the domain name, without intent for commercial gain to misleadingly divert consumers or tarnish the complainant's mark.

A number of UDRP proceedings have already been filed. They are listed at www.icann.org/udrp/proceedings-list.htm. You can view the facts, arguments, and decisions of cases decided under the Policy at the Providers' sites. Providers are required to make UDRP decisions available on the Web. The UDRP and Rules for using it are available online at www.icann.org/udrp/udrp.htm.

AN ICANN DISPUTE

The World Wrestling Federation (WWF) owns the trademark and service mark *World Wrestling Federation*. Michael Bosman registered the domain name worldwrestlingfederation.com with the Australia-based domain name registrar Melbourne IT. Three days later, Bosman offered to sell the domain name registration to the WWF for $1000. His letter to the WWF pointed out that this price was "far less than the thousands of dollars in legal fees, wasted time, and energy" that a cybersquatting lawsuit would consume. WWF filed a UDRP complaint against Bosman. Six weeks later, the Provider handling the dispute, WIPO, determined that Bosman had registered the domain name in bad faith. The WIPO decision is available on the WIPO site, www.wipo.org.

Choosing Your Remedy

If you believe that you have been the victim of a cybersquatter, here are some tips for determining whether an ACPA lawsuit or an ICANN UDRP complaint is your best choice for getting the cybersquatter's domain name registration cancelled or transferred to you:

- If you're seeking damages, choose an ACPA lawsuit. Damages are not available in a UDRP complaint procedure.

- If you're in a hurry, choose the UDRP complaint procedure. Litigation under ACPA will take much longer than the ICANN procedure.

- If the domain name owner is not using the domain name and has not yet offered to sell you the domain name, it's unclear whether you can use the UDRP complaint procedure. One arbitrator found bad faith use in those circumstances because the domain name registrant took active steps to conceal its identity and gave false contact information when registering. *Telstra Corp. Ltd. v. Nuclear Marshmallows*, available on the WIPO site. Bad faith registration alone (without use or an offer to sell) is clearly actionable under ACPA.

No Bad Faith

If someone has registered your trademark or company name as a domain name but you can't prove bad faith, you cannot use ACPA or the ICANN UDRP to get the domain name transferred to you or cancelled. You may be able to obtain a transfer or cancellation by suing the domain name owner for trademark infringement or dilution. These topics are discussed in the first section of this chapter and in chapter 15.

CHAPTER 17

PRIVACY POLICIES AND PROCEDURES

By *V. Scott Killingsworth*

I. Introduction

For e-commerce Web sites, having a privacy policy is no longer optional. Federal legislation, FTC enforcement, the European Union Data Protection Directive,[1] economic coercion, and consumer demand have all recently converged to create a new environment in which implementing a privacy policy is a business necessity for most, and legally advisable for all.

In principle, privacy policies are simple: if your Web site collects individually

---

The recipient of a J.D., Yale University, 1975, and a B.A., Yale University, 1972, Mr. Killingsworth is co-chair of the Intellectual Property and Technology Group of the Atlanta and Washington firm Powell, Goldstein, Frazer & Murphy, and advises clients on licensing, strategic alliances, e-commerce, and other technology-related business matters. He can be reached at (404) 572-6600 or at skilling@pgfm.com.

identifying information about visitors or customers, tell them how and why you collect the information, how it is used and to whom it is disclosed, and give them some choice in the matter. But the short history of personal privacy on the Web is already replete with examples of how treacherous the execution of this simple formula can be: Internet icons like Yahoo, DoubleClick, America Online, RealNetworks, and GeoCities, and major corporations like United Airlines, have all stumbled on privacy issues. The hazards are many: first, the emerging legal rules, self-regulation models, and Web-community norms are all moving targets; second, though consistent in thrust, the legal rules differ in important details; and third, there is a noticeable gap between what is legal and what may be necessary to avoid a public-relations disaster. Applying these fragmented, evolving principles to a Web-based business that is itself in constant flux can be like trying to thread a needle while roller skating on a boat in choppy seas.

This paper describes how to design a Web site privacy policy that will be effective both legally and in practice. It addresses specific issues that must be confronted in drafting and implementing a policy, and offers suggestions for avoiding pitfalls. But we begin with context: the business pressures that make a privacy policy necessary and the legal principles that apply.

II. Defining the Problem: "You have zero privacy anyway. Get over it."

Scott McNealy's impulsive remark to a roomful of reporters[2] could hardly be more politically incorrect, but it mirrors the perceptions of many on both sides of the privacy fence. On the one hand, some Web site operators have avidly exploited the Internet's special aptitude for harvesting, sifting, and remarketing information about visitors, often surreptitiously, with little if any respect for the wishes of the individuals involved. On the other, awareness of these zero-privacy practices has led many consumers to develop an abiding distrust of "the Internet,"[3] with consequent misgivings about disclosing personal data or doing business online.

Though concern about computers and privacy is nothing new,[4] the Internet offers unique temptations both for collectors of personal information and for individuals who are asked to reveal it. A department store or mail-order house may be able to deduce customer interests by tracking purchases, but on the Internet merchants can track not only what customers buy but also what else they look at and for how long. If the customer arrived at the merchant's site in the usual way, via a hyperlink from a referring site, the merchant's server logs will record the identity of the referring site, providing a source of additional clues about the customer's interests or browsing patterns. Instead of relying on hit-or-miss surveys to assess the efficiency of advertising in bringing customers to the store, Web merchants can receive a database-ready audit trail detailing which customers clicked on which ads on their way to the site. With the help of Web-based advertising networks that deliver cookies with their banner advertisements and thereby track browsing at all sites participating in the network, a Web site can learn about its visitors' browsing habits elsewhere on the Internet, their employer types (deduced from top-level domain names), the time of day they browse, and where they live.[5] Combined with personal demographic information gathered in a registration or transaction process—or purchased from third parties—and analyzed with sophisticated data-mining and predictive programs, this information can become a powerful marketing tool.[6] The process is tempting not only because the data is so valuable, but also because obtaining it is so easy. Virtually every "dotcom" start-up's business plan includes a section on the site's ability to construct and exploit demographic and psychographic[7] profiles of visitors, blurring the "fine line between good service and stalking."[8]

For consumers, the temptations to disclose information are many, from the convenience of ordering products online, to the benefits of registered membership in a free community or portal site (such as user-defined content, public or private discussion forums, etc.), to the personalized buying suggestions, and even third-party advertisements, that arrive as a result of making one's self known to a site. And again, it is so easy to disclose the information. The problem is that once the cat is out of the bag, it may be difficult to stop the resulting onslaught of marketing emails, savory and otherwise, and direct mail and telephone solicitations—especially if the Web site has shared the information with third parties.

As the Web has matured into a mainstream business channel, the need to strike a more appropriate balance between business and consumer interests has become plain. The backlash of mistrust provoked by some Web sites' cavalier treatment of personal information threatens to impede the growth of e-commerce, and so enlightened self-interest dictates that the business community focus on building consumer confidence in the Web. Privacy policies have become the centerpiece of this effort.

III. The Importance of Being Earnest

Of course, adopting a privacy policy is not enough; to protect the public and the Web site, the policy must be followed. This lesson was driven home by the Federal Trade Commission's (FTC) 1998 *GeoCities*[9] enforcement action, a watershed event that exemplified both the grounds for consumer privacy concerns, and the government's response to them. One of the ten most visited Web sites, GeoCities was a "virtual community" that hosted members' home pages and provided other services such as free electronic mail (email), clubs, and contests to its 1.8 million members. The membership application requested both mandatory and optional personal information, and included options as to whether the member wanted to receive specified marketing information. The site also promoted a club and contests for children, participation in each of which required the child to submit personal information and to establish a GeoCities home page.

The Web site included statements assuring members that their personal information would be shared with others only in order to provide members the specific advertising they requested, and that optional registration information would not be disclosed without the member's permission. Actually, the members' information had been sold or rented to third parties who used it for other purposes, including targeted advertising.[10] As to children, the FTC found that the Web site created the impression that GeoCities was collecting the contest and registration information, when in fact this was done by third parties hosted on its site.[11]

These blunders gave the FTC the platform it needed to make a public example,[12] and to put into practice its oft-stated views on how Web sites should handle personal privacy issues. The case settled with a consent order[13] that prohibited GeoCities from misleading consumers about its data collection, use or disclosure practices, and from misrepresenting who was collecting personal information. GeoCities agreed to post a privacy policy explaining what information is collected on the site, its intended use, what third parties might receive it, and how the member could access the information and have it erased from GeoCities' computers. In addition, GeoCities was required to obtain express parental consent before collecting personal information from children, and to delete all information previously collected unless the parents agreed otherwise.[14] The FTC's timing was politically astute: a week before the case was made public, the FTC had asked Congress to enact legislation protecting children's privacy online;[15] before the GeoCities order was officially issued, Congress had passed the Children's Online Privacy Protection Act of 1998 (COPPA).[16]

What is most legally interesting about *GeoCities* is that it is based entirely on misrepresentation. The FTC does not (except under COPPA) have authority either to require Web sites to post privacy policies, or to prescribe their content, but under Section 5 of the FTC Act it has broad enforcement power over "deceptive acts or practices."[17] If instead of saying one thing and doing another, GeoCities had made no promises at all, it might have avoided becoming the most notorious bad example in the history of online privacy.

IV. Why Volunteer for Liability?

As *GeoCities* shows, from a strictly legal perspective[18] McNealy's "zero-privacy" remark has much to recommend it as an eight-word privacy policy. As long as one is not catering to children, gathering information from European consumers,[19] or in an industry where information practices are already regulated,[20] the main source of liability exposure in this area is violating one's own policy, and the McNealy doctrine would be impossible to violate. Why should any business volunteer for potential liability by publicly adopting a higher privacy standard? Quite simply, one can't afford not to.

A. The New Confidence Game

Every Web-based business has a stake in consumer confidence. Even brands that already enjoy solid reputations have an interest in avoiding any taint from consumer fear, uncertainty, and doubt concerning the Web as a whole. And despite the spectacular growth of e-commerce, much doubt remains. Credible studies indicate that concern for privacy is the number one factor keeping non-Internet users off the Net,[21] and less than a quarter of all Web users have actually purchased anything online.[22]

The obvious product of this distrust is that people avoid disclosing personal information by opting against online transactions and Web site registration.[23] Less obvious but equally troubling for online marketers is the "garbage in" syndrome: in two recent surveys, over 40 percent of Americans who registered at Web sites admitted to providing false information some of the time, mainly because of privacy concerns; the figure for European registrants was over 58 percent.[24] Meanwhile, the market has responded to user privacy concerns with a variety of products and services designed to provide anonymous surfing and to block meaningful tracking of browsing behavior.[25] The message to marketers is clear: if you want useful and accurate data, earn it by assuring consumers that you will use it appropriately.

Posting a privacy policy can make an enormous difference in consumer confidence: in survey after survey, overwhelming majorities of Net users say that privacy policies are important,[26] or would matter to them in deciding whether to trade information for benefits,[27] or would increase their Internet usage,[28] purchases,[29] or information disclosure.[30] Moreover, as privacy policies become nearly universal,[31] the implicit message of *not* posting a policy may be that one should be assumed a "data bandit" until proven otherwise.[32]

Just as having no privacy policy can be a handicap, claiming the high ground with a conspicuously consumer-friendly policy can confer competitive benefits. People are especially sensitive about the release of their information by the original recipient to unnamed others.[33] Reacting to this sensitivity, many Web sites have adopted a black-box model that consolidates the marketing function for third-party products in the Web site so that consumers' identifying information need not be shared with the third-party advertisers. The outside vendor may specify group demographics for the targeted consumers but will not have access to an individual's information until an order is actually placed, and may not receive it even then.[34] A Web site that goes out of its way to identify itself in plain language as the consumer's privacy ally makes a powerful marketing statement—particularly if the contrast with competitors' indiscretions is explicit. Consider these excerpts from a musical instrument retailer's policy:

> *WHAT YOU DO WITH ZZOUNDS TODAY IS NOBODY ELSE'S BUSINESS. And we promise to keep it that way…Not all businesses respect their customer relationships like we do at zZounds. Many businesses, including other large music instrument retailers, are eager to share the information they have collected about you. Your trust and your privacy is for sale to the highest bidder…This will not happen when you shop at zZounds.*[35]

Indeed, taking this idea one step further, a growing market niche has developed around the business model in which the Web site openly bargains for Web users' demographic and psychographic profiles in return for a promise of limited anonymity, coupled with the privilege of sending targeted advertising to the users. The message of companies such as Juno[36] and MyPoints[37] is: tell us what we need to know to send you ads that will interest you, and we will keep your data confidential. To the extent that the marketing actually reflects the user's interests, advertisements will not be "junk mail" to the user, and they will be far more effective on a per exposure basis for retailers.

Finally, nothing undermines trust like a well-publicized betrayal. It has proven surprisingly easy for marketers, tightly focused on how information can be profitably used and sold, to misjudge (or be oblivious to) consumer reaction to new initiatives. Properly implemented, a privacy policy serves as an internal touchstone for a company's consumer information practices. As the standard for evaluating any change in these practices, the policy can help inoculate against the kind of ill-considered strategies that create public relations meltdowns.[38]

B. Seal Appeal

"Privacy Seal" programs such as those sponsored by TRUSTe[39] or BBBOnLine[40] may also win consumer confidence. Privacy counterparts to the Good Housekeeping and Underwriters' Laboratories seals, these programs bring the credibility of third-party assessment, verification, and dispute resolution to a Web site's information practices. These programs also require adherence to certain minimum standards in areas such as notice of information practices, consumer choice as to secondary uses[41] of the information and its transfer to third parties, consumer access to stored data, information security, and data integrity. Both organizations have special rules for sites targeted at children, consistent with those of COPPA.[42]

Both organizations require completion of self-assessment questionnaires that probe the site's information practices in great detail—a useful exercise for anyone preparing a privacy policy—and both impose strict license agreements and provide for ongoing compliance reviews.[43] BBBOnLine adds a mandatory, structured dispute resolution mechanism.[44] As of January 2000, TRUSTe had one thousand licensees, including all of the major portals, fifteen of the top twenty sites and approximately half of the top one hundred sites;[45] BBBOnLine rolled out its privacy seal in March of 1999, with approximately three hundred applications on file[46] and by January, 2000 had over two hundred sites enrolled.[47]

The potential of these seal programs to win consumer trust was illustrated by a 1999 survey in which Web users were shown twenty-seven certification marks used online, and asked to pick the two marks they were familiar with that most increased their trust of a Web site.[48] The BBBOnLine and TRUSTe marks were ranked second and third (behind only the Verisign symbol), with 36 percent of respondents ranking BBBOnLine[49] in their top two, and 31 percent naming the TRUSTe symbol.

For over four years the FTC has consistently encouraged industry self-regulation efforts such as these seal programs, which promise such benefits to the government as avoidance of the First Amendment issues that arise when the government attempts to control the flow of information, and conservation of limited government enforcement resources.[50]

C. Gorilla Marketing

As mentioned above, even the most trusted brands have a stake in public confidence in e-commerce generally, and in privacy protection as one of its components. The "800-lb. gorillas" of the Net are beginning to weigh in pointedly on the side of privacy policies. Recently the Internet's two largest advertisers,[51] IBM[52] and Microsoft,[53] announced that they would no longer advertise on Web sites that did not post privacy policies. A week after the Microsoft announcement, Disney's Go Network, which includes Disney.com, Infoseek, ABCNews.com, and ESPN.com, raised the ante by declaring that they would neither advertise on, nor accept advertising from, sites lacking a comprehensive privacy policy.[54]

Similar pressures are being exerted by trade associations such as the Direct Marketing Association (DMA), which required its 3,600 members to adopt its "Privacy Promise"[55] by July 1, 1999. This policy requires members to inform customers of their right not to have their personal information sold, rented, or exchanged; to honor consumer requests not to be contacted again by the member or not to have their information shared with others; and to consistently use the DMA's contact-suppression lists of consumers who have informed the DMA that they do not wish to receive direct-mail or telephone solicitations (an email suppression list is planned as well). In addition, the DMA has created an automated privacy policy generator[56] that can be used by its members or others to create a simple privacy policy. A number of other industry associations,[57] particularly in the banking and consumer marketing fields, recommend model information practice guidelines to their members.[58]

These "gorillas" are not proselytizing privacy wholly out of concern for individual rights or the credibility of the Internet; they see a bigger gorilla on the horizon. A political consensus on appropriate use of consumer information has arrived, and effective self-regulation (at the level of the individual company and of the Internet community as a whole) is probably the only way to head off federal privacy legislation, with its threat of inflexibility and bureaucratization. These companies know that the alternative to adopting a privacy policy is to have the government adopt one for them. The choice is not between whether to volunteer for liability or to avoid it; the choice is whether to define one's own standard or to accept whatever standard the political process may define. We turn now to the "Fair Information Practices" consensus, its history, and its gradual transformation into law.

V. Fair Information Practices

The consensus approach to personal information privacy is a market-based model that allows consumers to participate in decisions on disclosure and use of their personal information, within a framework of data security and integrity. As articulated by the FTC,[59] the elements of "Fair Information Practices" are notice, choice, access, security, and enforcement.

A. Notice

Consumers are entitled to clear and accessible notice of a Web site's practices of collecting, using, and disclosing personal identifying information, before the information is collected. Notice is the foundation on which the other principles operate, and accordingly the notice should address matters such as who is doing the collecting, what data is being collected and how it is being collected, how the data will be used, to whom it will or may be disclosed, and the consequences of refusing to give the information. The notice should also discuss the Web site's policies on choice, access, and security.

B. Choice

Consumers should be offered choice as to how their information is used beyond the purpose for which it was initially provided (e.g., to gain access to Web site features or to complete a transaction). Choice may be "opt-in" ("click here if you would like to receive valuable information from carefully selected business partners") or "opt-out" ("click here if you prefer *not* to receive junk mail from total strangers"). "Opt in" offers the stronger privacy protection because it establishes a default rule against disclosure and use.

The most important choice points are those concerning secondary uses by the Web site gathering the information (such as inclusion in the company's targeted mailing lists), and disclosure of the information to third parties.

C. Access

Consumers should have reasonable access to stored information about them[60] and an opportunity to correct inaccuracies or to have the data deleted.

D. Security

Web sites should take reasonable steps to protect the security of the data, both internally and vis-à-vis outsiders, and to ensure its integrity (freedom from alteration) and accuracy.[61]

E. Enforcement

These principles must be enforceable to be effective. The appropriate enforcement apparatus and the minimum standard of what enforceability means are at the heart of a spirited debate over whether self-regulation is sufficient[62] or additional federal legislation is needed. Undoubtedly, the FTC has pressed for universal adoption of privacy policies in part to bootstrap itself into *GeoCities*-style enforcement authority under section 5 of the FTC Act. Also, a key issue in the negotiations between the United States and the European Union (EU) over the EU Data Protection Directive[63] has been an EU requirement that enforcement include a right to money damages for those injured by privacy violations.

For young children, there is a codicil to the principles of notice, choice and access: Parents must receive the notice and exercise choice on behalf of young children, and parents should have access to the information on file about their children.

These five principles owe their current acceptance to both their considerable history and their flexibility. First presented in a 1973 study by the Department of Health, Education and Welfare,[64] they soon became the framework for the Privacy Act of 1974.[65] They were adopted as guidelines by the Organization for Economic Cooperation and Development (OECD)[66] in 1980, and with some important refinements, formed the basis of the EU Data Protection Directive. Lately, they have been strongly advocated by the Commerce Department and the FTC (the *GeoCities* order is a road map of Fair Information Practices) and have found their way into a number of laws and legislative proposals.

The flexibility that makes these principles so widely acceptable to consumer advocates, government, and industry alike could be equally well described as "vagueness," and the specter of endowing these principles with the force of law—to be further defined, refined, and expanded in the American way, through detailed regulations and endless litigation—is enough to make any businessperson an apostle of self-regulation. Self-regulation, after all, is simply the ability to decide for oneself what "reasonable" means.

VI. The Legal Landscape

Though America has recognized enforceable privacy rights in personal information for nearly a century,[67] the legal context for Web site privacy policies is, for the most part, new and rapidly evolving. Drafting a privacy policy means navigating a variety of United States statutes and legal principles of relatively narrow scope—a situation that has been described euphemistically as a "sectoral"[68] or "layered"[69] approach and realistically as a "patchwork" or "minefield"—as well as anticipating where United States and EU law may be headed. Without attempting a complete analysis, this section highlights the major legal issues that impact formulation of a privacy policy.

A. Privacy Torts

Although the common law of torts is not currently a major concern for the ordinary business practices of commercial Web sites, it cannot be ignored. The most relevant common law concept is invasion of privacy by public disclosure of private facts.[70] However, this cause of action arises only if the information revealed would be highly offensive or humiliating to a reasonable person, is of no legitimate public concern, *and* is disclosed widely enough to be "substantially certain to become . . . public knowledge."[71]

The case of naval officer Timothy McVeigh is a cautionary tale for online businesses in this area (although it is by no means clear that the elements of this tort were actually present in that case).[72] A Navy investigator duped an America Online (AOL) service representative into confirming that McVeigh was the person behind an AOL user profile that listed the user as being gay;[73] the Navy attempted to expel McVeigh from the service on that basis. For AOL, which settled out of court, the incident uncovered a need to redouble its staff education efforts on protection of members' privacy, including "scenario training" aimed at helping customer service representatives deal effectively with attempts to access member information via subterfuge.[74]

Looking ahead, Web site operators should be alert for cases which may lower the threshold of "public disclosure" in light of the ease of wide dissemination of data over the Web; but even if this occurs, the likelihood of tort liability for disclosure of ordinary marketing information seems remote. Sites that deal in especially sensitive information such as health status, mental illness, emotional or family problems, and sexual matters are at greater risk. Someday, someone who has ended up on a mailing list targeted at participants in anonymous discussion forums on masochism, obsessive-compulsive disorder, and Ivy League football is going to get mad enough to sue, and just might win.

For purposes of this article, the most important feature of tort law is that consent is a defense. In the tort context, it may be debatable whether submitting information on a Web site constitutes legally binding consent to the information practices stated in the Web site's privacy policy, but the argument is at least plausible. Web sites that deal with highly sensitive information, including those with anonymous or private discussion forums, typically have a clickwrap user agreement that can be integrated with the privacy policy to ensure valid consent.

B. The FTC Act

As the *GeoCities* discussion suggests, and the FTC seems to have publicly conceded,[75] the FTC's jurisdiction under the FTC Act is effectively limited to ensuring that a Web site's practices mirror its stated policies, if any. Previously, the FTC staff had asserted that even if no promises are made to the user, some information practices might be "inherently unfair" in the context of collection and release of information from children,[76] but this position seems moot in light of COPPA and is unlikely to be asserted as to data collected from adults. There is no private right of action under the FTC Act, so consumers seeking damages for privacy policy violations must find another theory of liability, such as contract.[77]

C. COPPA

Enacted in October 1998, COPPA applies to commercial[78] Web sites and online services that are targeted at children or that have actual knowledge that information is being collected from a child.[79] It codifies the FTC's Fair Information Practices as imposed in the *GeoCities* Consent Order, starting with the requirement of posting a privacy policy describing what information the site collects and how it uses and discloses that information.[80]

The cornerstone of COPPA is prior "verifiable parental consent"[81] to the collection, maintenance, and disclosure of information about children twelve and under. COPPA complements this initial parental "opt-in"[82] with a continuing "opt-out" right to stop further use or collection of information from the child[83] and also gives parents access rights to stored information.[84] Exceptions to the "verifiable parental consent" requirement accommodate the practicalities of getting the consent in the first place (how would you know whose parent to contact or how to contact the parents, unless you ask the child?) and allow isolated email contacts and actions necessary to protect the child's safety, to comply with the law, or to deal with Web site security issues.[85]

Covered Web sites are prohibited from extracting extraneous information from children as a prerequisite for entering an online contest or other activity[86] and are required to use "reasonable procedures to protect the confidentiality, security, and integrity of personal information collected from children."[87] Finally, the law provides for a "safe harbor" whereby a Web site will be deemed in compliance with COPPA if it complies with an industry self-regulatory program approved by the FTC.[88]

Enforcement of COPPA depends entirely on its implementing regulations; the only actual offense under the law is violation of the regulations.[89] The regulations,[90] which took effect April 21, 2000, address such issues as defining when a Web site is "targeted at children," what is considered "personal information," and how to notify parents and obtain verifiable parental consent. As to the latter, the regulations impose, on a transitional basis, a two-tier scheme for consent depending on the activities involved and the use the Web site intends to make of the information gathered. Until April 21, 2002, initial parental consent for internal uses of information by the Web site can be obtained via email, with follow-up confirmation via either email, postal mail, or telephone; but for disclosures to third parties and online activities such as personal home pages, message boards and chat rooms which inherently disclose information,[91] prior consent must be obtained by more reliable (and burdensome) means such as postal mail, use of a credit card, digital signature technology, a toll-free telephone bank with trained operators, or email containing a password issued by the site. After April 21, 2002, all consents must be obtained by the more rigorous means just listed.[92]

Equally important in the present context, the regulations impose specific requirements for the content and placement of the Web site's privacy policy.[93] The content requirements essentially mirror the structure of COPPA itself, requiring the Web site to disclose what information it collects and what it does with the information, and to advise visitors of their rights under COPPA.[94] The placement requirements are designed to ensure that the notice will be prominently displayed where it is most needed: on the site's home page and adjacent to each request for personal information.[95]

For most Web sites, the response to COPPA should be to avoid knowingly collecting information from young children, either by omitting age questions altogether or by providing data fields for age where 0-12 are invalid entries. These measures could be accompanied by a notice that the Web site does not wish to collect information from children twelve and under. For Web sites that actively cater to children, the law has ramifications not only for the privacy policy itself but also for site and database design. Like any privacy policy, COPPA sets a behavioral standard that the site operator must design its back-office systems to implement.

D. The Electronic Communications Privacy Act (ECPA)

Enacted in 1986 and hence not explicitly addressed to the Web as it exists today, the ECPA provides both criminal penalties and civil remedies, including punitive damages, for unauthorized interception or disclosure of electronic communications and unauthorized access to stored communications.[96] Parsing through the definitions reveals that the ECPA's reach may be greater than first appears. "Interception" means acquisition of the "contents" of a communication,[97] and "contents" is expansively defined to include "*any* information concerning the substance, purport, or meaning of that communication."[98] "Electronic communication" includes "any transfer of signs, signals, writing, images, sounds, data, *or intelligence of any nature*,"[99] a definition broad enough to encompass a browser request for a particular Web page, the transmission of a cookie, and other browser-server interactions.

The ECPA has obvious application to the monitoring or disclosure of emails, or of discussions in private forums or chat rooms, by a site that provides those services. Presumably the statute's exceptions permitting interception and disclosure by "parties to the communication"[100] exempt the collection, analysis, and disclosure of clickstream data by Web sites; however, in some contexts an argument could be made to the contrary.[101]

Exceptions also exist for interception and disclosure of electronic communications by third parties with the consent of a party to the communication.[102] As with tort law, it may be unclear whether simply posting a privacy policy that warns of monitoring or disclosure will lead to a conclusive presumption of consent.[103] Therefore, Web site operators contemplating monitoring or disclosure that might be questionable under ECPA should consider an auditable clickwrap consent.

E. Fair Credit Reporting Act (FCRA)

The FCRA[104] may apply to a Web site if it regularly collects and furnishes to others certain types of information[105] that may be used for purposes such as credit or insurance underwriting, employment decisions, or deciding whether to enter into a transaction with the person in question. These "consumer reports" may be used only for limited purposes, which do not include the marketing of any products other than insurance and credit. Even for the two industries in which consumer reports may be used for marketing, consumers must have an opportunity to opt out of receiving unsolicited insurance and credit offers.[106] An exception to FCRA that allows the use and reporting of one's direct "transactions and experience" with the consumer[107] would permit the sharing of most transaction information gathered by most Web sites from their customers. However, where a Web site merges its own data with data obtained from other sources and discloses the results, the exception would not apply.

Especially relevant to Web site privacy policies are several provisions requiring express consumer consent to particular disclosures (e.g., disclosures in connection with employment decisions or medical information). Similarly, an exemption for disclosures of consumer reports to company affiliates applies only if the consumer was clearly and conspicuously informed of the possibility of such disclosures and had an advance opportunity to opt out.[108]

Because the requirements of FCRA are complex, interpretive problems abound, particularly as to the distinction between a regulated "consumer report" and an unregulated "marketing profile."[109] Accordingly, any Web site that reports consumer information obtained from third parties should evaluate its information practices to determine whether the statute applies. If it does, it will have a significant impact on the Web site's information practices and privacy policy.

F. The European Union's Data Protection Directive

The EU Data Protection Directive sets minimum standards for personal information processing within the EU, and prohibits the transfer of this data to non-EU countries that do not provide "adequate" privacy protection.[110] Because most European nations have had comprehensive privacy statutes for some time, the United States, with its *ad hoc* or "sectoral" approach, has not been recognized as providing adequate protection.

In 1998, negotiations began between the EU and the U.S. Department of Commerce to remedy the discrepancy between existing U.S. standards for privacy protection and what is considered "adequate" privacy protection in the EU. In March 2000, the Department of Commerce and the European Commission reached an agreement on a set of "Safe Harbor" principles for U.S. companies.

If the "Safe Harbor" principles are adopted by the EU countries, EU data protection officials will treat U.S. companies that comply with the principles as if they are in compliance with the EU Directive. U.S. companies will be able to qualify for the "Safe Harbor" by joining a self-regulatory privacy program that adheres to the "Safe Harbor" principles or by developing their own privacy policies that conform with the principles. To obtain the benefit of the "Safe Harbor," a U.S. company will have to certify to the Department of Commerce or its designee that it adheres to the "Safe Harbor" principles. The company then must apply the principles to any information transferred from the EU after the certification date.

The Safe Harbor standards are similar to the FTC Fair Information Practices, but include important elaborations on those principles. First, the EU considers data concerning union membership, religious and political affiliation, medical condition, sexuality, and racial or ethnic origin to be especially sensitive, and therefore requires an express "opt-in" before this information can be disclosed to third parties or used for any purpose other than that for which it was originally collected. For all other personal information, there must be an "opt-out" opportunity to prohibit its use in marketing, either by the original recipient or by others to whom the data is transferred. When data is to be disclosed to third parties[111] pursuant to a privacy policy notice (as opposed to transfers with the explicit consent of the consumer), the transferor must ensure that the recipient also follows the Safe Harbor rules.

Other key provisions of the "Safe Harbor" principles address access to personal information and enforcement. The principles state that individuals must have access to personal information about them except where the burden or expense of providing access would be disproportionate to the risks to the individual's privacy, or where the rights of other persons would be violated. Enforcement mechanisms must include rigorous sanctions against companies that certify adherence to the principles but fail to comply with the principles.

The "Safe Harbor" principles and answers to "frequently asked questions" on the principles are available online at www.ita.doc.giv/td/ecom.

G. Financial Services Regulations

1. Internet-Specific Regulations. Reflecting the explosive growth of online banking, the Office of Thrift Supervision,[112] the Office of the Comptroller of the Currency,[113] and the FDIC[114] have all recently issued guidance to institutions under their supervision urging them to post privacy policies on transactional Web sites. For virtually all Web-banking accounts, the Electronic Funds Transfer Act[115] and implementing regulations[116] already require financial institutions to inform customers of the institution's policy on disclosing account information to third parties, including affiliates.

2. Gramm-Leach-Bliley Act. The 1999 Gramm-Leach-Bliley Act,[117] also known as the Financial Services Reform Act, represents a dramatic reshaping of U.S. regulation of financial institutions. Its main thrust is to repeal the Glass-Steagall Act[118] and to permit financial institutions to affiliate with securities broker-dealers, merchant banks, and insurance companies, as well as with a potentially wide variety of other businesses in financial or "complementary" fields.

Title V of the Act imposes substantive restrictions on the disclosure of personally identifiable financial information acquired by financial institutions, other than publicly available information.[119] It applies only to financial information, but applies to that information whether gathered online or offline and whether gathered directly from the consumer or from third parties.[120] Generally speaking,[121] this information may not be disclosed to unaffiliated third parties unless the consumer has been given notice of the institution's privacy policy, including conspicuous notice of any potential disclosure to third parties, and gives the consumer an opportunity to "opt out" of the third-party disclosures before they are made.[122] Notably, this restriction closes the door to banks' sales of their "transactions and experience" data to unaffiliated third parties, which was permissible under FCRA.[123] The Act also places restrictions on redisclosure of personal financial information received by third parties from financial institutions. Moreover, institutions are specifically prohibited from disclosing account numbers or access codes to third parties for use in telemarketing, direct mail marketing, or email marketing purposes. Furthermore, Gramm-Leach-Bliley does not preempt state laws that grant greater protections to personal information, so institutions and their attorneys formulating privacy policies are not relieved of the necessity of consulting state banking or general privacy laws.

All institutions (whether or not they disclose personal information) are required to formulate privacy policies and to provide them to each customer when the customer relationship is established and at least annually as long as the relationship continues.[124] Unlike COPPA, Gramm-Leach-Bliley does not require the institution to divulge the uses to which the information will be put, nor does the law grant the consumer any right of access to the information collected or require the privacy policy to discuss access.

The issue of disclosure to corporate affiliates was a major point of contention during the debates on Gramm-Leach-Bliley, as might be expected in connection with a law that would allow your heath insuror to affiliate with your bank and your broker. For the time being, the affiliates have won this battle: the law imposes no new restrictions on disclosure of information among corporate affiliates. However, the law does not expressly authorize such disclosures and it specifically does not override the provisions of FCRA relating to affiliates. The result would seem to be that financial institutions may exchange "transactions and experience" information with affiliates, as permitted by FCRA, but the exchange with affiliates of information sourced in part from third parties may require prior notice and an opt-out opportunity, if the information would otherwise constitute a "consumer report" and the institution is a "consumer reporting agency" under FCRA.[125]

Gramm-Leach-Bliley leaves many questions to be answered by implementing regulations, which because of the wide variety of institutions affected could be promulgated by a handful of different agencies.[126] Among the most provocative questions is that of what businesses will be considered "financial institutions." The law[127] defines this key term to mean institutions engaging in financial activities as described in Section 4(k) of the Bank Holding Company Act of 1956, a section replaced in its entirety by Section 103 of Gramm-Leach-Bliley. The primary function of the new section, which runs some ten single-spaced pages, is to define (and allow federal regulators to further define) the types of activities the new financial holding companies and their affiliates may engage in, and includes such broad terms as "indemnifying against loss," "providing investment advisory services," "providing any device or other instrumentality for transferring money or other financial assets," and "facilitating financial transactions for the account of third parties." That these descriptions, designed to expand the reach of permissible activities for financial institutions, should also serve as a snare for all other businesses engaged in these activities by designating them as "financial institutions," seems more likely a drafting error than an affirmative policy choice on the part of Congress, but only time and implementing regulations will tell whether this will be their effect.

Gramm-Leach-Bliley may be law now, but the privacy battle it spawned has merely changed venue. Before Gramm-Leach-Bliley was signed into law, twenty-three House members introduced H.R. 3320, the Consumer Right to Financial Privacy Act, which is still pending. This bill would rewrite Title V of Gramm-Leach-Bliley to treat affiliates the same as unrelated third parties;[128] to require affirmative opt-in for any disclosure to affiliates or third parties of personal financial information, or for any use of that information other than as necessary to effect, administer, or enforce the transaction for which it was gathered;[129] and to give consumers access to, and a right to dispute, information maintained about them.[130] In addition, the law would broaden (if possible) Gramm-Leach-Bliley's definition of "financial institution" to expressly include those engaging in activities that are "incidental or complementary to financial activities."[131]

H. Healthcare Laws

Medical records have long been recognized as deserving of special confidentiality, a recognition reflected in a longstanding proliferation of special-purpose confidentiality laws at both the state[132] and federal[133] levels. As medical records have moved wholesale into electronic form and their transmission over data networks has become routine, concern over medical privacy has grown in parallel and has begotten more legislative activity. According to one source, over three hundred bills relating to medical records confidentiality were introduced in state legislatures in 1999 alone.[134] In the federal arena, several comprehensive healthcare information privacy bills are currently pending in Congress,[135] but the most important development is the issuance of proposed privacy regulations[136] by the Department of Health and Human Services under the Health Insurance Portability and Accountability Act of 1996 (HIPPA).[137] HIPPA required issuance of such regulations if comprehensive federal legislation governing privacy of electronic medical records were not passed by August 21, 1999, and proposed regulations were published November 3.

The proposed regulations will apply directly to all individually-identifiable health information that is, or has been, maintained or transmitted in electronic form by health care providers, health plans, and health care clearinghouses;[138] indirectly they will apply to a much broader population, because when the directly-regulated entities disclose healthcare information to business partners such as subcontractors, practice management companies, auditors, accreditation agencies and the like, they are required to obtain confidentiality agreements from these recipients.[139]

The regulations restrict disclosure of health information other than for purposes directly related to treatment, payment for treatment, and internal operations of the regulated entity,[140] unless the patient affirmatively opts in to additional disclosures via a consent meeting seven specified criteria.[141] In addition, the regulations grant patients strong rights of access to their data,[142] including copying rights, along with the right to require correction of inaccurate or incomplete data.[143]

Unique to these regulations is a provision requiring the regulated entities to give an accounting to the patient of when, why, and to whom the patient's information has been disclosed, other than the core disclosures allowed by the regulations.[144] Finally, the regulations requires health care providers and plans to provide patients with a privacy policy which recapitulates the major elements of the regulations.

The HIPPA regulations do not establish uniformity in the treatment of medical information; as with Gramm-Leach-Bliley, state statutes and regulations are preempted only to the extent that they offer less protection to patients than the regulations. In effect, the regulations establish a lowest common denominator, albeit quite a high one. It remains to be seen whether this failure to establish a uniform regime for the protection of all medical data will give new impetus to the comprehensive bills now languishing in committee; in the meantime, affected entities have two years to adapt their systems and business processes before the HIPPA rules become final. As the increasing migration of healthcare information networks to the Web collides with the security, access and correction rights granted by the HIPPA rules, these rules will profoundly shape the future of health-data Web sites.

I. Other Sectoral Laws

Other sector-specific federal laws apply to information which could conceivably be gathered on a Web site but which today ordinarily is not, such as cable television subscriber records[145] and video rental data.[146]

J. The Online Privacy Protection Act of 1999

This bill[147] is not yet law, and the FTC is on record that it may not be needed.[148] But it is typical of the bills regulating privacy practices—the sticks to self-regulation's carrot—that are regularly introduced and reflect, to varying degrees, the FTC's Fair Information Practices.[149] This proposal would require commercial Web sites to post privacy policies and to implement the principles of choice, access, and security—essentially COPPA without the special protections for children. Like COPPA, the bill delegates regulatory authority to the FTC and, for industries exempt from FTC jurisdiction, assigns enforcement responsibility to the appropriate federal regulatory agencies (e.g., the Comptroller of the Currency for national banks). This bill and others like it serve as a warning that any site currently avoiding Fair Information Practices merely because none of the existing laws apply to it, may soon face the need to redesign its site, its practices, and its policies.

K. How It All Fits Together

It doesn't. What is most apparent about this loose assortment of laws is the combinatorial complexity resulting from their inconsistent treatment of every major variable. Some laws regulate only particular types of information, and only in the hands of certain classes of business, while others apply to all personally identifying information gathered from particular classes of person. Under some laws the method of collecting the information is critical; under others it is irrelevant. The boundary between opt-out and opt-in mandates shifts depending on the context. Some laws regulate both disclosure and use, others, only disclosure; some grant access rights and others do not; and some laws afford private remedies while others depend on enforcement by one or more of a gaggle of regulators. And the hoppers are full of proposals for change.

Because of the fragmented and overlapping quality of the laws in this field and the likelihood of equally fragmented, incremental change, it is generally impractical for a Web site to tailor its practices to applicable law as to each category of information. As a result, complying with the "highest common denominator"—the strictest rule applying to any information processed by the site—is usually necessary as to all information collected. It is enough to make one wonder whether the European model of comprehensive data-privacy laws may have its advantages after all.

VII. Doing the Thing Right

If adopting a privacy policy is "doing the right thing," it is no less imperative to "do the thing right." Two recurring points stand out in the discussion so far: first, a valid consent solves many problems; second, the key to avoiding liability is to have practice follow policy. With these principles in mind, and with an eye towards likely changes in one's own organization, a Web site can seize control of the risks and define the terms of its covenant with the public. For a very simple Web site, this may not be difficult, but as Web sites increase in complexity and the boundaries between them become less distinct, implementing a bulletproof policy may not be as easy as it looks.

A. Can't We Just Copy a Form?

Plenty of good privacy policies are available on the Web for copying, and TRUSTe, the Direct Marketing Association, and even the Organization for Economic Cooperation and Developmental host sites that will generate a customized draft of a privacy policy based on one's answers to a list of questions.

Why not just pick one of these policies and be done with it? Comparing any two sophisticated policies, or one generated by TRUSTe and one by the DMA, shows why: they're all different. A policy is functional only to the degree that it matches the business model and activities of the site, and deals with any special legal requirements that may apply. The permutations are as limitless as the creativity of Web site developers. And from a customer relations viewpoint, policy, practices, and the tone or personality of the notice may need to be tailored to the site's target audience (remember the zZounds example?[150]). The issues are complex enough that IBM has announced a new privacy policy consulting service, with basic workshops starting at $15,000,[151] and privacy audits (including systems reviews) by Big Five accounting firms can easily run into six figures.[152]

The way to create a policy that meets your site's distinctive needs is to use a process that ensures that all the relevant issues will be systematically addressed. Our recommended process includes four steps: (1) an Audit of current practices; (2) Goal Setting; (3) Policy Formulation, Drafting, and Site Design; and (4) Implementation and Maintenance. At each stage, participation and buy-in by each relevant constituency—marketing and sales, strategic planning, business development, information systems and Web site design, and legal—is critical. Experience suggests that none of these groups can reliably describe what the others are doing at any given time, much less predict what they will want to do or why; and hence any marketer who gives a proxy to the information systems department (or vice-versa) on issues of site design or policy probably deserves what they get. We will summarize the steps in this process and then return for a closer look at some important policy and drafting issues.

1. Audit. You can't formulate or document a policy unless you know exactly what your site does. Step one is to analyze how you collect, use, and disseminate information, both within your organization and with affiliates and other third parties. Every place information is collected and each way of collecting it—registration, contests, special offers, orders, mailing-list subscriptions, notification services and user customizations, as well as passive data-collection methods, such as cookies—needs to be catalogued, and the information collected should be identified.[153]

Once identified, the information must be traced to its destinations, internal and external. The following questions should be answered: How is the data analyzed or combined with data from other sources?[154] To whom is it available within your organization (including affiliates), and how are they authorized to use it? How do they *actually* use it? How do they *plan* to use it? It is helpful to divide the existing and anticipated uses for the data into primary uses (those necessarily incident to the purpose for which the information was collected), and secondary uses (those related to purposes different from those for which the information was collected).

With respect to primary uses, determine whether you outsource any portion of the function (such as order fulfillment or credit card verification). If you do, you must determine whether there are appropriate restrictions on the outsourcing party's use and disclosure of the data. Is data being collected that is *not* used, and if so, why?[155] This is also a good time to evaluate the physical and technical means used to keep the data secure.

If data is shared with third parties for secondary uses, what are those uses, and is there a contractual prohibition against unrelated uses and further disclosure? Are there means for detecting unauthorized use, such as "seeded" names in the data?[156] Do you have the right to remove a user from the third party's list upon request? Are there contracts requiring you to continue to provide any of these parties with data for a specified time, thus limiting your flexibility to implement more conservative data practices?

As Web pages become more elaborate and marketing and content partnerships more common, the boundaries within which a privacy policy applies may become indistinct. Therefore, you should review the site for co-branding or other joint marketing sections, frames of third-party content, and other third-party links where it may not be evident who is collecting the information. Then you should consider clarifying this by means of relabeling, alerts, conspicuous links to the relevant party's privacy policy, or a combination of these in order to clearly define your privacy "jurisdiction."[157] Where third parties are collecting data directly from your site (as opposed to your disclosing it to them), have you imposed contractual privacy rules in order to avoid guilt by association?

You should also search your site to locate all statements about the use of information collected or about privacy rights—especially isolated statements that should be folded into a comprehensive policy or eliminated altogether. One "rogue" statement can undo careful drafting elsewhere.[158] Be alert, as well, for statements that contradict one another. Last June, United Airlines found itself in a public-relations nightmare on this score when users noticed that what the Web site's privacy policy gave, the user agreement took away. Although the privacy policy pledged that United would not authorize any use of profile information except by the consumers themselves, the clickwrap "terms and conditions" statement said that by using the site, users gave their "express and unambiguous agreement"[159] that they had "no expectation of privacy"[160] resulting from the use of United's services. Further, through the clickwrap agreement, users gave their "express and unambiguous approval"[161] for United to use their personal information "for purposes of solicitations, promotions, and marketing programs."[162]

The audit phase concludes with an analysis of whether any special legal requirements apply as a result of any of three considerations: (1) the type of information collected (e.g., health status), (2) from whom it is collected (e.g., children or Europeans), or (3) how it is used or disclosed (e.g., credit reporting).

This analysis lays the groundwork for decisions on how to comply with, or become exempt from, those requirements.

2. Goal Setting. The next step is to consider what you really want to do with the data and with your Web site in the foreseeable future. This step can be skipped if the site meets your needs, but most audits result in ideas for improvement. If the site will be redesigned, new business models adopted or data practices changed, the privacy policy must reflect or anticipate these changes.

The major issue is the role of information collection and disclosure within the overall business plan; the fact that this exercise concerns data does not mean that the goal must be to collect as much data as possible and to maximize its use and disclosure. Do you want to position your site as a "privacy ally," to take a middle-of-the road stance, or to place emphasis on the other benefits your site offers, while maximizing your freedom to use consumer data? Could you win more business with less trouble by focusing on better customer service instead of emphasizing data mining? Are you willing to make strong commitments, or is your goal to minimize any possible liability?

Redesigns must also pass the practicality test: do you have the technical ability and financial strength to implement a data-management system reflecting the new business model? A potential redesign could include adding tags indicating when information was first collected (to track which version of an amended privacy policy applies) and for what purpose the information was collected (to distinguish between primary and secondary uses for that data), or to segregate data on children or EU residents and process it differently. Likewise, if your business has both online and offline data harvesting operations but uses a single company-wide database, you must either apply the Web site privacy policy to all data, even that gathered offline, or tag data according to its origin and design your systems to process it accordingly. The cost of redesigning back office data structures can be startling[163] and may far outweigh the benefits of a redesign that looks good on paper, especially if you are modifying a "legacy system" that was only recently installed. In that case, it may make more sense to scale back target-marketing ambitions and to adopt conservative data practices.

Finally, any redesign may reopen questions raised in the audit phase: would the new practices trigger special legal burdens, or require cooperation or new assurances from third parties to whom you disclose information?

3. Policy Development, Drafting, and Site Design. With the goals defined, the next step is to map out in detail how the Web site will handle data, and to reflect that map in a privacy policy and a site and data structure design. Again, coordination and feedback among technical, marketing, legal and other constituencies as the design progresses are critical to keep policy and practice from diverging.

The threshold question is whether to join one of the "privacy seal" programs, since doing so will both drive the policy development process and circumscribe the available policy options. These programs have many advantages; in particular they instill confidence without a "need to read" the privacy policy itself. But they also impose additional start-up and maintenance costs and demand certain minimum disclosures and practices that may not be required otherwise.[164] These programs have teeth; in addition to expulsion from the program for noncompliance, either BBBOnLine or TRUSTe could sue for breach of the promises in its licensing contract.[165] Worse, a failure to comply with BBBOnLine's dispute resolution mechanism may earn you a referral to the FTC. BBBOnLine may conduct an unscheduled inspection of your Web site, and TRUSTe uses technical means to detect any privacy policy changes you may implement. Be aware that these programs may also ratchet up their membership requirements from time to time.[166]

Most other policy issues involve choosing how the site will implement Fair Information Practices, a subject discussed separately below.

4. Implementation and Maintenance. The final step is implementing the new policy and data practices. At this point, human factors may be even more important than technical measures such as testing the database, setting security parameters, and protecting against hackers. The greatest risk of unauthorized use or disclosure comes from employees, and the greatest risk with employees is not malevolence but ignorance. Employees should be trained on the substance and importance of the new policy and held accountable for misuse or improper disclosure. In some cases separate employee-directed policies may be needed to complement the online policy, especially in organizations where there are many sources of personal data other than the Web site. Where Web site data is shared with affiliates, both the policy (or contractual restrictions) and employee awareness efforts should follow the data. In general, the more consistent data policies are across such an organization, the less likely a catastrophic mistake becomes.

Implementation may require establishing or amending contractual relationships with third parties. If the privacy policy gives assurances about third-party use of personal data, all existing third-party contracts should be reviewed for restrictions consistent with these assurances, and procedures should be in place to ensure imposition of privacy obligations in all new relationships with third-party users, including support contractors and outsourcers. Of course, if the data is valuable, contractual restrictions on use and further disclosure should be routine, though the "privacy" rubric may not be in evidence. Here the interests of the consumer and the collecting Web site are aligned because the former's privacy is the latter's confidential business information. Likewise, agreements for links or for framed or embedded third-party content may need to be modified to make sure that it will be obvious when a user has left your privacy policy's "jurisdiction."

Finally, management policies should require that any change to the Web site structure or data-entry screens, to the privacy policy, to third-party data sharing or partnering arrangements, or to the database structure or access rights, must be checked against the privacy policy considerations mentioned above (including legal review) and authorized by responsible executive management. If applicable, procedures should be established for notifying the privacy seal program of the change.

We turn now to a discussion of policy choices that must be made, and of some drafting opportunities and pitfalls.

VIII. Selected Policy and Drafting Issues: Implementing Fair Information Practices

The easy generalities of fair information practices must ultimately give way to concrete policies.[167] Here are some of the implementation issues to be considered.

A. Notice

A privacy policy should be conspicuous; if your policy is user-friendly, you want users to know it, and if your policy is aggressive, you don't want anyone to be able to claim they didn't see it. Ideally, the home page, every data-entry screen, and every invitation for the user to email information should include a prominent link to the policy. As to alerts or other signals that different policies will apply to linked sites and co-branded areas, a balance must be struck between the likelihood of user confusion in each case and design and clutter considerations. It may be useful to delegate this problem to the third parties involved.

In addition to the question of site boundaries vis-à-vis unrelated third parties, the notice should address the boundaries of the privacy policy as it relates to corporate affiliates, other operating divisions, and data gathered through sources other than the Web site.[168]

If you want to simplify your legal obligations by excluding data from sources like children or non-United States residents, or if access to parts of the site or special features is conditioned on disclosure of personal data, the notice should so state. If you match data submitted on the site with data from other sources to build a more complete profile, it may be appropriate to disclose this. Certainly, if the merged data is made available to third parties, this should be disclosed. If you intend to purchase supplemental data on consumers, bear in mind that doing so may require disclosing personal information (e.g., a list of names, social security numbers, or other unique identifiers) to the supplemental data vendor, and this will have to be disclosed in your privacy policy.

B. Choice

A major policy consideration is the extent to which user choice will be an all-or-nothing decision. For example, in order to register for special features on your site, *must* the user agree to secondary uses of the data submitted, or will you allow a user to register and veto secondary uses?[169] It may make sense to vary your rule depending on whether the primary use mainly benefits the Web site or the user; it would be foolish to condition a product sale upon consent to secondary use and third-party disclosure because some sales will be lost as a result, but conditioning contest entries upon such consent is a different story. The rule could also be varied among different secondary uses. For example, allowing use of demographic data for targeted banner ads may be required as a condition of registration, but the user could be permitted to opt out of disclosure to third parties.

Another issue is opt-out versus opt-in choice. The former will yield the most data since data flow continues until the user takes steps to stop it; the latter is best if you want to be perceived as a privacy ally. Opt-in decisions need to be easily reversible.

"Consent" is another word for choice. Where applicable law requires user consent, you must decide whether to rely on the theory that an opt-out scheme affords "implied consent," or whether to require opt-in with an audit trail to be on the safe side. COPPA and the EU Data Protection Directive foreclose this issue in some cases by requiring opt-in consent.

C. Access

A key question is exactly what data the user will have access to, the main distinctions being among data collected on the Web site, data collected or purchased elsewhere, and preference or profile data derived through analysis of the first two. The EU Data Protection Directive contains an exclusion for access to processed data where the processor's trade secrets would be exposed.[170] Companies with extensive operations outside of the Web site are well advised to make it clear that the policy's access provisions apply only to data collected on the Web site, unless subject to contrary legal requirements. By making this clear, a company avoids the burdensome obligation to seek out and make available all data in the company's possession concerning a particular consumer.[171]

With respect to passively collected data such as cookie or log file data, the question is whether to grant access at all, since this data may not be comprehensible without further processing.

D. Security

Policy questions as to security include how extensive your technical and human-factor security measures will be, and how much detail about those measures should be revealed to the public. An overly detailed description can both compromise the effectiveness of the security measures and unduly commit the Web site to these particular procedures.

E. Enforcement

What enforcement mechanisms will you allow or require users to pursue? The privacy seal programs impose their own requirements in this regard but do not limit other remedies for consumers. Limiting users' options for enforcement may be both prudent and achievable, as we will see in the next section.

IX. Contract Concepts

A. Is Your Privacy Policy a Contract? Are You Sure?

Considering enforcement leads to the question: what is the legal effect of a privacy policy? As between the Web site and the user, a privacy policy bears all of the earmarks of a contract, but perhaps one enforceable only at the option of the user. It is no stretch to regard the policy as an *offer* to treat information in specified ways, inviting the user's *acceptance*, evidenced by using the site or submitting the information. The Web site's promise and the user's use of the site and submission of personal data[172] are each sufficient consideration to support a contractual obligation. Under this analysis, users would have the right to sue and seek all available remedies for breach of the privacy policy, without the need for private rights of action under such regulatory statutes as the FTC Act.

But for the Web site, this contract may be a net full of holes, one that the Web site may get caught in but the user may easily slip through. Many popular Web sites use contractual concepts by making statements such as, "By using this site you agree to our privacy policy," or even riskier, "We may change our policy at any time, so check back here frequently; your continued use following the posting of a policy change constitutes consent to the new policy." These statements are sometimes contained in a privacy policy accessible only through a tiny link at the bottom of the home page that can be found only by actively scrolling down the page. Any Web site that relies on the binding effect of such a "contract," for example, by expanding its third-party disclosure of preexisting customer data,[173] is treading on dangerous ground. In such a case there is no independent evidence that the user assented to this "contract." In contrast, if the *user* wishes to enforce the contract, she has only to affirm that, in fact, she did read and accept the Web site's offer to protect her information and relied on its assurances when she entrusted the site with her personal information.

Of course, in order to claim the benefits of this contract, the user would have to acknowledge having accepted it, and this gives the Web site an opportunity to turn contractual obligation to its advantage by including protective provisions. But relying on acknowledgment by the consumer as a condition precedent to a contract claim does not solve the amendment problem mentioned above (where the contract assented to was the original one), nor does it afford protection against tort liability or generate a legally reliable consent when one is required by law.

B. Making It Legal

The more unavoidable the privacy notice, the less opportunity for a disgruntled user to claim that he did not see, read, or understand the privacy policy. At a minimum, links to the privacy notice should be conspicuously placed next to data-collection "submit" buttons.[174] But why not go a step further and ensure that a bilateral contract is in force? If a privacy policy is essentially a contract enforceable at the option of the user, there is no downside to making the contract mutual. The express assent manifested by a clickwrap agreement[175] offers valuable opportunities for moderating risk.

Clickwrap contracts are regularly formed on Web sites. When a purchase is made, the user is typically asked to agree to terms and conditions, and sites that allow user postings such as discussion forums and chat rooms usually require member agreements as a condition of registration. By incorporating the privacy policy into a clickwrap user agreement, or turning it into one, the Web site can potentially limit remedies and damages, exclude consequential damages, provide for notice of and a right to cure any breach, require mandatory dispute-resolution mechanisms such as a negotiation-mediation-arbitration sequence, specify governing law and forum, shorten the statute of limitations, extract representations from the user (e.g., as to nationality or age), provide for contingencies through a force majeure clause, and create clear evidence of binding consents or waivers.

Given the minimal money damages likely to result from any given privacy breach and the probability that most consumer complaints can be resolved with a sincere apology and a promise to do better (or to delete the information), it is fair to ask whether a contractual privacy policy is overkill. The two-word answer is: class actions. In the context of the Web, with its computerized user databases and instantaneous communication across a global network, a privacy-policy violation is more likely to involve 10,000 individuals than only one. Wherever individual damages are small, plaintiffs numerous, and fact patterns similar, class action attorneys will soon follow.[176] And they are not interested in apologies or data deletions unless they can be translated into fee dollars.

In *Hill v. Gateway 2000, Inc.,*[177] the Hills brought a warranty and RICO claim against Gateway and managed to get it certified as a class action. The

Gateway product had come with a shrink-wrap contract containing a mandatory arbitration clause, which the trial court refused to enforce. The Seventh Circuit reversed, enforced the arbitration clause, and nullified the class action certification. Since most arbitration rules do not accommodate class actions, an alternative dispute resolution clause such as that used by Gateway may effectively neutralize the class action threat.[178]

Another advantage of a bilateral contract is that it can provide a meaningful mechanism for amendment, should it ever be necessary to change the privacy policy in ways that might be considered adverse to the user. The example given previously, where the site warns of unilateral amendments and advises the user to check in periodically, might be viewed as less overreaching if a user can be shown to have expressly agreed to it. Also, it seems very likely that amendments would be enforceable if accompanied by a prior email to the user with an opportunity to opt out or delete his/her data rather than accept the change. Privacy expectations seem to be a one-way ratchet—the more users learn about corporate data practices, the more privacy they demand, and the more the legislative process grants privacy rights—but there are still many cases in which a user-unfriendly amendment might be desirable. Examples include situations where a privacy-oriented business model did not work, or where the Web site is acquired by another business with a different privacy policy.

C. Drafting Techniques

Whether or not a clickwrap agreement is adopted, contract drafting concepts such as coverage, clarity, caution and conciseness should be brought to bear on the privacy policy. The challenge is to be clear and concise, and to use plain language, without making overly broad or absolute promises. There is a difference between promising "your data is secure" and saying, "we use industry-standard security measures to protect your data." From the Web site's point of view, the former cries out for a protective list of exceptions—the many ways security can be compromised—but the latter speaks for itself. Should you say, "Your data will never be released without your consent," or "We will never authorize release of your data without your consent?" Perhaps it depends on how much you trust your systems, your security, and your employees. Confining promises to objective facts within the promisor's control is the heart of the drafting art.

A second important consideration involves identifying the necessary exceptions to the privacy promise. In the preceding example, exceptions would be needed for release under subpoena, search warrant, court order, civil investigative demand, or other compulsory process such as civil discovery. A cautious drafter might also except disclosures necessary to protect the Web site's rights or to prevent harm to other individuals; to identify persons who may be violating the law, the user agreement, or the rights of third parties;[179] and to cooperate with investigations of purported unlawful activities. In some cases routine disclosures to regulatory agencies, such as bank examiners, may also be necessary. Some Web site owners believe that they cover all of these situations with the statement that they will never *willfully* disclose personal information without consent.

As this article illustrates, privacy policies divide naturally into two components: fairly simple principles and detailed implementation of those principles. The former tend to be reassuring, the latter stupefying. Many of the better privacy policies take advantage of this division by beginning with the reassuring general principles and referring the reader to a list of "Frequently Asked Questions," or just an expanded discussion, for all of the details, qualifications, examples, explanations and exceptions.

D. Example: Boundary Conditions

The drafting principles of coverage and of caution can eliminate many legal problems with privacy policies because both principles address the issue of consistency between the written policy and the activities that it describes. We close with an illustration: the issue of boundaries, of where the policy applies and where it does not—an area where many privacy policies have foundered and where many more are ticking time bombs.

Coverage means identifying every place where a user might mistakenly assume that your privacy policy applies and preempting that false assumption. Using the results of the audit and policy formulation phases, the drafter would make clear who is collecting the data in co-branded or partner areas and whose privacy policy applies, warn users about outward links and framed third-party sites, and identify to what extent, if any, the site has imposed privacy requirements on these third-party sites. The data-gathering activities of banner ad cookies would also be mentioned and excepted.

A site that hosts third-party home pages under a common domain name should certainly mention that those pages are not covered by the host privacy policy, although this is seldom done. Some corporations maintain multiple sites under similar brands or domain names, or linked to one another as a network, but with different privacy policies. Since users would tend to assume that a company's sites would all share the same policy, the drafter would need either to consolidate the policies or to identify the different sites and warn the users that privacy policies may vary. Outsourcers such as employee-leasing companies or Web-hosting firms should be mentioned, along with their coverage by the policy or by narrower confidentiality agreements. And if a company wants to allow affiliated entities to use its customer data, it may wish to define the boundaries of its organization to include present and future affiliates[180] at the cost of having the policy apply to those as well.

If the privacy policy is intended to apply only to information gathered over the Internet, it should specifically exclude data collected through other means, such as data gathered by unrelated brick-and-mortar operations of the company or its affiliates and data purchased or leased from other parties. As mentioned earlier, in some industries (e.g., financial services), for some types of information (e.g., health information), and for some companies (e.g., those subject to the EU Data Protection Directive) common legal obligations will apply regardless of how the information was gathered, and for the sake of administrative simplicity it will be necessary to devise a common policy across the entire organization. Where this is not necessary, it may be unwise—at least if the Web site's privacy policy restricts the use of information meaningfully more than is required by law.

An example of the impact of careful boundary drafting is the RealNetworks incident in November 1999, when it was discovered that the company's RealJukebox software was transmitting to the company information about the users' music collections, unbeknownst to the users (and possibly unbeknownst to RealNetworks' senior management as well). RealNetworks was a TRUSTe licensee and TRUSTe promptly launched an investigation, ultimately determining that RealNetworks had not violated its online privacy policy because the information in question had not been gathered through its Web site. This led to the establishment by TRUSTe of a pilot program for privacy policies relating to software products, the first of which was adopted by RealNetworks.

The principle of caution looks to the future and anticipates change. The boundaries of an organization may shift over time, and yet in an environment where acquisitions and divestitures are announced daily, few privacy policies provide for this possibility.[181] Sharing information with a new parent, its other subsidiaries, a merged entity, or an acquired entity is not only common, but may be essential to the viability of many business combinations and so should be expressly foreshadowed in the privacy policy. Likewise, it may be wise to reserve the right to disclose or duplicate the customer database in order to sell the assets of an operating division.

X. Conclusion

An effective privacy policy expresses a delicate balance of marketing, legal, technical, and customer-relations issues, and successfully implementing a policy for a complex site can be challenging. Following the process suggested here should result in a privacy policy and information practices that are mirror images of one another, enabling the Web site to offer privacy assurances with confidence and to manage confidences with assurance.

CHAPTER 18

E-COMMERCE LAWS

In every state except Louisiana, a statute known as Article Two of the Uniform Commercial Code applies to all contracts for the sale of goods. In this chapter, we highlight some provisions of Article Two that are important for businesses involved in e-commerce. We also discuss "clickwraps," online contract terms that Web site users accept by "clicking" an acceptance button.

Other topics covered in this chapter include the Uniform Computer Information Transactions Act (UCITA), a proposed new law for transactions involving software and online information; sales tax; and, briefly, advertising laws.

The Uniform Commercial Code

After World War II, legal experts proposed that the states adopt a uniform set of legal rules to simplify, clarify, and modernize the laws regarding the sale of goods and other commercial transactions. These rules, known as the Uniform Commercial Code (UCC), are divided into "articles" that cover different types of commercial transactions.

Article Two of the Uniform Commercial Code applies to "transactions in goods." Forty-nine states, the Virgin Islands, and the District of Columbia have adopted it. Louisiana has not adopted it.

In those states that have adopted Article Two, the rules of Article Two displace general contract law (discussed in chapter 4) for all transactions in goods. Goods are defined as "all things (including specially manufactured goods) which are movable."

Ironically, Article Two of the UCC is not entirely uniform from state to state. California's version, for example, differs slightly from New York's version. For some provisions, the legal experts who drafted the rules gave the states a choice of several options. In addition, many state legislatures added their own variations for particular provisions. For sales to consumers, other federal and state consumer protection and warranty laws apply as well—the Magnuson-Moss Warranty Act, for example.

In international transactions, Article Two may be superseded by the United Nations Convention on the International Sale of Goods. This convention applies to a transaction if both parties are located in countries that have joined the convention, unless the parties have agreed that the convention will not apply. The United States joined the convention on January 1, 1988. Many important commercial states—France and Italy, for example—have joined the convention.

Article Two and E-Commerce

For Article Two to apply to a transaction, the transaction must involve "goods." If you are buying or selling goods over the Internet, Article Two applies, whether your transactions are business-to-consumer or business-to-business.

Virtually all courts apply Article Two's provisions to software transactions. Article Two does not apply to the licensing of information—but some courts, in the absence of other applicable laws, may apply it by analogy to licensing transactions. In states that have adopted UCITA (discussed later in this chapter), software and information licensing transactions will be governed by UCITA.

Merchant

Some of Article Two's provisions apply only to "merchants." A merchant is defined in Article Two as "a person who deals in goods of the kind or otherwise by his occupation holds himself out as having knowledge or skill peculiar to the practices or goods involved in the transaction...." If you are operating an e-commerce site, you are probably a merchant for the goods offered on the site.

Important Provisions of Article Two

Article Two governs the substantive rights of the parties to a transaction. Freedom of contract is the guiding principle of Article Two: The parties to a business transaction may, by agreement, modify most of Article Two's rules.

The balance of this chapter covers four provisions of Article Two that are important for those involved in e-commerce: the writing requirement for contracts, contract formation, warranties, and remedies.

The Writing Requirement

According to Article Two, a contract for the sale of goods for $500 or more is not enforceable "unless there is some writing sufficient to indicate that a contract for sale has been made between the parties" and it is signed by the party against whom enforcement is sought.

To satisfy Article Two's writing requirement, you don't need to get formal written contracts from those who agree to buy your products. (However, we recommend that you use written contracts for all your business relationships. See "Written Contracts," chapter 4.) All that is required is that the writing be "sufficient to indicate that a contract for sale has been made." Although courts have not addressed this issue, for online sales the writing requirement is probably met if you have a reproducible record of the terms of the agreement and a record of the user's response stored in the computer's memory. A record of a buyer's emailed response to your offer should also satisfy the requirement, so long as it is clear that the buyer intended to form a contract.

As for the requirement that the writing be "signed," pre-Internet Age case law makes it clear that a pen and ink signature is not required. Article Two states that the term "signed" includes "any symbol executed or adopted by a party with present intention to authenticate a writing." The courts have found names on telegrams and telexes and typewritten names to be signatures. Although courts have not yet addressed this issue, for online ordering, it seems logical that the buyer's filling in of his or her name on the order form should count as a signature. In an email, the buyer's typed name at the end of the email presumably counts as a signature. In fact, by analogy to the telegram and telex cases, the buyer's email symbol on the "from" line may count as a signature. The writing need not be signed by both parties, only by the party "against whom enforcement is sought."

EXAMPLE

West Coast Supply agreed to buy three hundred widgets from Widgets, Inc. for $40 each. When Widgets, Inc. attempted to deliver the widgets to West Coast Supply, West Coast Supply said it had changed its mind about buying the products. West Coast Supply and Widgets, Inc. did not have a written contract. However, Widgets, Inc. had an email from West Coast's purchasing manager that said, "West Coast Supply accepts your offer to sell us three hundred widgets for $40 per widget. Dan Brown, Purchasing Manager." If Widgets, Inc. sues West Coast Supply to enforce the contract, the email should satisfy Article Two's writing requirement. The email is sufficient to indicate that West Coast Supply and Widgets, Inc. had made a contract, and it was "signed" by West Coast Supply (through its purchasing manager), the party against whom Widgets, Inc. seeks to enforce the contract.

Something in writing is considered "insufficient" to indicate that a contract was made if it fails to state the quantity term for the sale. If the quantity is stated incorrectly in the writing, the contract can only be enforced for the quantity stated. Make certain that quantity is stated correctly in all written documentation on your sales transactions.

EXAMPLE

As in the previous example, Widgets, Inc. and West Coast Supply agreed orally that West Coast would buy three hundred widgets. The email from West Coast's purchasing manager says, "West Coast Supply accepts your offer to sell us two hundred widgets for $40 per widget." If West Coast denies that it actually agreed to buy three hundred widgets, Widgets, Inc. can only enforce the contract for two hundred widgets.

Something in writing is considered "sufficient" even if it omits terms that were agreed upon orally by the parties (such as price, delivery date, or payment terms).

If the buyer is a merchant as defined in Article Two (see "Merchant," earlier in this chapter), you may be able to satisfy Article Two's writing requirement by sending a "confirmation" of an oral agreement to the buyer within a reasonable time. If the buyer receives the confirmation, has reason to know the contents of the confirmation, and does not object within ten days of receipt of the confirmation, the confirmation will satisfy the writing requirement.

EXAMPLE

Widgets, Inc.'s salesperson and West Coast Supply's purchasing manager met and agreed orally that West Coast would buy three hundred widgets at $40 per widget from Widgets, Inc. The next day, the Widgets salesperson sent West Coast's purchasing manager an email that said, "I'm writing to confirm our oral agreement, made yesterday, that West Coast will buy three hundred widgets at $40 each." If the purchasing manager does not object to the email within ten days, Widgets' email probably satisfies Article Two's writing requirement.

To avoid disputes about whether or not the buyer is a merchant, whether the confirmation was sent in a reasonable time, and whether the buyer received the confirmation and had reason to know its contents, you should ask the buyer to email you back an acknowledgment that the buyer received the confirmation and agrees that the confirmation correctly summarized the agreement.

Exceptions to the Writing Requirement

There are three exceptions to Article Two's writing requirement that allow an oral agreement to be enforced. They are:

- If the other party admits in court testimony or in a court pleading that the contract was made.

- If payment has been made or accepted or the goods have been received and accepted.

- If the goods are specially manufactured for the buyer and not suitable for sale to others, and the seller has made a substantial beginning on manufacturing the goods before the buyer gives notice that it is repudiating the agreement.

Contract Formation

According to Article Two, unless otherwise indicated, an offer can be accepted "in any manner and by any medium reasonable in the circumstances." If an offer is made by email, it can be accepted by email. If made in another way, whether acceptance can be made by email depends on whether an email response is reasonable under the circumstances. Rather than putting yourself in the position of having to litigate this issue, it's best to ask, when you get an offer in another medium, whether you can accept by email.

According to the traditional common law of contracts, an offer can be accepted only on its exact terms. If the offeree's response to the offer is not a "mirror image" of the offer—for example, if the response includes terms that were not in the offer—the response becomes a counteroffer. A counteroffer terminates the original offer. (The basics of offer and acceptance are discussed in "Offer and Acceptance," chapter 4.) A contract can then be formed only if the original offeror accepts the counteroffer.

Article Two does not use the common law mirror image rule for contract formation. Instead, Article Two states that a "definite and seasonable expression of acceptance...operates as an acceptance even though it states terms additional to or different from those offered or agreed upon, unless acceptance is expressly conditional on assent to the additional or different terms."

EXAMPLE

Publisher offered to sell Eastern Books three hundred copies of Publisher's multimedia encyclopedia at $30 per copy. Eastern's purchasing manager responded by sending Publisher an email that said, "You've got a deal. Payment due in 120 days." Under the common law of contracts, the parties do not have a contract because the purchasing manager's response contains a new term, "payment due in

120 days," that was not part of the offer. However, because Article Two applies, Article Two's contract formation rule displaces the common law mirror image rule. According to Article Two's rule, Publisher and Eastern Books formed a contract. The purchasing manager's reply of "you've got a deal" is a "definite and seasonable expression of acceptance."

According to Article Two, when an acceptance contains terms that were not part of the offer, those additional terms are "proposals for addition to the contract." Between merchants (defined earlier in this chapter in "Merchants"), the additional terms become part of the contract unless one of these situations applies:

- The offer expressly limited acceptance to the terms of the offer.

- The additional terms would materially alter the contract.

- The offeror gives notice of objection to the additional terms.

EXAMPLE

In the previous example, the "payment due in 120 days" term in the purchasing manager's acceptance is a proposal for additional contract terms. Publisher and Eastern Books are both merchants. If Publisher does not object to the 120-day payment term, that term is part of the contract unless the term would "materially alter" the contract.

Whether an additional term materially alters a contract is a complex factual determination. That determination must be made after considering Article Two's "default rule" for that type of provision (if any), along with the custom in the industry and prior dealings between the parties (if any). In the last example, Article Two's default rule for when payment is due states that "unless otherwise agreed tender of payment is a condition to the seller's duty to tender and complete any delivery." Publisher, using that rule, might argue that giving Eastern Books 120 days to pay would materially alter the contract. Eastern Books, however, might have evidence that the custom in the publishing industry is to permit delayed payment by the buyer, or that in a previous contract, Publisher gave Eastern Books 120 days to pay.

Disputes arise frequently over whether additional or different terms contained in an acceptance are part of the contract. This is particularly true when contracts are formed by exchanging forms that contain "fine print" or "boilerplate" terms and conditions. For example, sales contracts are frequently formed based on an exchange of the seller's "quotation" and the buyer's "purchase order." Typically, the quotation contains terms designed to protect the seller's interests (for example, "payment due on receipt"). The purchase order contains different and additional terms designed to protect the buyer's interests ("payment due sixty days after buyer has had an opportunity to inspect and test the goods"). Try to avoid "battle of the forms" disputes because they are generally difficult and expensive to resolve.

If you are the offeror, read the offeree's response to your offer and immediately object to new terms that you do not view as part of your business deal with the offeree. Objections should be made in writing. In the example above, Publisher could have avoided a dispute over whether the 120-day payment term proposed by Eastern Books was part of the contract by objecting to that term. If you have sufficient bargaining power, another way to avoid these disputes is to state in your offers that acceptance is limited to the exact terms of your offer.

If you are an offeree and it is important to you that a contract include terms that were not in the offer, make your acceptance conditional on assent to your additional or different terms. By doing that, you are making a counteroffer. You will not have a contract unless the offeror accepts your counteroffer (see "Offer and Acceptance," Chapter 4).

EXAMPLE

Publisher offered to sell Eastern Books five hundred copies of Publisher's multimedia encyclopedia for $30 per copy. If Eastern Books' purchasing manager responded by saying, "We've got a deal, but only if you agree to pay shipping," that acceptance would be conditional on Publisher's assent to the additional term (it would really be a counteroffer to Publisher). If Publisher accepts the counteroffer, Publisher and Eastern Books have a contract. If Publisher does not accept the counteroffer, the parties do not have an enforceable contract.

Warranties

Article Two provides for four types of warranties in connection with the sale of goods:

- Express warranty.

- Implied warranty of merchantability.

- Implied warranty of fitness for particular purpose.

- Implied warranties of title and noninfringement.

You should be familiar with the ways in which express warranties arise. These and other warranties are discussed later in this chapter. For the three types of implied warranties, you should be aware that you are making these warranties every time you sell your product unless you take appropriate steps to exclude the warranties. If your products are being sold through a distributor, make certain that your distributor is aware of these warranties and how to exclude them.

Many manufacturers and sellers of consumer products exclude all of Article Two's implied warranties. Instead, they warrant only that the product will, for a limited period of time, be free from defects in materials and craftsmanship under normal use and service. In online transactions, warranty limitations are done through "clickwraps," discussed later in this chapter.

State consumer protection laws and the Magnuson-Moss Warranty Act must be considered in drafting warranty language. The Magnuson-Moss Warranty Act is a federal statute that applies to consumer products manufactured after July 4, 1975. Its purpose is to make warranties on consumer products more understandable and enforceable.

Express Warranties

A seller can create express warranties by making statements of fact or promises to the buyer, by a description of the goods, or by display of a sample or model. An express warranty can be created without using formal words such as "warranty" or "guarantee." All that is necessary is that the statements, description, or sample become part of the "basis of the bargain."

EXAMPLE

Software Seller told Client, "My product is 100 percent compatible with the other software you are using in your business." Even though Seller did not use the word "warranty," Seller's words created an express warranty. If Client buys Seller's product and it is not compatible with the accounting program Client is using, Seller will be liable to Client for breach of the express warranty.

To avoid making express warranties that you don't mean to make, you must be careful about what you say—and what your marketing representatives say—in marketing your products. While many written sales contracts include merger clauses (language purporting to exclude from the contract any prior promises made by the seller or seller's representatives that are not in the written contract), some courts have found that such language does not exclude Article Two express warranties. (Merger clauses are discussed in "Typical Contract Provisions," chapter 4.)

An affirmation of the value of the goods or a statement of the seller's opinion or commendation of the goods does not create a warranty.

EXAMPLE

Developer's ads state that Developer's computer game is "the most exciting game currently on the market." That statement does not create an express warranty. It is merely Developer's opinion about the game.

Implied Warranty of Merchantability

When a merchant (defined in "Merchant," earlier in this chapter) sells goods, a warranty that the goods are "merchantable" is implied in the contract unless that warranty is excluded. To be merchantable, goods must "pass without objection in the trade" and be "fit for the ordinary purposes for which such goods are used."

EXAMPLE

Big Company purchased a spreadsheet program that does not add correctly. The program is not merchantable because it is not fit for the ordinary purposes for which spreadsheets are used. Unless the seller excluded the implied warranty of merchantability for the sale, the seller gave Big Co. an implied warranty that the program was merchantable. The seller is liable to Big Co. for breaching the implied warranty of merchantability.

For many types of goods, merchantability has been defined through cases decided over a number of years. Grain, for example, has been held by courts to be merchantable only if it contains less than one-half percent of insect parts. For software and information products, though, the standards of merchantability have not yet been defined. While it is well known that software and software-based products generally contain "bugs" when they are sold, it is unclear how many bugs a product can contain and still be merchantable.

To avoid disputes over whether goods are merchantable, many manufacturers and sellers of goods exclude the warranty of merchantability. Article Two states that this warranty can be excluded only with language that mentions merchantability. If the exclusion is in writing (and it should be, for evidence purposes), the exclusion must be "conspicuous" (in a different typeface, type size, or color from the rest of the contract). This warranty can also be excluded by making it clear in the contract that the goods are sold "as is."

Implied Warranty of Fitness

The "implied warranty of fitness for particular purpose" is made by a seller when two factors are present:

■ The seller has reason to know of a particular purpose for which the buyer requires the goods.

■ The buyer relies on the seller's skill or judgment to select suitable goods.

EXAMPLE

Buyer told Software Vendor, "I'm relying on you to make sure that any software you sell me will run on my Model X laptop." Unless Software Vendor excluded the implied warranty that the software it sold to Buyer would run on Buyer's computer, Vendor made an implied warranty to Buyer that the software would run on Buyer's computer.

The implied warranty of fitness for particular purpose can be excluded through contract language that explicitly excludes this warranty. It can also be excluded by saying that "there are no warranties which extend beyond the description on the face hereof," or by selling products "as is."

Implied Warranties of Title and Noninfringement

Unless excluded, each contract for the sale of goods includes a warranty by the seller that the seller has the right to transfer title in the goods and that the buyer will get good title. The warranty of title can be excluded only by specific language or by circumstances that give the buyer reason to know that the person selling does not claim full title.

Unless otherwise agreed, a merchant (defined in "Merchant," earlier in this chapter) warrants that the goods sold do not infringe third parties' intellectual property rights. If the buyer furnishes specifications to the seller, the seller is not liable for an infringement claim arising out of the seller's compliance with the specifications.

If you breach the implied warranty of noninfringement, you will have to reimburse the buyer for the damages it pays to the intellectual property owner whose rights are infringed. The damages could far outweigh your profit on the sale.

EXAMPLE

Clothing Manufacturer sold some dresses to a clothing store for $3000. The fabric from which the dresses were made infringed a fabric design copyright owned by a third party. The copyright owner sued the clothing store for infringement, and the clothing store had to pay the copyright owner $30,000 in damages (the store's profits from selling the dresses). Because Clothing Manufacturer had sold the dresses to the clothing store with the implied warranty of noninfringement, Clothing Manufacturer had to reimburse the clothing store for the $30,000 in damages and for the costs of the lawsuit. (This example is based on an actual case.)

You can exclude this warranty or modify it, but most manufacturers and vendors do not do that (few are even aware of the existence of this warranty). Rather than exposing yourself to the unlimited liability of Article Two's implied warranty of noninfringement, you should exclude this warranty from your sales contracts, offering instead a limited warranty of noninfringement. (Three levels of noninfringement warranties are discussed in "Key Provisions in the Agreement," chapter 8.)

Remedies

According to Article Two, a buyer can obtain actual damages along with "incidental damages" and "consequential damages" from a seller who breaches a contract. (Breach of contract is discussed in "What Is a Contract?," chapter 4.) Incidental damages are those resulting from the seller's breach of contract, such as expenses incurred in inspecting and transporting rejected goods and obtaining substitute goods. Consequential damages include any loss that could not reasonably be prevented by the buyer that resulted from the buyer's requirements and needs that the seller knew about (or had reason to know about). Consequential damages also include damages for injury to person or property resulting from a breach of warranty.

EXAMPLE

Buyer, a mail-order catalog seller of personal care products, bought from Seller a telephone system for use in Buyer's mail-order business. Seller promised that the system would be installed and operational on January 2. Buyer, relying on that promise, disassembled its old phone system on January 1. The new phone system was not actually operational until February 10. As a result of the delay, Buyer lost $100,000 worth of orders. If Buyer could not reasonably have prevented the loss of the orders (for example, by arranging for an answering service to handle calls), Buyer has consequential damages of $100,000. If Buyer *did* prevent the loss of orders by having an answering service handle calls between January 2 and February 10, consequential damages are the cost of hiring the answering service.

Article Two states that a contract may provide for remedies "in addition to or in substitution for those provided in this Article and may limit or alter the measure of damages recoverable under this Article." Unless the contract remedy is the buyer's exclusive remedy, the buyer can choose from the Article Two remedies or the contractual remedy. Many manufacturers and sellers of products limit the buyer's remedy to repair of the defect in the product, replacement of the product, or refund of the purchase price.

Most product manufacturers and sellers try to exclude consequential damages because such liability exposes a seller to a risk of having to pay damages far in excess of the product's price. Consequential damages may be limited or excluded unless the limitation or exclusion is "unconscionable." The term "unconscionable" is not defined in Article Two, but many courts have used the definition created by one of the federal appellate courts: "Unconscionability has generally been recognized to include an absence of meaningful choice on the part of one of the parties together with contract terms which are unreasonably favorable to the other party." In the case of consumer goods, limitation of consequential damages for personal injury is assumed to be unconscionable.

If a seller excludes consequential damages or otherwise contractually limits remedies and then "circumstances cause the...remedy to fail of its essential purpose" (that is, leave the buyer with no real remedy), all of Article Two's normal remedies are available to the buyer, possibly even consequential damages.

EXAMPLE

Seller, a software supplier, installed a computer software system for the buyer but was unable to make the system operate reliably. The contract included a provision limiting the seller's liability to the contract price and excluding consequential damages. However, the trial court found that the seller's default was so fundamental that its consequential damages limitation was expunged from the contract, and the appellate court upheld that finding. *RRX Industries, Inc. v. Lab-Con*, 772 F2d 543 (9th Cir 1985).

To avoid such a determination, many manufacturers and sellers who limit the customer's remedy to repair or replacement also promise that they will refund the purchase price if the product cannot be repaired or replaced. The refund promise is a backup remedy.

UCITA

The National Conference of Commissioners on Uniform State Laws has drafted a proposed uniform law, the Uniform Computer Information Transactions Act (UCITA), for transactions involving "computer information" (defined as software, multimedia interactive products, data and databases, and online information). So far, only a few states have adopted UCITA. Whether UCITA will be widely adopted is unclear, because some industry segments and consumer groups are opposed to it.

UCITA contains provisions designed to validate electronic contracts. In states that adopt UCITA, it will be clear that electronic records are the equal of written records and that contracts can be formed electronically. According to UCITA, clicking an "I agree" button forms a contract if the party clicking the button has had an opportunity to review the terms.

Like Article Two, UCITA contains implied warranties. As in Article Two, the seller can disclaim these warranties. UCITA permits suppliers to prohibit reverse engineering (discussed in "When You Don't Need a License," chapter 9). It permits suppliers to use self-help measures to remotely disable their software if the contract is cancelled (after reasonable notice to the licensee).

Clickwraps

Clickwraps—online contract terms which site users accept by clicking an acceptance button—are used in online sales and software licensing transactions to define the terms of the transaction, disclaim warranties implied under Article Two of the Uniform Commercial Code, and limit the site owner's liability.

If you sell goods or license software or information on your Web site, you may want to use a clickwrap to define the terms and conditions that apply to sales or licenses. A clickwrap can be used whether delivery of the goods or software takes place online (as it often does with software and games) or offline (by mail or a package delivery company, as it generally does when goods are sold online).

Usually an e-commerce Web site has a separate order screen that deals with terms specific to the customer's order—what the customer is buying or licensing, the price or license fee, the payment terms, and the payment mechanism. General terms of sale that apply to all transactions are included in a clickwrap—delivery and return policies, support policies, product warranties and warranty disclaimers, and limitations on the seller's liability. In a "bricks and mortar" transaction, this information is often printed at the bottom of the customer's invoice or on the back of the invoice, or it's shrink wrapped inside the packaging containing the product or software the customer buys.

Some legal experts have questioned whether a purchaser is bound by terms that the purchaser did not have an opportunity to review prior to completing the transaction. This is often the case with shrink wrapped software (the card containing the warranty disclaimers and other use restrictions is shrink wrapped inside the box containing the product). Several shrink wrap cases are discussed in "Owning a Copy of a Work," chapter 3. Current thinking in the legal community is that clickwrap licenses have a better chance of being held enforceable than do shrink wraps. A well-designed clickwrap gives the licensee an opportunity to read the license and indicate acceptance prior to downloading (or, in the alternative, decline the transaction). In states that have adopted UCITA (discussed earlier in this chapter), clickwraps that meet certain standards form binding contracts.

For your online transactions, take advantage of the fact that the Web makes it possible for you to disclose the terms before the transaction is final. Make certain that your customers have an opportunity to review the terms before completing a transaction and to decline the transaction if they do not agree to the terms. They should be able to print the terms. It is a good idea to do something to draw the user's attention to the terms. Your e-commerce Web site should be set up so that a buyer or licensor is required to take affirmative action to show acceptance of the terms (such as clicking an "Accept" button or typing in words "I accept"). Our book *Internet Legal Forms for Business* contains a sample clickwrap agreement.

FORMING WEB CONTRACTS

You've seen language such as this on e-commerce sites: "*Please read this agreement carefully. To complete your order, you must accept the terms and conditions of this agreement by electronically checking the box marked 'I accept these terms and conditions.'*" Requiring the customer to check the "I accept" box is this site owner's way of getting the customer to take affirmative action to show acceptance of the terms, after having an opportunity to review the terms.

Sales Tax

Most states impose sales taxes on the sale of tangible personal property within the state. Sales tax is paid by the purchaser (you know this part). When "bricks and mortar" sellers sell goods, they must collect sales tax from purchasers and turn the sales tax revenues over to the state in which the store is located.

Sellers do not have to collect tax on Internet, telephone, and mail-order sales to customers in other states. Those sales are sales in interstate commerce. However, they do have to collect tax for Internet, telephone, and mail-order sales to customers in states where they have a physical presence (inventory or offices).

EXAMPLE

Bookco, a California-based business, sells books through the Bookco store located in San Francisco, through an "800" telephone order line, and from its Web site. Bookco must collect and pay sales tax on sales made in the store and on telephone and Web sales of goods shipped to a California address. It does not have to collect or pay sales tax for sales of goods shipped to other states.

Most states also have use tax (tax imposed by a state on the use within the state of goods that were purchased outside the state).

EXAMPLE

Jane, a resident of New York, purchased a book from Bookco's Web site. Bookco shipped the book to Jane in New York. Jane owes use tax to New York.

Are you worried now because you haven't been paying use tax to your state? Don't be. Most states do not try to collect use tax from state residents (except for cars, boats, and airplanes, and you pay the use tax on those items when you register them). However, an out-of-state seller must collect use tax for all states in which it has a physical presence.

EXAMPLE

Online Bookseller has "bricks and mortar" stores in California and Michigan. The distribution center for online sales is located in California. Online Bookseller must collect sales tax for store sales in California and Internet sales of goods shipped to California. It must also pay tax on store sales in Michigan and Internet sales of goods shipped to Michigan.

Technically, the tax on Michigan store sales is Michigan sales tax, and the tax on Internet sales of goods shipped to Michigan is Michigan use tax (which Online Bookseller must collect because it has a physical presence in Michigan). The sales and use tax rates are the same, though, and a single reporting form is used for reporting sales and use tax.

STATE COFFERS HURTING

Twenty-five percent of all state revenue comes from sales taxes, and 25 to 80 percent of local government revenue comes from sales taxes. With consumers shifting from shopping in physical stores to online shopping, state and local governments are worried and are trying to figure out what they can do about the situation.

A federal law passed in 1998, the Internet Tax Freedom Act, prohibits state and local governments from imposing new taxes on Internet access and multiple or discriminatory taxes on electronic commerce for three years beginning October 1, 1998. The act has no effect on state or local taxes "generally imposed and actually enforced" prior to October 1998.

If you are selling tangible personal property, chances are that you are required to collect sales tax in the state where your inventory is located. If you have a physical presence in other states, you are probably required to collect use tax for those states as well. Check with the appropriate state agency or your tax advisor about registering to collect sales tax (generally known as getting a seller's permit). The laws on what items are subject to sales tax vary from state to state. In some states, computer software is subject to sales and use tax whether it is delivered in tangible form (disk or CD-ROM) or online.

If you purchase goods for resale, you do not have to pay tax if you give the seller a resale certificate showing your seller's permit number.

Advertising Laws

The Federal Trade Commission Act states that unfair or deceptive practices in and affecting commerce and unfair methods of competition in and affecting commerce are unlawful. 15 USC § 45. The Federal Trade Commission's guide, "Advertising and Marketing on the Internet: The Rules of the Road," is available on the FTC's Web site, www.ftc.gov. Most states have their own laws regulating unfair and deceptive marketing and sales practices. In addition, there are federal and state laws regulating advertising in certain industries (securities, for example).

Section 43 of the federal Lanham Act states that anyone who, in commercial advertising, misrepresents the nature, characteristics, qualities, or geographic origin of his or another person's goods is liable in a civil action to those injured by the act. 15 USC § 1125(1)(B). Truthful comparative advertising is legal in this country, but some countries prohibit this type of advertising. Contests and sweepstakes are regulated in many states and countries.

For more information on advertising laws, visit the following Web sites: www.adlaw.com, www.webcom.com/~lewrose/home.html, www.lawpublish. com/sept.htm, and www.arentfox.com/quickGuide/businesslines.

CHAPTER 19

THE LAW OF ELECTRONIC COMMERCE IN CANADA

By John D. Gregory
Ministry of the Attorney General (Ontario), Toronto, Ontario, Canada

Canada has not stood aside from the computerization of the world in the past generation, or from the more recent move to global electronic commerce. Nor have we been immune from the legal concerns created by these developments. Our legal system[1] has shared some of the initiatives familiar in the United Nations and in the United States, while in other respects it has gone its own way. This paper will provide a quick overview of the main thinking in the field in recent years.

This paper uses the term "electronic commerce" in a broad sense, to extend

John D. Gregory, General Counsel, Policy Branch, Ministry of the Attorney General (Ontario), Canada. This paper was originally prepared for the Advanced Electronic Commerce Institute in the Georgetown University Law Center Continuing Legal Education program December 8–10, 1999. The views expressed here are not necessarily those of the Ministry of the Attorney General. Copyright 2000 by John D. Gregory.

to the use of electronic communications generally to affect legal relationships. However, much of the discussion here will focus on commercial law in particular.

I. The General Law

The legal concerns raised by e-commerce generally arise from form requirements, or what could be called "medium" requirements, i.e. (apparent) requirements that a particular medium of communication be used for legal effect. The law often presumes the presence of paper. What happens when one takes the paper away?

It is important to appreciate the border between legal requirements and prudent business practice. Many transactions are conducted with paper documents not because the law makes people do it that way but because people are accustomed to do it that way, or because it makes sense to do it that way. The letter X in pencil on a document is capable in law of constituting a signature. Nevertheless most people would not accept a check (what we in Canada call a cheque) signed only with an X. Likewise, oral contracts are often enforceable, but for high value transactions, especially with strangers, most people want to "get it in writing."

Where a medium is chosen for prudence and not for legal reasons, the parties are generally free to choose an electronic medium as well. The concern at this point is to judge the reliability of the electronic documents. Most of us do this with less confidence than with paper documents, since we count on centuries of experience in knowing what should or should not be done with writing on paper. There is a limit to how much the law can help settle questions of trustworthy practice, and a limit to how much the law should try to do so.[2]

That being said, there are numerous legal rules in Canada that appear to require a document on paper. These are generally statutes or regulations, not rules of common law. (The statutes of most Canadian jurisdictions are on line at http://www.acjnet.org/acjeng.html.) Many provinces have a Statute of Frauds that makes some kinds of transaction unenforceable without a memorandum in writing. Ontario's is typical, in some ways. See Revised Statutes of Ontario 1990 chapter S.19. British Columbia repealed its Statute of Frauds in 1958, Manitoba more recently. Parallel provisions sometimes appear in provincial Sale of Goods statutes, which are generally based on the English Sale of Goods Act of 1893. See e.g. the Sale of Goods Act, R.S.O. 1990 c. S.2, s. 5. Consumer protection legislation also tends to require executory contracts to be in writing. See for example the Consumer Protection Act, R.S.O. 1990 c. C.31, s. 19. These provisions can be barriers to appropriate use of electronic documents.

Statutes for more particular purposes also demand writing or signature or original documents, or use other language that suggests similar use of paper, such as "prescribed form" or "certified" or "under hand and seal" or "publicly displayed."

Over time the various jurisdictions (a compendious term to encompass the federal, provincial, and territorial governments) have enacted statutes and made regulations to resolve particular problems, or to permit particular uses of electronic documents. Ontario repealed writing requirements applicable to general sales contracts in 1994 (S.O. 1994 c.27 ss 54 and 55). The same province passed the Electronic Registration Act (Ministry of Consumer and Commercial Relations Statutes) 1991, S.O. 1991 c. 44, under which filings under the Personal Property Security Act (our version of UCC Article 9) have been done electronically for several years. Land registration is beginning to be done electronically in Ontario, using digital signatures, with the authority of legislation passed in 1994. See amendments to the Land Registration Reform Act made in S.O. 1994 c. 27 s 85. In 1998 British Columbia passed a statute to facilitate electronic filing of information with the provincial government (the Business Paper Reduction Act, S.B.C. 1998 c.26) and Saskatchewan did likewise (the Electronic Filing Act, S.S. 1998, c.E-7.21). Many more examples could be given.[3]

Such piecemeal and local initiatives are widely recognized to be inadequate to resolve the concerns among business people, governments, and the general public about the state of the law applicable to electronic communications. On the contrary, solving individual problems with narrowly focused statutes risks creating a patchwork of inconsistent legal rules that will make communications harder rather than easier, even within a single jurisdiction. The rest of this paper will deal with more widely applicable measures to remove statutory barriers to electronic commerce and to promote its use where appropriate.

II. Electronic Transactions

A. UNCITRAL Model Law

The international standard for removing statutory barriers to electronic commerce is the United Nations Commission on International Trade Law (UNCITRAL) Model Law on Electronic Commerce, recommended by the General Assembly for adoption in all member countries of the United Nations in 1996. (The text and the Guide to Enactment are at http://www.uncitral.org/english/texts/electcom/ml-ec.htm.) Canada participated in the preparation of the Model Law and has taken steps to implement it.

Here are the main characteristics of the Model Law. It is "minimalist," which is to say that it does not prescribe in detail how to create legally effective electronic documents; it is technology neutral, which is to say that it does not require the use of any particular technology to meet legal requirements; and it works by way of "functional equivalence," by which electronic documents are legally effective if they satisfy the same policy functions as the paper documents that the law requires. For more discussion of this approach and its application to particular kinds of requirement, see the Guide to Enactment of the Model Law.

In that context, the Model Law bars any discrimination against electronic documents (which it calls "data messages") on the sole ground that they are in electronic form. It cannot of course guarantee the legal effect of data messages, since a number of factors may prevent such an effect for any particular message. It can only ensure that the electronic form alone does not invalidate the message. The Model Law goes on to set out functional equivalents of "writing," "signature," and "original" documents. It also states that evidence shall not be inadmissible only because of its electronic form, under certain circumstances, and that people can retain electronic records to satisfy record retention rules.

Later articles of the Model Law provide for electronic contracts and regulate the attribution of data messages and the time and place of their sending and receipt, as well as the form of acknowledgments of receipt. Final articles validate electronic contracts for the carriage of goods, including otherwise negotiable documents of title such as bills of lading. Such documents must be unique, and provision must be made to prevent the coexistence of paper and electronic versions of the same obligations.

The Model Law has been implemented in a few countries, notably Singapore (http://www.cca.gov.sg/eta/salient_info.html), Australia (http://www. law.gov.au/ecommerce), and Colombia, and has inspired proposed legislation in Ireland (http://www.ecommercegov.ie), India, and Hong Kong. Several others are in the process of implementing it or are contemplating doing so. Useful sources of information on international developments in this field are the Internet Law and Policy Forum, http://www.ilpf.org, the McBride Baker Coles firm Web site, http://www.mbc.com/ecommerce.html, and the Baker & McKenzie firm Web site, http://www.bmck.com/ecommerce/

Canada and the United States have, of course, been active in considering the Model Law. In both cases their uniform law bodies have worked with the UNCITRAL text and put it into national statutory language. The Canadian work is described below, with references to parallel or divergent American provisions. The American uniform statute, the Uniform Electronic Transactions Act (UETA), was adopted by the National Conference of Commissioners on Uniform State Laws (NCCUSL) in July, 1999. See http://www.law.upenn.edu/ bll/ulc/ulc.htm#ueccta for the drafts and the final version, and http://www. webcom.com/legaled/ETAForum for a record of the discussions leading up to its adoption.

B. Uniform Electronic Commerce Act (UECA)

The Uniform Law Conference of Canada adopted the Uniform Electronic Commerce Act as of September 30, 1999, and recommended it for adoption by the member jurisdictions of the Conference—all the provinces and territories of Canada and the federal government. The Uniform Act is at http://www.law.ualberta.ca/alri/ulc/current/euecafa.htm. Since the federal government has declared its intention in the field through Part 2 of the Personal Information Protection and Electronic Documents Act, S.C. 2000 c.5 (formerly Bill C-6), it will not pick up the Uniform Act in its present form. The federal Act is described in the next part of this paper.

The UECA was developed by a working group assembled on the Internet, representing private and public sectors in Canada and a handful of foreign contributors, which reached over 150 participants by the middle of 1999. The group also met in person about four times a year for three years, with up to twenty people present at those meetings. In addition the Act was debated at the annual meetings of the Uniform Law Conference in 1998 and again in 1999.

The Uniform Act can be considered a minimalist response to the quest for certainty about the legal status of electronic communications and electronic records. It is minimalist for several reasons. First, the current law—statutes and common law and private law based on contracts—is capable of resolving a good number of questions on its own. Electronic messages, even on the Internet, do not present radically new questions in every field. Second, the technology underlying electronic records is changing rapidly, so attempts to prescribe specifically how to conduct legally effective communications risk obsolescence even before they come into force. Third, e-commerce is global in scope, and we do not want to take a seriously different approach from our major partners. As noted earlier, the international consensus today is to minimalism. See http://www.pkilaw.com for a list of minimalist statutes from around the world, along with those classified as more interventionist.

Scope

The Canadian Uniform Act applies not only to commercial transactions, but to all rules of law that are not excluded from it. That makes the list of exclusions important. Most of the list is itself a matter of international consensus, in that several of the laws that purport to enact the UN Model Law have similar exclusions. The Model Law contemplated that enacting countries would exclude some laws from its rules but did not specify any itself. Wills and testamentary trusts and dealings in land are common exclusions, as are negotiable instruments. The American UETA does not exclude negotiable instruments as such—section 16 deals in detail with "transferable records"—but many of the main provisions of the Uniform Commercial Code touching such documents are excluded.

In Canada we have also excluded powers of attorney for personal care (sometimes known as advance health care directives) and for the financial affairs of an individual. The concern with these kinds of documents was that they are often created by unsophisticated people, often without legal or technical advice. It was thought that there was too much risk of undetectable fraud or loss of integrity of data unless more specific security measures were provided, more than a uniform and fairly generic statute could give. There is no implication that any document excluded from the Uniform Act should never be created electronically. In Ontario we have a detailed scheme for electronic land transfers and registration, for example, but it rests on a particular set of statutory and regulatory rules to ensure that it works properly. See the Land Registration Reform Act R.S.O. c. L.4, as amended by S.O.1994 c.27 s. 85, and associated regulations. Operational details are at http://www.teranet.on.ca.

The scope section also provides that the Uniform Act yields to any other statute that expressly regulates, permits, or prohibits the use of electronic communication. The conference thought it inappropriate to override legislated standards, even if the standards are out of date or inadequate. The point of the Model Law is to remove barriers, not to reform the law where the barriers have already been addressed. However, the Act provides that using words like "in writing" or "signed" does not constitute a prohibition against using electronic communications, since otherwise this exclusion would undermine the operation of the Act itself.

One purpose of the Uniform Act is to permit the use of electronic documents without individually amending all the statutes that could bar their use in some way. In case a government learns after enacting the Act that some unnoticed statutory provision should not be subject to the general permission, the Act allows the addition of exclusions by regulation.

Consent

The Uniform Act does not require anyone to use or accept electronic documents. The Guide to Enactment of the Model Law says that the Model Law is not intended to compel the use of data messages, but the actual text is silent on the point. Section 6 of the UECA makes that clear. The UETA has a similar provision (section 5), drafted in even stronger terms, if anything. The Australian bill does likewise. The Uniform Act is intended to remove barriers where people want to use this technology. Since most electronic communications, and certainly most commercial transactions, will be on consent, this section does not undermine the Act, it simply confines it to where it should be. Consent to use electronic documents may be inferred from conduct, however; an express agreement is not needed. Otherwise there is too much risk of bad faith refusal.

Functional Equivalents

Many rules of law use language that requires, or appears to require, the use of documents on paper. When the UECA says "a requirement under [Ontario] law," it covers not just statutes and regulations but any other source of law. It also covers permissions to use electronic documents. See section 4. The Model Law and the Uniform Act expand these rules to cover documents in electronic form. They do so by creating "functional equivalents" to the paper documents. In other words, they do not simply define writing as including an electronic record, or define signature as including an electronic signature. This was thought too rigid an approach that risked including too many electronic records or allowing electronics in too many situations.

Rather, the law seeks to isolate the essential policy functions of the requirement and state how those functions can be achieved electronically. The basic form of the rule in the Act is therefore "where the law requires [paper], that requirement may be satisfied by an electronic record if [certain standards are met]." The standards themselves vary but of course are stated in general terms.

The principal effect of this approach is to turn questions of capacity ("Can I do this electronically?") into questions of proof ("Have I met the standard?"). Since meeting the standards is often a matter of agreement, this seems a useful contribution.

Writing

The basic function of writing is memory. The Uniform Act therefore says that a writing requirement can be satisfied by information in electronic form if the information is accessible so as to be usable for subsequent reference. This formulation rests on a fundamental principle of the Uniform Act: the electronic system does not have to be better than the paper system it replaces. Just as a paper document may last a long time or be destroyed quickly, so too the Uniform Act does not say how long the information has to be usable. If however there are other rules about the length of storage, for example in a record retention rule, then the electronic information would have to satisfy that rule, too. That is dealt with expressly in section 13.

In the United States, the UETA deals with the policy function of writing, as discerned in the Model Law, through the use of the term "record." This term was adopted by NCCUSL some years ago as a media-neutral term for some kinds of information. It is defined as "information that is inscribed on a tangible medium or that is stored in an electronic or other medium and is retrievable in perceivable form." The last quality is what ties it to the Model Law. (For a discussion of the principles in the term "record," see Patricia B. Fry, "X Marks the Spot: New Technologies Compel New Concepts for Commercial Law" 26 *Loyola L.A. Law Rev* 607 (1993).)

The Act deals with two other aspects of writing. If information has to be delivered, and not just be in writing, then section 8 requires that the information must be capable of being retained by the addressee. Just as I cannot deliver a paper document to you by simply showing it to you, I cannot deliver an electronic document by putting it on a Web site. It may be possible to have the main part of the information on a Web site if I give direct notice, say by email, that the information is there, if the person can download or print the information. The addressee must be able to decide how long to keep the information, without risk that the person providing it will alter or delete it. The principle of this provision came out of the Canadian Conference; the current language originated with NCCUSL. See section 8 of the UETA.

Sometimes the law requires information to be provided in a particular form. An electronic document can satisfy this requirement if the information is laid out in substantially the same form. It is not the intention here to prevent the use of formatting codes, such as are common in electronic data interchange systems. Information can be transmitted as economically as possible by electronic means. However, the practical display of the information should be recognizable as being the form required by law.

If the law requires a form of display or communication, then the electronic document has to satisfy that, under Article 15. For example, the capacity of a public place may have to be posted conspicuously in that place. The landlord's address may have to be displayed in the entry to a rental building. Information may have to be delivered by registered mail. While information in electronic form can meet these requirements - for example one could deliver a diskette by registered mail—the Act does not allow people to avoid them by using electronic documents. This provision was directly inspired by section 8(b) of NCCUSL's UETA.

Signature

In all its functional equivalence rules, the Uniform Act does not intend to change the substance of the existing law. It intends only to make the law media neutral, equally applicable to paper and to electronic documents. The definition of "electronic signature" therefore does not create a new legal "thing" with this name. Rather it says what the essential functions of any signature are. The essence of a signature is the intention with which it was made. The definition says that the electronic information must be made or adopted "in order to sign a document." The existing law about the appropriate intention, and how one proves it, continues in effect.

The purpose of defining electronic signature is to make clear that the electronic version does not have to "look like" a signature when it is displayed. It may be code or sound or symbol of any kind, if the intention is present. Likewise, a signature may travel apart from the document it signs, if the association with the document is clear. The signature may be in the document but also may not be. Also, the wording of the definition would allow one to contemplate an electronic signature applied to a document on paper, if the connection between them were clear.

Section 10 provides that a signature requirement can be met by an electronic signature. Unlike the Model Law, it does not go on to require that the electronic signature must be as reliable as is appropriate in the circumstances. The Canadian statute follows the UETA in this regard. At common law, and arguably in the Civil Law of Quebec as well, a method of signature on paper does not have to meet any test of reliability. If the association with a person is demonstrated and the intent to sign is demonstrated, the signature will be valid. Those elements will have to be shown in order to meet the definition of electronic signature. As noted earlier, the Uniform Act is not trying to make the law better, just neutral.

However, it is possible that the authority that imposed the signature requirement in the first place did have some degree of reliability in mind. In that case, subsection 10(2) allows that authority to make a regulation imposing the reliability standards of the Model Law.

This discussion hints at another key principle of the Uniform Act: there is a distinction between basic legal requirements and prudent business practices. A name typed on the bottom of an email may be a valid signature, but it may not be trustworthy enough for many people to want to rely on it in practice. What people want in practice will depend on many factors, including the context, the course of dealings of the parties, the use to which the signed document is to be put, and so on.

Originals

When the law requires a document in original form, it is seeking assurance of the integrity of the document, that it has not been altered. The Uniform Act reproduces this function in section 11. The notion of "original" is hard to apply to electronic documents, because of the way they are generated. The rule in section 11 would apply whether the document was first created on paper and later became electronic, say by scanning or faxing to an email system, or whether it was in electronic form at all times. (The requirement for original documents under the "best evidence" rule is covered in the Uniform Electronic Evidence Act, a separate statute adopted in 1998. See http://www.law.ualberta.ca/alri/ulc/acts/eeeact.htm. Evidence questions are discussed in Part III below.)

Copies

Copying electronic documents can be very easy. However, it is harder to understand how to comply electronically with a requirement to furnish a number of copies of a document. First, it is very difficult, as noted above, to distinguish between an original and a copy. Next, there are a number of ways in which one could provide, say, three copies: send the same email three times, attach the same text three times to one email, put three versions of the document onto a single diskette, remit three diskettes with one version of the document on each, and so on. To avoid this rather sterile discussion, section 14 of the Uniform Act provides that only a single version of the electronic document needs to be furnished to a single address, where the law requires copies. The recipient can decide how best to make the additional documents.

Government Documents

The Uniform Act contains a number of special provisions about documents sent to government. The concern is that governments receive a lot of information from a lot of people, many of whom are communicating involuntarily and with many of whom the government has no contract by which the methods of communication could be agreed. To protect the government from an overwhelming variety of formats and hardware, therefore, the provisions on consent require express consent by government, rather than implied consent. Moreover, the rules on providing information, on forms, on signatures, and on originals say that governments may impose their own technical requirements in order to satisfy these sections. Documents originating with government, however, would have to meet the general standards of the Act.

A very similar structure is found in the Australian Electronic Transactions Act, http://www.law.gov.au/ecommerce/. The U.S. uniform statute also has special provisions on government documents (sections 17 and 18). The Canadian federal act, formerly Bill C-6, requires a central register of designations and regulations for the use of electronic documents under federal law. The Uniform Act has no set requirement for communicating government choices, except that consent must be notified to people likely to be affected by it. See section 6.

Government is defined to include core government departments and agencies, but not Crown corporations (corporations owned by the government), which are thought to be more like commercial operations. Each enacting jurisdiction will have to decide on the appropriate scope for this definition. Likewise, municipal governments may need the same kind of protection against multiple formats, but it may be thought that the risk of hundred of inconsistent technical standards from hundreds of municipalities may require a more centralized solution.

Section 17 allows governments to use electronic communications for all their purposes. Section 16 provides for electronic forms, whether or not forms on paper are already prescribed (and whether or not the forms are used to submit information to government or between private parties). Section 18 authorizes incoming and outgoing payments to be electronic, if the main financial authority of the government consents.

Contracts

The Uniform Act follows the Model Law in providing some basic rules about electronic contracts. The volume of electronic commerce conducted under the present law may suggest that businesses are not much impeded by doubt about validity of such contracts. Nevertheless a few points are covered in the interests of greater certainty.

The main question about such contracts appears to be whether sending some kinds of electronic signals can show sufficient intent to be bound by contract. Section 20 says that an action in electronic form, including touching or clicking on an appropriately designed icon or place on a computer screen is sufficient to express any matter that is material to the formation or operation of a contract. A voice-activated response would also be effective.

Section 21 and 22 provide for the use of electronic agents. Electronic agents are defined as computer programs used to initiate an action or to respond to electronic documents without human intervention at the time of response or action. They have nothing to do with the law of agency, since they are machines that have no legal personality. The term is, however, widely accepted and not easily displaced by something clearer in law, such as "electronic device."

Section 21 makes it certain that contracts may be formed using electronic agents, on one side or on both sides.

Section 22 provides a solution for the "single keystroke error," where a human being makes a mistake in communicating with an electronic agent. Often such agents are not programmed to recognize messages intended to correct an error, e.g. "I didn't mean 100 widgets, I meant 10." The section makes these mistakes unenforceable if the procedures set out there are followed, unless the owner of the agent provides a method of preventing or correcting errors. It is not the role of legislation to say exactly what method must be used, as there may be many acceptable ways. Restating an order before processing it, with a note like "This is what you are ordering. Are you sure?" would probably be enough. This provision was borrowed largely intact from the UETA in the USA.

Attribution of Documents

Article 13 of the Model Law provides that data messages may be attributed to those who create them or who authorize their creation. This is of course the general law in Canada and the United States. The UETA (section 9(a)) and the Australian bill have similar provisions. The Canadian Conference thought this went without saying, so did not say it.

The Model Law goes on to provide a rule (the Guide to Enactment calls it a presumption) of attribution where certain agreed security procedures are used on data messages. NCCUSL attempted to devise similar rules, but they fell under severe criticism based partly on the fluidity of the technology available and partly on the likely sophistication of its users. Reports of the Drafting Committee meetings at the ETA Forum site can provide details (http://www.webcom.com/legaled/ETAForum/). In Canada we did not try to follow the Model Law on this point. Some of the current work of UNCITRAL on electronic signatures aimed to give more substance to the provisions of Article 13, but it is not clear that any such result will be achieved.

Sending and Receiving Electronic Documents

The Model Law has influenced the Uniform Act in determining where and when messages are sent and received. The location question is easier. The basic rule, subject to agreement of the parties, is that messages are sent from and received at the place of business of the sender or recipient. Subsidiary rules deal with multiple places of business or no place of business.

The rule helps separate the essence of the communication from the incidental aspects, such as the location of the server, or the location of the sender or recipient when he or she actually deals with the message. Thus someone with a business in Toronto who has an email account or a Web site with sympatico.ca does not have to worry about where sympatico's server is, and does not change the law relating to a transaction by sending or picking up messages while travelling out of the province.

There may be cases where the location of the server or other indicia of location remain important, of course, such as in deciding if one has a permanent establishment for tax purposes. Jurisdictional questions in electronic commerce are tricky. The rules in the Uniform Act will resolve a few but far from all. One may have different considerations in civil disputes, regulatory actions, and criminal prosecutions. The Uniform Law Conference has published a discussion of jurisdiction from a Canadian point of view at http://www.law.ualberta.ca/alri/ulc/currrent/ejurisd.htm.

The rule on the time of sending is relatively simple: the message is deemed sent when it leaves the control of the sender. If the sender and the addressee are on the same system, then the message is sent when it becomes accessible to the addressee.

The somewhat more difficult issue is time of receipt. The Model Law deems a message received when it reaches an information system in the control of the addressee. The American uniform statute requires that the addressee have designated or used the system for the purpose of the kind of message in question, before that rule applies. The UECA picks up the designation or use point, but makes receipt a presumption not a rule, as it is in the Model Law and the UETA. It was widely thought among the working group that the receipt of electronic messages is not reliable enough to support a rule that cannot be rebutted.

In the absence of a rule or presumption, the sender will have to demonstrate actual receipt. If senders need to be sure of receipt before taking further steps, they may have to ask for acknowledgments. It was not thought necessary to exclude the mailbox rule expressly. The Ontario Court of Appeal has recently held that a fax is received only on actual receipt, in other words the mailbox rule that applies to postal mail and telegrams does not apply. It followed the House of Lords in *Brinkibon v. Stahag Stahl*, [1983] 2 A.C. 34, in saying that there is no general receipt rule for electronic communications. *Eastern Power v. Azienda Communale Energia*, (1999), 178 Dominion Law Reports (4th) 409 (Ont.C.A.), http://www.ontariocourts.on.ca/ decisions/1999/September/eastern.htm. (I submit elsewhere that the mailbox rule should not apply to any electronic messages. See "Receiving Electronic Messages," 15 *Banking and Finance L.R.* No. 3 (2000).) The Uniform Act applies to all communications, not only to the acceptance of offers of contract.

Carriage of Goods

One of the last things that UNCITRAL added to the Model Law was a section on special transactions, namely those dealing with the carriage of goods. It was thought that these are very often international transactions, and they are subject to a number of special legal regimes and conventions. In particular they often rest on negotiable documents of title such as bills of lading. The general principles of the Model Law on nondiscrimination based on medium apply here too, but it was thought that particular rules were needed for negotiability and for the possibility that documents would be transferred from one medium to another when the document itself carried legal effect.

The Uniform Act has picked up these provisions. It has not spoken of "unique" documents, however, as it is not clear how to create a unique electronic document (though one can immobilize and time-stamp an electronic document.) Instead, the Uniform Act speaks of a document intended for one person and no other. Representatives of transport organizations have favored enacting these provisions, even though it is not clear yet what technology may be able to satisfy the requirements.

Next Steps

Adoption by the Uniform Law Conference does not, of course, make the Uniform Act law anywhere. It is up to the provincial and territorial legislatures to pass it into legislation, if they think those likely to benefit from the Act want it. A lobbying campaign may be needed, though the conference by its nature is not suited to lead one. The conference is largely made up of civil servants, unlike its U.S. counterpart. In the U.S., enactment of their uniform Act has begun, in ten states, starting in California. (The text of the implementing statutes can be traced most easily through the compendious sites mentioned above in Part II.A.) The momentum there may also influence Canadians who seek a legal regime that gives the same kind of certainty as our neighbors enjoy.

It may be noted that the government of Quebec will not be adopting the Uniform Act. The differences appear to be based on methods of expression of the principles, on which Quebec agrees with its neighbors: media and technology neutrality and flexibility. The responsible minister announced in September 1999 that he would be presenting comprehensive legislation in the near future to implement the UN Model Law in Quebec. The legislation has not been introduced as of mid-May 2000.

C. Federal Legislation on Electronic Documents

The Canadian federal government has passed the Personal Information Protection and Electronic Documents Act, known familiarly (and more economically) as Bill C-6. (The legislation is the same as Bill C-54 in the 1998–99 session of Parliament.) Bill C-6 was given Royal Assent on April 14, 2000, as S.C.2000 c.5. See http://www.parl.gc.ca/36/2/parlbus/chambus/house/bills/government/C-6/C-6_4/C-6_cover-E.html.

Bill C-6 contains provisions on personal privacy, electronic documents, and electronic evidence. Each part will be discussed in this paper in the appropriate place. Here we are concerned with Part 2 on electronic documents.

Part 2 of Bill C-6 applies to provisions of federal statutes and regulations that impose or seem to impose paper requirements. In Canada the federal government regulates interprovincial undertakings, like broadcasting, telecommunication, and railways, and certain prescribed sectors of the economy like banks and some other financial institutions. Most smaller businesses are subject to provincial legislation. Bill C-6 will also apply of course to communications between members of the public—businesses or individuals—and the federal government itself.

The legislation permits federal government departments and agencies to use electronic means to create, collect, receive, store, transfer, distribute, publish, or otherwise deal with documents or information whenever a federal law dos not specify the manner of doing so (section 33). In other words, the general permission here yields to existing or future specific form legislation, just as the Uniform Act does. It also permits federal departments to make electronic payments as the Receiver General specifies (section 34). Where forms are prescribed under federal law, electronic forms may be created or used for the purpose (section 35).

Part 2 sets up an opt-in scheme, by which certain media requirements can be met by electronic documents if the government department responsible for the requirement has designated the requirement to be covered by the statute and if it makes regulations at the time of designation to say how the electronic documents are to be created or dealt with. The designated provisions will appear in Schedules to the Act—statutes in Schedule B, regulations in Schedule C—so the public has a central point of reference to learn what provisions are in or out of the scheme. This format applies, for example, to writing requirements (section 41), signatures (section 43), copies (section 47), and the provision of information (section 40).

Most of these provisions were taken from the 1998 draft of the Uniform Electronic Commerce Act, which had a special section on government documents. The August 1998 version is on the Uniform Law Conference Web site, on the same page as the final Uniform Act. Since that time the Uniform Act changed its approach to government documents, as described above. However, the federal government has gone further than the Uniform Act in one important aspect. Several sections of Part 2 contemplate the use of a "secure electronic signature." For example, section 36 says that one can use a secure electronic signature to create a certificate signed by a minister or public official that is proof of a fact or admissible in evidence. Section 39 allows a secure electronic signature to serve as a seal, if the seal requirement has been designated under the Act. Affidavits may be made electronically if both deponent and commissioner of the oath sign with a secure electronic signature, under section 44 (which also requires designation and regulations as above.) Declarations of truth may be made with such signatures, in similar circumstances, under section 45. Witnesses may sign under similar conditions, according to section 46.

A "secure electronic signature" is not defined in the Bill, except as "an electronic signature that results from the application of a technology or process prescribed by regulations made under subsection 48(1)"(section 31). That subsection sets out the usual provisions for signatures of this type, originally designed by the National Institute of Science and Technology (NIST) in the United States, and since adopted or adapted in California, Illinois, and other states, and by UNCITRAL in its ongoing work on electronic signatures (http://www.uncitral.org/english/sessions/wg_ec/index.htm). Similar language is found in the European Union Directive on Electronic Signatures (http://europa.eu.int/comm/internal_market/en/media/sign/Dir99-93-ecEN.pdf), though there they are called "advanced electronic signatures.") A technology or process may be designated only if it can be proved (to the maker of the regulation, presumably) that

a) the electronic signature resulting from the use by a person of the technology is unique to the person;

b) the use of the technology or process by a person to incorporate, attach, or associate the person's electronic signature to an electronic document is under the sole control of the person;

c) the technology or process can be used to identify the person using the technology or process; and

d) the electronic signature can be linked with an electronic document in such a way that it can be used to determine whether the electronic document has been changed since the electronic signature was incorporated in, attached to, or associated with the electronic document.

The intention is that in the first instance the only technology to be designated is that of digital signatures certified through the Government of Canada Public Key Infrastructure, or that of systems cross-certified with the GOC PKI. More on that PKI can be found at http://www.cio-dpi.gc.ca/pki/Initiatives/initiatives_e.html. Some provincial governments are developing public key infrastructures as well, and they hope to be cross-certified with the federal PKI. This would help extend the reach of Bill C-6, since most provincial systems will probably issue digital signature certificates to a number of people in the private sector who could use them in dealing with the federal government as well (depending on the terms of the provincial implementation.)

In short, the federal approach is a cautious one, but it does remove the major statutory barriers to electronic commerce. It does so by empowering the government to make regulations when and as appropriate. The law contains no encouragement to adopt harmonized standards across government, though federal officials say that market forces and central planning of technology requirements will tend to harmonize the departments' approaches in any event. The Uniform Act does not purport to harmonize the standards applicable to incoming documents among government departments or agencies either. Outgoing electronic documents would be subject to the general rules of functional equivalence.

D. Promoting Electronic Transactions

The focus in Canada so far has been on removing legal barriers to electronic commerce. Few steps have been taken actively to promote it, or to resolve problems in particular sectors of business presented by electronic communications. No one in Canada has seriously proposed law reform along the lines of the Uniform Computer Information Transactions Act that was adopted by NCCUSL in the summer of 1999 (found at http://www.law.upenn.edu/library/ulc/ulc.htm#ucita). This statute, which was originally conceived of as a new article 2B to the Uniform Commercial Code, aims to prescribe the content and legal effect of licence agreements for information transferred by computer, mainly software (the actual scope was frequently altered).

It is not clear why there has been no interest in this. Perhaps software developers are content with the enforceability of their current contracts. Perhaps the main software developers in Canada are American, and they have been concentrating on U.S. law to start and will turn their attention northwards once the U.S. has got it right, from their point of view. Or maybe knowledgeable

Canadians are too aware of the fierce controversy that has surrounded the development of UCITA and want the dust to settle before taking any steps at home. See for example http://www.ucitaonline.com/ for accounts of the debates, position papers and the like.

As noted above with respect to the federal legislation, many provinces are developing a public key infrastructure. So far there is no consensus, or even coherent opinion, on what legislative framework would be needed to support the use of digital signatures (i.e. those created with public key cryptography) or private PKIs, beyond Bill C-6. No one is suggesting a Utah-like licensing regime, or even a more open-market approach like that in Illinois or California.

Consumer protection in electronic commerce has attracted some attention, on the other hand. Recently a business/consumer task force published guidelines on this subject, promoting education of all parties and standards for vendors and consumers engaging in online transactions. The guidelines are available at the Industry Canada e-commerce Web site, http://strategis.gc.ca/SSG/ca01182e.html. They are similar to, but not directly influenced by, the American Bar Association guidelines for "safe shopping" published in October 1999 at http://www.safeshopping.com. They are also intended to be consistent with consumer protection rules about to be promulgated by the Organization for Economic Cooperation and Development (OECD). See http://www.oecd.org/subject/e_commerce/

To date the consumer protection rules are only guidelines. It is expected that some form of relatively light-handed legislation will be developed as well, but nothing is yet public of the workings of a federal-provincial-territorial (FPT) working group on the subject that reports to the FPT Ministers responsible for Consumer Issues. That group has made efforts to ensure that its proposals will be consistent with the Uniform Electronic Commerce Act and designed to supplement rather than to displace it.

III. Electronic Evidence

The substantive rules of law may not hamper electronic commerce, but they will be of limited assistance to businesspeople unless the records of the electronic transactions can be fairly placed before the courts and administrative tribunals when disputes arise. Some work has been done in Canada in recent years on the law of evidence, to ensure the appropriate admission of computer-generated records. (It is extremely rare for legislation in Canada to deal with the *weight* of evidence once it is before the court. That issue is left to the judges.)

In practice, the courts have not been slow to recognize that businesses and governments keep their records on computers. Very few cases have refused to admit evidence on the ground that it was in electronic form. (The only case that comes to mind is *R. v Shepherd*, (1992), 97 Nfld & PEI L.R. 144 (Nfld S.C.).) As a result, litigation lawyers have often taken the view that no law reform is needed to promote the admissibility of electronic evidence. However, lawyers who are called on to advise clients on recordkeeping systems or on business communications issues generally have been more enthusiastic about legislative support on this issue. Some of the questions need more certain answers, in their view.

The Canadian law of evidence is largely based on the common law, except in Quebec. However, it is supplemented extensively by statutes at the federal and provincial (and territorial) levels. The Canada Evidence Act, R.S.C. 1985 c. C-5, applies to proceedings under federal statutes, notably the Criminal Code of Canada (criminal law is a federal responsibility in Canada), and in federally constituted administrative tribunals. Provincial evidence statutes, like the Ontario Evidence Act, R.S.O. 1990 c. E.23, govern civil proceedings in court and matters before provincially constituted administrative tribunals. The Civil Code of Quebec has a part on evidence, which applies to the same matters as the evidence statutes in other provinces. [4]

Electronic evidence, for the purposes of this discussion, refers to evidence of computer-generated records, mainly business records. It is a form of documentary evidence, which of course the courts have been dealing with for a long time. [5] This paper does not discuss computer simulations or computer-based analyses of statistics prepared for the purposes of particular litigation. These are forms of expert evidence to which quite different rules apply. Nor does it discuss the process of discovery of electronic documents in civil litigation. See the Gahtan book mentioned in the footnotes.

A. Principles of Documentary Evidence

Documentary evidence, including evidence in electronic documents, presents three legal problems. First, it is usually hearsay, rather than the direct testimony of a live witness under oath and available for cross-examination, which is the paradigm of good evidence in our court system. Second, such evidence needs to be authenticated, that is, identified in some authoritative way. Third, documents are subject to the "best evidence" rule, which generally requires that original documents be presented to the court, and that a good explanation be given if copies are to be admitted instead.

It should be noted that Canadian courts have not always kept these notions separate in their decisions. The tendency to merge the different concepts has made the area ripe for reform, in the view of the Uniform Law Conference's drafting committee. The degree of confusion might have allowed ambitious and careful counsel the opportunity to exploit the inadequacies of the case law to create some serious difficulties in judicial doctrine and thus add to the uncertainty about what documents were admissible and why.

i) Hearsay

The rules on hearsay are generally accepted to present no special problems for the admission of electronic records. The medium on which indirect evidence is stored does not alter the characteristics of that evidence as hearsay. As a result, the law dealing with the hearsay aspect of documentary evidence has been able to handle electronic records without difficulty. For example, the Ontario Evidence Act has a codification of the business records rule in section 35 that defines record this way: "includes any information that is recorded or stored by means of any device." Indeed the leading Canadian common law case on documents, *Ares v. Venner*, [1970] Supreme Court Reports 608, set out rules that could be applied as well to electronic as to paper records.

This kind of thinking led the Uniform Law Conference of Canada to omit rules on hearsay from the Uniform Electronic Evidence Act that it adopted in 1998 (http://www.law.ualberta.ca/alri/ulc/acts/eeeact.htm).

However, in the 1990s the Supreme Court of Canada has been developing the law of hearsay. The old rigid categories of exceptions to the rule, i.e. cases in which such evidence is admissible, are disappearing. The more recent formulations of the Supreme Court say that hearsay evidence is admissible when it is "necessary and reliable." (See *R. v. Khan*, [1990] 2 S.C.R. 531, *R. v. Smith*, [1992] 2 S.C.R. 915, *R. v. U. (F.J.)*, [1995] 3 S.C.R. 764.)

The necessity of hearsay evidence is not usually difficult to demonstrate, particularly in the field of documentary evidence, since the purpose of creating the documents in the first place is to preserve information beyond the capacity of human memory. Its reliability can be more contentious. However, documentary evidence has at common law been admitted on the ground that the manner in which it is created gives a "circumstantial guarantee of trustworthiness," in the words of Wigmore on Evidence, cited in J.D.Ewart, *Documentary Evidence in Canada* (Carswell 1984) p.13. Compare the language of the Civil Code of Quebec, noted below.

Electronic documents may tend to reopen the debate, however. The impermanence and the malleability of information in electronic form makes some electronic records unreliable. Others are, of course, thoroughly trustworthy, and technology offers many ways to give different degrees of assurance to them. It has been argued in Canada that the combination of electronic records and the restatement of the law of hearsay makes it necessary to develop new rules for the admission of such records in their character as hearsay. If these records are unreliable in different ways, then their reliability is a hearsay issue in a way it was not when that law was more bound in categories.

The main proponent of this point of view is Ken Chasse, who is much published on electronic evidence issues. See for example his opening contribution to the Uniform Law process in the 1994 Proceedings of the Conference, at http://www.law.ualberta.ca/alri/ulc/94pro/e94j.htm. He would prefer that the courts examine in detail the circumstances of the creation and retention of electronic records. The recommendations of his 1994 paper echo the procedures of the Ontario Court of Appeal in *R. v. McMullen*, (1978), 42 Canadian Criminal Cases (2d) 67, affd (1979), 100 Dominion Law Reports (3d) 671. This case has, however, been little followed since then.

The argument on the other side is twofold. First, the law does not investigate the actual abilities of the human beings that keep records, in order to apply the business records rule. Why should it investigate the inner workings of a computer? Second, "[t]he required circumstantial guarantee of trustworthiness flows from the presumption that businesses will create systems which ensure the reliability of their records. The nature of those systems, whether they involve computers or human beings, does not affect the reliability of that presumption."[6] (We are not talking here of records created with the prospect of litigation.)

As noted, the Uniform Electronic Evidence Act tends to the latter argument, at least in respect of hearsay, rather than Ken Chasse's more demanding recommendations. The debate is a reminder of the difficulty caused by using the same word "reliability" in several different contexts. It does not mean the same thing, or involve the same tests, when we are talking about authentication or best evidence. The quotation from Douglas Ewart's book in the preceding paragraph introduces yet another concept, of the reliability of a presumption (in effect, of reliability)! The Uniform Act tried to stay away from the word, if not the concept.

ii) Authentication

In the law of evidence, a document must be authenticated before it can be admitted. Authentication means the demonstration of what a document is and where it came from. There must be evidence, generally live and under oath, to authenticate a document. However, in practice this foundation evidence does not need to be extensive. The usual formulation is that it must be "sufficient to support a finding that the document is what it purports to be." One will note that the foundation evidence does not have to prove that the document *is* what it purports to be. That is a question of weight, after admission.

Canadian reported cases have seldom dealt at length with authentication. It seems however that wide-ranging inquiries about the reliability of a document do not often occur at the authentication stage. The question for law reformers was whether electronic documents needed an additional test.

The Uniform Electronic Evidence Act says no. On authentication it simply codifies the common law requirement noted above, that the foundation evidence be capable of supporting a finding of authenticity. See section 3. The intention, according to the commentary to the Uniform Act, is that the reliability of an electronic record should be tested only once to get the record admitted. This would happen under the rubric of the best evidence rule. Whether the wording of the Uniform Act will be sufficient to impose that limit remains to be seen.

iii) Best Evidence Rule

The third rule about documentary evidence, and indeed about all evidence, is that it must be the "best evidence" available. For documents, this has come to mean that the court wants to see an original document, or have a good explanation of why the original is not available. The problem with electronic documents is that the concept of "original" does not apply very easily, for at least two reasons. First, electrons are manipulated in many places to create a document, and they will leave traces, if not the whole document, in many of them. The random-access memory, the hard drive, disk drives, network backup tapes, and home as well as office computers—and one's colleagues computers if one can share screens during creation—can all be sites of electrons constituting the document. One is not necessarily more "original" than the other.

The second reason that "original" applies poorly is that copies are not distinguishable from the electronic file first created. The reason that a court (or anyone else) would want an original is to test its integrity. It is thought that changes will be easier to detect if they have been made on an original document. This makes sense for a text on paper, especially if written in ink by a pen. It does not make much sense for an electronic document. Electronic documents are made up of bits, which are mere instructions to run or not run an electric current. One version of an electronic document is likely as accurate as another, or just as likely to contain an alteration. (There are ways to increase one's confidence in the integrity of an electronic document, but they depend on its handling, not on its status as an original.)

Canadian courts have not always faced the best evidence rule in dealing with computer-generated records, and when they have done so, they have not been consistent. Some cases have found that the "original" was in a hard drive or central core of a mainframe computer, so the court had to be content with a copy printed out (*R. v. McMullen*, supra). Others have found that the printout was a display of the original that satisfied the demand for an original (*R. v. Vanlerberghe*, (1976), 6 Criminal Reports (3d) 222 (B.C.C.A.). Others have found that the printout was a "duplicate," which at least in the Canada Evidence Act has a higher status than a copy. The courts do not seem to have considered an electronic document shown to the court on a computer monitor from the "original" storage medium.

The UN Model Law provides that the admissibility of information shall not be denied on the sole ground of its electronic form, or on the ground that it is not in its original form, "if it is the best evidence that the person adducing it could reasonably be expected to obtain." This last part is in effect a restatement of the common law rule. Its formulation may have undesirable consequences, however. Someone who made electronic images of paper records could arguably not introduce the images into evidence without having destroyed the paper, since the courts may be inclined to consider the paper as the best evidence, if the paper is available. It may still be open to the proponent of the evidence to demonstrate that the images are as good as paper, but why should that be necessary? If the images can be demonstrated to be reliable, the paper should become irrelevant. One can destroy it to save storage costs, or keep it for historical reasons, or destroy parts and keep parts (though of course not for the purposes of the litigation, but for record-management reasons independent of the litigation.) This is not a question that should be resolved by the law of evidence.

The Uniform Electronic Evidence Act follows the principle of Article 8 of the Model Law on original generally, which makes clear that the policy function of requiring an original is to help ensure the integrity of the record, i.e. that it has not been altered. The Uniform Act says in section 4(1) that for an electronic record, the best evidence rule is satisfied "on proof of the integrity of the records system in or by which the data was recorded or stored." Note that it does not speak of "reliability"!

Proving the integrity of the record by the integrity of the system is fairly standard in U.S. law (in the federal and uniform rules, at least), but it has not been clearly established in Canada. In many cases there will be no other way to get at the integrity of the record than by referring to the system. The main other way to show integrity would be to have someone attest that the information in the record was accurate. However, if one had a live witness who could testify about the content of the document, one would not need the document. One could show integrity of a particular record by showing it had been securely encrypted in an appropriate way, but the encryption system is more likely to be part of a security system than devised for a single record.

The integrity of the recordkeeping system is not of course a guarantee of integrity of the individual record. However, the original nature of a document is also not a guarantee of its integrity. The best evidence rule works towards integrity, but does not ensure it. The drafting team for the Uniform Act wanted to replace the search for original with some equivalent hurdle to admissibility, but the team did not intend to make admission of evidence much more difficult than it should be, given the nature of electronic records.

For this reason, i.e. to avoid a lot of litigation on matters that would normally not be disputed, the Uniform Act contains a number of presumptions of integrity of a records system. The general presumption appears in section 5(a). The presumption is established by evidence that supports a finding that at all material times the computer system or other similar device was operating properly or, if it was not, that the fact of its not operating properly did not affect the integrity of that electronic record, and there are no other reasonable grounds to doubt the integrity of the electronic records system.

This looks like a test that appeared in an English statute from the 1960s, the Police and Criminal Evidence Act, section 69. The Uniform Act's language has been modified in light of later case law that dealt with the immaterial misfunction. The English test has been criticized as unnecessary, on the ground that the law already presumes that machines function as they are supposed to, unless the opposite is shown. (See Amanda Hoey's article at http://www.ncl.ac.uk/~nlawwww/1996/issue1/hoey1.html, and Consultation Paper 138 of the Law Commission, 1995, paragraphs 14.27 to 14.32.) It is far from clear that such a presumption operates in Canadian law, or if it does, that it would apply to computerized record systems. New types of machine generally have to prove themselves before the courts effectively, if not formally, shift the burden of proof about their reliability.

The second provision of section 5 creates a presumption of integrity of the records system if the record was recorded and stored by a party to the proceedings adverse in interest to the proponent of the record. It is hard to show the integrity of someone else's system. The person best able to demonstrate the lack of integrity is the person whose record it is. If a person claims that a record recorded and stored by it has no integrity, let that person prove that lack (or rebut the presumption at least). The presumption is limited to adverse parties, in order to prevent parties with the same interest from colluding by introducing each others' records to get the presumption.

The third provision creates a presumption in favor of the system of a stranger to the proceedings who created the record in the ordinary course of business. Bank records might be part of such a class. However, the records must not have been created or stored under the control of one of the parties, since that would call into question the independence that justifies the presumption. If the third party did create them under the control of the proponent, then the proponent should be able to fulfil the conditions for the first presumption, about the proper operation of the computer.

What is the strength of the presumption? The Uniform Act leads off section 5 with "in the absence of evidence to the contrary." To rebut the presumption the other party must bring evidence against the presumption, but need not disprove it. Once the presumption is rebutted, or if it cannot be established in the first place, both sides would have to bring evidence to allow the court to decide whether the recordkeeping system had sufficient integrity to justify admitting the record.

They can do this by reference to standards for the relevant system. Section 6 authorizes the court to consider "any standard, procedure, usage, or practice on how electronic records are to be recorded or stored, having regard to the type of business or endeavor that used, recorded, or stored the electronic record and the nature and purpose of the electronic record." Standards could be national technical standards, practices current in a particular industry, usages unique to the party seeking admission of its document, or rules agreed to by trading partners in an electronic data interchange relationship. The credibility of the standards is a matter for argument.

Canada has a national standard, approved by the Canada General Standards Board, on microfilm and electronic imaging as documentary evidence. This is CAN/CGSB-72.11-93. This is a complex standard that incorporates by reference a number of subsidiary standards, some of them American. One of the terms of the standard, adopted in 1993, is that it be reviewed for technical accuracy every five years. A working group of the CGSB has recently proposed very minor changes to this standard. More important, the group is developing a general standard for the admissibility of electronic records in general, and not just imaged records. This work will probably be completed during the year 2000.

Before leaving the subject of the best evidence rule, one should consider subsection 4(2) of the Uniform Act:

An electronic record in the form of a printout that has been manifestly or consistently acted on, relied upon, or used as the record of the information recorded or stored on the printout is the record for the purposes of the best evidence rule.

It makes sense for a printout to be included in the definition of electronic record, since it can be only the display of what is in the computer. What is in the computer may be the issue before the court. However, sometimes a document is created on a computer and printed and always used in its paper form. Most business correspondence falls into this class. Typewriters are rare in the modern office. Correspondence on paper is not. These letters are used at all material times as paper documents. If their content is at issue in a suit, it is the content of the letter, not the content of the computer where it originated, that is to be proved. The printout should be treated the same as a typewritten letter. Subsection 4(2) intends to ensure that result. The reasoning is supported by the decision of the Ontario Court of Appeal (upheld by the Supreme Court of Canada) in *R. v. Bell and Bruce*, (1982), 65 C.C.C. (2d) 377, where printouts of bank ledgers were held to be original records when the computer records had been erased and the paper records stored and relied on by the bank. The bank's reliance in practice on the paper records was the key to the decision, more than the absence of the electronic version.

B. Law Reform on Electronic Evidence

The Government of Canada was the first to introduce the Uniform Act into legislation. Part 3 of Bill C-6, the Personal Information Protection and

Electronic Documents Act referred to in the Electronic Transactions part of this paper, enacts the Uniform Act with a few changes in wording and structure to accommodate it to the Canada Evidence Act, where the Bill makes it section 31.1. The principal difference is that Bill C-6 inserts the possibility of establishing "evidentiary presumptions" of integrity and source, where electronic records have been signed with a "secure electronic signature," which was also described in the earlier part of this paper. These presumptions can be brought into force by regulation.

The Government of Ontario has recently enacted the Uniform Electronic Evidence Act almost verbatim, as new section 34.1 of the Ontario Evidence Act. The provisions are section 7 of the Red Tape Reduction Act, 1999, S.O. 1999 c.12. They are expected to be proclaimed in force in the late spring of 2000.

Two nonuniform statutes are worth noting. The first is the Civil Code of Quebec, in effect on January 1, 1994. Article 2837 says:

> Where the data respecting a judicial act [a type of legal document] are entered on a computer system, the document reproducing them makes proof of the content of the act if it is intelligible and if its reliability is sufficiently guaranteed....

Article 2838 contains presumptions:

> The reliability of the entry of the data of a juridical act on a computer system is presumed to be sufficiently guaranteed where it is carried out systematically and without gaps and the computerized data are protected against alterations. The same presumption is made in flavor of third persons where the data were entered into by an enterprise.

There appears to be no significant case law on these articles.

The second recent item of law reform is the Electronic Evidence Act of New Brunswick, S.N.B. 1996 c.52. This inserts a new section dealing with data evidence and electronic images. It sets up a system of affidavit support for the electronic evidence. Electronic images are admissible only if the paper originals have been destroyed in the usual course of business.

IV. Privacy

Electronic commerce has animated the long-standing debate about the protection of privacy. The ability to collect and manipulate personal information has expanded rapidly in the computer age, and even more quickly with Internet connections. Governments feel a good deal of pressure to protect that information, though the means and even the potential for success are debated.

The common law of Canada has not protected privacy reliably, though the courts in recent years have mentioned the importance of privacy in cases involving search and seizure rules and defamation. Several provinces of Canada have a statutory tort of invasion of privacy, though there is little litigation under those statutes. British Columbia's statute is at R.S.B.C. 1996 c.373; Saskatchewan's is at S.S. c. P24; Manitoba's at R.S.M. 1987 c. P125; and Newfoundland's at R.S.N. 1990 c. P-22. In 1994, after many years of discussion, the Uniform Law Conference adopted the Uniform Privacy Act, which would create such a statutory tort in any province or territory that enacted it. It has not attracted much interest.

A. Public Sector Privacy Protection

The federal government and most or all of the provinces have statutes protecting personal information in the public sector. See for example the Privacy Act, R.S.C.1985 c. P-21, and the Freedom of Information and Protection of Privacy Act, R.S.O. 1990 c. F.31 in Ontario. In general there is a public servant, reporting to the Legislature not the Executive, responsible for the enforcement of these statutes, and sometimes for comment on policy matters too. See for example the Web site of the Information and Privacy Commissioner of Ontario, who has published a number of analyses of electronic commerce: http://www.ipc.on.ca/. See also the federal Commissioner's site, http://www.privcom.gc.ca/, which provides links to all the provincial commissions.

B. Private Sector Privacy Protection

The earliest legislative initiative on privacy in the private sector came in Quebec. The Quebec Charter of Human Rights and Freedoms establishes a right to privacy. R.S.Q. 1977 c.C-12. The 1994 Civil Code also speaks of a basic right to privacy (Book 1 Chapter 3), and a separate statute, an act respecting the protection of personal information in the private sector, S.Q. 1993 c. 17, adds a regime of obligation and enforcement. Further information and the texts of the statutes themselves can be found at http://www.cai.gouv.qc.ca (in French). The five years or so since the law came into effect have not produced general controversy.

So long as only one province has legislation, it is of course easier for businesses to comply with the law. The risk of inconsistent laws across the country led the Uniform Law Conference to adopt a project to produce a Uniform Data Protection Act, so that harmonized and principled legislation would be available if the political demand arose. Policy documents and draft statutes were published in the annual Proceedings of the Conference from 1995 to 1998 (see http://www.law.ualberta.ca/alri/ulc/ under the reports of the annual meetings). The work has not been completed, for reasons to be noted in a moment.

Meanwhile the private sector itself moved to create standards for proper conduct in the matter. The Canadian Standards Association managed a private-public consultation process for some five years to develop the Model

Privacy Code, completed in 1996. The Code is described at and available for purchase from http://www.csa.ca. The main part of its text appears as Appendix A to the federal legislation, Bill C-6, discussed below.

The Code has been very successful in its adherents, its sectoral variants, and even its international influence, as the International Standards Organization has considered making an international standard based on the Code. The Code itself is a modern elaboration of the OECD Guidelines on the Protection of Personal Information that date from 1980. (The OECD Guidelines appear in the 1995 Proceedings of the Uniform Law Conference.)

The Government of Canada has decided, however, that a voluntary code of conduct, however well-received and however influential, was not satisfactory, for three reasons. See the privacy section of Canada's e-commerce strategy at http://e-com.ic.gc.ca/english/privacy/632d1.html#privup.

First, as a matter of social policy, individuals needed more consistent and enforceable protection than voluntary compliance with a code gave them.

Second, protecting privacy effectively will promote electronic commerce, which is good for the economy and Canadian competitiveness in global markets. Many studies show that individuals are worried about their privacy when they venture onto the Internet, and electronic commerce is restricted as a result.

Third, the European Union has published a Data Protection Directive that requires members states to restrict the export of personal information where the receiving country does not adequately protect that information. The Directive is at http://europa.eu.int/eur-lex/en/lif/dat/1995/en_395L0046.html. The United States has negotiated with the EU a qualification or exemption or substitute compliance (known as a "safe harbor" deal) with the Directive's standards. Canada is too small to have bargaining power for that kind of deal. As a consequence, the federal government thinks that Canada will simply have to enforce standards compatible with those in Europe, in order to preserve commercial communications with EU members.

As a result, the government of Canada has enacted the Personal Information Protection and Electronic Documents Act, S.C.2000 c.5. As noted earlier, it is available at http://www.parl.gc.ca/36/2/parlbus/chambus/house/bills/government/C-6/C-6_4/C-6_cover-E.html . Part 1 of the Act deals with privacy.

i) The Federal Legislation

Essentially the federal statute (still known as Bill C-6) enacts the CSA Model Code into law. The operating provisions of the Model Code are annexed as a Schedule to the Act. The incorporation process caused a few difficulties, because the Code contains language like "parties should do X" or "where appropriate, parties should do Y." Bill C-6 says that "the word 'should', when used in Schedule 1, indicates a recommendation and does not impose an obligation" (section 5(2)).

Part 1 of Bill C-6 aims to protect the privacy of individuals while recognizing the need of organizations to collect, use or disclose personal information "for the purposes that a reasonable person would consider appropriate in the circumstances" (section 3). Three definitions (in section 2) are important in understanding how the Bill would do that.

a) Application

First, the Act applies to "personal information," defined as "information about an identifiable individual, but does not include the name, title or business address of an employee of an organization." Second, its rules apply to "organizations," defined to include "an association, a partnership, a person and a trade union." As a result, the Act applies to the activities of individuals in their handling of personal information. Third, the Act applies (only) to commercial activity, defined as "any particular transaction, act or conduct or any regular course of conduct that is of a commercial character."

The Act governs "every organization in respect of personal information that…the organization collects, uses, or discloses in the course of commercial activity" (section 4). It also applies to information about employees of organizations that engage in "federal works and undertakings." The latter is a well-known expression in Canadian law, though Bill C-6 defines it as well. The expression covers the main activities that the federal government regulates under its most direct constitutional powers: banks, railways, broadcasters and telecommunications companies, marine enterprises, and some others.

The application of the Act to other kinds of commercial activity has been controversial. On its face it applies to interprovincial collection, use or disclosure of personal information for commercial purposes. Three years after it comes into force, it will apply to all commercial collection, use and disclosure of such information (section 30). In other words, it would apply to areas of activity that normally are under provincial jurisdiction. (The general heads of provincial jurisdiction under section 92 of the Constitution Act are "property and civil rights in the province"—92(13)—and "all matters of a merely local and private nature in the province"—92(16).)

The federal government claims that its broadly worded power over trade and commerce in Canada justifies its jurisdiction in this case, partly because of the borderless nature of electronic commerce. In Canada the trade and commerce power has generally been interpreted narrowly, unlike the Commerce Clause of the US Constitution. Opinions among constitutional scholars are divided about this extension in Bill C-6. In October 1998 the provincial and territorial Attorneys General unanimously asked the federal government to withdraw the Bill for further consultation on this point. Some challenge is probable when the legislation comes to be enforced against an otherwise provincially-regulated organization.

The Act allows the federal government to exempt an organization or activity from the Part if the organization or activity is covered by provincial legislation "that is substantially similar to this Part" (section 26(2)(b)). It is not clear just what this means, and the federal government has discretion whether to declare an exemption or not. The responsible Minister has announced that Quebec's legislation, mentioned above, does qualify and that an exemption will be granted under this provision at the appropriate time. This announcement has not weakened the Quebec government's opposition to the Act.

There are two important limits on the application of the Act in section 4(2). First, it does not apply to "any individual in respect of personal information that the individual collects, uses of discloses for personal or domestic purposes and does not collect, use or disclose for any other purpose " At least the Christmas card list and the wedding invitation list seem to be safe. It is not clear why this exception is needed, given the general application of the Act to commercial activity only.

Next, the Act excludes Aany organization in respect of personal information that the organization collects, uses or discloses for journalistic, artistic or literary purposes and does not collect, use or disclose for any other purpose." How this will work in practice is subject to some debate.

b) Operation

It is clear from the foregoing discussion that three distinct types of activity are covered: collection, use and disclosure. The Act sets out rules for all of them, and these rules are not the same for all. So the right of one organization to disclose information does not automatically give anyone the right to collect it. The consent of an individual to one organization to disclose his or her personal information does not necessarily constitute consent for another organization to collect it from the disclosing organization.

This is understandable in some cases. The right of an organization to disclose an individual's health information to a doctor does not create a right in anyone at all to collect the information from the organization that has it. This structure of the rules creates difficulty in other cases, though, if parties who deal with each other do not have equivalent rights about the same information when they both need it for a common purpose. At least one federal lawyer has spoken privately about "implied consent" in such cases, but the legislation does not support any such concept, and privacy commissioners in Canada are expected to be sceptical of it.

The basic obligation of an organization under the Act is to comply with the CSA Model Code as set out in Schedule 1 to the Act (section 5(1)). This is a set of principles about getting consent of the individual to collection, use or disclosure of his or her personal information, not using the information for purposes other than those disclosed at the time of collection, giving access to the information for purposes of verification and correction, and the like. As noted earlier, the principles are developed from the OECD Guidelines of 1980 that have influenced the European Union's Directive, Quebec's statute, and other common texts on the subject.

The Act goes on to restrict or focus the obligations. For example, section 6 says that the consent of an individual under clause 4.1 of the Schedule does not relieve the organization of the duty to comply with the obligations in the Schedule. Section 7 limits the cases in which personal information may be collected, used or disclosed without the consent of the individual. The three subsections of this section must be read closely, because as noted earlier, the right to collect does not imply the right to use or disclose, and vice versa. They override the rules in the relevant provisions of the Schedule, where inconsistent.

Here are some of the considerations in section 7. Subsection 7(a) gives permission to collect information "clearly in the interests of the individual," but then such information may be used "in respect of an emergency that threatens the life, health, or security of an individual"—a rather narrower idea than "clearly in the interests." There is a law enforcement exception, some ability to use personal information for scholarly purposes but only with advance notice to the Privacy Commissioner, and permission to use information if it is publicly available, but only if specified in the regulations. In other words, the presence of personal information on a public register does not give anyone an automatic right to use it for other purposes than those of the register. Subsection 7(c) has a longer list of permitted disclosures, though many with internal limits.

Section 8 spells out the terms on which an individual has access to his or her personal information, including how to apply for it, how soon the information has to be provided, at what cost, and so on. Section 9 has some limits to disclosure where third party personal information would be disclosed at the same time as the requester's information. Section 10 provides for disclosure in special format where the person with a right to access has a "sensory disability" as defined, within some reasonable limits.

c) Enforcement

Organizations have to designate someone to be responsible for its personal information policies, who can explain them to individuals who want to know and who can receive and deal with complaints (Principle 4.1 of Schedule 1 of Bill C-6). This may be a burden on smaller organizations, though no doubt the task would be done by someone with other responsibilities too.

Bill C-6 uses the federal government's Privacy Commissioner, an official independent of the Executive who reports to Parliament. (This relationship is unusual in a parliamentary system like Canada's and is used for officials with some kind of supervisory power over the Executive, like the Auditor-General or, in some provinces, the Ombudsman.) Complaints may be made to the

Commissioner, and in some cases notice of proposed use or disclosure of personal information must be given to the Commissioner. The Commissioner can initiate a complaint in some cases (section 11). He or she can investigate the complaints or respond to the notices, and may attempt to mediate a solution (section 12). The Commissioner may make a public report on the outcome of the investigation (section 13).

The Commissioner has no direct enforcement powers, however. Any request for mandatory enforcement is directed to the Federal Court of Canada, either by the complainant (section 14) or by the Commissioner (section 15). (The Federal Court is a statutory court that deals primarily with matters involving the federal government, plus a few specific matters like tax appeals, intellectual property and admiralty cases. It is not an equivalent to the federal court system in the United States.)

The Commissioner also has extensive "audit" powers, under 18 and 19 of the Act. He or she may do general research on privacy matters and publish them, and generally "promote the purposes of this Part" (section 24(d)).

The Commissioner may consult with and cooperate with a number of bodies, including provincial counterparts. This can pave the way for provincial enforcement of matters within provincial competence that are covered by the legislation.

d) Status

Part 1 of the Act, on privacy, will come into force on January 1, 2001, to give organizations time to set up systems to comply with it. It will apply to personal health information one year later, under section 31.1. As noted, its provisions come into force for intraprovincial commercial activity three years after that. (The provisions on electronic documents and electronic evidence came into force on May 1, 2000.)

ii) Provincial Legislation

No province has yet announced an intention to legislate on privacy in the private sector, apart of course from Quebec, which has legislation in place. A number of them are consulting, some more actively than others, on the prospects for such legislation. Why would the provinces legislate, when Bill C-6 will cover provincial ground in due course? Besides the desire to control one's own lawmaking and assert jurisdiction, the provinces may want to extend private sector rules beyond commercial activity to the "broader public sector," such as academic institutions or hospitals. Employee records of provincially regulated organizations are not covered by Bill C-6, only employee records of federal works and undertakings. Provinces might want to provide local enforcement mechanisms, using provincial courts or the provincial privacy commissioner. They might even want to try to harmonize the principles and operation of their current laws on public sector privacy with the new field of private sector privacy.

Naturally it would be helpful if provincial legislation were consistent with the federal statute. The federal statute will continue to operate unless the federal government judges that the provincial law is substantially similar. The declared extension of the federal legislation into provincial jurisdiction cast some doubt on the relevance of the proposed Uniform Data Protection Act, and that work has been suspended for the moment. Federal officials were leading the uniform project, and when their Bill was introduced, a provincial replacement became necessary, but in the circumstances, none has come forward. A brief report appears in the 1999 Proceedings at the Uniform Law Conference's Web site.

iii) Sectoral legislation

There is little privacy legislation on specific sectors of the economy. Ontario has its Consumer Reporting Act, R.S.O. c. C.33, which controls the use of personal information by credit agencies. Other provinces may have similar legislation.

The sector most likely to be covered by its own legislation is health. Canada's health care system is a mix of public and private organizations, largely but not entirely supported by public funds. There are for example no private hospitals in Canada, though there are private clinics for particular purposes. As a result, it is difficult to characterize transactions as commercial or noncommercial. Applying Bill C-6 to the health sector is very hard, which is one reason for the delay in its application to this sector.

The province of Manitoba recently passed The Personal Health Information Act, S.M. 1997 c.51, to deal with these challenges (though it was not incited by the federal bill, which was not then released.) Alberta, Saskatchewan, and Ontario have published consultation documents on protecting health care information. Ontario has released a draft of legislation for the purpose, though as of mid-May 2000 it had been withdrawn from the Web.

iv) Implications

The federal statute represents a dramatic change to how personal information must be handled in Canada, outside Quebec, which has had several years to get used to such rules. (Quebec's laws are based on similar principles but their specific application and their enforcement are not always the same.) Health sector legislation is likely to spread.

In short, the policy development process is in full swing in the privacy field. It is hard to predict the constellation of federal and provincial legislation in five years' time. It is certain that legislation will protect personal information more thoroughly than it does today, and that enforcement mechanisms will be available to those who are not happy with how their information is being treated. Anyone doing business in Canada will have to take account of such laws.

Foreign businesses that carry on their activities in Canada, or that even collect, use or disclose personal information in Canada, should expect to be affected by the legislation. Cross-border transfers of personal information are subject to the federal legislation as soon as it comes into force.

Canada is by far the largest trading partner of the United States. A good deal of that volume represents dealings between corporate subsidiaries. They may have to reexamine how they keep records of personal information of individuals in Canada.

V. Conclusion

Canada's legal system is evolving to accommodate the disappearance of paper from so many of our legal relationships (if not from our law offices). The common law is managing to deal with much of the change, and legislation at federal and provincial levels aims to increase the legal certainty and thus the confidence of Canadians to engage in electronic commerce. The main legislative developments have affected electronic transactions, electronic evidence, and individual privacy.[7]

Canada is very sensitive to the global nature of electronic commerce, and to its relative size. As a result, it participates actively in developing international standards and promotes harmonization efforts at home as well. The Uniform Law Conference of Canada, of which the federal government is a member, is working hard to ensure the greatest compliance possible with the best principles and best practices for the legal framework for electronic commerce. We share with the rest of the world the conviction that it is a work in progress.

CHAPTER 20

LINKING, FRAMING, AND CACHING

Web site links permit Web users to click their way from one Web site to another. Framing permits a Web site user to view material from another Web site within a "frame" on the original site. Caching is the creation of a copy of a Web site by storing data on a computer.

This chapter considers the legal questions currently raised by linking, framing, and caching.

LINKING

Linking is so common on the Web that the idea that a Web site owner might need permission to link to another site was once considered absurd. After all, it is linking that makes the Web a "web" of interconnected sites. In the Web culture, providing a link to another site generally has been viewed as a favor to the owner of the linked site, because providing a link increases traffic to the site.

However, the increasing commercialization of the Web and the availability of new technology (such as framing technology) have caused the assumption that linking does not require permission to be reexamined, especially in light of recent lawsuits (discussed below).

Currently, linking can take three forms:

- A simple text hyperlink to the home page of the linked site, implemented through HTML, in which a hypertext link is marked as a highlighted word or different-colored word on the linking site.

- A graphic hyperlink, in which a graphic (a logo or just a button) on the linking site alerts the user of the linking site to the existence of a link.

- Deep linking, a text hyperlink to an internal page of the linked site.

Other types of links may become possible as new technology becomes available.

In this section, we discuss whether permission is required for each type of linking. We also discuss Web site terms stating that permission must be obtained for linking, revenue-sharing linking agreements, and liability issues related to linking.

Text Hyperlinks

Copyright Infringement

When a Web site user clicks on a link to the home page of another site, the user is transferred to the linked site. To determine whether linking to a site without the permission of the site's copyright owner could be copyright infringement, we must ask whether linking is an exercise of any of the copyright owner's exclusive rights. (The exclusive rights are discussed in chapter 1).

Although few courts have ruled on this issue, linking does not appear to be an exercise of the copyright owner's exclusive rights. Here's why: Linking does not appear to involve reproduction or public display of the linked site—a user who follows a link is actually transferred to the linked site. Linking to the home page of another site also does not appear to be an exercise of the copyright owner's modification, distribution, or public performance rights. (An argument can be made that "deep linking"—linking to an internal page of the linked site—is an exercise of the modification right. This point is discussed in "Deep Linking," later in this section. Liability for linking to a site that contains infringing material is also discussed later in this section.)

Because linking to the home page of another site is not an exercise of any of the copyright owner's exclusive rights, copyright law does not require that permission be obtained for linking.

Nonetheless, many people consider it good manners to ask permission before linking to another site (particularly if the site says "ask permission before linking"). Some Web site owners may not want to be associated with your site or your products. We have included a simple Permission to Link agreement in appendix B (Form 5).

Other Rights

If a Web site says "ask permission before linking," it is possible that linking to the site without the owner's permission may be trespass. The auction site eBay used trespass law to obtain a preliminary injunction to keep Bidder's Edge from accessing ebay's computer system by an automated query program, robot, or Web crawler. (Bidder's Edge is an auction aggregator site designed to offer online buyers the ability to search for items across a number of auction sites.) Bidder's Edge maintained that it could not possibly trespass on eBay's Web site because the site is publicly accessible. The court—unlike the *Ticketmaster* court discussed later in this section—found this argument unconvincing because eBay's servers are private property "conditional access to which eBay grants the public." *eBay, Inc. v. Bidder's Edge, Inc.*, 2000 U.S. Dist LEXIS 7287 (ND Cal 2000). Although the *eBay* case is not a linking case, it is possible that the trespass theory could be applied to unauthorized linking.

Graphic Hyperlinks

For graphic hyperlinks, if you own or have the right to use the graphic, the same rule we just stated for text hyperlinks applies for graphic hyperlinks: Copyright law does not require you to get permission for a link to the home page of the linked site, but it is considered good manners to ask permission.

If you use a copyrighted graphic image from the linked site as the graphic hyperlink, you will be reproducing and displaying copyrighted material you do not own (the graphic). You need the copyright owner's permission to use the graphic image, unless your use of the graphic image is fair use.

> **EXAMPLE**
>
> John linked to the home page of a cartoon site, using an image of one of the cartoon characters as a graphic hyperlink. The cartoon character is protected by copyright. By using the image of the cartoon character on his site, John exercised the reproduction and display rights belonging to the cartoon character's copyright owner.

Deep Linking

Whether deep linking—linking to an internal page of the linked site—requires permission is unclear, as we'll explain. The cautious approach is to obtain permission for deep linking, particularly if the Web site to which you want to link states that you should obtain permission before linking.

Copyright Infringement

Whether deep linking is copyright infringement is unclear. An argument can be made that deep linking changes the way a Web user who follows a deep link to a linked site experiences the linked site. This could be viewed as an exercise of the linked site owner's modification right.

EXAMPLE

Ticketmaster Corp. operates a ticket-purchase Web site. The Ticketmaster site's home page contains banner ads, instructions on using the site, and a directory listing (and linking to) "event pages" within the Ticketmaster site. Tickets.com, Inc., another ticket-purchase Web site, provides links from its site to a number of event pages on the Ticketmaster site. A Tickets.com site user can click on one of these links and go directly to a Ticketmaster site event page, bypassing the Ticketmaster site's home page.

This example states the facts of the case *Ticketmaster Corp. v. Tickets.com Inc.*, 54 USPQ2d 1344 (CD Cal 2000). In *Ticketmaster*, the court, ruling on the defendant's motion to dismiss the lawsuit, held that linking does not involve a violation of the Copyright Act because no copying is involved. The court stated that linking is analogous to using a library's card index to get a reference to items. The court did not distinguish between linking to a site's home page and deep linking, nor did it address the question of whether deep linking is an exercise of the linked site owner's modification right. Subsequent cases may address the modification right issue.

Other Rights

Even if deep linking is not copyright infringement, linking without permission could violate other rights of the linked site's owner. Ticketmaster Corp. maintained that Tickets.com's deep linking was trespass to the Ticketmaster site and unfair competition. The court dismissed these two causes of action. Addressing the trespass claim, the court said, it "is hard to see how entering a publicly available Web site could be called a trespass, since all are invited to enter." As to the unfair competition claim, the court said that deep linking by itself, without confusion of source, did not necessarily involve unfair competition.

However, the court in the *Ticketmaster* case refused to dismiss three other causes of action:

- ■ **Copyright infringement.** Ticketmaster's copyright infringement claim was not dismissed entirely. Ticketmaster claimed that Tickets.com reproduced thousands of copies of interior Ticketmaster.com Web pages in order to extract data from them. This aspect of Ticketmaster's copyright infringement claim will go to trial.

- **"Passing off," false association, and false advertising claims.** Ticketmaster claimed that the Tickets.com site falsely suggested an association with Ticketmaster and gave misleading information. These issues will be tried.

- **Tortious interference with prospective business advantage.** The factual basis of this claim is that Tickets.com's links diverted Web users from the Ticketmaster site's home page, depriving Ticketmaster of ad revenue. Advertisers who pay for ads based on the number of "hits" to the Ticketmaster site's home page will not pay anything for people who enter the Ticketmaster site through a deep link from the Tickets.com site.

These claims may be raised in other deep linking cases as well. Another aspect of the *Ticketmaster* case, Ticketmaster's claim that Tickets.com wrongfully used factual information from the Ticketmaster site, is discussed in "When You Don't Need a License," chapter 9.

Requiring Permission

For all three types of linking, if a site to which you want to link states that you should get permission before linking to the site, it's best to obtain permission. (You can use Form 5, appendix B.) If you don't obtain permission, you could be liable for breach of contract.

EXAMPLE

Joan wants to link from her site to XYZ Company's site. The XYZ Company site's Terms of Use state that permission is required for linking to the site. The Terms also state, "If you do not accept the terms stated here, do not use the site." If Joan views the Terms of Use and then continues to use the site, she has accepted the terms. Her acceptance of the terms forms a contract with XYZ Company. Her failure to obtain permission before linking would be a breach of one of the contract's terms.

(Web site Terms of Use are discussed in "Terms of Use," chapter 12.) A number of sites' Terms of Use state that those wishing to link should obtain permission.

In *Ticketmaster*, the court dismissed Ticketmaster's breach of contract claim because it found that the way the Ticketmaster site presented its Terms did not create a binding contract with a site user. The site's Terms of Use page was an internal page. The site's home page contained a link to the Terms page, but the link was at the bottom of the home page. The court noted that site users did not have to view the Terms page before proceeding to an event page. There was no evidence that Tickets.com employees had viewed the Terms page. If they had, it is possible that they would be bound by the terms. The court indicated that it would revive the breach of contract claim if Ticketmaster introduced evidence at trial that Tickets.com employees knew about the terms and implicitly agreed to them.

Links to Your Web Site

If you want others to get permission before linking to your site, post a "request permission" notice prominently on your home page. If you prefer to include this notice in your Terms of Use document, the *Ticketmaster* case indicates that you can increase your chances of having your Terms of Use be held binding if you require users to show agreement to the terms (by clicking on "I agree") before going on. Making terms of use binding on site users is discussed in more detail in our book *Internet Legal Forms for Business*.

Revenue-Sharing Linking

Linking can promote commercial objectives such as a revenue-sharing arrangement between the owners of the linking and linked sites. In a revenue-sharing linking arrangement, the linking site's owner receives—as compensation for providing a link from the owner's site to another site—a percentage of the linked site's revenues (from product sales or advertising fees).

EXAMPLE

The owner of the portal site Adventure Travel agreed to provide a link from the Adventure Travel site to White Water Rafting's site. As compensation for the "referrals," White Water Rafting agreed to pay Adventure Travel 10 percent of the revenue from bookings by customers who entered the White Water Rafting site by way of the link from the Adventure Travel site.

The details of a revenue-sharing linking arrangement should be spelled out in a written linking agreement, which covers the duties and responsibilities of both parties, including such issues as link placement, exclusivity (limitations on links to competitors' sites), access to site user data, privacy policies, and site content control rights. Our book *Internet Legal Forms for Business* contains a revenue-sharing linking agreement.

Liability Issues

Linking may expose you to liability for wrongs done by the owner of the linked site under several legal theories. We'll discuss three.

Affiliation with Other Sites

Web viewers may get the impression that you are affiliated with the owners of sites to which your site links or is linked, with shared responsibility for the other sites' product and marketing claims. If your site contains links, it is a good idea to provide a statement in your Terms of Use or on your home page that:

- Your site provides links to sites not under your control.

- Links should not be interpreted as endorsements of the linked sites or the linked sites' products.

(The sample Terms of Use document in our book *Internet Legal Forms for Business* includes such a provision. Terms of Use documents are discussed in Chapter 12.)

Graphic Hyperlink Copyright Infringement

If you use a graphic from the linked site as a graphic hyperlink, you may be sued for copyright infringement if the linked site's owner does not own the copyright in the graphic.

EXAMPLE

Sue got permission from Z Software to use a graphic from Z Software's Web site as a graphic hyperlink from Sue's site to Z Software's site. Z Software does not own the copyright in the graphic; Artist does. Z Software did not get Artist's permission to use the graphic. Both Z Software and Sue have exercised Artist's rights of reproduction and display and are liable to Artist for copyright infringement. Z Software's grant of permission to Sue does not protect Sue from liability to Artist because Z Software does not own the copyright in the graphic.

Linked Site's Infringing Content

It is possible that a Web site owner who links to a site containing infringing material may be liable for contributory copyright infringement. Contributory copyright infringement is established when a defendant, with knowledge of another party's infringing activity, causes or materially contributes to the infringing conduct.

One court held that a Web site owner who linked to Web sites containing infringing material and made statements encouraging Web site viewers to visit the linked sites to view, download, and print out the material actively encouraged copyright infringement by site users. *Intellectual Reserve, Inc. v. Utah Lighthouse Ministry, Inc.*, 75 FSupp2d 1290 (D Utah 1999). However, the court stopped short of holding that merely linking to a site containing infringing material is contributory infringement.

Part of the Digital Millennium Copyright Act (DMCA) states that a "service provider" is not liable for monetary relief for linking to a site containing infringing material if the service provider, upon receiving notification of the claimed infringement, removes or disables access to the material. This provision is one of the "safe harbor" provisions of the DMCA, discussed in "Copyright Infringement," chapter 25. As we point out there, "service provider" is defined so broadly in the DMCA that the owner of any Web site that incorporates material posted by third-party site users would seem to be a "service provider" and thus eligible to take advantage of the immunity offered by the DMCA. For a discussion of what you must do to take advantage of the immunity provisions, see "Copyright Infringement," chapter 25.

FRAMING

Framing permits viewers of one Web site to view material from another Web site within a frame, without leaving the "framing" site. Framing changes the way the viewer experiences the framed site, because the frame on the framing site covers up part of the content of the framed site.

EXAMPLE

Futuredontics operated a Web site that advertised the company's dental referral business. Applied Anagramics, a dental marketing service, set up a Web site that framed the Futuredontics Web page within a frame that included the Applied Anagramics logo and information about Applied Anagramics.

Framing may be an exercise of the linked site owner's modification right. Do not frame another site without permission. In the case from which the example was drawn, *Futuredontics, Inc. v. Applied Anagramics, Inc.*, 45 USPQ2d 2005 (CD Cal 1998), the defendant, Applied Anagramics filed a motion to dismiss the copyright infringement suit filed against it by Futuredontics. The court refused to dismiss the case, holding that the framed site may constitute a derivative work (work created by modifying a copyrighted work). This case is still pending.

In another framing suit, *Washington Post Co. v. TotalNews*, several publishers sued TotalNews for copyright and trademark infringement for framing the publishers' news Web sites. The TotalNews site's frame covered up the framed site's ads. TotalNews filled the frame with its own ads. Viewers of the TotalNews site viewed content from a publisher's site but not the publisher's ads. The case was settled, with the defendant agreeing to link to—not frame—the plaintiffs' sites.

CACHING

Caching is the creation of a copy of a Web site by storing data on a computer. In this section, we'll discuss two types of caching: server-level caching and temporary caching.

Caching at the server level is done to facilitate quick linking to a popular site, to maximize site "uptime," and for security reasons (as part of a firewall). This type of caching is also called proxy caching. In copyright terms, caching a Web site is an exercise of the Web site copyright owner's reproduction and display rights.

The DMCA states that a service provider is not liable for monetary relief for caching material made available online by a third party and transmitted without modification through the service provider's system by and from that third party to someone else if the caching is carried out through an automatic technical process and the service provider complies with reasonable restrictions that the originating party places on use of the material. If the person who makes the material available online did so without the authorization of the copyright owner, the service provider must remove or disable access to the material upon receiving a notification of claimed infringement in order to take advantage of the immunity offered by the statute.

For information on what you must do to take advantage of the DMCA's immunity, see "Copyright Infringement," chapter 25. The DMCA provision's immunity does not apply to situations in which the service provider has selected material for caching, only to caching performed by an automatic technical process.

Temporary caching occurs within your computer's random access memory (RAM) when you view a Web site (your browser caches each Web page you visit in your computer's RAM). Most copyright attorneys believe it is not necessary (thank goodness!) to ask permission for this temporary caching before viewing a Web site. Presumably, by posting material, Web site owners grant Web viewers implied licenses for the RAM copy, without which viewers cannot access material on the Web.

LINKING VS. CACHING

To a Web site user, there doesn't seem to be any difference between clicking on an icon that will take the user to a linked site and clicking on an icon that will bring up a cached site for the user. You may wonder why copyright law requires that permission be obtained for caching but not for linking. The reason is that caching involves the creation of a copy of the cached site. Linking to a site does not involve the creation of a copy of the linked site.

CHAPTER 21

USING MUSIC ON THE WEB

In some respects, music copyright law differs from copyright law in general. Special features of music copyright law are discussed in this chapter.

We'll begin with a brief discussion of technologies for using music on the Web. It includes a primer on music copyright law and a section on licensing music for use on the Internet. At the end of the chapter, we'll discuss alternatives to licensing—recording your own version of a song, creating original music, using public domain music, and using music from music libraries.

Introduction

Currently, there are two ways in which music is being delivered over the Internet—"streaming," in which a Web user listens to music on a real-time basis (similar to listening to a radio broadcast), and "downloading," in which a copy of music is delivered to a Web user's hard drive.

Streaming technologies allow a Web site user to listen to music that is "served" from Web sites. These technologies allow "instant gratification"—the music can be heard immediately. The consumer must be online to listen to the music, which is not retained for later listening.

Streaming technologies are used by Webcasters to play audio music recordings from "playlists" created by Web site employees (the Web version of an AM or FM radio broadcast). Some of the Web sites that use streaming to deliver music are interactive, allowing Web site users to select the type of music or specific songs they want to hear. Streaming is also used to provide music for online films, games, music videos, and greeting cards and to add music to the mix of content on Web sites (to enhance content and advertising features).

Download technologies give consumers a music file that is accessible when the consumer wants it from the consumer's hard drive. The file must be downloaded to the hard drive of the consumer's computer before the consumer can listen to it.

Initially, the download market was dominated by MP3 format technology. Files in the MP3 format typically do not contain security measures to prevent unauthorized distribution of music. Newer download technologies provide copyright protection tools enabling the copyright owner to control whether the consumer is able to make copies. Information on some of these technologies is available at www.riaa.com/tech (part of the Recording Industry Association of America's Web site).

Some Web sites use both streaming and download technologies. For example, many Web retail music sites that offer digital downloads for sale allow the consumer to listen without charge to a streamed audio clip prior to purchase.

A Music Copyright Primer

A recording of a single song is generally protected by two copyrights: the copyright on the song, known as the musical composition copyright, and the copyright on the recording of the song, known as the sound recording copyright.

Musical Compositions

Original musical compositions are protected by copyright as soon as they are fixed in any tangible medium of expression. Most composers in this country assign their copyrights to a music publishing company in exchange for a percentage of all future royalties generated by licensing the composition.

As with other intellectual property, the owner of a copyrighted musical composition has the exclusive right to:

■ Reproduce and distribute the musical composition in sheet music and in phonorecords. Phonorecords are defined in the Copyright Act as "material objects in which sounds, other than those accompanying a motion picture or other audiovisual work, are fixed…and from which the sounds can be perceived, reproduced, or otherwise communicated, either directly or with the aid of a machine or device." 17 USC § 101.

■ Modify the composition to create derivative works based on the composition.

- Publicly display the composition.

- Publicly perform the composition.

(These are the same rights discussed in "The Exclusive Rights," chapter 1.)

Licensing

The music industry has its own licensing terminology, and it is helpful to know the terminology when dealing with music publishers:

- **Mechanical license.** A license to copy and distribute a song in the form of records, tapes, or compact discs or by "digital phonorecord delivery" (download from the Internet) is known as a mechanical license.

- **Synchronization license.** A license to copy and distribute music in synchronization with an audiovisual work is known as a synchronization license (also called a synch license).

- **Performance license.** A license to publicly perform a song is known as a performance license. There are two types of performance licenses: nondramatic and dramatic performance licenses. A dramatic performance of a composition is a rendition that is woven into and carries forward a plot and its action (for example, an opera).

- **Parody authorization.** Permission to modify the lyrics to a song is known as parody authorization. The music publisher's contract with the songwriter may require that the songwriter give consent for alterations.

While some music publishers handle their own music licensing, many publishers have authorized licensing rights societies to act as their licensing agent for certain types of licenses. In the United States, three organizations handle nondramatic performance rights licenses—the American Society of Composers, Authors, and Publishers (ASCAP), Broadcast Music, Inc. (BMI), and the Society of European Stage Authors and Composers (SESAC). The liner notes for a recorded musical composition will usually indicate whether ASCAP, BMI, or SESAC handles performance rights for the song-for example, "1989 Lucy Jones Music (BMI)." The Harry Fox Agency (established by the National Music Publishers Association) handles mechanical rights for many music publishers. Contact information for these organizations is given in "Licensing Music for the Internet," later in this chapter.

For most types of works, whether to permit third parties to use a copyrighted work is solely up to the copyright owner. However, once a musical composition has been recorded and phonorecords of the recording distributed to the public, any other person may obtain a license to make and distribute phonorecords of the work to the public for private use, including by means of a digital phonorecord delivery. 17 USC § 115. This compulsory mechanical license provision is discussed in "Licensing for the Internet," later in this chapter.

Sound Recordings

Once musical compositions are recorded, the resulting sound recording is a separate work. It has a copyright that is separate from the copyrights on the musical compositions used in the recording. The copyright on a sound recording covers the original expression added by the record developer in creating the recording—the way the musical composition is sung on the recording, the way it is played, the musical arrangement, the sound engineer's mixing, and so on. Contracts between recording artists and record companies generally provide that sound recording copyrights are owned by the record companies. In the United States, the owner of a sound recording copyright gives notice of copyright by using the ℗ symbol.

EXAMPLE

The Dixie Chicks' CD *Fly* contains a song called "Goodbye Earl." According to the CD's liner notes and packaging, the copyright in the song is owned by EMI Blackwood Music Inc./Rising Gorge Music. The copyright in the sound recording is owned by Sony Music Entertainment Inc.

The Copyright Act defines sound recordings as "works that result from the fixation of a series of musical, spoken, or other sounds regardless of the nature of the material objects, such as discs, tapes, or other phonorecords, in which they are embodied." 17 USC § 101. According to U.S. law, only original sound recordings fixed and published on or after February 15, 1972, are protected by copyright. Pre-1972 sound recordings are not protected under federal copyright law. However, they may be protected under state law.

The United States was one of the last major countries to provide copyright protection for sound recordings. In most other countries, copyright protection was made available for sound recordings prior to 1972.

Foreign-made sound recordings, until recently, were treated the same in the United States as U.S.-made recordings—that is, no protection for pre-1972 recordings. However, effective January 1, 1996, pre-1972 foreign sound recordings whose "source country" is a member of the Berne Convention or the World Trade Organization are protected by copyright in the U.S. (This change in the law is part of the GATT legislation discussed in "Public Domain Works," chapter 9.)

According to U.S. law, the owner of a sound recording copyright has the exclusive right to reproduce and distribute phonorecords of the copyrighted work and to prepare derivative works based on the copyrighted work. In the U.S., unlike in other countries, from 1972 through 1995, sound recording copyright owners did not have a public performance right. Since 1996, sound recording copyright owners in the U.S. have had a limited public performance right, the exclusive right to "perform the copyrighted work publicly by means of a digital audio transmission." 17 USC § 106. More than 60 countries provide a full performance right for sound recordings.

Licensing

The Digital Millennium Copyright Act created a compulsory license for certain types of digital audio transmissions, 17 USC § 114(d). This compulsory license is discussed later in this chapter, in "Licensing Music for the Internet."

Licensing of sound recordings is handled by the copyright owners (record companies). There are no licensing rights societies for sound recording copyright owners. However, the Recording Industry Association of America (RIAA) issues compulsory licenses for its members and provides information on licensing (www.riaa.com).

Myths About Music Use

Don't believe the following myths about music copying:

Myth #1: "Copying a small amount is okay."

Many people think that it is permissible to use three or four bars of a song or a thirty-second clip without getting permission from the copyright owner. This is not true. Copying a small amount of a work is copyright infringement if (1) what is copied is a qualitatively substantial portion of the copied work; and (2) the use is not fair use. In one case, the court held that the sounds "Brrr" and "Hugga Hugga" used in a rap song could be sufficiently creative to warrant copyright protection. *Tin Pan Apple v. Miller Brewing Co.*, 1994 WL 62360 (SD NY 1994).

Myth #2: "No licenses are needed to use a thirty-second audio clip on the Web. That's fair use."

Whether using an audio clip of recorded music on a Web site is fair use can only be decided on a case-by-case basis using the four factors discussed in "When You Don't Need a License," chapter 9. Contrary to what you may have heard, so far there is no special fair use rule permitting the use of thirty-second clips on the Web. Many record companies are currently choosing not to enforce their rights against those making use of thirty-second clips (although they are reserving their right to object). The company DiscoverMusic.com (www.discovermusic.com) has made arrangements with major record companies to provide song samples to Internet music retailers.

Myth #3: "Digital sampling is okay."

Digital sampling means extracting portions of a prior recording for use in a new recording using a device that can store the copied material in a computer's memory. This process may be copyright infringement of both the sound recording and the copied musical composition. In 1991, a Federal District Court in New York enjoined all sales of a rap artist's album because the artist had included a digital sample of three words and accompanying music taken from a recording of the Gilbert & Sullivan song, "Alone Again (Naturally)." *Grand Upright Music Ltd. v. Warner Bros. Records, Inc.*, 780 FSupp 182 (SDNY 1991). While some digital sampling may be noninfringing—using a two-note phrase or a single grunt from a background singer, for example—it is difficult to know where to draw the line between infringing and noninfringing sampling. (De minimus copying—copying a small amount—is discussed in "Myths," chapter 9.)

Myth #4: "It's okay to copy a song's melody so long as I don't copy the lyrics."

Using the melody of a copyrighted song without the lyrics is infringement if you don't obtain a license. The copyright on a song covers both the lyrics and the melody. The fact that you have not copied the entire copyrighted work (lyrics plus melody) does not excuse the copying of the protected melody.

Myth #5: "It's okay to copy a song's melody if I use new words with the melody."

When you add new words to a song, you are "reproducing" the melody and creating a derivative work based on the original song, violating the copyright owner's reproduction and modification rights. (These rights are discussed in "The Exclusive Rights," chapter 1.) To lawfully use the melody of a copyrighted song with new lyrics, you need a license to modify the work.

Myth #6: "I bought this compact disc, so it's okay for me to use streaming technology to add a clip from it to my Web site."

The purchase of a copy of a protected work does not give the purchaser permission to exercise the copyright owner's exclusive rights with respect to the work. In copyright law, ownership of a copy of a protected work or of a phonorecord is separate from ownership of the copyright rights. (This topic is discussed in "Owning a Copy of a Work," chapter 3.) A provision added to the Copyright Act by the Digital Audio Home Recording Act of 1992 states that consumers who make noncommercial use of a "digital audio recording device" or medium or "analog recording device" or medium cannot be sued for copyright infringement. 17 USC § 1008. This provision creates a limited exception to the copyright owner's reproduction right. It allows a consumer to copy a purchased music CD to create an audiotape version to use in the car, for example.

Streaming music over the Web is an exercise of the public performance right (see "Licensing Music for the Internet," later in this chapter).

Myth #7: "It's okay to secretly tape a live musical performance and show the performance on my Web site."

Unfixed musical performances are not protected by copyright (see "Standards," chapter 1). However, 17 USC § 1101 states that those who record live musical performances without the consent of the performers are liable to the performers for damages and other remedies. This law is known as the antibootlegging law. The law also prohibits the reproduction, distribution, and transmission of unauthorized recordings of live musical performances. In addition, using the taped performance would infringe the copyrights on copyrighted musical compositions being performed.

MUSICIAN'S PERSPECTIVE

Interested in the musician's perspective on music business and legal issues? Prentice Hall publishes *The Musician's Business and Legal Guide* (Mark Halloran, Esq., Editor).

Licensing Music for the Internet

To use recorded music on the Web, generally you will need licenses from the copyright owners for the musical compositions and sound recordings you use. The owner of the musical composition copyright cannot authorize you to copy the version of the song that is fixed in the sound recording. The owner of the sound recording copyright cannot authorize you to use the song.

What rights you need to license from the musical composition and sound recording copyright owners depends on whether you will be using streaming technology, download technology, or both. If you wish, you can use a rights clearance agency (also known as a rights and permission agency) to obtain the music licenses you need. A rights clearance agency will find out who owns the copyrights and whether licenses are available for your intended use. These agencies also will negotiate license fees and obtain licenses for you. Rights clearance agencies are discussed in "Rights Clearance Agencies," chapter 10. A list of these agencies is in appendix C.

Streaming

Musical Compositions

To stream music over the Internet, you'll need a public performance license from the owner of the musical composition. Streaming a musical composition is considered a public performance of the musical composition. Public performance licenses can be obtained from the licensing rights societies: ASCAP (www.ascap.com), BMI (www.bmi.com), and SESAC (www.sesac.com). Each of these organizations has an Internet license, and each has a Web site area giving information on Web licensing (www.ascap.com/weblicense, www.bmi.com/iama/webmaster, and www.sesac.com/web.htm). The Web licensing areas include a copy of the standard license agreement, rate information, and an email contact address for questions. These organizations grant only nonexclusive rights.

The ASCAP, BMI, and SESAC licenses are "blanket licenses" authorizing the licensee to use all the songs in the licensing organization's catalog. These licenses are more appropriate for Webcasting sites (or other sites or products involving the use of many musical compositions) than they are for the Web site or online product using only a small number of musical compositions. Public performance licenses can also be obtained on a song-by-song basis from the copyright owners for the compositions you want to use—the best approach if you plan to use clips from only a small number of musical compositions. Music libraries, discussed later in this chapter, may be able to provide you with appropriate music, simplifying this aspect of the licensing process.

You also will need to negotiate directly with copyright owners if your use is dramatic use. The performing rights societies only license nondramatic uses. Whether a use of music is dramatic or nondramatic must be determined on a case-by-case basis. A dramatic performance of a composition is a rendition that is woven into and carries forward a plot and its action (for example, an opera).

INTERNATIONAL RIGHTS

ASCAP, BMI, and SESAC license performance rights only for the United States. Similar organizations exist for other parts of the world. The Web site www.kohnmusic.com has links to some of the international performing rights societies. At the present, many U.S.-based licensees are not trying to obtain licenses to international rights, due to the complexity of doing so. They are obtaining only U.S. rights. Other U.S.-based licensees are using technological devices to limit access to their Web sites to U.S.-based users, thus avoiding the need for international licenses.

If you need to locate a copyright owner for a song and have a record, tape, or compact disc of the song, you may find the name of the copyright owner for the song in the liner notes (for example, "Sunny Day," by Susie Songwriter, Copyright 1992 XYZ Music, Inc.). The ASCAP, BMI, and SESAC Web sites contain searchable song databases (although the organizations do not guarantee the accuracy of the information), as does the Web site www.songfile.snap.com. You also can look up older songs by title in the *Catalog of Copyright Entries* to find out who registered the copyright. An assignment search will tell you whether the copyright has been assigned. (The Catalog and assignment searches are discussed in "Determining Who Owns the Copyright," chapter 10).

It is not possible to stream music directly from a CD. The CD must be copied into the hard drive of the Webcaster's (or other music provider's) computer—raising the question of whether streaming requires reproduction right permission in addition to public performance right permission. According to the "ephemeral recording" provision of the Copyright Act, if you have a public performance license for a composition, you do not need to separately license the reproduction right of the music if you are making only one copy of a particular transmission program embodying the performance and you meet three other conditions: (1) The copy is retained and used solely by the transmitting organization, and no further copies are made; (2) The copy is used solely for the transmitting organization's own transmissions or for purposes of archival preservation or security; and (3) The copy is destroyed within six months from the date the transmission program was first transmitted (or preserved exclusively for archival purposes). 17 USC § 112 (a). If you need more than one copy or do not meet the three conditions, you will need a reproduction license from the copyright owner or the Harry Fox Agency (discussed later in this section).

Whether you need a synch license depends on whether you will be using the music in synchronization with an audiovisual work. For example, a synch license would not be needed for Webcasting, but it would be needed for a streamed music video or animated cartoon (where the music is coordinated with performers' actions). The Harry Fox Agency handles synch licenses for many copyright owners. If the agency does not handle synch licenses for the music publisher whose music you want to use, you will need to get a license directly from the publisher.

Streaming does not require a mechanical license (license to make and distribute phonorecords). However, if you are offering downloads as well as streaming, you will need a mechanical license from the Harry Fox Agency, as discussed in "Downloads," later in this section.

Sound Recordings

Streaming an audio clip from recorded music is considered public performance of the sound recording by means of a digital audio transmission—an exercise of the sound recording copyright owner's limited public performance right. (This right is discussed earlier in this chapter, in "A Music Copyright Primer.") The Copyright Act provides a compulsory license provision for subscription and "eligible nonsubscription" Webcasting that meets certain criteria, including a limit on how many songs from one sound recording can be played in a three-hour period and how many songs in a row from a single artist can be played. 17 USC § 114(d)(2). These criteria are designed to prevent or at least deter listeners from making their own recordings from transmissions (instead of buying the material). They are listed at the "Web Licensing" section of the RIAA Web site (www.riaa.com/weblic/wlwcast.htm).

To operate under a statutory license, you must file an "Initial Notice" with the Copyright Office prior to making transmissions. The Copyright Office has posted a suggested form for the Initial Notice at www.loc.gov/copyright/licensing/format.html. Rates for the statutory license are to be set by a three-member arbitration panel to convene in late 2000. The process could take several years. The alternative is to negotiate your own licenses.

Webcasters that do not meet the criteria for the compulsory license must negotiate licenses with the RIAA or record companies, as discussed in "A Music Copyright Primer," earlier in this chapter. For more information on compulsory or negotiated licenses to use sound recordings, contact Steven Marks at RIAA (smarks@riaa.com, telephone 202-775-0101) or the licensing department at a record company.

The compulsory license is available only for transmissions whose primary purpose is to provide the public with audio or other entertainment programming (such as Web radio), not for transmissions whose primary purpose is to sell, advertise, or promote products or services other than sound recordings, live concerts, or other music-related events. 17 USC § 114(d)(2) and (j)(6) (definition of "eligible nonsubscription transmission"). If you are planning to use music to make your e-commerce site more interesting (not to sell or promote music), the compulsory license is not applicable. You need a negotiated license from the sound recording copyright owners.

The compulsory license is not available for "interactive services." 17 USC § 114(d)(2)(A)(i). An interactive service is one that enables a member of the public to receive a transmission of a program specially created for the recipient, or, on request, a transmission of a particular sound recording selected by the recipient. Special requests do not make a service interactive if the programming does not substantially consist of sound recordings that are performed within one hour of the request or at a time designated by the transmitting entity or the requesting party. 17 USC § 114(j)(7).

If a Webcaster qualifies for the compulsory public performance license or has a negotiated public performance license to use a sound recording, separate reproduction right permission is not needed to make one "ephemeral" copy of the sound recording if the conditions of Section 112(a) (discussed earlier in this section) are met. (The earlier discussion of Section 112(a) was in the context of musical compositions. However, that provision also applies to sound recordings.) If more than one copy is needed, a compulsory license is available. If the conditions of Section 112(a) are not met, separate reproduction permission must be negotiated.

Downloads

Musical Compositions

To provide downloads of musical compositions from recordings, you generally need a mechanical license authorizing you to reproduce and distribute the compositions. As we discussed earlier in this chapter, once a song has been recorded, anyone can get a compulsory license to record and distribute the song. Congress included provisions in the Digital Millennium Copyright Act stating that the compulsory mechanical license applies to "digital phonorecord deliveries" (deliveries by digital transmission). 17 USC § 115(a).

The current rate is stated on the Harry Fox Agency Web site, www.nmpa.org/hfa.html. Most record companies obtain mechanical licenses from Harry Fox rather than relying on the compulsory license "Notice of Intent" procedure of the Copyright Act. You may contact the Internet Licensing Information Department at Harry Fox by email at ihotline@harryfox.com. The phone number for the agency is (212) 370-5330.

If you are offering sample clips on your Web site, in addition to providing downloads, you need permission to exercise the public performance right— either blanket licenses from the performing rights societies (discussed earlier, in "Streaming") or song-by-song negotiated licenses with the owners of the musical composition copyrights.

Sound Recordings

To offer downloads, you also will need licenses from the sound recording copyright owners authorizing reproduction and distribution. No compulsory licenses are available, so licenses must be negotiated. You may also need artist and AFM permissions, as discussed earlier in this chapter. If you will be offering sample clips as well as downloads, you will need permission to exercise the public performance right in the sound recordings as well.

Licensing Tips

As with other types of works, before you begin negotiating for a license, you should know exactly what use you will make of the licensed music and disclose all your planned uses. (See "Determining What Rights You Need," chapter 10). You will need to provide detailed information before you are quoted a license fee (music publishers use the information on your planned uses in determining their fee).

If you want the right to use the music in more than one Web site or Web product, the license must explicitly give you that right. Consequently, the licensing agent needs to know what you want.

EXAMPLE

Developer obtained a license to use a five-second excerpt of Music Publisher's copyrighted song in Developer's online game, *Geek*. Developer later used the same excerpt in another game, *Geek 2*. Developer's use of the music in *Geek 2* is copyright infringement.

License Terms

The license should cover the following points:

■ Definition of the Web sites or products in which the music can be used (by title or by description or both). Pay careful attention to this provision. To be able to use the licensed music in future versions or in sequels, you must include future versions or sequels in this definition.

■ Authorized uses, including any limitations on the amount of the work that can be copied and used.

■ Consideration for the license, whether royalties, one-time fee, or some other form of consideration. If your use of a music clip is promotional, the record company may waive the fee.

■ Term (duration) of the license.

■ Whether the license is exclusive or nonexclusive. (These terms are defined in "Licenses," chapter 3.)

■ Warranties and indemnity. (See "Obtaining a License," chapter 10.) In chapter 10, we recommend that you try to get a warranty of noninfringement and an indemnity from all copyright owners who grant you licenses. Music publishers generally will give you only a limited indemnity in which their exposure is limited to the amount of the license fee.

Licensing is discussed in more detail in chapter 10.

After You Get a License

Once you have obtained a license, stick to its terms. Do only what you are authorized to do. Be careful to comply with all your license obligations, such as royalty payments. Failure to make royalty payments as required by the license may be material breach of contract. (Breach is discussed in "What Is a Contract?," chapter 4.) If you are required by the license to pay royalties every quarter and you have a quarter in which you make nothing and so owe no royalties, tell the licensor that no royalties are due for that quarter.

Other Music Options

In this section, we discuss music options other than licensing copyrighted musical compositions and sound recordings.

Recording Your Own Version

If you record your own version of a copyrighted musical composition, you will need a license from the musical composition's copyright owner. However, you will not need a license from a record company (you will not be using a sound recording). Whether you hire musicians or use a production service, you should get a written contract with an appropriate copyright assignment or work made for hire provision. (See "Copyright Ownership," chapter 6.)

The antibootlegging law mentioned in "Myths About Music Use," earlier in this chapter, prohibits making audio or video recordings of live musical performances without the consent of the performers. While it is possible that performer consent would be implied in a recording studio situation, cautious record producers are obtaining performance consents for recording sessions.

Musicians' union issues are covered in "Signing Collective Bargaining Agreements," chapter 22. If you are using a production service, your contract with the service should state who is responsible for paying any applicable American Federation of Musicians union fees—you or the production service.

SOUND-ALIKE RECORDINGS

In 1988, Bette Midler won a $400,000 judgment in federal court in California against an ad agency that used a sound-alike version of her hit, "Do You Want to Dance." *Midler v. Ford Motor Co.*, 849 F2d 460 (9th Cir 1988). The singer who recorded the sound-alike version—a backup singer for Ms. Midler—was instructed to sound as much as possible like the Bette Midler record. The court held that the ad agency had appropriated what was not theirs. You should not create sound-alike recordings without consulting an experienced attorney.

Creating Original Music

You may think that creating original music for your Web site or Web-based products is not practical because you don't know any composers, and you can't afford to pay for original music. Both of these assumptions are incorrect. Full-service music arranging and composing services with reasonable fees can be found in most major cities. You can find them by doing Web searches for "Music Arrangers and Composers" and similar terms and by consulting telephone book Yellow Pages and video industry directories.

A full-service arranging and composing facility can provide orchestration and production of the finished piece as well as composition. It can also create a sound recording (known in the music industry as a "master recording") of the original music. If the arranging and composing service will be creating the master, it is a good idea to get written consents from musicians and vocalists before the recording session begins.

Like your other production contracts, your agreement with a music arranging and composing service should take the form of a signed written contract (see "Written Contracts," chapter 4). The contract should spell out the rights and duties of each party to the agreement. The contract should cover the following points:

- Whether the arranging and composing service is obligated to compose; compose and arrange; or compose, arrange, and produce the master recording.

- Who will own the copyright in the music (and in the master recording, if one is to be made). If you obtain ownership of the copyrights in the music and in the master recording, you can use the music again in the future without worrying about copyright clearance and license fees (see "Using Works That You Own," chapter 9). To avoid future legal disputes with the arranging and composing service and to provide you with maximum flexibility, the contract should state that you will own all rights, including the copyrights, everywhere in the world and for all time. To ensure that you obtain ownership, your agreement should also contain a copyright assignment or work made for hire provision (see "Copyright Ownership," chapter 6).

- How much you will pay for the service's work and when payment is due.

- Who will pay any applicable American Federation of Musicians union fees, if the service is to create the master recording as well as compose and arrange the music. (See "Unions and Web Production," chapter 22.)

- Whether the agreement is assignable. If you are expecting the work to be done by particular individuals who are employed by the arranging and composing service, the contract should state that the work must be done by those individuals and that the service cannot assign its contract obligations to another party. (See "Contracts with Independent Contractors," chapter 6.)

Your contract with the arranging and composing service should include a warranty by the service that the material is original and does not infringe upon third parties' copyrights, trademarks, or other property rights. The contract should also include an indemnity provision. (Warranty and indemnity provisions are discussed in "Contracts with Independent Contractors," Chapter 6.)

Public Domain Music

If you can locate appropriate public domain music, you are free to use it—that is, you are free to record your own version of the public domain song. You cannot lawfully copy a public domain song as recorded on a copyrighted record, tape, or compact disc unless you get a license from the record company that owns the sound recording copyright.

EXAMPLE

Bay Multimedia plans to use excerpts from a 1987 recording of Bach's *Brandenberg Concerto No. 4* as background music in a Web film. The concerto is in the public domain, but Bay still needs a license from the record company that owns the sound recording copyright.

Copyrighted Arrangements

While you are free to use a public domain work, you cannot (unless you obtain a license) use a copyrighted *arrangement* of a public domain work. An arrangement of a public domain work is, if sufficiently original, a separate copyrightable work. (See the discussion of derivative works in "Public Domain Works," chapter 9). If you want to use the public domain elements of a copyrighted arrangement, you may need a musicologist to separate the public domain elements from the arrangement's copyrighted elements.

Finding Public Domain Music

You can sometimes find out whether a song is in the public domain by looking at the copyright notice. If the copyright date is earlier than January 1, 1923, the work is in the public domain. If the copyright date is January 1, 1923, or later, the song could still be in the public domain (for reasons discussed in "Public Domain Works," chapter 9).

Every major city has dealers that handle old sheet music. Try a Web search or Yellow Pages search for "sheet music" and similar terms. The Lincoln Center Library of the Performing Arts in New York City has an extensive collection of old songs. ASCAP and BMI catalogs—which include many copyrighted arrangements—indicate the public domain status of underlying works for arrangements. Here are four resource books that provide lists of public domain songs:

■ The ASCAP booklet, *ASCAP Hit Songs*

■ *Kohn on Music Licensing*, a book by Al Kohn and Bob Kohn (www.kohnmusic.com)

■ The *Mini-Encyclopedia of Public domain Songs* from BZ/Rights and Permissions (send an email to mini@bzrights.com for information on ordering it)

■ *PDR Music Bible* from Public Domain Report, www.footagesources.com/pdr/pdr.html

In searching for public domain works, don't be fooled by a recent copyright notice and date on what is actually an arrangement of a public domain work. For example, if a new arrangement of a public domain folk tune shows a 1993 copyright date, you cannot—without obtaining a license—use the new arrangement, but you can use the public domain version of the song.

If someone else has written lyrics for a public domain tune, you are free to write your own lyrics for that tune. Both of you are creating new derivative works based on a public domain tune. If you use an arranger or lyricist to create the new lyrics, make certain that your contract with the arranger or lyricist includes a copyright assignment or work made for hire provision (see "Copyright Ownership," chapter 6).

Using Music from Music Libraries

If you don't want to create your own music, deal with rights clearance, or pay license fees, and you can't find suitable public domain music, you may be able to obtain appropriate music from music libraries. A list of music libraries appears in appendix D.

Music libraries specialize in providing "cleared" music—music in which they own both the song and the sound recording copyrights. Many libraries now offer their material in digital audio form.

Make sure that the music library you choose can provide you with all the rights you need. Some music libraries grant only limited licenses to use the works they license. If you are using a "copyright-free" sample, read the fine print to make certain you can use the work as you plan to use it.

CHAPTER 22

UNION ISSUES

Many people who work in the entertainment industry are represented by unions. Performers in the movie and television industries are represented by the Screen Actors Guild (SAG) and the American Federation of Television and Radio Artists (AFTRA). Recording and radio artists are also represented by AFTRA. Film and television directors are represented by the Directors Guild of America (DGA). Screenwriters are represented by the Writers Guild of America (WGA) and musicians by the American Federation of Musicians (AFM). In addition, there are unions for technical workers.

The unions have collective bargaining agreements with many entertainment industry employers. A company that signs a collective bargaining agreement with a union must comply with the union's numerous rules concerning employee pay, benefits, and working conditions.

This chapter deals with two issues:

- ■ Signing collective bargaining agreements.

- ■ Reuse of material created by union members.

Signing Collective Bargaining Agreements

In mature sectors of the entertainment industry such as motion pictures and television, if you sign a union's collective bargaining agreement, you will be bound for the duration of the agreement (usually several years) to comply with all provisions of the agreement. The collective bargaining agreement's provisions on hiring, contracts, work conditions, and pay will, in effect, be "written in" to your contracts with people you hire to do work under those agreements. Those provisions will apply to all your productions during the term of the agreement.

Because the online film industry is new, the entertainment unions are currently taking a different approach to Web production companies—permitting them to sign on a "single picture" picture basis. The "single picture" approach means that if you sign, you will be bound by the terms of the agreement for the picture covered by the agreement, not for a term of several years.

Collective bargaining agreement requirements vary from union to union, because each agreement was negotiated separately by union representatives and industry representatives.

If You Don't Sign

Union members are prohibited from working for those who have not signed the union's collective bargaining agreement. A member of the Writers Guild of America, for example, is prohibited from accepting employment with or selling literary material to a nonsignatory. If you plan to hire screenwriters, performers, directors, or musicians, you may find that the most qualified people in these professions are union members. You will not be able to hire union members unless you sign collective bargaining agreements.

If You Sign

If you sign a collective bargaining agreement, you generally will not be permitted to hire nonunion members to do work that is within the scope of the agreement. (This is not true of the Writers Guild. See "Writer's Guild," later in this chapter.) For example, if you sign the Directors Guild agreement, you can hire a director who is not a member of the guild only if that director joins the guild.

Signing one union's collective bargaining agreement (SAG's, for example) does not mean that you have to use union members for work not covered by the agreement (electrical work, for example).

Unions and Web Production

The entertainment industry unions' collective bargaining agreements for Web and interactive productions are discussed in this section.

SAG and AFTRA

SAG (www.sag.org) and AFTRA (www.aftra.com) represent performers. Traditionally, SAG has represented motion picture performers, and AFTRA has represented radio and television performers and recording artists. However, over the years, the jurisdictional lines between the two unions have become blurred. At present, both unions consider the use of performers in the production of new material for new online works and CD-ROM products such as computer games an area of shared jurisdiction. (That means you can pick the union with which you want to sign.) Most professional performers belong to both SAG and AFTRA.

EXAMPLE

Developer plans to hire three performers to act in an online film production. If Developer wants to sign with one of the performers' unions (so he will be able to use union performers), he can sign with either SAG or AFTRA.

Some companies sign with both unions.

AFTRA has exclusive jurisdiction over recording artists. If you want to use an AFTRA recording artist in your project, you will have to sign an agreement with AFTRA.

SAG and AFTRA both have collective bargaining agreements for various industries (motion picture industry, television, industrial films, and CD-ROM production). Neither SAG nor AFTRA has yet developed a standard collective bargaining agreement for online productions. SAG and AFTRA rates for Web production work vary, as rates are currently being negotiated for each production.

SAG

SAG is currently negotiating separate agreements with each individual Web production company that asks to sign. These agreements incorporate some of the terms of SAG's Interactive Media Agreement, developed in the early 1990s to cover CD-ROM computer game production. Because online products have unique distribution issues, certain provisions in the Interactive Media Agreement are not appropriate for Web production. (The SAG Interactive Media Agreement and "frequently asked questions" concerning the agreement are online at www.sag.org/interactive.html.)

Allen Weingartner, Senior Administrator for Industrial/Interactive Contracts at SAG, has indicated that SAG is willing to be flexible with Web producers, granting one-year Web use rights for a union performer's work for a lower price than the performer pay rates that apply to film and television production. In certain circumstances, SAG may be willing to accept deferred pay contracts, allowing performers to work for less money up front if the performers receive an equity stake in the production.

For more information on signing with SAG, contact Allen Weingartner by email at Aweingartner@sag.org or by telephone at (323) 549- 6847

PLAN AHEAD

If you plan to use SAG or AFTRA performers in your Web productions, think carefully about how you plan to use the footage in which the performers are featured. Your agreement will give you the right to use the performers' performance in the specific product covered by your agreement with SAG or AFTRA. If you later decide you want to use the performance in other products, you'll have to obtain the performers' consent and pay them again. If you know that you will want to use the material in several different products, it makes sense to get "integration rights" (the right to include the material from the performers' performance in other products) when you sign your agreement.

AFTRA

AFTRA is currently using a short Experimental Internet Agreement with Web production companies. A copy of the Internet Agreement is included in appendix B (Form 13).

The Experimental Internet Agreement does not include standard pay rates. Rates are negotiated with each Web production company on a case-by-case basis and added to the standard agreement as appendix A.

AFTRA, like SAG, generally grants one-year Web use rights for a union performer's work. The pay rate for Web production work is generally lower than the performer pay rates that apply to film and television production. A Web producer who is willing to commit to an AFTRA agreement covering multiple productions generally receives a more favorable performer rate than a producer who is only signing the Interactive Agreement for a single short production.

According to Rebecca Rhine, West Coast Director for AFTRA, the current five-page Internet Agreement will likely evolve into a standard Internet Agreement with set minimum pay rates once a pattern emerges and larger content providers engage in bargaining with AFTRA. Web producers who want to have input into the provisions of this anticipated full agreement should get involved in the discussions with AFTRA now, she says, taking advantage of the window of opportunity to develop a model for the future.

For more information on signing with AFTRA, contact Rebecca Rhine by email at rrhine@aftra.com or by telephone at (415) 391-7510.

Writers Guild of America

The Writers Guild (WGA) is currently using a one-page contract with Web producers for material that is nonepisodic and does not resemble television programs. This contract, known as the Interactive Program Contract, covers writing for online use other than online news format reporting and other text-only material. It may be used on a per project, per writer basis.

The Interactive Program Contract does not set compensation rates. Compensation is to be determined by the Web producer and the WGA member hired by the producer. The contract simply requires a Web producer to pay 12.5 percent of the agreed-upon compensation to the guild's pension and health plans for the member who is hired. A developer can also hire a non-WGA writer under the contract, in order to permit the writer to earn membership points toward full WGA membership and become eligible for WGA pension and health benefits.

Web producers who are creating episodic material resembling television programs cannot use the one-page contract. They must sign a collective bargaining agreement with minimum rate provisions (cable television rates, most likely).

If you are interested in finding out more about the Writers Guild, contact Grace Reiner in the Contracts department of the Writer's Guild by email at greiner@wga.org or telephone at (323) 782-4501, or visit the WGA Web site a www.wga.org.

Directors Guild of America

The Directors Guild (DGA) is currently using a single-picture agreement called the Internet Pictures Sideletter with Web producers. According to Warren Adler, Western Executive Secretary for DGA, "Interactive movies are an exciting new business that promises to offer significant additional employment opportunities for DGA members."

The Internet Pictures Sideletter is available for pictures that will be exploited mainly on the Internet on free Web sites. Pictures made under the sideletter can be used on free Web sites for an unlimited period of time without the payment of any additional fees. However, if a picture that was made under the sideletter is exhibited in theaters, on free or pay television, on home video, or on airplanes, additional fees called residuals apply.

The sideletter does not set minimum compensation levels for DGA members. Compensation is to be negotiated between the employer and the DGA member. Certain provisions from existing DGA collective bargaining provisions are incorporated into the sideletter.

In addition to directors, DGA represents film production managers and assistant directors for film productions, and associate directors and stage managers for videotape productions. Generally, a signatory must hire a full DGA crew if the project involves work for the whole crew. However, the DGA is flexible about scaling down the hiring requirement for smaller productions.

If you are interested in finding out more about the Directors Guild or in signing a collective bargaining agreement with the DGA, contact Warren Adler by telephone at (310) 289-2003 or by email at warren@dga.org, or visit the DGA Web site at www.dga.org.

American Federation of Musicians

Most professional musicians belong to the American Federation of Musicians (AFM). The work of AFM musicians is being used on the Internet in many different contexts—including live "streaming" Webcast performances of music, music recorded specifically for Web sites, and music recorded for commercials used on the Internet.

If you want to use AFM musicians in a live Webcast or to record music for a Web site, you will need to sign a Special Letter of Agreement with the AFM. This Letter of Agreement will state how much you must pay the musicians and what Pension Fund and Health and Welfare Fund contributions you must make. For current rates, contribution requirements, and applicable conditions, see "Interactive/Multimedia Projects" at www.afm.org. (Go to AFM Departments, Electronic Media Services Division, then click on "Interactive/Multimedia.")

To obtain a Special Letter of Agreement or ask questions about the AFM, contact Sue Collins, Contract Administrator, Interactive/New Media, at the AFM's West Coast office by email (scollins@afm.org), telephone (323-461-3441, extension 202), or fax (323-462-8340). The information the AFM will need is stated at www.afm.org. To obtain information on pay scales and conditions for using AFM musicians to record music for commercials or to use existing commercials on the Internet, contact Callum Benepe in the Commercials Department at (323) 461-3441, extension 206.

PERMITTED USES

An AFM Special Letter of Agreement gives the producer named in the letter the right to use the AFM musicians' performance in a specific way—for example, the right to use up to five minutes of recorded music as menu music for a specific Web site, or the right to Webcast a live performance from a location in a specified city on a certain date at a certain time. If you want to use the musicians' work in more than one Web site or archive a Webcast, make that clear when you request your Special Letter of Agreement (and expect to pay more).

Reuse Provisions

Even if you don't sign a union collective bargaining agreement, the reuse provisions of these agreements will affect you if you want to use an excerpt from a movie or television show or from a master recording of music.

Reuse provisions fall into two categories:

- Reuse fees (fees for using preexisting material).

- Consent requirements.

The Directors Guild, Writers Guild, and American Federation of Musicians collective bargaining agreements all require that a signatory pay fees to union members involved in creating a work if that work (or a portion of it) is used in a different production.

EXAMPLE

Producer, a signatory to the Writers Guild collective bargaining agreement, owns the copyright in *Hotdog*, a motion picture that is based on a screenplay written by Victor, a member of the Writers Guild. Producer wants to use a portion of *Hotdog* in a new online game. Producer will have to pay Writers Guild reuse fees to Victor (even though Producer has already paid Victor for his work on the *Hotdog* screenplay).

SAG and AFTRA collective bargaining agreements require that a performer's consent be obtained before the photography or soundtrack of a performer's work is used in a picture or program in a medium other than the picture or program for which the performer was employed.

Other unions' agreements also have consent requirements.

Reuse fees and consent requirements are discussed in this section.

Reuse Fees

Fees paid for using a portion of an existing work are called "reuse fees" or "new use fees." Fees paid to use an entire program in a different market—to show an entire episode of a television program on the Internet, for example—are called "supplemental market fees."

The theory behind the reuse and supplemental market fee provisions is that using existing material takes away jobs that would be available if new material had been created instead. These fees are substantial.

The company for whom the performer did the work is actually responsible for paying the reuse fees. If the copyright has been assigned, the assignee generally assumes this obligation. Your licensor will either require you to pay these fees or add them to your license fee. Your license should include a warranty that any applicable union reuse fees have been paid. (See "Obtaining a License," chapter 10.)

If you want to use an excerpt from a work that was created before the 1950s, you should call the unions whose members were involved in the work and find out when the union's collective bargaining agreement reuse provisions went into effect. You may find that you can use the material without paying reuse fees, because the reuse provisions were not in effect when the work was made. Always check with the appropriate unions on this issue.

Consent Requirements

Several of the entertainment industry unions have consent requirements for the reuse of existing material. Those requirements are discussed in this section.

Performers

The SAG and AFTRA collective bargaining agreements for motion pictures, television, and interactive media state that no part of the photography or sound track of a performer can be used in a picture or program in any medium other than the picture or program for which the performer was employed without separately bargaining and reaching an agreement with the performer regarding payment for the reuse. These agreements also limit the extent to which a performance can be altered.

The performer is not permitted to consent to reuse at the time of original employment. Either you or the copyright owner will have to negotiate for the consent of performers who are shown or heard in clips you plan to use. To start the consent process, contact the appropriate union. For motion picture and film clips, contact SAG if the material was originally shot on film. Contact AFTRA if it originally was shot on videotape. The union will put you in touch with the performers' agents. If the clip you want to use shows a deceased performer, the union will put you in touch with the performer's executor.

The consent requirement does not apply to AFTRA non-network, nonprime time programs, but reuse fees apply to such programs. Contact AFTRA for more information.

Recording Artists

AFTRA represents recording artists as well as performers. If you want to use an excerpt from a master recording that involves the voice of an AFTRA recording artist, contact AFTRA to start the consent process.

OUTSIDE WORK

Union performers sometimes do work outside the jurisdiction of the union (outside the United States, for example, or in print media). The consent requirement discussed here does not apply to such work, only to work produced under a collective bargaining agreement.

Screenwriters

The Writers Guild's standard contract contains a unique "separation of rights" provision that gives the writer the right to retain certain rights in his or her script. Because of separation of rights, a Writers Guild member who no longer owns the copyright in a script he or she wrote may own certain rights that you need to license to lawfully use a clip of a movie or television program that is based on that script. Rights retained under the separation of rights provision can include the following rights:

- **Publication right**. This is the right to publish the work in any book, magazine, or periodical.

- **Sequel right**. This is the right to use the leading character or characters of a work for a different story in a television program or a motion picture.

- **Merchandising right**. This is the right to manufacture and to sell objects first fully described in the literary material.

If you want to use a film clip and the writer has retained any of these rights, you should get permission from the writer to use the clip (as well as a license from the copyright owner).

Directors

According to the Directors Guild Basic Agreement, a director must be consulted if a theatrical motion picture made by the director is edited for distribution in other media or licensed for videodisc or videocassette. In addition, some directors have a contractual right to approve alterations of the works they made.

Musicians

The American Federation of Musicians collective bargaining agreements state that use of an existing master recording in a new work requires the union's consent (in addition to the payment of fees for the new use, discussed in "Reuse Fees," earlier in this chapter). Information on the AFM's fee and consent requirements is available from Sue Collins and Callum Benepe, whose contact information is given in "Unions and Web Production," earlier in this chapter.

Other Legal Issues

In addition to dealing with union reuse requirements, if you plan to use film or television clips or excerpts of master recordings on the Web, you must obtain copyright licenses from all copyright owners and, for commercial use, you must get right of publicity releases from all performers shown or heard in the clip or excerpt. Clearing these rights can be complicated and expensive.

Licensing film and television clips is discussed in chapter 11. Copyright licenses are discussed in chapters 9 and 10. Music licenses are discussed in chapter 21.

CHAPTER 23

THE LAW OF EMAIL

Eric J. Sinrod & Jeffrey W. Reyna
Copyright 2000 by Eric J. Sinrod and Jeffrey W. Reyna

Introduction[1]

Electronic mail or email is by far the most prevalent medium of communication in cyberspace. Use of email in both commercial and noncommercial settings raises a slew of legal questions, the answers to many of which are still being developed. This chapter focuses on the legal issues surrounding email that are most relevant to the business enterprise. These areas include: (1) use of email as a marketing, commercial, or advertising tool, (2) issues associated with employee use of email and/or an employer's policies regarding permissible use and monitoring of employee email communications, and (3) issues surrounding the use of email in litigation (with an emphasis on discoverability of email and rules of evidence).

Eric J. Sinrod is a partner in the national law firm of Duane, Morris and Hecksher LLP. He can be reached at ejsinrod@duanemorris.com or eric@sinrodlaw.com. Jeffrey W. Reyna is a member of the eCommerce & Internet practice group at McCutchen, Doyle, Brown & Enersen LLP. He can be reached at jreyna@mdbe.com.

Commercial Use of Email and the Potential Pitfalls of Anti-"Spam" Laws

Overview

Email became a conduit for commercial activity on the Internet long before e-commerce came to be associated with polished Web storefronts. Today, businesses use email as an integral part of their Internet business model. For example, email has become an integral part of customer service operations for many online businesses, and is often used as an adjunct to, or even in lieu of, a toll-free customer service line. For some time, email has been used as an advertising and marketing tool. And, even though a wide range of marketing models that use email exist (e.g. unsolicited mass commercial emails vs. direct-response customer mailing lists), many individuals and legislators have come to focus on what is broadly defined as "spam."[2]

Though an exact definition of "spam" is elusive,[3] for purposes of our discussion we will define "spam" or "unsolicited commercial email" as unsolicited commercial email messages or advertisements of a commercial nature. Until recently, the battles waged over bulk emails had been the exclusive province of private regulation or self-help mechanisms. Various email filtering software products exist on the market today. At the same time, many private organizations have sprung up to deal with the "problem" of unsolicited commercial email.[4] These organizations' main purpose is to promote awareness of the problems associated with "spam" and lobby for legislative solutions. Others have taken matters into their own hands and created "blackhole lists" that block all email from Internet or IP addresses[5] that have been identified as sources of "spam."[6]

Currently, there is no federal legislation regulating unsolicited commercial email.[7] However, fourteen states have entered the fray and have enacted legislation directly regulating unsolicited commercial email. Of course, given the borderless nature of cyberspace, such piecemeal regulation is of limited effectiveness and raises a slew of regulatory problems and constitutional (jurisdictional) concerns.

Yet, any business that incorporates email into its operations needs to be aware of the extent to which state regulation and court decisions may impact the commercial use of email. In this section, we provide an analysis and overview of all state laws dealing with unsolicited commercial email and then briefly outline the actions courts have been willing to take in this area.

State Regulation of Unsolicited Commercial Email

Fueled by strong public opinion against "spam," states have led the rush to regulate the most egregious forms of unsolicited commercial email. As the chart at the end of this chapter demonstrates,[8] many of the state laws share common characteristics. For example, many states require that unsolicited commercial emails include specific language in the subject line, or contain instructions that recipients can follow to opt-out of receiving further emails. Many state laws also prohibit the falsification of email routing information or the use of another's domain name without authorization. Finally, many of the laws specifically include broad exceptions for emails sent pursuant to a preexisting relationship or with the consent of the recipient.

In this section, we provide a detailed analysis of each of the fourteen state laws regulating unsolicited commercial email.

California

California has enacted three pieces of legislation that deal with unsolicited commercial advertisements sent via email. Two of these regulate the content of unsolicited commercial emails and provide for civil enforcement. The third provides criminal penalties for unauthorized use of a domain name when sending commercial email. These statutes have formed the basis for one of the first successful actions for damages brought by an ISP against a sender of unsolicited commercial email.[9]

■ **Business & Professions Code §17538.4**

This provision prohibits the transmission of unsolicited commercial advertisements over email unless the sender includes in the email a toll-free telephone number and/or valid return email address which the recipient of the email can use to "notify the sender not to email any further unsolicited documents."[10] The unsolicited email must also include a statement indicating that the recipient can call the toll-free number or submit an email to the return address provided in order to request that the sender cease sending emails to any email address specified by the recipient.[11] The law specifically requires the sender of the email, once notified of the recipient's desire not to receive any further advertisements, to cease transmitting emails to that address.[12] Finally, unsolicited commercial email advertisements must include the characters "ADV:" as the first four characters of the subject line.[13]

This provision applies to any "unsolicited emailed documents...delivered to a California resident via an electronic mail service provider's service or equipment located" in California.[14] The definition of "unsolicited emailed documents" covers most messages sent with a commercial purpose,[15] but does not include messages that:

1. are sent to someone with which the sender has an "existing business or personal relationship," or

2. are sent at the request, or with the express consent, of the recipient.[16]

Finally, this statute allows any employer who owns more than one email address to notify the sender of unsolicited commercial advertisements to cease sending such emails to any or all of the employer-owned email addresses.[17]

■ Business & Professions Code § 17538.45

This provision in California law regulates the transmission of unsolicited commercial emails from another angle. Instead of focusing on the content of emails or a recipient's right to opt-out of further emails, this section provides that no unsolicited commercial emails can be sent in violation of an "electronic mail service provider's policy prohibiting or restricting the use of its equipment to deliver unsolicited electronic mail advertisements to its registered users."[18] As with Section 17538.4, this section defines "unsolicited electronic mail advertisement" to *exclude* any email that is sent pursuant to a preexisting business or personal relationship, or where the advertisement was sent at the request, or with the consent, of the recipient.[19]

This section allows an "electronic mail service provider" whose policies on unsolicited commercial emails were violated to bring a civil action against the sender. Such a provider can recover either the actual damages suffered as a result of the unsolicited commercial email or liquidated damages in the amount of $50 per email that violates this law, up to a maximum of $25,000 per day.[20]

In order to prevail, the email service provider must establish that the defendant had "actual notice" of the "service provider's policy on electronic mail advertising" and that the messages sent would use, or cause to be used, the service provider's equipment located in California.[21] With respect to the "actual notice" requirement, the California legislature found that the requirement of "actual notice" may be met, at some point in the future, if a technology was available which supplied notice by the mere act of sending an email message between the sending and receiving computers.[22]

■ Penal Code § 502

California has adopted a criminal computer crime statute that, in general, is intended to prevent "tampering, interference, damage, and unauthorized access" to computer data and computer systems.[23] With respect to email, this section makes it a criminal offense to:

"[k]nowingly and without permission use the Internet domain name of another individual, corporation, or entity in connection with the sending of one or more electronic mail messages, and thereby damag[ing] or caus[ing] damage to a computer, computer system, or computer network."[24]

A violation of this section is punishable by a fine of up to $250 for a first offense, and a fine of up to $5000 and/or up to a year imprisonment for subsequent violations.[25] This section also allows those harmed by this activity to bring a civil action for compensatory damages against any person convicted of a violation of this section.[26] Finally, any computer equipment used in the commission of an offense covered by this section is subject to forfeiture.[27]

Connecticut

Connecticut's law dealing with unsolicited commercial email went into effect on October 1, 1999. Public Act No. 99-160 is generally intended to prevent unauthorized access or tampering of computers, networks, and computer data.[28] The act makes it illegal to:

- ■ "Falsify or forge electronic mail transmission information or other routing information in any manner in connection with the transmission of unsolicited bulk electronic mail through or into the computer network of an electronic mail service provider or its subscribers."[29]

- ■ "[K]nowingly sell, give, or otherwise distribute or possess with the intent to sell, give, or distribute" any software that: is primarily designed to enable falsification of email routing information, has limited commercial purposes aside from falsifying such information, or is marketed for the purpose of falsifying email routing or transmission information.[30]

In addition to criminal penalties,[31] the act enables "any person" who suffered injury as a result of a violation of the act to bring a civil action in Connecticut Superior Court and recover damages[32] and enjoin further activity that violates the act.[33] The statute of limitations on such actions is two years.[34]

Finally, the act includes a separate jurisdictional clause that allows Connecticut courts to exercise personal jurisdiction over individuals charged with a violation of this section, so long as such individual "uses a computer…or a computer network…located within" Connecticut.[35]

Delaware

Delaware joined a number of other states that have enacted legislation dealing with unsolicited commercial email when it enacted amendments to its criminal laws, which became effective July 2, 1999.[36] Specifically, these amendments create the crime of "un-requested or unauthorized electronic mail or use of network or software to cause same."[37] In essence, the statute makes it a crime to intentionally or recklessly, and "without authorization" distribute "any unsolicited bulk commercial electronic mail[38]…to any receiving address or account under the control of any authorized user of a computer system."[39] However, the section exempts any communication that is either:

- ■ "sent between human beings,"
- ■ "when the individual has requested said information," or

■ a commercial email sent pursuant to a "preexisting business relationship."[40]

The act provides several liability exemptions for Internet service providers who merely transmit such messages through their network, or take actions in good faith to block the transmission of messages which the ISP believes are or will be sent in violation of the act.[41] The ISP also has the right to terminate the account of any user who it believes, in good faith, is violating this act.[42]

The act further makes it illegal to "falsify or forge" email transmission information,[43] or sell or distribute software that makes it possible to falsify or forge email transmission information.[44]

The act covers any conduct occurring outside of Delaware, so long as the recipient's email account belongs to a user located in Delaware "at the time he or she received the electronic mail" and the defendant was aware of the fact that the presence of a recipient in Delaware was a "reasonable possibility."[45]

Finally, the act also requires that all commercial email sent to an address in Delaware has to include information on procedures the recipient can follow to opt-out of further mailings. Failure to promptly honor opt-out requests is a criminal offense.[46]

Idaho

Idaho is one of the most recent entrants into the anti-spam legislation arena. Idaho's anti-spam law[47] prohibits the use of an "interactive computer service"[48] to send or transmit any "bulk electronic mail advertisement"[49] unless such email contains a "readily identifiable" email address the recipient can use to "send a request for declining such mail."[50]

Additionally, the law prohibits the transmission of bulk email advertisements that:

■ use a fictitious return email address;

■ misrepresent the origin of the email;

■ omit information regarding the point of origin or transmission path of the email; or

■ are sent to a recipient that has declined further email advertisements any time after five days since the recipient declined further emails.[51]

The law gives recipients of emails sent in violation of this section a civil right of action and opportunity to recover actual damages or statutory damages of $100 per advertisement or $1000.[52]

Finally, like many other state anti-spam laws, the Idaho law contains broad liability exemptions for ISPs and providers of email services.[53]

Illinois

Illinois' Electronic Mail Act[54] became effective January 1, 1999. The act contains both civil and criminal provisions intended to curtail the proliferation of "unsolicited electronic mail advertisements."[55] However, the definition of "unsolicited electronic mail advertisement" does not include email advertisements addressed to recipients with which the sender has a preexisting business or personal relationship or which were sent at the request, or with the consent, of the recipient.[56/]

The act prohibits sending unsolicited email advertisements that:

1. "use a third party's Internet domain name without permission…or otherwise misrepresent any information in identifying the point of origin or the transmission path of an electronic mail advertisement" or

2. contain "false or misleading information in the subject line."[57]

The act gives Illinois jurisdiction over any unsolicited email advertisements that are delivered to a resident of Illinois through an ISP's equipment located in Illinois.[58] The act allows ISPs and individuals who suffer damages as a result of a violation of the act to recover actual damages or statutory damages in the amount of $10 per unsolicited email advertisement, up to a maximum of $25,000 per day.[59] Finally, the act immunizes ISPs from any liability when they, in good faith, act to block the "receipt or transmission" of email advertisements that the ISP "reasonably believes" violate the act.[60]

Finally, the Electronic Mail Act amends Illinois law on computer tampering to include the offense of falsifying email transmission or routing information in connection with "unsolicited bulk electronic mail."[61] The act also makes it a computer tampering offense to "sell, give or otherwise distribute" software that is intended to accomplish the falsification of email routing or transmission information, is marketed for that purpose, and has no other commercially viable use.[62]

Iowa

In 1999, Iowa enacted legislation dealing with unsolicited bulk email—both commercial and non-commercial—that contains many of the attributes of laws enacted by other states. The law became effective on July 1, 1999. The Iowa law prohibits the use of an "interactive computer service"[63] to send "bulk electronic mail that the sender knows or has reason to know":

- "uses the name of a third party in the return address field without permission of the third party,"

- "misrepresents any information in identifying the point of origin of the transmission path of the electronic mail,"

■ "does not contain information identifying the point of origin or the transmission path of the electronic mail,"

■ in the case of unsolicited email advertisements, "does not…provide an electronic mail address readily identifiable in the advertisement to which the recipient may send a request for declining such electronic mail," and

■ "demonstrates a pattern of sending unsolicited advertisements to a recipient who has sent the person a request for declining such electronic mail following a reasonable time, which in no event shall be more than five business days, after the receipt by the person of such request."[64]

The act provides that both a recipient of emails sent in violation of the act, as well as an ISP who is injured by such a violation, can bring a civil action in Iowa against the sender of the unsolicited bulk email.[65] Individuals can recover damages of $10 per message, up to $500, while ISPs can recover up to $25,000.[66] Finally, a recipient may also obtain an injunction prohibiting the transmission of additional email advertisements covered by the act.[67]

As with many other state laws of this nature, the Iowa law does not impose liability on ISPs that merely transmit emails on behalf of its users and do not have specific knowledge of any violating email.[68] Moreover, ISPs who act in good faith to block emails that they reasonably believe violate the act will be immune from liability.[69]

Louisiana

The Louisiana law dealing with unsolicited commercial email[70] is fairly streamlined compared with other state regulation in this field. The Louisiana law contains two main provisions. First, it prohibits the transmission of an "unsolicited bulk electronic mail"[71] in violation of ISP policies.[72] Second, the act prohibits the use of a computer or network to "falsify or forge electronic mail transmission…or other routing information" in connection with unsolicited bulk electronic mail that is transmitted through an ISP computer network or an ISP subscriber's computer.[73] It is likewise prohibited to "sell, give, or distribute" software that is primarily designed to accomplish the falsification of email transmission or routing information.[74] A violation of either of these two provisions is subject to a fine of up to $5,000.[75]

Finally, the act specifically indicates that no provision is to be construed in a way that limits an ISP's ability to adopt contractual or technical measures "to prevent the transmission of unsolicited mail" in violation of the act.[76]

Nevada

Nevada was the first state to enact legislation dealing with unsolicited commercial email. The Nevada statute[77] became effective on July 1, 1998. As originally introduced, the Nevada statute would have made it illegal to send *any* unsolicited commercial emails that did not arise out of a preexisting business relationship. However, the final version allows the transmission of unsolicited commercial email within certain parameters.

The Nevada statute is fairly straightforward and contains two main provisions. First, the statute requires that any email that contains an advertisement[78] either:

- arise out of a preexisting business or personal relationship,

- be sent with the express consent of the recipient, or

- be "readily identifiable as promotional, or contain[] a statement providing that it is an advertisement, and clearly and conspicuously provide[]:

  1. The legal name, complete street address, and electronic mail address of the person transmitting the electronic mail; and

  2. A notice that the recipient may decline to receive additional electronic mail that includes an advertisement from the person transmitting the electronic mail and the procedures for declining such electronic mail."[79]

The act provides that the recipient of emails covered by the statute can recover the greater amount of actual damages suffered or $10 per email received, and can obtain an injunction blocking the transmission of additional emails.[80]

North Carolina

The North Carolina law[81] dealing with commercial use of email, which became effective on December 1, 1999, mirrors some of the central aspects of other state laws. The North Carolina law makes it illegal to send an "unsolicited bulk commercial electronic mail"[82] that is sent with the intent to "deceive or defraud" or contains forged email transmission or routing information and is sent in contravention of ISP policies governing unsolicited commercial email.[83] A violation of this section is treated as a crime of "computer trespass" and is punishable as either a misdemeanor or a felony, depending on the amount of "damage" to property that results from a violation.[84] In addition to criminal enforcement provisions, the act gives any individual injured as a result of a violation the right to sue and recover actual damages and costs.[85]

As with most other laws of its kind, the North Carolina statute provides liability safe harbors for ISPs who merely route emails without knowledge of potential violations.[86] Finally, the act gives North Carolina personal jurisdiction over any defendant who sends an "unsolicited bulk commercial electronic mail" that is involved in solicitation within the state, or whose products or services are used or consumed within the state during the "ordinary course of trade," or where such unsolicited commercial email was sent "into or within" North Carolina using an ISP's systems in contravention to ISP use policies.

Oklahoma

Oklahoma's unsolicited commercial email statute,[87] which went into effect on July 1, 1999, governs both the content of bulk emails and prohibits falsification of email routing information.

The first set of guidelines make it unlawful to send an email that:

1. "misrepresents any information identifying the point of origin or the transmission path of the electronic mail message;

2. does not contain information identifying the point of origin or the transmission path of the electronic mail message; or

3. contains false, malicious, or misleading information which purposely or negligently injures a person."[88]

Violation of this section is subject to a maximum civil penalty of $500.[89]

The second set of guidelines prohibits the sale or distribution of software that is primarily designed, marketed, or whose main purpose is to facilitate or enable the falsification of email transmission or routing information.[90]

The civil damage provision of the Oklahoma statute mirrors those in many other states, and enables individuals and ISPs to recover anywhere from $10 per message up to $25,000 per day.[91] Finally, the act grants Oklahoma courts jurisdiction over entities or individuals that transmit emails in violation of the Act to an email account in Oklahoma, or through a network located in Oklahoma.[92]

Rhode Island

The Rhode Island unsolicited commercial email statute[93] contains three main provisions.

First, the law makes forgery or tampering with email header or other routing information a violation of the law against computer trespass.[94] Sale or distribution of software that enables these prohibited acts is also an offense under the act.[95] As with other state laws in this area, Rhode Island law provides a liability safe harbor for ISPs who take contractual or technological steps to block unsolicited commercial emails that violate the law.[96] Violation of these provisions carries both criminal[97] and civil[98] penalties.

A separate and distinct provision in Rhode Island law governs the content of unsolicited email advertisements.[99] This provision requires that all unsolicited email advertisements contain either a valid toll-free phone number or return email address which the recipient can use to opt-out of further messages.[100] All emails covered by the act must also include a statement informing the recipient that he or she may use the toll-free number or email address to opt-out of receiving further messages to any address specified by the recipient.[101] Opt-out requests must be honored.[102]

Finally, the act also prohibits the fraudulent use of a third party's email address for the purpose of transmitting electronic mail.[103]

It is important to note that "commercial electronic messages" do not include messages sent pursuant to a preexisting business or personal relationship, or sent at the request, or with the express consent, of the recipient.[104]

Tennessee

Tennessee law governing unsolicited commercial email[105] incorporates some of the main "consumer protection" elements of similar state laws.

Every unsolicited commercial email transmitted in Tennessee must include the following information:

- ▪ a valid toll-free telephone number or return email address the recipient can use to opt-out of further mailings;

- ▪ a statement indicating that the recipient can use the toll-free telephone number or return email address to opt-out of further mailings; and

- ▪ the characters "ADV:" as the first four characters of the email subject line.[106]

Finally, the act prohibits the falsification of email transmission or routing information, or the use or sale of software that accomplishes the same.[107]

The act applies to all unsolicited bulk emails "delivered to a Tennessee resident via an electronic mail service provider's service or equipment located in [Tennessee]."[108] As with many other state laws on this subject, the Tennessee law gives an injured party the option of recovering either actual damages or statutory damages ranging from $10 per message up to $5000 per day.[109]

Virginia

While the prohibitions against unsolicited commercial email contained in Virginia law[110] are typical of many other similar state laws, Virginia's statute is unique in terms of its very broad jurisdictional reach, which could potentially apply to activities with only a tangential connection to Virginia.

Under Virginia law, it is unlawful to, "without authority,"[111] falsify email transmission or routing information in connection with the transmission of unsolicited bulk commercial email through the computer of an ISP or its customers.[112] It is likewise an offense to sell or distribute software that enables these activities.[113] Violations of these provisions carry both civil[114] and criminal[115] penalties similar to other laws we have examined in this chapter.

Finally—and most importantly—this law gives Virginia jurisdiction over any entity or individual who simply "uses"[116] a computer or computer network located in Virginia.[117] This is significant given the amount of email traffic that courses through the computers and computer networks of America Online—which is based in Virginia.

Washington

The State of Washington was another early adopter of legislation dealing with unsolicited commercial email. The current Washington law is a combination of laws enacted in early 1998 and then amended in 1999.[118]

The main provisions of Washington's law prohibit:

- sending unsolicited commercial emails that use a third-party domain without permission;

- sending an unsolicited commercial email containing false or misleading information in the subject line, or

- otherwise misrepresenting or obscuring email transmission or routing information.[119]

The Washington law imposes liability on both the sender of an email transmitted in violation of this title *and* on any person who "assists in the transmission" of such a message.[120] The law also provides that Washington may assert its jurisdiction in cases where an email message is either: (1) "sent from a computer located in Washington," or (2) "to an electronic mail address that the sender knows, or has reason to know, is held by a Washington resident."[121]

Finally, any ISP that blocks unsolicited commercial emails that it reasonably believes violate this chapter is immune from liability for such actions.[122]

Not only was Washington's anti-spam law one of the first to reach the books, but it was also one of the first to be challenged in court on constitutional grounds. In early 2000, an Oregon resident who was charged with violating Washington's anti-spam law succeeded in convincing a Washington trial court that the law is unconstitutional. In the case of *Washington v. Heskel,*[123] the trial court dismissed a case brought against the alleged spammer on grounds that Washington's anti-spam law was "unduly burdensome and restrictive" on interstate commerce, and that such burden outweighed any benefit the law may bring to Washington residents.[124] While this trial court decision does not invalidate the law, this case raises important questions about state regulation of a communications medium that is, by design, not contained by political boundaries.

West Virginia

The West Virginia statute governing unsolicited bulk email[125] makes it illegal to send unauthorized emails with the "intent to deceive or defraud."[126] The act also contains several provisions found in other state statutes dealing with unsolicited commercial email.

First, the statute makes it illegal to use a third party's domain without permission or otherwise misrepresent email routing or transmission information.[127] Second, the statute prohibits the transmission of unsolicited commercial emails with false or misleading information in the subject line.[128] Third, all such emails must "clearly provide the date and time the message is sent, the identity of the person sending the message, and the return electronic mail address of that person."[129] Finally, the statute contains an outright prohibition on the unauthorized transmission of emails that contain sexually explicit materials.[130]

The statute prohibits the sale, distribution, or possession of software whose main purpose is to facilitate or enable the falsification of email routing or transmission information.[131]

West Virginia can exercise jurisdiction over any individual who transmits messages in violation of the statute from a computer in West Virginia or with the knowledge (actual or constructive) that the recipient resides in West Virginia.[132]

Litigation over Unsolicited Commercial Email

Prior to the enactment of most state laws dealing with unsolicited commercial email, courts were called upon to decide disputes between ISPs and senders of bulk commercial email. In a series of well-known cases, ISPs were generally successful in enjoining or limiting the transmission of unsolicited commercial email over their network. ISPs have asserted a number of different legal theories in an effort to halt unsolicited commercial emails. Those theories vary, depending on the nature of the emails being transmitted. The legal theories most often asserted by ISPs include "trespass to chattels, conversion, service mark infringement or dilution,[133] fraud, unfair trade practices and unfair competition, and violation of the Electronic Communications Privacy Act[134] or the Computer Fraud and Abuse Act[135] ."[136]

In light of the fact that many sates have enacted statutes dealing with unsolicited commercial email,[137] a detailed discussion of the older cases dealing with this topic is not necessary. Moreover, a discussion of the different legal theories pursued by ISPs based on distinct factual scenarios—many involving fraudulent behavior—is likewise beyond the scope of our discussion. Those interested in learning about specific cases filed by ISPs against transmitters of unsolicited commercial email can find several resources on the Internet.[138]

However, there is one trend that has emerged in cases dealing with unsolicited commercial email that is worth discussing. Courts have been receptive to the theory that unsolicited commercial emails that are transmitted over their networks constitute a "trespass to chattels." One of the first cases to establish this theory was *CompuServe v. Cyber Promotions, Inc.*[139] The *CompuServe* court succinctly summed up the dispute when it said that "[d]efendants assert that they possess the right to continue to send these communications to CompuServe subscribers. CompuServe contends that, in doing so, the defendants are trespassing upon its personal property."[140] In analyzing CompuServe's trespass claim, the court noted that "trespass to chattels has evolved from its original common law application, concerning primarily the asportation of another's tangible property, to include the unauthorized use of personal property."[141] The court also noted that "[e]lectronic signals generated and sent by computer have been held to be sufficiently physically tangible to support a trespass cause of action."[142] With this legal foundation in mind, the court held that Cyber Promotions' transmission of unsolicited commercial emails through CompuServe's proprietary networks constituted a trespass because it exceeded CompuServe's consent and continued after repeated cease and desist demands.[143]

In 1999, a California trial court extended the trespass theory from the context of unsolicited commercial email to the context of noncommercial bulk emails. In *Intel v. Hamidi*,[144] the court entered a permanent injunction preventing Ken Hamidi, a former Intel employee, from sending emails to current Intel employees at Intel email addresses. The specifics of the case are as follows. Intel fired Ken Hamidi, an Intel engineer, in 1995. Thereafter, Hamidi began a vigorous email campaign of criticism against Intel and its employment practices. Of course, being a former Intel engineer, Hamidi waged his anti-Intel campaign in cyberspace. Hamidi set up a Web site to post his gripes with Intel and engaged in a systematic email campaign directed at Intel employees. On several occasions, Hamidi sent over 30,000 emails to Intel employees that were critical of Intel. Intel tried to fight back by sending cease-and-desist letters and employing technological measures to block Hamidi's emails. Both proved ineffective. Finally, Intel filed suit in California court alleging that Hamidi's emails constituted a trespass onto Intel's proprietary networks. Relying on the holding in *Cyber Promotions*, the court agreed and entered a permanent injunction barring Hamidi from sending further bulk emails to Intel addresses.[145] According to some commentators, this might be the first case in the country which applied the "trespass to chattels" theory in order to enjoin the transmission of noncommercial emails.[146] Other commentators have noted the application of the "trespass" theory to noncommercial emails raises serious First Amendment implications.[147] As we have noted previously, state legislation imposing restrictions on the transmission of commercial email will likely be reviewed for constitutionality under the intermediate scrutiny standard applied to most commercial speech.[148] Yet, absent state legislation on the topic of non-commercial unsolicited bulk email, courts will likely continue to allow private actors to use the trespass theory to protect their networks without raising First Amendment concerns that are in force when dealing with state actors.

Email in the Workplace

The pervasive use of email in the workplace raises several important legal questions for employers who provide email accounts to their workforce. Two inter-related issues that are of concern to any employer are: (1) the extent to which an employer can monitor employee email communications, and (2) potential liabilities an employer can incur from employees' use of an employer's email system. Though there is no overarching federal law that governs in this area, our aim in this section is to provide an analytical framework that surveys court decisions, common law, and statutes that provide a certain level of guidance to employers who provide email access for their employees on private company networks.

Monitoring Workplace Email Communications

The debate over employer monitoring of employee email communications has centered around the tension between an employee's right to privacy and an employer's need to control the workplace environment. An employer can have many reasons for monitoring employee email, including: observing and documenting employee workplace activities undertaken on behalf or in the course of business, protecting company property or trade secrets, and protecting against potential liability for employee activity conducted over email.[149] Employees, on the other hand, have asserted that the common law right to privacy protects their email communications from unwarranted monitoring by an employer.[150] This section describes the most prominent cases and statutes that employers should look to when seeking guidance on this subject.

Court Decisions Dealing With Email Monitoring in the Workplace

The issue of workplace email monitoring by employees has been dealt with in a couple of prominent published opinions and in some unpublished state trial court proceedings that have garnered the attention of the legal and business communities. Even though these cases were decided at the trial court level—and therefore have reduced precedential value—they are notable because they provide a window into the attitudes courts, employers, and employees are taking toward this issue.

   In one of the first published opinions providing some guidance on this issue, a U.S. District Court in Pennsylvania determined that the interception of email communications in the workplace did not constitute a substantial invasion of an employee's privacy. The court in *Smyth v. The Pillsbury Co.* was presented with a wrongful termination suit brought by an employee who was terminated after his employer intercepted emails in which the employee made inappropriate comments and made threats directed at other employees.[151] Plaintiff claimed that his termination was a violation of Pennsylvania public policy because the termination based on interception of his email communications violated "public policy which precludes an employer from terminating an employee in violation of the employee's right to privacy as embodied in Pennsylvania common law."[152] After analyzing other court opinions that looked at an employee's right to privacy in the workplace, the court determined that, "unlike urinalysis and personal property searches" an employee did not have "a reasonable expectation of privacy in email communications voluntarily made by an employee to his supervisor over the company email system."[153] The court further stated:

> [E]ven if we found that an employee had a reasonable expectation of privacy in the contents of his email communications over the company email system, we do not find that a reasonable person would consider the defendant's interception of these communications to be a substantial and highly offensive invasion of his privacy.[154]

Finally, the court held that "the company's interest in preventing inappropriate and unprofessional comments or even illegal activity over its email system outweighs any privacy interest the employee may have in those comments."[155]

Some commentators have criticized the holding in *Smyth v. The Pillsbury Co.* for a number of reasons, including the court's failure to fully balance the employee's right to privacy with the employer's legitimate business motives for email monitoring, and the court's determination that all workplace email communications carry with them a lowered expectation of privacy.[156] However, other courts analyzing the issue have come to similar conclusions.

In an unpublished opinion, the California Court of Appeal in *Bourke v. Nissan*[157] plaintiff's brought a claim for invasion of privacy based on their employer's interception of email messages that proved to be of a personal nature. Plaintiffs claimed that they had a reasonable expectation of privacy in their email communications based, in part, on the fact that their email accounts were password protected. Conversely, Defendant argued that no such expectation existed because Plaintiffs had signed a document acknowledging that the company had a policy preventing the use of email for personal purposes. Stating that Plaintiffs had no reasonable expectation of privacy in their email communications, the court granted summary judgment in favor of the defendant—which was affirmed by the Court of Appeals. In other unpublished decisions, California courts have affirmed an employer's right to monitor email communications in the workplace.[158] In fact, as recently as late 1999, the governor of California vetoed a bill that would have provided private employers with the duty to notify all employees before an employer monitored email communications in the workplace.[159]

Statutory and Common Law That May Impact an Employer's Right to Monitor Proprietary Email Systems

■ The Electronic Communications Privacy Act

The Electronic Communications Privacy Act (ECPA)[160] prohibits the unauthorized interception of electronic communications or electronic messages by any "provider of wire or electronic communication service"[161] irrespective of whether such interception is done when the communication is in transmission or in storage.[162] The ECPA imposes liability on any individual who "intentionally intercepts, endeavors to intercept, or procures any person to intercept or endeavor to intercept, any wire, oral, or electronic communication."[163] The ECPA does not specifically mention email as one of the "electronic communications" protected. However, courts have interpreted the ECPA's protections to extend to email communications.[164] Yet, even though email communications are covered by the protections of the ECPA, employers may be able to rely on statutory exceptions written into the ECPA in order to monitor their proprietary email networks.

According to what is commonly known as the "provider exception":

It [is] unlawful...for an operator of a switchboard, or an officer employee, or agent of a provider of wire or electronic communication service, whose facilities are used in the transmission of a wire or electronic communication, to *intercept, disclose, or use* that communication in the normal course of his employment while engaged in any activity which is a necessary incident to the rendition of his service or to the protection of the rights or property of the provider of that service.[165]

Therefore, an employer who provides a network for employees to transmit email communications (as opposed to outsourcing such services to an ISP) may intercept and monitor such email communications if it is done "in the normal course" of business and if such monitoring is "a necessary incident to the rendition of [the] service or to the protection of [an employer's] rights or property."[166] This exception would seem to apply irrespective of whether the email communications are intercepted in transit (which is difficult to do) or whether they are accessed from a network storage device (which is infinitely easier).[167] Some commentators have noted that an employer could use a variety of rationales to support the monitoring of email communications, including trade secret protection, or other legitimate business objectives.[168] Though no court has yet interpreted this exception in the context of workplace monitoring, an employer relying on this exception to circumvent the applicability of the ECPA should have an articulated email use policy that specifically addresses the compelling business need for such monitoring.

Finally, the ECPA also provides a broad exception in cases where a party to the electronic communication has provided prior consent to the interception[169] or access from storage[170] of electronic communications. While courts are sometimes willing to find implied consent based on the facts of a given case, an employer relying on this exception would be well served by seeking express consent from employees for email monitoring. In fact, one court has commented that the ECPA would be eviscerated "if consent would be routinely implied from the circumstances."[171] The act of announcing a policy of workplace email monitoring, in and of itself, will likely not suffice to provide a court with enough evidence for a finding of "implied consent."[172] However, announcing a monitoring policy is an important step employers can take in minimizing liability as a result of workplace email monitoring.

■ Common Law Tort of Invasion of Privacy

As we noted in Section III.A.1, employees have brought legal challenges to workplace email monitoring based on several theories, including the common law tort of invasion of privacy.[173] The common law tort of invasion of privacy can be segmented into four distinct torts:

1. unreasonable intrusion upon the seclusion of another;

2. misappropriation of another's name or likeness;

3. unreasonable publicity given to another's private life; and

4. publicity that unreasonably places another in a false light before the public.[174]

Of these four distinct torts, the one most relevant to workplace email monitoring is the tort of unreasonable intrusion upon the seclusion of another. This tort is committed when one intentionally intrudes upon the seclusion or solitude of another or that person's private affairs, by physical means or otherwise.[175] In order to be actionable, the intrusion must be highly offensive to the reasonable person.[176] As with any other intentional tort, consent is a bar to liability.[177] The determination of whether a workplace email monitoring policy runs afoul of these privacy protections will depend on whether an employee had a reasonable expectation of privacy and whether the employer has put forth a legitimate business purpose as the driving force behind the monitoring. While some courts have been willing to make blanket statements indicating that employees can never have a reasonable expectation of privacy in workplace email communications,[178] every employer should take heed of the potential liabilities posed by the dichotomy between employee privacy and legitimate business email use policies.

Potential Employer Liabilities for an Employee's Use of Workplace Email

An issue that is closely tied to workplace monitoring of email (and other online activities) is the fact that employers may, in some circumstances, be held liable for their employees' email activities. In addition, as we have seen in recent high profile litigation, and as more fully discussed in the following section, employee emails can often be used against the employer in the course of litigation. For purposes of this chapter, however, we will focus on the two most prominent ways an employer can be held liable for the acts of its employees while using email: defamation and copyright infringement.

Defamatory Material Transmitted or Posted By Employees

One area of concern for employers who provide employees with access to email is the possibility that employees will transmit defamatory emails through the employer's network or post such messages on the employer's Web site or electronic bulletin board. While no court has squarely dealt with an employer's liability in this context, employers who provide and maintain the computer network that carries employee email traffic can draw guidance from cases and statutes intended to address defamation liability for network or Internet service providers.

The Fourth Circuit in *Stratton Oakmont, Inc. v. Prodigy Services, Inc.,*[179] (subsequently overruled by Congress in the Telecommunications Act of 1996[180]) examined the issue of whether an ISP can be held liable for the defamatory messages posted on bulletin boards by its users. The court held that the ISP would be treated as a "publisher" for purposes of defamation liability because it took steps to regulate the content on its bulletin boards. The court further held that Prodigy's affirmative steps to monitor content transformed it into a "publisher," as opposed to a mere "distributor." Generally, distributors of defamatory material are held liable for the defamatory statements only if they know or have reason to know they are distributing defamatory content. Publishers, on the other hand, are held to a strict standard of liability for defamatory statements. Therefore, under this standard, finding Prodigy to be a publisher meant it was liable for the defamatory statements posted by its users.

The holding in *Stratton Oakmont* created an incentive for network providers or ISPs to turn a blind eye and refrain from monitoring content, lest they be considered publishers of defamatory content, as opposed to mere distributors. In response, Congress expressly overruled Stratton Oakmont when it enacted the Telecommunications Act of 1996.[181] Section 230(c) of the act explicitly carves out a liability exemption that states that "[n]o provider or user of an interactive computer service shall be treated as the publisher or speaker of any information provided by another information content provider."[182]

However, in order to qualify for the "good samaritan" liability safe harbors provided by Section 230(c), an employer must regulate or monitor the email traffic being transmitted over its network. Under Section 230(c)(2), an employer is required to monitor email or Internet communications in connection with "any action voluntarily taken in good faith to restrict access to or availability of material that the provider or user considers to be . . . harassing, or otherwise objectionable, whether or not such material is constitutionally protected."[183] The definition of "interactive computer service"[184] is broad enough to potentially include any employer who provides email or Internet access to multiple employees over a workplace network. Of course, as discussed in the previous section, any employer who takes advantage of this incentive to monitor email traffic over a workplace network in order to qualify for the "good samaritan" liability safe harbor must be mindful of the potential that employees may assert that some forms of monitoring invade the employee's common law right to privacy.

Copyright Infringement

Employers should also beware of incurring liability for copyright infringement based on employee use of email (or the Internet). Email and the Internet increase the ease with which copyrighted materials can be copied, transferred, and downloaded online. According to the Business Software Alliance, employees are "significant contributors to software piracy in the workplace."[185] In fact, copyright infringement can be as easy as attaching a copy of a program or file to an email in the workplace. An employer who provides and maintains the network and email server can potentially be held liable under theories of contributory infringement or vicarious liability for the infringing acts of its employees. Though no case has squarely dealt with the applicability of copyright infringement liability to employers in this context, several prominent decisions have examined potential liabilities for ISPs whose users transmit or post copyrighted material.

For example, the court in *Religious Technology Center v. Netcom* On-*Line Communications Services, Inc.*[186] held that an ISP can be held liable for contributory infringement when "with knowledge of the infringing activity, [the ISP] induces, causes or materially contributes to the infringing conduct of another."[187] Moreover, "providing the site and facilities for known infringing activity is sufficient to establish contributory liability."[188] Therefore, an employer who provides network services, including email, for its employees, will expose itself to contributory liability in the event it has knowledge of infringing activities and continues to provide email or network access to such employees.

Finally, courts have also held that an ISP can be found vicariously liable for copyright infringement for the activities of its subscribers where the ISP "(1) has the right and ability to control the infringer's acts, and (2) receives a direct financial benefit from the infringement."[189] Though employers will seldom receive a direct financial benefit from the infringing activities of its subscribers, employers should have in place a sound email use policy and a software use policy that both clearly indicate that the employer does not condone and will not tolerate acts of infringement.[190]

Email and Litigation

Introduction

Email can be powerful evidence. The convenience provided by email has led to its nearly ubiquitous use as a medium of communication, particularly in the workplace. However, the casual ease with which an email can be drafted and transmitted often leads to the creation of bits of evidence that can cause headaches when used by parties to a litigation. As one commentator has put it, "[c]ases involving electronic smoking guns are now legion."[191] Every individual or attorney involved in litigation needs to make the discovery of all electronic evidence, including email records, a key aspect of any sound litigation discovery strategy. In this chapter, we provide a brief overview of three main issues to consider when thinking of email (or other electronic evidence) in the context of litigation: discovery of email evidence, the admissibility of such evidence at trial, and destruction of email evidence (including the risks associated with sanctions for spoliation of evidence).[192]

Discovery of Email Evidence

Electronic evidence, including email records, is often discoverable in litigation. The Federal Rules of Civil Procedure specifically state that "documents," which include "data compilations from which information can be obtained, translated . . into reasonably usable form" are subject to discovery requests.[193] Therefore, any discovery request should include a specific request for documents stored in electronic or digital form—including email.[194]

Admissibility of Email Evidence

If you are lucky enough to find the "smoking gun" email, you then have to determine whether it will be admissible at trial. There are several obstacles to the admissibility of email (or other electronic) evidence.[195] These include: hearsay and its multiple exceptions, authenticity, and issues related to proving the content of the writing itself under the "original document" rule.

One of the first things to consider is whether the email in question meets the definition of hearsay.[196] Depending on the context, many statements contained in email communications will be considered non-hearsay because they do not meet the definition of hearsay. For instance, an email can be offered to establish something other than the truth of the matter asserted in the email.[197]

Another instance where the email statement will be considered to be non-hearsay will be when it contains an admission by a party opponent or one of the opponent's representatives.[198]

Assuming that the email meets the definition of hearsay, there are several exceptions to the hearsay rule that may make the email admissible. Given the ease and relative carelessness with which email messages are composed, any number of the following hearsay exceptions may suffice to make the email admissible: statement against interest,[199] present sense impression,[200] a recorded recollection,[201] and the business record exception.[202] While these exceptions will lend themselves to email communications that meet the definition of hearsay, other exceptions may be available depending on the circumstances of each case.

Once the party seeking to admit the email into evidence has cleared the hearsay hurdle, he or she must also show that the email is authentic.[203] Under the Federal Rules of Evidence, the proponent of the evidence must first put forth "evidence sufficient to support a finding that the matter in question is what its proponent claims."[204] Authentication can usually be accomplished by reaching a stipulation with the opposing party or producing competent testimony from either the sender or the recipient of the email in question.[205]

Finally, under the "best evidence" rule, printouts of email communications that "reflect the data accurately" will be considered "original" for purposes of the rule.[206] Therefore, a party seeking to "prove the content" of an email need only introduce a copy that accurately reflects the data contained in the original email communication.[207]

Spoliation of Email Evidence

Many companies and institutions have policies in place dealing with the routine destruction of electronic evidence, including backup copies of email, while other companies have no such policy in place. Irrespective of whether such policy is in place, it is important to keep in mind that, under some circumstances, the deletion of potential email evidence will subject a litigant to a range of sanctions—in some cases even when the deletion of the email took place before the commencement of litigation. Of course, a "sensible and consistently implemented [email] disposal policy significantly limits the possibility that sanctions will be imposed for spoliation, by negating an inference of willful intent."[208]

Both state and federal jurisdictions impose varying levels of civil and criminal sanctions for the intentional or negligent spoliation of evidence. Most jurisdictions impose a duty to preserve evidence upon a party that is "on notice that documents and information in its possession are relevant to litigation, or potential litigation, or are reasonably calculated to lead to the discovery of admissible evidence."[209] The point where a party is put on notice varies by

MAIN FEATURES OF STATE UNSOLICITED COMMERCIAL EMAIL LAWS

State	Opt-Out Procedures	Contact Info	"Adv" Labeling	No False Routing Info	No Software Designed To Falsify Routing Info	No Use of 3rd Party Domain w/o Permission	No False or Misleading Subject Line	No Violation of ISP Policies	No X-Rated Material	Date & Time Stamp
California	■	■	■							
Connecticut				■	■					
Delaware		■		■	■					
Idaho	■			■						
Illinois		■		■	■	■	■			
Iowa	■	■				■				
Louisiana	■			■	■			■		
Nevada	■	■	■	■						
North Carolina				■				■		
Oklahoma				■	■					
Rhode Island	■	■	■	■	■	■		■		
Tennessee	■	■		■	■					
Virginia				■	■	■	■			
Washington							■			
West Virginia		■		■	■	■	■		■	■

jurisdiction.[210] The sanctions that can be imposed for spoliation of evidence range from evidentiary presumptions to terminating sanctions.[211]

Given the inconsistency between jurisdictions over when the duty to preserve evidence arises, and the fact that electronic evidence (including email) can be easily destroyed, a party who seeks to preserve electronic evidence for discovery would be well-advised to send the opposing party a "preservation letter" or seeking a "preservation order" from the court in an effort to halt the destruction of relevant evidence at the earliest possible moment.[212]

CHAPTER 24

OTHER LEGAL ISSUES

In this chapter, we'll discuss three topics:

- Legal rules for using trademarks owned by others.

- The federal law prohibiting removal of copyright management information (information about the work's title, author, and owner, and terms for using the work).

- The federal law prohibiting circumventing access control devices (technological devices that limit access to a copy of a work).

Using Third-Party Trademarks

The basic rule about using trademarks owned by others is that you should not use trademarks owned by third parties if doing so would cause consumer confusion as to sponsorship or the source of goods or services.

EXAMPLE 1

Sam, a fan of the San Francisco Giants baseball team, set up a Web site called *The Official Giants Site.* Site users are likely to think Sam's site is sponsored by the Giants.

EXAMPLE 2

The MAPHIA bulletin board offered users free "bootleg" copies of *Sega*-brand electronic games. The *Sega* trademark appeared when one of the games obtained from the bulletin board was played. Some of the bulletin board versions of the games did not function as smoothly as genuine, commercially released copies, either because they were prerelease versions or because they contained errors. The court concluded that users were likely to confuse the unauthorized bulletin board copies of games with genuine *Sega* games. *Sega Enterprises Ltd. v. Maphia*, 857 F Supp 679 (ND Cal 1994).

The trademark law concept of "confusing similarity" is discussed in "Scope of Trademark Rights," chapter 15.

Naming famous brands in order to criticize them is not likely to cause consumer confusion.

EXAMPLE

Joe created a Web site called *Famous Company's Products Stink*. On the Web site, he uses Famous Company's brand names in referring to (and criticizing) Famous Company's products. Consumers are not likely to think Joe's Web site is the official site of Famous Company.

This type of use of another party's trademarks is generally considered fair use (sometimes called collateral use). Other types of trademark fair use are discussed later in this section.

Sometimes the names of well-known, high quality products are used without permission to promote other products—referring to game development software as the "Mercedes" of all game development software, for example. It is possible that such use of trademarks violates dilution laws, discussed in "Dilution," chapter 15. Noncommercial use of a mark (such as Joe's use of Famous Company's trademarks in the example immediately above) is not actionable under the federal dilution statute. Use of trademarks in news reporting and commentary is also not actionable under that statute.

In the rest of this section, we'll discuss fair use of trademarks, trademark parody, and rules under U.S. law for using third-party trademarks properly. At the end of the section, we'll look at using third-party trademarks as metatags and banner ad keywords.

Fair Use

Trademarks can be descriptive, suggestive, arbitrary, or fanciful. These terms are explained in "Choosing a Strong Trademark," chapter 15. For all types of marks, you are free to use the mark in good faith to describe the goods or services of a party or its geographic origin.

EXAMPLE

An auction site offering used computer equipment identifies the equipment being offered by the equipment manufacturers' brand names and product numbers ("Hewlett Packard Laser Jet 5L Printer," "Mitsubishi Diamond Pro Monitor"). Assuming the products are genuine, the site's use of the product manufacturers' trademarks is not infringement. This use is necessary to describe the goods being offered.

You are also free to use a third party's trademark to advertise that you sell or service lawfully acquired merchandise of that particular brand as long as you do not misrepresent that you are an authorized agent or otherwise connected with the trademark owner.

> **A scooter manufacturer, owner of the *Go-Ped* trademark, sued an unauthorized *Go-Ped* dealer for using "goped" as the back-end of the URL (www.idiosyn.com/goped) for a Web page on which the dealer posted criticism of the plaintiff. The court dismissed the trademark claims, holding that the defendant's use of the term was fair use because it was reasonably necessary to identify the product and did not imply plaintiff's sponsorship or endorsement. *Patmont Motor Works, Inc. v. Gateway Marine, Inc.,* 1997 US Dist LEXIS 20877 (ND Cal 1997).**

For a descriptive mark, you are free to use the mark in its descriptive sense.

EXAMPLE

Radio Channel Networks (RCN) tried to stop Broadcast.com from using the term "Radio Channel" on the Broadcast.com Web site. RCN claimed that it had trademark rights in the term based on prior use. The court held that the term "Radio Channel" was descriptive and that trademark law permitted Broadcast.com to use "Radio Channel" in a descriptive sense, to describe its own services. *Radio Channel Networks, Inc. v. Broadcast.com, Inc.,* 1999 WL 124455 (SDNY 1999), *aff'd,* 201 F3d 432 (2d Cir 1999).

In the United States, you are free to use your competitors' trademarks in truthful, substantiated comparative advertising. (False advertising is covered briefly in "Advertising Laws," chapter 18.) However, comparative advertising is illegal in some countries.

Trademark Parodies

Parody of a trademark, like copyright parody (discussed in "When You Don't Need a License," chapter 9), is considered fair use.

EXAMPLE

The creators of the character "Barney" filed a trademark infringement suit against an individual who put on a chicken costume and pummeled a Barney look-alike at baseball and basketball games. The court dismissed the suit on the basis that the defendant's performance was a parody. *Lyons Partnership v. Giannoulas,* 179 F3d 384 (5th Cir 1999).

Because this is a complex area of law (and one in which the courts have not been consistent), you should seek the advice of experienced trademark counsel if you are planning a trademark parody.

Association Issues

Some trademark owners may object if you show their trademarks on your Web site or online products without permission. The trademark owner may object to being associated with your Web site, business, or products. For example, Nabisco objected to the use of the *Marlboro* trademark on a billboard in the background of a video game. American Airlines objected to the use of its logo on planes in flight-simulation software. (American had exclusively licensed the use of the logo to another company for use in a flight-simulator product.)

Using Trademarks Properly

Avoid using a trademark as a noun. If a term becomes the generic word for goods of that type, it can no longer serve as a trademark because it is no longer capable of identifying a seller's products and distinguishing the seller's products from those manufactured and sold by others. "Escalator," "dry ice," and "aspirin" are former trademarks that lost their protection.

When you use third-party trademarks in text, take care to use the trademark as the owner uses it. When possible, use proper trademark notice (discussed in "Trademark Law," chapter 2), at least with the first most prominent use. In addition, you may want to add a line of text to make it clear that you do not claim ownership of third-party trademarks—for example, "Widget is a trademark of XYZ Company."

Trademarked Products

The use of actual images of actual goods bearing real trademarks in your Web site or products (for example, a photograph of an airplane with the United Airlines logo) is a gray area. (If you're selling the goods, it's okay to show them. As we discussed earlier in this section, in the U.S. you are free to use a third party's trademark to advertise that you sell lawfully acquired merchandise of that brand. Right now we're talking about showing goods you are *not* selling.)

Some trademark owners have taken the position that such use "associates" them with the product in which the images are used, and thus, gives them the right to grant or deny permission to use the images of trademarked goods. The national sports teams have been aggressive in asserting these rights. If you will be displaying an item that includes a national sports team's logo—for example, a *Giants* cap worn by an actor in a video clip—you should contact the team's licensing department about getting a license.

other legal
issues

As a general rule, get permission to use an image of a trademarked item if the item will be prominently featured or a prominent part of the story. (This is the same rule we give for showing copyrighted products, discussed in "Permits," chapter 7.) You should be particularly sensitive to such concerns when creating Web sites or products that are viewed as negative or critical about the industry in which the trademark owner is involved (for example, the use of images of airplanes with real logos in a game that includes plane crashes).

Trademarks as Links
It is unclear whether using a third party's trademark as a link button to the third party's site is trademark infringement. It may be fair use. In one case, plaintiffs claimed that the defendants' use of the plaintiffs' registered trademarks as hyperlinks to the plaintiffs' Web sites was trademark infringement (because it was likely to confuse the public as to whether the plaintiffs were associated with the defendants). The parties settled the case.

Using Third-Party Marks as Metatags
Metatags are HTML code used to describe the contents of a Web site. Search engines retrieve results for Web users by looking for metatags, keywords in domain names, and actual text on Web pages. The more often a term appears in the metatags for a site, the more likely it is that the Web page will be found in a search for that term.

Several court decisions have held that trademark law bars a Web site owner from using a trademark belonging to someone else as a metatag. In *Playboy Enterprises v. AsiaFocus International, Inc.*, 1998 WL 724000 (ED Va 1998), defendant AsiaFocus used Playboy Enterprises' federally registered trademark *Playboy* as metatags for the AsiaFocus site. The court held that AsiaFocus had intentionally misled viewers into believing that the AsiaFocus site was connected with or sponsored by Playboy Enterprises. It enjoined the defendant from continuing to use *Playboy* as a metatag.

The *Brookfield* case went even further, holding that using a competitor's trademark as a metatag was trademark infringement even if consumers were not misled about site sponsorship. In that case, the defendant West Coast Video was using Brookfield's federally registered trademark *moviebuff* in metatags of West Coast's site, westcoastvideo.com. The court noted that because the West Coast site's home page prominently displayed the West Coast Video name, it would be difficult to say that a consumer viewing the site would think he had reached Brookfield's site. Nonetheless, the court felt that defendant West Coast Video's use of *moviebuff* in metatags for its site was likely to result in initial interest confusion—meaning that the West Coast site would attract the initial interest of consumers looking for *moviebuff* (because search engines would provide the URL for westcoastvideo.com in response to searches for the keyword "moviebuff"). "Using another's trademark in one's metatags is much like posting a sign with another's trademark in front of one's store," the court said. *Brookfield Communications v. West Coast Entertainment Corp.*, 174 F3d 1036 (9th Cir 1999). (Another aspect of the *Brookfield* case, the conflict between domain name registrations and trademark rights, is discussed in "Registering Domain Names," chapter 16.)

METATAGS AND FAIR USE

Terri Welles, 1981 Playmate of the Year, used *Playboy* and *Playmate* as metatags for her own Web site (which is not affiliated with Playboy Enterprises). Playboy Enterprises sued her for trademark infringement and dilution. The court granted summary judgment in favor of Welles, holding that her use of the trademarks in metatags and on her site was fair use because there was no other way for her to identify herself and describe her services. 7 FSupp2d 1098 (SD Cal 1999).

Using Third-Party Trademarks as Keywords

A keyword is a term used in search engine queries to retrieve listings of Web sites with content related to the keyword. Many search engines sell the right to have a particular banner ad appear when a search engine user types in a certain keyword.

EXAMPLE

Someone who wants information on dogs might type in "dog" in the query box in a search engine. An online pet store might buy the right to have a banner ad advertising its site come up when a search engine user enters the word "dog."

Some search engines have sold banner ad rights for a trademarked term to someone other than the trademark owner.

EXAMPLE

The search engine Excite sold banner ad rights for the term *Estee Lauder* to a company called The Fragrance Counter, an online cosmetics retailer.

Whether this is trademark infringement is unclear. Several cases are pending. In these cases, the trademark owner's view is that the use of a trademark keyword in this manner diverts a customer who is looking for the trademark owner's site to a different Web site, diluting the mark.

Only one of the banner ad cases has been decided, *Playboy Enterprises, Inc. v. Netscape Communications Corp.* In that case, Netscape had sold banner ad rights to "playboy" and "playmate" to the operator of a hard-core pornography site. The court denied a preliminary injunction to Playboy Enterprises because it held that Netscape used the words "playboy" and "playmate" as "words in the English language rather than trademarks." 55 FSupp2d 1070 (CD Cal 1999). (The result might have been different had Netscape used a "made up" trademark that did not correspond to a word.)

Copyright Management Information

"Copyright management information" (CMI) is information conveyed in connection with copies or phonorecords of a copyrighted work, or performances or displays of a work, about the title, author, and owner of a copyrighted work and terms and conditions for the use of the work. The title page and copyright notice page of this book, for example, contain CMI.

Electronic copies of a work often include CMI in "digital watermarks." Digital watermark technology embeds CMI in digital files. Users with appropriate software can display the information and contact the copyright owner to get permission to use the work embodied in the file. Digital watermarks also can be used to detect unauthorized copying, by having Web crawlers locate watermarked content on the Web.

Section 1202 of the Copyright Act makes it illegal to remove or alter CMI, knowing or having reasonable grounds to know that to do so will induce, facilitate, or conceal infringement. Section 1202 is both a civil and a criminal law. A copyright owner can collect actual or statutory damages (up to $25,000 for each violation) from anyone who violates this provision. A willful violation of Section 1202 for purposes of commercial advantage or private financial gain is a crime. Section 1202 also makes it illegal to do the following things:

- Distribute altered CMI knowing that the copyright information has been altered and that the distribution will aid infringement.

- Distribute copies of works or phonorecords knowing that CMI has been altered and the distribution will aid infringement.

- Provide false CMI.

- Distribute or import for distribution false CMI.

Circumventing Access Control Devices

Access control devices limit who can view a copy of a work. (See "Protecting Your Material," chapter 12.) Section 1201(a) of the Copyright Act, effective October 29, 2000, prohibits the circumvention of access control devices. As with Section 1201, actual and statutory damages are available, and willful violation for purposes of commercial advantage or private financial gain is a criminal offense. Descrambling a scrambled work and decrypting an encrypted work are examples of acts that violate Section 1201.

Section 1201 contains limited exceptions permitting circumvention of access control devices for reverse engineering and encryption research. Nonprofit libraries, archives, and educational institutions are permitted to circumvent access control devices to determine whether they want to purchase or license the protected works. It is not a violation of Section 1201(a) to circumvent an access control device on a work that collects or disseminates personally identifying information under certain circumstances. The Copyright Office is currently involved in a rulemaking proceeding (mandated by Congress) to determine other exemptions.

Section 1201(a) does not prohibit the circumvention of copy control devices, just the circumvention of access control devices. (Copy control devices determine what uses a user can make of material, for example, whether the user can copy it, download it, or electronically distribute it.)

This statute also prohibits manufacturing, importing, offering to the public, or providing technology for circumventing access control devices under any of these three circumstances:

- The technology is primarily designed or produced for the purpose of circumventing access control measures.

- The technology has only limited commercially significant use other than circumvention.

■ The technology is marketed for use in circumventing copy protection measures. Examples are cable decoders and software piracy tools.

17 USC § 1201(b). This part of Section 1201 became law in 1998.

A SECTION 1201(b) CASE

Several motion picture studios sued to enjoin several defendants from posting on their Web sites a computer program that permits users to decrypt and copy the studios' copyrighted motion pictures from digital versatile disks. A preliminary injunction was granted to the plaintiffs. *Universal City Studios v. Reimerdes*, 2000 WL 678835 FSupp2d (SDNY 2000).

CHAPTER 25

SERVICE PROVIDER LIABILITY

In this chapter, we'll discuss whether an Internet service provider (ISP) or other provider of Internet access or facilities is liable for wrongs by a system user.

Here are three examples of this issue:

- **Example 1:** Dennis Erlich, a former Scientologist, posted 154 pages of copyrighted Church of Scientology materials to a Usenet Newsgroup. Is the operator of the bulletin board service (BBS) used by Erlich liable for copyright infringement? Is the BBS's Internet service provider, Netcom, liable? (This example is drawn from the *Religious Technology Center* case, discussed in "Copyright Infringement" in this chapter.)

- **Example 2:** Giantco's Web site has copyrighted text and graphics which Giantco's marketing department used without permission. Is Giantco's Web hosting company liable for copyright infringement because the material resides on the Web hosting company's system?

- **Example 3:** A consumer products review site posts product reviews submitted by site users. One user comment states that the manufacturer of a particular product is insolvent (an untrue statement). Is the owner of the consumer review site liable for defamation? What about the Web hosting company for the consumer review site?

The liability of the system user— Erlich in example 1, Giantco in example 2, and the consumer who submitted the comment in example 3—is discussed in other chapters. (Copyright infringement is discussed in chapters 1, 9, and 10 and defamation in chapter 7.)

Copyright Infringement

As you may know, in the 1990s, Internet service providers (ISPs) maintained that they should not be liable for copyright infringement by system users. "A telephone company is not liable when a telephone subscriber transmits infringing material by phone line to someone else," they stated. "We're in the same position as a telephone company: We just provide the facilities for storing and transmitting material." However, content owners and some legal experts maintained that ISPs are "electronic publishers"—and, like other publishers, are liable for providing infringing material.

In the case *Religious Technology Center v. Netcom On-Line Communication Services, Inc.* (the facts of which are given in example 1, in this chapter's introduction), the court held that ISP Netcom could be liable for contributory copyright infringement for postings made by a system subscriber after the copyright owner notified Netcom that the system subscriber was posting infringing material. 907 FSupp 1361 (ND Cal 1995). This case was settled before the judge made a final decision in the case (and before the federal law discussed in the rest of this section was enacted).

Liability Limitation

In October 1998, the Digital Millennium Copyright Act (DMCA) became law. Part of this law, the "Online Copyright Infringement Liability Limitation Act," creates "safe harbors," which ISPs, system operators, and other providers of Internet access and facilities can use to shield themselves from liability for monetary damages for transmitting, storing, caching, and linking to infringing material placed on the system by a third party. We'll discuss the transmission and storage safe harbor provisions in this section. The other two safe harbor provisions are discussed in "Linking" and "Caching," chapter 20.

Transmission Safe Harbor

According to the DMCA's "transmission" safe harbor, a service provider is not liable for copyright infringement damages when infringing material is transmitted or routed over its system if the transmission was initiated by a third party and the following conditions apply:

■ The transmission or routing was carried out by an automatic technical process without selection of material by the service provider.

- The service provider did not select recipients for the material (except as an automatic response to a third party's request).

- The service provider did not maintain a stored copy for longer than necessary to allow the transmission, and it did not maintain a stored copy accessible by nonrecipients.

- The content was not modified while it was transmitted.

17 USC § 512(a). Here's an example of how the transmission safe harbor shields Internet service providers and system operators from liability:

EXAMPLE

Pam posted copyrighted material belonging to the Church of Scientology on a computer bulletin board. John accessed the bulletin board from his home computer. For John to view Pam's postings on the bulletin board, those postings were automatically copied many times by computers belonging to a number of network providers. If the four conditions stated in the previous paragraph were met, the owners of these computers are not liable for copyright infringement damages (even though, technically, their computers engaged in copying the infringing material posted by Pam).

Storage Safe Harbor

According to the DMCA's "storage" safe harbor, a service provider is not liable for copyright infringement damages when infringing material is stored on the service provider's system by a system user under the following conditions:

- The service provider does not have actual knowledge that the material or an activity using the material is infringing.

- The service provider is not aware of facts or circumstances from which infringing activity is apparent.

- The service provider, if it has the right and ability to control the activity, does not receive a financial benefit directly attributable to the infringing activity.

- The service provider, upon receiving a notice of claimed infringement ("take down notice") by the copyright owner, removes the material or disables access to it.

17 USC § 512(c). Here's an example of the storage safe harbor:

EXAMPLE

Giantco's Web site has copyrighted graphics belonging to John. Giantco's marketing department used the graphics without John's permission. World Internet provides the Web hosting facilities for Giantco's Web site, so the infringing material is stored on and transmitted through World Internet's system. World Internet is not liable to John for damages for infringement if the four conditions stated in the previous paragraph were met.

In both examples, the party that posted infringing material (Pam in the first example, Giantco in the second one) is liable to the copyright owner for infringement damages. The DMCA does not protect the party that posted infringing material from damages for infringement.

SAFE HARBOR, NOT IMMUNITY

A photographer we know discovered that a number of his photographs had been posted, without his permission, on the "user postings" page of a computer "wallpaper" supplier's Web site. When the photographer asked the Web site's owner to remove the photographs, the owner said, "I'm not liable for infringing material posted by users of my site." That's not true. For the site owner to claim immunity under the DMCA, he would have to comply with the photographer's take down notice and meet the threshold requirements discussed later in this section.

Definition of Service Provider

For the storage safe harbor, "service provider" is defined as "a provider of online services or network access, or the operator of facilities therefore" or an entity offering transmission or routing for material specified by a user between points specified by the user. For the transmission safe harbor, only the second part of the definition applies. 17 USC § 512(k).

ISPs and online services are clearly service providers, but other providers of online facilities also appear to be within the definition—for example, portal sites, search engines, intranet owners and operators, educational institutions that provide online services for faculty and students, and membership organizations that provide online services and Internet access facilities for members.

In fact, the owner of any Web site that incorporates material posted by third-party site users would seem to be within the definition of "service provider" and thus eligible to take advantage of the safe harbors. If you operate a Web site that posts user submissions or has a chat room feature, you should make certain that you meet the threshold requirements to take advantage of the DMCA's provisions.

FOREIGN LAW

The DMCA's safe harbors are U.S. law. In other countries, there may be no parallel safe harbors or immunity for ISPs and other providers of Internet access and online facilities. The European Union is considering a copyright directive that will insulate ISPs from liability for transmission of infringing material, but it will be some time before that directive will become effective (and it is not as broad as the DMCA). Germany has a statute that immunizes ISPs from liability unless the ISP has actual knowledge of the infringement and can block it using technology.

Threshold Requirements

There are three threshold requirements a service provider must meet in order to take advantage of any of the DMCA's safe harbors. A service provider must:

■ Adopt and implement a policy of terminating the accounts of repeat infringers.

■ Inform subscribers and account holders of this policy.

■ Accommodate and not interfere with "standard technical measures" used by copyright owners to identify or protect copyrighted works. (Copyright management information and copy protection devices are discussed in chapter 24.)

If you want to be in a position to rely on a safe harbor provision, develop a policy of terminating repeat infringers and post it on your Web site.

To take advantage of the storage safe harbor, you must designate an agent to receive notices of claimed infringement. The agent must be an individual, not the title for a corporate officer (such as president or vice president).

We'll use a capital "A" when referring to a designated agent. The Agent designation information must be made available on the service provider's Web site and filed with the Copyright Office. The fee for filing the designation form with the Copyright Office is $20. It must be mailed to the Copyright Office, not transmitted by email.

The Copyright Office has posted a suggested format ("Interim Designation of Agent" and "Amended Designation of Agent") online at http://lcweb. loc.gov/copyright/onlinsp.

The Copyright Office also has posted a list of designated Agents at www.loc.gov/copyright/onlinsp/list/index.html.

Take Down Notices

The DMCA states that a notification of claimed infringement must be written and must contain this information:

- The signature of the rights owner (or person authorized to act on behalf of the owner).

- Identification of the copyrighted work claimed to have been infringed.

- Identification of the material that is claimed to be infringing (material that is to be removed).

- Information on how the service provider can contact the complaining party.

A notification of claimed infringement must include a statement that the signing party has a good faith belief that use of the material in the manner complained of is not authorized by the copyright owner, or its agent, or the law. It must also include a statement that the information in the notification is accurate, and under penalty of perjury, that the complaining party has the authority to enforce the owner's rights that are claimed to be infringed. Any person who knowingly materially misrepresents that material is infringing is liable to the alleged infringer, the copyright owner, and the service provider for damages, including attorney's fees. 17 USC § 512(f).

A notice that does not meet these requirements will not be considered in determining whether a service provider has actual knowledge of infringement or is aware of facts or circumstances from which infringing activity is apparent. 17 USC § 512(c)(3). However, if a deficient take down notice substantially complies with the information requirements for a notice but lacks a signature or the statements described in the previous paragraph, the service provider must promptly attempt to contact the person making the notification or takes other reasonable steps to help that person comply with all the requirements.

Liability for Removing Material

A service provider is not liable to any person for good faith removal of material claimed to be infringing, even if the material is ultimately determined to not be infringing. 17 USC § 512(g)(1). This is true even if the service provider has not received a take down notice.

If the service provider removes material posted by a subscriber pursuant to a take down notice, the service provider is immune from liability for removing the material only if it takes reasonable steps promptly to notify the subscriber that it has removed the material. If the service provider's designated Agent receives a "counter notice" from its subscriber stating that the material was removed as a result of mistake, the law's protection against liability to the subscriber applies only if the service provider replaces the removed material no sooner than ten business days and no later than fourteen business days after receipt of the counter notice. The service provider must send the complaining party a copy of the counter notification and inform that person that it will replace the removed material in ten business days. If, before the service provider replaces the material, the service provider receives a notice from the complaining party that it has filed a lawsuit in federal court seeking a restraining order against the subscriber, the service provider is not required to replace the material. 17 USC § 17(g)(2).

A DMCA CHECKLIST

In order to be able to take advantage of the DMCA's safe harbors, you should do the following:

- Adopt and implement a policy of terminating the accounts of repeat infringers.

- Inform subscribers and account holders of this policy.

- Accommodate standard technical measures used by copyright owners to identify or protect copyrighted works.

- Designate an Agent who will receive take down notices.

- Develop a procedure for receiving, reviewing, and acting on take down notices.

- Follow through on the procedure when you receive take down notices.

Removing material without having met the threshold requirements does not immunize you. Meeting the threshold requirements but not following through when you receive take down notices doesn't immunize you either.

Knowledge

The general rule in "agency" law is that an agent's knowledge of relevant facts is attributed to a principle. For example, a corporation will generally be deemed to "know" what its management knows. This principle is known as *respondeat superior*.

The DMCA provides a limited exemption from this principle for public and other nonprofit institutions of higher education. When a faculty member or graduate student who is an employee of such an institution is performing a teaching or research function, for purposes of the transmission and caching safe harbors, the faculty member or graduate student is considered to be a person separate from the institution (so the institution is not considered to "know" things just because the faculty member or graduate student knows them). For purposes of the storage and linking safe harbors, the faculty member's or graduate student's knowledge or awareness is not attributed to the institution if these three conditions apply:

■ The faculty member's or graduate student's infringing activities do not involve providing online access to instructional materials that were required or recommended within the preceding three-year period for a course taught by the faculty member or graduate student at the institution.

■ The institution has not, within the preceding three-year period, received more than two take down notices claiming infringement by the faculty member or graduate student.

■ The institution provides all users of its system with informational materials that describe and promote compliance with U.S. copyright law.

Materials used in distance learning courses would appear to be instructional materials required or recommended for a course. Thus, if a faculty member uses materials in violation of copyright laws in a distance learning course, the DMCA safe harbors are not applicable.

EXAMPLE

Ron, an art history professor, is currently teaching an online course for Central University. Ron has created an online compilation of images of copyrighted paintings for use by the students during class and for after-class review. He did not get permission from the copyright owners. Because the online compilation is instructional material for a course, Ron's knowledge that he has used the images without permission is attributed to Central University. (This doesn't mean that his use is infringement. It may be fair use.)

Distance learning is discussed in chapter 27.

When the DMCA Doesn't Apply

In this section, we'll discuss two situations in which the DMCA doesn't apply: (1) When material is placed on the system by the service provider rather than a system user; and (2) When the material is placed on the system by a system user, but the service provider cannot take advantage of a safe harbor provision.

Material Posted by Service Provider

When a service provider (or one of its employees) posts copyrighted material belonging to someone else on its Web site, without permission, the safe harbors do not apply.

EXAMPLE

Portal Site offers several reports on e-commerce. The reports were posted on the site by Portal Site's marketing director, who posted them without the copyright owners' permission. The DMCA does not protect Portal Site from liability for damages for copyright infringement. The reports were not stored on Portal Site's system at the direction of system users; they were stored by Portal Site. Portal Site is liable for infringement damages.

Safe Harbors Not Applicable

When material is placed on the service provider's system by a third-party user but the safe harbor provision does not apply, the service provider is not necessarily liable for infringement. Pre-DMCA legal principles (such as contributory infringement, applied in the *Religious Technology Center* case, discussed earlier in this section) apply. Congress stated that it was not changing the law of liability in passing the DMCA or negating any defenses to infringement, such as fair use.

EXAMPLE

Giantco's Web site has copyrighted graphics belonging to John. Giantco's marketing department used the graphics without John's permission. World Internet provides the Web hosting facilities for Giantco's Web site, so the infringing material is stored on and transmitted through World Internet's system. World Internet has not designated an Agent for receiving take down notices, so World Internet cannot claim immunity from infringement damages under the DMCA's storage safe harbor. That doesn't mean that World Internet is liable to John for infringement damages.

World Internet could be found liable to John for direct copyright infringement (for the automatic copying of John's material within World's computers and networks), for contributory infringement, or for vicarious infringement.

In the *Religious Technology Center* case, the judge noted that copying of the church's materials took place within Netcom's computer each time Dennis Erlich posted a message to the newsgroup (because a copy of each message was automatically made on Netcom's computer and stored there for several days). However, the judge held that Netcom was not liable for direct infringement because

Netcom did not take any affirmative act that directly resulted in copying the Church of Scientology's works (aside from setting up a system that copies and stores messages to get them from the sender to the Usenet). The judge stated that even though copyright is a strict liability statute, "there should still be some element of volition or causation which is lacking where a defendant's system is merely used to create a copy by a third party." *Religious Technology Center v. Netcom On-Line Communication Services, Inc.*, 907 FSupp 1361, 1370 (ND Cal 1995).

Contributory infringement is established when a defendant, with knowledge of another party's infringing activity, causes or materially contributes to the infringing conduct. The *Religious Technology Center* court found that Netcom could be liable for contributory infringement for postings made by Erlich after the church notified Netcom that Erlich was posting infringing material. If Netcom had knowledge of Erlich's infringement, as the church claimed, and failed to cancel infringing messages while there was still time to do so, that would constitute substantial participation in the distribution of the message. Netcom would then be liable for contributory infringement. (The case was settled, so we'll never know how these issues would have been decided at trial.)

Vicarious liability may be imposed where the defendant has the right and ability to supervise the infringing activity and a direct financial interest in the activities. A line of cases known as the "dance hall cases" holds that dance hall owners are liable for infringing performances by non-employee musicians because the owners were able to control the premises and received a direct financial benefit from the audience that paid to enjoy the infringing performance. In the *Religious Technology Center* case, the court held that Netcom could not have vicarious liability because Netcom did not receive a direct financial benefit from Erlich's infringement. At the time, the law in the Ninth Circuit (the appellate division for the court that decided the *Religious Technology Center* case) was that financial benefit meant a commission directly tied to the sale of the particular infringing material. However, a later Ninth Circuit case, *Fonovisa, Inc. v. Cherry Auction, Inc.*, 76 F3d 259 (9th Cir 1996), held that even fixed fees could count as financial benefit. Had the *Fonovisa* case been decided by the Ninth Circuit before the *Religious Technology Center* court rendered its opinion, the *Religious Technology Center* court probably would have ruled differently on the vicarious liability theory.

Benefit to Copyright Owners

The DMCA gives copyright owners a new way of stopping infringement: Copyright owners who find their text, graphics, photos, or other copyrighted material used on the Web without their permission can contact the ISP or other service provider for the offending Web site and request that the service provider remove the material.

EXAMPLE

One day, while Sue was surfing the Web, she found her copyrighted graphics on High Tech Company's marketing Web site. Sue did not give High Tech permission to use her graphics. High Tech's ISP is Superb Internet. Using the DMCA, Sue sends Superb Internet a notification of claimed infringement. Superb removes Sue's graphics from High Tech 's Web site (knowing that by doing so, it shields itself from liability to Sue for copyright infringement, assuming it has met the threshold requirements).

Sue can still recover damages for copyright infringement from High Tech Company. The DMCA gives her an additional remedy, that of having the material taken off the Web.

Preparing a Take Down Notice

It's a good idea to review copyright law's ownership rules (discussed in chapter 3) before filing a notification of claimed infringement. If you are not the copyright owner or owner of an exclusive right, you should not sign a notification of claimed infringement unless the owner has authorized you to act for it.

EXAMPLE

If Sue (in the example immediately above) created the graphics "borrowed" by High Tech as part of her job while working for Big Company, Big owns the copyright. Sue does not. Unless Sue has received permission from Big to enforce Big's rights, Sue should not sign or send a notification to Superb Internet complaining about High Tech's use of the graphics. Sue's rights are not being infringed by High Tech's use of the material.

Liability for Other Wrongs

In this section, we address the issue whether an ISP or other provider of Internet access or online facilities is liable for other wrongs by a system user—defamation, misappropriation of the right of privacy, and trademark and patent infringement.

Defamation

Defamation protects an individual against the dissemination of falsehoods about the individual. The question considered here is whether an ISP or other provider of Internet access or facilities is liable when a system user posts material that defames someone else (or a company).

EXAMPLE

A consumer products review site posts product reviews submitted by site users. Jack submitted a product review which states that the manufacturer of the product is insolvent and its president is a convicted felon (untrue statements). Is the owner of the consumer review site liable for defamation? What about the Web host for the consumer review site?

Defamation law distinguishes between original publishers, distributors, and common carriers. Whether the Web site owner and the Web host are liable for defamation depends in part on whether these parties acted as publishers, distributors, or common carriers.

Here are the basic rules:

- **Publishers:** Actual publishers of books, magazines, and newspapers are generally liable for republication of defamatory material because they are deemed to have acquired knowledge of the content provided by third parties through the process of editing and producing their publications for sale.

- **Distributors:** One who merely delivers or transmits defamatory material previously published by someone else is liable for having published defamatory material only if they knew or had reason to know that the material was false and defamatory. Libraries and booksellers fall into this category.

- **Common carriers:** Common carriers—a telephone company, for example—are immune from liability for defamatory content carried by their equipment.

It is difficult to apply these rules to cyberspace because many of the players perform multiple functions (for example, an online news service with an interactive Web page and a bulletin board). However, a provision in the 1995 Communications Decency Act appears to resolve the issue for ISPs. That provision states that "[n]o provider or user of an interactive computer service shall be treated as the publisher or speaker of any information provided by another information content provider." 47 USC § 230(c)(1). "Interactive computer service" is defined as "any information service, system, or access software provider that provides or enables computer access by multiple users to a computer service, including specifically a service or system that provides access to the Internet." "Information content provider" is defined as "any person or entity that is responsible, in whole or part, for the creation or development of information provided through the Internet or any other interactive computer service."

In the example, the Web hosting company appears to be an interactive computer service. It is not liable for the defamatory posting. The same is probably true of the Web site owner.

EARLIER LAW

At the time the Communications Decency Act went into effect, there were two cases dealing with system operator and service provider liability for defamation by users. In *Stratton Oakmont, Inc. v. Prodigy Services Co.,* 1995 N.Y. Misc. LEXIS 229 (NYSCt 1995), the plaintiff, a securities investment bank, sought to hold Prodigy liable for allegedly defamatory statements made about Stratton by an unknown Prodigy subscriber on Prodigy's financial bulletin board, "Money Talk." The court held that Prodigy was liable as a "publisher" because Prodigy exercised content control. Money Talk discussions were facilitated by "bulletin board leaders" who participated in discussions and had the ability to delete posted messages believed to be in bad taste or grossly repugnant to community standards or harmful to maintaining a harmonious online community. Stratton Oakmont withdrew the suit in exchange for a statement from Prodigy that Prodigy was sorry that a subscriber had posted messages accusing Stratton Oakmont of fraud. In *Cubby v. CompuServe,* 776 FSupp 135 (SD NY 1991), CompuServe was sued for allegedly defamatory statements made about the plaintiffs on CompuServe's "Rumorville" bulletin board. The court held that CompuServe was merely a distributor because it had no more editorial control over bulletin board material than does a public library, bookstore, or newsstand (CompuServe contracted with another company to review and control the contents of the bulletin board). Because the plaintiffs failed to show that there was a genuine issue as to whether CompuServe knew or had reason to know of the allegedly libelous statements, the court granted summary judgment for CompuServe.

Trademark and Patent Infringement

Whether ISPs and system operators are liable for trademark, patent, and trade secret infringement or right of publicity and privacy violations by system users is unclear. There are no safe harbor laws for these types of infringement. The DMCA is limited to copyright infringement.

A service provider is not liable for a third party's cybersquatting use of a domain name that is identical to or confusingly similar to a trademark protected under the Anticybersquatting Consumer Protection Act (ACPA). A provision in ACPA states that "[a] person shall be liable for using a domain name [in violation of ACPA] only if that person is the domain name registrant or the registrant's authorized licensee.

ACPA is discussed in "Cybersquatting," chapter 16.

Liability for Other Wrongs by Users

Whether system operators and service providers will be held liable for user wrongs other than copyright infringement and defamation is also being debated.

The Federal Trade Commission's current view on liability for unfair and deceptive practices is that a third party (such as a system operator or service provider) should be held liable for a user's unfair or deceptive message only when the third party "knew or should have known" that the message was unfair or deceptive and failed to take appropriate action. In 1994, the FTC investigated fraudulent ads posted on America Online by a credit repair operation and prosecuted the author of those messages, not AOL (AOL cooperated with the FTC).

FOREIGN LAW

Remember that the Communications Decency Act is U.S. law. In other countries, ISPs and other providers of Internet access and online facilities may be considered "publishers" of material posted by system users. In March 2000, a British court required an ISP to pay libel damages to a British physicist, Laurence Godfrey, who was defamed when an unknown user posted a bulletin board message and falsely attributed the message to Godfrey. The court held that the ISP was liable for defamation because Godfrey informed the ISP that he was not the author and asked the company to remove it. He did not receive a response.

CHAPTER 26

PROTECTING YOUR INTELLECTUAL PROPERTY RIGHTS

Much of this book has been devoted to how to avoid infringement of others' intellectual property rights. The focus of this chapter is on how you can maximize your own intellectual property protection.

To review the basic principles of copyright law, refer to chapter 1. The basic principles of patent law, trademark law, and trade secrets law are discussed in chapter 2. Additional information about trademark law is in chapter 15.

Copyright Protection

For Web software and content and online products, copyright law is the primary source of intellectual property protection. As a copyright owner, you have the exclusive right to:

- Reproduce your work.

- Modify your work to create new works (known as derivative works).

- Distribute your work.

- Publicly display your work.

- Publicly perform your work.

(These rights are defined in "The Exclusive Rights," chapter 1.)

Anyone who wants to exercise any of these exclusive rights in your work needs a license from you. For your own material, you get to be on the other side—the licensor side—of the rights clearance process described in chapters 9 and 10.

Register Early

Copyright protection attaches automatically when an original work of authorship is "fixed." However, the Copyright Act provides an incentive for "timely" registration: To ensure that you can get statutory damages in an infringement suit, you must register your work within three months after first publication of the work.

Statutory damages are damages of $750 to $30,000, "as the court considers just." For "willful infringement," a court can award statutory damages up to $150,000. An act is willful if the infringer knew the act was an infringement of copyright.

"Publication" is defined as distribution of copies to the public by sale, rental, lease, or lending. 17 USC § 101. An offer to distribute copies to a group of persons for further distribution or performance is also publication.

"PUBLICATION" OF ONLINE MATERIAL

Making material available on the Web is not distribution of a "copy" of the material, as we discussed in "When You Need a License," chapter 9. Making material available on the Web is public display of the material, but public display does not constitute publication. 17 USC § 101. For an unpublished work, statutory damages and attorney's fees are available only if the infringement began after the effective date of copyright registration. To be safe, we recommend that if you want to preserve your right to get statutory damages and attorney's fees, you should file registration applications promptly after the material is available for public access on the Web.

Early registration also makes you eligible to receive an award of attorney's fees (in the court's discretion). If your work has not been published or if it is registered more than three months after first publication, then statutory damages and attorney's fees are available only for infringements that began after the date of the registration.

If you don't register your copyright, your damages in an infringement suit may be limited to the actual damages that you can prove (how much money you lost as a result of the infringement) and any profits of the infringer that are not taken into account in computing your actual damages. It may be difficult to prove your actual damages and the infringer's profits.

More importantly, if you don't register your copyright within three months of the first publication, you may not be entitled to recover attorney's fees. Even if you can prove your actual damages and the infringer's profits, the total may be too low to cover your legal fees for the lawsuit.

409

protecting
your
intellectual
property
rights

EXAMPLE

Defendant used ten seconds of content from Developer's "published" CD-ROM computer game in a new online computer game. Developer sued Defendant for copyright infringement. Developer had registered the copyright on the game within three months of first publication of the game. Developer opted for statutory damages and asked the court for attorney's fees. The court awarded Developer $10,000 in statutory damages and the entire cost of its legal fees in the case ($15,000). If Developer had not been eligible to opt for statutory damages and receive attorney's fees, it might not have been worth it to file the lawsuit. Developer would have had difficulty proving that it had any damages from Defendant's use of ten seconds of Developer's work or that Defendant had profited from using ten seconds of Developer's work. Additionally, Developer probably would not have received enough in damages to cover its attorney's fees.

ATTORNEY'S FEES FOR SUCCESSFUL DEFENDANTS

A court can award attorney's fees to a successful defendant in a copyright infringement case. *Fogerty v. Fantasy, Inc.*, 114 SCt 1023 (1994).

The other reasons to register the copyright in a work are as follows:

■ If you are a U.S. citizen, you *will* have to register your work before filing a copyright infringement suit. Citizens of foreign countries whose works are protected in the U.S. by the Berne Convention are exempt from this requirement. Expedited registration costs $500. Regular registration costs $30. (These fees are effective through June 30, 2002.)

■ If you have registered your work, someone who wants permission to use it or buy it will be able to find you by obtaining a Copyright Office registration search. (Copyright Office searches are discussed in "Determining Who Owns the Copyright," chapter 10.)

- If you intend to assign your copyright, give a lender a security interest in your copyright, or grant exclusive licenses, the other party to the transaction will probably want to record the transaction in the Copyright Office and so will insist that the copyright be registered. The benefits of recording a transaction are discussed in "Assignments" and "Licenses," chapter 3. Recording the transaction gives constructive notice only if the copyright is registered and the copyright registration number is included on the recorded document (see "Obtaining a License," chapter 10).

- A certificate of registration made within five years of the first publication of the work is legal evidence of the validity of the copyright and of the facts stated in the certificate of registration. If you registered within five years of first publication, the defendant in an infringement suit has the burden of proof in challenging the validity of your copyright (for example, by claiming that your work was not original) or your ownership of the copyright.

Registration Procedure

To register your work, you have to fill out a two-page registration application form and mail it to the Copyright Office in Washington, D.C. You must include the required deposit of copies of your work (see "Deposit Requirements," later in this chapter) and a check for the registration fee ($30).

ELECTRONIC REGISTRATION

The Copyright Office is currently testing an electronic registration, recordation, and deposit system called "CORDS" (see www.loc.gov/copyright/cords/cords.html), but electronic registration is not yet available for anyone other than test project participants.

The Copyright Office has an informational circular to guide you through the application process, Circular 66, *Copyright Registration for Online Works*. Information circulars are available online at www.loc.gov/copyright/circs. You may also want to look at Circular 61, *Copyright Registration for Computer Programs*; Circular 65, *Copyright Registration for Automated Databases*; Circular 55, *Copyright Registration for Multimedia Works*; and Circular 14, *Copyright Registration for Derivative Works*.

Which Form?

For administrative purposes, the Copyright Office has divided copyrightable works into different classes. It provides registration application forms for these classes. There is no special application form for online works. You have to choose one of these forms:

411

protecting
your
intellectual
property
rights

- Literary works, including software (Form TX).

- Pictorial and graphic works (Form VA).

- Audiovisual works (Form PA).

Use the form that corresponds to the predominant material in the work you are registering.

If you want to register the copyright in a Web site that is predominantly text and software, use Form TX. If you want to register the copyright in a Web site that is primarily photographs, use Form VA. If you want to register the copyright in an online game (an audiovisual work), use Form PA. Do not file multiple forms for the same work unless you need separate registrations for components, as discussed later in this section.

DON'T SWEAT FORM SELECTION

Except for sound recordings, which must be registered on Form SR, a work may actually be registered on any form. Which form you choose does not affect the scope of your copyright protection (which arises automatically) or whether you will be entitled to the benefits of registration.

Obtaining Forms

The Copyright Office registration application forms and instructions are available in Adobe Acrobat PDF format on the Copyright Office's Web site at www.loc.gov/copyright/forms. You need an Adobe Acrobat Reader on your computer to view and print the forms. The Reader is available for free from Adobe Systems. The Copyright Office "forms" Web page has a link to the Adobe site.

The forms must be printed on 81-inch by 11-inch paper head to head (so that the top of page 2 is directly behind the top of page 1) using both sides of a single sheet of paper. An application made on a photocopied blank form is acceptable if it meets these criteria. You can also receive forms by mail by calling the Copyright Office's Forms Hotline at (202) 707-9100. If you're not sure what forms and circulars you want, call the Copyright Office's general information number: (202) 707-3000, or consult the Information Circulars and other information available on the Copyright Office's Web site (www.loc.gov/copyright).

Use black ink or a typewriter to fill out your application form. You also can fill out the form online (see "Fill-in Forms Instructions" at www.loc.gov/copyright/forms/fill.html), but you then have to print and mail the form to the Copyright Office (complying with the printing instructions stated in the preceding paragraph).

How to Fill Out Form TX

Here's a space-by-space explanation of how you fill out Form TX. (Forms VA and PA require basically the same information.)

SAMPLE FORM TX

We've included a sample filled-out Form TX at the end of this chapter. The sample registration application seeks copyright registration for a Web site called *Adventure Travel Site*. We chose Form TX for this work because the site contains more text (articles on trips and travel destinations) than photos. The Web site is a work made for hire created by employees of the site owner, ABC Travel, Inc.

Front Page

Top right corner: Don't put anything here. This space is for the Copyright Office staff.

Space 1: Title: The Copyright Office will register and index your work under this title. If your Web site or online product already has a name (such as Adventure Travel Site), use that name. If it doesn't, chose a name.

Space 2: Author:

Works created by individuals: For a work created by an individual author or authors, list the names of the individuals and add the requested birth date, death date, and nationality information.

Works made for hire: If the work is a work made for hire (see "The Work Made for Hire Rule," chapter 3), list the employer or hiring party as the "author." (ABC Travel, Inc. is the author of the *Adventure Travel Site* because the site is a work made for hire.) For works made for hire, do not list contributing employees or independent contractors as authors. (Copyright law does not consider them authors, as we explained in "The Work Made for Hire Rule," chapter 3.)

Nature of Authorship: For each author, you must describe the "nature of authorship" (nature of material created by the author in which copyright is claimed). Identify the type of work contributed by the author, using terms that refer to copyrightable works such as "text," "artwork," "photographs," "music," or "software code." For the sample application, the nature of authorship is "text, art, software, and photographs." Circular 66 states that you should not use these terms: user interface, format, layout, design, lettering, concept, or game play.

If you have licenses to use copyrighted works owned by others, do not put the licensors' names in space 2. Your licensors are not authors of the work that you are applying to register (and your copyright doesn't cover the work protected by their copyrights). You will mention the types of preexisting works that are included in your work in another section of the application (space 6).

Space 3: Year in which creation was completed: Give the date of completion of the version of the work that you are applying to register.

Date and nation of first publication: As we noted earlier in this section, a public display of a work does not constitute publication. If your material is available only online (you are not distributing physical "copies"), your work is not "published." Circular 66 acknowledges that the "definition of 'publication' in the U.S. copyright law does not specifically address online transmission." If you decide that your work has been published (because physical copies have been distributed), give the complete date and nation of first publication in space 3b. If the work has not been published, leave this space blank.

Space 4: Copyright claimants: Unless you acquired the copyright in the work by assignment (see "Assignments," chapter 3), you are both the author and the claimant. Put your name and address here. This information tells potential licensees where to reach you.

If you acquired the copyright by assignment, explain how you acquired the copyright (for example, "by written assignment from the author"). You must indicate that you acquired all of the author's U.S. copyright rights (not just permission to use the work).

Second Page

Space 5: Previous registration: Leave this space blank unless an earlier version of the work has been registered, in which case you have to justify filing a new registration application.

Space 6: Derivative work or compilation: If the work you are registering includes preexisting works—for example, text, graphics, and photographs—you need to fill out space 6. If all of the components of the work you are registering were newly created for this work, you can skip this space. If your work incorporates preexisting works, identify them in space 6a. You can identify them by title or by type of work ("previously published graphics, text, and photographs").

In space 6b, state what new material you have added to the preexisting material to create your copyrighted work—for example, "original graphics, text, and software, and compilation and editing of preexisting material."

NOTE: If you are using Form PA or Form VA, if you created your work by simply collecting and assembling preexisting materials or data, your work is a compilation and you don't have to fill out space 6a. You just have to explain in space 6b what has been compiled—for example, "a compilation of various photographers' photographs of Depression-era poverty scenes with soundtrack consisting of excerpts of musical compositions composed during the Depression." Your goal here is to convince the Copyright Office that there's sufficient originality in your selection, arrangement, and coordination of the material to justify copyright protection. (See "Standards," chapter 1.) If your work is a derivative work, as most Web sites and online products are, you need to fill out spaces 6a and 6b.

Spaces 7, 8, and 9: Deposit account, correspondence, and certification: Unless you have a deposit account with the Copyright Office, leave space 7a blank and attach a check for $30 payable to the Register of Copyrights. You can open a deposit account if you have twelve or more transactions each year with the Copyright Office.

Put your address and other contact information in space 7a, unless someone else (a copyright attorney, for example) will be handling any questions the Copyright Office staff might have about your application. In space 8, check the appropriate box, print or type your name and fill in the date, and sign below the typed or printed name. If you are signing as agent of a corporation (president, for example), check the box "authorized agent of " and fill in the corporation's name in the blank. Type and sign your own name, though, in the "typed or printed name and date" and "handwritten signature" blanks.

Fill out space 9, the mailing label for your certificate. It will be several months before you receive your certificate. Your registration is effective as of the date the Copyright Office receives your properly completed application, deposit, and check.

Deposit Requirements

For online works other than computer programs, databases, and works fixed in CD-ROM format, you have two deposit options:

- Deposit a computer disk containing the entire work plus representative portions in a format that can be examined by the Copyright Office (printout, audiocassette, or videotape).

- Deposit a reproduction of the entire work (printout, audiocassette, or videotape).

If the work is published both online and by the distribution of physical copies, follow the deposit requirement that applies to the physical copy. For example, if a work is published in the form of books and online, deposit two copies of the printed book. For most types of works, the deposit requirement is two copies of the work (one copy if the work is unpublished).

For computer programs, follow the deposit requirements stated in Circular 61. For databases, follow the deposit requirements stated in Circular 65. For CD-ROM works, the deposit requirement is one complete copy of the CD-ROM package. A complete copy is defined as all of the following items:

- The CD-ROM.

- The operating software.

- Any manuals that go with the material.

- A printed version of the work embodied in the CD-ROM, if the work is fixed in print as well as in a CD-ROM.

Separate Registrations for Components

You are not required to file separate copyright registrations for the original individual components of your work (the music, graphics, video footage, software, and so on). The copyright registration on the work as a whole covers the components. There are two exceptions to this rule: one for stand-alone components and one for exclusively licensed components.

Stand-Alone Components

Stand-alone components are components that are (or could be) a separate commercial product and that you intend to exploit apart from your work as a whole. An example is a software engine that you use in your Web-based product but also intend to exploit separately by licensing it to other Web developers. You should file a separate registration on a stand-alone component to make it easier to identify the component for licensing purposes.

WEB SITE CHANGES

Many Web site owners change their Web sites frequently. Material added after you submit a registration application is not covered by the registration. However, it is protected by copyright (because copyright protection arises automatically when a work of authorship is "fixed"). There is no group registration procedure available to cover Web site updates. Separate registrations (and filing fees) are required. However, some online works may be automated databases. For automated databases, a group of updates covering up to a three-month period within the same calendar year may be combined in a single registration (see Circular 65). Group registration is available for online serials and daily newsletters. See Circular 62 and Circular 62a.

415

protecting
your
intellectual
property
rights

Exclusively Licensed Components

You don't own the copyright in a component for which you have an exclusive license. (This term is defined in "Licenses," chapter 3.) However, the Copyright Act gives you the right to register a work for which you have an exclusive license. You may wish to do so if you believe that it is likely that the exclusively licensed component will be infringed apart from your work as a whole.

Copyright Notice

Copyright notice consists of three elements:

- The copyright symbol ©, the word "Copyright," or the abbreviation "Copr."

- The year of first publication of the work.

- The name of the copyright owner.

The use of copyright notice is optional in the United States. However, there are good reasons for using copyright notice:

- Using notice informs the public—and potential infringers—that the work is copyrighted.

- Notice tells those who might want to get licenses to use your work who owns the copyright (at the time of the publication of the copy with notice).

- In an infringement suit, an infringer who had access to a copy containing notice cannot use an "innocent infringement" defense. This defense, if successful, could result in the court's lowering your statutory damages (discussed in "Register Early," earlier in this chapter).

- It's difficult to prove "willful" infringement (and get increased statutory damages) if copies of your work don't contain the copyright notice.

- Using notice will get you protection for your work in the few countries that still require the use of notice (countries that are not members of the Berne Convention).

Many people don't understand the rights of copyright owners under the Copyright Act. For example, some people don't know that buying a copy of a copyrighted work doesn't give them permission to copy the work. (This topic is discussed in "Owning a Copy of a Work," chapter 3.) You should consider adding your own "warning statement" to your material. For example, you could include a statement, "No part of this work may be reproduced in whole or in part in any manner without the permission of the copyright owner."

International Copyright Protection

As was noted in "International Protection," chapter 1, American authors automatically receive copyright protection in countries that belong to the Berne Convention and the Universal Copyright Convention. Most major countries belong to one of these conventions. You don't need to register your copyrights in Berne or UCC countries to receive copyright protection in those countries. You *do* need to use copyright notice on copies of your work that are distributed in countries belonging to the UCC, but not to Berne.

Bolivia and Honduras require a unique form of copyright notice: "All rights reserved." If you plan to distribute your products in these countries, add that phrase at the end of your copyright notice.

Patent Protection

If your product involves technology that is novel and nonobvious, you may be able to patent it. You should see a patent attorney without delay (and certainly before you publicly distribute or display your product). By delaying, you risk losing your right to get a patent. The basics of patent law are discussed in "Patent Law," chapter 2.

Trademark Protection

Trademark law provides protection for words, symbols, slogans, and product configurations that are used in marketing products and services. The basics of trademark law are discussed in "Trademark Law," chapter 2. Choosing a trademark is discussed in chapter 15.

Although you can obtain trademark ownership and limited trademark protection in the United States simply by using a trademark in connection with your products, you should obtain federal registrations of your trademarks to receive maximum trademark protection. There are several benefits to federal registration:

- A federal registration gives you rights in your trademark throughout the United States, even in geographical areas in which you are not currently using your trademark (see "Trademark Law," chapter 3).

- A federal registration is legal evidence of your ownership of the mark and your exclusive right to use it in interstate commerce.

- Federal registrants can file infringement suits in federal court.

- Federal registrants can have U.S. Customs bar the importation of goods bearing infringing trademarks.

■ Federal registrants enjoy expanded remedies against counterfeited goods, and they are eligible to receive awards of attorney's fees (in the court's discretion) in infringement actions.

If you plan to spend significant amounts of money advertising your product, you should seriously consider federal registration.

If you are planning on coming out with a line of products, you should consider registering a "house mark" that you can use on your entire product line. "Adobe" is an example of a house mark used by its owner, Adobe Systems, Inc., on the various items in the owner's product line (for example, *Adobe Illustrator* and *Adobe Photoshop*).

Trademark protection can be lost by the action or inaction of the trademark owner, whether or not there is a federal registration. To maintain trademark protection, you as the trademark owner must do the following things:

■ **Continuously use the mark.** A trademark must be used continuously to avoid loss of rights. A federally registered trademark is assumed to be abandoned if it is not used for a period longer than two years. Once a mark has been abandoned, the trademark owner loses the priority date of the original registration or adoption of the mark.

■ **Monitor third-party use.** A trademark owner has a duty to prevent third parties from using the trademark to designate a class of products (rather than the owner's products). A trademark owner's failure to prevent confusing use of the trademark can result in the mark becoming generic and unprotectible. "Aspirin," "escalator," and "thermos" are examples of trademarks that became generic and lost their protection.

■ **Exercise quality control over licensees.** Trademarks can be licensed to third parties for their use. However, the trademark owner must exercise quality control over third-party use of the trademark to ensure that the trademark indicates a consistent level of quality of goods or services. The failure to exercise quality control can result in a loss of rights.

■ **Avoid improper assignment of the mark.** Trademarks can only be assigned with the associated goodwill of the business in which they are used. An attempt to assign a trademark without the goodwill destroys trademark rights.

Trade Secret Protection

Trade secret law protects valuable product and business information that is not generally known. The basics of trade secret law are discussed in "Trade Secret Law," chapter 2.

While developers and publishers don't need to register their trade secrets to establish protection, trade secret protection is lost if reasonable efforts are not made to keep the information from becoming generally known. Measures to maintain secrecy include such steps as marking documents as confidential; restricting employees' and outsiders' access to materials or areas of the company; and requiring employees, independent contractors, and visitors to sign nondisclosure agreements (sometimes called "confidentiality agreements"). Trade secrets can be licensed to others without losing protection if the licensees are required to maintain the confidentiality of the trade secrets.

419

protecting
your
intellectual
property
rights

Nondisclosure Agreements

A nondisclosure agreement should state the following:

- What information is to be considered confidential information.

- How confidential information must be treated (for example, whether the receiving party can disclose the information to all employees and consultants or only to certain employees).

- The duration of the obligation to keep the information confidential.

Generally, confidential information is defined in one of these two ways: as information that is marked confidential by its owner or as information that the receiving party knows or should know is confidential. If you use the first definition, you need to include a method for identifying confidential information disclosed orally or by exhibition.

Generally, the following types of information are specifically excluded from the definition of confidential information:

- Information that is in the public domain at the time it is disclosed to the receiving party.

- Information that later enters the public domain (but not through the fault of the receiving party).

- Information that is required to be disclosed by a court or government.

- Information that is received from a third party without restrictions on disclosure.

Information that is independently developed by the receiving party (in addition to being received as a disclosure from the other party) is sometimes excluded from the definition as well. Some agreements require the party claiming that information is not confidential under this exception to bear the burden of proving that the party independently developed the information.

A sample nondisclosure agreement is included in appendix B (Form 1).

FEE CHANGES

Fees are effective through June 30, 2002. After that date, check the Copyright Office Website at www.loc.gov/copyright or call (202) 707-3000 for current fee information.

FORM TX

For a Nondramatic Literary Work
UNITED STATES COPYRIGHT OFFICE

REGISTRATION NUMBER

_____

TX _____ TXU

EFFECTIVE DATE OF REGISTRATION

_____

Month _____ Day _____ Year _____

DO NOT WRITE ABOVE THIS LINE. IF YOU NEED MORE SPACE, USE A SEPARATE CONTINUATION SHEET.

1

TITLE OF THIS WORK ▼

Adventure Travel Site

PREVIOUS OR ALTERNATIVE TITLES ▼

PUBLICATION AS A CONTRIBUTION If this work was published as a contribution to a periodical, serial, or collection, give information about the collective work in which the contribution appeared.   **Title of Collective Work ▼**

If published in a periodical or serial give: **Volume ▼**   **Number ▼**   **Issue Date ▼**   **On Pages ▼**

2

a

NAME OF AUTHOR ▼

ABC Travel, Inc

DATES OF BIRTH AND DEATH
Year Born ▼   Year Died ▼

Was this contribution to the work a "work made for hire"?
☑ Yes
☐ No

AUTHOR'S NATIONALITY OR DOMICILE
Name of Country
OR { Citizen of ▶ _____
Domiciled in ▶ _____

WAS THIS AUTHOR'S CONTRIBUTION TO THE WORK
Anonymous?   ☐ Yes ☑ No
Pseudonymous? ☐ Yes ☑ No
If the answer to either of these questions is "Yes," see detailed instructions.

NATURE OF AUTHORSHIP Briefly describe nature of material created by this author in which copyright is claimed. ▼
text, art, software, and photographs

NOTE

Under the law, the "author" of a "work made for hire" is generally the employer, not the employee (see instructions). For any part of this work that was "made for hire" check "Yes" in the space provided, give the employer (or other person for whom the work was prepared) as "Author" of that part, and leave the space for dates of birth and death blank.

b

NAME OF AUTHOR ▼

DATES OF BIRTH AND DEATH
Year Born ▼   Year Died ▼

Was this contribution to the work a "work made for hire"?
☐ Yes
☐ No

AUTHOR'S NATIONALITY OR DOMICILE
Name of Country
OR { Citizen of ▶ _____
Domiciled in ▶ _____

WAS THIS AUTHOR'S CONTRIBUTION TO THE WORK
Anonymous?   ☐ Yes ☐ No
Pseudonymous? ☐ Yes ☐ No
If the answer to either of these questions is "Yes," see detailed instructions.

NATURE OF AUTHORSHIP Briefly describe nature of material created by this author in which copyright is claimed. ▼

c

NAME OF AUTHOR ▼

DATES OF BIRTH AND DEATH
Year Born ▼   Year Died ▼

Was this contribution to the work a "work made for hire"?
☐ Yes
☐ No

AUTHOR'S NATIONALITY OR DOMICILE
Name of Country
OR { Citizen of ▶ _____
Domiciled in ▶ _____

WAS THIS AUTHOR'S CONTRIBUTION TO THE WORK
Anonymous?   ☐ Yes ☐ No
Pseudonymous? ☐ Yes ☐ No
If the answer to either of these questions is "Yes," see detailed instructions.

NATURE OF AUTHORSHIP Briefly describe nature of material created by this author in which copyright is claimed. ▼

3

a

YEAR IN WHICH CREATION OF THIS WORK WAS COMPLETED This information must be given in all cases.
2000 ◀ Year

b

DATE AND NATION OF FIRST PUBLICATION OF THIS PARTICULAR WORK Complete this information ONLY if this work has been published.
Month ▶ _____ Day ▶ _____ Year ▶ _____
◀ Nation

4

COPYRIGHT CLAIMANT(S) Name and address must be given even if the claimant is the same as the author given in space 2. ▼

ABC Travel, Inc.
100 Lake Street
Any City, CA 99999

See instructions before completing this space.

TRANSFER If the claimant(s) named here in space 4 is (are) different from the author(s) named in space 2, give a brief statement of how the claimant(s) obtained ownership of the copyright. ▼

DO NOT WRITE HERE
OFFICE USE ONLY

APPLICATION RECEIVED
_____

ONE DEPOSIT RECEIVED
_____

TWO DEPOSITS RECEIVED
_____

FUNDS RECEIVED
_____

MORE ON BACK ▶   • Complete all applicable spaces (numbers 5-9) on the reverse side of this page.
• See detailed instructions.   • Sign the form at line 8.

DO NOT WRITE HERE

Page 1 of _____ pages

DO NOT WRITE ABOVE THIS LINE. IF YOU NEED MORE SPACE, USE A SEPARATE CONTINUATION SHEET.

PREVIOUS REGISTRATION Has registration for this work, or for an earlier version of this work, already been made in the Copyright Office?

☐ Yes ☑ No If your answer is "Yes," why is another registration being sought? (Check appropriate box.) ▼

a. ☐ This is the first published edition of a work previously registered in unpublished form.

b. ☐ This is the first application submitted by this author as copyright claimant.

c. ☐ This is a changed version of the work, as shown by space 6 on this application.

If your answer is "Yes," give: **Previous Registration Number** ▶   **Year of Registration** ▶

5

DERIVATIVE WORK OR COMPILATION

Preexisting Material Identify any preexisting work or works that this work is based on or incorporates. ▼

Previously published graphics, text, and photos.

a

6

Material Added to This Work Give a brief, general statement of the material that has been added to this work and in which copyright is claimed. ▼

Original graphics, text, and software, and compilation and editing of preexisting material

b

See instructions before completing this space.

DEPOSIT ACCOUNT If the registration fee is to be charged to a Deposit Account established in the Copyright Office, give name and number of Account.

Name ▼   **Account Number** ▼

a

7

CORRESPONDENCE Give name and address to which correspondence about this application should be sent.   Name/Address/Apt/City/State/ZIP ▼

Susan Something
ABC Travel, Inc.
100 Lake Street
Any City, CA 99999

b

Area code and daytime telephone number ▶   Fax number ▶

Email ▶ susans@abct.com

CERTIFICATION* I, the undersigned, hereby certify that I am the

Check only one ▶

☐ author
☐ other copyright claimant
☐ owner of exclusive right(s)
☑ authorized agent of ABC Travel. Inc.

Name of author or other copyright claimant, or owner of exclusive right(s) ▲

of the work identified in this application and that the statements made by me in this application are correct to the best of my knowledge.

8

Typed or printed name and date ▼ If this application gives a date of publication in space 3, do not sign and submit it before that date.

Susan Something   Date ▶ May 15, 2000

Handwritten signature (X) ▼

X _

Certificate will be mailed in window envelope to this address:	Name ▼ ABC Travel, Inc. Attention: Susan Something
	Number/Street/Apt ▼ 100 Lake Street
	City/State/ZIP ▼ Any City, CA 99999

YOU MUST:
• Complete all necessary spaces
• Sign your application in space 8

SEND ALL 3 ELEMENTS
IN THE SAME PACKAGE
1. Application form
2. Nonrefundable filing fee in check or money order payable to *Register of Copyrights*
3. Deposit material

MAIL TO:
Library of Congress
Copyright Office
101 Independence Avenue, S.E.
Washington, D.C. 20559-6000

As of July 1, 1999, the filing fee for Form TX is $30.

9

*17 U.S.C. § 506(e): Any person who knowingly makes a false representation of a material fact in the application for copyright registration provided for by section 409, or in any written statement filed in connection with the application, shall be fined not more than $2,500.

June 1999—200,000   ♻ PRINTED ON RECYCLED PAPER   ☆U.S. GOVERNMENT PRINTING OFFICE: 1999-454-879/49
WEB REV: June 1999

CHAPTER 27

DISTANCE LEARNING ISSUES

Distance learning is any form of education in which the instructor and the students are separated from each other by time and/or space. In this chapter, we'll cover copyright issues in online learning and several other forms of distance learning. Because some distance learning courses include classroom teaching components and the use of photocopied course packs as supplemental materials, we'll cover those topics as well.

Copyright ownership of distance learning materials created by instructors is currently a hot topic at a number of educational institutions. We'll discuss various approaches to the ownership issue. Library copyright issues are covered at the end of the chapter.

Copyright law basics are covered in chapter 1, and the basic rules of copyright ownership are covered in chapter 3. The liability of educational institutions when they provide Internet access and facilities for faculty and students is covered in "Copyright Infringement," chapter 25.

Introduction

Much of the content being used in distance learning materials—text, graphics, photographs, music, film clips—is protected by copyright. (Copyright protection for these types of works is discussed in "Types of Works Protected by Copyright," chapter 1, and in chapter 11.) There are a number of myths about how copyright law applies to distance learning and to educational use of copyrighted materials in general. Don't make the mistake of believing these myths:

Myth #1: "Educators and libraries are exempt from the copyright law."

There is no general exemption from the copyright law for educators or libraries. There *are* two narrow statutory exceptions to the copyright owner's exclusive rights that permit libraries, nonprofit educational institutions, and governmental bodies to use copyrighted material without permission in certain ways and under certain conditions. However, these exceptions, discussed later in this chapter, are limited and of little help to distance educators and to librarians interested in creating electronic "reserve rooms."

Myth #2: "Copyright law doesn't apply to nonprofit organizations."

It does. There is no general exemption from the copyright law for nonprofit organizations.

Myth #3: "Any educational use is fair use."

Educational use of copyrighted material by a nonprofit educational institution may be fair use. It is not necessarily fair use. Educational use of material by a for-profit enterprise is not likely to be fair use. See "Fair Use," later in this chapter.

Myth #4: "Copyright owners never sue educators."

This is not true. For examples, see "Suits Against Educators," below. Generally, both the educator and the educational institution are liable if the educator's use of copyrighted material is infringement.

It would be a serious mistake to assume that content owners do not object to unlicensed uses of their material in distance learning materials. In fact, many content owners see distance learning as a new market for their content, and some are themselves creating distance learning course materials. Furthermore, as the Copyright Office observed in its 1999 *Report on Copyright and Digital Distance Education*, many content owners are concerned about the increased risk of unauthorized "downstream" uses when works are used online. Once a student obtains access to materials, it is generally easy for the student to distribute multiple copies to people who are not in the course. *Report on Copyright and Digital Distance Education*, p. 12. (The report is available online, in PDF format, at the Copyright Office's Web site, www.loc.gov/copyright.)

SUITS AGAINST EDUCATORS

In *Marcus v. Rowley,* a public school teacher who owned the copyright on a booklet on cake decorating sued another public school teacher who used a substantial portion of the plaintiff's booklet in her own booklet. The court found that the use was not fair use. 695 F2d 1171 (9th Cir 1983). In *Encyclopedia Brittanica Educational Corp. v. Crooks,* a public school system's taping of off-the-air broadcasts of educational programs (for permanent retention and use by the school system) was held to not be fair use. 542 FSupp 1156 (WD NY 1982).

Myth #5: "It's okay to photocopy copyrighted material for course packs or classroom handouts."

There is no general exception to the Copyright Act's reproduction right for teacher copying.

Copying for course packs or classroom use may be fair use, but it is not necessarily fair use. This topic is discussed later in this chapter, in "Course Packs and Photocopying."

Myth #6: "If I find something on the Web, it's okay to use it without getting permission."

Much of the material on the Web is protected by copyright, and the usual rules about using copyrighted material apply. This topic is discussed in "Taking Material from the Web," chapter 9.

The Reality

Educators need to be familiar with copyright law and to respect the rights of copyright owners. If an educator wants to use copyrighted material in a way that would be an exercise of the copyright owner's exclusive rights (reproduction, modification, distribution, public performance, and public display), the educator should get permission from the copyright owner, if the narrow statutory exceptions do not apply and the use is not fair use.

Other laws discussed in this book must also be considered. For example, electronic "field trips" may require releases from individuals who will be shown, location releases and permits for filming on private and public property, and permission to show copyrighted works. These topics are discussed in "The Right of Publicity" and "Permits," chapter 7.

Educators do not need permission to do the following things:

■ To make fair use of copyrighted material (discussed later in this chapter).

■ To use copyrighted material in noninfringing ways (see "When You Don't Need a License," chapter 9).

■ To use material that is in the public domain (see "Public Domain Works," chapter 9).

■ To use works created by federal government officers and employees as part of their official duties (see "Types of Works Protected by Copyright," chapter 1).

Online Learning Materials

Using copyrighted material in online learning materials is an exercise of the copyright owner's reproduction right and public performance or public display right.

EXAMPLE 1

Sue, who teaches a college course in music theory, created an online version of her course. In the online course, Sue uses sound clips of copyrighted musical compositions to illustrate concepts. The use of the sound clips in the online course is an exercise of the public performance rights in the musical compositions and sound recordings. (Music copyright law is covered in chapter 21.)

EXAMPLE 2

Ron, an art history professor, has created an online compilation of images of copyrighted paintings, for use by the students during class and for after-class review. The use of the images in the online compilation is an exercise of the public display right in the paintings (and probably in the photographs of the paintings as well, if Ron did not take the photographs that he scanned to create digital images used in the online compilation).

(The public display and public performance rights are discussed in more detail in "When You Need a License," chapter 9.)

Creating and transmitting online learning materials also requires the exercise of the reproduction right. The work used (the sound clips in the first example, the images of the paintings in the second example) must be copied ("uploaded") to a server prior to transmitting it to recipients. Furthermore, a number of transient copies must be made as part of the technical process of transmitting the material over a network to the recipients' computers, and the recipients' computers must make RAM copies. When Sue and Ron (from the previous examples) create and transmit their online materials, they must exercise the reproduction right in the copyrighted material they are using in those materials.

Thus, the use of copyrighted materials in online training materials requires the exercise of the copyright owner's reproduction right and public display or public performance right. As we explain in "When You Need a License," chapter 9, you need a license to exercise these rights, unless a specific exemption in the Copyright Act makes a license unnecessary or the use is fair use. In the rest of this section, we'll discuss Section 110(2) of the Copyright Act, which may eventually be amended to make licenses for uses of certain types of works in online learning materials unnecessary. As currently written, Section 110(2) is not helpful for online learning uses of copyrighted material, because it does not provide an exemption from licensing for all the rights needed. We'll also discuss fair use and licensing for online educational materials.

Section 110(2)

Section 110 of the Copyright Act permits instructors in nonprofit educational institutions to publicly perform and display copyrighted material without permission in face-to-face classroom teaching (discussed later in this chapter, in "Face to Face Teaching") and in the course of transmissions. The provision is a limited exception to the copyright owner's public performance and display rights.

"Transmission" is defined broadly enough in the Copyright Act to cover online delivery. According to Section 101 of the Copyright Act, to transmit a performance or display is to communicate it by any device or process whereby images or sounds are received beyond the place from which they are sent." For Section 110(2) to apply, three conditions must be met:

■ The performance or display must be a regular part of the systematic instructional activities of a nonprofit educational institution or governmental body.

■ The performance or display must be directly related to and of material assistance to the teaching content of the transmission.

■ The transmission must be made primarily for reception in classrooms or similar places normally devoted to instruction, or reception by persons to whom the transmission is directed because their disabilities or other special circumstances prevent their attendance in classrooms or similar places normally devoted to instruction, or reception by government officers or employees as part of their duties.

Many online learning courses meet these three conditions. Even for such courses, though, Section 110(2) is inapplicable. As we explained earlier in this section, creating and transmitting online learning materials requires the exercise of the reproduction right and the public display or public performance right. Section 110(2) only permits educators to exercise the public display and performance rights, not the reproduction right.

The Copyright Office has recommended to Congress that Congress amend Section 110(2) and another provision of the Copyright Act to add the right of reproduction (and possibly distribution) to the extent these rights must be exercised in order to transmit a performance or display already authorized by the exemption. It also has recommended that the third condition for using Section 110(2) be eliminated, because the goal of distance education is to permit instruction to take place anywhere, whether or not the students' circumstances prevent them from attending traditional classroom classes.

Under current law, where the performance right is concerned, Section 110(2) applies only to the transmission of nondramatic literary and musical works. For the display right, it applies to all types of works, including dramatic literary and musical works, audiovisual works, and sound recordings. A number of educators urged the Copyright Office to recommend that the public performance aspect of Section 110(2) be expanded to include all categories of copyrighted works. The Copyright Office found there were valid reasons for preserving the exclusion of these additional types of works and valid reasons to change the policy. It suggested a compromise: Amending Section 110(2) to allow performances of limited portions of works in these additional categories—a film clip or a sound clip, for example.

Fair Use

Even without a specific distance learning exemption in the copyright law, educators can use copyrighted material in online learning materials without getting licenses—if their use is fair use. Whether a distance learning use of copyrighted material is fair use must be determined on a case-by-case basis by considering four factors: (1) the purpose and character of the use; (2) the nature of the copyrighted work; (3) the amount and substantiality of the portion used in relation to the copyrighted work as a whole; and (4) the effect of the use upon the potential market for or value of the copyrighted work. (These are the same four factors discussed in "When You Don't Need a License," chapter 9.) There are no decided cases involving fair use in the distance learning context.

Nonprofit Educational Use

If the use is nonprofit educational use, the first factor favors a finding of fair use. However, if two of the other factors go the other way—for example, if most of a copyrighted work is copied to create a market substitute for the copyrighted work, as in the *Marcus v. Rowley* case (discussed earlier in this chapter)—the use may not be fair use.

A teacher's use of a small part of a copyrighted work for traditional fair use purposes of comment or criticism on the work or to illustrate a lesson is probably fair use. The Copyright Office stated in its report that fair use is particularly likely where the work that is used is itself the subject of study in the class, only illustrative portions are used, and the risks of unauthorized access and "downstream" dissemination to those not taking the course are controlled.

If you are using a music clip in an online course on music theory to illustrate a concept you are covering, that may be fair use. If you use the same clip as background music to add "sex appeal" to your course materials, a court could characterize your use as use for entertainment rather than educational use.

If a copyrighted work is being used in such a way as to have a significant negative effect on the potential market for or value of the protected work (the fourth factor), the use is likely to be found to be unfair. A number of content owners are currently developing systems for making digitized versions of their content available for licensing for online use. Because online material is easily copied and distributed downstream, they may feel that even an isolated unauthorized use of their material exposes them to many additional unauthorized uses, resulting in a significant impact on their digital licensing market.

If the material you create for use within your nonprofit educational institution will also be distributed through commercial channels, don't rely on fair use. Any commercial provider of distance learning materials will expect to see licenses authorizing you to use third-party content.

For-Profit Providers

A number of for-profit educational institutions and commercial providers are creating and supplying online learning materials, and nonprofit institutions are partnering with for-profit companies to create courses. As the Copyright Office noted in its report:

> While mainstream education in 1976 [when the Copyright Act was passed] was the province of nonprofit institutions, today the lines have blurred. Profit-making institutions are offering distance education; nonprofits are seeking to make a profit from their distance education programs; commercial entities are forming partnerships with nonprofits; and nonprofits and commercial ventures are increasingly offering competitive products. (*Report on Copyright and Digital Distance Education*, p.153.)

If you are creating course materials for a for-profit educational institution or a commercial vendor of distance learning material, it is not wise to rely on fair use. On the first factor, your use is more likely to be deemed commercial use rather than educational use, making it difficult to win on fair use. (See "When You Don't Need a License," chapter 9, for a discussion of the importance of this first factor in the fair use analysis.) A consultant used by the Copyright Office in developing its report found that for-profit corporations believe that they cannot rely on fair use, so they obtain licenses to use copyrighted materials in the courses they develop. Hinds, *Marketplace for Licensing in Digital Distance Education*, p. 26. (The Hinds paper is included with the downloadable copy of the Copyright Office's *Report on Digital Distance Education.*)

Whether fair use applies when a nonprofit educational institution and a for-profit provider or vendor work together to create online learning materials is unclear. It is not wise to rely on fair use in this situation. Fair use probably does not apply to a for-profit division created by a nonprofit educational institution.

Corporate Training

If you are creating online learning materials for use within a for-profit company, your use is likely to be considered commercial use rather than fair use. See "Fair Use and Commercialism," below. You should get licenses. This is true even if the materials will only be used on the company's intranet. Do not make the mistake of thinking that intranet use does not require licenses. (See "Myths," chapter 9.)

FAIR USE AND COMMERCIALISM

In *American Geophysical Union v. Texaco*, the question was whether it is unlawful for a profit-seeking corporation, Texaco, to make unauthorized copies of copyrighted scientific journal articles for use by the company's scientists. (Texaco's library circulated original copies of a number of scientific journals and invited researchers to make their own photocopies.) Texaco claimed the researchers were copying for research purposes. The court, however, viewed the use as commercial use because a researcher's copying served to facilitate his or her research, which led to the creation of new products and to profits for Texaco. The court concluded that the copying was not fair use. 37 F3d 881 (2d Cir 1994).

Guidance on Fair Use

As one university counsel has said, relying on fair use is "a tricky road fraught with legal land mines." Lucien Capone III, university counsel, University of North Carolina at Greensboro, *Copyright and Distance Learning*, available at *www.uncg.edu/cha/UNIVERSITY_COUNSEL/FAQ/distlrn.html*. In its report, the Copyright Office stated that because there is so much confusion and misunderstanding about the fair use doctrine, Congress should provide some clarification, including examples of digital uses that are likely to qualify as fair use. *Report on Digital Distance Education*, p. 162. Congress has not yet done so. However, there have been other attempts to provide guidance.

In the mid-1990s, the Clinton Administration's Information Infrastructure Task Force requested that copyright owners and educators come together in a Conference on Fair Use (CONFU) to negotiate guidelines establishing "safe harbors" that educators could rely on in using copyrighted material for nonprofit educational purposes. (An earlier use of this type of process led to the development of Classroom Photocopying Guidelines, discussed later in this chapter, in "Course Packs and Photocopying.") Working groups were established to develop guidelines for distance learning, multimedia, electronic reserves, interlibrary loan, and image collections. Draft guidelines were created. None of the guidelines was formally adopted by CONFU. Nonetheless, some nonprofit educational institutions have incorporated them into their own intellectual property policies, and some library and educational associations and content owners have endorsed them.

The Educational Fair Use Guidelines for Distance Learning were never adopted by CONFU because a number of CONFU participants were not satisfied with them. For the most part, the Distance Learning Guidelines do not apply to asynchronous learning, only to live interactive distance learning classes (a teacher in a live class with all or some of the students at remote locations). The only provision relevant to asynchronous distance learning is a provision allowing an educator to record classes that include the performance of an entire copyrighted work, retaining the recorded copy for up to fifteen consecutive class days for viewing by students enrolled in the course.

The focus of the Educational Multimedia Fair Use Guidelines is stored educational multimedia products (CD-ROM products) rather than online learning materials. The Educational Multimedia Guidelines were created by the Consortium of College and University Media Centers (CCUMC) and adopted by the CONFU working group on multimedia. They address online learning in a limited way, stating that educators may use multimedia materials created pursuant to the guidelines for remote instruction to students located at remote sites if there are technological limitations on access to the network and program and the technology prevents the making of copies of the copyrighted material. If the educational institution's technology cannot prevent duplication, the material can only be used for a period of fifteen days after its initial real-time remote use in the course. The Educational Multimedia Guidelines are posted at www.sju.edu/~lees/FU-guidelines.html.

The Educational Fair Use Guidelines for Digital Images state that nonprofit educational institutions and other nonprofit institutions engaged in educational activities may digitize material in their existing analog collections during a seven-year transitional period beginning December 31, 1996, but only for use while permission to digitize the material is being sought. For newly acquired images, these guidelines authorize digitization to support educational purposes unless the images are readily available in usable digital form at a fair price. Digitized images may be used on the institution's secure electronic network for one academic term and retained in digital form while permission is being sought.

A number of educational institutions have created their own guidelines on fair use of copyrighted material, and some of these documents are available online—for example, the University of Texas policy, www.utsystem.edu/OGC/ Intellectual Property/, and the Indiana University Policy, www.iupui.edu/ ~copyinfo/fupolicy.html. The Educause Web site, www.educause.edu, also has copyright and fair use information for educators.

Licensing for Online Courses

Online licensing is available for some types of content. This topic is discussed in "Licensing Agents" and "Stock Houses and Libraries," chapter 10. According to the Copyright Office's report, those publishers that produce the types of works for which educators constitute a major market are far along in the process of developing online rights management systems. Other suitable material may be available from stock houses and media libraries.

If you have acquired material marketed specifically for creating distance learning materials, hopefully your license to use these materials will include the rights you need. Read the license to make certain it does. See "When You Need a License," chapter 9, and "Determining What Rights You Need," chapter 10.

In addition to copyright licenses, you may need releases from individuals who are shown or discussed in your online learning materials (including students). If your online learning materials include photos or video shot on public or private property, you may need location releases. These topics are discussed in "The Right of Publicity," "The Right of Privacy," and "Permits," chapter 7. If your materials will show trademarks, you may need permission from the owner of the trademark. See "Using Third-Party Trademarks," chapter 24.

Other Types of Distance Learning Materials

In this section, we'll discuss copyright issues raised by types of distance learning materials other than online course materials and course packs. We cover instructional videos, CD-ROM products, videoconferencing, and instructional television.

Instructional Videos

Making an instructional video requires attention to copyright law and other laws. It may require getting film permits and "right of publicity" releases.

Copyright Law

If you will be using copyrighted content owned by third parties in your video—music clips and film clips, for example—unless your use is fair use, you need to obtain licenses to reproduce and publicly display or perform that content. If you perform (play) a copyrighted musical composition in a video, unless fair use applies, you need permission from the copyright owner. You may be able to find suitable public domain music. (See "Public Domain Music," chapter 21.)

The Section 110(1) and (2) "educational use" statutory exceptions do not apply to the production of instructional videos, since the videos are neither face-to-face teaching (Section 110(1)) or performances in the course of transmissions (Section 110(2)).

Other Laws

To avoid claims that your video violates an individual's right of privacy and publicity, get a release from any person whose image, name, or voice is used. (See "The Right of Publicity" and "The Right of Privacy," chapter 7.) This includes students (for minors, get a parent to sign the release). If a teacher is making the video but the institution is to own the copyright (see "Copyright Ownership" in the first section of this chapter), the institution should get a release from the teacher. To avoid defamation claims, follow the suggestions made in "Defamation" chapter 7.

If you are going to shoot photographs or video on private property, get a location release from the property owner. If you will be shooting on public property, you may need a permit from a government authority. If your shots will show a work that is protected by copyright—a painting, for example—you may need permission from the copyright owner. These topics are discussed in "Permits," chapter 7. If your video will show trademarks, you may need permission from the owner of the trademark. See "Using Third-Party Trademarks," chapter 24.

CD-ROM Products

Creating an educational interactive multimedia CD-ROM product requires attention to the same legal issues involved in instructional video production. As with instructional videos, neither the Section 110(1) exception (face-to-face teaching) nor the Section 110(2) exception (performances in the course of a transmission) applies. The Educational Multimedia Guidelines, discussed earlier in this chapter, while not law, may provide guidance if you choose to rely on fair use.

Videoconferencing

Videoconferencing (like traditional classroom teaching and online learning materials) can involve the public performance or display of copyrighted material.

For example, the instructor whose teaching is being transmitted to students by videoconferencing equipment could read from a prose work or recite a poem or play a musical composition on the piano.

Videoconferencing is within the Copyright Act's definition of "transmission." For videoconferencing by nonprofit educational institutions or governmental bodies, Section 110(2), discussed earlier in this chapter, in "Online Learning Materials," may eliminate the need for a license for displays of all types of works and for public performances of nondramatic literary and musical works. If Section 110(2) applies, Section 112(b) permits the educational institution to keep up to thirty copies of the videoconference program without infringing the copyright owners' reproduction rights. The copies must be destroyed within seven years from the date of the class.

If Section 110(2)'s conditions cannot be satisfied or works other than nondramatic literary and musical works are to be performed, fair use may apply. If it does not, licenses must be obtained. Section 110(2) would not permit an instructor to act out a play (performance of a dramatic work), perform an opera (performance of a dramatic musical work), show a motion picture, or perform a choreographic work.

Instructional Television

Instructional television can be one way (teacher to students) or two way (with response from the students).

As with videoconferencing, for nonprofit educational institutions or governmental bodies, Section 110(2) may apply. If Section 110(2) doesn't apply, a "compulsory license" (license for which the fee is set by the Copyright Royalty Tribunal) may be available under Section 118(d) if the program is to be transmitted over a noncommercial educational broadcast station. Section 118(d) states that a public broadcasting entity may, by paying the compulsory license fee established by the Copyright Royalty Tribunal, publicly perform or display certain types of works —published nondramatic musical, pictorial, graphic, and sculptural works—on a noncommercial educational broadcast station.

A "public broadcasting entity" is defined in Section 118(g) as "a noncommercial educational broadcast station" or any nonprofit institution engaged in noncommercial educational broadcasting. A noncommercial educational broadcast station is defined as a television or broadcast station eligible to be licensed, or licensed, by the FCC, as a noncommercial educational broadcast station and which is owned and operated by a public agency or a nonprofit foundation, or a television or radio broadcast station owned and operated by a municipality which transmits only noncommercial programs for educational purposes.

Face-to-Face Teaching

Section 110(1) of the Copyright Act states that the performance or display of a copyrighted work in the course of face-to-face teaching activities by a nonprofit educational institution in a classroom or similar setting devoted to instruction is not infringement. This exception applies to all types of copyrightable works. It permits instructors and students in a nonprofit educational institution to do the following things in classroom teaching:

- Act out a drama.

- Read a poem or prose work.

- Play or sing a musical work.

- Show a motion picture.

- Show an interactive multimedia CD-ROM.

- Display text or pictorial material by a projector.

Without Section 110(1), an educator would need the copyright owner's permission to do these things, (unless the use is fair use). The first five activities are exercises of the copyright owner's public performance right. The last activity is an exercise of the public display right. (Display is also covered by another exception, Section 106(5), which gives the owner of a copy lawfully made, or any person authorized by the owner, the right to display the copy publicly, either directly or by projection of no more than one image at a time, to viewers present at the place where the copy is located.)

In the case of a motion picture or other audiovisual work, the Section 110(1) exception does not apply if the copy was not lawfully made and the person responsible for the performance knew or had reason to believe that it was not lawfully made. Generally, an educator who acquires a videotaped copy of a motion picture from a legitimate source will have no difficulty with this element of the exception.

The Section 110(1) exception applies to the public performance right only. It does not authorize a nonprofit school to copy a copyrighted work into "fixed" instructional materials created by the school.

EXAMPLE

John, a high school music and drama teacher at a nonprofit school, made a video for use in his classes. In the video, John performs several copyrighted songs on various instruments and acts out a copyrighted monologue. Section 110(1) does not authorize John's use of the songs or the monologue in the video, just in a "live" class. However, John's use of the songs in the video may be fair use.

Face-to-face teaching, according to the legislative history, requires that the instructor and pupils be in the same building, but not necessarily in the same room. The exception does not apply to the use of copyrighted material in instructional television broadcasts, fixed videos or CD-ROM products, long distance videoconferencing, or online instruction.

The performance cannot be open to outsiders; it must be limited to the pupils and the instructors (including guest instructors). The exception does not apply to performances by actors, singers, or instrumentalists brought in from outside the school to put on a program.

Because the teaching activities must take place in "a classroom or similar place devoted to instruction," performances in an auditorium or stadium during an assembly, a graduation ceremony, a class play, or a sporting event (where the audience is not confined to members of a particular class) are outside the scope of the exception. The exception applies to use of the material in teaching activities only—not for entertainment or as a reward for good behavior.

Course Packs and Photocopying

Many distance learning courses include "course packs"—teacher-selected compilations of journal articles, book excerpts, magazine articles, and original content created by the instructor which are photocopied and provided to the students enrolled in a course. The Copyright Office's report states that policy and practice at most educational institutions require that copyrighted material included in course packs be licensed, particularly in the aftermath of the two cases summarized in "Course Packs in the Courts."

COURSE PACKS IN THE COURTS

In *Basic Books v. Kinko's,* a number of publishers claimed that Kinko's infringed their copyrights when Kinko's copied excerpts from their copyrighted books (chosen by professors) for course packets for college students. Kinko's claimed its use of the excerpts was fair use and that the copying was for educational purposes. The court noted that the use of the course packets by the students was educational. However, it held that the use of the packets in the hands of Kinko's employees was commercial, because Kinko's made money on the packets. It concluded that the copying was not fair use. 758 FSupp 1522 (SDNY 1991). A later course pack case against a commercial copy service, *Princeton University Press v. Michigan Document Services,* 99 F3d 1381 (6th Cir 1996), also concluded that the copy service's copying was not fair use. Although neither of these decisions involved course pack copying by a nonprofit education institution, many university counsels and administrators became concerned about liability and instituted licensing requirements even for course pack copying done "in-house."

The Copyright Clearance Center, www.ccc.com, handles permission grants for photocopying rights for many publications. Its Academic Permissions Center has recently started licensing electronic course packs as well. Other licensing agents are listed in appendix D. Some commercial copy services will also obtain permissions for course pack photocopying.

There is no statutory exception in the Copyright Act that authorizes teachers to photocopy copyrighted material for research or for classroom use. However, in 1976, representatives of educational institutions and the Association of American Publishers reached an agreement on the Guidelines for Classroom Copying. The guidelines are intended to state the minimum standards of educational fair use. While they are not law, courts are highly likely to respect them, holding that copying which is within the limits of the Guidelines is fair use.

The guidelines cover two topics: (1) single copying for teachers; and (2) multiple copies for classroom use. They apply only to "not-for-profit" educational institutions. The guidelines should not be relied upon for course pack copying because they state that they do not permit copying to create or replace or substitute for anthologies or to substitute for the purchase of books, reprints, or periodicals. A teacher cannot rely on the guidelines to continue to copy the same item from term to term (for repeated use, the teacher should request permission to copy the material). The Guidelines can be found online at www.utsystem.edu/OGC/IntellectualProperty/clasguid.htm.

The guidelines have been criticized as being too restrictive for classroom situations at the university and graduate level. The American Library Association (ALA) recommends that university-level faculty members needing to exceed the guideline's limits should "not feel hampered" by the guidelines (although the ALA recommends that faculty members attempt a "selective and sparing" use of photocopied, copyrighted material). ALA "Model Policy Concerning College and University Photocopying for Classroom, Research, and Library Reserve Use" (1982), online at www.musiclibraryassoc.org/copyright/guidere.htm.

The ALA takes the position that most single-copy photocopying for a teacher's personal use in research "may well constitute fair use"—even when it involves a substantial portion of a work. As for multiple copying for classroom use, the ALA takes the position that an instructor's photocopying practices should not have a significant detrimental impact on the market for the copyrighted work (the fourth fair use factor). The ALA recommends restricting the use of an item to one course. It warns against repeatedly copying excerpts from one periodical or author without getting permission.

Ownership of Course Materials

Most of the material currently in use in online training is original content developed by instructors and staff members at educational institutions. *Marketplace for Licensing in Distance Digital Education*, p. 13. In this section, we'll discuss ownership of intellectual property rights for distance learning materials created by employees of educational institutions. (When course materials are created for commercial providers by employees or independent contractors, the general copyright ownership rules covered in chapters 3, 5, and 6 apply.)

Under copyright law's ownership rules, when an employee creates material within the scope of the employment, the employer owns the copyright. This rule is known as the work made for hire rule. (See "The Work Made for Hire Rule," chapter 3, and "Works Made by Employees," chapter 5.) Many faculty members are employees of the institutions at which they teach. Applying this ownership rule, it would appear that the copyright in materials created by an individual faculty member within the scope of employment is owned by the institution.

EXAMPLE

Helen, a professor employed at Gavel Law School, created a computer simulation game to help her students learn the rules of evidence. According to copyright law, if Helen created the game within the course of her employment, Gavel owns the copyright.

The institution does not own the copyright for material created outside the scope of employment.

EXAMPLE

If Helen (from the previous example) wrote a science fiction novel on weekends and evenings, Gavel probably does not own the copyright in the novel, because writing the novel was probably outside the scope of Helen's employment with Gavel.

Whether material was created within the scope—or outside the scope—of employment may be a difficult question. For example, if a professor writes a textbook, is that work done within the scope of employment? If it is, according to the copyright law's work made for hire rule, the copyright on the textbook—and the right to commercially exploit it—belong to the institution.

ACADEMIC COPYRIGHT OWNERSHIP DISPUTES

There are few reported cases on ownership of materials created by academics. One case held that a word processing manual written by high school teachers may have been created outside the scope of the employment. *Hays v. Sony Corp. of America,* **847 F2d 412 (7th Cir 1987).**

University Ownership Policies

Most colleges have adopted intellectual property ownership policies, which state that copyrights in works created by faculty members belong to the faculty member. As we pointed out in the introduction to chapter 3, the work made for hire rule and the other copyright ownership rules are default rules, which apply if the parties do not reach their own agreement on ownership.

Even in the absence of a policy, many academics take the position that academic tradition allows faculty members to own copyrighted works not necessary for classroom instruction (for example, textbooks, scholarly articles, musical compositions, and works of fine art). The American Association of University Professors, in its *Statement on Copyright* states that "it has been the prevailing academic practice to treat the faculty member as the copyright owner of works that are created independently and at the faculty member's own initiative for traditional academic purposes."

Distance education, however, is raising new concerns on the part of university administrators, causing them to revisit their institutions' ownership policies. Here's why:

> [M]ost colleges have adopted policies relinquishing the copyright back to the author. This has been done for several reasons including providing an incentive to faculty, as a recruitment tool, and because the college's investment of resources is relatively small. Additionally, there is usually only a small market for those materials, and the college has not lost much by giving the copyright to the author. In contrast, the college's investment of resources in the development of a distance learning course may be great, and the potential market for the course is much expanded over the traditional classroom. —Lucien Capone, *Copyright Law and Distance Learning.*

The questions being raised by administrators include the following:

■ Is it fair for a faculty member to get ownership of material that is created with the help of instructional designers employed by the university and expensive university equipment?

■ Should the university have to pay license fees to use materials created by a faculty member using university resources? As one university policy review document states, "The cost to acquire rights to use scholarly works created on our campuses are escalating at a pace that far exceeds our libraries abilities to acquire them." University of Texas System, *Revising the Intellectual Property Policy and Other Administrative Policies Involving Intellectual Property*, available at www.utsystem.edu/ OGC/IntellectualProperty/rrrevise.htm.

■ If the faculty member who created the materials leaves the institution, will the university still be able to use the material?

■ Is it permissible for a faculty member to create materials for a commercial online course that competes with the university's course offerings?

■ Does the university need permission to use in other courses the online materials created by a faculty member for the faculty member's course?

Faculty members have new concerns as well, such as the following:

■ If I create an online course or other distance learning materials, can I take the material with me if I move to another institution?

■ Is the course mine to exploit commercially, or do I have to share royalties with the university?

■ Can the university grant a commercial provider rights to distribute material I created?

■ If my materials include patentable components, does the university's patent policy apply? (Patent policies generally state that patent rights belong to the university, with part of the royalties going to the faculty member.)

■ Will the university administration and my department chair understand how much time and effort are involved in developing an online course? Will they compensate me for that time or give me release time to create a course?

■ Who has the right to alter the content of an online course or create an updated version? (This concern is both a copyright ownership concern and an academic freedom concern.)

■ Can I record my lectures and use them as a component of an online course I develop for a commercial publisher of distance learning materials?

Those most familiar with these issues urge that universities develop ownership policies for distance learning materials as soon as possible, in order to avoid disputes. Some universities have already done so, in some cases changing their general policies to give the university limited rights in all types of faculty-created materials, and in other cases developing special policies for distance learning materials. Here are some examples:

- **New general policies.** At the University of Texas, a proposal to change the University's general policy is being considered. The existing version of the University of Texas Intellectual Property Policy states that the Board of Regents will not assert an interest in faculty-authored works unless the work is commissioned by the system or a component institution of the system or is a work created by an employee who was specifically required to produce it. The proposed new version states the board "retains certain rights in the works as set forth in the Policy and Guidelines for Management and Marketing of Copyrighted Works." *Revising the Intellectual Property Policy and Other Administrative Policies Involving Intellectual Property, available at www.utsystem.edu/OGC/IntellectualProperty/rrrevise.htm.* The draft policy for the University of Nevada, Las Vegas states that when an invention or copyrightable work is developed by UNLV personnel using significant UNLV resources "such as facilities, materials, equipment, personnel, funds," UNLV will own the intellectual property rights. *UNLV Intellectual Property Policy Draft*, available at www.unlv.edu/courses/policy/intelprop.html.

- **Special Policies for Distance Learning.** The University of North Texas has adopted a special policy for distance learning materials. For works created with minimal or insubstantial resources, the university has a nonexclusive educational license to use the materials as part of a UNT course. For works created with substantial university resources, both the university and the faculty member can market the material outside the university, sharing royalties according to a negotiated formula. The university owns all intellectual property rights in works created by an employee who was under contract to develop a specific product. *Distributed Learning: Creation, Use, Ownership, Royalties, Revision and Distribution of Electronically Developed Course Materials, available at* www.unt.edu/legalaffairs/distributed_learning.htm.

The American Association of University Professors (AAUP) takes the position that the traditional rule on ownership (the faculty member owns material he or she creates) should apply to distance learning materials. *Special Committee on Distance Education and Intellectual Property Issues, www.aaup.org/ipguide.htm.* However, the AAUP states that a collective bargaining agreement or institutional policy may allow for institutions to use works created by faculty members without charge for educational and administrative purposes within the institution.

Works Created by Contractors

When online courses are created by an independent contractor, a different rule applies: The independent contractor owns the copyright unless the institution gets an assignment of the copyright or unless the parties agree in writing to treat the work as a work made for hire (this only works for certain types of works). See "Copyright Ownership," chapter 6.

Part-time instructors and adjuncts may be independent contractors rather than employees. Whether a worker is an employee or an independent contractor must be determined by weighing thirteen factors (see "Who is an Employee?," chapter 5, and "Who is an Independent Contractor?," chapter 6). As a general rule, if the institution does not treat the instructor as an employee for tax and employee benefits purposes, it will be difficult for the institution to establish that the instructor is an employee for copyright ownership purposes.

Joint Ownership

If a work is created by two or more teachers who are employees of an institution that has a policy of giving intellectual property ownership to teachers, the teachers may jointly own the copyright. If the institution's rule is that the institution owns the copyright, the teachers are not owners (the institution is). If two or more independent contractor-type teachers work together to create a work, they may jointly own the copyright. See "Joint Authorship and Ownership," chapter 3.

Student Contributions

A student is not an employee of the school. A student is generally the author and the copyright owner for the material he or she creates. See "Initial Ownership," chapter 3. A student's contributions to distance learning materials are owned by the student, unless there is an agreement transferring ownership to the supervising faculty member or educational institution.

Commercial Distribution

If you are interested in finding a distributor or publisher for distance learning materials that you (or instructors affiliated with your educational institution) have created, here are some points to consider:

- **Copyright ownership**: If there's doubt as to whether the institution or the instructor owns the materials, the publisher will want this issue clarified (or will require assignments or licenses from both parties, possibly with royalty-splitting). The same is true if several individuals have helped create the materials (creating conflicting claims of ownership or claims of joint ownership).

- **Use of third-party material**: The publisher will want to see licenses to use third-party material and warranties of noninfringement. (See "Key Provisions in the Agreement," chapter 8, and "Additional Publisher Issues," chapter 13.) If you relied on fair use (or were unaware that you might need licenses), the publisher may lose interest unless you can get licenses (and it's much better to get them before you use the material). Licensing is discussed in chapters 9 and 10.

- **Releases and permits**: If you didn't get releases from individuals whose image, name, or face are shown, or didn't get filming permits for locations or permission to show copyrighted objects, the publisher may lose interest. These topics are discussed in chapter 7.

- **Rights granted**: Be cautious about granting an assignment of your copyright to a publisher. An assignment is a complete transfer of copyright ownership. (See "Assignments," chapter 3.) If you assign the copyright and a better deal comes along, you're stuck (even if the publisher to whom you granted the assignment is not pushing your product and you're getting no royalties). You will not be able to use components of the product in other projects unless you get a license back. (See "Key Provisions in the Agreement," chapter 8, and "Assignment or License?," chapter 13.) You won't even be able to use the product in your own courses unless you get a license back (that would be an exercise of the public performance right for course materials you no longer own). Be cautious about a broad exclusive license for the same reasons. A narrow exclusive license will generally be better for you.

Web product distribution agreements are discussed in chapter 13.

Library Copyright Issues

In this section, we will discuss two library copyright issues, the right of a library to reproduce copyrighted works and electronic reserves.

Reproducing Copyrighted Works

The Copyright Act gives a copyright owner the exclusive right to reproduce the copyrighted work in copies (see "The Exclusive Rights," Chapter 1). Section 108 of the act, however, creates a narrow exception to the reproduction right for libraries, giving them a limited right to reproduce or distribute copyrighted works for archival purposes and replacement purposes and to fulfill a user's request for a copy. In addition, libraries have a limited right to reproduce a work during the last twenty years of the work's copyright term. This provision was added to Section 108 when Congress extended the term of copyright. (See "Public Domain Works," chapter 9.)

Section 108 applies only if three conditions are met: (1) the reproduction or distribution is without any purpose of direct or indirect commercial advantage; (2) the library's collections are open to the public or are available to persons doing research in a specialized field (not just to researchers affiliated with the library); and (3) the reproduction or distribution of the work includes a notice of copyright. A library in a profit-making institution can rely on Section 108 so long as the reproduction or distribution itself is not commercially motivated.

A library may make three copies of an unpublished work from its collections for the purposes of preservation and security or for deposit for research use in another library that meets the "open collection" requirement. Section 108(b). Unpublished works are works that have not been distributed to the public by sale or other transfer of ownership, or by rental, lease, or lending (dissertations and student papers, for example).

A library may make three copies of a published work for the purpose of replacing a copy that is damaged, deteriorated, lost, or stolen—but only, if the library has, after reasonable efforts, determined that a replacement cannot be obtained at a fair price. Section 108(c).

A library may make a copy of one article from a periodical issue or a collection (or a small part of any other copyrighted work such as a book) at the request of a library user if three additional conditions are met: (1) the copy becomes the property of the user; (2) the library has had no notice that the copy would be used for any purpose other than private study, scholarship, or research; and (3) the library displays prominently at the place where orders are accepted, and includes on its order form, a warning of copyright. Section 108(d). A library may make a copy of an entire work at a user's request if it has determined, after a reasonable investigation, that a copy cannot be obtained at a fair price. Section 108(e). According to the legislative history for Section 108, a "reasonable investigation" would include inquiries to commonly known U.S. trade sources (wholesalers, distributors, bookstores) and to the publisher or author.

During the last twenty years of the term of copyright of a published work, a library or archives, including a nonprofit educational institution, may reproduce, distribute, display, or perform the work in facsimile or digital form for purposes of preservation, scholarship, or research. The provision is inapplicable if the work is subject to normal commercial exploitation, if a copy can be obtained at a reasonable price, or if the copyright owner provides notice pursuant to regulations developed by the Copyright Office of either of those facts.

Digital Copies

Copies made under the authority of Section 108 may be facsimile or digital. The "preservation" exemption authorizes a library to make a digital copy only if the work is not otherwise distributed in digital format and is not made available to the public in that format outside the library premises. The "replacement" exemption authorizes a digital copy only if the digital copy is not made available to the public in digital format outside the premises of the library in lawful possession of the digital copy.

Types of Works

The exception permitting library copying at the request of a user does not apply to musical works, pictorial works, graphic works, sculptural works, or motion pictures or other audiovisual works (except for audiovisual news programs). It is primarily applied to literary and dramatic works (but it is also applicable to pantomimes and choreographic works, sound recordings, and architectural works).

All types of works can be copied for purposes of preservation or replacement. All types of works can be copied during the last twenty years of the work's copyright term.

Systematic Reproduction

The reproduction right given to libraries under Section 108 is limited to "the isolated and unrelated reproduction or distribution of a single copy...on separate occasions." A library cannot rely on Section 108 to justify systematic reproduction or distribution of single or multiple copies.

Taken literally, the prohibition against systematic reproduction and distribution could be read to prohibit copying for interlibrary loan arrangements (the lending of materials or copies of materials by one library for use by patrons of another library). However, Congress added a proviso to the prohibition against systematic reproduction. The proviso states that the prohibition does not prevent a library from participating in interlibrary arrangements that do not have the effect of substituting for a subscription or purchase of copyrighted works.

To determine what should constitute requesting journal articles (the most commonly requested material) in such quantities as to substitute for a subscription, Congress sought the help of the National Commission on New Technological Uses of Copyright Works (CONTU). CONTU decided that the rule should be that the requesting library may not ask for more than five copies of an article published in a given periodical during the five years prior to the date of the reproduction request. This rule is known as the "suggestion of five."

Electronic Reserves

Electronic reserve systems are created by scanning printed materials into a database system. Many electronic reserve systems permit students with passwords to access the material from any computer. They are replacing the traditional "reserve desk" where students in a course could check out supplemental material chosen by the teacher.

Whether materials may be included in electronic reserves without a license is unclear. According to the report on licensing in digital distance education that was included with the Copyright Office's *Report on Copyright and Digital Distance Education*, only a minority of institutions with electronic reserves obtain licenses to copy and display the material. *Marketplace for Licensing in Digital Distance Education*, p. 12. Some systems include only public domain materials. Other institutions rely on fair use.

Section 108 does not apply, because it does not authorize a library to make a copy *before* it gets a user request (other than for archival or replacement purposes), only to satisfy a user's request. Also, Section 108 does not authorize a library to keep a copy of the material requested by a user (the copy must become the property of the user). Many publishers maintain that licenses are required.

Most libraries now license their most frequently requested works in digital format. Whether material licensed by an institution in digital format can be made available in an electronic reserve room system is governed by the license. For tips on reviewing rights grants in licenses, see the *Software and Database License Agreement Checklist*, available at www.utsystem.edu/OGC/IntellectualProperty/dbckfrm1.htm.

THE U.S. LEGAL SYSTEM

In the United States, laws are made at the federal and state levels. Laws adopted by legislative bodies—Congress and state legislatures—are called "statutes."

The federal and state courts enforce statutes. They also create law.

This chapter describes some of the basic concepts of our legal system, and the roles played by legislatures and courts.

Federal Statutes

The U.S. Constitution gives Congress to power to enact federal laws ("statutes") on certain subjects.

The Copyright Act (discussed extensively in chapter 1) is one example of a statute adopted by Congress. Congress's power to enact the Copyright Act stems from Article I, Section 8, of the Constitution, which authorizes Congress to establish laws giving "authors and inventors the exclusive right to their respective writings and discoveries" to encourage progress in the arts and sciences. The "commerce clause" of the Constitution (which concerns interstate commerce) is generally viewed as giving Congress broad power to regulate matters affecting interstate commerce—trademarks used in interstate commerce, for example.

Federal lawmaking begins when a member of the Senate or the House of Representatives introduces a bill. Most bills are referred to standing committees (for example, the House Committee on the Judiciary) and to subcommittees for study. Bills are later brought before the Senate or House for debate and vote. Differences between the Senate and House versions of a bill are resolved in joint conference committees. Information on pending federal bills is available online at http://thomas.loc.gov.

After the House and Senate have approved a uniform version of the bill, the bill is sent to the President. If the president signs the bill, it becomes law. If the president vetoes the bill, it becomes law only if the Senate and House override the veto. This requires the consent of two-thirds of the members of the Senate and House.

State Statutes

State legislatures can pass laws on matters for which they share jurisdiction with Congress. Trademark law is an example of a shared jurisdiction. In other matters, the federal government has taken exclusive jurisdiction. Copyright is an example: The Copyright Act prohibits the states from granting copyright-like protection.

States can also pass laws on matters in which the Constitution does not grant jurisdiction to the federal government. State lawmaking occurs through a process that is similar to the federal process.

The Courts

The courts enforce statutes and interpret them. They also invalidate unconstitutional statutes, and make law in areas not covered by statutes. Here are some examples of the four main roles played by our courts:

■ **Enforcement.** The Copyright Act gives a copyright owner the exclusive right to reproduce the owner's work. A copyright infringement suit is an example of court enforcement of a statute. (Copyright infringement is discussed in "Infringement," chapter 1.)

■ **Interpretation.** According to the Copyright Act, the copyright in a work created by an employee within the scope of his or her employment is owned by the employer. The Copyright Act does not define the term "employee." The Supreme Court case that defines the term is an example of court interpretation of a statute. (That case is discussed in "The Work Made for Hire Rule," chapter 3.)

■ **Invalidation.** The courts invalidate unconstitutional laws. Unconstitutional laws are laws that conflict with provisions of the Constitution. The Constitution is the supreme law of the United States. Many "constitutionality" cases involve claims that a law violates the Constitution's Bill of Rights (the first ten amendments). For example, in *Roe v. Wade*, the Supreme Court invalidated a state statute restricting women's access to abortion. According to the court, the statute violated a pregnant woman's constitutional right of privacy.

- ■ **Making Law.** The courts create the law for "common law" subject areas. Common law covers areas not covered by statutes. In many states, for example, individuals' rights of privacy and publicity (discussed in "Defamation, Publicity, and Privacy Laws," chapter 7) are protected under common law rather than under statutory laws.

Types of Courts

There are several types of courts. The federal and state court systems consist of two levels of courts: trial courts and appellate courts. Cases are tried in trial courts. Appellate courts review the decisions of the trial courts. (Appellate and trial courts are discussed in "Civil Lawsuits," later in this chapter.)

The federal court system is divided into thirteen judicial circuits. Eleven of the circuits are numbered. Each of the numbered circuits contains more than one state. The Ninth Circuit, for example, covers California, Oregon, Washington, Idaho, Nevada, Arizona, Alaska, and Hawaii. The 12th and 13th circuits are the District of Columbia Circuit and the Federal Circuit. The Federal Circuit handles appeals in patent cases and Claims Court cases.

Each federal circuit has one appellate court. These courts are known as Courts of Appeals or Circuit Courts. The Supreme Court reviews the decisions of the Courts of Appeals.

Each federal circuit is divided into judicial districts. A district can be as small as one city or as large as an entire state. The trial courts are known as the United States District Courts.

Jurisdiction

The federal courts have jurisdiction over cases involving federal statutes (the Copyright Act, for example) and other "federal questions." They also have jurisdiction over cases in which the party filing the suit and the party being sued reside in different states. This type of federal jurisdiction is known as "diversity" jurisdiction.

Other types of cases must be brought in state court.

Civil and Criminal Cases

A criminal case is brought by the federal government or a state to prosecute a defendant (the party sued) for violations of the government's criminal laws. Murder and burglary are examples of violations of criminal laws. If the defendant in a criminal case is found guilty by the jury, he or she is sentenced by the court to serve a jail sentence or pay a fine as punishment for the crime.

A civil case is a case brought by one party (the "plaintiff") against another party (the "defendant") to resolve a legal dispute involving rights based on statutory law or common law. A copyright infringement case is an example of a civil case involving statutory law. A suit seeking damages for a writer's breach of a contract (in which the writer promised to create a script for a online movie but failed to do so) is an example of a civil case involving common law rights. (Breach of contract is discussed in "What Is a Contract?," chapter 4.)

While certain violations of the Copyright Act and the Lanham Act (the federal trademark statute) are criminal violations, most Internet legal disputes are civil cases.

Civil Lawsuits

There are several stages in civil lawsuits, from initiation to trial and then on to stages of appeal. We'll discuss these stages in this section.

Initiation

A civil lawsuit is initiated when the plaintiff files a "complaint" against the defendant alleging that the defendant has wronged the plaintiff in some way recognized by the law. In most civil lawsuits, the plaintiff asks the court to award the plaintiff "damages" (a remedy for the defendant's wrongdoing—usually money) or to order the defendant to do something.

The defendant responds to the allegations in the complaint by filing an "answer" (a document in which the defendant admits or denies the complaint's allegations and states defenses). The defendant can also file a "counterclaim" against the plaintiff (allegations that the plaintiff has wronged the defendant).

Trial

If the parties do not "settle" the case (reach their own agreement on how to resolve the dispute), the case eventually goes to trial. In most types of civil cases, the Constitution gives the parties a right to a jury trial. The role of the jury is to decide questions of fact. However, in some complex cases, the parties choose to dispense with the jury and have the case decided by the judge.

Appeal

If the losing party in a civil lawsuit is not satisfied with the decision of the trial court, the losing party can appeal the case to the appropriate appellate court.

In the federal court system, the appeal generally must be filed with the Court of Appeals for the judicial circuit in which the trial was held. A case tried in the United States District Court for the Northern District of California, for example, must be appealed to the Court of Appeals for the Ninth Circuit.

An appellate court's job in reviewing a trial court's decision is to look for "mistakes of law" made by the trial court. Appellate courts do not "second guess" factual issues decided by trial courts. In our legal system, factual issues are supposed to be resolved by the jury, not by the appellate court. So long as there is adequate factual evidence to support the verdict, an appellate court will not reverse a trial court's decision or "remand" the case (send it back to the trial court for retrial) unless they find that the trial court made a "mistake of law."

Filing an appeal is probably a waste of money unless a losing party can reasonably hope to convince the appellate judges that there is insufficient evidence to support the trial court's decision, or that the trial court misapplied the law.

EXAMPLE

Plaintiff's lawsuit alleges that Defendant infringed the copyright on Plaintiff's song by copying the melody of the song. The jury found that Defendant did not infringe Plaintiff's copyright. If the jury reached its decision after being told by the judge that a song's melody is not protected by copyright (a mistake in the applicable law, copyright law), Plaintiff has a good basis for appeal. However, if the jury reached its decision after listening to Defendant's song and concluding that the melody of Defendant's song is not similar to the melody of Plaintiff's song, Plaintiff does not have a strong basis for appeal. (Whether or not the songs have similar melodies is a factual determination.)

Appellate courts generally issue written opinions explaining how they reached their conclusions on whether to affirm (uphold), reverse, or remand a case. These opinions are important parts of the development of the law because our legal system is based on "precedent" (reliance on previously decided cases). (The role of precedent is discussed in "Precedent," later in this chapter.)

Supreme Court Review

There are two ways to get a case reviewed by the U.S. Supreme Court: by appeal and by certiorari. The losers in certain types of cases—for example, cases involving claims that state statutes are unconstitutional —have a right to appeal to the Supreme Court.

For most cases, though, there is no right of appeal to the Supreme Court. However, a party who has lost a case at the federal Court of Appeals level can file a petition for certiorari with the Supreme Court. A petition for certiorari is a document explaining why the Supreme Court should review a case. If the Supreme Court grants certiorari, the appeal proceeds. If the Court denies it, the Court of Appeals' decision stands.

Thousands of petitions for certiorari are filed each year and most are denied. The Supreme Court is likely to grant certiorari on a case only if the case involves a matter of national interest or the Court believes that it must decide the case to resolve conflicts among the Circuit Courts and create uniformity in federal law.

Precedent

An appellate court's decision on an issue is binding on lower courts in the appellate court's jurisdiction. Thus, an appellate court's decisions are "precedent" that the lower courts in the appellate court's jurisdiction must follow (apply).

EXAMPLE

In *Effects Associates v. Cohen,* 908 F2d 555 (9th Cir 1990), the United States Court of Appeals for the Ninth Circuit held that the grant of a nonexclusive copyright license can be implied from the copyright owner's conduct. This decision is binding on the federal district courts located in the Ninth Circuit. Those courts are not free to decide that a nonexclusive copyright license cannot be implied from conduct.

A lower court's decision is not binding on a higher court. In fact, appellate courts frequently reverse decisions made by trial courts to correct the trial courts' "mistakes of law."

Because the United States Supreme Court is the "highest court in the land," the Supreme Court's decisions are binding on all courts in the United States.

EXAMPLE

In *Community for Creative Nonviolence v. Reid,* 490 US 730 (1989), the Supreme Court decided how to apply the Copyright Act's "work made for hire" rule to works created by independent contractors. That decision is binding on all courts in the United States. (Work made for hire is discussed in "The Work Made for Hire Rule," chapter 3.)

A court's decision may "be persuasive" outside its region. For a decision to "be persuasive" means that other courts, while not compelled to follow it, choose to follow it. For example, if the Court of Appeals for the Eleventh Circuit has never decided whether a nonexclusive copyright license can be implied from the copyright owner's conduct but the Ninth Circuit has, the Eleventh Circuit may reach the same conclusion as the Ninth Circuit when it decides that issue because it believes that the Ninth Circuit's decision was correct.

Earlier court decisions are generally "followed" by the deciding court in all later cases involving the same issue. For example, if the Ninth Circuit decides a case that involves the same legal issues that were involved in a previous case, it is likely to decide those issues as it did in the previous case.

The reliance that our courts put on previously decided cases in deciding new cases is known as *stare decisis.* That is Latin for "let the decision stand."

The doctrine of *stare decisis* does not prevent a court from "overruling" its own previously decided cases. However, the doctrine discourages rapid and radical changes in the law. As Supreme Court Justice William O. Douglas once wrote in the *Columbia Law Review*, "*stare decisis* provides some moorings so that men may trade and arrange their affairs with confidence....It is the strong tie which the future has to the past."

The doctrine of *stare decisis* is the reason that an attorney performs legal research hoping to find cases supporting the attorney's position on a legal issue.

Finding the Law

Because law is made by the courts on a precedent basis following the doctrine of *stare decisis*, and also made by Congress and the state legislatures, knowing the law on a given topic generally requires a review of both statutory law and case law.

Statutes

Federal and state statutory laws can be found by consulting published "codifications" of laws in law libraries maintained by law schools, law firms, courts, and bar associations. To find a federal law such as the Copyright Act, for example, you would look in the United States Code, which is divided into "titles." Many statutory laws can be found online. The FindLaw Web site, www.findlaw.com, has links to a number of law sites. Federal and state statutory laws can also be obtained online for a fee from Westlaw or Lexis, two computerized legal research services.

Recently adopted laws may not be included in the published codifications of statutes or in online postings. While the publishers of these codifications add new material regularly (in "pocket parts" inserted at the back of appropriate volumes), even the pocket parts may not include laws adopted in the most recent session of the legislature.

Court Decisions

Court decisions (also known as "case law") can be found in publications called "reporters." Many courts now have Web sites on which they post new decisions. The FindLaw site has links to court sites.

Westlaw and Lexis provide online "keyword" research assistance. "Digests" that divide decide cases into topics are also helpful for locating relevant cases. Other research resources help lawyers determine whether cases in which they are interested have been reversed by a higher court or overruled (modified by a later decision of the same court).

This book contains "citations" for a number of cases relating to matters discussed in this book. The citations use the standardized abbreviations for the names of "reporters." For example, 490 US 730 refers to volume 490, page 730 in the *United States Reports* (one of three publications for U.S. Supreme Court cases). Law library staff members generally can "decode" citations for you and point you toward the reporters you need, if you are doing research in a law library.

Various publishing companies publish "annotated" statutory codes, which bring statutes and relevant court decisions together in one source. West Publishing Company, for example, publishes the *United States Code Annotated (USCA)*, which lists the court decisions enforcing or interpreting each provision of the United States Code.

Arbitration

The parties to a dispute sometimes choose to resolve a dispute through arbitration rather than through court litigation. In arbitration, a dispute is resolved by a neutral arbitrator rather than by a judge or jury.

Arbitration is generally quicker and cheaper than court litigation. Specially qualified arbitrators are often used to resolve technical disputes.

Both parties must agree to submit their dispute to arbitration. Many contracts require that disputes be resolved through arbitration rather than through litigation.

In the United States, many arbitration cases are handled by arbitrators approved by the American Arbitration Association, which has offices in a number of cities. Arbitration is similar to a trial in that both parties present their cases to the arbitrator, who renders a decision. Appeals of arbitrators' decisions are generally possible only if the arbitration was conducted improperly.

Government Offices and Agencies

Government offices and agencies play an important role in our legal system. The Copyright Office and the U.S. Patent and Trademark Office are the key federal government offices for Internet legal issues. The Copyright Office is discussed in "Copyright Protection," chapter 26. The U.S. Patent and Trademark Office is discussed in "Patent Law" and "Trademark Law," chapter 2.

FORM CONTRACTS

These contracts should be considered samples rather than "model" agreements that will fit all of your needs. You should review them (and the chapters to which they relate) to understand the issues that you need to address.

The contracts included here may not fit your needs in a particular transaction. Consult with an experienced attorney prior to using any of these contracts.

You will find these contracts in electronic form on the disk that came with this book (attached to the inside back cover of the book).

These contracts are provided for your personal use in your business or law practice or use by your company. You may reproduce them, modify them, or scan them. They may not be reproduced or modified for use by third parties without the permission of the authors.

If you need an additional copy of the forms disk, you may order one from our Web site (www.laderapress.com), by calling our order line (800-523-3721), or by faxing the order form at the back of the book to (810) 987-3562. Request the forms diskette for the *Internet Law and Business Handbook*. The cost is $15, including shipping within the United States. Express delivery is available for an additional fee.

Our book *Internet Legal Forms for Business* contains additional form contracts. For a list, see our Web site or the information on *Internet Legal Forms for Business* included at the end of this book.

FORMS

FORM 1   NONDISCLOSURE AGREEMENT

This agreement is used when one party (called "Provider" in the agreement) is disclosing confidential information to another party (called "Recipient") during discussions of a potential business project. The agreement permits the information to be used only for evaluation. Revise the first sentence in Article 2 if the information is to be used for other purposes (such as development of a Web site).

NONDISCLOSURE AGREEMENT

This nondisclosure agreement ("Agreement") is entered into as of _____ ("Effective Date") by and between _____ ("Provider") and _____ ("Recipient"). Provider and Recipient are engaged in discussions in contemplation of or in furtherance of a business relationship. In order to induce Provider to disclose its confidential information during such discussions, Recipient agrees to accept such information under the restrictions set forth in this Agreement.

1. Disclosure of Confidential Information. Provider may disclose, either orally or in writing, certain information which Recipient knows or has reason to know is considered confidential by Provider relating to _____ ("Provider Confidential Information"). Provider Confidential Information shall include, but not be limited to, trade secrets, know-how, inventions, techniques, processes, algorithms, software programs, schematics, software source documents, contracts, customer lists, financial information, sales and marketing plans and business plans.

2. Confidentiality. Recipient agrees to maintain in confidence Provider Confidential Information. Recipient will use Provider Confidential Information solely to evaluate the commercial potential of a business relationship with Provider. Recipient will not disclose the Provider Confidential Information to any person except its employees or consultants to whom it is necessary to disclose the Provider Confidential Information for such purposes. Recipient agrees that Provider Confidential Information will be disclosed or made available only to those of its employees or consultants who have agreed in writing to receive it under terms at least as restrictive as those specified in this Agreement. Recipient will take reasonable measures to maintain the confidentiality of Provider Confidential Information, but not less than the measures it uses for its confidential information of similar type. Recipient will immediately give notice to Provider of any unauthorized use or disclosure of the Provider Confidential Information. Recipient agrees to assist Provider in remedying such unauthorized use or disclosure of the Provider Confidential Information. This obligation will not apply to the extent that Recipient can demonstrate that:

    (a) the Provider Confidential Information at the time of disclosure is part of the public domain;

(b) the Provider Confidential Information became part of the public domain, by publication or otherwise, except by breach of the provisions of this Agreement;

(c) the Provider Confidential Information can be established by written evidence to have been in the possession of Recipient at the time of disclosure;

(d) the Provider Confidential Information is received from a third party without similar restrictions and without breach of this Agreement; or

(e) the Provider Confidential Information is required to be disclosed by a government agency to further the objectives of this Agreement, or by a proper court of competent jurisdiction; provided, however, that Recipient will use its best efforts to minimize the disclosure of such information and will consult with and assist Provider in obtaining a protective order prior to such disclosure.

3. Materials. All materials including, without limitation, documents, drawings, models, apparatus, sketches, designs and lists furnished to Recipient by Provider and any tangible materials embodying Provider Confidential Information created by Recipient shall remain the property of Provider. Recipient shall return to Provider or destroy such materials and all copies thereof upon the termination of this Agreement or upon the written request of Provider.

4. No License. This Agreement does not grant Recipient any license to use Provider Confidential Information except as provided in Article 2.

5. Term.

(a) This Agreement shall terminate ninety (90) days after the Effective Date unless terminated earlier by either party. Provider may extend the term of the Agreement by written notice to Recipient. Either party may terminate this Agreement, with or without cause, by giving notice of termination to the other party. The Agreement shall terminate immediately upon receipt of such notice.

(b) Upon termination of this Agreement, Recipient shall cease to use Provider Confidential Information and shall comply with Article 3 within twenty (20) days of the date of termination. Upon the request of Provider, an officer of Recipient shall certify that Recipient has complied with its obligations in this Section.

(c) Notwithstanding the termination of this Agreement, Recipient's obligations in Article 2 shall survive such termination.

6. General Provisions.

(a) This Agreement shall be governed by and construed in accordance with the laws of the United States and of the State of _____ as applied to transactions entered into and to be performed wholly within _____ between residents of that state. Except as provided in Section 6(b), any dispute arising out of or relating to this Agreement, or the breach, termination or validity thereof, will be submitted by the parties to arbitration, to take place in, by the American Arbitration Association under the commercial rules then in effect for that Association except as provided in this Section. All proceedings will be held in English and a transcribed record prepared in English. Depositions may be taken and discovery obtained in any such arbitration proceedings in accordance with California Code of Civil Procedure Sections 1283.05 and 1283.1, which is incorporated herein by this reference. Judgment upon the award rendered by the arbitrator(s) may be entered in any court having jurisdiction thereof.

(b) Notwithstanding Section 6(a), Provider shall have the right to obtain a preliminary relief on any equitable claim in any court of competent jurisdiction, where such judgment is necessary to preserve its property and/or proprietary rights under this Agreement.

(c) Any notice provided for or permitted under this Agreement will be treated as having been given when (a) delivered personally, (b) sent by confirmed telex or telecopy, (c) sent by commercial overnight courier with written verification of receipt, or (d) mailed postage prepaid by certified or registered mail, return receipt requested, to the party to be notified, at the address set forth below, or at such other place of which the other party has been notified in accordance with the provisions of this Section. Such notice will be treated as having been received upon the earlier of actual receipt or five (5) days after posting.

(d) Recipient agrees that the breach of the provisions of this Agreement by Recipient will cause Provider irreparable damage for which recovery of money damages would be inadequate. Provider will, therefore, be entitled to obtain timely injunctive relief to protect Provider's rights under this Agreement in addition to any and all remedies available at law.

(e) Neither party may assign its rights under this Agreement.

(f) This Agreement may be amended or supplemented only by a writing that is signed by duly authorized representatives of both parties.

(g) No term or provision hereof will be considered waived by either party, and no breach excused by either party, unless such waiver or consent is in writing signed on behalf of the party against whom the waiver is asserted. No consent by either party to, or waiver of, a breach by either party, whether express or implied, will constitute a consent to, waiver of, or excuse of any other, different, or subsequent breach by either party.

(h) If any part of this Agreement is found invalid or unenforceable, that part will be amended to achieve as nearly as possible the same economic effect as the original provision and the remainder of this Agreement will remain in full force.

(i) This Agreement constitutes the entire agreement between the parties relating to this subject matter and supersedes all prior or simultaneous representations, discussions, negotiations, and agreements, whether written or oral.

IN WITNESS WHEREOF, the parties have executed this Agreement as of the Effective Date.

"RECIPIENT":   "PROVIDER":

By:_____   By: _____

_____   _____
Typed name   Typed name

_____   _____
Title   Title

Address: _____   Address: _____

_____   _____

_____   _____

_____   _____

461

web site
development
and
maintenance
agreement

FORM 2   WEB SITE DEVELOPMENT AND MAINTENANCE AGREEMENT

This Web site development and maintenance agreement is used to have a Web site developed and maintained on the Internet. It provides that the access to the Internet will be furnished by a separate Internet service provider who is not party to this agreement.

WEB SITE DEVELOPMENT AND MAINTENANCE AGREEMENT

This Agreement is entered into by and between _____ ("Client") and _____ ("Developer") on the _____(the "Effective Date").

RECITALS

WHEREAS, Developer has experience in developing and maintaining Web sites for third parties;

WHEREAS, Client wishes to have Developer create a Web site for Client and maintain such Web site for Client, and Developer is interested in undertaking such work.

WHEREAS, Client shall employ a separate company to host its Web site.

NOW, THEREFORE, in consideration of the promises and mutual covenants and agreements set forth herein, Client and Developer agree as follows:

Section 1

DEFINITIONS

1.1 **Beta version** means a working version of the Web Site recorded in executable form on the specified medium with any necessary supporting software and data, which has been fully tested by Developer prior to delivery and which Developer believes in good faith to be bug free and to fully implement all functions called for in the Specifications.

1.2 **Client content** means the material provided by Client to be incorporated into the Web Site, as listed on Schedule "C".

1.3 **Development Schedule** shall be as set forth in Schedule "B" to this Agreement which lists the deliverable items contracted for ("Deliverables") and the deadlines for their delivery. Payment Schedule shall be as also set forth in Schedule "B".

1.4 **Developer Tools** means the software tools of general application, whether owned or licensed to Developer, which are used to develop the Web Site.

1.5 **Documentation** means the documentation for the software developed by Developer specifically for the Web Site and other material which implement the Web Site. Source materials are part of the Documentation.

1.6 **Enhancements** means any improvements to the Web Site to implement new features or add new material. Enhancements shall include modifications to the Web Site Content to make the Web Site operate on a Server System of a new ISP.

1.7 **Error** means any failure of the Web Site (i) to meet the Specifications and/or (ii) to operate with the Server System.

1.8 **Final version** means a non-copy protected and unencrypted disk master of the final version of the Web Site, recorded in executable form on the specified medium with any necessary supporting software and data, as to which all development work hereunder, and corrections to the Beta Version, have been completed and which meets the Specifications.

1.9 **ISP** means an Internet Service Provider which maintains the Web Site on the World Wide Web portion of the Internet. The ISP may change from time to time.

1.10 **Specifications** for the Web Site shall be as set forth in Schedule "A " to this Agreement.

1.11 **Source Materials** means (i) all documentation, notes, development aids, technical documentation and other materials provided to Developer by Client for use in developing the Web Site, and (ii) the source code, documentation, notes and other materials which are produced or created by Developer during the development of the Web Site, in such internally documented form as is actually used by Developer for development and maintenance of the Web Site.

1.12 **Server System** means the hardware and software system owned or licensed by the ISP.

1.13 **Web Site Content** shall mean (i) the graphic user interface, text, images, music and other material of the Web Site developed by Developer under this Agreement which is visible to World Wide Web browsers and (ii) software (including cgi scripts and perl scripts) developed by Developer under this Agreement to implement the Web Site. Web Site Content shall not include Developer Tools.

1.14 **Web Site** means the site to be developed for Client on the graphic portion of the Internet known as the World Wide Web which is described in the Specifications.

Section 2

DEVELOPMENT AND DELIVERY OF DELIVERABLES

2.1 Development; Progress Reports. Developer shall use its best efforts to develop each Deliverable in accordance with the Specifications. Developer shall first prepare a design for the Web Site. This design shall include drawings of the user interface, a schematic of how to navigate the Web Site, a list of hyperlinks and other components. All development work will be performed by Developer or its employees at Developer's offices or by approved independent contractors who have executed confidentiality and assignment agreements which are acceptable to Client. Developer agrees that no development work shall be performed by independent contractors without the express written approval of Client. Each week following execution of this Agreement during which any development and/or testing hereunder remains uncompleted, and whenever else Client shall reasonably request, Developer shall contact, or meet with Client's representative, and report all tasks completed and problems encountered relating to development and testing of the Web Site. During such discussion or meeting, Developer shall advise Client in detail of any recommended changes with respect to remaining phases of development in view of Developer's experience with the completed development. In addition, Developer shall contact Client's representative promptly by telephone upon discovery of any event or problem that will materially delay development work, and thereafter, if requested, promptly confirm such report in writing.

463

web site
development
and
maintenance
agreement

2.2 Delivery. Developer shall deliver all Deliverables for the Web Site within the times specified in the Development Schedule and in accordance with the Specifications.

2.3 Manner of Delivery. Developer agrees to comply with all reasonable requests of Client as to the manner of delivery of all Deliverables, which may include delivery by electronic means.

2.4 Delivery of Source Materials. Upon request by Client, but in no event later than the delivery of the Final Version, Developer shall deliver to Client all Source Materials.

Section 3

TESTING AND ACCEPTANCE; EFFECT OF REJECTION

3.1 Testing and Acceptance Procedure. All Deliverables shall be thoroughly tested by Developer and all necessary corrections as a result of such testing shall be made, prior to delivery to Client. Upon receipt of a Deliverable, Client shall have a period of ____ days within which to test the item (the "Acceptance Period") and to notify Developer in writing of its acceptance or rejection based on its test results with respect thereto. If Client has not given notice of rejection within the Acceptance Period, the Deliverable will be deemed to be accepted. No delivery of a Deliverable shall be considered complete unless and until Client has received all Documentation necessary to support the use and modification of the Deliverable. If Client accepts the Deliverable, the milestone payment for that Deliverable (set forth in Schedule "B ") is then due.

3.2 Correction. If Client requests that Developer correct errors in the Deliverable, Developer shall within ____ days of such notice, or such longer period as Client may allow, submit at no additional charge a revised Deliverable in which such Errors have been corrected. Upon receipt of the corrected Deliverable, Client shall have an additional ___ days to test the Deliverable and either (1) accept it (making the milestone payment set out in Schedule "B"); or (2) request that Developer make further corrections to the Deliverable to meet the Specifications and repeat the correction and review procedure set forth in this Paragraph 3.2. In the event Client determines, in its sole discretion, that the Deliverable continues to include Errors after three attempts at correction by Developer, Client may terminate this Agreement.

Section 4
OTHER OBLIGATIONS OF DEVELOPER

4.1 Web Site Warranty. Developer represents and warrants that the Web Site (1) will be of high quality and free of defects in material and workmanship in all material respects; and (2) will conform in all respects to the functional and other descriptions contained in the Specifications. For a period of one year after the date of acceptance of the Final Version by Client (the "Warranty Period"), Developer agrees to fix at its own expense any Errors. EXCEPT AS STATED IN SECTION 8.1, DEVELOPER DISCLAIMS ALL IMPLIED WARRANTIES, INCLUDING WITHOUT LIMITATION, THE WARRANTIES OF MERCHANTABILITY, NON-INFRINGEMENT OF THIRD PARTY RIGHTS, AND FITNESS FOR A PARTICULAR PURPOSE.

4.2 Web Site Support. Developer also agrees to provide Client with the support services stated in Schedule "D" to maintain and update the Web Site on the World Wide Web during the Warranty Period at no cost to Client. Such assistance shall not exceed _____ hours per calendar month.

4.3 Maintenance Period. After the expiration of the Warranty Period, Developer agrees to provide Client with the services stated in Schedule "D", at Client's option, for _____ years after the last day of the Warranty Period (the "Maintenance Period") for an annual fee of _____. Such maintenance shall include correcting any Errors or any failure of the Web Site to conform to the Specifications. Maintenance shall not include the development of Enhancements at the time of the notice.

4.4 Enhancements. During the Maintenance Period, if Client wishes to modify the Web Site, it may request that Developer provide a bid to provide such Enhancements. Developer shall provide Client a first priority on its resources to create the Enhancements over any other third party with the exception of obligations under contracts with third parties existing on the date of the notice. Such services shall be provided on a time and materials basis at the most favored price under which Developer provides such services to third parties.

Section 5
PROPRIETARY RIGHTS

5.1 Client's Ownership Rights. Developer acknowledges and agrees that except as stated in Section 5.3, the Web Site Content and Documentation, including but not limited to images, graphic user interface, source and object code, and any documentation and notes associated with the Web Site are and shall be the property of Client. Title to all intellectual property rights including but not limited to copyrights, trademarks, patents and trade secrets in the Web Site Content and Documentation is with, and shall remain with Client.

5.2 Assignment of Rights. Except as provided in Section 5.3, Developer hereby irrevocably assigns, conveys and otherwise transfers to Client, and its respective successors and assigns, all rights, title and interests worldwide in and to the Web Site Content and Documentation and all copyrights, trade secrets, patents, trademarks and other intellectual property rights and all contract and licensing rights, and all claims and causes of action of any kind with respect to any of the foregoing, whether now known or hereafter to become known. In the event Developer has any rights in and to the Web Site Content or Documentation that cannot be assigned to Client, Developer hereby unconditionally and irrevocably waives the enforcement of all such rights, and all claims and causes of action of any kind with respect to any of the foregoing against Client, its distributors and customers, whether now known or hereafter to become known and agrees, at the request and expense of Client and its respective successors and assigns, to consent to and join in any action to enforce such rights and to procure a waiver of such rights from the holders of such rights. In the event Developer has any rights in and to the Web Site Content or Documentation that cannot be assigned to Client and cannot be waived, Developer hereby grants to Client, and its respective successors and assigns, an exclusive, worldwide, royalty-free license during the term of the rights to reproduce, distribute, modify, publicly perform and publicly display, with the right to sublicense through multiple tiers of sublicensees and assign such rights in and to the Web Site Content and the Documentation including, without limitation, the right to use in any way whatsoever the Web Site Content and Documentation. Developer retains no rights to use the Web Site Content and Documentation except as stated in Section 5.3 and agrees not to challenge the validity of the copyright ownership by Client in the Web Site Content and Documentation.

5.3. Ownership of Components. Developer will retain copyright ownership of the following material: _____ ("Retained Components"). However, Developer grants to Client a royalty-free, worldwide, perpetual, irrevocable, nonexclusive license, with the right to sublicense through multiple tiers of sublicensees, to use, reproduce, distribute, modify, publicly perform, and publicly display the Retained Components on the Web Site or any Web site operated by or for Client and related marketing material.

5.4 Power of Attorney. Developer agrees to execute, when requested, patent, copyright, or similar applications and assignments to Client, and any other lawful documents deemed necessary by Client to carry out the purpose of this Agreement. Developer further agrees that the obligations and undertaking stated in this Section 5.4 will continue beyond the termination of this Agreement. In the event that Client is unable for any reason whatsoever to secure Developer's signature to any lawful and necessary document required to apply for or execute any patent, copyright or other applications with respect to the Web Site Content and Documentation (including improvements, renewals, extensions, continuations, divisions or continuations in part thereof), Developer hereby irrevocably designates and appoints Client and its duly authorized officers and agents as his agents and attorneys-in-fact to act for and in his behalf and instead of Developer, to execute and file any such application and to do all other lawfully permitted acts to further the prosecution and issuance of patents, copyrights or other rights thereon with the same legal force and effect as if executed by Developer.

5.5 License to Web Site Content and Client Content. Client grants to Developer a nonexclusive, worldwide license to reproduce and modify Client Content and the Web Site Content to develop and maintain the Web Site.

5.6 Internet Access. Client shall be responsible for obtaining access to the Internet through an ISP. Developer shall not be responsible for such access and shall not be considered a party to the agreement between ISP and Client. Although the Web Site will be hosted by the ISP, the ISP will not be a party to this Agreement nor will it be a third party beneficiary of this Agreement.

5.7 Licenses to Third-Party Content. _____ shall be responsible for obtaining and paying for any necessary licenses to use third-party content other than the third-party content listed on Schedule "C" as Client Content. Client shall be responsible for obtaining and paying for any necessary licenses to use third-party content listed on Schedule "C".

5.8. Licenses to Developer Tools. Developer shall be responsible for obtaining licenses for and paying license fees for any Developer Tools used in this project that are not owned by Developer.

5.9. Licenses to Use Other Software. _____ shall be responsible for obtaining a license to use _____ software and for paying license fees for such software.

5.10 Client's Domain Name. Client's domain name, _____, shall remain the sole property of Client. Developer acknowledges that Developer has no right to use Client's domain name other than in connection with the Web Site development and maintenance project covered in this Agreement.

Section 6
PAYMENT

6.1 Payment Schedule. The fees set forth in Schedule "B" shall be paid as provided in such Schedule.

6.2 Maintenance Fees. If Client chooses to have Developer perform maintenance and support service during the Maintenance Period, the annual fee stated in Section 4.3 shall be due thirty (30) days prior to the commencement date of each year of the Maintenance Period.

6.3 Taxes. Developer shall be responsible for the payment of all sales, use and similar taxes.

6.4 Expenses. Except as expressly stated in this Agreement or in a later writing signed by Client, Developer shall bear all expenses arising from the performance of its obligations under this Agreement.

Section 7
CONFIDENTIALITY

7.1 Confidential Information. The terms of this Agreement, the Source Materials and technical and marketing plans or other sensitive business information, including all materials containing said information, which are supplied by Client to Developer or developed by Developer in the course of developing the Web Site are the confidential information ("Confidential Information") of Client.

7.2 Restrictions on Use. Developer agrees that except as authorized in writing by Client: (i) Developer will preserve and protect the confidentiality of all Confidential Information; (ii) Developer will not disclose to any third party, the existence, source, content or substance of the Confidential Information or make copies of Confidential Information; (iii) Developer will not deliver Confidential Information to any third party, or permit the Confidential Information to be removed from Developer s premises; (iv) Developer will not use Confidential Information in any way other than to develop the Web Site as provided in this Agreement; (v) Developer will not disclose, use or copy any third party information or materials received in confidence by Developer for purposes of work performed under this Agreement; and (vi) Developer shall require that each of its employees who work on or have access to the Confidential Information sign a suitable confidentiality and assignment agreement and be advised of the confidentiality and other applicable provisions of this Agreement.

7.3 Limitations. Information shall not be considered to be Confidential Information if Developer can demonstrate that it (i) is already or otherwise becomes publicly known through no act of Developer; (ii) is lawfully received from third parties subject to no restriction of confidentiality; (iii) can be shown by Developer to have been independently developed by it without use of the Confidential Information; or (iv) is authorized in writing by Client to be disclosed, copied or used.

7.4 Return of Source Materials. Upon Client's acceptance of the Final Version, or upon Client's earlier request, Developer shall provide Client with all copies and originals of the Web Site Content, Client Content and Source Materials, as well as any other materials provided to Developer, or created by Developer under this Agreement. Not later than seven (7) days after the termination of this Agreement for any reason, or if sooner

467

web site
development
and
maintenance
agreement

requested by Client, Developer will return to Client all originals and copies of the Confidential Information, Web Site Content, Client Content and Source Materials, as well as any other materials provided to Developer, or created by Developer under this Agreement, except that Developer may retain one copy of the Web Site Content and Source Materials, which will remain the Confidential Information of Client, for the sole purpose of assisting Developer in maintaining the Web Site. Developer shall return said copy to Client promptly upon request by Client.

Section 8

WARRANTIES COVENANTS AND INDEMNIFICATION

8.1 Warranties and Covenants of Developer. Developer represents, warrants and covenants to Client the following:

(a) Developer has the full power to enter into this Agreement and perform the services provided for herein, and that such ability is not limited or restricted by any agreements or understandings between Developer and other persons or companies.

(b) Any information or materials developed for, or any advice provided to Client, shall not rely or in any way be based upon confidential or proprietary information or trade secrets obtained or derived by Developer from sources other than Client unless Developer has received specific authorization in writing to use such proprietary information or trade secrets.

(c) Except to the extent based on Client Content used as licensed to Developer in Section 5.5 and on licenses obtained by Client pursuant to Sections 5.7 and 5.9, the use, public display, public performance, reproduction, distribution, or modification of the Web Site Content and Documentation does not and will not violate the rights of any third parties, including, but not limited to, copyrights, trade secrets, trademarks, publicity, privacy, and patents. The use of the Developer Tools in the Web Site Content and Documentation does not and will not violate the rights of any third parties, including but not limited to, copyrights, trade secrets, trademarks, publicity, privacy, and patents.

(d) Its performance of this Agreement will not conflict with any other contract to which Developer is bound, and while developing the Web Site, Developer will not engage in any such consulting services or enter into any agreement in conflict with this Agreement.

(e) The Web Site Content and the Documentation was created solely by Developer, Developer's full-time employees during the course of their employment, or independent contractors who assigned all right, title and interest worldwide in their work to Contractor.

(f) Developer is the owner of all right, title and interest in the tangible forms of the Web Site Content and Documentation and all intellectual property rights protecting them. The Web Site Content and

Documentation and the intellectual property rights protecting them are free and clear of all encumbrances, including, without limitation, security interests, licenses, liens, charges or other restrictions.

(g) Developer has maintained the Source Material in confidence.

(h) The Web Site Content and the Documentation is not in the public domain.

8.2 Developer's Indemnity. Developer agrees to defend, indemnify and hold harmless Client and its directors, officers, its employees, sublicensees, and agents from and against all claims, defense costs (including reasonable attorneys' fees), judgments and other expenses arising out of or on account of such claims, including without limitation claims of:

(a) alleged infringement or violation of any trademark, copyright, trade secret, right of publicity or privacy (including but not limited to defamation), patent or other proprietary right with respect to the Web Site Content or Documentation unless based on the use of the Client Content or on licenses obtained by Client pursuant to sections 5.7 and 5.9;

(b) any use of confidential or proprietary information or trade secrets Developer has obtained from sources other than Client;

(c) any negligent act, omission, or willful misconduct of Developer in the performance of this Agreement; and

(d) the breach of any covenant or warranty set forth in Section 8.1 above.

8.3 Obligations Relating to Indemnity. Developer's obligation to indemnify requires that Client notify Developer promptly of any claim as to which indemnification will be sought and provide Developer reasonable cooperation in the defense and settlement thereof.

8.4 Client's Indemnification. Client agrees to defend, indemnify, and hold harmless Developer and its directors, officers, its employees and agents from and against all claims, defense costs (including reasonable attorneys fees), judgments and other expenses arisng out of the breach of the following covenants and warranties:

(a) Client possesses full power and authority to enter into this Agreement and to fulfill its obligations hereunder.

(b) The performance of the terms of this Agreement and of Client's obligations hereunder shall not breach any separate agreement by which Client is bound.

(c) The use, public display, public performance, reproduction, distribution, or modification of Client Content in accordance with the license granted to Developer in Section 5.5 does not and will not violate the rights of any third parties including, but not limited to, copyrights, trade secrets, trademarks, publicity, privacy, and patents. The use of third-party licensed material obtained by Client pursuant to Sections 5.7 and 5.9, if within the scope of the license, does not violate the rights of any third parties, including, but not limited to, copyrights, trade secrets, trademarks, publicity, privacy, defamation, and patents.

8.5 Obligations Relating to Indemnity. Client's obligation to indemnify requires that Developer notify Client promptly of any claim as to which indemnification will be sought and provide Client reasonable cooperation in the defense and settlement thereof.

Section 9

TERMINATION

9.1 Termination for Non-Performance or Delay. In the event of a termination of this Agreement by Client pursuant to Paragraph 3.2 hereof, Client will have no further obligations or liabilities under this Agreement. Client will have the right, in addition to all of its other rights, to require Developer to deliver to Client all of Developer's work in progress, including all originals and copies thereof, as well as any other materials provided to Developer by Client or third parties, or created by Developer under this Agreement. Developer may keep any milestone payments which have been paid or are due under Schedule "B", and such payments shall be deemed payment in full for all obligations of Client under this Agreement, including full payment for all source code, object code, documentation, notes, graphics and all other materials and work relating to the portion of the Web Site and the assignment or licenses of rights relating to the Web Site which has been completed as of the time of termination.

9.2 Termination for Convenience. Client shall have the right at any time to terminate this Agreement upon fifteen (15) days notice by giving written notice of termination to Developer. Developer shall immediately cease all work on the Web Site. In the event of such termination, Client's entire financial obligation to Developer shall be for then accrued payments due under the Development Schedule, plus the prorated portion of the next payment, if any, due with respect to items being worked on but not yet delivered at the time of termination. The pro-rata payment shall be calculated by determining what percentage of the total work required for the next milestone has been completed by the date of Developer's receipt of the termination notice.

9.3 Automatic Termination. This Agreement will be terminated automatically, without notice, (i) upon the institution by or against Developer of insolvency, receivership, or bankruptcy proceedings or any other proceedings for the settlement of Developer's debts; (ii) upon Developer making an assignment for the benefit of creditors; or (iii) upon Developer's dissolution.

Section 10
GOVERNING LAW AND DISPUTE RESOLUTION

10.1 Arbitration. The parties agree to submit any dispute arising out of or in connection with this Agreement to binding arbitration in _____ before the American Arbitration Association pursuant to the provisions of this Section 10.1, and, to the extent not inconsistent with this Section 10.1, the rules of the American Arbitration Association. The parties agree that such arbitration will be in lieu of either party's rights to assert any claim, demand or suit in any court action, (provided that either party may elect either binding arbitration or a court action with respect to obtain injunctive relief to terminate the violation by the other party of such party's proprietary rights, including without limitation any trade secrets, copyrights or trademarks). Any arbitration shall be final and binding and the arbitrator's order will be enforceable in any court of competent jurisdiction.

10.2 Governing Law; Venue. The validity, construction, and performance of this Agreement shall be governed by the laws of the state of _____, and all claims and/or lawsuits in connection with agreement must be brought in _____.

Section 11
MISCELLANEOUS PROVISIONS

11.1 Notices. For purposes of all notices and other communications required or permitted to be given hereunder, the addresses of the parties hereto shall be as indicated below. All notices shall be in writing and shall be deemed to have been duly given if sent by facsimile, the receipt of which is confirmed by return facsimile, or sent by first class registered or certified mail or equivalent, return receipt requested, addressed to the parties at their addresses set forth below:

If to Developer:

_____

_____

_____

Attn: _____

If to Client:

_____

_____

_____

Attn: _____

11.2 Designated Person. The parties agree that all materials exchanged between the parties for formal approval shall be communicated between single designated persons, or a single alternate designated person for each party. Neither party shall have any obligation to consider for approval or respond to materials submitted other than through the Designated Persons. Each party shall have the right to change its Designated Person from time to time and to so notify the other in writing of such change. The initial Designated Person for Client is _____ and for Developer is_____.

11.3 Entire Agreement. This Agreement, including the attached Schedules which are incorporated herein by reference as though fully set out, contains the entire understanding and agreement of the parties with respect to the subject matter contained herein, supersedes all prior oral or written understandings and agreements relating thereto except as expressly otherwise provided, and may not be altered, modified or waived in whole or in part, except in writing, signed by duly authorized representatives of the parties.

11.4 Force Majeure. Neither party shall be held responsible for damages caused by any delay or default due to any contingency beyond its control preventing or interfering with performance hereunder.

11.5 Severability. If any provision of this Agreement shall be held by a court of competent jurisdiction to be contrary to any law, the remaining provisions shall remain in full force and effect as if said provision never existed.

11.6 Assignment. This Agreement is personal to Developer. Developer may not sell, transfer, sublicense, hypothecate or assign its rights and duties under this Agreement without the written consent of Client. No rights of Developer hereunder shall devolve by operation of law or otherwise upon any receiver, liquidator, trustee, or other party. This Agreement shall inure to the benefit of Client, its successors and assigns.

11.7 Waiver and Amendments. No waiver, amendment, or modification of any provision of this Agreement shall be effective unless consented to by both parties in writing. No failure or delay by either party in exercising any rights, power, or remedy under this Agreement shall operate as a waiver of any such right, power, or remedy.

11.8 Agency. The parties are separate and independent legal entities. Developer is performing services for Client as an independent contractor. Nothing contained in this Agreement shall be deemed to constitute either Developer or Client an agent, representative, partner, joint venturer or employee of the other party for any purpose. Neither party has the authority to bind the other or to incur any liability on behalf of the other, nor to direct the employees of the other. Developer is an independent contractor, not an employee of Client. No employment relationship is created by this Agreement. Developer shall retain independent professional status throughout this Agreement and shall use his/her own discretion in performing the tasks assigned.

11.9 Limitation on Liability; Remedies. Except as provided in Section 8 above with respect to third party indemnification, neither party shall be liable to the other party for any incidental, consequential, special, or punitive damages of any kind or nature, including, without limitation, the breach of this Agreement or any termination of this Agreement, whether such liability is asserted on the basis of contract, tort (including negligence or strict liability), or otherwise, even if either party has warned or been warned of the possibility of any such loss or damage.

IN WITNESS WHEREOF, this Agreement is executed as of the Effective Date set forth above.

473

web site
development
and
maintenance
agreement

CLIENT: DEVELOPER:

_____   _____

By:_____   By:_____

_____   _____

Name _____   Name _____

Its: _____   Its: _____

Title _____   Title _____

SCHEDULE A
SPECIFICATIONS (attach)

SCHEDULE B
DEVELOPMENT AND PAYMENT SCHEDULE

Contract Signing: _____   Payment due: _____

DELIVERABLES

	Due Date	Payment Due Upon	Acceptance by Client

Delivery of Web Site Design

Delivery of Beta Version

Delivery of Final
Version /Source Materials

TOTAL PAYMENT:

Bonus. Client agrees to pay Developer a bonus of $_____ which shall be payable to Developer in the event Developer delivers a Final Version of the Web Site which is acceptable to Client prior to _____.

SCHEDULE C
CLIENT CONTENT

ITEM: OWNER:

_____   _____

_____   _____

_____   _____

SCHEDULE D
MAINTENANCE AND SUPPORT SERVICES

SCHEDULE E
DEVELOPER'S CREDIT

FORM 3   TEXT LICENSE AGREEMENT

This form assumes that the text is being licensed for nonexclusive use. It also assumes that the text being licensed is already in existence. If a writer is being hired to create text, use Form 7.

TEXT LICENSE AGREEMENT

This agreement is made and entered into by and between _____ ("Licensor") and _____ ("Licensee") on the _____ (the "Effective Date").

NOW, THEREFORE, in consideration of the promises and mutual covenants and agreements set forth herein, the parties agree as follows:

1. DESCRIPTION OF WORK BEING LICENSED: _____(the "Work").

2. DESCRIPTION OF PROJECTS OR PRODUCTS TO WHICH LICENSE APPLIES: _____ (the "Project").

3. GRANT OF RIGHTS: For good and valuable consideration, the receipt and sufficiency of which are hereby acknowledged, Licensor hereby grants to Licensee a nonexclusive license to reproduce, digitize, modify for editorial purposes for use on the Project (without destroying the integrity or meaning of the Work), publicly display, and distribute the Work as part of the Project and any advertising and promotion related to the Project. If the Project includes an internal network, this license includes the right of employees of Licensee and its subsidiaries to copy the work from the network for Licensee's internal business purposes. If the Project includes a Web site, this license includes the right to permit users of the Web site to reproduce one copy of the Work for their personal, noncommercial use, and Licensee shall so state in its Web site conditions of usage. This license shall not include the right to use the Work independently of the Project or advertising and promotion related thereto. The rights granted herein shall not confer in Licensor any rights of ownership in the Project, including, without limitation, the copyright thereto, all of which shall be and remain the exclusive property of Licensee, except that Licensor shall retain copyright in the Work.

4. CREDIT: In consideration of the rights granted to Licensee, and provided the Work is used in the Project, Licensee agrees to give Licensor credit in writing in the Project in substantially the following form:
_____
Any inadvertent failure to provide credit shall not be deemed a breach of this Agreement.

5. LICENSE FEE: In further consideration of the rights granted to Producer herein, Producer shall pay to Licensor the sum of $ _____.

6. TERM: This license begins on _____ and ends on _____.

7. WARRANTIES: Licensor represents and warrants that:

(a) The Work was created solely by him, his full-time employees during the course of their employment, or independent contractors who assigned all right, title and interest worldwide in their work to Licensor or Licensor has obtained sufficient rights to grant the license stated in Section 3;

(b) Licensor is the owner of all right, title and interest in the tangible forms of the Work and all intellectual property rights protecting them or has the right to grant the license in Section 3. The Work and the intellectual property rights protecting them are free and clear of all encumbrances, including, without limitation, security interests, licenses, liens, charges or other restrictions which conflict with the license in Section 3;

(c) The use, public display, public performance, reproduction, distribution, or modification of the Work does not and will not defame any third parties or violate the rights of any third parties in the Work including, but not limited to, copyrights, publicity and privacy;

(d) The Work is not in the public domain;

(e) Licensor has full power and authority to make and enter into this Agreement.

8. INDEMNIFICATION: Licensor agrees to defend, indemnify, and hold harmless Licensee and their officers, directors, employees and agents, from and against any claims, actions or demands, including without limitation reasonable legal and accounting fees, alleging or resulting from the breach of the warranties in Section 7. Licensee shall provide notice to Licensor promptly of any such claim, suit, or proceeding and shall assist Licensor, at Licensor's expense, in defending any such claim, suit or proceeding.

9. GENERAL PROVISIONS: This Agreement will be governed by and construed in accordance with the laws of the United States and the State of _____ as applied to agreements entered into and to be performed entirely within that state between residents of that state. This Agreement, including any Exhibits to this Agreement, constitutes the entire agreement between the parties relating to this subject matter and supersedes all prior or simultaneous representations, discussions, negotiations, and agreements, whether written or oral. The Agreement may not be modified except by written instrument signed by both parties. No term or provision hereof will be considered waived by either party, and no breach excused by either party, unless such waiver or consent is in writing signed on behalf of the party against whom the waiver is asserted. No consent by either party to, or waiver of, a breach by either party, whether express or implied, will constitute a consent to, waiver of, or excuse of any other, different, or subsequent breach by either party. Licensee may assign its rights and obligations under this Agreement. This Agreement will be for the benefit of Licensee's successors and assigns, and will be binding on Licensor's heirs,

legal representatives and permitted assignees. If any dispute arises between the parties with respect to the matters covered by this Agreement which leads to a proceeding to resolve such dispute, the prevailing party in such proceeding shall be entitled to receive its reasonable attorneys' fees, expert witness fees and out of pocket costs incurred in connection with such proceeding, in addition to any other relief to which it may be entitled. All notices, requests and other communications required to be given under this Agreement must be in writing, and must be mailed by registered or certified mail, postage prepaid and return receipt requested, or delivered by hand to the party to whom such notice is required or permitted to be given. Any such notice will be considered to have been given when received, or if mailed, five (5) business days after it was mailed, as evidenced by the postmark. The mailing address for notice to either party will be the address shown on the signature page of this Agreement. Either party may change its mailing address by notice as provided by this Section. The following provisions shall survive termination of this Agreement: Sections 7 and 8.

This Agreement is effective as of the date _____ .

By: _____   By: _____

_____   _____
Typed name   Typed name

_____   _____
Title   Title

Address: _____   Address: _____

_____   _____

_____   _____

FORM 4   PHOTO AND VIDEO LICENSE AGREEMENT

This form is appropriate for photo licensing and simple video licensing—for example, for getting permission to use footage owned by an independent video producer, as well as footage from travel videos, corporate training and marketing videos, media libraries, or stock houses. Licensing footage from motion pictures and television series is much more complex and involves multiple levels of licenses, fees, and performer permissions, as discussed in "Licensing Film and Television Clips," chapter 11.

This form assumes that the material is being licensed for nonexclusive use and is already in existence. If a photographer or video producer is being hired to shoot photos or footage, use Form 7 (and the photographer or producer should obtain privacy releases, Form 10, if releases are needed).

PHOTO AND VIDEO FOOTAGE LICENSE AGREEMENT

This agreement is made and entered into by and between _____("Licensor") and _____("Licensee") on the _____ (the "Effective Date").

NOW, THEREFORE, in consideration of the promises and mutual covenants and agreements set forth herein, the parties agree as follows:

1. DESCRIPTION OF WORK BEING LICENSED: _____ _____(the "Work").

2. DESCRIPTION OF PROJECTS OR PRODUCTS TO WHICH LICENSE APPLIES: _____(the "Project").

3. GRANT OF RIGHTS: For good and valuable consideration, the receipt and sufficiency of which are hereby acknowledged, Licensor hereby grants to Licensee a nonexclusive license to reproduce, digitize, edit without destroying the historical integrity or compromising the images, publicly perform, publicly display, and distribute the Work in the Project and in any advertising and promotion related to the Project. If the Project includes an internal network, this license includes the right of employees of Licensee and its subsidiaries to copy the work from the network for Licensee's internal business purposes. If the Project includes a Web site, this license includes the right to permit users of the Web site to reproduce one copy of the Work for their personal, noncommercial use, and Licensee shall so state in its Web site conditions of usage. This license shall not include the right to use the Work independently of the Project or advertising and promotion related thereto. The rights granted herein shall not confer in Licensor any rights of ownership in the Project, including, without limitation, the copyright thereto, all of which shall be and remain the exclusive property of Licensee, except that Licensor shall retain copyright in the Work.

4. CREDIT: In consideration of the rights granted to Licensee, and provided the Work is used in the Project, Licensee agrees to give Licensor credit in writing in the Project in substantially the following form:

_____

Any inadvertent failure to provide credit shall not be deemed a breach of this Agreement.

5. LICENSE FEE: In further consideration of the rights granted to Producer herein, Producer shall pay to Licensor the sum of $_____.

6. TERM: This license begins on _____ and ends on _____.

7. WARRANTIES: Licensor represents and warrants that:

   (a) The Work was created solely by him, his full-time employees during the course of their employment, or independent contractors who assigned all right, title and interest worldwide in their work to the Licensor or Licensor has obtained sufficient rights to grant the license in Section 3;

   (b) Licensor is the owner of all right, title and interest in the tangible forms of the Work and all intellectual property rights protecting them or has the right to grant the license in Section 3. The Work and the intellectual property rights protecting the Work are free and clear of all encumbrances, including, without limitation, security interests, licenses, liens, charges or other restrictions which conflict with the license in Section 3;

   (c) The use, public display, public performance, reproduction, distribution, or modification of the Work does not and will not defame any third parties or violate the rights of any third parties in the Work including, but not limited to, copyrights, trademarks, publicity and privacy;

   (d) The Work is not in the public domain;

   (e) The grant of the licenses in Section 3 to the Work does not require the payment of any fees to any third parties (including, without limitation, SAG, AFTRA, or Writer's Guild fees);

   (f) Licensor has full power and authority to make and enter into this Agreement.

8. INDEMNIFICATION: Licensor agrees to defend, indemnify, and hold harmless Licensee and their officers, directors, sublicensees, employees and agents, from and against any claims, actions or demands, including without limitation reasonable legal and accounting fees, alleging or resulting from the breach of the warranties in Section 7. Licensee shall provide notice to Licensor promptly of any such claim, suit, or proceeding and shall assist Licensor, at Licensor's expense, in defending any such claim, suit or proceeding.

9. GENERAL PROVISIONS: This Agreement will be governed by and construed in accordance with the laws of the United States and the State of _____ as applied to agreements entered into and to be performed entirely within that state between residents of that state. This Agreement, including any Exhibits to this Agreement, constitutes the entire agreement between the parties relating to this subject matter and supersedes all prior or simultaneous representations, discussions, negotiations, and agreements, whether written or oral. The Agreement may not be modified except by written instrument signed by both parties. No term or provision hereof will be considered waived by either party, and no breach excused by either party, unless such waiver or consent is in writing signed on behalf of the party against whom the waiver is asserted. No consent by either party to, or waiver of, a breach by either party, whether express or implied, will constitute a consent to, waiver of, or excuse of any other, different, or subsequent breach by either party. Licensee may assign its rights and obligations under this Agreement. This Agreement will be for the benefit of Licensee's successors and assigns, and will be binding on Licensor's heirs, legal representatives and permitted assignees. If any dispute arises between the parties with respect to the matters covered by this Agreement which leads to a proceeding to resolve such dispute, the prevailing party in such proceeding shall be entitled to receive its reasonable attorneys' fees, expert witness fees and out of pocket costs incurred in connection with such proceeding, in addition to any other relief to which it may be entitled. All notices, requests and other communications required to be given under this Agreement must be in writing, and must be mailed by registered or certified mail, postage prepaid and return receipt requested, or delivered by hand to the party to whom such notice is required or permitted to be given. Any such notice will be considered to have been given when received, or if mailed, five (5) business days after it was mailed, as evidenced by the postmark. The mailing address for notice to either party will be the address shown on the signature page of this Agreement. Either party may change its mailing address by notice as provided by this Section. The following provisions shall survive termination of this Agreement: Sections 7 and 8.

This Agreement is effective as of the date _____.

By: _____   By: _____

_____   _____
Typed name   Typed name

_____   _____
Title   Title

Address: _____   Address: _____

_____   _____

_____   _____

_____   _____

FORM 5   PERMISSION TO LINK

Use this agreement to:

- ■ Get permission *from* another Web site owner to link from your site to the owner's site; or

- ■ Grant permission *to* another Web site owner authorizing a link from the other owner's site to your site.

The party granting permission is the "Grantor." The party receiving permission is the "Grantee."

PERMISSION TO LINK

_____ ("Grantor") has a Web site located at http://_____ ("Grantor's Web site").

_____ ("Grantee") has a Web site located at http://_____ ("Grantee's Web site").

Grantor hereby grants Grantee permission to provide a hypertext link from Grantee's Web site to the home page of Grantor's Web site.

Neither party shall be liable to the other party for the content of its Web site or links on its Web site to other Web sites.

Grantee acknowledges that Grantor may terminate this Permission at any time with or without cause by giving notice to Grantee in the following manner: _____.

If this Grant is terminated, Grantee must remove the hypertext link to Grantee's Web site within _____days of receiving the notice.

This Agreement is governed by the laws of the State of _____, excluding its conflict of laws principles. This Agreement is the entire understanding between the parties relating to the link referenced here and supersedes all prior or contemporaneous understandings, whether written or oral.

By: _____   By: _____

_____   _____
Typed name   Typed name

_____   _____
Title   Title

Address: _____   Address: _____

_____   _____

_____   _____

_____   _____

FORM 6   EMPLOYEE NONDISCLOSURE AND ASSIGNMENT AGREEMENT

This agreement is used to ensure that an employee maintains the employer's information in confidence and assigns to the employer all proprietary rights developed during the term of the employment. It also prohibits the employee from engaging in employment, consulting jobs, or other activity in a business competitive with the developer.

The agreement should be signed on an employee's first day of work. The "employee" is referred to in the first person (as "I"). The employer is referred to as "Company."

EMPLOYEE NONDISCLOSURE AND ASSIGNMENT AGREEMENT

This Agreement is intended to set forth in writing my responsibility to ("Company"). I recognize that Company is engaged in a continuous program of research, development, and production respecting its business, present and future. As part of my employment with Company, I have certain obligations relating to inventions that I develop during my employment.

In return for my employment by Company, I acknowledge and agree that:

1. Effective Date. This agreement ("Agreement") shall be effective on _____ , the first day of my employment with Company.

2. Confidentiality. I will maintain in confidence and will not disclose or use, either during or after the term of my employment, any proprietary or confidential information or know-how belonging to Company ("Confidential Information"), whether or not in written form, except to the extent required to perform duties on behalf of Company. Confidential Information refers to any information, not generally known in the relevant trade or industry, which was obtained from Company, or which was learned, discovered, developed, conceived, originated or prepared by me in the scope of my employment. Such Confidential Information includes, but is not limited to, software, technical and business information relating to Company's inventions or products, research and development, production processes, manufacturing and engineering processes, machines and equipment, finances, customers, marketing, and production and future business plans and any other information which is identified as confidential by Company. Upon termination of my employment or at the request of my supervisor before termination, I will deliver to Company all written and tangible material in my possession incorporating the Confidential Information or otherwise relating to Company's business. These obligations with respect to Confidential Information extend to information belonging to customers and suppliers of Company who may have disclosed such information to me as the result of my status as an employee of Company.

3. Work Products.

3.1 Definition of Work Products. As used in this Agreement, the term "Work Product" means any new work of authorship, new or useful art, discovery, contribution, finding or improvement, whether or not patentable, and all related know-how. Work Product includes, but is not limited to, all storylines, characters, computer software, designs, discoveries, formulae, processes, manufacturing techniques, inventions, improvements, and ideas.

3.2 Disclosure of Work Products and Assignment of Proprietary Rights.

(a) The "Company Work Product" is defined as any Work Product that I may solely or jointly conceive, develop or reduce to practice during the period of my employment, (i) that relates, at the time of conception, development, or reduction to practice of the Work Product, to Company's business or actual or demonstrably anticipated research or development; (ii) that was developed, in whole or in part, on Company's time or with the use of any of Company's equipment, supplies, facilities, or trade secret information; or (iii) that resulted from any work I performed for Company. I will promptly disclose and describe to Company all Company Work Product.

(b) (i) I hereby irrevocably assign, convey and otherwise transfer to Company, and its respective successors and assigns, all rights, title, and interests worldwide in and to the Company Work Product and all proprietary rights therein, including, without limitation, all copyrights, trademarks, design patents, trade secret rights, moral rights, and all contract and licensing rights, and all claims and causes of action of any kind with respect to any of the foregoing, whether now known or hereafter to become known.

(ii) In the event I have any right in and to the Company Work Product that cannot be assigned to Company, I hereby unconditionally and irrevocably waive the enforcement of all such rights, and all claims and causes of action of any kind with respect to any of the foregoing against Company, its distributors and customers, whether now known or hereafter to become known and agree, at the request and expense of Company and its respective successors and assigns, to consent to and join in any action to enforce such rights and to procure a waiver of such rights from the holders of such rights.

(iii) In the event I have any rights in and to the Company Work Product that cannot be assigned to Company and cannot be waived, I hereby grant to Company, and its respective successors and assigns, an exclusive, worldwide, royalty-free license during the term of the rights to reproduce, distribute, modify, publicly perform and publicly display, with the right to sublicense and assign such rights in and to the Company Work Product including, without limitation, the right to use in any way whatsoever the Company Work Product.

483

employee
nondisclosure
and
assignment
agreement

(iv) I retain no rights to use the Company Work Product and agree not to challenge the validity of the ownership by Company of the Company Work Product.

(v) I do not assign or agree to assign any Work Product created by me prior to my employment by Company.

(c) Unless I specifically state such an exception in Exhibit A, if I use Work Product that I created prior to my employment with Company during my employment with Company, I grant an irrevocable, nonexclusive, royalty-free, worldwide license to Company, with the right to sublicense, to reproduce, modify, distribute, publicly perform and publicly display such works as part of Company's products.

(d) I recognize that Work Product relating to my activities while working for Company and conceived or made by me, alone or with others, within one year after termination of my employment may have been conceived in significant part while employed by Company. Accordingly, I agree that such Work Products shall be presumed to have been conceived during my employment with Company and are to be assigned to Company as a Company Work Product unless and until I have established the contrary. I agree to disclose promptly in writing to Company all Work Product made or conceived by me for one (1) year after my term of employment, whether or not I believe such Work Product is subject to this Agreement, to permit a determination by Company as to whether or not the Work Product should be the property of Company. Any such information will be received in confidence by Company.

3.3 Nonassignable Work Products. This Agreement does not apply to any Work Product which qualifies fully as a nonassignable invention under the provisions of Section 2870 of the California Labor Code.

4. Company's Materials. Upon termination of my employment with Company or at any other time upon Company's request, I will promptly deliver to Company, without retaining any copies, all documents and other materials furnished to me by Company or prepared by me for Company.

5. Competitive Employment. During the term of my employment with Company, I will not engage in any employment, consulting, or other activity in any business competitive with Company without Company's written consent.

6. Non-solicitation. During the term of my employment with Company and for a period of two (2) years thereafter, I will not solicit or encourage, or cause others to solicit or encourage, any employees of Company to terminate their employment with Company.

7. Acts to Secure Proprietary Rights.

7.1 Further Acts. I agree to perform, during and after my employment, all acts deemed necessary or desirable by Company to permit and assist it, at its expense, in perfecting and enforcing the full benefits, enjoyment, rights and title throughout the world in the Company Work Product. Such acts may include, but are not limited to, execution of documents and assistance or cooperation in the registration and enforcement of applicable patents and copyrights or other legal proceedings.

485

employee
nondisclosure
and
assignment
agreement

7.2 Appointment of Attorney-In-Fact. In the event that Company is unable for any reason whatsoever to secure my signature to any lawful and necessary document required to apply for or execute any patent, copyright or other applications with respect to any Work Product (including improvements, renewals, extensions, continuations, divisions or continuations in part thereof), I hereby irrevocably appoint Company and its duly authorized officers and agents as my agents and attorneys-in-fact to execute and file any such application and to do all other lawfully permitted acts to further the prosecution and issuance of patents, copyrights or other rights thereon with the same legal force and effect as if executed by me.

8. No Conflicting Obligations. My performance of this Agreement and as an employee of Company does not and will not breach any agreement to keep in confidence proprietary information, knowledge or data acquired by me prior to my employment with Company. I will not disclose to Company, or induce Company to use, any confidential or proprietary information or material belonging to any previous employer or other person or entity. I am not a party to any other agreement which will interfere with my full compliance with this Agreement. I will not enter into any agreement, whether written or oral, in conflict with the provisions of this Agreement.

9. Survival. Notwithstanding the termination of my employment, Section 3.2 and Articles 2, 6, and 7 shall survive such termination. This Agreement does not in any way restrict my right or the right of Company to terminate my employment at any time, for any reason or for no reason.

10. Specific Performance. A breach of any of the promises or agreements contained herein will result in irreparable and continuing damage to Company for which there will be no adequate remedy at law, and Company shall be entitled to injunctive relief and/or a decree for specific performance, and such other relief as may be proper (including monetary damages if appropriate).

11. Waiver. The waiver by Company of a breach of any provision of this Agreement by me will not operate or be construed as a waiver of any other or subsequent breach by me.

12. Severability. If any part of this Agreement is found invalid or unenforceable, that part will be amended to achieve as nearly as possible the same economic effect as the original provision and the remainder of this Agreement will remain in full force.

13. Governing Law. This Agreement will be governed by and construed in accordance with the laws of the United States and the State of California

as applied to agreements entered into and to be performed entirely within California between California residents.

14. Choice of Forum. The parties hereby submit to the jurisdiction of, and waive any venue objections against, the United States District Court for the District of _____ and the Superior and Municipal Courts of the State of _____ , _____ County, in any litigation arising out of the Agreement.

15. Entire Agreement. This Agreement, including all Exhibits to this Agreement, constitutes the entire agreement between the parties relating to this subject matter and supersedes all prior or simultaneous representations, discussions, negotiations, and agreements, whether written or oral. This Agreement may be amended or modified only with the written consent of both me and Company. No oral waiver, amendment or modification will be effective under any circumstances whatsoever.

16. Assignment. This Agreement may be assigned by Company. I may not assign or delegate my duties under this Agreement without Company's prior written approval. This Agreement shall be binding upon my heirs, successors, and permitted assignees.

EMPLOYEE:

_____   _____
Date   Signature

                                 _____
                                 Printed Name

COMPANY:

_____   _____
Date   By

                                 _____
                                 Title

487

employee
nondisclosure
and
assignment
agreement

LIMITED EXCLUSION NOTIFICATION

THIS IS TO NOTIFY you in accordance with Section 2872 of the California Labor Code that the above Agreement between you and Company does not require you to assign to Company, any invention for which no equipment, supplies, facility or trade secret information of Company was used and which was developed entirely on your own time, and (a) which does not relate (1) to the business of Company or (2) to Company's actual or demonstrably anticipated research or development, or (b) which does not result from any work performed by you for Company. This limited exclusion does not apply to any patent or invention covered by a contract between Company and the United States or any of its agencies requiring full title to such patent or invention to be in the United States.

I ACKNOWLEDGE RECEIPT of a copy of this notification.

_____
Signature

_____
Printed Name of Employee

_____
Date

WITNESSED BY:

_____
Company Representative

_____
Date

EXHIBIT A
Prior Work Products

FORM 7   CONTENT DEVELOPMENT AND TRANSFER AGREEMENT

When Web content is created by a freelancer (also known as an independent contractor) for a client, a contract is important for two reasons: (1) to clarify and document the two parties' understanding about their respective obligations and rights; and (2) to deal with the issue of who will own the copyright in the material created by the freelancer.

Use this form if you are planning to use the services of a freelancer to create graphics, photographs, text, or music for your Web site or online products. For a more general independent contractor agreement, see Form 14.

CONTENT DEVELOPMENT AND TRANSFER AGREEMENT

THIS AGREEMENT ("Agreement") is entered into by and between _____ (the "Client") and _____ (the "Contractor") on the_____(the "Effective Date").

NOW, THEREFORE, in consideration of the promises and mutual covenants and agreements set forth herein, the parties agree as follows:

1. Engagement of Services. Contractor agrees to perform services for client as follows:_____ ("Project"). Contractor may not subcontract or otherwise delegate its obligations under this Agreement without Client's prior written consent. Contractor agrees to perform the services in a professional manner and to complete the Project by _____.

2. Compensation.

2.1 Fees and Approved Expenses. Client will pay Contractor the fee of _____ for services rendered by Contractor pursuant to this Agreement. Contractor will not be reimbursed for any expenses incurred in connection with the performance of services under this Agreement, unless those expenses are approved in advance and in writing by Client or listed in Exhibit A as Reimbursable Expenses.

2.2 Payment Due. Client will review the Work Product within _____ days after receiving it from Contractor to ensure that it meets the Project requirements stated in Section 1. If Client does not give written notice of rejection to Contractor within that time period (describing the reasons for the rejection in reasonable detail), the Work Product will be deemed to be accepted. Client will pay Contractor for services and will reimburse Contractor for previously approved expenses within _____ days after acceptance.

3. Independent Contractor Relationship. Contractor and Client understand, acknowledge, and agree that Contractor's relationship with Client will be that of an independent contractor and nothing in this Agreement is intended to or should be construed to create a partnership, joint venture, or employment relationship.

4. Trade Secrets and Confidential Information.

4.1 Third-Party Information. Contractor represents that his performance of all of the terms of this Agreement does not and will not breach any agreement to keep in confidence proprietary information, knowledge or data of a third party, and Contractor will not disclose to Client, or induce Client to use, any confidential or proprietary information belonging to third parties unless such use or disclosure is authorized in writing by such owners.

4.2 Confidential Information. Contractor agrees during the term of this Agreement and thereafter to take all steps reasonably necessary to hold in trust and confidence information which he knows or has reason to know is considered confidential by Client (Confidential Information). Contractor agrees to use the Confidential Information solely to perform the Project hereunder. Confidential Information includes, but is not limited to, technical and business information relating to Client's inventions or products, research and development, manufacturing and engineering processes, and future business plans. Contractor's obligations with respect to the Confidential Information also extend to any third party's proprietary or confidential information disclosed to Contractor in the course of providing services to Client. This obligation shall not extend to any information which becomes generally known to the public without breach of this Agreement. This obligation shall survive the termination of this Agreement.

5. Ownership of Work Product.

5.1 Definition. "Work Product" means the works of authorship conceived or developed by Contractor while performing the Project services.

5.2 Assignment. Contractor hereby irrevocably assigns, conveys and otherwise transfers to Client, and its respective successors and assigns, all rights, title and interests worldwide in and to the Work Product and all copyrights, contract and licensing rights, and claims and causes of action of any kind with respect to any of the foregoing, whether now known or hereafter to become known (except as stated otherwise in Section 5.3). In the event Contractor has any rights in and to the Work Product that cannot be assigned to Client, Contractor hereby unconditionally and irrevocably waives the enforcement of all such rights, and all claims and causes of action of any kind with respect to any of the foregoing against Client, its distributors and customers, whether now known or hereafter to become known and agrees, at the request and expense of Client and its respective successors and assigns, to consent to and join in any action to enforce such rights and to procure a waiver of such rights from the holders of such rights. In the event Contractor has any rights in and to the Work Product that cannot be assigned to Client and cannot be waived, Contractor hereby grants to Client, and its respective successors and assigns, an exclusive, worldwide, royalty-free license during the term of the rights to reproduce, distribute, modify, publicly perform and publicly display, with the right to sublicense through multiple tiers of sublicensees, and the right to assign such rights in and to the Work Product including, without limitation, the right to use in any way whatsoever the Work Product. Contractor retains no rights to use the Work Product except as stated in Exhibit B and agrees not to challenge the validity of the copyright ownership by Client in the Work Product.

5.3. Ownership of Components. Contractor will retain copyright ownership of the following components: _____ ("Retained Components"). However, Contractor grants to Client a royalty-free, worldwide, perpetual, irrevocable, nonexclusive license, with the right to sublicense through multiple tiers of sublicensees, to reproduce, distribute, modify, publicly perform and publicly display the Retained Components on any Web site operated by or for Client and in marketing material.

5.4 Power of Attorney. Contractor agrees to assist Client in any reasonable manner to obtain and enforce for Client's benefit copyrights covering the Work Product in any and all countries. Contractor agrees to execute, when requested, copyright, or similar applications and assignments to Client, and any other lawful documents deemed necessary by Client to carry out the purpose of this Agreement. Contractor further agrees that the obligations and undertaking stated in this Section 5.4 will continue beyond the termination of Contractor's service to Client. If called upon to render assistance under this Section 5.4, Contractor will be entitled to a fair and reasonable fee in addition to reimbursement of authorized expenses incurred at the prior written request of Client. In the event that Client is unable for any reason whatsoever to secure Contractor's signature to any lawful and necessary document required to apply for or execute any patent, copyright or other applications with respect to any Work Product, Contractor hereby irrevocably designates and appoints Client and its duly authorized officers and agents as his agents and attorneys-in-fact to act for and in his behalf and instead of Contractor, to execute and file any such application and to do all other lawfully permitted acts to further the prosecution and issuance of copyrights or other similar rights thereon with the same legal force and effect as if executed by Contractor.

6. Return of Client's Property. Contractor acknowledges that Client's sole and exclusive property includes all documents, such as drawings, manuals, notebooks, reports, sketches, records, computer programs, employee lists, customer lists and the like in his custody or possession, whether delivered to Contractor by Client or made by Contractor in the performance of services under this Agreement, relating to the business activities of Client or its customers or suppliers and containing any information or data whatsoever, whether or not Confidential Information. Contractor agrees to deliver promptly all of Client's property and all copies of Client's property in Contractor's possession to Client at any time upon Client's request.

7. Warranties. Contractor represents and warrants that:

   (a) The Work Product was created solely by him, his full-time employees during the course of their employment, or independent contractors who assigned all right, title and interest worldwide in their work to Contractor.

   (b) Contractor is the owner of all right, title and interest in the tangible forms of the Work Product and all intellectual property rights protecting them. The Work Product and the intellectual property rights protecting them are free and clear of all encumbrances, including, without limitation, security interests, licenses, liens, charges or other restrictions;

   (c) Contractor has maintained the Work Product in confidence.

   (d) The use, reproduction, distribution, or modification of the Work Product does not and will not violate the rights of any third parties in the Work Product including, but not limited to, copyrights, trade secrets, trademarks, publicity and privacy.

   (e) The Work Product is not in the public domain.

   (f) Contractor has full power and authority to make and enter into this Agreement.

8. Indemnification. Contractor agrees to defend, indemnify, and hold harmless Client, their officers, directors, sublicensees, employees and agents, from and against any claims, actions or demands, including without limitation reasonable legal and accounting fees, alleging or resulting from the breach of the warranties in Section 7. Client shall provide notice to Contractor promptly of any such claim, suit, or proceeding and shall assist Contractor, at Contractor's expense, in defending any such claim, suit or proceeding.

9. General Provisions. This Agreement will be governed by and construed in accordance with the laws of the United States and the State of _____ as applied to agreements entered into and to be performed entirely within that state between residents of that state. This Agreement, including any Exhibits to this Agreement, constitutes the entire agreement between the parties relating to this subject matter and supersedes all prior or simultaneous representations, discussions, negotiations, and agreements, whether written or oral. The Agreement may not be modified except by written instrument signed by both parties. No term or provision hereof will be considered waived by either party, and no breach excused by either party, unless such waiver or consent is in writing signed on behalf of the party against whom the waiver is asserted. No consent by either party to, or waiver of, a breach by either party, whether express or implied, will constitute a consent to, waiver of, or excuse of any other, different, or subsequent breach by either party. Contractor may not assign its rights or obligations arising under this Agreement without Client's prior written consent. Client may assign its rights

and obligations under this Agreement. This Agreement will be for the benefit of Client's successors and assigns, and will be binding on Contractor's heirs, legal representatives and permitted assignees. If any dispute arises between the parties with respect to the matters covered by this Agreement which leads to a proceeding to resolve such dispute, the prevailing party in such proceeding shall be entitled to receive its reasonable attorneys' fees, expert witness fees and out-of-pocket costs incurred in connection with such proceeding, in addition to any other relief to which it may be entitled. All notices, requests and other communications required to be given under this Agreement must be in writing, and must be mailed by registered or certified mail, postage prepaid and return receipt requested, or delivered by hand to the party to whom such notice is required or permitted to be given. Any such notice will be considered to have been given when received, or if mailed, five (5) business days after it was mailed, as evidenced by the postmark. The mailing address for notice to either party will be the address shown on the signature page of this Agreement. Either party may change its mailing address by notice as provided by this Section. The following provisions shall survive termination of this Agreement: Sections 4, 5, 6, 7 and 8.

This Agreement is effective as of _____, 19____.

By: _____   By: _____

_____   _____
Typed name   Typed name

_____   _____
Title   Title

Address: _____   Address: _____

_____   _____

_____   _____

_____   _____

EXHIBIT A
Reimbursable Expenses

EXHIBIT B
Contractor's License to Use the Work Product

FORM 8   ASSIGNMENT AGREEMENT (WITH REPRESENTATIONS)

This agreement is used for an assignment of copyright. It includes standard representations about ownership and other important issues.

The party granting the assignment is referred to as the "Assignor." The party receiving the assignment is referred to as the "Assignee."

ASSIGNMENT AGREEMENT (WITH REPRESENTATIONS)

THIS AGREEMENT ("Agreement") is dated as of _____ by and between _____ ("Assignor") and _____ ("Assignee).

NOW THEREFORE, the parties agree as follows:

1. Assignor hereby irrevocably assigns, conveys and otherwise transfers to Assignee, and its respective successors, licensees, and assigns, all right, title and interest worldwide in and to the Work and all proprietary rights therein, including, without limitation, all copyrights, trademarks, design patents, trade secret rights, moral rights, and all contract and licensing rights, and all claims and causes of action of respect to any of the foregoing, whether now known or hereafter to become known. In the event, Assignor has any right in the Work which cannot be assigned, Assignor agrees to waive enforcement worldwide of such right against Assignee, its distributors, and customers or, if necessary, exclusively license such right worldwide to Assignee, with the right to sublicense. These rights are assignable by Assignee.

2. Assignor represents and warrants that: (a) the Work was created solely by Assignor, Assignor's full-time employees during the course of their employment, or independent contractors who assigned all right, title and interest in their work to Assignor; (b) Assignor is the owner of all right, title and interest in the tangible forms of the Work and all intellectual property rights protecting them; (c) the Work and the intellectual property rights protecting them are free and clear of all encumbrances, including, without limitation, security interests, licenses, liens, charges or other restrictions; (d) the use, reproduction, distribution, or modification of the Work does not and will not violate the rights of any third parties in the Work including, but not limited to, trade secrets, publicity, privacy, copyrights, and patents; (e) the Work is not in the public domain; and (f) Assignor has full power and authority to make and enter into this Agreement. Assignor agrees to defend, indemnify, and hold harmless Assignee, its officers, directors and employees for any claims, suits or proceedings alleging a breach of these warranties.

3. Assignor agrees that he or she will take all actions and execute any and all documents as may be requested by Assignee, at Assignee's expense, from time to time, to fully vest in Assignee all rights, title and interests worldwide in and to the Work.

4. In consideration of the foregoing, Assignee agrees to pay to Assignor the
   sum of _____ Dollars ($_____).

ASSIGNEE: ASSIGNOR:

By: _____   By: _____

_____   _____
Typed name   Typed name

Address: _____   Address: _____

_____   _____

_____   _____

_____   _____

FORM 9   ASSIGNMENT: SHORT FORM

This agreement is used to record a copyright assignment in the Copyright Office. In order for the recorded agreement to qualify as "constructive notice" of the transfer, the work's copyright must be registered and the recorded agreement must include either the registration number or title of the copyrighted work (see "Obtaining a License," chapter 10).

This short form assignment can also be used to record an assignment of less than all rights in the work (for example, an assignment of audiovisual rights or motion picture rights).

The agreement can be modified to use for recording an exclusive copyright license in the Copyright Office.

ASSIGNMENT: SHORT FORM

The Assignor _____ ("Assignor") for good and valuable consideration, the receipt of which is acknowledged, grants to _____ ("Assignee"), its successors and assigns all right, title and interest in the copyrightable work named _____ ("Work") owned by Assignor. Assignor authorizes the recordation of this notice with the Copyright Office. The registration number of the Work is _____.

ASSIGNOR: ASSIGNEE:

By: _____   By: _____

_____   _____
Printed name   Printed name

Address: _____   Address: _____

_____   _____

_____   _____

_____   _____

FORM 10 RELEASE

This release is used to obtain the right to use a person's image, name, or voice in a photograph or video footage. It is a general release applicable to all media and products. Some releases are more limited—for example, they may limit the use of an image to a particular product or prevent the modification of the image.

RELEASE

1. GRANT OF RIGHTS: For valuable consideration received, I hereby grant to _____ ("Grantee") the absolute and irrevocable right and permission, throughout the world, in respect of the photographs or video footage ("the Material") that it has, has taken, or has had taken of me or in which I may be included with others:

   (a) To use, reuse, publish, and republish, and otherwise reproduce, digitize, edit, modify, distribute, publicly display, and publicly perform the same, in whole or in part, individually or in conjunction with other photographs or videos, and in conjunction with any copyrighted matter, in any and all media now or hereafter known, for illustration, promotion, art, advertising and trade, or any other purpose whatsoever; and

   (b) To use my name in connection with the Material if it so chooses.

2. RELEASE: I hereby release and discharge Grantee from any and all claims and demands arising out of or in connection with the use of the photographs or footage, including without limitation any and all claims for defamation, invasion of privacy, and misappropriation of my right of publicity.

3. COPYRIGHT IN THE MATERIAL: I acknowledge that I have no claim to the copyrights in the Material. The copyright owners have the right to copyright the Material in their own names or otherwise and to use, assign, and license the Material throughout the world, including any rights I might have.

4. ASSIGNMENT OF RELEASE: Grantee may sell, assign, license or otherwise transfer all rights granted to it hereunder. This authorization and release shall also inure to the benefit of the heirs, legal representatives, licensees, and assigns of Grantee, as well as the person(s) (if any) for whom it took the photographs.

5. **GRANTOR'S REPRESENTATIONS:** I am of full age and have the right to contract in my own name. I have read the foregoing and fully understand the contents thereof. This release shall be binding upon me and my heirs, legal representatives and assigns. I further release Grantee from any responsibility for injury incurred during the photography session.

Signed: _____

Date: _____

Address: _____

City, State, Zip: _____

Phone: _____

Social Security #: _____

FORM 11   LOCATION AGREEMENT

This agreement is used to obtain the right to enter onto property to photograph it or film it and the right to use the photographs or film in a motion picture, product, or project.

LOCATION AGREEMENT

_____ ("Grantor") hereby grants to _____ ("Company") and its employees, contractors, agents, independent producers, and suppliers, permission to enter upon and use the property, both exterior and interior, located at: _____ ("Property"); and also the right to reproduce the Property, elsewhere, including the name, signs and identifying features thereof, accurately or otherwise, for the purpose of photographing by means of film, videotape, or otherwise, and recording certain scenes for the motion picture, product, or project _____ ("Project").

The permission herein granted shall be for one or more days beginning on or about _____ (subject to change on account of weather conditions or changes in production (schedule)) and continuing until completion of all scenes and work required and shall include permission to reenter the Property for the purpose of making added scenes and retakes ("Additional Use").

Company may place all necessary facilities and equipment, including temporary sets, on the Property and agrees to remove same after completion of work and leave the Property in as good condition as when received, reasonable wear and tear from uses permitted herein excepted. Signs on the Property may, but need not be, removed or changed, but, if moved or changed, must be replaced.

Company agrees to use reasonable care to prevent damage to the Property, and will indemnify the owner and all other parties lawfully in possession of the Property and hold each of them harmless from any claims and demands of any person or persons arising out of, or based upon personal injuries, death or property damage resulting directly from any act of negligence on Company's part in connection with the work hereunder.

All rights of every kind in and to all photographs and sound records made hereunder (including but not limited to the right to exhibit any and all scenes photographed or recorded at and of the Property or reproduction of the Property throughout the world) shall be and remain vested in Company, its successors, assigns and licensees, and neither the owner nor any tenant, or other party now or hereafter having an interest in the Property, shall have any right of action against Company or any other party arising out of any use of said photographs and/or sound recordings whether or not such use is or may be claimed to be defamatory, untrue, or censurable in nature and hereby waives any and all rights of privacy, publicity, or any other rights of a similar nature in connection with the exploitation of any such photography or soundtrack.

In full consideration of the above, Company shall pay Grantor the sum of
_____ and for Additional Use, if any, the sum
of _____. If the charge herein is on a daily rate,
such charge shall be made only for days on which photography actually occurs
on the Property. Payment will be made on or before the date of filming.

The commencement date above contemplated and any obligations of the parties shall be postponed for a period equal to the period of any act of God, fire,
strike or other labor controversy, law or other governmental regulation which
hinders or prevents Company's normal business operations or production of
the Project, plus such additional period of time as Company may reasonably
require to recommence production of the Project.

Should Company elect not to use said Property for filming purposes, written
notice will be given prior to filming date releasing all parties from any obligations mentioned above.

The provisions, if any, contained in Schedule "A" attached hereto shall be
deemed a part of this Agreement.

The undersigned warrants that the undersigned has the full right to enter into
this Agreement and that the consent of no other party is necessary to effectuate
the full and complete permission granted therein.

Signed: _____
　　　　　　[Grantor]

For Company: _____

SCHEDULE A

Company shall have the right to use the Property for the following number of
days and purposes commencing on or about _____.

DAYS   PURPOSE

_____   Preparation

_____   Photography

_____   Striking/Clean Up

Should Company require additional days' use of the Property for any of the
purposes set forth, Grantor grants Company the right to use the Property for
such additional days.

FORM 12   QUITCLAIM

This letter is used in community property states to "quitclaim" any rights which a spouse may have in a copyright. (See "Community Property," chapter 3.)

QUITCLAIM

Dear [Husband/Wife]:

Your spouse is assigning all rights (including the copyright) in _____ ("Work") to _____ (Assignee"). Under certain interpretations of the law, you may have partial ownership rights in the Work. In order to avoid any doubt and in consideration for our payment to [Husband/Wife], you agree to assign all of such rights, if any, in the Work to Assignee and to quitclaim all rights in the Work. Please indicate your agreement by signing below. Thank you for your assistance.

Sincerely yours,

Developer Company

Read and Agreed:

_____

Date: _____

FORM 13 AFTRA EXPERIMENTAL INTERNET AGREEMENT

This is the agreement AFTRA is currently using with Web production companies. It is discussed in "Signing Collective Bargaining Agreements," chapter 22.

DRAFT
AFTRA Experimental Internet Agreement

Made and entered into as of _____ by and between the AMERICAN FEDERATION OF TELEVISION AND RADIO ARTISTS a voluntary organization, organized and existing under the laws of the State of New York, and having its principal office at 260 Madison Avenue, New York, New York 10016 (hereinafter called "AFTRA"), and _____ (hereinafter called "Producer").

This Agreement confirms the understanding of the parties regarding the terms and conditions of employment by the Producer of Performers engaged to render services for exhibition on _____ .

1. TERM: This Agreement shall begin on _____, and end on December 31, 2000. Either party may serve notice of termination not less than sixty (60) or more than ninety (90) days prior to the expiration date above. At least sixty (60) days prior to the end of the term of this Agreement, AFTRA and the Producer shall commence to negotiate in good faith with respect to a new Agreement.

2. SCOPE: This Agreement applies to all elements, both visual and audio, produced by the Producer for exhibition on the Internet including, but not limited to, exhibition on specific Web sites, and to all persons seen or heard on such elements ("Performers"). The Producer hereby recognizes AFTRA as the exclusive collective bargaining agent for all Performers engaged by Producer throughout the United States subject to the provisions of Sections 9(a) of the National Labor Relations Act, as amended.

3. DEFINITIONS:

   Web site: A location on the World Wide Web identified by a unique URL or Uniform Resource Locator comprised of any computer or computer systems on the Internet.

   Internet: A worldwide system of interconnected networks and computers.

4. MINIMUM SCALE: Performers shall be paid no less than the rates set forth in Appendix A for work performed under this Agreement.

5. PRODUCTION REPORTS: Within ten (10) calendar days of any performance date, Producer shall submit a report to AFTRA detailing the work performed by each Performer, which shall include, for each day of work: 1) the type of performance (e.g. acting, voice-over, singing, background, etc.), 2) the date on which the performance occurred, 3) the name

and social security number of the Performer, and 4) the total amount paid to the Performer.

6. PAYMENT: Payments due under this Agreement shall be made to Performer's designee or the AFTRA _____ Local office not later than _____ calendar days after the Performer's services were rendered, subject to the deduction of such taxes and withholdings as are authorized or required by law. All required payments for additional compensation (e.g., reuse) shall also be made no later than _____ days after the right to such payment arises. If the Producer fails to make full and timely payment as provided herein, cumulative non-creditable penalty payments of Four Dollars ($4.00) per day shall accrue indefinitely and shall be added to the compensation due and payable to the Performer for each business day that the payment is delinquent. All payments shall be accompanied by a detailed breakdown of the earnings included in the payment.

7. HEALTH AND RETIREMENT: Producer shall contribute to the AFTRA Health and Retirement Funds an amount equal to twelve and one-tenth percent (12.1%) based on the total gross compensation paid to all Performers covered by this Agreement, including Performers employed directly or indirectly, as, for example, through a *for services only* (fso) corporation. AFTRA Health and Retirement contributions shall be made separately to the AFTRA H&R Funds, P.O. Box 19260, Newark, NJ 07195-0260 with written confirmation of this payment provided to the AFTRA _____ Local office. Producer hereby agrees to be bound by the AFTRA Pension and Welfare Funds Agreement and Declaration of Trust, dated November 16, 1954 which Agreement and Declaration of Trust, as amended, is hereby ratified and confirmed and is made a part of this Agreement with the same force and effect as though fully set forth herein.

8. ARBITRATION: Should any dispute as to the interpretation, application, or claimed violation of this Agreement and/or any personal services agreement arise, AFTRA shall advise the Producer in writing. If the parties are unable to resolve the matter, either party may submit it to arbitration within one (1) year from the date of the original notification. Arbitration shall be conducted in the state of California under the rules of the American Arbitration Association (AAA) or Federal Mediation and Conciliation Service (FMCS). Each party shall bear its own arbitration expenses and equally bear the fees of the arbitrator and the service utilized. The decision of the arbitrator on matters submitted shall be final, binding, and conclusive upon all parties.

9. MINIMUM TERMS: The Producer agrees that the terms herein are the minimum terms and conditions which govern the employment of Performers employed or otherwise engaged by the Producer. The Producer agrees that no Performer will be employed on terms and conditions less favorable to that Performer than those set forth herein. The Producer agrees that

the Producer shall seek no waiver of any provision in this contract from any Performer nor shall any such waiver be effective unless and until AFTRA consents to it. The Producer further agrees that nothing in this Agreement shall be deemed to prevent any Performer from negotiating for or obtaining better terms than the minimum terms provided for herein.

10. WARRANTY AND RECOGNITION: AFTRA warrants that it represents, for collective bargaining purposes, a majority of the Performers engaged by the Producer to render services for such programs described herein, recorded on video tape or by any other means or methods except recordation by motion picture film photography.

11. UNION SECURITY: It is agreed that during the term of this Agreement, the Producer will employ and maintain in its employment only such persons covered by this Agreement as are members of AFTRA in good standing, or shall make application for membership on the thirtieth (30th) day following the first day of employment hereunder or the date of execution of this Agreement, whichever is the latter, and thereafter maintain such membership in good standing as a condition of employment. For the purpose of this provision "good standing" shall mean the payment of uniform initiation fees and periodic dues in accordance with AFTRA policy as periodically amended.

12. CODES OF FAIR PRACTICE: The use anywhere other than on the specific Internet location or registered domain name designated herein of any material produced under this Agreement, except as explicitly stipulated in Appendix A, shall be subject to the consent of the Performer. Bargaining for such use shall begin at the terms and conditions contained in the AFTRA agreement applicable to such material and/or use.

    In the event the Producer does not secure the prior consent of the Performer as described in this Paragraph 12, and thereafter utilizes any material covered by this Agreement, the terms and conditions of the applicable AFTRA Code then in effect shall apply, except the Producer shall be obligated to pay not less than triple the applicable rates set forth in such Code. Performer may elect not to accept such triple scale payment and may either arbitrate, pursuant to Paragraph 8, Arbitration, or take legal action.

13. NO DISCRIMINATION: Neither the Producer nor AFTRA shall discriminate in any manner against a Performer because of race, creed, color, gender, religion, age, place of national origin, veteran-status, sexual orientation, union activity or disability (provided the disability does not impair the ability of the Performer to perform the required work).

14. SUCCESSORS AND ASSIGNS: This Agreement shall be binding on and inure to the benefit of the parties, their representative successors and assigns. The Producer agrees that if there is a transfer or sale of the material produced under this Agreement to a third party, it will incorporate into the contract with the purchaser(s) a requirement that said purchaser(s) will be bound by the terms and conditions of this Agreement and shall thereby assume all rights and responsibilities of Producer under this Agreement.

15. APPLICABLE LAWS; SEPARABILITY: If there are any valid provisions of law applicable to this document which are in conflict herewith, the provisions of this document which are in conflict shall be deemed modified in conformity with the provisions of such applicable laws.

16. TRANSFER OF RIGHTS: Upon the sale, transfer, assignment, license, lease, agreement to distribute or other disposition by the signed Producer hereunder of its rights in any recorded Program produced hereunder, Producer shall not be responsible to AFTRA or to any Performers for any payments thereafter due with respect to replays, reruns, supplemental markets, foreign, or any other payments due hereunder, if both Producer and transferee execute and comply with a standard Transfer of Rights Agreement. In the event the Producer and transferee do not enter into such Transfer of Rights Agreement and have such Agreement approved by AFTRA, Producer shall remain liable for all reuse, supplemental and all other payments to Performers hereunder. Written notice and a copy of the above-referenced assumption agreement will be given to AFTRA by Producer within thirty (30) days of each sale, transfer or assignment, license or other disposition of any material which is subject to this code.

17. RATIFICATION: This Agreement is subject to final approval by AFTRA's National Board of Directors or it's designated committees.

ACCEPTED AND AGREED:
FOR THE PRODUCER:

Date: _____

Name (print): _____

Title: _____

Address: _____

FOR AFTRA:

Date: _____

Name (print): _____

Title: _____

Address: _____

APPENDIX A

Performers engaged to render services for _____ to be utilized on _____ shall be engaged under the following terms and conditions:

1. ON-CAMERA PERFORMERS:

    Day Players

    Three-Day Players

    Weekly Players

    Extras

    Stand-Ins

2. OFF-CAMERA PERFORMERS:

    Voice-Over Performers (4-hour day)

    One Hour/One Voice*

    *Requires the engagement of additional Performers at standard rates.

3. OVERTIME:

    All On-Camera Performers shall receive overtime at the rate of time and one-half for all hours worked beyond eight (8) in a day, forty (40) in a week and for sixth and seventh days. All On-Camera Performers shall receive overtime at the rate of double-time for all hours worked beyond twelve (12) in a day.

    All Off-Camera Performers shall receive overtime at the rate of time and one-half for all hours worked beyond four (4) in a day, twenty (20) in a week and for sixth and seventh days.

    Overtime shall be calculated by dividing the Performer's actual daily rate by the number of hours allowed for such rate.

4. USE PERIODS:

    Upon payment of the fee(s) referenced herein, Producer may utilize material for a period not to exceed _____. For exhibition in excess of the aforementioned period, Performers shall be paid _____, which payment shall allow an additional use period of _____.

5. ADDITIONAL PROVISIONS:

    Agents Commission of ten percent (10%)

    Rest Periods

    Wardrobe

    Meal Periods

    Individual Contracts

FORM 14   INDEPENDENT CONTRACTOR AGREEMENT

This agreement is used when the independent contractor will perform a simple project for the hiring party. The agreement assumes that the project is one that does not include detailed milestones and acceptance provisions. In the agreement, the hiring party is referred to as "Company."

INDEPENDENT CONTRACTOR AGREEMENT

THIS AGREEMENT ("Agreement") is entered into by and between _____ ("Company"), a _____ corporation, and the undersigned (the "Contractor").

1. Engagement of Services. Contractor agrees to perform services for Company as follows:

   ("Project"). Company selected Contractor to perform these services based upon Company's receiving Contractor's personal service. Contractor may not subcontract or otherwise delegate its obligations under this Agreement without Company's prior written consent. Contractor agrees to perform the services in a professional manner.

2. Compensation.

2.1 Fees and Approved Expenses. Company will pay Contractor the fee set forth in Exhibit A for services rendered by Contractor pursuant to this Agreement. Contractor will not be reimbursed for any expenses incurred in connection with the performance of services under this Agreement, unless those expenses are approved in advance and in writing by Company.

2.2 Timing. Company will pay Contractor for services and will reimburse Contractor for previously approved expenses within thirty (30) days of the date of Contractor's invoice.

3. Independent Contractor Relationship. Contractor and Company understand, acknowledge, and agree that Contractor's relationship with Company will be that of an independent contractor and nothing in this Agreement is intended to or should be construed to create a partnership, joint venture, or employment relationship.

4. Trade Secrets—Intellectual Property Rights.

4.1 Disclosure.

   (a) Contractor agrees to disclose promptly in writing to Company, or any person designated by Company, every invention, including but not limited to computer programs, processes, know-how and other copyrightable material, that is conceived, developed, made or reduced to practice by Contractor within the scope of the Project.

   (b) Contractor represents that his performance of all of the terms of this Agreement does not and will not breach any agreement to keep in confidence proprietary information, knowledge or data of a third party and Contractor will not disclose to Company, or induce Company to use, any confidential or proprietary information belonging to third parties unless such use or disclosure is authorized in writing by such owners.

(c) Contractor represents that any inventions or copyrighted works relating to Company's actual or anticipated business or research and development which Contractor has conceived, developed, made, or reduced to practice at the time of signing this Agreement, have been disclosed in writing to Company and attached to this Agreement as Exhibit B. These inventions and copyrighted works are not assigned to Company. However, if Contractor uses such inventions or copyrighted works in the Project, Contractor grants to Company a royalty-free, worldwide, perpetual, irrevocable, nonexclusive license, with the right to sublicense, to reproduce, distribute, modify, publicly perform and publicly display such inventions and copyrighted works in Company's products based on the Project.

4.2 Confidential Information. Contractor agrees during the term of this Agreement and thereafter to take all steps reasonably necessary to hold in trust and confidence information which he knows or has reason to know is considered confidential by Company ("Confidential Information"). Contractor agrees to use the Confidential Information solely to perform the project hereunder. Confidential Information includes, but is not limited to, technical and business information relating to Company's inventions or products, research and development, manufacturing and engineering processes, and future business plans. Contractor's obligations with respect to the Confidential Information also extend to any third party's proprietary or confidential information disclosed to Contractor in the course of providing services to Company. This obligation shall not extend to any information which becomes generally known to the public without breach of this Agreement. This obligation shall survive the termination of this Agreement.

4.3 No Conflict of Interest. Contractor agrees during the term of this Agreement not to accept work or enter into a contract or accept an obligation, inconsistent or incompatible with Contractor's obligations or the scope of services rendered for Company under this Agreement.

4.4 Assignment of Work Product.

(a) "Work Product" means the storyline, characters, computer software, designs, discoveries, works of authorship, formulae, processes, manufacturing techniques, inventions, improvements and ideas solely or jointly conceived, developed or reduced to practice during the Project. Contractor hereby irrevocably assigns, conveys and otherwise transfers to Company, and its respective successors and assigns, all rights, title and interests worldwide in and to the Work Product and all proprietary rights therein, including, without limitation, all copyrights, trademarks, design patents, trade secret rights, moral rights, and all contract and licensing rights, and all claims and causes of action of any kind with respect to any of the foregoing, whether now known or hereafter to become known. In the event Contractor has any rights in and to the Work Product that cannot be assigned to Company, Contractor hereby unconditionally and irrevocably waives the enforcement of all such rights, and all claims and causes of action of any kind with respect to any of the foregoing against Company, its distributors and customers, whether now known or hereafter to become known and agrees at the request and expense of Company and its respective successors and assigns to consent to and join in any action to enforce such rights and to procure a waiver of such rights from the holders of such rights. In the event Contractor has any rights in and to the Work Product that cannot be assigned to Company and cannot be waived, Contractor hereby grants to Company, and its respective successors and assigns, an exclusive, worldwide, royalty-free license during the term of the rights to reproduce, distribute, modify, publicly perform and publicly display, with the right to sublicense and assign such rights in and to the Work Product including, without limitation, the right to use in any way whatsoever the Work Product. Contractor retains no rights to use the Work Product and agrees not to challenge the validity of the ownership by Company in the Work Product.

(b) Contractor agrees to assist Company in any reasonable manner to obtain and enforce for Company's benefit patents, copyrights, and other property rights covering the Work Product in any and all countries. Contractor agrees to execute, when requested, patent, copyright, or similar applications and assignments to Company, and any other lawful documents deemed necessary by Company to carry out the purpose of this Agreement. Contractor further agrees that the obligations and undertaking stated in this Section 4.4(b) will continue beyond the termination of Contractor's service to Company. If called upon to render assistance under this Section 4.4(b), Contractor will be entitled to a fair and reasonable fee in addition to reimbursement of authorized expenses incurred at the prior written request of Company.

(c) In the event that Company is unable for any reason whatsoever to secure Contractor's signature to any lawful and necessary document required to apply for or execute any patent, copyright or other applications with respect to any Work Product (including improvements, renewals, extensions, continuations, divisions or continuations in part thereof), Contractor hereby irrevocably designates and appoints Company and its duly authorized officers and agents as his agents and attorneys-in-fact to act for and in his behalf and instead of Contractor, to execute and file any such application and to do all other lawfully permitted acts to further the prosecution and issuance of patents, copyrights or other rights thereon with the same legal force and effect as if executed by Contractor.

4.5 Return of Company's Property. Contractor acknowledges that Company's sole and exclusive property includes all documents, such as drawings, manuals, notebooks, reports, sketches, records, computer programs, employee lists, customer lists and the like in his custody or possession, whether delivered to Contractor by Company or made by Contractor in the performance of services under this Agreement, relating to the business activities of Company or its customers or suppliers and containing any information or data whatsoever, whether or not Confidential Information. Contractor agrees to deliver promptly all of Company's property and all copies of Company's property in Contractor's possession to Company at any time upon Company's request.

4.6 Warranties. Contractor represents and warrants that:

(a) The Work Product was created solely by him, his full-time employees during the course of their employment, or independent contractors who assigned all right, title and interest in their work to Contractor;

(b) Contractor is the owner of all right, title and interest in the tangible forms of the Work Product and all intellectual property rights protecting them The Work Product and the intellectual property rights protecting them are free and clear of all encumbrances, including, without limitation, security interests, licenses, liens, charges or other restrictions except as set forth in Exhibit C;

(c) Contractor has maintained the Work Product in confidence;

(d) The use, reproduction, distribution, or modification of the Work Product does not and will not violate the rights of any third parties in the Work Product including, but not limited to, trade secrets, trademarks, publicity, privacy, copyrights, and patents;

(e) The Work Product is not in the public domain;

(f) Contractor has full power and authority to make and enter into this Agreement.

4.7 Performance. Contractor represents and warrants that for a period of _____ following acceptance of the Work Product (i) the _____will be free from defects in workmanship and materials under normal use, and (ii) that the _____ will perform in accordance with the specifications in Exhibit A.

4.8 Indemnification. Contractor agrees to defend, indemnify, and hold harmless Company, their officers, directors, sublicensees, employees and agents, from and against any claims, actions or demands, including without limitation reasonable legal and accounting fees, alleging or resulting from the breach of the warranties in Section 4.6. Company shall provide notice to Contractor promptly of any such claim, suit, or proceeding and shall assist Contractor, at Contractor's expense, in defending any such claim, suit or proceeding.

5. Termination—Noninterference with Business.

5.1 Termination by Company. Company may terminate this Agreement for material breach at any time upon fifteen (15) days prior written notice to Contractor. Company also may terminate this Agreement immediately in its sole discretion upon Contractor's material breach of Article 4 and/ or Section 5.3 of this Agreement and/or upon any acts of gross misconduct by Contractor directly affecting this Agreement or the independent contractor relationship.

5.2 Termination by Contractor. Contractor may terminate this Agreement for material breach at any time upon fifteen (15) days prior written notice to Company.

5.3 Noninterference with Business. During and for a period of two (2) years immediately following termination of this Agreement by either party, Contractor agrees not to solicit or induce any employee or independent contractor to terminate or breach an employment, contractual or other relationship with Company.

6. General Provisions. This Agreement will be governed by and construed in accordance with the laws of the United States and the State of _____ as applied to agreements entered into and to be performed entirely within _____ between residents of that state. This Agreement, including all Exhibits to this Agreement, constitutes the entire agreement between the parties relating to this subject matter and supersedes all prior or simultaneous representations, discussions, negotiations, and agreements, whether written or oral. No term or provision hereof will be considered waived by either party, and no breach excused by either party, unless such waiver or consent is in writing signed on behalf of the party against whom the waiver is asserted. No consent by either party to, or waiver of, a breach by either party, whether express or implied, will constitute a consent to, waiver of, or excuse of any other, different, or subsequent breach by either party. Contractor may not assign its rights or obligations arising under this Agreement without Company's prior written consent. Company may assign its rights and obligations under this Agreement. This Agreement will be for the benefit of Company's successors and assigns, and will be binding on Contractor's heirs, legal representatives and permitted assignees. If any dispute arises between the parties with respect to the matters covered by this Agreement which leads to a proceeding to resolve such dispute, the prevailing party in such proceeding shall be entitled to receive its reasonable attorneys' fees, expert witness fees and out-of-pocket costs incurred in connection with such proceeding, in addition to any other relief to which it may be entitled. All notices, requests and other communications required to be given under this Agreement must be in writing, and must be mailed by registered or certified mail, postage prepaid and return

receipt requested, or delivered by hand to the party to whom such notice is required or permitted to be given. Any such notice will be considered to have been given when received, or if mailed, five (5) business days after it was mailed, as evidenced by the postmark. The mailing address for notice to either party will be the address shown on the signature page of this Agreement. Either party may change its mailing address by notice as provided by this Section. The following provisions shall survive termination of this Agreement: Article 4 and Section 5.3. This Agreement is effective as of the date _____ and will terminate on the date _____, unless terminated earlier in accordance with Section 5 above.

COMPANY: CONTRACTOR:

By: _____   By: _____

Title: _____   Title: _____

Address: _____   Address: _____

EXHIBIT A
PROJECT AND SPECIFICATIONS

EXHIBIT B
PRIOR WORK PRODUCT DISCLOSURE

EXHIBIT C
EXCEPTIONS

FORM 15   WORK FOR HIRE AGREEMENT

This agreement is used to acquire copyright rights in independent contractors' works that are eligible for treatment as specially commissioned "works made for hire." (See "The Work Made for Hire Rule," chapter 3, and "Copyright Ownership," chapter 6.) The hiring party is referred to as "Company."

To be effective, the agreement must be signed by both parties before the contractor starts work on the project. The agreement includes a "back-up" assignment to guard against the limitations of work made for hire agreements. (These limitations are discussed in "Copyright Ownership," chapter 6.)

The agreement also includes representations about ownership and other important issues.

WORK FOR HIRE AGREEMENT

THIS AGREEMENT ("Agreement") is dated as of _____ by and between _____ ("Contractor") and _____ with its principal place of business at _____ ("Company").

WHEREAS, Contractor has been asked to create certain material described on Exhibit A (the "Work") for Company;

And WHEREAS the parties intended that Company be the owner of all rights in the Work. The agreement will confirm such understanding.

NOW THEREFORE, the parties agree as follows:

1. The Work is a commissioned "work for hire" owned by Company. If the Work is determined not to be a "work for hire" or such doctrine is not effective, the Contractor hereby irrevocably assigns, conveys and otherwise transfers to Company, and its respective successors, licensees, and assigns, all right, title and interest worldwide in and to the Work and all proprietary rights therein, including, without limitation, all copyrights, trademarks, design patents, trade secret rights, moral rights, and all contract and licensing rights, and all claims and causes of action of respect to any of the foregoing, whether now known or hereafter to become known. In the event Contractor has any right in the Work which cannot be assigned, Contractor agrees to waive enforcement worldwide of such right against Company, its distributors, and customers or, if necessary, to exclusively license such right worldwide to Company with the right to sublicense. These rights are assignable by Company.

2. Contractor represents and warrants that: (a) The Work was created solely by him, his full-time employees during the course of their employment, independent contractors who assigned all right, title and interest in their work to Company; (b) Contractor is the owner of all right, title and interest in the tangible forms of the Work and all intellectual property rights protecting them; (c) The Work and the intellectual property rights protecting them are free and clear of all encumbrances, including, without

limitation, security interests, licenses, liens, charges or other restrictions; (d) The use, reproduction, distribution, or modification of the Work does not and will not violate the rights of any third parties in the Work including, but not limited to, trade secrets, publicity, privacy, copyrights and patents; (e) The Work is not in the public domain; and (f) Contractor has full power and authority to make and enter into this Agreement. Contractor agrees to defend, indemnify and hold harmless Company, its officers, directors and employees for any claims, suits or proceedings alleging a breach of these warranties.

3. Contractor agrees that he or she will take all actions and execute any and all documents as may be requested by Company, at Company's expense, from time to time to fully vest in Company all rights, title and interests worldwide in and to the Work.

4. In consideration of the foregoing, Company agrees to pay to Contractor the sum of _____ Dollars ($_____).

CONTRACTOR: COMPANY:

By: _____   By: _____

EXHIBIT A
(Attach description of the Work)

RIGHTS CLEARANCE AGENCIES, SEARCH FIRMS, AND LICENSING AGENTS

This appendix lists rights clearance agencies, search firms, and licensing agents that can help you clear rights to use third-party content. (Clearing rights is covered in chapter 10.)

Rights clearance agencies will clear rights and obtain licenses for you. They are described in "Rights Clearance Agencies," chapter 10.

Search firms help you find out who owns copyrights and other intellectual property rights in third-party works. They will not assist you in obtaining the rights to use third-party works in your project. Search firms should be used when you are performing the "clearance" work yourself. (See "Determining Who Owns the Copyright," chapter 10.)

Licensing agents have authority to grant licenses on behalf of content owners.

This list of agencies, firms, and individuals has been compiled from a variety of sources. None of them paid to be listed in this book, and we don't endorse any of them. If you use them, make sure they have experience relevant to your particular project.

RIGHTS CLEARANCE AGENCIES

Jill Alofs
Total Clearance
Mill Valley, CA
www.totalclear.com
Telephone: (415) 389-1531

Burning Bright Enterprises
Santa Barbara, CA
www.burning-bright.com
Telephone: (805) 957-1199

Cherchez L'Image
Outremont, Quebec, Canada
cherchezimage@aol.com
Telephone: (514) 277-5144

Clearance Consultants
Los Angeles, CA
Telephone: (310) 441-2600

The Content Company
c/o Richard Curtis Associates, Inc.
New York, NY 10021
www.curtisagency.com
Telephone: (212) 772-7363

Copyright Clearinghouse, Inc.
Burbank, CA
Telephone (818) 558-3480

deForest Research
Hollywood, CA
www.deforestresearch.com
Telephone: (213) 469-2271

MPI Clearance Services
Tarzana, CA
http://home.earthlink.net/~rshenson

The Permissions Group
Glenview, IL
www.permissionsgroup.com
Telephone: (847) 635-6550

The Rights Company
Toronto, Ontario, Canada
www.therightscompany.com
Telephone: (416) 203-3547
    ext. 202

Barbara Zimmerman
BZ/Rights & Permissions, Inc.
New York, NY
www.bzrights.com
Telephone: (212) 924-3000
Fax: (212) 769-9224

For additional music clearance
rights organizations, see
www.kohnmusic.com/articles/
clear.html

COPYRIGHT SEARCH FIRMS

Government Liaison Services
Arlington, VA
www.glstm.com
Telephone: (800) 642-6564

Prentice Hall Legal and Financial Services
Albany, NY
Telephone: (800) 833-9848
(handles trademark searches as well)

Robert G. Roomian, Esq.
Alexandria, VA
roomian@mciworld.com
Telephone: (703) 690-6451

Thomson & Thomson Copyright Research Group
Washington, DC
www.thomson-thomson.com
Telephone: (800) 356-8630

XL Corporate Services
New York, NY
Telephone: (800) 221-2972
(handles copyright filings and trademark searches as well)

Trademark Search Firms
Coresearch
New York, NY
Telephone: (800) 732-7241

Thomson & Thomson
N. Quincy, MA
www.thomson-thomson.com
Telephone: (800) 692-8833
Fax: (617) 786-8273

LICENSING AGENTS

TEXT:

Copyright Clearance Center, Inc.
Danvers, MA
www.copyright.com
Telephone: (978) 750-8400

Copyright Direct
Contoocook, NH
www.copyrightdirect.com
Telephone: (603) 746-3102

Icopyright, Inc.
Renton, WA
www.icopyright.com
Telephone: (425) 430-4555

Publication Rights Clearinghouse
National Writers Union
New York
www.nwu.org/prc/prchome.htm
Telephone: (212) 254-0279

MUSIC PERFORMING RIGHTS:

American Society of Composers, Authors & Publishers (ASCAP)
Chicago, Los Angeles, Nashville, New York
www.ascap.com/weblicense/
    webintro.html
Telephone: (212) 621-6271

Broadcast Music, Inc. (BMI)
Burbank, Nashville, New York:
www.bmi.com/iama/webcaster/
    index.asp
Telephone: (800) 258-5813 (ask to speak to an Internet Licensing representative)

Society of European Stage Authors & Composers (SESAC)
Nashville, New York
www.sesac.com/web.htm
license@sesac.com

MUSIC MECHANICAL LICENSES:

The Harry Fox Agency
New York
www.nmpa.org/hfa.html
Telephone: (212) 370-5330
clientservice@harryfox.com

PHOTOGRAPHS:

The Media Photographers' Copyright Agency
Philadelphia
www.mpca.com
Telephone: (215) 451-2767

STOCK HOUSES AND OTHER CONTENT SOURCES

Stock houses and music and sound libraries are described in "Stock Houses and Libraries," chapter 10. This list was obtained from a variety of sources, including trade shows, advertisements, search engine listings, and recommendations. We have chosen to provide you the largest set of choices, rather than screening the entries. Consequently, you have the responsibility to ensure that they can provide you with the materials you need for your project. None of these firms paid to be listed here, and we don't endorse any of them. To obtain your own list, do an Internet search for "sound libraries," "music libraries," "stock footage," and "stock photos." Licensing agents, listed in appendix C, can also provide stock content.

If you license content from one of these sources, make sure your license covers all the rights you need for your intended use (see "Determining What Rights You Need," chapter 10).

MUSIC AND SOUND LIBRARIES

Creative Support Services
Los Angeles, CA
www.cssmusic.com
Telephone: (800) HOT-MUSIC

FirstCom Music
Carrollton, TX
www.firstcom.com
Telephone: (800) 858-8880

Killer Tracks
Hollywood, CA
www.killertracks.com
Telephone: (800) 877-0078

LicenseMusic
San Francisco, CA
www.licensemusic.com
Telephone: (415) 543-2470

MPI Media Group
Orland Park, IL
www.mpimedia.com
Telephone: (708) 460-0555

OGM Production Music
Hollywood, CA
www.ogmmusic.com
Telephone: (800) 421-4163

Pro Music
Boca Raton, FL
www.promusic.com
Telephone: (800) 322-7879

SoperSound Music Library
Palo Alto, CA
www.sopersound.com
Telephone: (800) 227-9980

Valentino, Inc.
Elmsdorf, NY
www.tvmusic.com
Telephone: (800) 223-6278

FILM/VIDEO CLIPS

Adventure Pictures
San Francisco, CA
www.adpix.com
Telephone: (415) 552-8094

Archive Films
New York, NY
www.archivephotos.com
Telephone: (800) 447-0733

BBC Library Sales
(various cities)
www.bbcfootage.com

CBS News Archives
New York, NY
Telephone: (212) 975-2875

Cinema Network (CINENET)
Simi Valley, CA
www.cinenet.com
Telephone: (805) 527-0093

Energy Film
Los Angeles, CA
www.energyfilm.com
Telephone: (818) 508-1444

The Film Vault
Frankenmuth, MI
www.thefilmvault.com
Telephone: (517) 652-FILM

Filmbank
Burbank, CA
www.filmbank.com
Telephone: (818) 841-9176

Filmstock Research
Australia
www.filmstock.com/au
Telephone: (612) 9556-2833

Fish Films Footage World
Studio City, CA
www.footageworld.com
Telephone: (800) 442-0550

Footage.Net
Hanover, NH
www.footage.net
Telephone: (603) 643-0288

Footage Now Productions
Beverly Hills, CA
www.footage-now.com
Telephone: (888) 695-0779

Grinberg Film Libraries
New York, Los Angeles
www.grinberg.com
Telephone: (212) 397-6200
(213) 464-7491

Image Bank
(various cities)
www.imagebankfilm.com

Imageways
New York, NY
www.imageways.com
Telephone: (800) 862-1118

Kesser Stock Library
Miami, FL
www.kesser.com
Telephone: (800) STK-FTGE

NBC News Video Archive
New York, NY
Telephone: (212) 664-3797

Video Tape Library, Ltd.
Los Angeles, CA
www.videotapelibrary.com
Telephone: (213) 656-4330

WYWH Stock Footage
www.wywhstock.com
Telephone: (818) 569-5876

WPA Film Library
www.wpafilmlibrary.com

PHOTO STOCK HOUSES

AP Photo Archive
(Associated Press bureaus, various
    cities)
www.apwideworld.com
Telephone: (212) 621-1930

Archive Photos
New York, NY
www.archivephotos.com
Telephone: (800) 447-0733

Artville
Madison, WI
www.artville.com
Telephone: (608) 243-5956

Corbis Corporation
Bellevue, WA
www.corbis.com
Telephone: (206) 649-3344

Corel Corporation
Toronto, Ontario Canada
www.corel.com/products/
    clipartandphotos/index.htm
Telephone: (613) 728-8200

Digital Stock
Encinitas, CA
www.digitalstock.com
Telephone: (800) 260-0444

John T. Fowler
Ottawa, Canada
www.magma.ca/~fowler
Telephone: (613) 256-4056

FPG International
New York, NY
www.fpg.com
Telephone: (877) 4FPG-WEB

The Image Bank
Seattle, WA
www.imagebank.com
Telephone: (877) 932-7497

The Image Works
Woodstock, NY
www.theimageworks.com
Telephone: (800) 475-8801

Index Stock Photography, Inc.
New York, NY
www.indexstock.com
Telephone: (800) 729-7466

Liaison International, Inc.
New York, NY
www.liaisonintl.com
Telephone: (800) 488-0484

Photo Researchers, Inc.
New York, NY
www.photoresearchers.com
Telephone: (800) 833-9033

Photos To Go
New York, NY
www.photostogo.com
Telephone: (212) 929-4844

Picture Network International
Arlington, VA
Telephone: (703) 807-2780

Sharpshooters, Inc.
Miami, FL
www.sharpshooters.com
Telephone: (800) 666-1266

The Stock Market Photo Agency
New York, NY
www.stockmarketphoto.com
Telephone: (212) 684-7878

The Stock Solution
Salt Lake City, UT
www.tssphoto.com
Telephone: (801) 363-9700

Tony Stone Images
(various cities)
www.tonystone.com
Telephone: (800) 234-7880

SuperStock
Jacksonville, FL
www.superstock.com
Telephone: (904) 565-0066

UNIONS, GUILDS, AND OTHER ORGANIZATIONS

This appendix provides contact information for union and guild representatives with responsibility for online productions.

Contact information for the music licensing organizations ASCAP, BMI, SESAC, and the Harry Fox Agency is listed in appendix C.

American Federation of Musicians (AFM)
www.afm.org
Sue Collins, Los Angeles
    (interactive productions)
Telephone: (323) 461-3441
    ext. 202
Email: scollins@afm.org

Callum Benepe, Los Angeles
    (Internet commercials)
Telephone: (323) 461-3441
    ext. 206

American Federation of Television and Radio Artists (AFTRA)
www.aftra.com
Rebecca Rhine, San Francisco
Telephone: (415) 391-7510
Email: rrhine@aftra.com

Directors Guild of America (DGA)
www.dga.org
Warren Adler, Los Angeles
Telephone: (310) 289-2003
Email: warren@dga.org

Screen Actors Guild (SAG)
www.sag.org
Allen Weingartner, Los Angeles
Telephone: (323) 549-6847
Email: Aweingartner@sag.org

**Writers Guild
of America (WGA)**
www.wga.org
Grace Reiner, Los Angeles
Telephone: (310) 782-4501
Email: greiner@wga.org

ENDNOTES

Endnotes for Chapter 17

1. Council Directive 95/46, 1995 O.J. (L 281) 31 [hereinafter EU Data Protection Directive].

2. P. Sprenger, "Sun on Privacy: 'Get Over It,'" *Wired News* (Jan. 26, 1999) http://www. wired. com/news/politics/story/17538.html. McNealy is the chairman and CEO of Sun Microsystems, which is both the developer of the Java programming language used to implement applets in Web browsers and a member of the Online Privacy Alliance.

3. Because similar personal information may be shared with a number of sites, and because there is a delay between the initial disclosure of information and the onset of such aggravations as unsolicited electronic mail (email) messages, the exact source of the privacy invasions is often hidden from the consumer. This disconnection between cause and effect can lead to a "one bad apple" syndrome whereby the actions of a small number of irresponsible Web sites may be attributed to the Internet as a whole.

4. Many of the privacy concerns and principles discussed in this article can be traced to a 1973 study by the Department of Health, Education and Welfare, Secretary's Advisory Committee on Automated Personal Data Systems, Records, Computers, and the Rights of Citizens. According to a 1992 survey, over two-thirds of Americans believed that "the present uses of computers are an actual threat to personal privacy" and that "if privacy is to be preserved, the use of computers must be sharply restricted in the future." *Equifax-Louis Harris Consumer Privacy Survey*, Equifax Executive Summary 1992 ¶4 (visited Nov. 3, 1999) http://www.privacyexchange.org/iss/surveys/eqfx. execsum.1992.html.

5. See http://www.doubleclick.com/advertisers/network/boomerang/reporting.htm for an explanation of reports available to advertisers subscribing to DoubleClick's "Boomerang" service, including answers to such questions as "What are your customers' interests? Where do your customers work? When are your customers online? and Where do your customers live?" According to DoubleClick, all of this information is collected anonymously http://www.doubleclick.com/advertisers/network/ boomerang/privacy.htm, but see note 7 below. (All sites visited January 29, 2000.)

6. Consumers who voluntarily submit personally identifying information to Web sites that participate in DoubleClick's Abacus Alliance may find that this information is disclosed to DoubleClick and then associated with the anonymously gathered data about its Web browsing generally (described above), unless they specifically opt out at each participating site visited, http://www.doubleclick.net/company_info/ about?doubleclick/ privacy/ (visited January 29, 2000). DoubleClick apparently offers an opt-out cookie that is effective throughout its network, but on January 29, 2000 the author received only error messages when attempting to activate this feature at http://www.douleclick.net/company_info/about_doubleclick/privacy/ privacy2htm#optout.

7. This Orwellian-sounding term refers to an analysis of attitudes, interests, and opinions as distinct from mere demographic data; such an analysis can bring improvement in predictive success.

8. Tara Lemmey, president of Narrowline (now executive director of the Electronic Frontier Foundation), quoted in Esther Dyson, "Privacy Protection: Time to Think and Act Locally and Globally," *Release 1.0*, (April 1998) http://www. edventure.com/release1/0498body.html.

9. In the Matter of GeoCities, a corporation, FTC File No. 9823015 http://www.ftc.gov/os/1999/9902/ 9823015cmp.htm.

10. *Id.*

11. *Id.*

12. The FTC action and proposed settlement were first announced in early June 1998, in SEC filings in connection with GeoCities' upcoming public offering that August. GeoCities, Corp., SEC Form S-1 Registration Statement (June 12, 1998) http://www.sec.gov/Archives/ edgar/data/1062777/0001017062-98-001328.txt.

13. GeoCities, FTC Docket No. C-3850 (decision and order) (February 5, 1999) http://www.ftc.gov/ os/1999/9902/9823015d%260.htm.

14. Regarding children's issues, a similar settlement was reached in May 1999 with Liberty Financial Companies; *see In re* Liberty Fin. Cos., FTC File No. 9823522 (agreement containing consent order), (visited September 28, 1999) http://www.ftc.gov/os/1999/9905/lbtyord.htm.

15. *Privacy Online: A Report to Congress*, FTC report (June 4, 1998) http://www.ftc.gov/reports/ privacy3/index.htm [hereinafter *Privacy Online*] was sent to Congress June 4, 1998.

16. Child Online Privacy Protection Act of 1998, 15 USC §§ 6501-6506 (1998) [hereinafter COPPA].

17. 15 USC § 45 (1998).

18. In this instance "legal perspective" seems oxymoronic: despite what law school teaches, business is about much more than avoiding every possible risk.

19. See *infra* Part VI.F (discussing the EU Data Protection Directive).

20. Industries with regulated information practices include healthcare, banking, video rentals, cable television, and telecommunications.

21. Detailed results can be viewed at "Business Week/Harris Poll: Online Insecurity," *Business Week* (last modified March 5, 1998) http://www.businessweek.com/1998/11/b3569107.htm [hereinafter *Online Insecurity*].

22. Louis Harris and Assoc., Inc. & Alan F. Westin, "Privacy and American Business," and Price Waterhouse, Inc., "E-Commerce & Privacy Survey" (June 1998) http://www. privacyexchange.org/iss/surveys/ecommsum.html (stating that 23 percent of Internet users have purchased online, whereas the *Business Week/Harris Poll* put the figure at 22 percent).

23. *See Online Insecurity*, *supra* note 22 (finding that despite the benefits of registering at Web sites, 59 percent of Internet users *never* do).

24. "Georgia Institute of Technology, Graphics Visualization and Usability Center's 9th WWW User Survey" (April 1998) http://www.cc.gatech.edu/user_surveys/survey-1998-04/graphs/general/q46.htm.

25. Examples of such products include anonymous proxy servers for browsing privacy and anonymous email remailing services.

26. Louis Harris & Assoc., Inc. and Alan F. Westin, *supra* note 23 (noting that 91 percent of net users and 96 percent of those who buy products or services online call privacy policies "important" or "very important." For computer users who are not yet online, the figure was 94 percent).

27. A. Westin, "Freebies" and "Privacy: What Net Users Think" (visited September 28, 1999) http://www.privacyexchange.org/ iss/surveys/sr990714.html (reporting on a February 1999 poll by Opinion Research Corp. for Privacy & American Business).

28. See *Online Insecurity*, *supra* note 22 (finding that 62 percent of respondents would increase their Internet usage).

29. See *id.* (finding that 57 percent of respondents would increase their amount of purchases).

30. "TRUSTe/Boston Consulting Group Consumer Survey" (visited October 8, 1999) http://www.truste.org/webpublishers/ pub_bottom.html states that information practice policy statements make it two to three times more likely that a consumer will provide personal information to a Web site; 56 percent of users in the *Business Week/Harris Poll*, *supra* note 22, indicated that a privacy statement would make it more likely for them to register at a Web site.

31. Approximately 65 percent of commercial Web sites in March 1999 included some form of information practices statement, in contrast to only around 14 percent of commercial Web sites in the previous year. Further, virtually all of the top 100 sites include some information practices statement, with eighty-one sites boasting a more or less comprehensive privacy policy. The first figure is from Mary J. Culnan, "Georgetown Internet Privacy Policy Survey: Report to the Federal Trade Commission" (March 1999), which evaluated 361 "dotcom" sites selected randomly from the top 7,500 sites. The 14 percent figure is from *Privacy Online*, *supra* note 16, an FTC study of 1,400 sites. While these two studies are not direct equivalents, the trend towards adopting privacy policies is undeniable. The data on the top 100 sites is from Professor Culnan's study, "Privacy and the Top 100 Sites: Report to the Federal Trade Commission" (June 1999) sponsored by the Online Privacy Alliance. While these upbeat figures mask wide variation in adherence to recognized privacy principles, they all support the present point that a site without a policy increasingly stands out from the crowd.

32. See Lorrie Faith et al., "Beyond Concern: Understanding Net Users' Attitudes About Online Privacy," *AT&T Labs-Research Technical Report* TR 99.4.1 (March 25, 1999) http://www.research.att. com/library/trs/TRs/99/99.4/99.41/Survey-TR-19990325.htm [hereinafter *Beyond Concern*] (citing Christine Hine & Juliet Eve, "Privacy in the Marketplace," 14(4) *The Information Society* 253, 261 (1998) for the proposition that where a Web site does not explain the purposes for which it gathers and uses personal information, consumers are likely to concoct their own unfavorable opinions about the Web site's intentions).

33. See *Beyond Concern*, *supra* note 33 (finding that sharing data with third parties was the most important criterion users evaluate in deciding whether to reveal information to a Web site).

34. Respond.com has even adapted the reverse-auction model as a "black box"; the buyer fills out a form specifying the desired product and the desired price, Respond.com sends an email with this information (absent the buyer's identity) to its list of registered retailers, collects the replies and forwards them to the buyer. The buyer can then follow up with a vendor if she wants to accept its offer. The "middleman" feature not only preserves anonymity, it also enables Respond.com to collect its fees, which are based not on sales but on the number of e-mails to which the given vendor replies. See, e.g., (visited September 29, 1999) http://www.respond. com/overview/index.html (providing an outline of the black-box-auction model).

35. zZounds.com http://www.zZounds.com/discover.music?page=privacy&z=493782266316.

36. "Welcome to Juno" (visited October 25, 1999) http://www.juno.com. A recent Juno advertisement (targeted to online advertisers, rather than to consumers) states that "nearly 7 million Juno subscribers have filled out a member profile with more in-depth personal questions than your mother asks."

37. See "Welcome to The MyPoints Program" (visited September 29, 1999) http://www.mypoints.com (explaining that MyPoints participants are offered redeemable points—an Internet version of trading stamps— when they participate in MyPoints promotions or buy in response to MyPoints offers. A recent advertisement claims better than a 20 percent response rate to MyPoints email advertising campaigns).

38. See, e.g., Alex Nash, "Yahoo Retracts Unlisted Home Addresses," *CNET News.com* (April 25, 1996) http://news.cnet.com/news/0-1005-202-311165.html (describing the consumer outrage and Yahoo's rapid retreat when it was learned that Yahoo's new People Search service disclosed some 85 million unlisted home addresses and telephone numbers).

39. "TRUSTe" (visited September 29, 1999) http:www.truste.org.

40. "BBBOnLine" (visited September 29, 1999) http://www.bbonline.org.

41. A "secondary use" is a use of information for a purpose other than that for which it was originally disclosed, such as use in a direct-marketing campaign of a mailing address originally obtained for product shipment.

42. See "BBBOnLine: The Children's Privacy Seal" (visited September 29, 1999) http://www.bbbonline.org/ businesses/privacy/child_privacy.htm (stating that BBBOnline's seal requirements are based on COPPA); "TRUSTe License Agreement Rev. 5.0," Appendix C (last modified June 25, 1999) http://www.truste.org/webpublishers/pub_selfassessment.html (stating that TRUSTe's children guidelines are based on COPPA).

43. See "BBBOnLine: Privacy Program Eligibility Criteria" (visited November 2, 1999) http://www.bbbonline.org/businesses/ privacy/eligibility.html. (covering requirements for BBBOnLine Privacy Seals); "TRUSTe License Agreement Rev. 5.0" (last modified August 8, 1999) http://www.truste.org/ webpublishers/pub_agreement.html (requiring licensees to agree to particular and comprehensive rules before awarding Privacy Seals).

44. See "BBBOnLine: Privacy Program Eligibility Criteria," *supra* note 44 (disclosing requirements to which a business must agree in order to qualify for a BBBOnLine Privacy Seal).

45. "TRUSTe Approves 1000th Web Site," TRUSTe press release, January 12, 2000, http://www.truste.org/about/ about_1000th.html.

46. Press Release, "BBBOnLine's New Privacy Seal Program Opens for Business" (March 17, 1999) http:// www.bbbonline.org/about/press/3-17-99.htm.

47. "BBBOnLine Approved Privacy Participants" (visited January 26, 2000) http://www.bbbonline.org/businesses/ privacy/approved.html.

48. Cheskin Research and Studio Archetype/Sapient, "eCommerce Trust Study," at 16 (January 1999) http://www.studioarchetype.com/cheskin/html.

49. At the time, the BBBOnLine privacy seal program was not in effect; the seal in question was BBBOnLine's Reliability Seal, which relates to business practices other than privacy, but it is probably safe to assume that the organization's privacy seal would garner comparable responses.

50. Debra Valentine, "About Privacy: Protecting the Consumer on the Global Information Infrastructure," 1 *Yale Symp. on L. & Tech.* 4, at para. IV, B.1 (1998).

51. See Maryann Jones Thompson, "Tech Firms Still Top List of Net Advertisers," *The Industry Standard* (May 20, 1999) http://www.thestandard.com/metrics/display/

0,1283,894,00.html [hereinafter The Industry Standard] (ranking advertisers for 1998; Microsoft was first and IBM second with combined advertising expenditures of $63.4 million).

52. Kim Girard, "IBM To Pull Web Ads Over Privacy Concerns," *CNET News.com* (March 31, 1999) http://www.news.cnet.com/news/0-1005-200-340588.html?tag=st.cn.1fd2.

53. "Microsoft Pushes Net Privacy Policy" (June 23, 1999) http://www.msnbc.com/news/283255.asp.

54. "Disney and Go Network Institute Comprehensive New Advertising Policy to Promote Industry Adoption of Online Privacy Standards" (June 29, 1999) http://www.info.infoseek.com/press/06-29-99_policy.html. The Go Network is one of the top five Web sites, and The Industry Standard, *supra* note 52, ranked its constituent Infoseek as the sixth largest advertiser on other Web sites in 1998.

55. "Privacy Promise" (visited October 2, 1999) http://www.the-dma.org/pan7/pripro22.html.

56. "DMA Will Help You Create Your Own Company's Online Privacy Policy" (visited October 2, 1999) http://www.the-dma.org/pan7/dmers7c1-policy.shtml.

57. See "Privacy Online: A Report to Congress: at 54 n.73 (visited October 2, 1999) http://www.ftc.gov/ reports/privacy3/index.htm (listing eleven associations that submitted guidelines or principles for the FTC's consideration).

58. See *id.* app. E (reporting the submitted guidelines).

59. *Id.* at 7-11. Many other organizations have modeled their recommended information practices on the FTC list. See, e.g., Online Privacy Alliance, *Guidelines for Online Privacy Policies* (visited October 2, 1999) http://www.privacyalliance.org/resources/ppguidelines.html (including headings of notice, choice, access, and security); *Elements of Effective Self-Regulation for Protection of Privacy* (visited October 2, 1999) http://www.ecommerce.gov/staff.htm (including headings of notice, choice, access, security, and enforcement).

60. This simple requirement conceals difficult questions about the practicality and necessity of disclosing to a consumer such database-resident information as their clickstream records, or the inferences drawn from that data by use of analysis programs. Likewise, questions abound as to the obligation to disclose to consumers information about them that has been acquired from third-party sources.

61. On January 21, 2000, the FTC announced the appointment of a forty-member Advisory Committee on Online Access and Security to advise the FTC staff on policy issues surrounding the issues of what constitutes "reasonable access" and "adequate security." The committee's Final Report is available online at www.ftc.gov/acoas/papers/finalreport.htm. Interestingly, the FTC's COPPA regulations on security and integrity have a Sphinxlike brevity (16 C.F.R. § 312.8), so the Advisory Committee may well be a harbinger of expanded COPPA regulations on this point.

62. The Online Privacy Alliance, a consortium of over eighty companies and associations involved in e-commerce, advocates that self-regulation via third-party privacy seal programs is sufficient. However, it takes pains to say that complaint-resolution processes of seal programs should not prevent the consumer from pursuing "other available legal recourse." Online Privacy Alliance, *Effective Enforcement of Self-Regulation* (visited October 3, 1999) http://www.privacyalliance.org/resources/enforcement.html.

63. See discussion *infra* Part VI.F (discussing the EU Data Protection Directive).

64. See *supra* note 5 (discussing the 1973 study).

65. 5 USC § 552a (1974).

66. OECD, *Guidelines for the Protection of Personal Data and Transborder Flows of Personal Data* (1980).

67. As early as 1905, the Supreme Court of Georgia had recognized the right to privacy as against misappropriation of one's likeness. *Pavesich v. New England Life Ins. Co.*, 122 Ga. 190, 50 S.E. 18 (1905).

68. See, e.g., *Privacy Online, supra* note 16, at endnote 160; letter from Ambassador David L. Aaron, Undersecretary of Commerce for International Trade, to industry representatives on the subject of proposed Safe Harbor principles under the EU Data Protection Directive (November 4, 1998) http://www.ita.doc. gov/ecom/aaron114.html.

69. *OPA White Paper: Online Consumer Data Privacy in the United States* (November 19, 1998) http://www.privacyalliance.org/resources>.

70. Restatement (Second) of Torts § 652D (1976).

71. *Id.* at comment a. This standard is seldom met in ordinary business transactions. For example, in *Tureen v. Equifax, Inc.*, 571 F2d 411, 419 (8th Cir 1978), Equifax's disclosure of the plaintiff's medical underwriting history to her health insurer, at the insurer's request, was held not to be sufficiently "public" for an invasion of privacy cause of action.

72. *McVeigh v. Cohen*, 983 F.Supp 215 (DDC 1998).

73. Philip Shenon, "Navy and America Online Settle Case on Gay Privacy," *N.Y. Times*, June 12, 1998, available at http://www.nytimes.com/library/tech/98/06/cyber/articles/12navy.html.

74. *Id.* In related litigation, the Navy was found to have violated both its own "don't ask, don't tell" policy and the Electronic Communications Privacy Act. *McVeigh*, 983 FSupp at 220-21.

75. *Prepared Statement of the Federal Trade Commission "Consumer Privacy on the World Wide Web": Hearings Before the Subcommittee on Telecommunications, Trade and Consumer Protection of the House Committee on Commerce*, 105th Cong. n.23 (1998) (statement of Robert M. Pitofsky, Chairman of FTC): "[The FTC Act] grants the Commission authority to seek relief for violations of the Act's prohibitions on unfair and deceptive practices in and affecting commerce, an authority limited in this context to ensuring that Web sites follow their stated information practices."

76. Letter from Jodie Bernstein, Director, Bureau of Consumer Protection, Federal Trade Commission, to Center for Media Education (July 15, 1997) http://www.ftc.gov/os/1997/9707/cenmed.html.

77. See *infra* Part IX (discussing Contract Concepts).

78. Nonprofit organizations are exempt, just as they are exempt from the FTC Act.

79. E.g., by virtue of information entered in an "age" field in the data-collection screen.

80. COPPA, *supra* note 17, § 1303(b)(1)(A)(i).

81. "Verifiable parental consent" is defined *id.* § 1302(9).

82. *Id.* § 1303(b)(1)(A)(ii).

83. *Id.* § 1303(b)(1)(B)(ii).

84. *Id.* § 1303(b)(1)(B)(i), (iii).

85. COPPA, *supra* note 17, § 1303(b)(2).

86. *Id.* § 1303(b)(1)(C).

87. *Id.* § 1303(b)(1)(D).

88. *Id.* § 1304. Since the approved programs would have to mirror the requirements of the law and the underlying factual questions of compliance would be essentially the same with or without the safe harbor, it is not immediately obvious what *substantive* difference the safe harbor makes, but it does show a willingness by the government to outsource some of its compliance-enforcement work to industry groups, where the industry groups would no doubt prefer that it reside.

89. *Id.* § 1303(a)(1).

90. 16 C.F.R. pt. 312, issued October 20, 1999.

91. 16 C.F.R. § 312.2 defines "disclosure" as including any means of making personal information publicly available, such as "public posting through the Internet, or through a personal home page posted on a Web site or online service; a pen pal service; an electronic mail service; a message board; or a chat room."

92. 16 C.F.R. § 312.5(b)(2).

93. 16 C.F.R. § 312.4(b).

94. 16 C.F.R. § 312.4(b)(2).

95. 16 C.F.R. § 312.4(b)(1).

96. 18 USC §§ 2510-2522, 2701-2711 (1994).

97. *Id.* § 2510(4).

98. *Id.* § 2510(8) (emphasis added).

99. *Id.* § 2510(12) (emphasis added).

100. *Id.* § 2511(2)(d).

101. Suppose a Web site, as a result of monitoring browser requests to its server, tags an individual as a regular participant in a closed forum on "Living with a Diabetic." The explicit communication from the browser is merely to access a page with a particular address, and the Web site is a party to that communication with the presumptive right to disclose it. However, given the known subject-matter of discussions in the forum, does disclosure to a marketer of the nature of the page requested constitute an interception and disclosure of the broadly defined "contents" of the user's communications *within* the forum, communications to which the Web site operator is *not* a party?

102. 18 USC § 2511(2)(d), (3)(b)(ii) (1994).

103. See *Griggs-Ryan v. Smith*, 904 F2d 112 (1st Cir 1990) (finding that consent to the recording of telephone calls is presumed where the landlady informed a tenant that all incoming calls would be recorded). With privacy policies, the question is: what if the user claims not to have seen the policy?

104. 15 USC §§ 1681-1681t (1994 & Supp. III 1997).

105. 15 USC § 1681a(d) provides that covered information includes information "bearing on a consumer's credit worthiness, credit standing, credit capacity, character, general reputation, personal characteristics, or mode of living."

106. *Id.* § 1681b(3).

107. 15 USC § 1681a(d)(2)(A)(i).

108. *Id.* § 1681a(d)(2)(A)(iii).

109. This distinction is the subject of *Trans Union Corp. v. FTC*, 81 F3d 228 (DC Cir 1996), where the Federal Circuit held that targeted marketing lists were not necessarily "consumer reports" even though they were created from data originally gathered to be used in conventional credit reports, on the dubious grounds that the routine inclusion of this data in credit reports did not prove that particular data was actually expected to be used as a factor in credit decisions when it was collected. The court remanded to the FTC for further factual determinations, and an FTC Administrative Law Judge made the required factual determination and held Trans Union in violation of FCRA. *In re Trans Union Corp.*, No. D-9255 (July 31, 1998). Trans Union appealed the order to the full Commission, which affirmed the Administrative Law Judge's decision and ordered Trans Union to stop selling consumer report information in the form of target marketing lists to marketers who lack an authorized purpose for receiving them under the Fair Credit Reporting Act. 2000 WL 234561 (F.T.C.). The Commission's opinion, dated March 1, 2000, is available on the FTC's Web site, www.ftc.gov.

110. For a general discussion of the history of United States-EU discussions over the application of the "adequacy" test to the United States, see Scott Killingsworth & Brett Kappel, "Safe Harbor in Muddy Waters? Commerce Department Proposes Voluntary Principles for Compliance with EU Data Protection Directive," 1 *E-Commerce Law Report* 2 (December 1998/January 1999).

111. It would appear that under the EU Data Protection Directive, affiliates of the collector of the information would be considered "third parties" if they are not processing the data on behalf of the collector, which would mean the individual must be given opt-out privileges to prevent proposed transfers to these affiliates. EU Data Protection Directive, *supra* note 2, art. 2, §(f). The Draft Safe Harbor does not adopt the Data Protection Directive's definitions, however, and uses the flexible and undefined term "organization" to describe the collector of data.

112. Office of Thrift Supervision News Release, "Thrifts Urged to Post Privacy Policies as Part of Transactional Web Sites" (June 10, 1999) http://www.ots.treas. gov/docs/77939.html.

113. Office of the Comptroller of the Currency Advisory Letter 99-6, *Guidance to National Banks on Web Site Privacy Statements* (May 4, 1999) http://www.occ.treas. gov/ftp/advisory/99-6.txt.

114. FDIC Financial Institution Letters, *Electronic Commerce and Consumer Privacy* (August 17, 1998) http://www.fdic.gov/news/news/financial/1998/fil19886b.html; FDIC Financial Institution Letters, *Online Privacy of Consumer Personal Information* (last modified July 17, 1999) http://www.fdic.gov/news/news/ financial/1998/fil19886b.html.

115. 15 USC §§ 1693-1693r (1994), specifically § 1693c(9). The law applies to all accounts with an electronic funds transfer feature.

116. 12 C.F.R. § 205.7(b)(9) (1999); Federal Reserve Board Official Staff Commentary, 12 C.F.R. § 205.7(b)(9)-1 (1999).

117. S.900, enacted November 12, 1999 (hereinafter "Gramm-Leach-Bliley").

118. 12 USC § 377.

119. What information is considered "publicly available" is to be defined by implementing regulations, Gramm-Leach-Bliley § 509(4)(B).

120. Compare with COPPA, which applies to information only if it is gathered both online and from a child, but applies to all information linked to the child's identity.

121. Gramm-Leach-Bliley includes a number of exceptions to the third-party disclosure rule for such practical matters as using third parties to help fulfill a transaction between the consumer and the institution, or to market to the consumer on behalf of the institution, in each case under a confidentiality agreement; to enforce obligations of the consumer; to protect against fraud; to comply with law or respond to legal process, etc.

122. Gramm-Leach-Bliley § 502.

123. In hearings on the bill, the FTC had testified that the sale by financial institutions of their direct "transactions and experience" data "raises serious privacy concerns." Federal Trade Commission, *Prepared Statement of the Federal Trade Commission before the Subcommittee on Financial Institutions and Consumer Credit Committee on Banking and Financial Services, United States House of Representatives on Financial Privacy, the Fair Credit Reporting Act, and H.R. 10* (visited July 21, 1999).

124. *Id.* § 503.

125. See the discussion of FCRA *supra* part VI.E.. This treatment of financial institution affiliates only seems Byzantine; in fact it is merely labyrinthine. The provisions of FCRA addressing disclosures to affiliates (§ 603(d)(2)(A)(iii) of FCRA, 18 U.S.C § 1681a(d)(2)(A)(iii)) are in the form of exceptions to the definition of a "consumer report." Hence disclosures permitted by this section would be otherwise prohibited by FCRA only if, but for these

exceptions, the information would constitute "consumer reports" a definition that itself partakes not only of the nature of the information included but also the purposes for which it is gathered or used. Moreover, FCRA's prohibitions apply principally to "consumer reporting agencies," those who for a fee regularly furnish consumer reports.

126. Gramm-Leach-Bliley § 504 requires the Federal banking agencies, the National Credit Union Administration, the Secretary of the Treasury, the Securities and Exchange Commission and the FTC to prescribe regulations, after consultation with the National Association of Insurance Commissioners. The FTC's rule on Privacy of Consumer Financial Information is posted on the FTC site, www.ftc.gov. It is effective November 13, 2000, with full compliance expected by the FTC beginning July 1. 2001. The banking agencies' rule is posted at www.occ.treas.gov/ftp/regs/npr0203.pdf.

127. *Id.* § 509(3).

128. H.R. 3320, § 502.

129. *Id.* § 502(b)(1) and § 508(6).

130. *Id.* § 503(a)(4) and (5).

131. *Id.* § 508(3).

132. See, e.g., O.C.G.A. § 24-9-40 (1993) (medical records generally); O.C.G.A. § 33-21-23 (1992) (HMO records); O.C.G.A. § 31-8-114 (1996) (long-term care facility records); O.C.G.A. § 24-9-47 (1990) (AIDS records); O.C.G.A. § 37-3-166 (1995) (mental health records); O.C.G.A. § 31-22-4 (1996) (sexually transmitted and communicable disease clinical laboratory tests).

133. See, e.g., Health Insurance Portability and Accountability Act of 1996, P.L. 104-191, codified at 29 U.S.C. § 1181 (Supp. III 1997) (mandating security systems for the electronic transmission of health data); 42 C.F.R., § 482.24 (1998) (governing hospitals' medical records confidentiality practices); 42 U.S.C. § 290dd-3 (1994) (relating to alcohol and drug abuse records) (omitted in the general revision of this part by Pub. L. No. 102-321).

134. C. Bowman, "Uneven State Medical-Record Laws Offer Potential Pitfalls for Health Plans," *BNA Health Law Reporter*, November 11, 1999, at p.1787.

135. E.g., Medical Information Privacy and Security Act, H.R. 1057, 106th Cong. (1999) (introduced March 10, 1999); the Health Information Privacy Act, H.R. 1941, 106th Cong. (1999) (introduced May 25, 1999); Medical Information Protection and Research Enhancement Act of 1999, H.R. 2470, 106th Cong. (1999) (introduced July 12, 1999).

136. 64 Fed. Reg. 59918.

137. Health Insurance Portability and Accountability Act of 1996, *supra* note 133.

138. A heath care clearinghouse is an organization that translates health care records from nonstandard formats into standard electronic formats; an example would be a billing intermediary.

139. One of the more interesting attributes of these confidentiality agreements is that the patients concerned must be made express third-party beneficiaries. HIPPA provides no private right of action, and the question whether a private right of action should be created is among the major issues that have so far derailed passage of comprehensive health information privacy legislation, but this bit of regulatory finesse shows that there is more than one way to create a private right of action.

140. 64 Fed. Reg. 60053.

141. 64 Fed. Reg. 60056.

142. 64 Fed. Reg. 60059.

143. 64 Fed. Reg. 60060.

144. *Id.*

145. Cable Communications Policy Act of 1984, 47 USC § 551 (1994).

146. Video Privacy Protection Act, 18 USC § 2710 (1994). Statements that certain types of transactions do not occur on the Internet are often short-lived. In January 2000, Blockbuster Inc. announced that it had acquired the exclusive right to distribute the MGM film library over the Internet. "MGM, Blockbuster to Develop Internet Movie Delivery," Reuters, January 18, 2000, accessed via *CBS MarketWatch.com*. Query whether pay-per-view streaming video transactions over the Internet would fall within the protection of the Video Privacy Protection Act, which contemplate the delivery of "video cassette tapes or similar audio visual materials."

147. The Online Privacy Protection Act of 1999, S. 809, 106th Cong. (1999).

148. Federal Trade Commission, *Self-Regulation and Privacy Online: A Report to Congress* (visited July 21, 1999) http://www.ftc.gov/os/1999/9907/privacy99.pdf. While advocating continued monitoring of the progress of self-regulation and refusing to rule out the eventual need for online privacy legislation, the report concluded that "legislation to address online privacy is not appropriate at this time." *Id.* at *12. The FTC reversed that position in its May 22, 2000 report to Congress, *Privacy Online: Fair Information Practices in the Electronic Marketplace*, available on the FTC site, www.ftc.gov. In this later report, the FTC recommends that Congress pass legislation to ensure a minimum level of privacy for online consumers, establishing "basic standards of practice for the collection of information online."

149. See, e.g., Children's Privacy Protection and Parental Empowerment Act of 1999, H.R. 369, 106th Cong. (1999) (this bill is not confined to Internet contexts and would generally regulate use of personal information on children under 16); Electronic Rights for the 21st Century Act, S. 854, 106th Cong. (1999) (an omnibus e-privacy bill that would, *inter alia*, amend the ECPA to limit circumstances under which an electronic communications service can reveal subscriber information); the Internet Growth and Development Act of 1999, H.R. 1685, 106th Cong. § 201 (1999) (requiring commercial Web sites to post privacy policies); Personal Information Privacy Act of 1999, H.R. 1450, 106th Cong. § 7 (1999) (amending FCRA to prohibit selling "transactions and experience" information about a person without that person's consent and regulating commercial use of social security numbers); Social Security On-Line Privacy Act of 1999, H.R. 367, 106th Cong. § 2 (1999) (prohibiting "interactive computer services" (apparently meaning Internet Service Providers) from disclosing users' social security numbers and related information).

150. See *supra* note 36 and accompanying text (quoting the zZounds Web site).

151. Jeff Partyka, "IBM Advises on Online Privacy" (July 16, 1999) http://www.pcworld.com/pcwtoday/article/ 0,1510,11830.00.html.

152. A. Lash, "Privacy, Practically Speaking," *The Industry Standard* (August 2-9, 1999) http://www. thestandard.com/articles/display/0,1449,563,co.html. The article mentions three audits costing $200,000 or more, and one program that involves quarterly follow-up inspections at $20,000 per inspection. For the record, legal costs are an order of magnitude lower.

153. For a more complete discussion of audit methods and procedures, see S. Killingsworth, "Making it Legal: A Checklist for Web Site Privacy Audits," *E-Commerce Law Report*, Vol. 2, No. 1 (October 1999), p. 15.

154. The BBBOnLine privacy program requires disclosures of whether data gathered on the Web site is merged with data from other sources, since this data-matching can multiply both the original data's usefulness to the Web site and the sense of intrusion into the user's privacy. Better Business Bureau, *Sample Privacy Notice* (visited October 4, 1999) http://bbbonline.org/businesses/privacy/sample.html.

155. Compiling sensitive data just because it is available, with no particular use in mind, is inadvisable since there is no immediate benefit to having it and there is always a risk of inappropriate use or disclosure.

156. Seeding refers to the practice of inserting into a mailing list fictional or coded names

with addresses that lead back to the party who compiled the list, to provide a practical means for that party to monitor the use of the list.

157. For Web sites directed at children, the BBBOnLine privacy seal program requires the use of alerts to warn the user when a link leads out of the Web site; this exceeds the requirements of COPPA and the COPPA regulations. Better Business Bureau, *supra* note 43.

158. This may have been GeoCities' problem—the statements cited by the FTC were not in a single, comprehensive privacy policy, but were scattered among its New Member Application Form, its Free Member E-mail Program Web page, and one issue of its World Report newsletter. GeoCities, FTC Docket No. C-3850 (decision and order) (Feb. 5, 1999) http://www.ftc.gov/os/1999/99/9823015d%260.htm.

159. T. Wolverton, "United Sends Mixed Privacy Messages," *CNET News.com* (June 4, 1999) http://news.cnet.com/news/0-1007-200-343254/htm.?tag=st.cn.1fd2.

160. *Id.*

161. *Id.*

162. *Id.* At this writing, no explanation for how this occurred had been made public; it is entirely possible that the privacy policy was the later and more authoritative expression of United's intent and that there was simply an administrative oversight in failing to conform the user agreement to it.

163. One recent project that included a new "opt-out" database cost $250,000. Lash, *supra* note 156.

164. For example, both BBBOnLine and TRUSTe regulate use of personally identifiable information obtained from persons other than the data subject. Further, as mentioned earlier, *supra* note 161, on children's sites BBBOnLine requires either posting an alert when a link leads to another site where the same privacy rules do not apply, or avoiding altogether links to other child-directed sites that do not follow "core privacy standards." Better Business Bureau, *supra* note 43.

165. It is intriguing to note that the BBBOnLine license agreement does not include a "no third-party beneficiary" clause, so conceivably a consumer—for whose benefit the program presumably exists—might be able to sue for damages under that agreement if it were advantageous to do so. Better Business Bureau, *supra* note 44.

166. Effective June 30, 1999, TRUSTe added to its license agreement new data security requirements and a requirement that consumers have the opportunity to correct inaccurate data. Additionally, a provision for mandatory opt-out for secondary uses and third-party disclosures was added effective August 30, 1999. "Changes In TRUSTe License Agreements," *TRUSTe Reporter* (Spring 1999) http://www.truste.org/ newsletter/spring99.html#02.

167. As with any legal drafting problem, there are legitimate questions as to just how detailed and specific a privacy policy should be, but implementing any policy requires more focus than the fair information practices formulations provide.

168. See *infra* Part IX.D for a detailed discussion of these issues.

169. Both BBBOnLine and TRUSTe require that users be allowed to "opt-out" of disclosure of their information to third parties for secondary uses. While an "opt-out" is also required for secondary uses by the Web site operator, both seal programs allow the operator some latitude in defining what a "secondary use" is in the privacy policy. *TRUSTe License Agreement Rev. 5.0*, § 4.A. (June 25, 1999) http://www.truste.org/webpublishers/ pub_agreement.html; *BBBOnLine Eligibility Criteria* (visited October 31, 1999) http://www. bbbonline.org/businesses/privacy/eligibility.html. The current EU Safe Harbor draft seems to offer similar flexibility. Draft Safe Harbor, *supra* note 112. The FTC's formulation of the Choice principle suggests that consumers should always have a choice as to secondary uses. *Privacy Online*, *supra* note 16.

170. The scope of the Draft Safe Harbor exclusion is subject to ongoing debate. Draft Safe Harbor, *supra* note 112.

171. The EU Data Protection Directive and the Draft Safe Harbor apply to all information an organization maintains on an individual, so organizations subject to those rules will not be able to limit the application of the privacy policy, or of the policy's access rules, to information gathered through the Web site.

172. The online economy leaves no doubt that user "eyeballs" and data have market value to most Web sites.

173. Notably, both BBBOnLine and TRUSTe require that a Web site apply to personal data the privacy policies that were in effect when the data was collected, effectively outlawing "bait and switch" privacy promises by their licensees. *See BBBOnLine Eligibility Criteria, supra* note 44; *Privacy Policy Assessment Questionnaire*, Section E1 (visited October 31, 1999) http://www.bbbonline.org/businesses/privacy/assess-html.html. Both the Eligibility Criteria and the Assessment Questionnaire are incorporated by reference into *BBBOnLine's Participation Agreement* (visited October 31, 1999) http://www.bbbonline. org/download/license.PDF. See also *TRUSTe License Agreement Rev. 5.0, supra* note 43, at Schedule A, § 4.F (for an additional example). However, these policies have not prevented some licensees from using the "implied consent to policy change" techniques outlined in this article.

174. BBBOnLine requires a link to the privacy policy on every page in which data is collected. *BBBOnline Eligibility Criteria, supra* note 44, §§ "Eligible Sites." The proposed regulations implementing COPPA require similar notice on sites aimed at children. COPPA, Prop. Regs § 312.4(B).

175. Like shrink-wrap software licenses, clickwrap agreements have now received express judicial sanction. *Hotmail Corp. v. Van Money Pie, Inc.*, 47 U.S.P.Q.2d (BNA) 1020 (ND Cal 1998).

176. See S. Junnarkar, "DoubleClick Accused of Unlawful Data Use," *CNET News.com* (January 28, 2000) http://news.cnet.com/category/0-1005-200-1534533.html, quoting Jason Catlett, the founder of Junkbusters, a resource site for privacy-protection measures, as follows: "Based on previous experience...these class-action lawyers follow privacy advocates like ambulance chasers. I think it is inevitable that we will see more suits filed." The article reports on a class-action suit arising out of the DoubleClick acquisition of Abacus, described in note 188 *infra*.

177. 105 F3d 1147 (7th Cir 1997), *cert. denied* 522 U.S. 808 (1997). New York has also upheld Gateway's shrink-wrap arbitration clause as against a class action. See *Brower v. Gateway 2000, Inc.*, 676 NYS2d 569 (NY AppDiv 1998).

178. For a more detailed discussion of the *Gateway* case and its implications for class actions, see J. T. Westermeier, "How Arbitration Clauses Can Help Avoid Class Action Damages," *Computer Law Strategist*, September 1997, at 1.

179. The identification of persons anonymously posting either false information about a publicly traded stock, or inside information, are examples of this exception.

180. Under the Draft Safe Harbor, *supra* note 112, and the EU Data Protection Directive, *supra* note 2, affiliates may be considered "third parties" despite any attempt to characterize them otherwise.

181. See Wendy Marinaccio, "Privacy Advocates Blast DoubleClick Merger," *CNET News.com* (June 21, 1999) http://www.news.cnet.com/news/0-1005-200-343915.html?tag=st.cn.1fd2. (reporting on the outcry against the acquisition of a market research company by one of the Web's premier advertising companies, allowing DoubleClick's 1,300 advertising Web sites to potentially exchange data with Abacus's collection of 1,100 catalog companies). The merger closed November 23, 1999, with results outlined at note 7 *supra*. It is doubtful, of course, that any privacy policy provision would have prevented this essentially political reaction.

Endnotes for Chapter 19

1. Canada has a federal system much like that of the United States, but run on British Parliamentary lines rather than with a formal division of powers as in the U.S. The authority of the ten provinces, the three territories, and the federal government is sometimes allocated differently than in the U.S. Most provinces and the territories, and for many purposes the federal government, have what we call "Anglo-Canadian law", i.e. based on English common law as modified by our courts and our legislation over the years. The province of Quebec is a civil law jurisdiction. Much of its private law is governed by the Civil Code of Quebec, which was fundamentally revised effective in 1994. Remarks in this paper about Canadian law should be taken with caution in their application to Quebec, unless specifically noted. Provincial laws vary across the country, too, of course.

2. See Amelia H. Boss, "Searching for Security in the Law of Electronic Commerce", 23 *Nova L.R.* 585 (1999).

3. See John D. Gregory, "Solving Legal Issues in Electronic Commerce", 32 *Can Business L.J.* 84 (1999) for further discussion.

4. The leading text on evidence in Canada is Sopinka, Lederman, Bryant, *The Law of Evidence in Canada*, Butterworths, 2d Edition, 1999. See also Alan Gahtan, *Electronic Evidence*, Carswell, 1999.

5. See J.D.Ewart, *Documentary Evidence in Canada*, Carswell, 1984.

6. These arguments are stated in J.D. Ewart, *Documentary Evidence in Canada*, supra note 5, at page 67.

7. There has been no taste in Canada to restrict the use of encryption for commercial or personal purposes. Canada is a member of the Wassenaar group that has made certain international commitments on the subject. The federal government's encryption policy is on line at http://strategis.ic.gc.ca/crypto.

Endnotes for Chapter 23

1. An earlier version of this chapter appeared as a two-part article in the *Journal of Internet Law*. See "The Eye of the High Tech Storm: The Law of Email," 3:8 *Journal of Internet Law* 1 (February 2000) & 3:9 *Journal of Internet Law* 1 (March 2000).

2. See, e.g., Paul Hoffman, "Unsolicited Bulk Email: Definitions and Problems," available at http://www.imc.org/ube-def.html.

3. See Faye Jones, "Spam: Unsolicited Commercial Email by Any Other Name," 3 *Journal of Internet Law* 1, 2 (1999).

4. Chief among these organizations is the Coalition Against Unsolicited Bulk Email (CAUCE). CAUCE can be found at http://www.cauce.org.

5. An IP, or Internet protocol address, is a unique 32-bit numeric address consisting of a set of numbers separated by dots (e.g. 206.112.192.104). IP addresses are given to any computer that is connected to the Internet.

6. The most famous of these is the Real-time Blackhole List (RBL), which is operated by the Mail Abuse Prevention System. It can be found at http://maps.vix.com/rbl/. For a recent discussion of the ongoing debate over the regulation of unsolicited commercial email, see Deborah Scoblionkov, "Direct Mail Double Cross," SALON.COM, November 12, 1999, available at: http://www.salon.com/tech/feature/1999/11/12/spam/index.html.

7. In the 1999–2000 congressional legislative session, several bills directly dealing with unsolicited commercial email were introduced in Congress: H.R. 1686, H.R. 1910, H.R. 2162, H.R. 3024, H.R. 3113, and S. 759. In 2000, one anti-spam bill appeared to gain the most legislative momentum. HR 3113, the Unsolicited Electronic Mail Act of 1999, would require that every unsolicited commercial email contain a valid return address and would require senders to honor "opt-out" requests. In addition, HR 3113 would prohibit the forgery of email

header information. Moreover, the law would enable ISPs to seek civil judgments against senders of spam in violation of posted ISP email policies, as well as enable individual recipients to seek damages. As of this writing, none have been enacted.

8. See Main Features of State Unsolicited Commercial Email Laws.

9. See "California ISP Sues Spammer and Wins," August 2, 1999, available at http://www.slashdot.org/articles.99/08/02/129213.shtml (recounting a small ISP's recovery of $600 in damages against a spammer for the "unauthorized use of its network.").

10. Cal. Business & Professions Code § 17538.4(a)(2).

11. Cal. Business & Professions Code § 17538.4(b).

12. Cal. Business & Professions Code § 17538.4(c).

13. Section 17538.4(g). Unsolicited email advertisements which deal with materials that may only be "viewed, purchased, rented, leased, or held in possession by an individual eighteen years of age and older" must include the characters "ADV:ADLT" as the first characters of the subject line. *Id.*

14. Cal. Business & Professions Code § 17538.4(d). "Electronic mail service provider" is defined to mean "any business or organization qualified to do business in this state that provides individuals, corporations, or other entities the ability to send or receive electronic mail through equipment located in this state and that is an intermediary in sending or receiving electronic mail." *Id.*

15. This includes "any emailed document or documents consisting of advertising material for the lease, sale, rental, gift offer, or other disposition of any realty, goods, services, or extension of credit." Section 17538.45(e).

16. Section 17538.4(e)(1) - (2).

17. Section 17538.4(h).

18. Cal. Business & Professions Code § 17538.45(b) & (c).

19. Section 17538.45(a)(2)(A) - (B).

20. Section 17538.45(f)(1). The email service provider may also recover reasonable attorney's fees. *Id.*

21. Section 17538.45(f)(3).

22. Section 17538.45(f)(3)(B).

23. California Penal Code § 502(a).

24. California Penal Code § 502(c)(9).

25. California Penal Code § 502(d)(4).

26. California Penal Code § 502(e).

27. California Penal Code § 502(g).

28. Connecticut Public Act 99-160, Section 1.

29. Public Act 99-160, Section 1(b)(7).

30. Public Act 99-160, Section 1(c).

31. Public Act 99-160, Section 1(d).

32. Public Act 99-160, Section 2(b). A person can recover either the actual damages suffered as a result of such activity, or statutory damages of $10 for each unsolicited bulk email transmitted in violation of this section, up to $25,000 per day. *Id.* at Section 2(b). The act allows email service providers to recover the same measure of damages. *Id.* at Section 2(c).

33. Public Act 99-160, Section 2(a).

34. Public Act 99-160, Section 2(f).

35. Public Act 99-160, Section 4(a).

36. Delaware Code, Title 11, Sections 937 & 938.

37. *Id.* at Section 937.

38. "Commercial Electronic Mail" or "Commercial Email" are defined to mean "any electronic mail message that is sent to a receiving address or account for the purposes of advertising, promoting, marketing, or otherwise attempting to solicit interest in any good, service, or enterprise." Section 931(17).

39. *Id.* at Section 937(a).

40. *Id.*

41. *Id.*

42. *Id.*

43. Section 937(b).

44. *Id.* This provision mirrors other state laws in this respect, and covers software that is primarily designed to accomplish falsification of routing information, that has only "limited commercially significant purpose" aside from such falsification, or is marketed for the purpose of falsifying such transmission information. Section 937(c).

45. Section 937(d).

46. Section 938(a).

47. Idaho Code, Chapter 6, Title 48, Section 603E.

48. "Interactive computer service" is defined as "an information service, system or access software provider that provides or enables computer access by multiple users to a computer server, including specifically a service or system that provides access to the Internet, and such systems operated or services offered by a library or an educational institution." *Id.* at 48-603E(1)(c).

49. "Bulk electronic mail advertisement" is defined as "an electronic message containing the same or similar advertisement, which is contemporaneously transmitted to two (2) or more recipients, pursuant to an Internet or intranet computer network." *Id.* at 48-603E(1)(a).

50. *Id.* at 48-603E(2).

51. *Id.* at 48-603E(3).

52. *Id.* at 48-603E(4).

53. *Id.* at 48-603E(5)(a) - (d).

54. Ill. Public Act 91-0233 (1999).

55. *Id.* at Section 5.

56. *Id.*

57. *Id.* at Section 10(a).

58. *Id.* at Section 10(b).

59. *Id.* at Section 10(c) - (d).

60. *Id.* at Section 10(g).

61. Illinois Criminal Code, Sections 16D-2 & 16D-3. Specifically, it is a crime in Illinois to "knowingly and without the authorization of a computer's owner . . . falsif[y] or forge electronic mail transmission information or other routing information in any manner in connection with the transmission of unsolicited bulk electronic mail through or into the computer network of an electronic mail service provider or its subscribers." Section 16D-3(a)(5).

62. *Id.* at 16D-3(a-5).

63. The act defines "interactive computer service" to mean "an information service, system, or access software provider that provides or enables computer access by multiple users to a computer server, including specifically a service or system that provides access to the Internet, and such systems operated or services offered by a library or an educational institution." Iowa Code, Chapter 714D.1(1)(e).

64. *Id.* at Chapter 714D.1(2)(a) - (e).

65. *Id.* at Chapter 714D.1(3).

66. *Id.* at Chapter 714D.1(3)(a) - (b).

67. *Id.* at Chapter 714D.1(4).

68. *Id.* at Chapter 714D.1(6). In addition, email accessed on an electronic bulletin board is not covered by the act, nor does the act cover email advertisements sent as a condition of providing free email or Internet access. *Id.*

69. *Id.*

70. Louisiana Revised Statutes, Section 14:73.1 (1999).

71. "Unsolicited bulk electronic mail" is defined as "any electronic message which is developed and distributed in an effort to sell or lease consumer goods or services and is sent in the same or substantially similar form to more than one thousand recipients." *Id.* at § 73.1(13).

72. *Id.* at § 73.6(A). However, noncommercial emails or emails sent "from an organization to its members" are not covered by this prohibition. *Id.*

73. *Id.* at § 73.6(B).

74. *Id.*

75. *Id.* at § 73.6(C).

76. *Id.* at § 73.6(D).

77. Nevada Revised Statutes, Section 41.705 - 735.

78. The act defines "advertisement" to mean "material that advertises for commercial purposes the availability or the quality of real property, goods, or services; or is otherwise designed or intended to solicit a person to purchase real property, goods, or services." *Id.* at Section 3.

79. *Id.* at Section 7.

80. *Id.*

81. North Carolina General Statutes, §§ 14-453 (definitions), 14-458 (main prohibitions), 1-539.2A (damages), and 1-75.4 (jurisdiction).

82. "Unsolicited" does not include emails "addressed to a recipient with whom the initiator has an existing business or personal relationship and not sent at the request of, or with the express consent of, the recipient." *Id.* at § 14-453(10).

83. *Id.* at § 14-458(a)(6).

84. *Id.* at § 14-458(b).

85. *Id.* at §§ 14-458(c), 1-539.2A(a) (any person suffering injury as a result of a violation can recover actual damages, including lost profits, or statutory damages ranging from $10 per message to $25,000 per day).

86. *Id.* at § 1-539.2A(a).

87. Oklahoma Statutes, Title 15, Section 776.1.

88. *Id.* at § 776.1(A)(1) - (3).

89. *Id.* at § 776.1(B).

90. *Id.* at § 776.1(E).

91. *Id.* at § 776.2.

92. *Id.* at § 776.3.

93. Rhode Island General Law, Title 11, Chapter 52 & Title 6, Chapter 47.

94. § 11-52-4.1(7).

95. § 11-52-4.1(8).

96. *Id.*

97. The criminal penalties for a violation of this provision are: misdemeanor: up to a $500 fine and/or up to one year imprisonment; felony: up to a $5,000 fine and/or up to five years imprisonment. *Id.* at § 11-52-5(a) - (b).

98. Individuals and ISPs injured by a violation of this act can recover either actual damages or statutory damages ranging from $500 per violation up to $25,000 per day. *Id.* at § 11-52-6.

99. Title 6, Section 47.

100. § 6-47.2(a).

101. § 6-47.2(b).

102. § 6-47.2(c).

103. § 6-47.2(d).

104. § 6-47.2(e)(1) - (2).

105. Tennessee Code Annotated, Title 47, Chapter 18.

106. *Id.* at Section 2 (a)–(e). If the email deals with material which cannot be "bought or possessed by those under eighteen, the first four characters of the subject line must be "ADV:ADLT." *Id.*

107. *Id.* at Section 2 (g).

108. *Id.* at Section 2 (f).

109. *Id.* at Section 2 (i).

110. Virginia Code, Title 8.01, Chapter 9, §8.01-328.1B; Title 10.2, Chapter 5, Article 7.1, §§ 10.2-151.2, 10.2-151.4 & 10.2-151.12.

111. "Without authority" is defined to include any use of an ISP's network in violation of that ISP's policy regarding the transmission of unsolicited bulk electronic mail. § 18.2-152.2.

112. § 18.2-152.4(A)(7).

113. § 18.2-152.4(B).

114. § 18.2-152.12.

115. § 18.2-152.4(C).

116. A "use" is defined to include, among other things, "attempt[ing] or caus[ing] a computer or computer network to perform or to stop performing computer operations." § 18.2-152.2.

117. § 8.01-328.1(B).

118. Revised Code of Washington, Title 19, Chapter 19.190 *et seq.*

119. §§ 19.190.020 and 19.190.030.

120. § 19.190.101(1); § 19.190.020(1).

121. § 19.190.020(1). A person will be held to know that "the intended recipient of a commercial electronic mail message is a Washington resident if that information is available, upon request, from the registrant of the Internet domain name contained in the recipient's electronic mail address." §19.190.020(2).

122. § 19.190.050.

123. Superior Court of Washington, County of King, No. 98-2-25480-7 SEA.

124. See Peter Lewis, "Anti-spam email suit tossed out," *Seattle Times*, Marrch 14, 2000, at A1.

125. West Virginia Code, Chapter 46A, Article 6G.

126. § 46A-6G-2.

127. § 46A-6G-2(1).

128. § 46A-6G-2(2).

129. § 46A-6G-2(3).

130. § 46A-6G-2(4).

131. § 46A-6G-4.

132. § 46A-6G-2.

133. 15 USC § 1125.

134. 18 USC § 2510 *et seq.*

135. 18 USC § 1030 *et seq.* (1994).

136. Faye Jones, "Spam: Unsolicited Commercial Email by Any Other Name," 3 *Journal of Internet Law* 1, 4 (1999); see also Cathryn Le, "How Have Internet Service Providers Beat Spammers?," 5 *Rich. J.L. & Tech.* 9 (Winter 1998).

137. See Section II.B.

138. A detailed list and description of cases pursued by AOL against "spammers" can be found at: http://legal.web.aol.com/email/jeaol/index.html. A list of cases involving major ISPs can be found at: http://www.jmls.edu/cyber/cases/spam.html#cs-cp.

139. 962 FSupp 1015 (SD Oh 1997) (order entering preliminary injunction in favor of CompuServe). The final consent order between CompuServe and Cyber Promotions in this case is available at: http://www.jmls.edu/cyber/cases/cs-cp3.html.

140. 963 FSupp at 1019.

141. *Id.* at 1021 (citing Prosser & Keeton, Prosser and Keeton on Torts, § 14, 85-86 (1984)).

142. *Id.* (citing *Thrifty-Tel, Inc. v. Bezenek*, 46 Cal App 4th 1599, 1567 (1996); *State v. McGraw*, 480 NE2nd 552, 554 (Ind 1985); *State v. Riley*, 846 P2d 1365 (Wash 1993)).

143. *Id.* at 1028.

144. California Superior Court, County of Sacramento, Case No. 98AS05067, 1999 WL 450944 (1998).

145. *Id.* The court's order granting a permanent injunction can be accessed at Ken Hamidi's FACE Intel Web site, and is available at http://www.intelhamidi.com/permamentinjunction.htm.

146. See Jones, *supra*, note 120 at 4.

147. See "Developments—The Law of Cyberspace: The Long Arm of Cyber Reach," 112 *Harvard Law Review* 1610 (1999).

148. See *supra*, Section II.A.

149. See Myrna L. Wigod, "Privacy in Public and Private Email and On-Line Systems," 19 *Pace Law Review* 95, 97-98 (1998).

150. See, e.g., *Smyth v. The Pillsbury Co.*, 914 FSupp 97 (ED Pa 1996).

151. *Smyth v. The Pillsbury Co.*, 914 FSupp at 98-99, n.1 ("Defendant alleges in its motion to dismiss that the emails concerned sales management and contained threats to "kill the backstabbing bastards" and referred to the planned holiday party as the "Jim Jones Koolaid affair.").

152. *Id.* at 100.

153. *Id.* at 101.

154. *Id.*

155. *Id.*

156. See, e.g., Rod Dixon, "Windows Nine-to-Five: *Smyth v. Pillsbury* and the Scope of an Employee's Right of Privacy in Employer Communications," 2 *Virginia Journal of Law and Technology* 4 (1997).

157. Cal. Court of Appeal, Case No. B068705 (1993).

158. See, e.g., *Shoars v. Epson*, Los Angeles Superior Court, No. YC003979 (1991); *Flannagan v. Epson*, Los Angeles Superior Court, No. SCW112749, *appeal denied*, 994 Cal. LEXIS 3670 (1994).

159. See Brad Marlowe, "You Are Being Watched: Think You Can Outsmart Big Brother?," *PC/Computing*, December 1, 1999, at 84; Clint Swett & Eric Young, "Davis Supports Firms on Secret Email Monitoring," *Sacramento Bee*, October 14, 1999, at F2.

160. 18 USC §§ 2510 - 2520 (1994).

161. *Id.* at § 2511(2)(a)(i).

162. *Id.* at § 2511.

163. *Id.* at § 2522(1)(a).

164. See, e.g., *Steve Jackson Games, Inc. v. United States Secret Service*, 36 F3d 457 (5th Cir 1994); *Wesley College v. Pitts*, 974 FSupp 375 (D Del 1997).

165. *Id.* at §2511(2)(a)(i) (emphasis added).

166. *Id.*

167. *Id.* at § 2701(c)(1).

168. See, e.g., Mark S. Dichter & Michael S. Burkhardt, "Electronic Interaction in the Workplace: Monitoring, Retrieving and Storing Employee Communications in the Internet Age," available at: http://www.mlb.com/speech1.htm.

169. 18 USC § 2511(2)(d).

170. *Id.* at § 2702(b)(3).

171. *Watkins v. L.M. Berry & Co.*, 704 F2d 577, 580 (11th Cir 1983).

172. See, e.g., *Deal v. Spears*, 980 F2d 1153, 1156-57 (8th Cir 1992) (analyzing the implied consent exception in the context of telephone monitoring).

173. For a more detailed discussion of the parameters of this tort as it may apply to the workplace, see Dichter & Burkhardt, *supra*, note 170.

174. Restatement (Second) of Torts, § 652A.

175. Restatement (Second) of Torts, § 652B.

176. See *Smyth v. The Pillsbury Co.*, 914 FSupp at 100 (analyzing Pennsylvania's version of the tort).

177. See Dichter & Burkhardt, *supra*, note 170.

178. See, e.g. *Smyth*, 914 FSupp at 101.

179. 1995 N.Y. Misc LEXIS 229 (Sup Ct NY 1995).

180. The Telecommunications Act of 1996, 47 USC § 230.

181. *Id.*

182. 47 USC § 230(c)(1).

183. 47 USC §230(c)(2)(A).

184. The act defines "interactive computer service" to mean "any information service, system, or access software provider that provides or enables computer access by multiple users to a computer server, including specifically a service or system that provides access to the Internet . . ." 47 USC § 230(f)(2). For an interpretation of the application of the "good samaritan" provision to ISPs, see *Zeran v. America Online*, 129 F3d 327 (4th Cir 1997); *Blumenthal v. Drudge*, 992 FSupp 44 (D Colo 1998).

185. Business Software Alliance, "Employer Beware" (press release), September 16, 1999, available at http://www.bsa.org (describing survey results indicating that employees routinely download copyrighted software from the Internet and share the programs with employees in the workplace).

186. 907 FSupp 1361 (ND Cal 1995).

187. *Id.* at 1373.

188. *Fonovisa, Inc. v. Cherry Auction, Inc.*, 76 F3d 259 (9th Cir 1996) (emphasis added).

189. *Netcom*, 907 FSupp at 1375.

190. For example, the Business Software Alliance recommends that the following sample language in connection with software use policies: According to applicable copyright law, persons involved in the illegal reproduction of software can be subject to civil damages and criminal penalties including fines and imprisonment. (Organization) does not condone the illegal duplication of software. (Organization) employees who make, acquire, or use unauthorized copies of computer software shall be disciplined as appropriate under the circumstances. Such discipline may include termination. Business Software Alliance, *The BSA Guide to Software Management: An Essential Step-by-Step Reference Manual.*

191. Michael Overly, "Finding the Needle in the Haystack: Discovering Electronic Evidence," February 17, 1997, available at http://www.collegehill.com/ilp-news/overly1.html.

192. A detailed discussion of the impact electronic forms of evidence has on litigation strategies is beyond the scope of this chapter. This topic is covered by other works on the use of electronic evidence in litigation. See *id.*; Matthew J. Bester, "A Wreck on the Info-Bahn: Electronic Mail and the Destruction of Evidence," 6 *CommLaw Conspectus* 75 (1998); *Moore's Manual of Complex Litigation*, § 21.446.

193. Fed. R. Civ. P. 34(a); see also *Crown Life Ins. Co. v. Craig*, 995 F2d 1376, 1383-84 (7th Cir 1993) (stating that electronic data is properly discoverable under federal rules).

194. One commentator has proposed sample language for defining "writing" to include electronic evidence: "Writing'" includes, but is not limited to, data stored in a computer or similar device, data stored on removable magnetic or optical media (e.g., magnetic tape, floppy disks, and recordable optical disks), backup copies of data, *email*, data used for electronic data interchange, audit trails, digitized pictures and video (e.g., data stored in MPEG, JPEG, and GIF formats), digitized audio, and voice mail. *Overly*, supra, *note 193.*

195. For purposes of this discussion, we assume that the email evidence meets the threshold relevancy requirement. See Fed. R. Evid. 104.

196. Under the Federal Rules of Evidence, hearsay is defined as: [A] statement, other than one made by the declarant while testifying at the trial or hearing, offered in evidence to prove the truth of the matter asserted. Fed. R. Evid. 801(c).

197. Common examples of non-hearsay are "verbal acts" which are offered, not for the truth of the matter asserted, but because the act of making the statement itself has some independent legal significance. "If the significance of an offered statement lies solely in the fact that it was made, no issue is raised as to the truth of anything asserted, and the statement is not hearsay." Fed. R. Evid. 801(c), Advisory Committee Note to Subdivision (c) (1972). Common examples of statements that are non-hearsay due to their independent legal significance are statements offered to show that the parties reached terms to a contract or that the speaker made a defamatory statement. As we have discussed in the context of an employer's potential liability for employees acting through workplace email, defamation is a likely candidate for employer liability.

198. Fed. R. Evid. 801(d)(2).

199. Fed. R. Evid. 804(b)(3) (exception applies if the statement must be contrary to declarant's interest when made, and the declarant must be "unavailable" to testify at trial).

200. Fed. R. Evid. 803(1).

201. Fed. R. Evid. 803(5).

202. Fed. R. Evid. 803(6).

203. Fed. R. Evid. 901.

204. Fed. R. Evid. 901(a).

205. For other illustrative means of authenticating a document, see Fed. R. Evid. 901(b).

206. Fed. R. Evid. 1001(3).

207. *Id.*; see also Fed. R. Evid. 1002.

208. Richard F. Ziegler & Seth A. Stuhl, "Spoliation Issues Arise In Digital Era," *National Law Journal*, February 16, 1998, at B9.

209. *Wm. T. Thompson Co. v. General Nutrition Corp.*, 593 FSupp 1443, 1445 (CD Cal 1984); *Gomez v. Acquistapace*, 50 Cal App 4th 740, 747 (1996) (party is guilty of intentional spoliation of evidence when it "destroys an object which might constitute evidence in a lawsuit with the purpose of harming the lawsuit, or when harm to the lawsuit is substantially certain to follow.").

210. *Compare Turner v. Hudson Transit Lines, Inc.*, 142 FRD 68, 72-73 (SD NY 1991) (the service of a complaint or a discovery request suffices to put a party on notice) *with Gomez*, 50 Cal App 4th at 747 (defense of spoliation available where party shows that the spoliating party knew that "harm to the lawsuit was substantially certain to follow.").

211. See, e.g., *Cedars-Sinai Medical Center v. Superior Court*, 18 Cal 4th 1, 11 (1998).

212. See Overly, *supra*, note 193.

INDEX

ABOUT THE AUTHORS

J. DIANNE BRINSON teaches Internet Law in the University of California-Berkeley Extension's Webmaster Certification Program and San Jose State University's Internet Education Institute. A former law school professor, she obtained her law degree from Yale Law School. With Mark Radcliffe, she is the author of three earlier well-received books on multimedia and Internet law: *Multimedia Law Handbook, Multimedia Law and Business Handbook*, and *Internet Legal Forms for Business*.

MARK F. RADCLIFFE practices Internet law with the California-based law firm Gray Cary Ware & Freidenrich. A graduate of Harvard Law School, he was named one of the "100 Most Influential Attorneys in the United States" by the *National Law Journal* in 1997. He has been quoted on Internet legal issues in *The New York Times, The Wall Street Journal*, and other publications.

UPDATES

As you probably know, the law of the Internet is still developing. (Every day, the news media run articles on some aspect of Internet law, such as privacy policies, domain name disputes, and linking issues.) As this book goes to press, many legal issues are still unresolved, as we note in the book. New laws are being passed, and cases dealing with crucial issues are being decided. **For information on new developments and how to obtain updates to this book, check our Web site, www.laderapress.com.**

If you would like for us to send you information on new publications, please email us at Laderapres@aol.com or fill out a "guest book" form on our Web site.

ADDITIONAL INTERNET LEGAL FORMS AVAILABLE

Ladera Press also publishes the book *Internet Legal Forms for Business*. The current version of this book includes the following sample contracts:

- Web Site Terms of Use

- Internet Advertising Contract

- Chat Room Agreement

- Internet Use Policy

- Clickwrap Agreement

- Revenue-Sharing Linking Agreement

- Domain Name Assignment Agreement

The book also includes several sample contracts that are included in the *Internet Law and Business Handbook*—a Content Development and Transfer Agreement, Content Licenses, Web Site Development Agreement, and Permission to Link. For each sample contract, we explain why the contract is used and provide an issues checklist and negotiating tips.

The price of the *Internet Legal Forms for Business* book is $24.95 plus $5 shipping (California residents, add 8.25% sales tax). Shipping to Canada is $6. Shipping to other foreign countries is $15.

The forms from *Internet Legal Forms for Business* are available on disk for $12. (The disk does not include the explanatory material, checklists, or negotiating tips, just the forms.) U.S. shipping is included in the price. For foreign orders, there is no additional charge for shipping the disk if the disk is purchased with the book. If the disk alone is purchased, the foreign shipping charge for the disk is $10.

For UPS 2d Day Air delivery in the United States, add $10 to the regular shipping fee (add $15 for delivery to Alaska or Hawaii). For express shipping to foreign countries, please contact Port City Fulfillment for information on charges (fulfillment@portcity.com, telephone (810) 989-9500, fax (810) 987-3562).

To order: visit our Web site, www.laderapress.com; call (800) 523-3721; or use the order form from this book.

NEED ADDITIONAL COPIES?

Additional copies of *Internet Law and Business Handbook* and copies of *Internet Legal Forms for Business* are available by phone, mail, fax, and from our Web site. Use the product and shipping information below and the order form on the following page to complete your order.

To Order by Mail

Send order information to:
Ladera Press
c/o Port City Fulfillment
408 Grand River
Port Huron, MI 48060

To Order by Fax

Fax order to (810) 987-3562

To Order by Phone

Have your credit card handy and call (800) 523-3721
Outside the U.S.: call (810) 989-9500

To Order Online

Visit our site at www.laderapress.com

LADERA PRESS PRODUCTS

Internet Law and Business Handbook (includes forms disk)	$44.95
Handbook Forms disk	$15.00
Multimedia Contracts Book	$89.95
Multimedia Contracts on Diskette (PC or Macintosh)	$99.95

Prices subject to change without notice.

Shipping

Please allow 2–3 weeks for delivery.
WITHIN THE UNITED STATES: $7.00 for first book & $4.00 for each additional book.
TO CANADA OR MEXICO: $9.00 per book.
TO OTHER FOREIGN COUNTRIES (U.S. Mail, Air Mail, Book Rate): $25.00 per book.
No charge for shipping disk orders.

In a Rush?

UPS 2ND DAY DELIVERY IS AVAILABLE: For delivery in the continental United States, add $10.00 to the regular shipping fee. For delivery to Alaska or Hawaii, add $15.00 to the regular shipping fee.

Ladera Press Order Form

Use this form to order additional Ladera Press products.

TO ORDER BY MAIL: Complete the form and mail to:
   Ladera Press
   c/o Port City Fulfillment
   408 Grand River
   Port Huron, MI 48060

TO ORDER BY FAX: Complete the form and fax to (810) 987-3562.

TO ORDER BY PHONE: Have your credit card handy and call (800) 523-3721.

Name _____

Title _____ Email address: _____

Company _____

Address _____

City _____ State _____ Zip _____

Telephone _____ Fax _____

Method of payment: ❑ Check enclosed   ❑ Visa   ❑ Mastercard

Credit Card Account Number: _____

Expiration Date: _____

Signature _____

Quantity	Item	Price	Total
	Subtotal		
	8.25% Sales Tax (CA Residents)		
	Shipping (see preceding pages)		
	UPS 2nd Day $10/$15		
	TOTAL		

Please allow 2–3 weeks for delivery.